Frame Work

CULTURE, STORYTELLING, AND COLLEGE WRITING

Gary Colombo

Los Angeles City College

Bonnie Lisle

University of California, Los Angeles

Sandra Mano

University of California, Los Angeles

Bedford Books   Boston

For Bedford Books

President and Publisher: Charles H. Christensen
General Manager and Associate Publisher: Joan E. Feinberg
Managing Editor: Elizabeth M. Schaaf
Developmental Editor: Jane Betz
Editorial Assistant: Maura Shea
Production Editor: John Amburg
Copyeditor: Barbara Sutton
Text Design: Claire Seng-Niemoeller
Cover Design: Ann Gallager
Cover Art: Nancy Crow, *Color Blocks # 33,* 1993. By courtesy of C & T Publishing, from the book *Improvisational Quilts.* Photograph by J. Kevin Fitzsimmons.

Library of Congress Catalog Card Number: 96–86767

0 9 8 7 6
f   e   d   c   b   a

For information write: Bedford Books, 75 Arlington Street, Boston, MA 02116
(617–426–7440)

ISBN: 0–312–10334–4

Acknowledgments

Preface for Instructors

A Fresh Approach to Writing

Four years ago we began working on a new approach to composition instruction for entering college students. We wanted to develop an approach that would be process oriented and revision based, but that would also incorporate recent insights concerning the impact of culture on language and writing. *Frame Work* is the result of that experiment in curricular design. Recent research in anthropology, linguistics, cognitive science, and women's and ethnic studies suggests that our understanding of the world is mediated by story frames—culturally constructed narrative patterns that filter, organize, and interpret all of our experiences. The concept of the story frame offers a powerful alternative to pedagogies based on personal/academic or narrative/analytic oppositions. A story frame approach to composition allows students to appreciate the impact that culture and craft have on even the most personal memoir; it also helps students see that narrative patterns underlie and organize the most abstract academic analysis. The story frame approach in *Frame Work* gives writing instructors a new language for teaching composition, a language that demystifies academic discourse by reconnecting it with the kind of storytelling students practice naturally every day.

Critical Thinking in Cultural Contexts

Frame Work moves from familiar narrative forms to more complex academic analysis. As students work through the book, they use the story frame approach to explore how the many cultures they participate in influence their development as thinkers and writers. *Frame Work* invites students to examine the interrelations of cultural narratives and identity, write essays based on readings and their own experience, assess the demands of writing in academic contexts, and revise their essays. Throughout, students are encouraged to question how the "official stories" of the cultures they belong to shape their identities, their ideas, and their responses to the works they read. *Frame Work* helps students see that critical thinking extends beyond classroom walls and that every act of critical analysis involves serious self-examination as well as critical appraisal of the cultural stories that shape us and our ideas.

Academia 101

Students often come to college unsure about how they fit into the intellectual culture of higher education. *Frame Work* explicitly addresses the assumptions, values, and expectations that students are likely to encounter when they join the college community. Specially designed chapters titled "Academically Speaking" challenge students to consider the power—and the limitations—of academic writing; they address student expectations about what academic discourse is supposed to "look" and "sound" like; and they encourage students to compare academic styles of thinking and writing with styles available in other cultural contexts. *Frame Work* also introduces students to the complexities of theoretical thinking and helps them appreciate the dialogical nature of academic discourse. Approaching academia as one of many cultures helps demystify it, particularly for those students who may consider themselves "outsiders" in a perplexingly new intellectual environment.

Highlighting Language and Voice

Frame Work places issues of language and voice at the center of the composition curriculum. Because the stories that make up a culture are inseparable from the voice they're told in, we've built *Frame Work* around questions of language and identity. As they work through the text, students will explore the genesis of the many different "Englishes" they speak and map the different speech communities they belong to. They'll consider their home languages as well as the languages they learn on the street, at work, in school, and from the media. *Frame Work* encourages students to experiment with different voices and to evaluate for themselves the impact that language standardization has on their identity and their development as academic writers.

Diversity in Principle

Because the idea of cultural diversity lies at the heart of our approach to composition, *Frame Work* weaves a broad selection of readings into its cultural storytelling approach to college writing. Each chapter contains several readings that complement the text's rhetorical apparatus—in all some thirty-six selections, including stories, essays, and poems by students, scholars, and professional writers. Most of the selections we've included are by authors who stand outside the dominant culture, and more than half are by women. We've also made it a principle to feature a diverse range of rhetorical styles and forms. In fact, you may be surprised at the amount of professional academic writing you'll find here: we've included selections by anthropologists, psychologists, biologists, educators, and historians because students need to see models of academic inquiry in action if they're expected to enter "the conversation of ideas" that's associated with thinking and writing in the academic disciplines.

An Emphasis on Process and Revision

In each section of the book, *Frame Work* offers a "Revision Workshop" built around student responses to one or more of the writing assignments in that section. Complete chapters devoted to revision, these workshops blend example, discussion, and activities to help students rethink their own writing. Throughout the book, writing process and revision skills are taught in the context of specific assignments. Among other topics covered, students learn how to shape effective introductions and conclusions, how to develop paragraphs and build solid transitions, how to analyze and respond to different audiences, how to quote and paraphrase from sources, and how to evaluate and marshal evidence—all in relation to writing problems they are currently encountering. Journal assignments, classroom activities, and essay options help students gain confidence as they write, revise, and collaborate with their peers.

Acknowledgments

A good textbook depends on the labor of many hands, and *Frame Work* is no exception. During the months we've spent on this project, we've relied time and again on the encouragement and critical insight of many friends and colleagues. We owe special thanks to Karen Rowe and the participants in the Curriculum Writing Integration Project seminars at UCLA for sparking ideas that led us to explore a story-based approach to composition. In addition, the UCLA Multicultural Studies Committee deserves recognition for the support it provided during the early phases of this project. Certainly, we couldn't have attempted a book like this without the guidance of a whole group of dedicated reviewers. We'd particularly like to thank Sonia Apgar, University of Minnesota—Twin Cities; Meg Carroll, Rhode Island College; Cynthia Cox, Belmont University; Helen Fox, University of Michigan—Ann Arbor; Robert Foreman, Pasadena City College; Min-Zhan Lu, Drake University; Denice Martone, New York University; Brendan Pieters, Santa Fe Community College; Stephen Rufus, Salt Lake City Community College; Randy Woodland, University of Michigan—Dearborn; Susan Young, LaGuardia Community College/CUNY. We also owe a debt of gratitude to the amazingly patient and supportive staff of Bedford Books. We'd like to thank our editor Jane Betz for helping us discover the rhetoric we always wanted to write amid the collage of ideas included in our earliest drafts. We also owe thanks to John Amburg, who guided us expertly through production; to Donna Dennison, who designed a cover we all admire; and to Maura Shea and John E. Sullivan. And of course, no Bedford acknowledgment would be complete without a deep bow of appreciation to Chuck Christensen and Joan Feinberg, who remain steadfast supporters of new approaches to the composition classroom. Lastly, we want to thank Elena Barcia, Roy Weitz, and Morris Mano, who were loving enough to stand by us while we spun this latest story together and forbearing enough to listen when we insisted on telling them what it was all about.

Introduction for Students

Why Storytelling?

Exposition: What a chilly, uninviting word. It's hard to get excited about studying something called exposition. For generations, composition teachers have labored to interest students in the intricacies of the expository essay, but all too often students have responded by concluding that exposition is what's left over when you squeeze all the life—and all the story—out of a piece of writing. There's a chance you've already bumped into this traditional composition classroom distinction. Narrative writing is portrayed as personal and down-to-earth; it focuses on people, actions, events and objects; and it typically follows a straightforward time sequence. Narrative writing assignments range from no-brainers like how you spent your summer vacation to imaginative challenges like creating your own science fiction adventure. In short, narrative writing involves storytelling. Expository writing, by contrast, is typically seen as impersonal, abstract, and conceptual—serious academic stuff like explaining the structure of DNA, interpreting the meaning of a novel, or analyzing the causes of the Spanish-American War. If you've survived writing assignments like these, you too may feel that narrative writing is fun and expository writing is hard work; that narrative taps your creativity while exposition requires rigor and discipline; that narrative belongs to you while while exposition is strictly for teachers.

In reality, though, the distinction between storytelling and expository writing is never this clear-cut. Stories and storytelling are central to the way that all people understand and interpret their experiences. People tell stories to make sense of the world and to explain their actions and ideas. If you try to suppress the storytelling instinct college writing is bound to become a mystifying, even an impossible, task. *Frame Work* is dedicated to the idea that storytelling forms the foundation of *all* writing, including the "serious" expository and analytical writing demanded in many college classrooms.

Of course, the idea of writing a bunch of stories might feel just as intimidating as the idea of writing abstract analytical essays. After all, what if you're not the creative, storytelling type? Where are you going to get all this inspiration from? Worries like these generally stem from the erroneous idea that storytelling involves a type of "creative" or expressive writing that "wells up" from deep within the writer's psyche. But *Frame Work* suggests a different way to think about stories. We all possess a wealth of cultural stories, stories that shape our ideas, values, and tastes—stories that we inherit from the many different cultures we participate in. In effect, we don't create stories so much as they create us. Our stories come *to* us: we hear them around kitchen tables, at holiday gatherings, on neighborhood streets, and on the job. The readings and the writing assignments you'll encounter in *Frame Work* encourage you to become critically aware of the way these cultural stories shape your own ideas, attitudes, and beliefs.

Cultural Frames and Quilting

For an example of what we mean by cultural stories, take another look at the quilt, created by Nancy Crow, that's pictured on the front cover of this book. Most people who've grown up in the United States already have some general knowledge about quilts. You might know, for instance, that in the past quilts were often made by groups of women working collaboratively during a quilting "bee." You might know that quilts were "pieced" from bits of old clothes and other fabric and that the patterns used in quilting were passed down from generation to generation. Equipped with this general knowledge framework or *story frame* for quilting, you'd probably have no trouble recognizing the pattern of colorful patches on our cover for what it is, and not assume that it's just an abstract pattern of random stripes. An even more detailed story frame would be possessed by someone who was part of the "culture" of quilting—someone who is an experienced quilter or a collector of quilts. An experienced quilter might recognize the work on our cover as a variation on the traditional "log cabin" pattern and might even wonder why its piecing is so "irregular" and "uneven." But to fully appreciate the significance of Nancy Crow's achievement, you've got to have other cultural story frames at your disposal. You have to recognize, for example, that her art is deliberately playful. Crow isn't interested in simply reproducing traditional quilting patterns and motifs; she's using — and breaking — quilting traditions to express a personal sense of movement, energy, and rhythm. In short, you're likely to understand Crow's work better if you're also familiar with improvisational art forms like jazz or modern painting. If you don't know the stories embedded in these contemporary artistic cultures, you might end up assuming that Crow just couldn't get her sewing to come out straight.

Since all perception is shaped by the cultural knowledge you bring to it, in-depth understanding almost always involves expanding that knowledge by crossing cultural boundaries. *Frame Work* invites you to hone your abilities as a cultural border crosser. Learning to operate in a new culture means learning the stories that it contains, and this kind of cultural awareness is particularly important when you're entering unfamiliar cultural territory. The intellectual culture of American higher education can be a distressing puzzle for many first-year students. Attitudes and expectations about your work, your behavior, your relation to authority — even about your language and the way you speak — can be disturbingly unclear. A major part of *Frame Work* is devoted to guiding you as you negotiate your way among the new customs and values you'll encounter in college. We'll explore what professors in the United States typically expect of themselves and of their students, and we'll contrast these expectations with alternative approaches to thinking and writing. By explicitly examining the story frames that dominate intellectual inquiry in the United States, we hope to take some of the mystery out of your entry into college, and we hope to help you become an effective and critically aware member of the culture of higher education.

Speaking of Pieces

Frame Work is divided into four major sections. The first part, "The Power of Stories," introduces the role that stories and storytelling play in shaping our ideas and identities. Here you'll begin exploring the interaction between stories, story frames, and the cultures they're associated with. The second section, "How Stories Shape Us," takes up the challenge of telling stories across cultural boundaries. In this section you'll consider the difference between story frames and stereotypes and you'll experiment with techniques for "listening" across cultural borders. "Framing Language," the book's third section, invites you to consider the many different "Englishes" you speak and to think seriously about how the cultures you participate in affect your development as a writer. The last section, "Framing Ideas: Analytic Storytelling," focuses exclusively on the role that storytelling plays in college-level academic analysis. Here you'll learn about the "official stories" that dominate our perceptions and interpretations. You'll also be invited to enter into the conversation of ideas that characterizes academic thinking by critically analyzing the work of established scholars.

Each major section of the book is further subdivided into four chapters. Within each section, the first chapter introduces key ideas and concepts necessary to understanding the section's central theme. The second chapter expands on these key ideas, typically with readings that offer alternative perspectives or that explore cultural complications. It's in these introductory chapters that you'll read about the role that story frames play in cross-cultural conflicts, about the relationship between story frames and stereotypes, or about culturally dominant "official stories" that channel thought and make it difficult to perceive alternative points of view. These introductory chapters also provide you with reading and study skills necessary for extended writing assignments—things like brainstorming techniques, note-taking strategies, hints for conducting successful interviews, and approaches to critical reading.

The third chapter of each section applies ideas introduced earlier to the culture of American higher education. In these chapters, titled "Academically Speaking," you'll have the chance to consider how teacher authority influences the way you tell and censor stories in school and how the stories told in college culture differ from those told in the home cultures you inhabit. You'll be invited to experiment with writing in different voices and styles for different audiences, and you'll have the opportunity to observe how academic writers use stories and storytelling to build their own theories and analyses.

The fourth and final chapter of each section is a "Revision Workshop" that introduces specific approaches for revising your major papers. These Revision Workshops will help you strengthen your essays by providing you with strategies for shaping effective paragraphs, introductions, and conclusions. They'll offer hints about how to select and use evidence and how to quote effectively. They'll guide you as you structure more complicated comparisons and shape your own academic analyses. They'll even invite you to take chances and break some of the so-called rules of composition. We've devoted a fourth of the book to these revision activities because we're convinced that writers learn best when they have the chance to rethink and rewrite their work. Revision Workshops also include many opportunities for collaborative learning because thinking and writing are often more productive when you work with others than when you struggle in isolation. Learning to appreciate the strengths and weaknesses in another person's paper is often the first step toward learning how to improve your own writing and thinking.

Opportunities for Writing

Frame Work offers you a variety of opportunities to try your own hand at storytelling and academic analysis. Each of the book's four sections contains two major "Essay Options." Typically, each Essay Option gives you the choice of several individual writing topics, each topic responding to one or more of the readings appearing earlier in the section. These Essay Options lie at the heart of *Frame Work*'s approach to writing. Think of them as a laboratory where you can experiment with the concepts and ideas you encounter in the text. As you work through these major assignments you'll be asked to write your own family stories, to interview people of different cultures, to compare the different speech communities you belong to, and to explore alternative ways of analyzing media images, personal conflicts, and historical events. Because they usually require more than a week to complete, we recommend that you plan on tackling only one Essay Option per section. However, you'll probably want to read through both options before you decide on the one that's right for you.

You'll also find ample opportunity for shorter, more informal excursions into writing in *Frame Work*. After every reading selection we've included a series of "Discussion Questions" that can be reviewed in small groups or answered in learning logs. These questions are meant to deepen your understanding of the readings and help you apply some of the concepts we'll be introducing. In addition, most reading selections in the book are followed by "Journal Options" that offer suggestions for productive entries in reading response journals. We've designed these Journal Options to help you prepare for the more ambitious Essay Options that follow. Often you'll find that we'll ask you to return to a journal topic as a starting point for brainstorming a more extensive essay. As with the Essay Options, we've included more Journal Options than you're likely to complete in a single term, so your class or your instructor may want to approach them selectively. There are also a number of "Optional Activities" throughout the book that can be used as the focus of collaborative group work or as points of departure for informal writing assignments.

Readings

One of the first things you'll notice about the readings in *Frame Work* is their diversity. As you browse through the book you'll find selections by writers representing a wide range of cultural and ethnic backgrounds. In the first section, for example, you'll read about a young Italian American teenager who decides to "go bad," about the meaning of storytelling in Laguna-Pueblo tribal culture, and about the role that stories play in the memories of a Mormon family's Christmas. You'll follow along as a four-year-old African American ventures into the icy atmosphere of a parochial school classroom; you'll hear how a Japanese American writer celebrates and shapes the stories told about his grandparents; and you'll learn about the meaning of *Las Mañanitas* in Mexican American culture. *Frame Work* includes a variety of perspectives not because it's politically correct or pedagogically fashionable, but because the notion of cultural story frames is central to our approach to college writing. Communicating is easy as long as you're talking to someone who knows all of your cultural stories; but venturing across cultural borders can become a serious intellectual and emotional challenge. The diverse reading selections we've included are meant to help you develop your own skills as a writer and cultural border crosser.

Frame Work also provides readings that feature a variety of different voices, styles, and purposes. As you might expect, the book's early chapters are dominated by personal stories that will probably strike you as relatively straightforward and easy to comprehend. But as you begin to explore the conventions of academic thinking and writing, you'll encounter more complicated analytic and interpretive readings. These more formal academic selections are likely to stretch your reading skills: you may not have trouble with a straightforward narrative, but an academic analysis of the impact of gender on biological theories of sexual reproduction may leave you breathless. To help you decipher these demanding academic texts, we've provided tips and techniques for active reading, note-taking, and the use of reading response journals. The discussion questions and journal options that follow the reading selections will help you to connect readings with your own experiences and to deepen your comprehension through collaborative learning activities. And, particularly in the "Academically Speaking" chapters, we've tried to explain, as explicitly as possible, the conventions that are often associated with academic thinking and writing in the United States.

Of course, not all academic writing is dull, dense, or deadeningly abstract. Although some scholarly prose deserves this reputation, academic writing at its best is smart, lively, and deeply engaged in issues that matter. *Frame Work* encourages you to see academic thinking as real "critical" thinking—thinking that's capable of making a difference and changing the world. That's why we've included readings that challenge the "official stories" told in academic disciplines such as anthropology, sociology, history, and biology; and it's also why we've tried to offer examples of solid scholarly writing that test the limits of academic discourse. We want you to see that effective writers, even those who work in the confines of academic culture, are always ready to challenge the expectations of their audience. We want you to move beyond the idea that there's a single "correct" model of academic writing, so that you can also "enter into the conversation" of competing stories and story frames that underlies academic discourse.

Finally, because about a half century of collective experience has taught us that nothing helps students more than clear examples of effective student writing, we've filled the "Revision Workshop" chapters with sample revisions of real student papers. In some cases, we've included multiple drafts of a whole essay so that you can see how a paper develops during the revision process. Elsewhere, we include selected passages, ranging from a paragraph to a page, as examples of how you might structure an introduction, shape an effective paragraph, or marshall evidence in support of an interpretation. These student-authored readings offer you live examples of how students have approached the "Essay Options" outlined in each of the book's four sections. But they are also meant to do more: the student writing featured in *Frame Work* gives you a first-hand view of someone like yourself, someone who is learning to adapt to, and even to challenge, the story frames of a new intellectual culture.

Contents

Chapter 2

Shaping Stories

Chapter 3

Academically Speaking: Writing for Teachers

Chapter 4   **Revision Workshop: Engaging the Reader**   **96**

PART TWO   *How Stories Shape Us*   *113*

Chapter 5   **Cultural Collisions**   **115**

Chapter 8   **Revision Workshop: Writing for Others**   **197**

Chapter 12   **Revision Workshop: Shaping Structure, Shaping Voice**   **290**

Index of Authors and Titles

PART ONE

The Power of Stories

Discovering Stories

Nine-thirty, Thursday night. Through the bedroom door Anita hears the fading laugh track of *Friends*. She thinks of her brother in the other room, then she tries to refocus her attention on the blank sheet of paper on her desk. The assignment is to write a character analysis of Celie in Alice Walker's *The Color Purple*, the novel she's been reading in her English class. For over a week she has pored over notes, reread chapters, and put off this moment. After dinner she forced herself away from her family to sit at her desk, writing out sentences as they occurred to her until she couldn't tell what she was saying or where her ideas were going.

After four or five false starts, she wanders into the kitchen to get a soda and call a friend.

"Hi, Jill. You working on the essay?"

"Yeah, but I'm getting nowhere. I don't know what she wants. Every time I start to write I end up retelling the story, and Ms. Moore already told us she doesn't want us to summarize the plot."

"Yeah, well I sure wish I knew what it was she wanted."

"I ran into Eddie yesterday. He just heard about that scholarship he was applying for. They're going out to celebrate tonight. Anyway, he said that all Moore wants is for you to focus on a single idea about Celie, you know, the 'thesis.' Just put it in the first paragraph and then support it in the next three. The last paragraph's the conclusion where you sum it all up."

"I know. That's what she said last week in class, but I just can't seem to make it all work. Must be brain-dead or something. So where was Eddie going to party?"

"I think they were heading down to the village. He's really lucky to get that scholarship. He can pick and choose where he wants to go from now on."

"Yeah, well, all I know is if I don't get this paper done, I'm going nowhere. Maybe if I outline it again, I'll figure out what to say. You know, I really hate this. I can never figure out what to do."

Anita returns to the empty pages on her desk. By the time she's ready to give up, she's pushed herself through five paragraphs that sound as if they were written by somebody else. A few days later the essay comes back, and although her teacher has explained in her comments that it is disorganized, unfocused, repetitive, and lacking a clear point of view, Anita finds herself wondering just what it is that Ms. Moore really wants.

This is a question that has troubled generations of college students. For many, academic writing is an exercise in frustration. Often it seems to boil down to a handful of rules and simple but sometimes contradictory formulas: put your main idea in the opening paragraph, don't give away all your ideas at once, put in lots of interesting details, don't ramble on, make your writing as personal as possible, never use "I." This litany of advice gets passed along from decade to decade, but the only result for many students is loss of sleep and a rapidly eroding sense of self-worth. Some, like Anita, try to follow all the rules only to discover that they still haven't "got it." Sometimes they feel that they could write better if only they had a bigger and more impressive vocabulary, or if they understood all the possible uses of the comma. They may not understand what academic writing is all about, but they've already accepted the notion that it must be made of rules. For these students, writing in school can become an alienating—even humiliating—experience, one that stands between them and their academic success.

Writing as Storytelling

Academic writing may strike many students as a kind of mystery simply because it is often made to seem mysterious. The rules, conventions, formulas, strategies, and techniques that clutter so many writing courses can transform academic writing into a foreign and forbidding activity. This mystification of academic writing starts from the moment that we set it apart from the way we communicate our thoughts and feelings a hundred times a day. From the moment we wake up each morning until the moment we go to sleep each night, we all engage in the oldest form of verbal communication: we all tell stories. When you answer a friend who asks you what you did last night, or explain why you were late for an appointment, you're weaving a story: out of all that you saw, felt, heard, tasted, smelled, did, and thought you're selecting certain facts and details, maybe exaggerating some of them slightly and omitting others, arranging them in a particular order to make a particular point for a particular purpose. That's basically what you do when you write an academic essay. Although you may not recognize it at first, good academic writing involves good storytelling, and storytelling is something all of us have been doing since we first learned to talk.

In fact, stories have been around since talking itself. Before there were novels or soap operas, even before the idea of writing came into being, people told stories. Much of what we now consider to be the world's greatest literature and philosophy—Homer's *Iliad* and *Odyssey,* great religious books like the Torah, the New Testament, the Qu'ran, and the Hindu Vedas—originated with stories told and retold through generations of storytellers and listeners. Every cultural group has its mythology—ancient stories that explain the birth of the cosmos, the creation of life, the diversity of nature, and the genesis of good and evil. Every nation has its heroes and legends—stories that offer models of behavior and moral strength. Stories are the way we make sense of our lives: by telling them we tell ourselves who we are, why we're here, how we came to be what we are, what we value most, and how we see the world.

Ten thousand years ago people passed knowledge from generation to generation through stories told around campfires. Today, although the medium may have changed, we still tell stories for many of the same purposes. We used a brief story to begin this chapter to illustrate the problems that students have with academic writing. Within that brief story Jill tells Anita another story about their mutual friend Eddie and how he recently won a scholarship. And that story leads to two more: one about Eddie's educational plans and another about his plans for celebrating. Stories grow out of stories, surrounding us in a web of storytelling that connects us to our friends, family, and culture. Every conversation we engage in every day, like Anita's conversation with Jill, is actually a network of interconnected stories: we tell stories in response to the stories we hear, and our listener tells us stories in return. We are so completely immersed in this constant process of story creation and storytelling that we scarcely notice it; it's automatic and unconscious.

Whether you know it or not, by the time you enter college you're already an expert storyteller. You bring with you a wealth of knowledge about what makes a story worth telling, how to shape an experience into story form, which stories are appropriate in which situations, and how to revise stories for different purposes and audiences. Unfortunately, many students also bring along a set of rigid expectations and assumptions about storytelling and academic writing. We tend to think of stories and storytelling either as child's play or as mindless entertainment: stories are the things you tell to kids to quiet them down or what you see on the soaps or at the movies. College is a place for more serious matters like thinking and learning. The irony, as we'll see in greater detail later on, is that stories are the way that humans learn best. Storytelling is the basic tool we use for making sense of our world.

OPTIONAL
ACTIVITIES

Exploring Stories

To begin exploring your own assumptions about stories and storytelling, try a few of the following activities. As you work through them let your imagination run wild—don't be hemmed in by any "rules" or conventions you may associate with "good" storytelling.

1. Working in small groups, choose characters and a basic situation for a story. Then have the group tell or write a story using these elements. You can share these with the class and discuss what features or qualities make one story seem more "storylike" than another. Which features seem to give a story its "storiness"?
2. Try your hand at collective storytelling. Working in small groups, build a story by having each group member contribute one line. Go around the group until the story seems complete, or until you reach an agreed upon number of contributions. When you're finished, share your group's collective story with the class and then discuss which group's story seems the most interesting. What makes it stand out from the rest?
3. Try to keep track of and summarize all the stories you tell or are told over the next twenty-four hours. Remember that the stories we hear every day are rarely told in formal situations; they may crop up during informal conversations, in class lectures, or in a phone call to a friend. During your next class, work in small groups and compare the stories you have collected with those of your classmates. Follow up by trying to reach a consensus about what exactly a "story" is.

Stories, Meaning, and Memory

The central importance of stories in human affairs is reflected in the role that storytelling plays in academic thinking. While the role of stories may seem obvious in a field like history, we are accustomed to think of science as just the opposite of storytelling: science is supposed to be based on observable fact; data, not stories, are the stuff of modern scientific inquiry. But nearly every field of contemporary scientific research is actively engaged in storytelling. Anthropologists collect and analyze the stories of tribal peoples to decipher the values and beliefs of their cultures. Psychologists piece together fragments of an individual's personal history from the stories reported in therapy sessions. Biologists try to make sense of the diversity of species by weaving the data of fossil remains into stories of evolution. Epidemiologists trace the story of the origin and history of disease. Astrophysicists seek to draw everything they know about the cosmos together into a story that will explain the nature of all matter and the beginning of the universe. Even computer scientists are fascinated with storytelling: some believe that stories offer a key to the way the mind works, the secret behind the way human brains store and use information.

Stories are essential to thinking because they help us to organize our knowledge of the world in a special way. When we tell a story, we do much more than convey the "facts." Instead of merely reporting information, we *shape* what we know; we select and manipulate the "facts" of our experience and use them to construct a framework that gives them meaning. Stories provide networks of actions, characters, events, ideas, feelings, and values; they weave relationships between all the individual "facts" of our experience, just as they build relationships between ourselves, our friends, and our families. And it is the network of interrelationships provided by the story that gives the facts of our lives meaning. Here's a classic illustration. Quickly read the following paragraph and then try to summarize as much of it as you can.

> With hocked gems financing him, our hero bravely defied all scornful laughter that tried to prevent his scheme. Your eyes deceive you, he had said, an egg not a table correctly typifies this unexplored planet. Now three sturdy sisters sought proof, forging along sometimes through calm vastness, yet more often over turbulent peaks and valleys. Days became weeks as many doubters spread fearful rumors about the edge. At last, from nowhere, welcome winged creatures appeared, signifying momentous success.[1]

If you had some trouble keeping the facts of this confusing little narrative straight, it's probably because you didn't recognize the story behind it. Try reading it again, this time with the following title as a hint: "1492." Once you know the story, the individual elements of the paragraph begin to make sense: the "hocked gems" become the jewels that, according to

[1] Dooling and Lachman, "Academic Learning and Retention," in *Introductory Psychology* (Lexington, Mass.: Morris K. Holland, 1981), p. 99.

legend, Queen Isabella sold to finance Columbus's voyage. The "three sturdy sisters" translate into the *Nina,* the *Pinta,* and the *Santa Maria,* the three ships of Columbus's expedition. All of the passage's obscure images and ideas snap into clear focus once we understand the story.

The brain, like a good detective, is constantly trying to weave stories out of the clues of our experience. Unless they find their way into a story, the facts of our lives—the isolated events that happen to us and the individual people we meet—fade and are forgotten. Try, for a moment, to remember what you were doing a year ago today. Or what you had for dinner just a week ago. Chances are you can't, unless you were doing—or eating—something particularly interesting or unusual. The mind doesn't bother filing away commonplace events or insignificant encounters. We tend to remember only the things and people that strike us as important or unusual—the ones that fall outside or disrupt the daily flow of our experience. You may not recall what you were doing on a given day a few weeks ago, but you probably remember quite vividly the first day you ever held a job or the first time you went on a date. It's the firsts, the exceptions, and the anomalies that catch our attention—the things that don't fit the patterns of our expectations. When we're surprised or caught off guard or even just interested in something that happens or someone we meet, we start to weave a story around them; we transform the raw "event" into an "experience" and begin to make sense of it by telling and retelling it to friends, family—even to ourselves in our memories and dreams.

The mind engages in this process of pattern-making and storytelling because we have to learn from our experiences. Imagine how difficult life would be if you always felt as disoriented and awkward as you may have on that first date or first day of work. Fortunately, we do learn lessons about what to expect and what to do in these and other new situations. Our minds are full of such lessons—stories that explain why something happened or why someone did or said what they did in a particular situation. That's why some of the best personal stories have to do with critical decisions and life choices: we all have done things that we need to understand and that need to be explained to others. Telling the story of these critical turning points is how we give them meaning and how we come to understand our own motives and desires.

The following selection, "Trouble," by Beverly Donofrio, offers a case in point. Taken from Donofrio's autobiography *Riding in Cars with Boys* (1990), this excerpt describes an important turning point in the author's adolescence, the moment she decided to become a "bad girl." A high school dropout, Donofrio became a mother at seventeen, married her high school boyfriend, and divorced him a few years later, when he couldn't kick his addiction to drugs. Living on welfare payments, she returned to school at a community college and eventually graduated with her B.A. from Wesleyan University. She went on to earn an M.A. from Columbia University and to write for popular magazines like *Rolling Stone, Cosmopolitan,* and *Sports Illustrated.* Donofrio (b. 1950) lives and continues to write in Orient, New York.

Before Reading

Spend a few minutes thinking about the title: What kinds of "trouble" do most kids get into during their teens? What typically leads them into trouble? Can you think of any turning points you've experienced in your own life?

Trouble
Beverly Donofrio

Trouble began in 1963. I'm not blaming it on President Kennedy's assassination or its being the beginning of the sixties or the Vietnam War or the Beatles or the make-out parties in the fallout shelters all over my hometown of Wallingford, Connecticut, or my standing in line with the entire population of Dag Hammarskjold Junior High School and screaming when a plane flew overhead because we thought it was the Russians. These were not easy times, it's true. But it's too convenient to pin the trouble that would set me on the path of most resistance on the times.

The trouble I'm talking about was my first real trouble, the age-old trouble. The getting in trouble as in "Is she in Trouble?" trouble. As in pregnant. As in the girl who got pregnant in high school. In the end that sentence for promiscuous behavior, that penance (to get Catholic here for a minute, which I had the fortune or misfortune of being, depending on the way you look at it) — that kid of mine, to be exact — would turn out to be a blessing instead of a curse. But I had no way of knowing it at the time and, besides, I'm getting ahead of myself.

By 1963, the fall of the eighth grade, I was ready. I was hot to trot. My hair was teased to basketball dimensions, my 16 oz. can of Miss Clairol hairspray was tucked into my shoulder bag. Dominic Mezzi whistled between his teeth every time I passed him in the hallway, and the girls from the project — the ones with boys' initials scraped into their forearms, then colored with black ink — smiled and said hi when they saw me. I wore a padded bra that lifted my tits to inches below my chin, and my father communicated to me only through my mother. "Mom," I said. "Can I go to the dance at the Y on Friday?"

"It's all right with me, but you know your father."

Yes, I knew my father. Mr. Veto, the Italian cop, who never talked and said every birthday, "So, how old're you anyway? What grade you in this year?" It was supposed to be a joke, but who could tell if he really knew or was just covering? I mean, the guy stopped looking at me at the first appearance of my breasts, way back in the fifth grade.

In the seventh grade, I began to suspect he was spying on me, when I had my run-in with Danny Dempsey at Wilkinson's Theater. Danny Dempsey was a high school dropout and a hood notorious in town for fighting. I was waiting in the back of the seats after the lights dimmed for my best friend, Donna Wilhousky, to come back with some candy when this Danny Dempsey sidled up to me and leaned his shoulder into mine. Then he reached in his pocket and pulled out a knife, which he laid in the palm of his hand, giving it a little tilt so it glinted in the screen light. I pressed my back against the wall as far away from the knife as I could, and got goosebumps. Then Donna showed up with a pack of Banana Splits and Mint Juleps, and Danny Dempsey backed away. For weeks, every time the phone rang I prayed it was Danny Dempsey. That was about the time my father started acting suspicious whenever I set foot out of his house. He was probably just smelling the perfume of budding sexuality on me and was acting territorial, like a dog. Either that or maybe his buddy Skip Plotkin, the official cop of Wilkinson's Theater, had filed a report on me.

Which wasn't a bad idea when I think of it, because I was what you call boy crazy. It probably started with Pat Boone when I was four years old. I went to see him in the movie where he sang "Bernadine" with his white bucks thumping and his fingers snapping, and I was in love. From that day on whenever "Bernadine" came on the radio, I swooned, spun around a couple of times, then dropped in a faked-dead faint. I guess my mother thought this was cute because she went out and bought me the forty-five. Then every day after kindergarten, I ran straight to the record player for my dose, rocked my head back and forth, snapped my fingers like Pat Boone, then when I couldn't stand it another second, I swooned, spun around, and dropped in a faked-dead faint.

I was never the type of little girl who hated boys. Never. Well, except for my brother. I was just the oldest of three girls, while he was the Oldest, plus the only boy in an Italian family, and you know what that means: golden penis. My father sat at one end of the table and my brother sat at the other, while my mother sat on the sidelines with us girls. You could say

I resented him a little. I had one advantage though — the ironclad rule. My brother, because he was a boy, was not allowed to lay one finger on us girls. So when his favorite show came on the TV, I stood in front of it. And when he said, "Move," I said, "Make me," which he couldn't.

But other boys could chase me around the yard for hours dangling earthworms from their fingers, or call me Blackie at the bus stop when my skin was tanned dirt-brown after the summer, or forbid me to set foot in their tent or play in their soft-, kick-, or dodgeball games. They could chase me away when I tried to follow them into the woods, their bows slung over their shoulders and their hatchets tucked into their belts. And I still liked them, which is not to say I didn't get back at them. The summer they all decided to ban girls, meaning me and Donna, from their nightly softball games in the field behind our houses, Donna and I posted signs on telephone poles announcing the time of the inoculations they must receive to qualify for teams. On the appointed day they stood in line at Donna's cellar door. Short ones, tall ones, skinny and fat, they waited their turn, then never even winced when we pricked their skin with a needle fashioned from a pen and a pin.

By the summer of 1963, my boy craziness had reached such a pitch 10 that I was prepared to sacrifice the entire summer to catch a glimpse of Denny Winters, the love of my and Donna's life. Donna and I walked two miles to his house every day, then sat under a big oak tree across the street, our transistor radio between us, and stared at his house, waiting for some movement, a sign of life, a blind pulled up or down, a curtain shunted aside, a door opening, a dog barking. Anything. Denny's sister, who was older and drove a car, sometimes drove off and sometimes returned. But that was it. In an entire summer of vigilance, we never saw Denny Winters arrive or depart. Maybe he had mononucleosis; maybe he was away at camp. We never saw him mow the lawn or throw a ball against the house for practice.

What we did see was a lot of teenage boys sitting low in cars, cruising by. Once in a while, a carload would whistle, flick a cigarette into the gutter at our feet, and sing, "Hello, girls." Whenever they did that, Donna and I stuck our chins in the air and turned our heads away. "Stuck up" they hollered.

But we knew the cars to watch for: the blue-and-white Chevy with the blond boy driving, the forest-green Pontiac with the dark boy, the white Rambler, the powder-blue Camaro, the yellow Falcon. I decided that when I finally rode in a car with a boy, I wouldn't sit right next to him like I was stuck with glue to his armpit. I'd sit halfway there — just to the right of the radio, maybe.

My father, however, had other ideas. My father forbade me to ride in cars with boys until I turned sixteen. That was the beginning.

"I hate him," I cried to my mother when my father was out of the house.

"Well, he thinks he's doing what's best for you," she said.   15

"What? Keeping me prisoner?"

"You know your father. He's suspicious. He's afraid you'll get in trouble."

"What kind of trouble?"

"You'll ruin your reputation. You're too young. Boys think they can take advantage. Remember what I told you. If a boy gets fresh, just cross your legs."

It was too embarrassing. I changed the subject. "I hate him," I repeated.   20

By the time I turned fourteen, the next year, I was speeding around Wallingford in crowded cars with guys who took corners on two wheels, flew over bumps, and skidded down the road to get me screaming. Whenever I saw a cop car, I lay down on the seat, out of sight.

While I was still at Dag Hammarskjold Junior High School, I got felt up in the backseat of a car, not because I wanted to exactly, but because I was only fourteen and thought that when everybody else was talking about making out, it meant they got felt up. That was the fault of two girls from the project, Penny Calhoun and Donna DiBase, who were always talking about their periods in front of boys by saying their *friend* was staying over for a week and how their *friend* was a *bloody mess*. They told me that making out had three steps: kissing, getting felt up, and then Doing It. Next thing I knew, I was at the Church of the Resurrection bazaar and this cute little guy with a Beatles haircut sauntered up and said, "I've got a sore throat. Want to go for a ride to get some cough drops?" I hesitated. I didn't even know his name, but then the two girls I was with, both sophomores in high school, said, "Go! Are you crazy? That's Skylar Barrister, the president of the sophomore class." We ended up with two other couples parked by the dump. My face was drooly with saliva (step one) when "A Hard Day's Night" came on the radio and Sky placed a hand on one of my breasts (step two). Someone must've switched the station, because "A Hard Day's Night" was on again when his hand started moving up the inside of my thigh. I crossed my legs like my mother said, but he uncrossed them. Lucky for me, there was another couple in the backseat and Sky Barrister was either too afraid or had good enough manners not to involve them in the loss of my virginity or I really would've been labeled a slut. Not that my reputation wasn't ruined anyway, because sweetheart Sky broadcast the news that Beverly Donofrio's easy—first to his friends at the country club and then, exponentially, to the entire town. Hordes of boys called me up after that. My father was beside himself. I was grounded. I couldn't talk on the phone for more than a minute. My mother tried to intervene. "Sonny," she said. "You have to trust her."

"I know what goes on with these kids. I see it every day, and you're going to tell me?"

"What's talking on the phone going to hurt?" my mother asked.

"You heard what I said. I don't want to hear another word about it. You 25 finish your phone call in a minute, miss, or I hang it up on you. You hear me?"

I heard him loud and clear, and it was okay with me—for a while, anyway, because my love of boys had turned sour. Sophomore year in high school, my English class was across the hall from Sky Barrister's and every time I walked by, there was a disturbance—a chitter, a laugh—coming from the guys he stood with. My brother was the captain of the football team and I wished he was the type who'd slam Sky Barrister against a locker, maybe knock a couple of his teeth out, but not my brother. My brother was the type who got a good-citizenship medal for never missing a single day of high school.

Meanwhile, his sister began to manifest definite signs of being a bad girl. My friends and I prided ourselves on our foul mouths and our stunts, like sitting across from the jocks' table in the cafeteria and giving the guys crotch shots, then when they started elbowing each other and gawking, we shot them the finger and slammed our knees together. Or we collected gingerbread from lunch trays and molded them into shapes like turds and distributed them in water fountains.

The thing was, we were sick to death of boys having all the fun, so we started acting like them: We got drunk in the parking lot before school dances and rode real low in cars, elbows stuck out windows, tossing beer cans, flicking butts, and occasionally pulling down our pants and shaking our fannies at passing vehicles.

But even though we were very busy showing the world that girls could have fun if only they'd stop acting nice, eventually it troubled us all that the type of boys we liked—collegiate, popular, seniors—wouldn't touch us with a ten-foot pole.

One time I asked a guy in the Key Club why no guys liked me. "Am I 30 ugly or stupid or something?"

"No." He scratched under his chin. "It's probably the things you say."

"What things?"

"I don't know."

"You think it's because I don't put out?"

"See? You shouldn't say things like that to a guy."   35

"Why?"

"It's not right."

"But why?"

"I don't know."

"Come on, is it because it's not polite or because it's about sex or be-   40
cause it embarrasses you? Tell me."

"You ask too many questions. You analyze too much, that's your problem."

To say that I analyzed too much is not to say I did well in school. Good
grades, done homework—any effort abruptly ended in the tenth grade,
when my mother laid the bad news on me that I would not be going to college. It was a Thursday night. I was doing the dishes, my father was sitting
at the table doing a paint-by-numbers, and we were humming "Theme
from Exodus" together. My mother was wiping the stove before she left for
work at Bradlees, and for some reason she was stinked—maybe she had her
period, or maybe it was because my father and I always hummed while I did
the dishes and she was jealous. Neither of us acknowledged that we were
basically harmonizing. It was more like it was just an accident that we were
humming the same song. Our favorites were "'Bye 'Bye Blackbird," "Sentimental Journey," "Tonight," and "Exodus." After "Exodus," I said, "Hey,
Ma. I was thinking I want to go to U Conn instead of Southern or Central.
It's harder to get into, but it's a better school."

"And who's going to pay for it?"

It's odd that I never thought about the money, especially since my parents were borderline paupers and being poor was my mother's favorite
topic. I just figured, naively, that anybody who was smart enough could go
to college.

"I don't know. Aren't there loans or something?"   45

"Your father and I have enough bills. You better stop dreaming. Take
typing. Get a *good* job when you graduate."

"I'm not going to be a secretary."

She lifted a burner and swiped under it. "We'll see," she said.

"I'm moving to New York."

"Keep dreaming." She dropped the burner back down.   50

So I gritted my teeth and figured I'd have to skip college and go straight
to Broadway, but it pissed me off. Because I wasn't simply a great actress, I
was smart too. I'd known this since the seventh grade, when I decided my
family was made up of a bunch of morons with lousy taste in television. I
exiled myself into the basement recreation room every night to get away
from them. There were these hairy spiders down there, and I discovered if I

dropped a Book of Knowledge on them they'd fist up into dots, dead as doornails. Then one night after a spider massacre, I opened a book up and discovered William Shakespeare—his quality-of-mercy soliloquy, to be exact. Soon I'd read everything in the books by him, and then by Whitman and Tennyson and Shelley. I memorized Hamlet's soliloquy and said it to the mirror behind the bar. To do this in the seventh grade made me think I was a genius. And now, to be told by my mother, who'd never read a book in her life, that I couldn't go to college was worse than infuriating, it was unjust. Somebody would have to pay.

That weekend my friends and I went around throwing eggs at passing cars. We drove through Choate, the ritzy prep school in the middle of town, and I had an inspiration. "Stop the car," I said. "Excuse me," I said to a little sports-jacketed Choatie crossing Christian Street. "Do you know where Christian Street is?"

"I'm not sure," he said, "but I think it's that street over there." He pointed to the next road over.

"You're standing on it, asshole!" I yelled, flinging an egg at the name tag on his jacket. I got a glimpse of his face as he watched the egg drool down his chest and I'll remember the look of disbelief as it changed to sadness till the day I die. We peeled out, my friends hooting and hollering and slapping me on the back.

Issues for Discussion

1. What did being a "bad girl" mean to the adolescent Donofrio? How has the idea of what it means to be a "bad girl" changed since the 1960s, when Donofrio was growing up? Why has it changed?
2. What different motives led Donofrio to her decision to break the rules? How else might she have coped with her situation? What advice would you have given her at this stage in her life? Why?

Active Reading: Keeping a Reading Journal

When someone tells you a story, it's natural to respond by telling a similar story of your own. A friend may tell you how close he came to having an accident on the way to school because he was so worried about the math test you're both facing in the afternoon. You'd probably respond by telling him a story about a close call you once had or a story that reflects your concern about the test. We signal our understanding of the stories we hear by sharing similar stories of our own. When you read Anita's story at the beginning of this chapter, you may have recognized yourself or someone you know in her struggle with Ms. Moore's academic writing assignment. If you were asked to express your understanding of Anita's predicament, you'd probably share that experience by telling your story. Of course, there's always the chance that you've never experienced any trouble at all with academic writing and never known anyone who did. In that case you might not be able to grasp Anita's problem; you wouldn't understand her feelings and her predicament. We understand other people's stories when we are reminded of similar stories of our own, and we demonstrate our understanding by sharing these stories with them. We call this congenial give-and-take of stories a conversation.

One way to become a better reader is to become a better conversationalist. Most people assume that reading is a passive process, a matter of simply decoding the words on the page. Sure, they may take the time to "go over" every line—they might even use a marker to highlight passages—but when they're done they have difficulty recalling and comprehending the material they've read. Successful readers, by contrast, read actively. They approach each reading as if it were a partner in a good conversation, not like a sack of potatoes about to be peeled. Active readers enter a relationship with the text; they respond to it, they don't simply process it. As they read they actively work to discover connections between their own experiences and the ideas, events, characters, and situations they encounter in the reading. Above all, active readers are good listeners. Like expert conversationalists, they have learned the value of empathetic listening. They listen carefully to the ideas and details in the text, but they also listen for the ideas, experiences, feelings, and reactions that rise up within themselves in response to it. Perhaps this is why so many students haven't developed the knack of reading actively: they spend so much energy trying to solve the riddle of the text that they forget to listen carefully to their own responses.

One of the best ways to practice active reading is to keep a reading journal. All it takes is a notebook, and almost any kind will do. A reading journal gives you a place to converse with your reading on a regular basis, a place where you can practice listening to all the voices within you—all the ideas, memories, and feelings—that make up your reactions. Every time you finish a reading, take a few minutes to explore your response. Here are a few techniques you may want to experiment with in your journal:

- Tell a story or a series of stories that connect your personal experience with the reading.

- Write an entry in which you explore and explain a particularly strong personal reaction.

- When words fail you, try drawing a picture or a cartoon of your response. (Some students find that drawing helps them discover complex intellectual reactions; when they try to explain their drawings, they put feelings and ideas into words that they hadn't originally recognized as their own.)

- Generate a list of questions that hit you as you read, and then try to imagine how the author would answer them.

- Write an imaginary conversation between yourself and the author.

- Write a letter to the author, and then imagine her reply.

- Create a collage of images that expresses your reaction.

- Write a skit, a poem, or a song.

There are no rules for keeping a reading journal. No one can give you a method or a series of steps that will help you "listen" to your own responses. Be outrageous and personal. Experiment with any form of expression that helps you connect with the reading.

Even if your teacher occasionally collects and reads it, try to remember that your journal is primarily meant for you. The surest way to stifle your own personal response to a reading is to imagine that you're performing for a clench-jawed English teacher who's about to redline every grammar and spelling error. Don't aim at producing perfect mini-essays or neat summaries of your reading. Your journal should be as free, as informal, and as full of personal response as possible. Think of your journal as a place to experiment, to do whatever it takes to jog your memory and make personal connections with your reading. It's even good to let your mind wander: some of the most creative thinking happens when you sit back, relax, and just let your mind roam from association to association—just as long as you get in the habit of always bringing your musings back to link up in some way with the reading at hand.

JOURNAL OPTIONS

Responding to "Trouble"

This is a good time to use your reading journal to respond to Beverly Donofrio's "Trouble." You may want to try one or more of the options offered below.

1. Write a letter to Beverly Donofrio in which you express your personal reaction to the story she tells in "Trouble." If you felt sympathy for her situation—or rage or disgust or pity—try to put it into words. Let her know how you feel about her decision to go "bad." Do you empathize with her

story—and perhaps even recognize some of your own experiences in hers? Or do you think she's just being immature?

2. Write the story of a boy or girl you knew during your adolescence who, like Donofrio, decided to go "bad." What did they do? What happened to them? What was their situation like? To what extent did it resemble Donofrio's? What do you think motivated them to do the things they did?

3. Write the story of what will happen to Donofrio from this point on in her life. Where will she be and what will she be doing at eighteen? At twenty-eight? What will happen to her? Compare these with versions written by other members of your class.

Cultural Stories: Story Frames and Scripts

One reason stories like Beverly Donofrio's account of her adolescent troubles are interesting and effective is that they convey experiences that many people can understand: they contain characters, events, ideas, or situations that are easily recognized. It's possible—perhaps even likely—that you never self-consciously decided to be "bad" in the same way as Donofrio, but that doesn't stop you from appreciating her story or comprehending her motives. Even if you were blessed with the kindest, most sympathetic parents and grew up in a home that provided all the opportunities you could want, you still might find it easy to grasp the gist of Donofrio's story—its general meaning or significance—because it resembles a type of story line that is common in Western culture: the story of a headstrong individual who rebels against oppressive authority. It's a story at least as old as the Declaration of Independence and the Boston Tea Party and one that is enacted again and again in a society that places a high value on individualism and independence: it appears in classic American novels like Mark Twain's *The Adventures of Huckleberry Finn* and Toni Morrison's *Sula,* on television shows like *Roseanne* and *The Simpsons,* and in innumerable Hollywood films featuring loner/rebel/heroes, ranging from *Shane* to the latest cop/spy action-adventure extravaganza.

The story of the young rebel is such a staple of Western culture that most Americans easily recognize its basic elements: the protagonist is a misunderstood misfit—someone who is out of step with the powers that be— police, government, or family. Often she is talented in a way that makes her stand out or that reveals to her the pettiness or the poverty of her surroundings. Unlike the others around her, she wants more out of life or is aware of a higher meaning or purpose. She instigates conflict, but she typically does so to resist the authorities or the injustices she encounters—never purely for the sake of violence or for personal gain. Although she makes mistakes and occasionally goes too far, her special abilities and independence lead her to success.

Common cultural stories like this are often referred to as story frames, story schemata, or scripts. Every one of us has mastered a huge inventory of these story frames, literally thousands of basic story outlines that organize our knowledge of the world and help us negotiate our way through it. When you go out to eat, you take along a set of well-defined expectations about the people you will meet, the events that will occur, and the role you will be expected to play. Most adults, for example, have a set of mental scripts for getting service in a restaurant: we adopt certain roles and behaviors depending on whether we're ordering fast food at a takeout window, waiting in the foyer of a formal four-star restaurant, or just dropping by the local family-run spaghetti house. These expectations are part of our restaurant story frames—the scripts that tell us how to act and what to expect from others in the "story" of eating out. Each situation demands a certain level of formality, a certain style and vocabulary—even a particular set of "lines" and actions. Moreover, we expect the other players in each of these story frames to live up to their part of the bargain: we expect them to play out their roles in a way that fulfills our expectations. You might get a warm hug from Mario every time you walk into Luigi's, but the same warm hug might be disconcerting coming from the cashier at McDonald's or the tuxedoed headwaiter at Chez Hélène. And you'd probably be just as uncomfortable if your professor strolled into class one day in a dirty T-shirt and cutoffs and started asking probing questions about what you'd done over the weekend. Story frames are important because they tell us what to expect from others and what others expect from us. Without them the world wouldn't make sense.

But not all story frames are as simple and situation-specific as the scripts that tell us how to order lunch. We all have story frames that apply to more personal and more meaningful situations and relationships. From the stories we hear as children and the lessons we learn in school—at the blackboard and on the playing field; from the anecdotes we're told by family members and the "stories" we see enacted again and again by parents, siblings, and friends; from the TV shows we watch, the books we read, and all the other sources of information at our disposal we gather story frames that tell us tales about who we are. These larger story frames tell us about what it means to be a child, how children are expected to relate to parents and caretakers, and how guardians should treat their children. As we grow and mature, we absorb scripts that tell us what to expect from and how to act around the authorities in our environment—teachers, police, and other representatives of institutionalized power. We learn the roles that men and women are expected to play and what it means to be a brother, a sister, a son, a daughter, a husband, a wife, a lover. We even learn, as Donofrio did, what it means to be a "bad girl" and how that differs from being a "bad boy." Such story frames do more than help us predict the behavior of others in a limited situation: they tell us who we are and who we are expected to become. They provide us with roles we struggle with as we define our personalities and shape our identities.

Seen in this way, story frames represent a pact that each of us unconsciously enters into with the cultures we grow up in, a pact that allows us to live in what seems to be a relatively comprehensible and meaningful world, but only by specifying, to a certain extent, the roles we must play in it. Every culture elaborates its own variations on story frames about mothering, fathering, masculinity, femininity, and all of the other critical social roles that human beings assume. In some contemporary American cultures, for example, the story frame for fathering might include assisting at a birthing class, helping in the delivery, changing diapers, helping with night feedings, helping with homework, and even cooking a couple of nights a week. In more traditional cultures it's possible that men would not welcome or be welcomed in many of these roles. Neither approach is intrinsically right or wrong, better or worse: they simply reflect differences in expectation.

Culture, then, is the master storyteller: our cultural heritage affects the way we tell our own stories and the way we understand and respond to the stories we hear. To become part of a culture means mastering the stories and story frames that define it. Unless you are able to adopt a culture's essential stories and scripts as your own, your actions and attitudes will always mark you as an outsider. This is the daunting task facing every child at birth: growing up means more than maturing biologically; it means learning the stories and story frames of all the cultures you participate in. Perhaps this is why children have such a natural affinity for stories and storytelling. They have a deep, perhaps even inborn, craving to hear stories—whether they're told by parents, siblings, teachers, or television.

In the next reading, Leslie Marmon Silko discusses the importance of cultural stories—stories that she remembers hearing as a child growing up on a Pueblo Indian reservation. As Silko points out in this essay, originally delivered as an address to the English Institute at Johns Hopkins University, storytelling in a tribal setting serves a multitude of important purposes. Born in Albuquerque, New Mexico, in 1948, Leslie Marmon Silko grew up in a family that traces its roots to Mexican, Anglo-American, and Laguna Pueblo Indian cultures. The winner of a MacArthur Foundation "genius" grant, she is best known for stories, novels, and poems that focus on conflicts between tribal peoples and dominant American culture. Her most recent publication, *Almanac of the Dead* (1992), is a massive novel that weaves the history of an American Indian family with the past, present, and future history of the North American continent. Silko currently lives in Tucson, Arizona.

Before Reading

Think of one or two stories you heard growing up that you might classify as "cultural stories." What were they about? What did you learn from them?

Language and Literature from a Pueblo Indian Perspective
Leslie Marmon Silko

Where I come from, the words that are most highly valued are those which are spoken from the heart, unpremeditated and unrehearsed. Among the Pueblo people, a written speech or statement is highly suspect because the true feelings of the speaker remain hidden as he reads words that are detached from the occasion and the audience. I have intentionally not written a formal paper to read to this session because of this and because I want you to hear and to experience English in a nontraditional structure, a structure that follows patterns from the oral tradition. For those of you accustomed to a structure that moves from point A to point B to point C, this presentation may be somewhat difficult to follow because the structure of Pueblo expression resembles something like a spider's web—with many little threads radiating from a center, criss-crossing each other. As with the web, the structure will emerge as it is made and you must simply listen and trust, as the Pueblo people do, that meaning will be made.

I suppose the task that I have today is a formidable one because basically I come here to ask you, at least for a while, to set aside a number of basic approaches that you have been using and probably will continue to use in approaching the study of English or the study of language; first of all,

This "essay" is an edited transcript of an oral presentation. The "author" deliberately did not read from a prepared paper so that the audience could experience firsthand one dimension of the oral tradition—non-linear structure. Her remarks were intended to be heard, not read.

I come to ask you to see language from the Pueblo perspective, which is a perspective that is very much concerned with including the whole of creation and the whole of history and time. And so we very seldom talk about breaking language down into words. As I will continue to relate to you, even the use of a specific language is less important than the one thing—which is the "telling," or the storytelling. And so, as Simon Ortiz has written, if you approach a Pueblo person and want to talk words or, worse than that, to break down an individual word into its components, ofttimes you will just get a blank stare, because we don't think of words as being isolated from the speaker, which, of course, is one element of the oral tradition. Moreover, we don't think of words as being alone: words are always with other words, and the other words are almost always in a story of some sort.

Today I have brought a number of examples of stories in English because I would like to get around to the question that has been raised, or the topic that has come along here, which is what changes we Pueblo writers might make with English as a language for literature. But at the same time I would like to explain the importance of storytelling and how it relates to a Pueblo theory of language.

So first I would like to go back to the Pueblo Creation story. The reason I go back to that story is because it is an all-inclusive story of creation and how life began. Tséitsínako, Thought Woman, by thinking of her sisters, and together with her sisters, thought of everything which is, and this world was created. And the belief was that everything in this world was a part of the original creation, and that the people at home realized that far away there were others—other human beings. There is even a section of the story which is a prophesy—which describes the origin of the European race, the African, and also remembers the Asian origins.

Starting out with this story, with this attitude which includes all things,   5
I would like to point out that the reason the people are more concerned with story and communication and less with a particular language is in part an outgrowth of the area [pointing to a map] where we find ourselves. Among the twenty Pueblos there are at least six distinct languages, and possibly seven. Some of the linguists argue—and I don't set myself up to be a linguist at all—about the number of distinct languages. But certainly Zuni is all alone, and Hopi is all alone, and from mesa to mesa there are subtle differences in language—very great differences. I think that this might be the reason that what particular language was being used wasn't as important as what a speaker was trying to say. And this, I think, is reflected and stems or grows out of a particular view of the story—that is, that language *is* story. At Laguna many words have stories which make them. So when one is telling a story, and one is using words to tell the story, each word

that one is speaking has a story of its own too. Often the speakers or tellers go into the stories of the words they are using to tell one story so that you get stories within stories, so to speak. This structure becomes very apparent in the storytelling, and what I would like to show you later on by reading some pieces that I brought is that this structure also informs the writing and the stories which are currently coming from Pueblo people. I think what is essential is this sense of story, and story within story, and the idea that one story is only the beginning of many stories, and the sense that stories never truly end. I would like to propose that these views of structure and the dynamics of storytelling are some of the contributions which Native American cultures bring to the English language or at least to literature in the English language.

First of all, a lot of people think of storytelling as something that is done at bedtime—that it is something that is done for small children. When I use the term storytelling, I include a far wider range of telling activity. I also do not limit storytelling to simply old stories, but to again go back to the original view of creation, which sees that it is all part of a whole; we do not differentiate or fragment stories and experiences. In the beginning, Tséitsínako, Thought Woman, thought of all these things, and all of these things are held together as one holds many things together in a single thought.

So in the telling (and today you will hear a few of the dimensions of this telling) first of all, as was pointed out earlier, the storytelling always includes the audience and the listeners, and, in fact, a great deal of the story is believed to be inside the listener, and the storyteller's role is to draw the story out of the listeners. This kind of shared experience grows out of a strong community base. The storytelling goes on and continues from generation to generation.

The Origin story functions basically as a maker of our identity—with the story we know who we are. We are the Lagunas. This is where we came from. We came this way. We came by this place. And so from the time you are very young, you hear these stories, so that when you go out into the wider world, when one asks who you are, or where are you from, you immediately know: we are the people who came down from the north. We are the people of these stories. It continues down into clans so that you are not just talking about Laguna Pueblo people, you are talking about your own clan. Within the clans there are stories which identify the clan.

In the Creation story, Antelope says that he will help knock a hole in the earth so that the people can come up, out into the next world. Antelope tries and tries, and he uses his hooves and is unable to break through; and it is then that Badger says, "Let me help you." And Badger very patiently uses his claws and digs a way through, bringing the people into the world. When the Badger clan people think of themselves, or when the Antelope people think of themselves, it is as people who are of *this* story, and this is *our* place, and we fit into the very beginning when the people first came, before we began our journey south.

So you can move, then, from the idea of one's identity as a tribal person into clan identity. Then we begin to get to the extended family, and this is where we begin to get a kind of story coming into play which some people might see as a different kind of story, though Pueblo people do not. Anthropologists and ethnologists have, for a long time, differentiated the types of oral language they find in the Pueblos. They tended to rule out all but the old and sacred and traditional stories and were not interested in family stories and the family's account of itself. But these family stories are just as important as the other stories—the older stories. These family stories are given equal recognition. There is no definite, pre-set pattern for the way one will hear the stories of one's own family, but it is a very critical part of one's childhood, and it continues on throughout one's life. You will hear stories of importance to the family—sometimes wonderful stories—stories about the time a maternal uncle got the biggest deer that was ever seen and brought back from the mountains. And so one's sense of who the family is, and who you are, will then extend from that—"I am from the family of my uncle who brought in this wonderful deer, and it was a wonderful hunt"—so you have this sort of building or sense of identity.

There are also other stories, stories about the time when another uncle, perhaps, did something that wasn't really acceptable. In other words, this process of keeping track, of telling, is an all-inclusive process which begins to create a total picture. So it is very important that you know all of the stories—both positive and not so positive—about one's own family. The reason that it is very important to keep track of all the stories in one's own family is because you are liable to hear a story from somebody else who is perhaps an enemy of the family, and you are liable to hear a version which has been changed, a version which makes your family sound disreputable—something that will taint the honor of the family. But if you have already heard the story, you know your family's version of what *really* happened that night, so when somebody else is mentioning it, you will have a version of the story to counterbalance it. Even when there is no way around it—old Uncle Pete did a terrible thing—by knowing the stories that come out of other families, by keeping very close watch, listening constantly to learn the stories about other families, one is in a sense able to deal with terrible sorts of things that might happen within one's own family. When a member of one's own family does something that cannot be excused, one always

10

knows stories about similar things which happened in other families. And it is not done maliciously. I think it is very important to realize this. Keeping track of all the stories within the community gives a certain distance, a useful perspective which brings incidents down to a level we can deal with. If others have done it before, it cannot be so terrible. If others have endured, so can we.

The stories are always bringing us together, keeping this whole together, keeping this family together, keeping this clan together. "Don't go away, don't isolate yourself, but come here, because we have all had these kinds of experiences"—this is what the people are saying to you when they tell you these other stories. And so there is this constant pulling together to resist what seems to me to be a basic part of human nature: when some violent emotional experience takes place, people get the urge to run off and hide or separate themselves from others. And of course, if we do that, we are not only talking about endangering the group, we are also talking about the individual or the individual family never being able to recover or to survive. Inherent in this belief is the feeling that one does not recover or get well by one's self, but it is together that we look after each other and take care of each other.

In the storytelling, then, we see this process of bringing people together, and it works not only on the family level, but also on the level of the individual. Of course, the whole Pueblo concept of the individual is a little bit different from the usual Western concept of the individual. But one of the beauties of the storytelling is that when something happens to an individual, many people will come to you and take you aside, or maybe a couple of people will come and talk to you. These are occasions of storytelling. These occasions of storytelling are continuous; they are a way of life.

Storytelling lies at the heart of the Pueblo people, and so when someone comes in and says, "When did they tell the stories, or what time of day does the storytelling take place?" that is a ridiculous question. The storytelling goes on constantly—as some old grandmother puts on the shoes of a little child and tells the child the story of a little girl who didn't wear her shoes. At the same time somebody comes into the house for coffee to talk with an adolescent boy who has just been into a lot of trouble, to reassure him that *he* got into that kind of trouble, or somebody else's son got into that kind of trouble too. You have this constant ongoing process, working on many different levels.

One of the stories I like to bring up about helping the individual in crisis is a recent story, and I want to remind you that we make no distinctions between the stories—whether they are history, whether they are fact,

15

whether they are gossip—these distinctions are not useful when we are talking about this particular experience with language. Anyway, there was a young man who, when he came back from the war in Vietnam, had saved up his Army pay and bought a beautiful red Volkswagen Beetle. He was very proud of it, and one night drove up to a place right across the reservation line. It is a very notorious place for many reasons, but one of the more notorious things about the place is a deep arroyo behind the place. This is the King's Bar. So he ran in to pick up a cold six-pack to take home, but he didn't put on his emergency brake. And his little red Volkswagen rolled back into the arroyo and was all smashed up. He felt very bad about it, but within a few days everybody had come to him and told him stories about other people who had lost cars to that arroyo. And probably the story that made him feel the best was about the time that George Day's station wagon, with his mother-in-law and kids in the back, rolled into that arroyo. So everybody was saying, "Well, at least your mother-in-law and kids weren't in the car when it rolled in," and you can't argue with that kind of story. He felt better then because he wasn't alone anymore. He and his smashed-up Volkswagen were now joined with all the other stories of cars that fell into that arroyo.

Again there is a very beautiful little story. It comes from far out of the past. It is a story that is sometimes told to people who suffer great family or personal loss. I would like to read that story to you now, and while I am reading it to you, try to listen on a couple of levels at once. I want you to listen to the usage of English. I came from a family which has been doing something that isn't exactly standard English for a while. I come from a family which, basically, is intent on getting the stories told; and we *will* get those stories told, and language *will* work for us. It is imperative to tell and not to worry over a specific language. The imperative is the telling. This is an old story from Aunt Suzie. She is one of the first generations of persons at Laguna who began experimenting with our notion of English—who began working to make English speak for us—that is, to speak from the heart. As I read the story to you, you will hear some words that came from Carlisle. She was taken from Laguna, New Mexico, on a train when she was a little girl, and she spent six years at Carlisle, Pennsylvania, in an Indian school, which was like being sent to prison. But listen and you will hear the Carlisle influence. This is a story that is sometimes given to you when there has been a great loss.

This took place partly in old Acoma and Laguna. Waithia was a little girl living in Acoma. One day she said, "Mother, I would like to have some yastoah to eat." Yastoah is the hardened crust of corn meal mush that curls up. The very name *yastoah* means sort of "curled up," you know, dried, just as mush dries on top. She said, "I would like to have some yastoah," and her mother said, "My dear little girl, I can't make you any yastoah because we haven't any wood, but if you will go down off the mesa, down below, and pick up some pieces of wood, bring them home and I will make you some yastoah." So Waithia was glad and ran down the precipitous cliff of the mesa. Down below, just as her mother told her, there were pieces of wood, some curled, some crooked in shape, that she was to pick up and take home. She found just such wood as these.

She went home and she had them in a little wickerlike bag. First she called to her mother as she got home and said, "Mother, upstairs." The Pueblo people always called "upstairs" because long ago their homes were two or three stories, and that was their entrance, from the top. She said, *"Naya, deeni!* Mother, upstairs!" And her mother came. The little girl said, "I have brought the wood you wanted me to bring." She opened her little wicker basket and laid them out and they were snakes. They were snakes instead of the crooked pieces of wood, and her mother said, "Oh, my dear child. You have brought snakes instead." She says, "Go take them back and put them back just where you got them." The little girl ran down the mesa again. Down below to the flats. And she put those snakes back just where she got them. They were snakes instead, and she was very much hurt about this, and she said, "I am not going home. I am going away to the beautiful lake place and drown myself in that lake, Kawaik *bunyanah,* to the west. I will go there and drown myself."

So she started off, and as she came by the Enchanted Mesa, Kátsima, she met an old man, very aged, and he saw her running, and he said, "My dear child, where are you going?" She said, "I am going to Kawaik and jump into the lake there." "Why?" "Well, because," she says, "my mother didn't want to make any yastoah." And the old man said, "Oh, no, you must not go my child. Come with me and I will take you home." He tried to catch her, but she was very light and skipped along, and every time he would try to grab her she would skip faster away from him.

So he was coming home with some wood on his back, strapped to his back and tied with yucca. He just let that strap go and let the wood fall. He went as fast as he could up the cliff to the little girl's home. When he got to the place where she lived, he called to her mother, *"Deeni!* Upstairs!" "Come on up." And he says, "I can't. I just came to bring you a message. Your little daughter is running away. She is going to Kawaik to drown herself in the lake there." "Oh, my dear little girl!" the mother said. So she busied herself around and made her the yastoah she loved so much. Corn mush, curled at the top. She must have found enough wood to boil the corn meal and make the yastoah.

And while the mush was cooling, she got the little girl's clothing, she got the little dress and all her other garments, little buckskin moccasins that she had, and put them in a bundle, too—probably a yucca bag. And she started down as fast as she could on the east side of Acoma. There used to be a trail there, you know. It's gone now. But it was accessible in those days. And she followed, and she saw her way at a distance—saw the daughter—she kept calling: "Tsumatusu, my daughter, come back. I have got your yastoah for you." But the little girl did not turn. She kept on ahead, and she cried. And what she cried is the song: "My mother, my mother, she didn't want me to have any yastoah. So now I am going to go away and drown myself." Her mother heard her cry and said, "My little daughter, come back here." "No," and she kept a distance away from her.

And they came nearer and nearer to the lake that was here. And she could see her daughter now, very plain. "Come back, my daughter, I have your yastoah." And no, she kept on, and finally she reached the lake, and she stood on the edge. She tied a little feather in her hair, which is traditional: in death they tie this little feather on the head. She carried a little feather, the girl did, and she tied it in her hair with a little piece of string, right on top of her head she put the feather. Just about as her mother was to reach her, she jumped into the lake. The little feather was whirling around and around in the depths below.

Of course the mother was very sad. She went, grieved, back to Acoma and climbed her mesa home, and the little clothing, the little moccasins she brought, and the yastoah. She stood on the edge of the mesa and scattered them out. She scattered them to the east and west, to the north and to the south—in all directions and where every one of the little clothing and the little moccasins and shawls and yastoah [fell], all of them turned into butterflies, all colors of butterflies! And today they say that Acoma has more beautiful butterflies: red ones, white ones, blue ones, yellow ones. They came from this little girl's clothing.*

Now that is a story that anthropologists would consider to be a very old story. The version I have given you is just as Aunt Suzie tells it. You can occasionally hear some English she picked up at Carlisle—words like "precipitous." You will also notice that there is a great deal of repetition, and a little reminder about yastoah and how it was made. There is a remark about the cliff trail at Acoma—that it was once there, but is there no longer. This story may be told at a time of sadness or loss, but within this story many other elements are brought together. Things are not separated out and put

*Copyright © 1981 by L. M. Silko in *Storyteller,* a Richard Seaver Book.

into separate categories; all things are brought together. So that the reminder about the yastoah is valuable information that is repeated, a recipe, if you will. The information about the old trail at Acoma reveals that stories are, in a sense, maps, since even to this day there is little information or material about trails that is passed around with writing. In the structure of this story the repetitions are, of course, designed to help you be able to remember. It is repeated again and again, and then it moves on. There is a very definite pattern that you will hear in these pieces. . . .

As the old people say, "If you can remember the stories, you will be all right. Just remember the stories." And, of course, usually when they say that to you, when you are young, you wonder what in the world they mean. But when I returned—I had been away from Laguna Pueblo for a couple of years, well more than a couple of years after college and so forth—I returned to Laguna and I went to Laguna-Acoma high school to visit an English class, and I was wondering how the telling was continuing, because Laguna Pueblo, as the anthropologists have said, is one of the more acculturated pueblos. So I walked into this high school English class and there they were sitting, these very beautiful Laguna and Acoma kids. But I knew that out in their lockers they had cassette tape recorders, and I knew that at home they had stereos, and they were listening to Kiss and Led Zeppelin and all those other things. I was almost afraid, but I had to ask—I had with me a book of short fiction (it's called *The Man to Send Rain Clouds* [New York: Viking Press, 1974]), and among the stories of other Native American writers, it has stories that I have written and Simon Ortiz has written. And there is one particular story in the book about the killing of a state policeman in New Mexico by three Acoma Pueblo men. It was an act that was committed in the early fifties. I was afraid to ask, but I had to. I looked at the class and I said, "How many of you heard this story before you read it in the book?" And I was prepared to hear this crushing truth that indeed the anthropologists were right about the old traditions dying out. But it was amazing, you know, almost all but one or two students raised their hands. They had heard that story, just as Simon and I had heard it, when we were young. That was my first indication that storytelling continues on. About half of them had heard it in English, about half of them had heard it in Laguna. I think again, getting back to one of the original statements, that if you begin to look at the core of the importance of the language and how it fits in with the culture, it is the *story* and the feeling of the story which matters more than what language it's told in.

One of the other advantages that we have enjoyed is that we have always been able to stay with the land. The stories cannot be separated from geographical locations, from actual physical places within the land. We were not relocated like so many Native American groups who were torn away from our ancestral land. And the stories are so much a part of these places that it is almost impossible for future generations to lose the stories because there are so many imposing geological elements. Just as Houston Baker was speaking about the mesas—there are such gigantic boulders—you cannot *live* in that land without asking or looking or noticing a boulder or rock. And there's always a story. There's always at least one story connected with those places. . . .

Dennis Brutus talked about the "yet unborn" as well as "those from the past," and how we are still *all* in *this* place, and language—the storytelling—is our entryway of passing or being with them, of being together again. When Aunt Suzie told her stories, she would tell a younger child to go open the door so that our esteemed predecessors may bring in their gifts to us. "They are out there," Aunt Suzie would say. "Let them come in. They're here, they're here with us *within* the stories." 20

I last visited her about four months ago. She is 106, and so if you walk into the room and try to ask her how many years she was at Carlisle Indian School—a direct question—she says she doesn't remember. But if you just let her speak her mind, everything that she says is very clear. And while I was there, she said, "Well, I'll be leaving here soon. I think I'll be leaving here next week, and I will be going over to the Cliff House." She said, "It's going to be real good to get back over there." I was listening, and I was thinking of her house at Paguate, at Paguate village, which is north of Laguna. And she continued on, "Well" (and she gave her Indian name) "my mother's sister will be there. She has been living there. She will be there and we will be over there, and I will get a chance to write down these stories I've been telling you." And it wasn't until she said it was her mother's sister who would be there that I realized she wasn't talking about dying or death at all. She was talking about "going over there," and she meant it as a journey, a journey that perhaps we can only begin to understand through an appreciation for the boundless capacity of language which, through storytelling, brings us together, despite great distances between cultures, despite great distances in time.

Issues for Discussion

1. How do the Laguna Pueblo Indians view stories and language according to Silko? How does their view differ from the view commonly held by non-Indian peoples? How does their view compare to the view of stories in your family or culture?
2. What different uses do stories serve in Laguna Pueblo culture? Can you think of instances when you have seen stories used in similar ways? Do stories seem to fulfill different functions in different cultures?

J O U R N A L
O P T I O N

Cultural Roots

Write a full version of one of your own cultural stories—a story that connects you with your "tribe," your culture, your roots.

Active Reading: Taking Notes

Understanding always involves expectation and recognition. It's easy to understand Beverly Donofrio's story because it refers to so many well-known scripts and story frames: most Americans have well-developed sets of expectations about the kinds of experiences an American teenager goes through, and most have fairly clear expectations about what it means to be a "bad girl," to have an authoritarian father, or to grow up poor in a small town. If you recognize these story frames in Donofrio's reminiscence, you'll probably feel as if you've "understood" her. "Trouble" is no trouble to read if you have all the scripts you need to grasp the point of her story.

But what happens when you read a text that's less accessible than Donofrio's memoir, and you don't get the point? A selection like Silko's description of Laguna Pueblo storytelling is challenging for at least two reasons. First, it's structurally complicated: it contains several sections or segments each composed of different types of writing and each serving different purposes. Second, it contains story frames that may not be entirely familiar. A Laguna Pueblo tribal member might not have any difficulty interpreting the transformation of Waithia's clothes into butterflies, but how can you begin to appreciate a text that falls outside your immediate experience? One response to a challenging reading like Silko's is to decode it sentence by sentence in the hopes of squeezing the meaning out. But reverting to mechanical decoding won't help you move beyond the surface of what Silko is saying. To grasp the point of her essay and to comprehend its structure and its deeper meaning, you have to discover a way to help you grasp all of its structural complexity and a way to help you "get reminded" of similar stories from your own experience despite the unusualness of Silko's ideas and experiences.

Skilled readers usually rely on one or more note-taking techniques to help them cope with such challenging readings. Engaging a text actively by making notes in the margins as you read helps you to "see" the way the structure of the text breaks down because as you take notes you leave behind a permanent "map" or model of its content. It can also encourage you to make personal connections and associations with the ideas in the text even if they seem, at first, relatively unfamiliar. Here are a few common approaches to note-taking—approaches you can apply to your reading of Silko.

Dialoguing.   Underlining and highlighting can be very useful, but only if you use these techniques judiciously and only if you follow up by making some careful explanatory notes in the margins of your reading. Here's a simple rule of thumb: whenever you highlight a passage, make a quick note in the margin that indicates why the passage is significant. Maybe one of Silko's stories reminds you of one of your own: jot down a note in the margin to capture the memory. Maybe your story differed from Silko's in an interesting or significant way: jot that down too. You might find yourself wondering about an idea, action, or attitude Silko presents: put your curiosity into words by asking a question and record it in the margin as well. Or you may just want to note that a particular idea or image excites you (or repulses you): an exclamation point and a couple of explanatory words will do the trick. Dialoguing in the margins like this is more than just an aid to memory. It actually helps make the reading yours. The more you add your own ideas and reactions to the text you're reading, the more meaning you are apt to discover in it. The more you compare your own thoughts, memories, and ideas with those of the author, the more likely you'll be to grasp the nuances of the author's argument. To discover what the author is thinking, you've got to explore your own thinking first. You can't begin to understand a reading until you have listened carefully and taken note of your own responses. Dialoguing with the author in margins is the best way to begin this process.

Glossing.   This is a more formal approach to note-taking, more focused on the text and the parts that make it up. When you gloss a reading, you work through it systematically, trying to extract the main idea or the main point of each paragraph. Once you feel confident that you've grasped the main idea of a particular paragraph or section, you jot it down in the form of an index or label in the margin—just a few descriptive words capturing the essence of the section. The first paragraph of Silko, for example, seems to address the way that language is used within an oral as opposed to a written tradition. You might want to gloss it by noting in the margin "Structure of English in Oral Trad." or just "English in Oral Trad."

Some readings require that you gloss them paragraph by paragraph, each paragraph introducing a relatively distinct and well-developed idea or topic. Most often, however, you'll find that the reading breaks down into larger sections, some sections developing a single idea over the space of several paragraphs. A single gloss would work, for example, to describe each of the stories that Silko relates in her selection. You probably wouldn't want to bother labeling each paragraph, because the individual actions they contain just don't seem all that important. A word of caution, however: your glossing is only as good as the labels that you place in the margins. These need to capture the main idea or topic of the section in language that's as descriptive and specific as possible. It wouldn't help much to label Silko's first paragraph as "Traditions" or "Language Differences." Nor would it be much use to gloss the stories she tells as "Story #1," "Story # 2," "Story # 3," and so forth. You'll have more success if you use detailed and descriptive labels like "Creation Story" or "Smashed VW."

The power of glossing lies in its ability to help you grasp the overall structure of a piece of writing: once you finish labeling each section, it's easier to see the relationship between the author's ideas—your marginal glosses give you a concise index of the selection's main points. Glossing is also a powerful aid to memory. If you have glossed Silko effectively, you should be able to return to it after a few weeks and quickly refresh your memory about the content of every passage simply by reviewing your notes. Glossing creates a marginal summary of the reading, a miniature map that you can return to when it comes time for you to remember and to write.

Translating.   When you read college-level material you're bound to encounter passages that seem so foreign and incomprehensible that you simply don't have a clue to their meaning, main idea, or purpose. Generally, this happens when you encounter a new story frame—a script that falls outside your experience and that, therefore, seems either mysterious or nonsensical. When this happens, one thing to do is to translate the passage into terms that make sense to you. Most students have no trouble understanding the story that Silko tells about the young man who wrecks his VW. This is a story frame we all recognize: we've all broken valuable things at one time or another, and we know how a mistake in judgment can lead to an accident that leaves us feeling alone in our foolishness. No need for translation here. But the story Silko tells about "a great loss"—the story about Waithia and her mother—may not at first seem as transparent. After all, how many of us have ever seen firewood turn into snakes or run away to throw ourselves in a lake because we didn't get to eat the cornmeal mush we asked for? How are we to interpret the fact that Waithia's clothing turns into butterflies at the story's end? What could this story mean to the Pueblo Indians who have been telling it and learning from it for centuries?

One way to begin answering these questions is to translate the story's essential elements into terms that make sense in our culture. Waithia's story comes from a culture that is closer to nature than contemporary urban American culture; it's a world where magical powers fill even the most common objects, where miracles are placed on the same level as mush. How would this story read if we were to translate its characters and events into contemporary terms? What would motivate a girl living in contemporary New York or Los Angeles to leave home in despair? What would such a young woman want so badly? What would she go out to do to get it? By translating Waithia's story into a story frame you are more familiar with, you have a better chance of grasping its meaning and importance. You'll find it handy to carry out translations like this whenever you meet sentences or passages that stump you. Just take a moment or two and write them out in the margin of your reading.

O P T I O N A L
A C T I V I T Y

Collaborative Note-Taking

Work in pairs and reread Silko's essay in class to apply the note-taking approaches we've been discussing. To save time, you may want to underline, dialogue, and gloss only the first three or four pages for practice. Read through the selection paragraph by paragraph, stopping after each to discuss how you'd handle it. Compare the lines you'd highlight, the marginal dialoguing notes you'd make, and your glosses. When your approach to a section differs from your partner's, try to explain what led you to make the notes you did. Finally, spend about ten minutes working together to translate the Waithia story. Try to retell the entire story in modern terms. When you're finished, share your updated version with the class and explain what you think the story means.

CHAPTER 2

Shaping Stories

Family Stories and Identity

Silko's creation story and the story of Waithia are ancient cultural tales, passed down from generation to generation for perhaps thousands of years. Stories like the VW anecdote that Silko relates may not have a distinguished historical pedigree, yet they can still have tremendous importance for teller and listener. Every family tells stories about its past, stories that create a sense of relatedness between family members, a sense of shared experience and shared values. Family stories may feature distant figures—a great-grandparent or a great-uncle or great-aunt whose exploits are enacted in an almost mythic past. Or they may center on memories of immediate family members: the stories of our own childhood adventures told by parents or siblings play a critical role in the formation of our personal memories and personalities. Families are the bridge that connects us to our culture. The people who raise us and fill our households provide a cast of characters that fleshes out the story frames we adopt from our cultural context: we learn what it means to play the part of a woman from many different story frames, but all of the scripts we adopt involving women are influenced by the roles played by our mothers and grandmothers. Family stories tell us a great deal about who we are and who we can be: at their best they provide us with models of what we might someday become; at their worst they can become snares of negativity and judgment that threaten to imprison us.

But the shaping power of stories is a two-way process. Just as the stories we grew up with shape us and our perceptions, so do we also build and express our own sense of self by shaping the stories we tell. Earlier we noted that the events in our lives may be forgotten if they are not incorporated in and told as stories. These story memories are themselves shaped by the story frames and scripts available in our culture and by our own individual interests and goals. The version of that first date or first day on the job that you remember may, in fact, only vaguely resemble the version recalled by those who suffered it with you. In your version of the events, you've selectively "forgotten" hundreds of details and amplified or even created many others. In fact, many of our personal memories are completely created from the general story frames we keep on file: think back to last year's Thanksgiving dinner: you can probably describe it, but it's also likely that much of the detail you include comes from a general script you possess for the "Thanksgiving Celebration" and not from that particular holiday feast at all. Memory, like all storytelling, is essentially a creative process.

Of course, when we listen to a parent, aunt, or uncle tell a story, it may be easy to forget that family stories, like all stories, are carefully constructed artifacts. The events, characters, situations, actions, ideas, values, and beliefs they contain are all carefully chosen, embellished, and edited to fit the purpose of teller and listener. Family stories, like any other stories, are never a matter of simple historical fact. The following two selections illustrate the power *and* the artfulness of personal family stories. In the first, David Mura offers stories about his Japanese American immigrant grandparents and their experience in the relocation camps of World War II. In the second, by Phyllis Barber, we hear another story about a grandfather — this time in the context of a Mormon celebration of Christmas. Both stories demonstrate how the teller honors and edits the memory of a grandparent to create a past that makes the present more bearable — or simply more enjoyable.

David Mura (b. 1952) is a poet and novelist who has won national acclaim for his examination of what it means to be Asian American. In *Turning Japanese* (1991), the source of the story that follows, Mura chronicles a year spent searching for his roots in contemporary Japan. Phyllis Barber's cultural roots, by contrast, lay half a world away. Born in Henderson, Nevada, in 1943 and raised in a traditional Mormon family, Barber has been a homemaker, community volunteer, professional pianist, cabaret dancer, teacher, and freelance writer. Her story originally appeared in *How I Got Cultured: A Nevada Memoir* (1992), which explores the tensions she faced as a devout young Mormon who wanted to "make it" in the world of art and entertainment.

Before Reading

Try to remember a story that's repeated in your family about one of your grandparents. How much of it strikes you as fiction, how much as fact? Summarize it in your journal and try to speculate about why it became a permanent part of your family history.

Family Stories
David Mura

In my early twenties, during the summers, I sometimes visited my aunt, whose small house in Stamford looks out on Long Island Sound and is wedged in between the larger mansions of rich businessmen and executives. The foundation of my aunt's house was once a playhouse for the children of the next-door mansion, and even though many additions have been made, the house retained for me an air of childhood fantasy. After I first read *The Great Gatsby,* I sometimes imagined my aunt's house as the carriage house in which Nick Carraway resides, next to the mansion of the fabled, mysterious Mr. Gatsby.

But it was more than my aunt's house which entranced me. My aunt and her roommate, who was an artist and an illustrator of children's books, lived a life informed by New York City, where my aunt worked as a manager for a Japanese restaurant, a life filled with talk of Broadway shows, ballet, and the opera. When she was younger, my aunt had worked for a Broadway producer, had met Katharine Hepburn, had watched Eugene O'Neill direct *The Iceman Cometh.* She had gone to parties in the Village where people like Jackson Pollock, Frank O'Hara, and e.e. cummings appeared.[1]

From classical records to Japanese pottery and prints, from children's books to various Japanese foods, my aunt's house was filled with objects exotic to me, that embodied some alternative to my parents' all-American suburbia of bridge, golf, and television. She was the only person in my family with books like Robert Lowell's *Lord Weary's Castle* and W. C. Williams's *Paterson* in her bookcase. Her roommate, Baye, was Japanese, and their house was the one place where I heard Japanese spoken with any frequency.

---

[1]**parties . . . appeared:** Greenwich Village in New York City was a mecca for artists and writers in the 1930s, 40s, and 50s.

So: In this archetypical scene I am setting, I am sitting after dinner with my aunt Ruth and Baye and Susie. I am asking my aunt about her childhood, about my grandparents. I ask because my father never talks of the past, nor does my mother. At home, when I have tried to bring up the subject of the camps, my father has simply said, "I had fun in the camps. Back in L.A., after school, I had to work in my father's nursery. In the camps I could go out and play baseball." My mother replies that she does not remember, she was too young, it wasn't all that important. Only my aunt will talk about the camps, about the past, about her parents. On these visits, I listen to story after story. Sometimes they are humorous, such as the time she was on a pass from camp and was walking through the town of Jerome, Arkansas, and some ladies on a porch, drinking mint juleps, called out to her, "Dear, are you Anna May Wong? You look like Anna May Wong."

Other stories invoked generational differences, such as the time my aunt asked my grandfather to sign the loyalty oaths. She believed the Nisei needed to prove they were good Americans, she wanted to believe she could be a part of the country. My grandfather looked at her and said, "When they let me out of here, then I'll sign up," and walked away.   5

In my mind, these stories took on a legendary quality. Japanese are not necessarily known for their oral tradition, and though my aunt was an adequate storyteller, I don't think I was impressed by the way she told these stories. No, I loved them because they were a clear link to the past that my parents had not provided. Just as importantly, the stories had a certain romantic cast. They pictured my grandfather as a certified character, a somewhat lazy and fun-loving man, who liked to gamble, smoke cigars, and play the Japanese biwa, who wrote haiku until a stroke kept him from holding a brush ever again. He cried when this happened, and he went upstairs and stayed in his room for a week. In making this legend, I choose to ignore my father's resentment of the work his father made him do, or the scene in the back yard with my grandfather brandishing the board like a weapon above my father's head.

In my aunt's stories, my grandmother was pictured as a seer, a ghostlike creature with an eye for the future and the other world. In one of these stories, it's the thirties, their time of prosperity before the war, when they lived in a small house in west L.A. (today, a freeway runs through it). I see my grandmother shaking my grandfather awake. It is just before dawn, the light in the room is blue as a flame. He waves her away. He's naturally a late sleeper, and perhaps he was down in Japan Town the night before, playing hana or poker, drinking sake with his cronies. But my grandmother keeps shaking him. Even in the cool before day, she is sweating, her eyes and face muscles squeezed tight, as if she has just taken a bite of a lemon. "What is it now?" he asks.

"You mustn't go out today," she says.

"Why? Just let me sleep."

"No, listen to me," and she tells him of her dream. Like a pitcher knocked from the table, it spills about chaotically, it makes no sense. Images of blood, of broken glass, of his face in pain.

"Baka-rashii," he mutters. She is a worrier, he thinks, always has been, has never embraced the world as he has, has never learned English, never ventures far from the confines of their neighborhood and the other Japanese families that surround them like a cocoon, like cotton batting.

He leaves for the day, ignoring her pleas, drives off in his shiny silver Packard, bought with who knows what funds. He has the tastes and work habits of a rich man's son.

Now she wakes my father, who is ten at the time. Instructs him to go to the temple. Gives him change to place in the box there. Tells him to light a stick of incense, to give prayers to the Buddha. He must save his father. They must pray for him.

My father comes back. Two hours later, she sends him to the temple again. And later, again. Again.

It is getting dark now, the sky is beginning to take on the colors of fire and blood. Farther west, like a red-hot coin fresh from a forge, the sun is dipping into the cooling waters.

Her husband still has not appeared. One, two, three hours. Finally, just before midnight, a sound of steps on the porch. She rushes to the door.

She sees the bandages first, the shock of white cloth wrapped around his forehead. He is angry, wincing from pain. She can see a pinkness beginning to seep through the cloth. He has had an accident, his car has been totaled.

"Don't ever," he says, "don't ever tell me your dreams again."

Several years later, during the war, they are in the relocation camp at Jerome. A summer that seems swimming in dampness, the heat seeps up from the swamps nearby, films the air, pours out of their bodies. Mosquitoes, fireflies, tiny gnats, moths hover at the screens until the lights are turned off. In barrack after barrack, the families are cramped together, with clothes for partitions, with paper-thin boards. They hear each other's snores, the arguments between husband and wife, fathers and sons, mothers and daughters; they hear the sound of love cries, of a baby bawling. There's the smell of shoyu, wafts from the benjo downwind. Outside, in the rifle towers, the privates are bored. One tosses a cigarette over the edge. It falls, scattering flakes of ash, tiny red sparks.

Suddenly my grandmother wakes screaming. She has seen it, her sister's   20
house in Tokyo. It started with a whooshing sound, then the wailing of sirens. Streaks of light through the sky, boom after boom reverberating. House after house catching on fire. My grandmother sees it all, the flames peeling the paper walls like skin, the pine and cedar boards rippling with flames, her sister trapped in a ring of white heat, succumbing to the smoke, fainting.

And then my grandfather is holding her, yanking her back and forth, trying to understand what she is saying. It is like holding an infant wakened in the night; it is like holding a ghost.

Near the end of the war, more than a year later, she receives a letter detailing her dream, her sister's death.

The night my aunt told me this story was the night her roommate, Baye, told me about living in Tokyo during the war. I had known Baye since I was a child—she was almost a second aunt—but she had never talked much to me about the past. Spurred perhaps by my aunt's story, I started to ask Baye questions. I knew she had had a baby during the war, that she had married a man with tuberculosis, against her family's wishes, but I wanted to know more.

"I remember once we were walking in the hills," said Baye. She was sipping tea near the picture window, which looked out on the blackness of the waters below, the sound of the tide moving out. Her hair is salt and pepper, in a bowl cut; her body is small, beginning to bend at the shoulders. She has the hopping, quick movements of a sprite, a pixie, though she can also possess the petulance of a youngest daughter. "I was pregnant, and we had this apple, because I was pregnant. And I was so happy. We halved the apple and ate it, and it was the most delicious apple I have ever tasted. I think that was the most happiest moment of my life."

And then she told me of the time when the firebombs came. She could   25
hear the sirens going off. Her husband roused her. Part of their house was already on fire. He and the maid would try to douse the flames. She was to take the baby to the shelters.

"So I picked up the baby in my blanket and I went out the door. But I was so panicked, I ran around the house. I could see the firebombs falling down the street. I went back to the door and opened it. My husband asked me why I wasn't going to the shelter. I didn't know. It was like a dream. I ran around the house again and came back. And then again."

Baye was laughing as she told me this. She couldn't believe how silly she had been, she said.

"And then I was running through the streets. And the bombs were falling in front of me, and it was almost as light as day. They looked like light bulbs, one after the other, falling from the sky. All of the houses were in flames. I jumped to the side of the road, into this ditch, and it was wet at the bottom. The blanket was wet too, the baby had gone shi-shi, and I realized I'd forgotten her diapers. I was so angry, diapers were such a luxury, they were almost as precious as gold, and now they were probably lost in the fire. I was so wet and tired, and I wanted to die, to just give up and lie there in that ditch. But then I felt this sucking at my breast. The baby was trying to eat. And I thought, Well, if she can do that, if she wants to live, I guess I can."

When Baye finished, my aunt Ruth said, "You know, I've lived with you for fifteen years and I never heard that story." My aunt, Susie, and I were all aware that both Baye's husband and child had died of tuberculosis before the end of the war.

I don't remember if this was the night my aunt Ruth told me about 30 how my grandmother had once suspected that my grandfather was cheating on her. I recall that my aunt mentioned something about a white woman named Evelyn, and how my aunt didn't know if she was the one my grandmother suspected. At any rate, when my grandmother had that premonitory dream, she woke up my grandfather with a knife blade pressed to his throat. "If you ever . . ." she said, and left the sentence unfinished, as Japanese often do.

Stories

Phyllis Barber

TOMMY AND HERMAN'S FAMOUS STORY

When relatives gathered on Christmas night at our two-story house facing hills of sand instead of drifts of snow, my father and his brother, Tommy, never failed us.

Ritual was the first order of business, however. We had to pray over the food on our buffet table before we scooped and plucked and mathematically figured how to fill a plate to capacity. The children found places to sit cross-legged on the floor, the adults on the sofa or a kitchen chair brought into the living room. Everyone balanced clear-glass hostess plates on their laps, careful not to spill the raspberry punch or topple quivering jello salad and stacks of sliced ham, roast beef, and cheese arranged between halves of Mother's feather-light rolls.

"Herman, you lucky dog," Tommy said. "How did you ever find this woman who could produce such beautiful food!"

"Herman's not a dog," my mother said from across the room, her literal mind offended.

"This food is good," Aunt Grace agreed and pressed her lips together as 5 if she hadn't put enough lipstick on the upper lip and was making last-minute repairs. "That's the one thing Thora sure knows how to do."

Mother looked half pleased, then half hurt. She was constantly wary of Grace's tongue, and at the moment seemed busy interpreting her words. Had she said my mother only knew how to do one thing, nothing else?

"True enough," said Uncle Elwin, whose only entree into Christmas night conversations was to express his appreciation for Mother's cooking. The rest of the time, he stayed tight by his wife Raity's side.

At the back of this small talk was a sense the evening would soon light up. After the dirty plates were collected and Mother's candy was set out in cut-glass dishes, the uncles loosened their belt buckles one notch, and everyone waited for Tommy and Herman to begin.

"Well, you know," Uncle Tommy began, "we weren't always perfect." Everyone laughed, no matter how many times they'd heard him use that line for openers, and everyone settled back in their seats, comforted that the Christmas night story was coming and that things never changed.

Sitting on the floor with my cousins, I leaned against the sofa's seat 10 cushions between Uncle Tommy's and Aunt Grace's legs, also content to know I was about to hear the famous tale of my father and Uncle Tommy almost blowing up the side of a mountain in Ruth, Nevada.

"We'd fallen in with a ring of thieves," Tommy said, "something like Ali Baba. You know that story, don't you?"

"They were the same boys we played with every day, actually," my father, an honest man, said. "I was the smallest one," he continued. "Those big boys lifted me up and pushed me through the window of the munitions shed on the side of the mountain. 'It's in the box with three Xs,' they said as they pushed me into that dark, spider-infested shed. 'Don't throw it out, though, just hand it to us.'

"I fumbled around until my eyes adjusted to the dusky light and then saw those three big Xs staring back at me like a poison label on a pharmacy bottle. I pulled the screwdriver out of my back pocket and wedged the lid open. The dynamite looked like cardboard-covered candles with wicks—a thousand of them, it seemed. 'Hurry up,' I heard them whispering like hoarse coyotes.

"I stood on my tiptoes to pass the dynamite over the ledge, then realized I was too short to pull myself up and over the window. 'Get me outta here,' I yelled. They told me to shut up quick, then yanked on my arms and dragged me over that ledge. If I think about it much, I can still feel the pains in my stomach where those splinters scraped my skin."

"And then," Uncle Tommy, the relay runner standing ready with an open mouth, lifted the baton from my father's hand, "we crawled up over rocks, almost losing our footing, almost sliding back down the hill on that loose gravel, but we were like lizards, our bellies scraping over boulders and brambles. Sweat running down our faces, mixing with the dust so close to our noses."

"It was Don Belknap who set the cap and blew the fuse," my father retrieved the telling. "He was the biggest one of all of us, eighteen, which meant he got sent to prison, not reform school. You should have seen the people bust out of those houses below us when they were suddenly besieged with those rolling rocks and clouds of dust."

"Boulders," Tommy said, lifting his arms to recapture the story again. "Gigantic boulders rolling down toward Ruth, gaining speed. I never in my life wanted so much to be an eagle so I could fly to some crevice to hide deep down inside where no one could see me. Boy, were those people mad. One man even ran outside with a gun."

"A gun?" Aunt Grace said, slapping her knees so heartily I felt a breeze on my neck. "That's a new twist. But then, you two have to have at least one new twist every year. Right, Tom?"

Tommy ignored Grace. "Damn rights," he said. "I just never mentioned it before."

"I don't remember that part either." My father folded his arms and looked sideways at Tommy.   20

"Well," Tommy said, sliding to the front of the sofa cushions, leaning further into the story, not looking at my father, "I do. You must not have noticed it in all the excitement. The sheriff and some men of the town came roaring up that hill like bulls in a fury. They picked us up by the back of the pants and carried us under their arms like we were Christmas hams."

"You're Christmas hams all right," Aunt Grace said, and I turned to watch her throw her brightly painted face back to laugh. I laughed, too, always happy for an opportunity to laugh with the irreverent Aunt Grace who opened forbidden doors. So did my cousins and Uncle Elwin.

"My stomach was still hurting from the window ledge," my father said, interrupting our laughter too soon. "When I got picked up and carried by my belt, I thought I might die right then and there."

"And you should have seen our dad when we arrived home," Tommy said. "Grandpa to you nieces and nephews. He was a picture of the Black Death — black in the face, unbuckling his belt to take us out to the chicken yard where we stacked wood. He must have lashed me with that belt over fifty times. He was one mad José."

"You sure about that?" Grace asked. "Your numbers seem different every year."   25

"Well, maybe not quite that many." Tommy frowned.

"Maybe two or three?" My father smiled a cat-got-a-mouse smile.

"They were going to send me up," Tommy slid away from any answers, "but Mother pleaded with the judge. She told him she'd make us do dishes for a year and feed those stupid chickens who smothered each other when they got too cold and tried to keep warm. She never let us forget our crime, kept telling us how lucky we were to be at home and not in some wild animal cage with iron bars on the windows."

"They didn't consider me a candidate," my father said, snatching a piece of peanut brittle from the bowl on the coffee table. "Lucky for me, I was too young."

"Well, I was sure in big trouble there for a while," Tommy said. "Lucky   30
Mother had such a convincing way with the law."

For a moment, I thought I heard some unlikely emotion in Tommy's voice, but then, both my father and Tommy grabbed handfuls of Mother's fruitcake, toffee, and peanut brittle. I stretched forward to the same plate and pinched a slab of fruitcake with the most gumdrops visible — yellow, orange, green, and red all together in the same piece. My lucky night.

Everyone else followed suit, and we sat in a momentary lull, listening to the sound of teeth crunching candy.

Sitting quietly between Aunt Grace's and Uncle Tommy's legs, I was wishing we could go back inside the story and that the story would go on and on and never end because when it ended, we were all the same people sitting in the same squared-off, tiny living room with the tall metal gas heater crowding the space. We were something different inside a story; we had possibilities other than the ones in this yellow plastered room. And I wondered if some of the other relatives were wishing the story would end, just for once, with as big a bang as it started.

Every year I kept hoping everyone except Tommy would be quiet. Then the story could really become a story, and something more awful or miraculous could happen to Tommy and my father in Ruth, Nevada, just once. Maybe they'd have to go to reform school where they'd be forced to eat thin gruel for breakfast and dig up old highways with pickaxes. Or maybe a gigantic boulder would be rolling perilously close to a house in Ruth, Nevada, and an angel with wings would appear out of nowhere and lift the boulder into the air in the nick of time.

But even with the same, anticlimactic ending, there was something soothing about the story, maybe because it was always the same with a few minor variations. Maybe everyone was relieved the story wasn't worse and the law had been merciful to two men we loved.

"Wouldn't be Christmas without your candy," Uncle Tommy told my 35 mother when he stood up to pass the caramels to the cousins who couldn't reach the coffee table without social embarrassment. "Wouldn't be Christmas at all."

"Wouldn't be Christmas without your stories," my mother told him as he leaned down to buss her on the cheek. . . .

THE KING OF STORIES

The doorbell rang. Everyone was surprised because the Christmas night party at Herman and Thora's was almost over. The clock said nine-thirty. Consensus had been growing that it was time for everyone to be getting home and let the curtain drop on Christmas for yet another year.

When the doorbell rang, my father opened the door, and the king of stories came into the living room like a prince, a duke, a man of royal blood: my grandfather in a rare appearance.

He hadn't brought his new wife, Helen. She'd been waiting a long time for him, pursuing Grandpa when Grandma was still in place. Helen was convinced Grandpa needed her and only her, and she'd finally captured him. But Raity, Herman, and Tommy weren't ready to forget the

woman who'd mothered them, changed their diapers, taught them to tie
shoes. They wanted Christmas to resurrect their mother's laughter, even if
it had been bittersweet. They wanted the memory of their mother's eyes
even if they had to look at Raity's eyes to be reminded—those uncertain
windows unable to hide her hesitation or her apology for taking up space
on earth.

So Grandpa came alone. 40

"We were wrapping things up," my father said, "but there's still some of
Thora's candy left."

"Just as well," Grandpa said. "I can't stay for long. I left Helen by herself."

He was a little man, squat in some ways, not in others. Sometimes he
seemed imperious, as if he'd been crowned king once upon a time. At other
times he seemed to be running after the crown that had rolled off his head
one day. Without his crown, he was a commoner. But even though he
never found it, he didn't shed his courtly ways or forget he was king of stories. He could shine the inside of a story into pure gold.

"Always a story," my mother said in disgust because of the way
Grandpa didn't pay much mind to his wife, who was sick with melancholia,
the way he'd stay out late at night drinking, telling stories to people too
drunk to care. "Always a story," about where he'd been and what he'd been
doing when he explained to his wife at 2:00 A.M. One story built upon another, a house of stories upon stories, floor after floor, stacks of stories, and
who could ever tell where the truth was in all that flurry of stories?

Aunt Raity and Uncle Elwin scooted over from their places on the sofa. 45
"Sit here, Dad," Raity said, patting the cushion. "How's my little daddy?"
She squeezed his bicep as he sat down and then rested her head on his
shoulder for a brief second.

"Fine as things will allow," he said, straightening the knees of his
trousers, but then he was back up again, center floor. "Children," he said.
"Do you want me to tell you about the time I was selling eggs and had to
balance my way across a railroad trestle? Or do you want me to tell you
about my favorite chicken who fell down the outhouse hole and squawked
like a mighty condor until. . . ."

"What about the one about the cow that showed up out of nowhere?"
my mother said.

"Well, all right," Grandpa said. "If you insist." He cleared his throat and
held up his hands as if he were preparing to conduct his audience. Then he
closed his eyes for a minute to concentrate before he began with words.

All of us children were looking up at the man standing in the middle of
the floor on the beige sculptured carpet. He seemed to have a glow on him,

almost as if emanating from a portable spotlight he carried with him for occasions such as this. He was a man who'd seen the world and lived to tell about it; he was a mystery man we'd heard about in whispers—a man who bought a new car when he hadn't paid for the one he had, a man who had enemies because they owed him money, a man who came home late at night and made our grandmother cry. We'd heard the whispers.

"He acts like he's been drinking again," Grace whispered to Tommy as she tapped her right foot close to my knee. They forgot me sitting at their feet, privy to their clandestine commentary. "He never shows up on Christmas night. What's he doing here now?"

"Shhh," Tommy said. "He's ready."

Grandpa stood in the middle of our living room as if he were a treasure to be revered and appreciated, a wild turkey spreading its tail, a man alive because he had an audience to validate him, saying, "Yes, yes, you are the king." Still looking for his crown.

"As you children know," he began, his eyes still closed, "we never had much money when I was a little boy. There were eleven of us, not counting Mom and Dad."

"You sure you don't want to sit down, Fon?" my mother asked.

"No, no. I like to stand when I tell stories." His eyes were opening. "My mother was a real stickler for the church, you know. She followed every admonition given her by the authorities, one of them being tithing. My dad wasn't quite so attached to the principle, but he could see how upset she was when he told her they'd better not pay their tithing this one particular month. They didn't have it to pay.

"Well, as you might imagine, Mother went into a tailspin, crying like a reed pipe in the wind, wailing how the Lord would take care of them if only they had enough faith. Where was his faith? She was going to take their last money to the bishop then and there. Right that minute.

"My father could see she had her mind made up, so he said he'd walk with her over to the bishop's. They had nothing to lose, he guessed, except they wouldn't be able to feed their children now. He hadn't done well by them, he confessed as they walked.

"When they handed the bishop an envelope with the last of their money in it, they didn't say it was all they had. They paid as if this was the smallest pittance possible in their vast fortune raining down from heaven above. The bishop smiled and said, 'The windows of heaven shall open onto you. The sun will shine so bright you'll wish you had a windowshade to pull down. Bless you, my faithful brother and sister.'"

"Wasn't that just before his dad did himself in?" Grace whispered more quietly than I'd ever heard anyone whisper and still hear it.

50

55

Grandpa pulled at his jaw, stopped to think about something, his mind 60
stretching further out of the room than before. Raity's eyes were moist, as
well as my father's. My mother looked at all the children, pleased we were
all tuned in, rapt witnesses to this finer moment of our grandfather.

"Well, for two days we didn't have anything to eat. Mother was afraid
to borrow from the neighbor again, so we chewed on the last of the wheat
we'd stored in the basement. Chewed it like chewing gum. Speaking of
gum, Tom, why do you chew it the way you do? It doesn't become you."

Tommy was startled. I could feel his body react because I was leaning
against the side of his leg. "Sorry, Dad." He pulled the gum out of his mouth
and wrapped it in a corner of scratch paper he had in his shirt pocket.

"Just about the time our stomachs were gnawing like rats in an empty
loft, this brown and white cow wanders up to our door. I mean up to our
door, not into the yard. She walks up and talks to us with a long moo. No
rope was hanging on her. She didn't look like any of the neighbors' cows.
She was new to our eyes. We'd never seen her in anyone's pasture. And she
was ready to milk. Full and tight, her teats spread out like swollen fingers.

"'Whose cow is that?' my mother asked.

"'Nobody's I know of,' my father said. 'Fon, you run around to all the 65
neighbors in this part and ask if any of them are missing a cow.'

"Well, I ran as fast as wind around the neighborhood, then ran back to
the house with the good news. And nobody came looking for that cow, either. Not one person. That cow was probably brought to our door by one of
the Three Nephites. Led right to our door by the Lord's anointed."

He held his hand in the air with his last word. No one spoke while his
hand stayed in the air, the fingers pointing upward in praise of God. He
held us as if we were an orchestra whose strings he didn't want to stop vi-
brating. Then he closed his hand and thumped his heart once with his fist.

"And with that," he said after a slight pause, "I must go back home. I wish
you all a happy new year. I wish you all faith. I wish you all peace. May one of
the Nephites help you if you're in need and the angels smile upon you."

I hated the end of his story. He knew how to weave the words and his
hands and his eyes together into the magic requisite for a tale. His story was
the only one being told on earth while he told it. His was the last word.

Everyone broke into clusters, shaking hands, kissing cheeks, wishing 70
"Merry Christmas" one last time before it was too late. I watched my
mother put her arm around Grandpa. "Thank you for that beautiful story,
Fon. You touch my heart every time you tell it. Thank you, and please tell
Helen we missed her."

"Hypocrites," I heard Grace whispering as she gathered her skirt to
stand up and while her red-patent shoes squeaked. I still sat on the floor

with my back resting on the sofa's seat cushions. "Both Thora and your dad. Can you believe she can say she missed Helen or that he can tell a story like that and not tell the whole story. Then he walks out of here and lives the way he does."

"Be quiet, Grace," Tommy said. "Have a little respect for the man."

"Respect! Him?"

"He's my father."

"But he's so full of bull, even you say so."   75

"He's my father."

And Grandpa walked the full circle of relatives, saying goodnight to his children, then looking each of us grandchildren straight in the eyes and telling us to have faith like his mother had faith, then we'd be able to find the way.

"The windows of heaven will open for you," he said to me as he held my hand in his, not letting me act on the impulse to escape. "Everything will be given to you; all will be understood. You are a good girl, aren't you, Phyllis? Obedient to God's and your parents' word, aren't you?"

I shook my head yes, trying not to show the shame I was feeling in this act of supposed affection between a grandfather everyone whispered about behind his back and his granddaughter who heard all the whispers. The words of his story, the whisperings I heard, Grace's words, all were liquid in my head. What manner of man was standing before me? Whose hand did I hold? Which stories were the true stories? Could I kneel and ask God which?

Standing outside the stories, I could feel them colliding with each   80
other. They tumbled from everyone's mouth and filled my ears until I was confused by them. But every time I was inside a story, there was no confusion, only the clarity of a tale spun and the sound of the spinning wheel.

So as I held my grandfather's hand, the only thing I could think to say was, "Will you come back sometime and tell us another story?"

"You like my stories?" he said.

"I do."

It was Christmas. All was calm, all was bright. The cardboard story of peace on earth was arranged on top of our Baldwin spinet—an awed Joseph, a round yon Virgin kneeling over the glow of her heavenly child. I'd felt the same sense of love when the Holy Ghost slipped through my ceiling not so many years ago.

Filled with this serenity, I smiled at my grandfather. I held his hand   85
until we became another story, he and I. He was the king of stories, and now I was the queen at his side. My grandfather could be anything I wanted him to be. He was safe with his hand in mine.

Issues for Discussion

1. What is the "point" of these two family stories? What attracts Mura and Barber to these two men?
2. In what ways do you sense that Mura and Barber are editing the pictures they present of their grandfathers? What are they enhancing? What, do you suppose, are they selectively forgetting?
3. How might Mura's grandmother or Barber's Aunt Grace rewrite their accounts of the men in these stories? Whose, do you think, would be the most accurate? Why?

J O U R N A L   O P T I O N S

People and Places from Your Past

1. Write a couple of stories based on "legendary" figures in your family — grandparents, great-uncles or great-aunts, or other figures in your family's past who seemed to have some special significance in your family's collective memory.
2. Describe a place you remember from your childhood, a place like Mura's Aunt Ruth's home that is steeped in fantasy for you — or simply a place that is associated with any strong feeling or memory from your childhood.

The Writing Process

Anyone who has ever tried to write has at least occasionally suffered from writer's block. We all know the symptoms: breaking out in a cold sweat when you see a blank page; prolonged staring into empty space; ideas that come in fits and starts and seem to evaporate whenever you try to capture them in words. Writer's block often grows out of the assumptions we bring to the task of writing — out of the story we've learned to tell ourselves about the academic writing process. Many students come to college believing that good writers are born, not made: according to the script they bring with them, the good writer sits down the night before a paper is due, thinks for a bit until she knows what she wants to say, and then simply says it, from start to finish, all in a well-formed, neatly executed, and thoughtful essay. Meanwhile, the rest of us gasp for air and pray that another idea will please come soon.

The trick to coping with writer's block is to change your story about how good writing happens. Experienced writers know that writing is never a neat or effortless activity. More often than not, productive writing grows out of a messy, muddled-looking process involving scattered notes, pictures, diagrams, multiple drafts, cross-outs, cartoons, arrows, cuts and pastes, and constant questioning. We tend to think of writing as a matter of simple self-expression because one of our dominant cultural stories tells us that we are individuals, and individuals are people who know what they think and feel. Once you know what you think, all you have to do is translate those well-formed thoughts and feelings into words. But in many ways it makes better sense to see writing as a process of constant discovery: sometimes you have to brainstorm ideas for pages or even crank out a couple of formless, meandering "junk" drafts before you stumble onto the story you want to tell. If you adopt a discovery approach to writing, you acknowledge that you don't just think up ideas and then express them in clear prose. Instead, you try to engage yourself in a dialogue: you venture an idea on paper, follow it as far as it will take you, let yourself be reminded of another idea—even if it's a little off the track—follow it for a while, reread, and get reminded again of an even better idea. Maybe you add these ideas up into a coherent paper; maybe you discard the first ones and build your essay around a whole new approach. The important thing is to find ways to stimulate this process of dialogical thinking. You may find it helpful to think of writing as a process that can be divided into the following four stages.

Prewriting. This is the common term for the first step. Prewriting includes anything you do to generate ideas before you actually begin formal drafting—although writers typically employ prewriting techniques throughout the writing process. Prewriting is the messiest, most creative phase of the process: it begins with taking notes while you read—like the marginal glosses and dialoguing we discussed earlier (see pp. 32–33). It also involves things like brainstorming, clustering, listing, and doing inventories, storyboards, cartoons, and diagrams—just about anything that will get ideas and associations coming. Some writers develop habitual prewriting strategies that help them to generate ideas without what appears to be a formal process: they may have routines for taking, reviewing, and categorizing notes that stimulate them to ask questions and begin thinking dialogically. They may discuss their ideas with friends and make discoveries through the give-and-take of conversation. They may experiment with ideas while they jog, work out, or even when they sleep. Most writers, however, use a pencil and paper in prewriting so they'll have a record of their thoughts. Prewriting is frequently the most complicated—and the longest—stage of the writing process. Skipping it is a sure way to invite writer's block.

Composing.   Composing begins when you start to do a formal draft. Some writers have special rituals connected with composing. They may prefer to write drafts with a favorite pencil or pen, or they may insist on working with a word processor. Some writers compose best in the quiet of a library; others may prefer the din of a café or a dormitory commons. The important part about composing is to remember that discovery continues even during this phase. Some writers, for instance, find that they inevitably grasp the "real" idea that lurks behind their writing only after they attempt a formal draft. If that's the case for you, you'll want to get to composing sooner than most writers—probably by attempting a couple of "junk" drafts fairly early in your process (see p. 61).

Revising.   This is perhaps the most misunderstood component of the writing process. When asked to revise their writing, students often think they're supposed to correct grammar and spelling mistakes—or perhaps change a word or phrase here and there—to make the paper "read" better. But revision usually means more than simple correction. When accomplished writers revise an essay or a book, they literally try to "resee" it—to reconsider or re-envision its organization, focus, and approach. Revision gives you the chance to reshape your first draft in light of the ideas you discover while writing. Like prewriting, revision occurs throughout the writing process: every time you look back over a sentence or paragraph you've just drafted and rewrite to clarify an idea or add emphasis, you're revising. It's often a good idea, though, to postpone revision until you've got at least the semblance of a full draft; if you indulge in too much self-criticism early in your process, you may discourage the kind of creative risk-taking you need to get ideas flowing.

Editing.   Revision focuses on substantial changes in your paper; editing is more concerned with the mechanics of writing. After you've finished revising and you feel satisfied with your essay's shape and logic and the development of your ideas, you can take the time to look more carefully at issues of grammar, punctuation, and spelling.

J O U R N A L
O P T I O N S

Exploring Your Writing Process

Your writing process may vary depending on the topic (Is it a subject you're comfortable with or one that will require some serious reading and research?), the type of writing task involved (Are you writing a formal essay, a technical report, or an editorial argument?), and the writing situation (Is it an in-class essay, a term paper, or a personal letter?). To help you begin to develop a model of your writing processes, write journal responses to the following questions:

1. Think about the journal assignment you completed in response to the family stories by David Mura and Phyllis Barber. How would you describe the process you went through to complete it? Did you just sit down and write, or did you think first about your experiences? Did you make notes and rearrange them in some way?

2. Now think about a time in the past when you wrote a formal essay. How would you describe the process you used at that time? In general, what do you typically do to get started when you write formal academic papers? What do you do when you get stuck? How do you get going again? Do you have a special place where you like to prewrite or compose? How does your general writing process compare with the model presented above? How much effort do you usually dedicate to prewriting, composing, revising, and editing?

Follow up: When you've completed these journal entries, share them in small groups or with the entire class. To get an idea of the range of strategies available, you might want to list the various types of activities and techniques different students use when they write in different situations. Afterwards, discuss the effectiveness of your own strategies. Do they usually seem productive? What would you like to change the next time you write a formal essay?

ESSAY OPTIONS

Family Stories

Now it's time for you to transform one of your own stories into a more formal academic paper. The following assignment invites you to use the informal journal entries you did earlier in this chapter as points of departure for a more developed essay. Choose only one topic to focus on — perhaps the one you most enjoyed writing about in your journal. Before you begin writing — or even thinking — about your choice, be sure to read the section "Approaches to Pre-Writing" that follows this assignment.

Topic 1. The readings in this chapter focus on family stories. Most families tell and retell favorite stories that create an informal history of family experiences — stories of courtship, marriage, moving to a new place or country, legendary characters, unusual relatives, or strange occurrences. Write a paper in which you relate a family story of your own and explain its significance to you. Be sure to provide the reader with the background information she may need to understand your story and its meaning. For inspiration, review the family stories by David Mura (p. 37) and Phyllis Barber (p. 42).

Topic 2. For some families, particular customs, traditions, or holidays have a special meaning. Most cultures have ceremonies that commemorate special events: coming of age, important historical occasions, religious experiences. In addition, many cultures make special days of "namedays," birthdays, or wedding anniversaries. Write a paper in which you describe and explain the importance of one of the traditional customs, holiday celebrations, or ceremonies in which you participate. It might be one you particularly enjoy or even one you dislike. Think about the background information your reader may need to understand this event and your feelings about it. For examples, take a look at Phyllis Barber's "Stories" (p. 42) or D'Andra Galarza's "Las Mañanitas" (p. 99).

Topic 3. Think of a time from your childhood or adolescence that defined a turning point in your life—a moment when something happened that changed your life or when you decided to make a significant life change. Write a paper in which you tell the story of this turning point, detailing the circumstances that led up to it, the way it changed you, and the impact it's had on your life. Be sure to explain what this experience has meant to you and include enough detailed information so that your reader can understand your story's importance. Beverly Donofrio's "Trouble" (p. 9) and Reginald Lockett's "How I Started Writing Poetry" (p. 76) offer possible models.

Approaches to Prewriting

Before beginning work on one of these topics, take a few minutes to consider how to get started. There is no single prewriting technique that works equally well for everyone. Your goal in prewriting is to generate as many ideas as you can, without worrying about how they fit together or where they lead. Anything you do that leads you to "discover" a detail, a memory, or an idea is worth the effort. Below you'll find a few standard prewriting strategies. As you work on this first full paper, experiment with these techniques to see which work the best for you. You might decide that you like them all, you might find different strategies useful in different contexts, or you might come up with new strategies on your own. The important thing is to make your own approach to prewriting as rich and as productive as you can.

Brainstorming.   When you brainstorm you list any thought that comes to mind about your topic. The purpose of brainstorming is to generate a lot of ideas as quickly as possible. You want to work fast when brainstorming because speed helps you overcome the mental censors that stifle creativity. Try to get your ideas down as fast as you can write; don't take time to think or to critique them. And try to fill a whole page or more if you can. If Beverly Donofrio were brainstorming the story she tells in "Trouble," she might generate a list that looks something like this:

Donna & "inoculations"

Dag Hammarskjold H.S.

Pat Boone — "Bernadine"

1963

beehive hair & fake tatocs

Miss Clairol (16 oz.)

pregnant

Cop/Dad

NO COLLEGE!

basement books

Shakespeare, Whitman, Tennyson, and the gang

hairy spiders

N.Y. dreaming vs. typist nightmare

Ma cooks and cleans and Bradlees

brother = golden penis = Mr. Citizen

Church Bazaar w/ Skylar Barrister

Danny Dempsey & his wicked knife

cruisin & moonin

night I egged the Choatie

crotch shots

fake turds in H2O fountains

Key Club guy: too much thinking

Once you've generated as many ideas as possible, you should look your list over and decide which ideas you want to keep. The primary goal of brainstorming is to get lots of ideas down on paper, but often you'll find that many of the ideas you spew out during a productive session are repetitious, off the topic, or just plain boring. Before moving on, you'll want to winnow these out from the "keepers."

Next, you'll want to try to discover relationships between the items remaining in your list by grouping them into categories. Grouping related ideas and events will help you begin to shape your thinking into topics — broader, thematically related ideas that you may eventually develop into paragraphs or larger segments of your paper. Here are a few groupings that might naturally emerge from the brainstorming we've imagined for Donofrio's "Trouble":

Dreams	Bad Behavior	Family
basement books	cruisin & moonin	Cop/Dad
Shakespeare	egging the Choate kid	Ma cooks/cleans/Bradlees
Whitman	Skylar Barrister	brother = golden penis =
Tennyson	fake turds	Mr. Citizen
New York	crotch shots	
College		

At this point you may decide to revisit certain items for a second round of brainstorming. Donofrio, for example, might decide to zoom in on her father, because he plays an important role in her story, and to generate a secondary list that would include the following:

SuperCop

Mr. Veto

going nuts over boy phone calls

painting-by-numbers

dinner seating arrangement

surveillance

always humming

She might also do second rounds of brainstorming for ideas that don't fit neatly into any particular category but that still seem too important to discard. Thus, a second round on the idea of "1963," might look something like this:

Kennedy assassinated

the Beatles

cold war

Vietnam

make out parties

Dominic Mezzi

push-up bras

Every round of brainstorming produces more and more details for you to think and write about. And every round leads to the possibility of additional rounds and the generation of additional key ideas.

After you've detailed your brainstorming, you'll want to step back and consider the relationship that underlies the various groups of ideas and events you've produced. The few groups we've created from our imaginary brainstorming of Donofrio's "Trouble"—"Dreams," "Dad = SuperCop," and "Bad Behavior"—already begin to suggest that hers is a story about a young woman who decides to "go bad" as an act of rebellion against a family that's unsympathetic to her dreams. The relationships you discover among these groupings gives you your story frame—the logical structure of events, actions, and causes and effects—that underlies the story you want to tell. And this framework in turn gives your story its shape, its point, and its purpose.

Once you've discovered your story frame, you may want to reconsider the sequence of ideas and events you initially generated. Memory is rarely a straightforward, orderly process; we tend to recollect ideas and events through patterns of association and not in strict chronological order. The memory of the night when Donofrio's parents told her she couldn't go to college might have popped into her head just after she thought about her father, but as she rereads her brainstorming she might reorder these events in a way that seems more logical—and more effective—given the story she's trying to tell. Instead of talking about this important moment in the middle of her story, she might decide to postpone it until the end, when it would have more impact. In the same way, although she remembers Danny Dempsey and his knife toward the end of brainstorming, it might make better sense to mention this event as an example of her early career as a "bad" girl and rebellious adolescent. Taking the time to reconsider the order of the ideas you brainstorm will help you to organize your thinking before you begin to write and may even suggest the beginnings of an outline of your paper.

Clustering. Clustering is a graphic strategy for generating ideas that provides an alternative to listing. Sometimes your ideas just won't present themselves in neat—or even messy—lists of associations. Clustering frees you from this straight-line approach and helps you see how ideas might relate to each other. Begin by writing down a central word or idea. Circle it, and then continue by surrounding it with other words that it suggests. Again, don't worry about the quality of your ideas at this point; just get them down. Once you've surrounded your original concept, repeat this process, trying now to come up with as many associations as you can for each of the words or concepts you've just created. Eventually, you'll end up with a spreading "cluster" of ideas that radiates out from your central concept. If Leslie Marmon Silko had used this approach to prepare for "Language and Literature from a Pueblo Indian Perspective," the results of her efforts might have looked something like this:

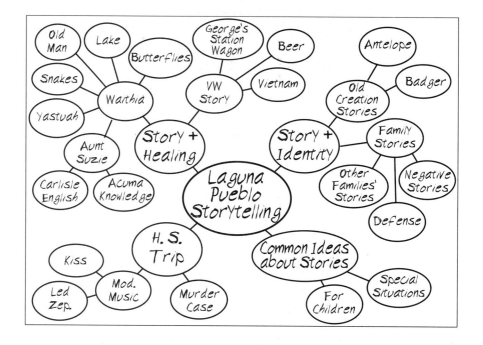

As you can see, clustering can be extended all the way down to the level of very specific detail. Our imagined clustering of Silko's essay branches from the concept of storytelling, to the meaning of storytelling from a Pueblo Indian perspective, to the idea of story as a source of healing, to the stories told by Aunt Suzie, to the specific story of Waithia. And even at this level, clustering can continue to generate details like Waithia's desire for yastoah, her quest for firewood, her drowning, the old man who sees her, and the transformation of her clothing into butterflies. The power of clustering lies in its ability to help you generate layers of detail and to see how these details interrelate. Just remember that clustering is always a "work-in-progress": as you generate more and more ideas, you may want to revise your clustering diagram by redrawing lines to show emerging and changing relationships.

Talking Draft.   Some writers find that they can clarify their ideas better when they try to explain them to someone else. The process of explanation —itself a kind of storytelling—can help you discover relationships and ideas you hadn't seen before. Try this approach by talking through your main idea for your essay with a classmate. Your partner can give you feedback, ask questions when clarification is needed, and make suggestions for improvement. In the following example of a talking draft dialogue, Mariel is having trouble writing about a turning point in her life. Her conversation with José gives her insight about her topic and helps her to recognize its complexity.

> *Mariel:* I'm thinking of writing about the time I got lost on the freeway and I was afraid to get off because I didn't think I was driving through a good neighborhood, and I was afraid . . .
>
> *José:* Why were you afraid?
>
> *Mariel:* I don't know . . . I guess I had heard bad things about that part of town . . . I guess I was afraid of getting lost.
>
> *José:* Did you think you could ask someone for directions?
>
> *Mariel:* I was afraid to, so I just keep on driving. It was daytime, and I really don't know why I was so afraid. I guess I just thought it was kind of a really dangerous area, and I was afraid to ask for help, so I ended up going way out of my way. But maybe I was right not to stop. There's a lot of crime in that area.
>
> *José:* It sounds like a complicated decision. Why do you want to write about this?
>
> *Mariel:* Well, at first I wanted to talk about how the city has become so dangerous. But now that I think about it, maybe I want to talk about how my fears kept me from asking for help and how that makes me feel about myself and my city. What's the future going to hold for us if we're always afraid of other people? On the other hand, maybe there are reasons to be afraid. I'll have to work on this.

You can experiment with a talking draft by dividing into pairs in class, but most writers find that they talk through their ideas best in a more relaxed atmosphere. The natural setting for a talking draft is over a cup of coffee or a soda in your college cafeteria, in a dormitory commons, or at a café or restaurant off campus.

Freewriting.   Like brainstorming and clustering, freewriting is an approach that can help you discover what you are thinking at an unconscious level. If you're having trouble generating ideas—or even settling on a topic—it sometimes helps to dive directly into the process of writing. To start a freewrite, sit down with paper and pencil and give yourself five to ten minutes to write whatever comes into your head about your topic. You can write anything: the only rule is not to stop writing during the time you've allotted. If you get stuck, you can write "Now, I'm stuck" or something to that effect, and write about why or how it feels to be stuck until you get back on track. When the time is up, stop and review what you've written. You might want to make additional notes at this point, or try another bout of freewriting based on the results of your first round. Freewriting is an important prewriting strategy, because thinking is rarely a top-down process: we hardly ever think of a complete thought and then translate it into words. More often than not, our ideas percolate up to consciousness, appearing in half-sentences and phrases before they take shape on paper as whole ideas. If you've had the experience of discovering a really good idea just as you finish a paper, you'll understand how this happens. In a sense, freewriting is a way to stimulate the process of discovery through drafting without the hassle of writing an entire essay.

Drawing.   Scientists have recently confirmed what elementary school students have known for decades—that different people think in different ways. Exclusively verbal prewriting strategies like brainstorming may work well for students who relate to the world through words. But verbal approaches may only frustrate those who tend to "see" and not "say" ideas and relationships. If you're a visual thinker, you may want to experiment with graphic approaches to generating and organizing your ideas. Instead of brainstorming key words and concepts, try covering a whole page or two with drawings or cartoons that capture your ideas on the subject. Let your mind—and your pencil—wander much in the way you would when you brainstorm or freewrite. Then sit back and review what you've drawn, trying to create captions that begin to translate your ideas into words. Once you've generated some ideas on your topic, you may want to experiment with possible organizational strategies by drawing them as "storyboards." Start by dividing a sheet of paper into two-inch squares. Beginning at the top left corner, draw the sequence of your story—or your essay—so that you can see where it is going and how its various episodes and sections fit together. Again, just as with brainstorming and freewriting, don't worry about the quality of your drawings: stick figures and two-dimensional symbols will do.

Junk Draft.   No matter how much prewriting they do, some writers freeze the moment they sit down to write the first formal draft of their essay. This makes sense because most of us are still developing and refining our ideas as we write: plunging into a "formal" draft can make us worry about grammar, sentence structure, and all the other formal aspects of writing that can kill creativity. The junk draft offers a way around this dilemma. You can forget about "correctness" and feel free to experiment with ideas in a junk draft because you know that you are going to throw much of it away. When you do a junk draft, work as quickly as you can: you may not want to force yourself to compose as swiftly as you would for a freewrite, but you do want to sketch out the basic sections of the paper as quickly as possible. Don't worry about sentence shape and mechanics at this point. Don't bother to erase or "white out" botched sentence openings; just cross them out and keep on going. Try to focus on your ideas and the details that will get them across to the reader. Once you're finished, you have something concrete to work with, develop, and eventually revise. Now is the time to review what you've written and to decide what to save and what to throw away. A good junk draft can also help you to see what sections of your paper need more details and what changes you may need to make in the paper's overall organization. Just remember that a junk draft, like a freewrite, is part of your discovery process: as you reread and begin planning a formal draft of your paper, let yourself pursue new ideas and even play with new approaches to your topic. Creative ideas and fresh insights have a way of emerging unexpectedly once you get the hang of junk drafting.

Outlines.   In the past, many writing teachers insisted that students write elaborate outlines before they began a paper. Often this demand for a formal outline stimulated little more than a bad case of writer's block, because, as we've already mentioned, many writers discover what they want to say only through the process of trying to say it. But that doesn't mean that outlines are a waste of time—not if you outline at the right stage of your writing process. Informally jotting down a sequence of ideas during prewriting can help you design the organization of your essay and see how your ideas relate to one another at an early stage. By moving key words or topics around in an informal outline, you can try out different organizational strategies. A more detailed outline may also be helpful, particularly for longer essays, but many writers find it wise to wait until they've completed a junk draft before outlining. At this point, outlining becomes a revision strategy: after finishing your junk draft, gloss each paragraph with a sentence or word that summarizes its content. Then review these glosses to see if the resulting order is logical. If you can think of alternative orderings that would be easier for your reader to understand, use them as the basis for a formal outline before writing the next draft.

J O U R N A L
O P T I O N

Analyzing Your Prewriting Process

Return to the Essay Options (p. 53) and review the topics suggested there. As you begin working on your paper, remember that one of your purposes should be to experiment with a number of prewriting options. Use your journal to keep track of the approaches you try and to evaluate how well each works for you. Also make notes on the approaches that you invent for yourself. When you finish a formal draft of your paper, share the result of your observations with the class. Which strategies seemed the most productive for you? Which helped you generate and organize ideas most effectively? What approaches would you like to try when you work on future papers? What suggestions do you have for your classmates?

CHAPTER 3

Academically Speaking: Writing for Teachers

Telling Tales in School

School is an incredibly rich source of scripts and stories: we can all tell tales about the time we struggled with a particularly troublesome homework assignment. And like Calvin in the cartoon, most of us have encountered at least one "Zorg Despot" in the classroom. School stories are important because they shape our expectations about what it means to be a successful or unsuccessful student—about what constitutes "proper" attitudes, behavior, and forms of expression. And perhaps the most important school story of all is the story we learn about the relationship between students and teachers. Everyone who comes to college enters with a set of mental models describing the way teachers act, the roles they play, the kinds of people they tend to be, and the demands they are likely to make. All of us absorb stereotypes about teachers and professors from popular culture and the other subcultures we belong to. We all grow up hearing stories about "hard" teachers and "easy" teachers from friends and family, and we pick up a sizable chunk of teacher lore from the characters we see on television shows and in the movies. But a good number of our mental models of teachers as readers comes from direct prior experience. Some students may begin their college careers thinking of the teacher as a kind of "pal"—a sympathetic and supportive friend who is always ready to encourage new ideas or hear about their feelings and experiences. Students who bring this model of the teacher reader to college—perhaps because a high school instructor played this role for them—may feel comfortable getting words down on paper but may also find it difficult to adjust to the formality of college-level discourse. Other students may enter college seeing the teacher reader as a kind of correction machine, a red pencil in pants. The way you tell the story of the "typical teacher" may contain values and beliefs that can help you achieve your academic goals, but it may also foster attitudes about learning and writing that aren't very effective in college.

Almost everyone has known a teacher who has, for better or worse, made a difference in her life. The following school story by Audre Lorde offers a case in point. As you read this memoir of Lorde's early experiences learning to read, try to "listen" for memories about important classes and teachers that arise from your own educational experiences. Born in New York in 1934, Audre Lorde grew up in a West Indian immigrant household. She worked as a librarian and as a professor of English at Hunter College. Her first book of poetry, *The First Cities* (1968), explores the impact of race and racism on African Americans. In *Zami: A New Spelling of My Name* (1982), the source of this selection, Lorde offers her "biomythography"—the account of her own development as an artist, activist, lesbian, and African American. Lorde died in 1992.

Before Reading

Write a brief entry in your journal about the earliest experiences you can remember that involved reading and writing. Tell about the setting of these experiences: Were they in school or at home? Do you recall learning to read and write from your teachers, parents, siblings? What feelings do these memories evoke?

From *Zami: A New Spelling of My Name*
Audre Lorde

When I was five years old and still legally blind, I started school in a sight-conservation class in the local public school on 135th Street and Lenox Avenue. On the corner was a blue wooden booth where white women gave away free milk to Black mothers with children. I used to long for some Hearst Free Milk Fund milk, in those cute little bottles with their red and white tops, but my mother never allowed me to have any, because she said it was charity, which was bad and demeaning, and besides the milk was warm and might make me sick.

The school was right across the avenue from the catholic school where my two older sisters went, and this public school had been used as a threat against them for as long as I could remember. If they didn't behave and get good marks in schoolwork and deportment, they could be "transferred." A "transfer" carried the same dire implications as "deportation" came to imply decades later.

Of course everybody knew that public school kids did nothing but "fight," and you could get "beaten up" every day after school, instead of being marched out of the schoolhouse door in two neat rows like little robots, silent but safe and unattacked, to the corner where the mothers waited.

But the catholic school had no kindergarten, and certainly not one for blind children.

Despite my nearsightedness, or maybe because of it, I learned to read at   5
the same time I learned to talk, which was only about a year or so before I started school. Perhaps *learn* isn't the right word to use for my beginning to talk, because to this day I don't know if I didn't talk earlier because I didn't know how, or if I didn't talk because I had nothing to say that I would be allowed to say without punishment. Self-preservation starts very early in West Indian families.

I learned how to read from Mrs. Augusta Baker, the children's librarian at the old 135th Street branch library, which has just recently been torn down to make way for a new library building to house the Schomburg Collection on African-American History and Culture. If that was the only good deed that lady ever did in her life, may she rest in peace. Because that deed saved my life, if not sooner, then later, when sometimes the only thing I had to hold on to was knowing I could read, and that that could get me through.

My mother was pinching my ear off one bright afternoon, while I lay spreadeagled on the floor of the Children's Room like a furious little brown toad, screaming bloody murder and embarrassing my mother to death. I know it must have been spring or early fall, because without the protection of a heavy coat, I can still feel the stinging soreness in the flesh of my upper arm. There, where my mother's sharp fingers had already tried to pinch me into silence. To escape those inexorable fingers I had hurled myself to the floor, roaring with pain as I could see them advancing toward my ears again. We were waiting to pick up my two older sisters from story hour, held upstairs on another floor of the dry-smelling quiet library. My shrieks pierced the reverential stillness.

Suddenly, I looked up, and there was a library lady standing over me. My mother's hands had dropped to her sides. From the floor where I was lying, Mrs. Baker seemed like yet another mile-high woman about to do me in. She had immense, light, hooded eyes and a very quiet voice that said, not damnation for my noise, but "Would you like to hear a story, little girl?"

Part of my fury was because I had not been allowed to go to that secret feast called story hour since I was too young, and now here was this strange lady offering me my own story.

I didn't dare to look at my mother, half-afraid she might say no, I was too bad for stories. Still bewildered by this sudden change of events, I climbed up upon the stool which Mrs. Baker pulled over for me, and gave her my full attention. This was a new experience for me and I was insatiably curious.

Mrs. Baker read me *Madeline,* and *Horton Hatches the Egg,* both of which rhymed and had huge lovely pictures which I could see from behind my newly acquired eyeglasses, fastened around the back of my rambunctious head by a black elastic band running from earpiece to earpiece. She also read me another storybook about a bear named Herbert who ate up an entire family, one by one, starting with the parents. By the time she had finished that one, I was sold on reading for the rest of my life.

10

I took the books from Mrs. Baker's hands after she was finished reading, and traced the large black letters with my fingers, while I peered again at the beautiful bright colors of the pictures. Right then I decided I was going to find out how to do that myself. I pointed to the black marks which I could now distinguish as separate letters, different from my sisters' more grown-up books, whose smaller print made the pages only one grey blur for me. I said, quite loudly, for whoever was listening to hear, "I want to read."

My mother's surprised relief outweighed whatever annoyance she was still feeling at what she called my whelpish carryings-on. From the background where she had been hovering while Mrs. Baker read, my mother moved forward quickly, mollified and impressed. I had spoken. She scooped me up from the low stool, and to my surprise, kissed me, right in front of everybody in the library, including Mrs. Baker.

This was an unprecedented and unusual display of affection in public, the cause of which I did not comprehend. But it was a warm and happy feeling. For once, obviously, I had done something right.

My mother set me back upon the stool and turned to Mrs. Baker, smiling. 15

"Will wonders never cease to perform!" Her excitement startled me back into cautious silence.

Not only had I been sitting still for longer than my mother would have thought possible, and sitting quietly. I had also spoken rather than screamed, something that my mother, after four years and a lot of worry, had despaired that I would ever do. Even one intelligible word was a very rare event for me. And although the doctors at the clinic had clipped the little membrane under my tongue so I was no longer tongue-tied, and had assured my mother that I was not retarded, she still had her terrors and her doubts. She was genuinely happy for any possible alternative to what she was afraid might be a dumb child. The ear-pinching was forgotten. My mother accepted the alphabet and picture books Mrs. Baker gave her for me, and I was on my way.

I sat at the kitchen table with my mother, tracing letters and calling their names. Soon she taught me how to say the alphabet forwards and backwards as it was done in Grenada. Although she had never gone beyond the seventh grade, she had been put in charge of teaching the first grade children their letters during her last year at Mr. Taylor's School in Grenville. She told me stories about his strictness as she taught me how to print my name.

I did not like the tail of the Y hanging down below the line in Audrey, and would always forget to put it on, which used to disturb my mother greatly. I used to love the evenness of AUDRELORDE at four years of age, but I remembered to put on the Y because it pleased my mother, and because, as she always insisted to me, that was the way it had to be because that was the way it was. No deviation was allowed from her interpretations of correct.

So by the time I arrived at the sight-conservation kindergarten, braided,   20
scrubbed, and bespectacled, I was able to read large-print books and write my name with a regular pencil. Then came my first rude awakening about school. Ability had nothing to do with expectation.

There were only seven or eight of us little Black children in a big classroom, all with various serious deficiencies of sight. Some of us were crosseyed, some of us were nearsighted, and one little girl had a patch over one of her eyes.

We were given special short wide notebooks to write in, with very widely spaced lines on yellow paper. They looked like my sister's music notebooks. We were also given thick black crayons to write with. Now you don't grow up fat, Black, nearly blind, and ambidextrous in a West Indian household, particularly my parents' household, and survive without being or becoming fairly rigid fairly fast. And having been roundly spanked on several occasions for having made that mistake at home, I knew quite well that crayons were not what you wrote with, and music books were definitely not what you wrote in.

I raised my hand. When the teacher asked me what I wanted, I asked for some regular paper to write on and a pencil. That was my undoing. "We don't have any pencils here," I was told.

Our first task was to copy down the first letter of our names in those notebooks with our black crayons. Our teacher went around the room and wrote the required letter into each one of our notebooks. When she came around to me, she printed a large A in the upper left corner of the first page of my notebook, and handed me the crayon.

"I can't," I said, knowing full well that what you do with black crayons   25
is scribble on the wall and get your backass beaten, or color around the edges of pictures, but not write. To write, you needed a pencil. "I can't!" I said, terrified, and started to cry.

"Imagine that, a big girl like you. Such a shame, I'll have to tell your mother that you won't even try. And such a big girl like you!"

And it was true. Although young, I was the biggest child by far in the whole class, a fact that had not escaped the attention of the little boy who sat behind me, and who was already whispering "fatty, fatty!" whenever the teacher's back was turned.

"Now just try, dear. I'm sure you can try to print your A. Mother will be so pleased to see that at least you tried." She patted my stiff braids and turned to the next desk.

Well, of course, she had said the magic words, because I would have walked over rice on my knees to please Mother. I took her nasty old soft smudgy crayon and pretended that it was a nice neat pencil with a fine point, elegantly sharpened that morning outside the bathroom door by my father, with the little penknife that he always carried around in his bathrobe pocket.

I bent my head down close to the desk that smelled like old spittle and rubber erasers, and on that ridiculous yellow paper with those laughably wide spaces I printed my best AUDRE. I had never been too good at keeping between straight lines no matter what their width, so it slanted down across the page something like this: A

        U

          D

            R

              E

The notebooks were short and there was no more room for anything else on that page. So I turned the page over, and wrote again, earnestly and laboriously, biting my lip, L

       O

         R

        D

          E

half-showing off, half-eager to please.

By this time, Miss Teacher had returned to the front of the room.

"Now when you're finished drawing your letter, children," she said, "Just raise your hand high." And her voice smiled a big smile. It is surprising to me that I can still hear her voice but I can't see her face, and I don't know whether she was Black or white. I can remember the way she smelled, but not the color of her hand upon my desk.

Well, when I heard that, my hand flew up in the air, wagging frantically. There was one thing my sisters had warned me about school in great detail: you must never talk in school unless you raised your hand. So I raised my hand, anxious to be recognized. I could imagine what teacher would say to my mother when she came to fetch me home at noon. My mother would know that her warning to me to "be good" had in truth been heeded.

Miss Teacher came down the aisle and stood beside my desk, looking down at my book. All of a sudden the air around her hand beside my notebook grew very still and frightening.

"Well I never!" Her voice was sharp. "I thought I told you to draw this   35
letter? You don't even want to try and do as you are told. Now I want you to turn that page over and draw your letter like everyone . . . " and turning to the next page, she saw my second name sprawled down across the page.

There was a moment of icy silence, and I knew I had done something terribly wrong. But this time, I had no idea what it could be that would get her so angry, certainly not being proud of writing my name.

She broke the silence with a wicked edge to her voice. "I see." she said. "I see we have a young lady who does not want to do as she is told. We will have to tell her mother about that." And the rest of the class snickered, as the teacher tore the page out of my notebook.

"Now I am going to give you one more chance," she said, as she printed another fierce A at the head of the new page. "Now you copy that letter exactly the way it is, and the rest of the class will have to wait for you." She placed the crayon squarely back into my fingers.

By this time I had no idea at all what this lady wanted from me, and so I cried and cried for the rest of the morning until my mother came to fetch me home at noon. I cried on the street while we stopped to pick up my sisters, and for most of the way home, until my mother threatened to box my ears for me if I didn't stop embarrassing her on the street.

That afternoon, after Phyllis and Helen were back in school, and I was   40
helping her dust, I told my mother how they had given me crayons to write with and how the teacher didn't want me to write my name. When my father came home that evening, the two of them went into counsel. It was decided that my mother would speak to the teacher the next morning when she brought me to school, in order to find out what I had done wrong. This decision was passed on to me, ominously, because of course I must have done something wrong to have made Miss Teacher so angry with me.

The next morning at school, the teacher told my mother that she did not think that I was ready yet for kindergarten, because I couldn't follow directions, and I wouldn't do as I was told.

My mother knew very well I could follow directions, because she herself had spent a good deal of effort and arm-power making it very painful for me whenever I did not follow directions. And she also believed that a large part of the function of school was to make me learn how to do what I was told to do. In her private opinion, if this school could not do that, then it was not much of a school and she was going to find a school that could. In other words, my mother had made up her mind that school was where I belonged.

That same morning, she took me off across the street to the catholic school, where she persuaded the nuns to put me into the first grade, since I could read already, and write my name on regular paper with a real pencil. If I sat in the first row I could see the blackboard. My mother also told the nuns that unlike my two sisters, who were models of deportment, I was very unruly, and that they should spank me whenever I needed it. Mother Josepha, the principal, agreed, and I started school.

My first grade teacher was named Sister Mary of Perpetual Help, and she was a disciplinarian of the first order, right after my mother's own heart. A week after I started school she sent a note home to my mother asking her not to dress me in so many layers of clothing because then I couldn't feel the strap on my behind when I was punished.

Sister Mary of Perpetual Help ran the first grade with an iron hand in   45
the shape of a cross. She couldn't have been more than eighteen. She was big, and blond, I think, since we never got to see the nuns' hair in those days. But her eyebrows were blonde, and she was supposed to be totally dedicated, like all the other Sisters of the Blessed Sacrament, to caring for the Colored and Indian children of america. Caring for was not always caring about. And it always felt like Sister MPH hated either teaching or little children.

She had divided up the class into two groups, the Fairies and the Brownies. In this day of heightened sensitivity to racism and color usage, I don't have to tell you which were the good students and which were the baddies. I always wound up in the Brownies, because either I talked too much, or I broke my glasses, or I perpetrated some other awful infraction of the endless rules of good behavior.

But for two glorious times that year, I made it into the Fairies for brief periods of time. One was put into the Brownies if one misbehaved, or couldn't learn to read. I had learned to read already, but I couldn't tell my numbers. Whenever Sister MPH would call a few of us up to the front of the room for our reading lesson, she would say, "All right, children, now turn to page six in your readers." or, "Turn to page nineteen, please, and begin at the top of the page."

Well, I didn't know what page to turn to, and I was ashamed of not being able to read my numbers, so when my turn came to read I couldn't, because I didn't have the right place. After the prompting of a few words, she would go on to the next reader, and soon I wound up in the Brownies.

This was around the second month of school, in October. My new seatmate was Alvin, and he was the worst boy in the whole class. His clothes were dirty and he smelled unwashed, and rumor had it he had once called Sister MPH a bad name, but that couldn't have been possible because he would have been suspended permanently from school.

Alvin used to browbeat me into lending him my pencil to draw endless pictures of airplanes dropping huge penile bombs. He would always promise to give me the pictures when he was finished. But of course, whenever he was finished, he would decide that the picture was too good for a girl, so he would have to keep it, and make me another. Yet I never stopped hoping for one of them, because he drew airplanes very well.

He also would scratch his head and shake out the dandruff onto our joint spelling book or reader, and then tell me the flakes of dandruff were dead lice. I believed him in this, also, and was constantly terrified of catching cooties. But Alvin and I worked out our own system together for reading. He couldn't read, but he knew all his numbers, and I could read words, but I couldn't find the right page.

The Brownies were never called up to the front of the room; we had to read in anonymity from our double seats, where we scrunched over at the edges, ordinarily, to leave room in the middle for our two guardian angels to sit. But whenever we had to share a book our guardian angels had to jump around us and sit on the outside edge of our seats. Therefore, Alvin would show me the right pages to turn to when Sister called them out, and I would whisper the right words to him whenever it came his turn to read. Inside of a week after we devised this scheme of things, we had gotten out of the Brownies together. Since we shared a reader, we always went up together to read with the Fairies, so we had a really good thing going there for a while.

But Alvin began to get sick around Thanksgiving, and was absent a lot, and he didn't come back to school at all after Christmas. I used to miss his dive-bomber pictures, but most of all I missed his page numbers. After a few times of being called up by myself and not being able to read, I landed back in the Brownies again.

Years later I found out that Alvin had died of tuberculosis over Christmas, and that was why we all had been X-rayed in the auditorium after Mass on the first day back to school from Christmas vacation.

I spent a few more weeks in the Brownies with my mouth almost shut during reading lesson, unless the day's story fell on page eight, or ten, or twenty, which were the three numbers I knew.

Then, over one weekend, we had our first writing assignment. We were to look in our parents' newspaper and cut out words we knew the meaning of, and make them into simple sentences. We could only use one "the." It felt like an easy task, since I was already reading the comics by this time.

On Sunday morning after church, when I usually did my homework, I noticed an ad for White Rose Salada Tea on the back of the *New York Times Magazine* which my father was reading at the time. It had the most gorgeous white rose on a red background, and I decided I must have that rose for my picture—our sentences were to be illustrated. I searched through the paper until I found an "I," and then a "like," which I dutifully clipped out along with my rose, and the words "White," "Rose," "Salada," and "Tea." I knew the brand-name well because it was my mother's favorite tea.

On Monday morning, we all stood our sentence papers up on the chalk-channels, leaning them against the blackboards. And there among the twenty odd "The boy ran," "it was cold," was "I like White Rose Salada Tea" and my beautiful white rose on a red background.

That was too much coming from a Brownie. Sister Mary of PH frowned.

"This was to be our own work, children," she said. "Who helped you   60
with your sentence, Audre?" I told her I had done it alone.

"Our guardian angels weep when we don't tell the truth, Audre. I want a note from your mother tomorrow telling me that you are sorry for lying to the baby Jesus."

I told the story at home, and the next day I brought a note from my father saying that the sentence had indeed been my own work. Triumphantly, I gathered up my books and moved back over to the Fairies.

The thing that I remember best about being in the first grade was how uncomfortable it was, always having to leave room for my guardian angel on those tiny seats, and moving back and forth across the room from Brownies to Fairies and back again.

This time I stayed in the Fairies for a long time, because I finally started to recognize my numbers. I stayed there until the day I broke my glasses. I had taken them off to clean them in the bathroom and they slipped out of my hand. I was never to do that, and so I was in disgrace. My eyeglasses came from the eye clinic of the medical center, and it took three days to get a new pair made. We could not afford to buy more than one pair at a time, nor did it occur to my parents that such an extravagance might be necessary. I was almost sightless without them, but my punishment for having broken them was that I had to go to school anyway, even though I could see nothing. My sisters delivered me to my classroom with a note from my mother saying I had broken my glasses despite the fact they were tied to me by the strip of elastic.

I was never supposed to take my glasses off except just before getting 65
into bed, but I was endlessly curious about these magical circles of glass that
were rapidly becoming a part of me, transforming my universe, and remaining movable. I was always trying to examine them with my naked, nearsighted eyes, usually dropping them in the process.

Since I could not see at all to do any work from the blackboard, Sister
Mary of PH made me sit in the back of the room on the window seat with
a dunce cap on. She had the rest of the class offer up a prayer for my poor
mother who had such a naughty girl who broke her glasses and caused
her parents such needless extra expense to replace them. She also had
them offer up a special prayer for me to stop being such a wicked-hearted
child.

I amused myself by counting the rainbows of color that danced like a
halo around the lamp on Sister Mary of PH's desk, watching the starburst
patterns of light that the incandescent light bulb became without my
glasses. But I missed them, and not being able to see. I never once gave a
thought to the days when I believed that bulbs were starburst patterns of
color, because that was what all light looked like to me.

It must have been close to summer by this time. As I sat with the dunce
cap on, I can remember the sun pouring through the classroom window
hot upon my back, as the rest of the class dutifully entoned their Hail Marys
for my soul, and I played secret games with the distorted rainbows of light,
until Sister noticed and made me stop blinking my eyes so fast.

Issues for Discussion

1. Why does Lorde fall in love with reading under the tutelage of Mrs. Augusta Baker? What attracts her to reading in the first place? What qualities make Mrs. Baker an effective and memorable "teacher"?
2. How do Lorde's kindergarten and first-grade teachers compare with
   Mrs. Baker? How would you describe their relationship to their students? What "lessons" about reading, writing, and learning do they
   teach through their attitudes and actions?

OPTIONAL
ACTIVITY

Teacher Stories

Work together in small groups to draw a quick, collective visual representation
of the student-teacher relationship. After you've finished, share these images
with the class and explain the messages they contain about students, teachers,
and the roles they play in education.

Writing to Authority

The stories we tell ourselves about teachers and students are important because the teacher-student relationship offers one of our first models for the complicated interaction of reader and writer. After all, for many of us a teacher is the first person who reads the words we commit to paper. Unfortunately, teachers like Audre Lorde's Sister MPH remind us that, first and foremost, teachers are authorities: even though most American public schools banned corporal punishment sometime in the 1970s or 1980s, the cultural script that most of us have for "teacher" still contains traces of the stern disciplinarian whose primary mission is to maintain order and guarantee "correctness." Particularly when you're writing a paper, it's hard not to see your instructor as a kind of "grammar cop," an enforcer who represents the rules of the English language and is unflaggingly dedicated to hunting down and annotating your every "mistake." Once the words you've struggled so hard to put down on paper have been judged and graded by a teacher, it's almost impossible to imagine that writing involves something more than trying to figure out what your teacher "wants."

Even humane and dedicated instructors have a hard time getting beyond the image of teacher as authority figure. Today, public education in this country is beset by many problems: overcrowded classrooms, lack of resources, overworked and stressed-out teachers, and increasing violence in schools. Under these conditions, teachers often are forced to concentrate on training students to conform, to complete tasks, and to behave in a manner that will not disrupt the class. Students can even be rewarded with good grades for just following the rules and completing assignments. There isn't much time for experimentation, creativity, or critical thinking. Teachers often praise writing that gets the job done—writing that is clear and predictable with few grammatical errors—because they may not have the time or the resources to allow students to take risks, to experiment, and to try again. It's no wonder, then, that many students enter college with the impression that good thinking and good writing are relatively straightforward and predictable affairs: follow the rules, get your work in on time, and everything will be OK. Good writers, according to this script, are just students who have learned to behave themselves on paper.

We don't mean to suggest that writing shouldn't be well organized and grammatically correct. But we do want to suggest that there is room for risk taking in academic writing. In fact, in many college courses, being safe and doing only what's expected may not get you very far: you're expected to think independently and creatively, take risks, and try out new ideas. That's when expectations about teachers can seriously mislead you: if you focus too much on getting a good grade and "doing what the teacher wants," you're bound to have trouble doing—or thinking—anything that's really interesting, and perhaps even worse, you're likely to lose track of any motive or interest you might have in putting words on paper. Writing for an academic audience can thus put you in a paradoxical situation: the best academic work shows that the writer has a good command of the rules or conventions of her discipline but at the same time is bold enough to challenge those rules and conventions in interesting ways.

We'll explore this paradox more fully in later chapters, but first let's take a look at one writer's story of how he was inspired to break the rules. In the following essay, Reginald Lockett describes how he became a poet after encountering a teacher who made him question his preconceptions about writing for class. Lockett (b. 1949) might have seemed unlikely material for a poet when he was growing up on the streets of West Oakland, California, but since graduating from San Francisco State University with a master's degree in English, he has been published in more than fifty anthologies and journals. His most recent volume of poetry, *Where the Bird Sings Bass,* appeared in 1995. Currently, Lockett teaches creative writing at San Jose City College.

Before Reading

Break into small groups and take ten minutes to brainstorm the "rules" of writing you have learned, directly or indirectly, in school through the years. What kinds of advice did teachers offer about dealing with specific words, acceptable topics, paragraph organization, grammar, spelling, the writing process, and so forth? How do the rules you learned compare with those your classmates learned? Are they consistent or contradictory? If you find inconsistencies, how might you explain them?

How I Started Writing Poetry
Reginald Lockett

At the age of fourteen I was what Richard Pryor over a decade later would call "going for bad," or what my southern-bred folks said was "smellin' your pee." That is, I had cultivated a facade of daring-do, hip, cool, con man bravado so prevalent among adolescent males in West Oakland. I "talked that talk and walked that walk" most parents found downright despicable. In their minds these were dress rehearsals of fantasies that were Popsicles that would melt and evaporate under the heat of blazing hot realities. And there I was doing the pimp limp and talking about nothing profound or sustaining. All I wanted to do was project that image of being forever cool like Billy Boo, who used to wear three T-shirts, two slipover sweaters and a thick Pendleton shirt tucked neatly in his khaki or black Ben Davidsons to give everybody the impression that he was buffed (muscle bound) and definitely not to be messed with. Cool. Real cool. Standing in front of the liquor store on 35th and San Pablo sipping white port and lemon juice, talking smack by the boatloads until some real hoodlum from Campbell Village (or was it Harbor Homes?) with the *real* biceps, the sho-nuff triceps and sledgehammer fists beat the shirt, both sweaters, the T-shirts and pants right off of Billy Boo's weak, bony body.

Herbert Hoover Junior High, the school I attended, was considered one of the toughest in Oakland at that time. It was a dirty, gray, forbidding looking place where several fights would break out every day. There was a joke going around that a mother, new to the city, mistook it for the Juvenile Detention Center that was further down in West Oakland on 18th and Poplar, right across the street from DeFremery Park.

During my seventh-grade year there were constant referrals to the principal's office for any number of infractions committed either in Miss Okamura's third-period music class or Mrs. George's sixth-period math class in the basement where those of us with behavioral problems and assumed learning disabilities were sent. It was also around this time that Harvey Hendricks, my main running buddy, took it upon himself to hip me to everything he thought I needed to know about sex while we were doing a week's detention in Mrs. Balasco's art class for capping on "them steamer trunks" or "suitcases" under her eyes. As we sat there, supposedly writing "I will not insult the teacher" one hundred times, Harvey would draw pictures of huge tits and vaginas, while telling me how to rap, kiss and jump off in some twanks and stroke. Told me that the pimples on my face were "pussy bumps," and that I'd better start getting some trim or end up just like Crater Face Jerome with the big, nasty-looking quarter-size pus bumps all over his face.

Though my behavior left a lot to be desired, I managed to earn some fairly decent grades. I loved history, art and English, and somehow managed to work my way up from special education classes to college prep courses by the time I reached ninth grade, my last year at Hoover. But by then I had become a full-fledged, little thug, and had been suspended—and damn near expelled—quite a few times for going to knuckle city at the drop of a hat for any real or imagined reason. And what an efficient thief I'd become. This was something I'd picked up from my cousins, R.C. and Danny, when I started hanging out with them on weekends in San Francisco's Haight-Ashbury. We'd steal clothes, records, liquor, jewelry—anything for the sake of magnifying to the umpteenth degree that image of death-defying manhood and to prove I was indeed a budding Slick Draw McGraw. Luckily, I was never caught, arrested and hauled off to Juvenile Hall or the California Youth Authority like so many of the guys I ran with.

Probably through pressure from my parents and encouragement from my teachers and counselors, I forced myself to start thinking about pursuing a career after graduation from high school, which was three years away. Reaching into the grab bag of professional choices, I decided I wanted to become a physician, since doctors were held in such high esteem, particularly in an Afro-American community like West Oakland. I'd gotten it in my head that I wanted to be a plastic surgeon, no less, because I liked working with my hands and found science intriguing. Then something strange happened.   5

Maybe it was the continuous violence, delinquency and early pregnancies that made those Oakland Unified School District administrators (more than likely after some consultation with psychologists) decide to put a little Freudian theory to practical use. Just as I was grooving, really getting into this fantastic project in fourth-period art class, I was called up to the teacher's desk and handed a note and told to report to a classroom downstairs on the first floor. What had I done this time? Was it because I snatched Gregory Jones' milkshake during lunch a couple of days ago and gulped it down, savoring every drop like an old loathsome suck-egg dog, and feeling no pain as the chump, big as he was, stood there and cried? And Mr. Foltz, the principal, was known to hand out mass suspensions. Sometimes fifteen, twenty, twenty-five people at a time. But when I entered the classroom, there sat this tall, gangly, goofy-looking white woman who wore her hair unusually long for that time, had thick glasses and buckteeth like the beaver on the Ipana Toothpaste commercials. Some of the roughest, toughest kids that went to Hoover were in there. Especially big old mean, ugly Martha Dupree who was known to knock out boys, girls, and teachers when she got the urge. If Big Martha asked you for a last-day-of-school kiss, you'd better give it up or make an appointment with your dentist.

When Miss Nettelbeck finally got our attention, she announced that this was a creative writing class that would meet twice a week. Creative writing? What the hell is creative writing a couple of us asked. She explained that it was a way to express what was on your mind, and a better way of getting something off of your chest instead of beating up your fellow students. Then she read a few poems to us and passed out some of that coarse school-issue lined paper and told us to write about something we liked, disliked, or really wanted. What I wanted to know was, did it have to be one of "them pomes." "If that's how you want to express yourself, Reginald," she said. So I started racking my brain, trying to think about what I liked, didn't like and what I really wanted. Well, I liked football, track and Gayle Johnson, who would turn her cute little "high yella" nose up in total disgust everytime I tried to say something to her.

I couldn't stand the sight—not even the thought—of old monkey-face Martha. And what I really wanted was either a '57 Buick Roadmaster or a '56 Chevy with mag wheels and tuck 'n' roll seats that was dropped in the front like the ones I'd seen older dudes like Mack's brother, Skippy, riding around in. Naw, I told myself, I couldn't get away with writing about things like that. I might get in some more trouble, and Big Martha would give me a thorough asskicking for writing something about mashing her face in some dough and baking me some gorilla cookies. Who'd ever heard of a poem about cars? One thing I really liked was the ocean. I guess that was in my blood because my father was then a Master Chief Steward in the Navy, and, when I was younger, would take me aboard ships docked at Hunter's Point and Alameda. I loved the sea so much that I would sometimes walk from my house on Market and W. MacArthur all the way to the Berkeley Pier or take a bus to Ocean Beach in San Francisco whenever I wasn't up to no good. So I wrote:

> I sit on a rock
> watching
> the evening tide
> come in.
> The green waves travel
> with the wind.
> They seem to carry
> a message of
> warning, of plea
> from the dimensions
> of time and distance.

When I gave it to Miss Nettelbeck, she read it and told me it was good for a first attempt at writing poetry, and since there was still some time left in the period, I should go back to my seat and write something else. Damn! These teachers never gave you any kind of slack, no matter what you did and how well you did it. Now, what else could I think of to write about? How about a tribute to Miss Bobby, the neighborhood drag queen, who'd been found carved up like a Christmas turkey a week ago? Though me, Harvey and Mack used to crack jokes about "her" giving up the boodie, we still liked and respected "her" because she would give you five or six dollars to run an errand to the cleaners or the store, never tried to hit on you, and would get any of the other "girls" straight real quick if they even said you were cute or something. So I wrote:

> Bring on the hustlers
> In Continental suits
> And alligator shoes.
> Let ladies of the night
> In short, tight dresses
> And spiked heels enter.
> We are gathered here
> To pay tribute to
> The Queen of Drag.
>
> What colorful curtains
> And rugs!
> Look at the stereo set
> And the clothes in the closet.
> On the bed, entangled
> In a bloody sheet,
> Is that elegant one
> Of ill repute
> But good carriage
> Oh yes! There
> Was none like her.
> The Queen of Drag.

When she read that one, I just knew Miss Nettelbeck would immediately write a referral and have me sent back upstairs. But she liked it and said I was precocious for someone at such an innocent age. Innocent! When was I ever innocent? I was guilty of just about everything I was accused of doing. Like, get your eyes checked, baby. And what was precocious? Was it something weird? Did it mean I was queer like Miss Bobby? Was I about to go to snap city like poor Donny Moore had a year ago when he suddenly got up and started jacking off in front of Mr. Lee's history class? What did this woman, who looked and dressed like one of them beatniks I'd seen one night on *East Side, West Side,* mean? My Aunt Audry's boyfriend, Joe, told me beatniks were smart and used a lot of big words like precocious so nobody could understand what they were talking about. Had to be something bad. This would mess with me for the rest of the week if I didn't ask her

10

what she meant. So I did, and she told me it meant that I knew about things somebody my age didn't usually know about. Wow! That could only mean that I was "hip to the lip." But I already knew that.

For some reason I wasn't running up and down the streets with the fellas much anymore. Harvey would get bent out of shape everytime I'd tell him I had something else to do. I had to, turning punkish or seeing some broad I was too chinchy to introduce him to. This also bothered my mother because she kept telling me I was going to ruin my eyes if I didn't stop reading so much; and what was that I spent all my spare time writing in a manila notebook? Was I keeping a diary or something? Only girls kept diaries, and people may start thinking I was one of "them sissy mens" if I didn't stop. Even getting good grades in citizenship and making the honor roll didn't keep her off my case. But I kept right on reading and writing, looking forward to Miss Nettelbeck's class twice a week. I stopped fighting, too. But I was still roguish as ever. Instead of raiding Roger's Men's Shop, Smith's and Flagg Brothers' Shoes, I was stealing books by just about every poet and writer Miss Nettelbeck read to the class. That's how I started writing poetry.

Issues for Discussion

1. What risks does Lockett take in the poems he writes for Miss Nettelbeck? What kind of response does he expect?
2. Which of the rules that you brainstormed before reading does Lockett follow in this essay and which does he break? Does his violation of some common rules (for instance, using slang) make his story easier or harder to read, more or less engaging?
3. Some of the risks Lockett takes might appeal to some readers but offend or alienate others. How did you respond to his use of profanity? His references to women's bodies as sex objects?
4. How would you describe Lockett's "voice"—the tone and style of speech that comes through his essay? What image does it evoke of him as a person? To what extent does his voice add to your enjoyment of the essay?

ESSAY OPTIONS

School Stories

The following topics invite you to write a paper in which you tell one of your own school stories. Choose one to focus on, and be sure to experiment with some of the prewriting strategies you learned in Chapter 2 (p. 54) before you begin to write.

Topic 1. Write a story about a school experience that was important to you or that changed you in an important way. Try to focus on a single specific event in your educational career—a crucial incident that shaped your attitude toward learning, a moment of particular insight or growth in your life as a student, or a difficult or humorous transition to a new school. What happened? How did this experience affect you, and why was it significant? Lockett's essay provides an example of this kind of story, as does Audre Lorde's account of her experience in first grade (p. 65).

Topic 2. Write a story focusing on a teacher who had an important impact on your life and your attitudes toward learning. It might be a teacher who changed your way of thinking in some significant way—or one, like Audre Lorde's Sister MPH, who made your life miserable. Try to describe this figure in as much detail as you can, offering specific examples of how terrific—or painful—they were in class. Again, Lorde and Lockett offer examples.

Risky Business

Calvin and Hobbes   by Bill Watterson

Regular readers of Calvin and Hobbes immediately know why Calvin's "creative pieces" get him in trouble with school authorities: many strips detail his wildly active fantasy life, in which his teacher appears as a hideous, drooling space monster. But while Calvin may not be an entirely typical student, he identifies a tension that many writers struggle with. Being too conscious of external rules and expectations can stifle creativity and thwart your ability to take the risks that are essential to good thinking and writing ("How can you be creative when someone's breathing down your neck?"). On the other hand, there are potential dangers in ignoring your audience entirely; your creative efforts may not get you referred to a psychiatrist, but they could earn you a low grade and a warning to "Please follow directions!"

Like Calvin, Lockett faces the problem of striking a balance between pure self-expression and what he thinks will be acceptable to his audience. When Miss Nettelbeck gives the assignment, Lockett initially assumes that she (like other teachers) has particular "rules" about what she wants to see in student writing; yet she insists that the writing reflect only "how you want to express yourself." Lockett mentally reviews the things he likes, dislikes, and really wants, and he quickly concludes, "I couldn't get away with writing about things like that." He still can't believe that the kinds of topics that interest him are appropriate for the classroom, and he's afraid to take a big risk: "Who'd ever heard of a poem about cars?" His first effort is a compromise, a poem about the ocean. He does like the sea, but it's also a conventional subject of serious literature—something he can assume Miss Nettelbeck would find acceptable. After she praises the poem, he takes a much bigger risk, assuming she will be shocked and outraged by the story of Miss Bobby. The risk pays off when she responds even more warmly to this poem.

Risks aren't always rewarded, though. Would every audience respond as Miss Nettelbeck did? Was Lockett right to believe that even she wouldn't have appreciated a poem about a '56 Chevy or Big Martha's ugly face? How do you know what kinds of risks to take, and when? Unfortunately, there's no simple answer to such questions, but here are some preliminary suggestions for finding your own balance.

Taking Risks

- *Go wild in prewriting.* Make the most of informal writing opportunities by using journal entries, brainstorming, freewriting, junk drafts, and so forth to cut loose and try things you've never considered or dared to do before.

- *Try several different approaches.* Always push yourself to come up with more than one option, whether it's two ways to introduce or conclude your essay, three possible methods of telling a story, or several different positions you could take on an issue. Once you've come up with some options, consider each one carefully; even if an idea seems a little crazy at first, play it out for a while instead of dismissing it right away.

Evaluating Risks

- *Give yourself time to reflect and revise.* Let your experiments "cool off" for a while and then reconsider them. Sometimes a paragraph that seemed absolutely brilliant at 3:00 A.M. looks dismal the next afternoon; conversely, a page that you cranked out in sheer panic and desperation may turn out to have some real promise when you return to it with a clearer mind.

- *Test your ideas on a real audience.* When you've done some writing, even if it's still rough, get feedback from your peer response group, tutor, TA, or professor. Professional writers rely heavily on such "test marketing": just glance at the acknowledgments page of any book by a serious writer (academic or otherwise) and see how many colleagues, friends, editors, and family members she thanks for reading manuscript drafts and making suggestions. You'll have more chances to practice reading and responding to each other's writing in the revision workshop coming up in the next chapter. Meanwhile, we'd like to introduce you to the read-around—an enjoyable way to share writing in class and get some quick feedback on your work.

**OPTIONAL
ACTIVITY**

The Read Around

Working with a short piece of informal writing or a draft, code your paper with a three-digit number that you'll remember easily (for example, the last three digits of your phone number or student ID). Get into groups of five or six and exchange your group's set of papers with another group's set, so that you'll be reading papers that were *not* written by anyone in your own group.

Distribute the new set of papers so that every member of your group has one paper to read. Now quickly read the paper in your hand and, on a piece of scratch paper, jot down the code number and a word or two that will remind you what the passage is about or how you felt about it. The whole point of the read around is to move quickly, so read fast and keep your notes simple.

When you've read and made a note for the first paper, pass it to the person on your right. Keep reading and responding until everyone in the group has read every paper in the set. Then take about five minutes to try to come to a consensus about which paper you liked best. Someone from each group can read aloud to the class the paper her group selected, and the group can explain why they found this piece moving, enjoyable, or entertaining. If you like, you can also try to decide as a class on your favorite piece among those that were read aloud.

Establishing Expectations: Writing for Readers or Super-Readers?

Good writing may have a lot in common with good storytelling, but there's remarkably little similarity between face-to-face communication and what goes on between a writer and a reader. When you talk to someone, you can usually take a lot for granted: talking to a friend, a relative, a teacher, or an employer, you can assume that your listener understands a great deal about you and what you have to say. You don't have to explain the point or the significance of the stories that you tell any more than you have to take up a lot of time providing background information. Most of this is simply "understood"—it's embedded in the situation you find yourself in and in your personal relationship with the friend, parent, teacher, or boss you're talking to. So, when you arrive at your apartment and your roommate asks you how it went, you don't have to bother expounding on your motives for speaking or the point you're about to make. You just talk and tell the story of your day. If problems of comprehension do occur, you have the luxury of stopping in mid-sentence to explain exactly what you mean or what actually happened—or to show your listener with a glance or gesture what you really think.

But when you write, you lose this immediate connection with your audience; in fact, you lose the ability to assume that your reader understands any of your motives, aims, or purposes. By definition, writing is long-distance communication. The writer commits her ideas and feelings and experiences to paper, knowing that she won't be there when it's read—knowing in advance that she won't have the luxury of monitoring the reader's responses as she speaks. Unfortunately, many beginning writers continue to work with the model of communication they know the best—the conversational model. They write as if they were talking face to face with someone they know pretty well. When they write, they continue to assume that the reader understands almost everything they have in mind, including the purpose behind their writing and the points they are trying to make. In a sense, they write as if they were addressing not a reader but a "super-reader," a kind of reader-psychic who knows what they have to say even *before* they say it. Super-reader syndrome shows up in the assumptions that writers make about what readers need to know: if you *assume* your reader already understands the purpose of your paper, you may feel that explaining it would be boringly obvious; if you *assume* your reader grasps how hideous your third-grade teacher really was, you might think that detailed explanation would be a waste of time. Perhaps that's why super-reader syndrome shows up so clearly in the way that many writers approach introductions and in their use of details.

Introductions and Expectations

Introductions are especially sensitive to super-reader syndrome because they provide readers with essential background information about an essay's purpose and focus. If a writer unconsciously assumes her reader already knows this essential information, chances are she'll either produce abbreviated introductions that are almost useless to real readers or no introduction at all. Here's a sample introductory paragraph similar to many that we've seen in student drafts of family stories:

```
My grandparents grew up on the East Coast. Even
though their families had very little money during the
Great Depression, they had the chance to go to college.
That's where they met. After they graduated, they decided
to get married. That was when they were at the ripe old
age of 25.
```

Reading this introduction is a lot like trying to make sense of a conversation you eavesdrop on halfway through: the words make literal sense, but you have little understanding of what they mean in the larger context of the conversation—or, in this case, of the essay in question. As a reader, you know the paper has to have something to do with the early lives of the author's grandparents, but you have little clear idea about what the paper will focus on, what the author wants to say or is attempting to accomplish through it. Apparently, the writer *assumes* that the reader already knows all of this important information and that she can just push ahead with the story she wants to tell.

Some students appear to remedy this problem by adding more detail to their introductory paragraphs. Here's an example modelled on a paper describing a family tradition:

```
It is a tradition to have Christmas dinner at my
Aunt's house. She always does the cooking and hosts this
special holiday feast. I live in the Valley with my
brother, so we drive across town to be with the rest of
the family in L.A. My Aunt cooks the best food of anyone I
know, and I always love going to her house to eat. The
scene is always festive when everybody arrives. We take
off our hats and coats, the new ones we bought for this
```

```
special occasion, and greet each other with hugs and
kisses. It isn't often that we all get together, so we
have to catch up on family news and hear about who's going
to school, who's got a new job, and who's getting ready to
get married. This is a very happy day for all of us. While
my Aunt is cooking, a bunch of us usually gather around
the kitchen table and watch her work. I love to see the
way she zips from counter to counter, checking the turkey,
heating up a pan of gravy, or mashing potatoes. My father
and my uncles don't just stand or sit around like most men
do on family occasions; they get busy and help out by set-
ting the table or by carrying steaming platters into the
dining room. My Uncle Charles always wants to know how my
classes are going, and I have plenty to tell him . . .
```

The writer may have crammed in more detail, but the reader still has no clear idea about *why* this story of one family's Christmas dinner is being told or where it's going. Again, instead of giving the reader the information she needs to appreciate the point of the paper, the writer plunges into the story, assuming that the reader understands the purpose of all the information that is to follow.

Of course, students who write paragraphs like these might object at this point and argue that they assumed the reader understood the purpose and point of their essays because their primary reader was, in fact, their English teacher—the very person who cooked up the assignment in the first place. And, unfortunately, they'd be right. One of the biggest obstacles to becoming an accomplished writer is the typical student-teacher relationship. After all, aren't teachers supposed to know more than students? Can't you assume that they understand the topics they assign even better than you do? For at least twelve years, you've been taught to see the teacher as an authority, as someone who knows more than you do about a particular topic. That's why you listen to teachers in the first place, isn't it? But while it's safe to assume that your biology professor understands the composition of cytoplasm better than most students—or that your English teacher may have a richer understanding of literature or the composing process—it is fatal to *assume* that she or any other instructor or reader automatically understands the ideas, events, or experiences you write about. Seeing your teacher as a super-reader—as an unquestionable authority who understands the intent of every paragraph and every line—is a pre-scription for writing disaster.

In a face-to-face conversation the purpose of a story is usually determined by its context. When you tell your roommate how lousy your day was, the purpose of your speaking is established by the time of day, the fact you just walked into your dorm room, and the question your roommate just asked you. But an essay, unlike a conversation, exists outside of a ready-made con-text. When you jump into a story without providing any orientation to your topic or purpose, you sound to your reader as incoherent—and even as weird—as a stranger who launches into a detailed account of his life while riding next to you on a bus. It's up to you, the writer, to establish the context of your story for the reader by orienting him to your topic, purpose, and point. Here are a few more sample introductions. Compare them to the super-reader introductions you read above. What different kinds of information do they provide? Which one strikes you as the best? What might you do to im-prove them in the next revision? These introductory paragraphs were written by Kevin Mong, Cesar Rodriguez, and Gabriela Nuñez, all students at UCLA.

Sample Introduction #1

```
     Immigrants from all over the world have come to the
United States to better themselves and their posterity.
Each immigrant has a story to tell, for each has added a
piece of himself to this mosaic puzzle we call America.
Similarly, my family has their own story to divulge be-
cause the story greatly defines who we are. We feel that
it is important for future generations to know our story--
to know the hardships and sacrifices that we, as immi-
grants, had to go through in order to come to America, so
that they can better appreciate the lives that their an-
cestors made possible for them.
```

Sample Introduction #2

```
                   My Influential Person
     When I entered my first school year in the United
States during the third grade, seeing my teacher for the
first time was not pleasant. Mr. Hamilton was a very tall
and strict-looking man; his six foot frame intimidated
```

everybody in the class. He had a very deep voice that seemed to come straight out of a horror movie. This man meant business: he addressed the class by telling us that there was to be no screwing around near him; he said, "Horse-playing belongs at home, we come to school to learn." With these words, he left us speechless, anticipating the worst to come. Coming from a foreign country, I was not really familiar with the English language. Entering a new school with people I had never seen before was really uncomfortable and stepping into a classroom with a teacher that did not look very friendly were two inconveniences I had to deal with during my first year. But as the year passed, this teacher whom I thought was very strict started to show that he was "human" after all.

Sample Introduction #3

A Shattered Life, A Second Chance

I live in a city that seems to be possessed by demons. There's not one day that goes by that I don't hear about a drive-by shooting, a gang related death, or just an innocent bystander getting shot for being at the wrong place at the wrong time. The echoing sounds of the fading sirens that can be heard through my bedroom window every night make me wonder if there is any hope out there. I hear about crime every day, I see it all the time, and worst of all I have lived this all my life. South Central L.A.: the city of crime, the infested city of gangsters-- my home.

I fool myself by saying that I have learned to adjust, but I don't think anyone can ever adjust to the constant reminder of death. The truth is, I can't take this any longer. My parents came to this country in pursuit of a better life for themselves as well as their children. They wanted to further our choices and opportunities.

Their main ambition was to give us a brighter and better future, but living in this city scares me sometimes. I'm tired of wondering if I will live to see tomorrow.

It was only four years ago when I received my wake-up call. I was fourteen years old. It was a time to enjoy life and to discover new things. Instead, I was shattered by the devastating news that my boyfriend, who happened to be a gangster, had been killed by a rival gang member. That day is so vivid in my mind. And the pain that I felt then, I still feel today.

Specific Details: Moving beyond Code Phrases

The super-reader syndrome shows up not only in the way writers structure introductions but also in the assumptions they make about how much detail to include in their papers. Can you conjure up the feeling of a really good conversation? You get going, telling a friend the story of how bad your first period class was, and you can actually "feel" understanding as it passes between the two of you. No need to detail how pathetic your instructor's attempts were to "liven up the class"—your friend has been there and seen that before. But when you write, it can be disastrous to *assume* your reader has this kind of "intuitive" understanding of your experiences, ideas, and feelings. In fact, effective writers frequently assume the opposite: they assume that the reader can't understand their ideas or their experiences unless they literally re-create their experiences for them in words.

The key to this ability to re-create experience in words is detail. Beverly Donofrio's story "Trouble," for example, is packed with details—details that not only give you a vivid image of what she's talking about but that convey a great deal (more than she tells us directly) about her dreams, her life, and her family relationships. Let's take a close look at this description of herself in the third paragraph of her story:

By 1963, the fall of the eighth grade, I was ready. I was hot to trot. My hair was teased to basketball dimensions, my 16 oz. can of Miss Clairol hairspray was tucked into my shoulder bag. Dominic Mezzi whistled between his teeth every time I passed him in the hallway, and the girls from the project—the ones with boys' initials scraped into their forearms then colored with black ink—smiled and said hi when they saw me. I wore a padded bra that lifted my tits to inches below my chin, and my father communicated to me only through my mother.

This short passage is rich with specific images: the huge hair, the hair-spray can, the whistling admirer, the makeshift tatoos, the padded bra. Notice that Donofrio doesn't just say, "My hair was really big," the way you might in conversation. This is where words have to make up for all those visual cues you depend on when you're face to face with your audience: talking to a friend about your "big hair," you'd probably sketch how big with your hands as you spoke, perhaps without even being conscious that you were gesturing. Here Donofrio gives us a precise (and funny) verbal picture instead—"basketball dimensions." Notice, too, that she mentions not just "a can of hairspray" but "my 16 oz. can of Miss Clairol hairspray." Her specificity helps us to *see* the teenage Donofrio much more clearly, letting us know indirectly, for example, that she lugged an enormous shoulder bag (how else could a one-pound can of hairspray be neatly "tucked" inside?). What do the other details in this short passage—the girls from the project, the push-up bra, her father's behavior—tell you about her and her family?

Writers who assume that readers comprehend their experiences tend to write in "code phrases"—vague or highly generalized statements and descriptions that do little more than hint at the events, scenes, and situations they have in mind. For example, if you write, "My fifth-grade teacher was really bad," you may assume that the statement is perfectly clear. In your own mind, "really bad" is a code phrase that encompasses all your specific, dreadful memories of fifth grade: being ridiculed for not knowing the right answer, filling out endless dittoed exercise sheets, having to raise your hand to go to the bathroom, and so forth. A super-reader, if such a thing existed, might be able to intuit your intentions and "fill in" all of these missing details, but an average reader can't. "Really bad" could just as easily refer to a wide range of failings, from bad breath and body odor to drug abuse; perhaps, too, the strict disciplinarian you loathed is someone else's notion of the ideal teacher. You never know what different values and story frames a reader will associate with a particular code phrase.

When you're talking face to face, you can get away with code phrases: if your listener doesn't understand exactly what you mean, she can ask for an explanation. Sometimes, too, tone and body language help listeners interpret the code; for example, if your roommate tells you that she thinks Raul down the hall is "really nice" you can usually figure out by the way she says it whether she means that he's a sweet, nerdy guy who's willing to share his lecture notes with her or he's drop-dead gorgeous and she's aching to go out with him.

But writing is a different matter. Writers who have fallen into the habit of assuming their reader understands their code phrases often turn out papers that amount to little more than a stream of generalizations: asked to describe an important educational experience, a writer suffering from super-reader syndrome might build a whole essay out of relatively vague statements like this:

```
High school was a really enjoyable period in my life.
I hung around with a great group of kids. We were always
in and out of trouble, but somehow we always managed to
end up O.K. My teachers were great. There was one, Mr.
Phillips, who was a particular favorite. He had a really
important impact on my life. I'll never forget what a cool
guy he was.
```

Highly general writing like this isn't just imprecise—it's downright boring. Detail is what makes your experiences and ideas interesting—and valuable—for others; it's the specific event, the fine-grained picture, and the dramatic incident that catches a reader's attention and clarifies your meaning. That's why experienced writers usually follow general statements with clear, detailed examples and illustrations. Beverly Donofrio doesn't simply tell us that she became a "bad girl," she illustrates her "badness" by telling us several specific stories about how she paraded around her school with her beehive hairdo, how she used to moon people from the window of her car, and how she once splattered a stranger with an egg just because he was lucky enough to go to prep school. Leslie Marmon Silko does much the same thing: she makes a general statement about how storytelling in her culture serves to create tribal identity, and she immediately follows it by telling a specific tribal creation story. Next she tells us that Laguna Pueblo storytelling works to bring people together as individuals, and again she pauses to relate the story of a specific event—action by action—involving a young man who smashes up his VW. Good writing—whether it's personal storytelling or the kind of analytic writing you're expected to do in college—always moves back and forth between generalization and specific illustrative detail.

Audre Lorde's depiction of Sister MPH offers another clear example of how expert writers use detailed stories to bring generalizations to life. Lorde tells us directly that her teacher was a "strict disciplinarian," but she doesn't stop there: she then goes on to flesh out this statement by telling how Sister MPH wanted Lorde dressed in thin clothing so she would "feel the strap" on her behind when punished. She continues her portrait of this rigidly authoritarian teacher by explaining how Sister MPH divided the class into "Fairies" and "Brownies," filling the latter group with "baddies" who refused to follow the rules that governed her class. To drive her point home she relates the story of a particular "baddie" named Alvin, "the worst boy in the whole school," who becomes Lorde's friend and ally against Sister MPH before he dies of tuberculosis. Experienced writers understand that they have to "translate" their code phrases into specific scenes, dramatic examples, or particular illustrations in order to get their meanings across to their all-too-human readers.

Making Memories

It's hard to move beyond code words and phrases because that's the way we typically remember things: the brain doesn't usually store away all the specific details of every scene and event we've experienced. Unless a memory records a first-ever experience or one that's particularly traumatic or exceptional in some other way, we usually retain only a general impression of it. Sure, you might be able to recall your first day in kindergarten in remarkable detail: you might even be able to conjure up the smells of the classroom, the exact sound of your teacher's voice, the precise feeling you had when you were praised or blamed for something you did. But it's less likely that you'll recall what happened two months later in such fine-grained detail. Why is it, then, that writers have amazing memories? Phyllis Barber is able to remember not just little details about Christmas at her mother's house—things like the peanut brittle her father ate from a bowl on the living room coffee table—she can even retell other people's stories in minute detail, right down to the sweat that ran down her father's nose and the "boulders and brambles" he and her uncle crawled over to get clear of the explosion they set off when they were kids. David Mura has an equally prodigious memory; here's how he describes the sky on the evening of his grandfather's car wreck:

> It is getting dark now, the sky is beginning to take on the colors of fire and blood. Farther west, like a red-hot coin fresh from a forge, the sun is dipping into the cooling waters.

And here's his description of the Japanese relocation camp where his parents and grandparents were sent during World War II:

> In barrack after barrack, the families are cramped together, with clothes for partitions, with paper-thin boards. They hear each other's snores, the arguments between husband and wife, fathers and sons, mothers and daughters; they hear the sound of love cries, of a baby bawling. There's the smell of shoyu, wafts from the benjo downwind. Outside, in the rifle towers, the privates are bored. One tosses a cigarette over the edge. It falls, scattering flakes of ash, tiny red sparks.

Mura could easily have written, "It is getting late now. The sky turns red and the sun goes down," or "Life in the relocation camps was really awful," but instead he offers us detailed visual pictures that put us directly into the scene or situation he's describing. How do these writers do it? How does Barber remember every detail of her father's and grandfather's stories, and how does Mura know about the guards and their cigarettes? After all, he wasn't even born when his parents were in the camps!

The key to memory is imagination. When Mura and Barber began to write their family stories, they probably began with only a general mental "outline" specifying the events that happened and who did what to whom. It's possible they could recall a few specific features of what they had seen or heard in the past. But most likely they "built up" the basic outlines provided by their memories into fully realized stories by adding specific details of their own. Barber may not, in fact, be able to remember every word her father said, but she probably does know enough about the basic outline of his story and western terrain to *imagine* how he told it. Mura couldn't have personally experienced what he describes in his family stories, but he probably has learned enough about the relocation camps through family stories, reading, and in school—*and* enough about prison camps in general—to create a convincing image of one in his story. Both writers combine memories, personal experience, general knowledge, and imagination to create clear, highly detailed pictures for their readers—pictures that help to support the point of their stories even if they are not 100 percent historically accurate. Good storytellers aren't limited by the natural limitations of memory: they build up details imaginatively when they need them to illustrate and dramatize the point they want to make.

OPTIONAL
ACTIVITIES

Discovering Details

Here are a couple of activities that will help you add specific details to your writing.

Translating Code Phrases

Rewrite the numbered sentences on the next page, filling in the kinds of specific details that you would associate with the underlined code words or phrases. For example, depending on what your notion of a "really bad" teacher is, you might translate this sentence:

"My fifth-grade teacher was really bad."

like this:

My fifth-grade teacher was a tyrant in tweed, who thwacked our heads with his walnut-sized insignia ring whenever we mispronounced a word.

or like this:

> My fifth-grade teacher just didn't want to be bothered; if we were quiet and well-behaved, we got good grades—even if we couldn't read.

or like this:

> My fifth-grade teacher reeked of stale cigarette smoke, looked hung over, and dozed at his desk while we struggled through our workbook assignments unassisted.

Now try your hand at revising the following sentences, spelling out for the reader the precise images the underlined code phrases call up in your mind:

1. Aunt Graciela was always <u>nice</u> to us kids.
2. Our first apartment in Portland was <u>pretty small.</u>
3. The New Year festivities are <u>fun</u> for the whole family.
4. Last weekend I saw a <u>really super</u> movie.
5. Ninth grade was really <u>a terrible time</u> for me.

After you've taken a shot at reworking each of these vague super-reader sentences, trade papers with a partner or share your efforts with the class. How much variation do you see in different writers' interpretations of each code word or phrase?

Visualizing Details

Try creating your own detailed images by means of visualization. Return to one of the stories you've written in your journal and pick out a passage that seems to rely on vague code words or phrases. Then close your eyes and focus on the scene or situation the passage refers to, trying to remember or reconstruct every detail and sensation you can associate with it. For example, if you referred to "my lucky jeans," picture the slash in the left knee, the fraying cuffs, the color and feel of the fabric, the way they fit, the way you felt when you put them on, the experience that convinced you they were lucky. If your passage focuses on how rigid and authoritarian your third-grade teacher was, try to re-create a day in his class—from the ringing of the first bell down to the feeling you got when he called your name. Once you've developed a clear picture in your mind, quickly write down all these details. Try to get at least a full page of description. Now reread what you've written, selecting and refining the details that best convey the mood or the theme you want to emphasize in your story. Compare your results with those of your classmates.

CHAPTER 4

Revision Workshop:
Engaging the Reader

Revision: Why Bother?

Once you've got a draft on paper, you may feel that your job is done. But
for most successful writers, the first draft is just the beginning: revision is
where much of the serious work of writing takes place. As we mentioned
earlier, many people have the mistaken idea that revising a paper means fix-
ing the spelling and putting the commas in the right place. We suspect that
this misconception comes from years of experience writing papers for
teachers who seemed obsessed with such details. "Three misspelled words
means an automatic F!" Sound familiar? If so, you may need to revise your
ideas about revision. Checking the grammar and spelling and tidying the
margins is what we call editing. And while editing is essential, you should
try not to spend too much time on it until the very end, *after* you've spent
as much time as you can on the bigger task of revising. Revision literally
implies reseeing, looking again with fresh eyes. So revision means thinking
hard and thinking big: going back to rewrite the introduction because you
came up with some good new ideas as you wrote; gritting your teeth and
throwing out a paragraph you sweated over because you realize that it
doesn't fit; adding details and examples to clarify the point you're making;
reordering sentences and paragraphs to make your ideas "flow" more
smoothly; and so forth.

Why this emphasis on revision? Like most things, it has a lot to do with
culture. Linguist John Hinds distinguishes between cultural traditions that
stress "reader responsibility" and those that emphasize "writer responsibil-

ity." In reader-responsibility cultures, it's understood that the reader of an essay or article is primarily responsible for interpreting the writer's message. The writer in such a culture may be able to assume that readers share particular values or knowledge, so that general references to common themes or traditions require little explanation. Readers may also value subtlety and ambiguity and enjoy the challenge of making their own connections between ideas. This means that many of the things we agonize over when we revise—clearly linking each sentence to the next, choosing words that leave the least room for misinterpretation, demonstrating how every point is related to the main idea—are less crucial to writers in a reader-responsibility culture. Hinds notes that these writers often produce only one draft, rather than laboring through multiple revisions. It's not that the writers are careless or lazy; it's just that their readers have different expectations: in fact, a writer who spelled things out too explicitly would be seen as dull, unsophisticated, or even insulting to the reader's intelligence.[1]

However, cultures that believe in writer responsibility assume that it's the writer's job to make everything clear and unambiguous: if the reader gets confused or lost, the writer isn't doing as good a job as she should. So it becomes the writer's responsibility to try to imagine what difficulties a reader might have and to revise in order to make the reader's task as effortless as possible. The cultural tradition in the United States, according to Hinds, places the burden of clarity on the writer. In a society as large and culturally diverse as ours, we can't always assume that our readers will be familiar with the customs and ideas that seem like "common knowledge" to us. Moreover, the dominant culture in the United States favors a kind of hard-headed Yankee practicality: straightforwardness, accuracy, and "nailing things down" are generally held up as positive values. There are exceptions to this rule: for instance, poetry in English often demands a high level of reader responsibility, and art historians tend to be more tolerant of ambiguity than do mathematicians. But in general, U.S. college students live in an intensely writer-responsibility culture, shaped not only by the directness of American communication style but by most scholars' high regard for "scientific" precision.

Because revision is the heart of effective writing in a culture like this, we'll ask you to take part in a series of revision workshops. In this first workshop, you'll work on developing and focusing one of the drafts you wrote earlier. We've included a revision case study to show you how a particularly

[1]"Reader vs. Writer Responsibility: A New Typology," in *Writing across Languages: Analysis of L2 Text,* ed. Ulla Connor and Robert B. Kaplan (Reading, Mass.: Addison-Wesley, 1987).

successful student writer added and selected details to clarify the theme of her family story. Throughout this chapter, we'll ask you to test your writing on an audience—your classmates—and we'll suggest focused activities to help you read and respond to each other's writing effectively.

Revision Case Study: Making Details Work

What makes a story tellable? It's obvious that we don't bother telling our friends or family members everything that happens to us every day. Good stories, like good essays, generally have a point: we tell them because they convey something significant about us, our acquaintances, our worlds. The point of the story gives it focus and shape—it's what makes a story recognizable and understandable to an audience. For example, in her memoir (p. 9), Beverly Donofrio doesn't just relate random details about her adolescence; instead, she tells the recognizable story of how a good girl went bad when she rebelled against authority. Her story has a point—and has cultural significance—because it's built around a story frame that Americans might expect to find in relation to the topic of growing up. This conceptual framework or theme focuses her memoir by selectively limiting the events and details that she includes. Given the focus of her story, it wouldn't make sense if she plunged into a long account of teen hairstyles in the 1960s or if she began to talk about some of the "nice" things she did for her father or friends during those years. These details might, in fact, be part of her adolescent memories, but they wouldn't fit the story she's trying to tell. They wouldn't support or develop her point.

Even a complex essay like Leslie Marmon Silko's analysis of storytelling in Pueblo Indian culture (p. 21) needs a clear sense of focus. Although Silko refuses to take a traditional approach to writing and speaking—the approach that "moves from point A to point B to point C"—she still builds her essay around a story frame. She tells the story of the complex web of connections that link language, stories, landscape, and people in Pueblo culture. All of the details she includes, all of the stories she tells in the course of her essay, are included because they clarify this central idea or theme.

If you're lucky, the story you want to tell in your essay will become clear early in the writing process, during prewriting, or even as you read through the assignment. Often, however, you won't find the focus of your essay until you've worked through at least one complete draft: sometimes it's only through the process of writing itself that you discover the story you really want to tell. The following student essay, "Las Mañanitas," illustrates how revision can strengthen a paper by sharpening its focus and enriching the details used to develop it. Because the revisions in this case are all additions to the original text, we have simply highlighted the added portions rather than reprinted the entire text. The writer, D'Andra Galarza, composed this moving account of her mother's forty-fifth birthday celebration for a writing class that was linked to an introductory course in Chicana/o studies.

STUDENT
WRITING

Las Mañanitas
D'Andra Galarza

Being a fourth generation Chicana is not an easy thing. Why couldn't I be first or even second? When I say I'm fourth generation, I feel people want to ask, "Why does it even matter anymore?" By the fourth generation, our language has changed from all Spanish to all English with a few sprinkles of Spanglish. The Chicana/o culture that was, takes on an entirely new meaning. The stories that were passed down in prior generations have ceased and the tradition that once was so rich is scarce.

I take my culture very seriously. The rest of my family doesn't necessarily think the same way about these matters or perhaps we, as a family, would value and celebrate our culture on a regular basis. The family has been in Southern California for many generations and has adapted very much to American ways. Consequently today, many of our Mexican traditions and customs cease to exist. However, one tradition I value so much that has continued to thrive but has lessened significantly in the last few years is Las Mañanitas.

Five years ago, when my mother turned forty-five, our family held a Las Mañanitas celebration for her, one that will live in my memory and my heart forever. At 5:30 a.m. my entire family (which is very big) as well as many good friends congregated at a church about a half mile from my mother's house. My parents are divorced, but even relatives from my father's side were invited to the celebration--in Chicana/o and Latina/o culture, <u>si eres familia, eres familia siempre</u>.

It was a brisk, windy, November morning. As each one of us arrived, there was a warm hug and thermos of coffee to greet us. There was such laughter as we tried to keep warm because it was such a ridiculous time to be awake on a cold November morning. The excitement mounted as more of us came together in love and in anticipation of this great celebration. The most important members of our celebration finally arrived-- the mariachis. The mariachis were essential to our celebration; they would lead us in singing "Las Mañanitas" to my mother. When we had all arrived at the church, we started the walk to my mother's house. There must have been fifty of us walking up the block. What a sight we had to be, fifty Chicanos in a predominantly white neighborhood walking up the block with the mariachis in tow, including the pobrecito bass player who had to carry his huge bass all the way up the block (not to mention that he had partied a little too much the night before because that morning at 5:30 he was wearing sunglasses). As we walked up the street, an old man who had come out to get his morning paper shouted, "Hey, where ya going?" One of my cousins answered, "We're going to las mañanitas." "To a what?" he said, we all died laughing.

As we approached my mother's house, we started singing, "Estas son Las Mañanitas que cantaba el Rey David hoy por ser dia de tu santo te las cantamos a ti. Despierta mi bien despierta mira que ya amanecio ya los pajaritos cantan la luna ya se metio." We must have sung the entire song when finally the lights in my mother's bedroom came on. Completely surprised, she came outside, with her bathrobe on and tears in her eyes, to find her entire family and friends celebrating her on her forty-fifth year as a woman, a mother--my mother, a friend, a wife, and a Chicana. How we celebrated that cool November

5

morning. We ate menudo and steaming hot corn tortillas with butter. We had pan dulce, beer, and Bloody Marys. The mariachis played until at least 12:00 noon.

This was not merely a birthday celebration: this was a celebration of who we are and where we came from. This was a celebration of life--our lives as Chicanas/os. As we sang, ate, and drank together as a family on that morning, I could feel a bond with each one of my family members. The second, third, fourth and even fifth generations were all together celebrating a tradition that had been in our culture for hundreds of years.

My family members and I are all extremely different in the way we view culture and tradition. Our lifestyles are very different in theory and in practice. My co-fourth-generationers don't put the same emphasis that I do on maintaining our cultural and familial traditions. For this reason, when we do have a Las Mañanitas celebration, it is exceptionally special. As a family we have become so assimilated and so ingrained in our American culture that we forget we have a duo-culture. Only one side of our bi-culturalism seems to be in practice. We live every day forgetting we are Chicanas/os because by now we fit in "perfectly" . . . or so we think. We live every day forgetting our responsibilities to La Raza and to our children in remembering and passing on the undisputable fact that we are, indeed, Chicanas/os. When I mention cultural importance to my family they think I am getting on my "Chicano Power" soapbox. My parents' generation experienced life from the barrio. Although there are some very fond memories of having grown up in a Chicana/o neighborhood this image also represents extreme economic and social hardships for them. The economic and social mobility my parents, aunts, and uncles have been able to achieve and provide for their children is representative of their being able to find their notch in American culture, a place that was made up of the sweat, tears, and dreams of their parents. Going "back" to reclaim cultural pride is regression to many of them and they would much rather look forward than behind. Looking back can be very painful because what was can never be experienced again in the same way. Assimilation and acculturation do not happen without cost. The previous culture has to be modified greatly and at some point almost forfeited entirely otherwise the individual will always be in turmoil over identity. In the case of my family, it is evident that years of being here have eroded our past to an almost unrecognizable present. This must be one of the reasons why as a child I remember my Tio Jimmy telling me if anyone asked I was to tell them I was an American!

I remember that morning so well. The pride of being a Chicana/o was in the face of each of my family members as we stood out in the cold singing and reliving a tradition that our great-great-grandparents had celebrated also. I wondered what prior generations would have thought if they could have seen how this tradition had transcended their time and their country. I wondered what they would have thought if they had been able to see how much their family had grown and changed. Since my ancestors' time, the family had become a mixture of colors, cultures, and expressions, and yet, the bond I felt with my family was not just a bond of love, which was very much present, but it was a bond of Chicana/o love. As we stood out in the front yard singing, we knew we were different, a difference to be proud of. Although no one spoke of it, we felt in our hearts the struggle that had gone on in our ancestors' time and even in the time of our parents, for it was that very struggle which enabled us to bring such a tradition to a neighborhood which had never experienced anything like this before or since my family's celebration. Our marginality could not be denied at the moment of singing, as we stumbled through the words of Las Mañanitas with our broken Spanish, humming the parts we didn't know. My mother's second husband, Mike, conducted our singing with his hands. We laughed because he didn't know the words or even what a mañanitas was. The friends or family members who had married into the family and were not Chicana/os smiled through the ritual of singing. I don't think they could fully understand the meaning of having your family wake you with a song on your birthday, but we were glad they wanted to share in this celebration with us. As the mariachis broke into "Happy Birthday" we all joined in. We cheered and hooted in old Mexicano tradition to onlooking neighbors who were probably wondering what we were doing. Each one of our hearts soared because at that moment we remembered, we all remembered who we really were.

We haven't had a celebration like this since my mother's. We all get very wrapped up in our own lives and responsibilities, and we forget that retaining culture and tradition is work. It is a conscious effort every day to remind ourselves of our humble heritage and to remember the struggle La Raza went through so we can now do many of the things we take for granted, like my writing this paper for this class at UCLA. Thirty years ago this would have been almost unheard of. As I looked at my aunts and uncles that day I realized how far they had come since their barrio childhoods. My Tio Ronnie is one of the best criminal attorneys in Orange County, my Tio Jimmy is a very successful contractor, my mother and Mike had just bought this beautiful little house that was entirely their own, and my sister had presented me with a beautiful nephew and godson, Devin. As I held Devin in my arms, I clung to him tightly. His light brown hair shown in the early morning sunlight. His skin, which looked even more pale compared to my olive-tone arms that were embracing him, was evidence of his duo-heritage. I held him close and whispered, "Mijo, please

remember today, please remember this is part of who you are."
He looked up at me and said, "Hi, Nina."

I'm not living my life in the past by wanting tradition   10
and culture as an important part of my life for myself and my
family. I simply want to retain the beauty that we as a people have created together. I want to treasure these traditions so that I may better understand who I am. I want to remember how far we as Raza have come, and I want to remember
where we are and where we have to go, in order to fully understand my being as a Chicana. As we make our way through
the dominant system that allows no time or space for individuality, we need ways in which we can be grounded so that we
remember who we are. The memory of this celebration in all
its simplicity reminds me of a simpler time and place when
the family was the institution and the quality of life was
much greater.

Las Mañanitas is always so beautiful when we celebrate
together as a family. At events like this I always remember my
Grandma Jennie, who was killed in a car accident when I was
just a year old. She had single-handedly raised five kids, including my mother, and saw her husband drink himself to death.
After her kids had all left home and gotten married, she had a
chance at life again; she was killed shortly thereafter. My
mother was only twenty-two. I could see the tears form in my
mother's and my aunt's eyes as my uncle played a song on the
accordion he said "Was one of Mama's favorites." I often wonder how different the family would be if she was here to share
these times with us. I have been told what a wonderful woman
my grandmother was; she sang and loved to speak Spanish. Since
I was a child I always associated Spanish with her image. Before I learned Spanish, I asked someone the words to Las
Mañanitas. When they told me the words, I cried. I had never
heard a song celebrating birth with such unequivocal beauty as

"Las Mañanitas." Because it is in Spanish, I also associate it with death--my grandmother's. I still cry when I hear it. It is one of the few songs in Spanish I recall hearing as a child. It is one of the few direct links to our Mexicana/o culture that is still very much alive in my family today. It is one of the few direct links to my grandmother that I will ever have. It is one of the few songs in Spanish (or in English) that carry with them memories of the closeness, love, and struggle we have experienced as a family and as La Raza. Siempre hay esperanza. No lo olvide familia.

Developing and Focusing a Draft

In the previous chapter you worked on translating general code phrases into more precise language. Skillful writers do more than simply add details wherever they can, though. They select details carefully in order to focus attention on important ideas and develop those ideas more fully. Galarza's revision clearly illustrates this kind of selection.

Galarza tells a good story; details like her description of the hung-over bass player make the scene come alive for the reader. But this is more than a simple account of her mother's Las Mañanitas celebration: it's also a perceptive analysis of how the family's cultural traditions are changing as every generation becomes more Americanized. Her first two paragraphs introduce her dilemma as a fourth-generation Chicana: "When I say I'm fourth generation, I feel people want to ask, 'Why does it even matter anymore?'" By the fourth generation, she points out, the language and traditions her family brought from Mexico have nearly been lost through adaptation to "American ways." One of the few remnants of Mexican culture to survive has been the celebration of Las Mañanitas. In both drafts, Galarza's introduction stresses how Americanized the family has become, yet in the original version her account of the celebration itself focused almost exclusively on its most traditional elements—the food, the music, the customs that link the family to its Mexican heritage. In effect, the details in this first draft conflicted with the theme. It was as if the writer were trying to tell two different stories at the same time—the story of how her family had preserved its cultural heritage and the story of her family's loss of traditional ways.

Galarza's revisions enhance both the story of the celebration and the discussion of cultural change. By adding the descriptions of her uncles, her stepfather, her nephew, and her grandmother, she paints a richer portrait of her family and of the emotional significance Las Mañanitas holds for her. These same details also support the essay's focus on cultural change within the family: the memory of her Spanish-speaking grandmother, the images of her professionally successful uncles, her stepfather (who cheerfully conducts the singing without understanding the Spanish words), and her light-skinned nephew—all these details underline the story Galarza is telling about cultural change. Notice, too, how the added details give you a deeper understanding of the writer's values, her feelings about family and culture. For instance, her description of her parents' generation (paragraph 7) expresses both pride in the hard work and sacrifice that led them to succeed economically and regret at the cultural price that they paid in the process. In the revised final paragraph, Galarza gathers all the strands of the story together in an extended reflection on her grandmother. Grandma Jennie's strength assured the family's survival and ultimate success in their adopted country, yet the language and cultural memory that she represents to Galarza have nearly vanished except in the celebration and song of "Las Mañanitas": "It is one of the few direct links to our Mexicana/o culture that is still very much alive in my family today. It is one of the few direct links to my grandmother that I will ever have." In the revision, Galarza includes the intimate memory of her grandmother to illustrate the point she is trying to make: instead of simply saying that this celebration reminds her of the "closeness, love, and struggle" her family has experienced, she offers us a detailed picture of all these qualities, captured in the story of her grandmother.

The ability to distinguish details that work hard from those that don't is crucial to successful academic analysis. What's impressive about Galarza's revision, then, is not just the number of details she includes but how much those details accomplish—sharpening the focus, developing the analysis, and enhancing the voice of the essay. The contrast between her grandmother and the younger family members (uncles, stepfather, nephew) clearly illustrates the cultural changes she mentions in the first paragraph, thus developing and supporting the theme instead of contradicting it. While there are many other details she could have included (the names of everyone who attended the celebration, what they all looked like, what they wore, the jokes and small talk they exchanged), these wouldn't have had the same kind of impact because they wouldn't have helped her develop the central point of the story—the tension between her family's gradual adaptation to American culture and her strong sense of the importance of maintaining a Chicana/o identity.

OPTIONAL
ACTIVITY

Sample Revision for Discussion

Here are the opening paragraphs of a paper by another student writer, Yolanda Davis, in both draft and revised form. Work in pairs or groups to identify and discuss the changes she has made in the revision. How does her use of details differ in the two versions? How do the added details work to develop or clarify the purpose of the essay?

Draft

Juneteenth

The Fourth of July is celebrated nationwide as a day of liberation from the tyranny of England. In my family we celebrate June nineteenth, or Juneteenth as it is called, instead. Juneteenth is a day of jubilation for many African Americans, as it is the day on which two years after the signing of the Emancipation Proclamation by Lincoln, slaves in Eastern Texas were told of their independence. With freedom in their hands and newfound hope in their hearts, the ex-slaves onset an all-day annual "holiday" filled with baseball, political speeches, square dancing, and general socializing. It is important to me because the observance of this event continues a cultural tradition and perpetuates racial identity, thus instilling in me the self-love, respect, and pride necessary to survive in American Society.

The year was 1988. I was eleven years old and attending my first Juneteenth picnic. There was an abundance of food. I ate barbequed ribs, baked beans, mustard greens, potato salad, and watermelon when I first arrived. My second plate not only consisted of the before mentioned items, but also barbequed chicken, rice, corn on the cob, sweet potato pie, German chocolate cake, and two tall glasses of Kool-Aid. I was so full when I finally arrived

home. I was full of the music of my people--there were
African musicians there--full of the profound speakers who
made me question the given idealogies of my ancestors,
full of the culture I never knew I had. I even learned the
three legends of the delay of the news. . . .

Revision

Juneteenth

July fourth is celebrated nationwide as a day of liberation from the tyranny of England. In my family, however, we celebrate June nineteenth, or Juneteenth as it is
called, instead. Juneteenth is a day of jubilation for
many African Americans, as it is the day on which two
years after the signing of the Emancipation Proclamation
by Lincoln, slaves in Eastern Texas were told of their release. With freedom in their hands and newfound hope in
their hearts, the ex-slaves launched an all-day celebration filled with baseball games, political speeches,
square dancing, and general socializing. It's important to
me because the observance of this event continues a cultural tradition and perpetuates racial identity, thus instilling in me the self-love, respect, and pride necessary
to survive in American society.

I didn't attend a Juneteenth celebration prior to
1988. As my mother explained, I wasn't taken earlier because I was too young to understand the importance of
the day. My grandmother and mother often went back south
to these celebrations. They would return filled with stories of how great it was. Dreams I had about Juneteenth--
visions of clowns, rides, pizza, and all the ice-cream I
could eat--paraded in my head. I had to partake in this
festival. When I was finally allowed to go, I was initially disappointed. There were no clowns or pizza. The

celebration took place in a park. African masks adorned the trees. Barbeque and incense (black love) filled the air. The performers were dressed in traditional African wardrobe--buba (blouse) and lappa (wrap skirt)--and some even wore headwraps. Cowrie shell necklaces, bracelets, and anklets jingled from the feet of the dancers as they gave thanks to their God. The live drums called to my soul, begging, pleading for me to dance. Resistance was futile as I became enrapt by the beat. I stood in the midst of the park awed, totally taken by my environment. I ate barbequed ribs, baked beans, mustard greens, potato salad, and watermelon when I first arrived. My second plate not only consisted of the aforementioned items, but also barbequed chicken, rice, corn on the cob, sweet potato pie, German chocolate cake, and two tall glasses of Kool-Aid. I was so full when I finally arrived home. I was full of the music of my people--full of my heritage.

I used to think my history began with slavery. I believed my ancestors' black dialect came about only because we were mentally inferior to our white "massas," and that that was the closest we could come to "real" English. I never knew we contributed to the building of this nation and carried the load of America on our backs. I never knew the myriad injustices committed against our people. New knowledge replaced my ignorance, and understanding of the past removed hatred of everything black, including myself. Now I embrace and love my people, my color, and myself. This is why the observance of Juneteenth is important. It teaches the younger generation the beauty of their culture.

The history behind Juneteenth hinges on three theories. . . .

Responding to Another Writer's Draft

The rest of this chapter will guide you through the process of revising your draft and helping your classmates with their revisions. If you haven't worked in peer response groups before, you may feel a little unsure at first about your own or your classmates' ability to give advice about writing. Isn't that the teacher's job? Up to a point, yes. But your instructor, no matter how expert, is only one reader, and won't notice everything; getting responses from other readers will give you more perspectives on your writing. Besides, one point of peer response is to help you become less dependent on the teacher, to improve your ability to help yourself. Before we get started, though, here are some general principles you need to keep in mind in order to make peer response productive for you.

Don't sweat the small stuff. Since your purpose is to substantially *revise* your work, not merely edit it, we'll ask you to avoid commenting on or correcting each other's spelling, punctuation, and grammar. When you spend time fussing over the spelling of a word or the placement of a comma it's easy to neglect larger issues, like whether the writer's ideas make sense. Besides, at this stage of the writing process, you'd most likely be wasting your time: Why spend ten minutes laboring over a sentence to make it grammatically perfect only to realize later that it's irrelevant and has to be thrown out entirely? So try your best, at least for now, to turn off that nagging grammar censor in your mind; don't pay attention to errors unless they interfere with your understanding of the draft.

Be diplomatic. Because writing is a very personal thing, all writers feel at times that criticism of something they struggled to put on paper is really an attack on *them.* If someone says "This paragraph is boring" it's easy to assume that means "You're a boring person." So when you respond to a draft, avoid judgmental language and concentrate instead on detailing your responses to the draft as fully as possible. For example, instead of telling the writer that his fifth paragraph is deadly dull, try saying, "I lost interest in paragraph five because . . . " and then spell out your reasons. Likewise, instead of telling the writer that her anecdote about Uncle Phong's practical joke is pointless, ask her how the incident relates to her earlier remark that her family is too serious, or explain why the inconsistency confused you. Focusing on *your* experience of the paper can help make the writer less self-conscious about criticism and can also help her to see her work from a new perspective.

Don't forget the praise. Everyone needs some encouragement, so take every opportunity to tell the writer she's done something well. Remember, though, that your goal is not just to make her feel good but to help her understand and use her strengths consistently; so, like your criticisms, your praise should be as specific as possible. Instead of simply writing "Great paragraph!" or "I like this," try to spell out in detail what it is that you're responding to.

Revising Your Draft: Focus and Details

Now it's time to try the real thing. The following activities were designed to help you focus your draft and develop specific details that enhance your essay. Before you begin, you'll need to get into revision groups, exchange drafts, number each paragraph in the margin, and prepare a "revision response sheet" for each paper you'll read. To make these sheets, just take out a separate sheet of paper and write the name of the writer, the title of the draft, and your name at the top.

Focusing

- First, read up to the point where you think the introduction ends. Mark the spot where you stopped and then take a few minutes to think about what expectations the writer has set up for you, the reader. What seems to be the general topic of the paper so far? From what you've read, what do you think the specific focus or purpose of the paper will be? Where do you expect the writer to go from here? Write a brief response to these questions on your revision response sheet. If the writer's purpose or direction is unclear to you, write a note explaining what you find confusing.

- Now go back to the beginning of the draft and read through to the end without stopping. When you finish, take a few minutes to reconsider the paper's focus: Did the rest of the story confirm the expectations that were set up in the introduction, or did the paper seem to shift focus to another idea or topic? Did the writer make the significance of the story clear by the end of the paper? Write a brief response, explaining what you see as the central focus or purpose of the paper as a whole.

- Next look at the individual paragraphs in the draft and write a short response to each one on your revision sheet. Which paragraphs or passages work best to develop the central theme or focus of the paper as you identified it? Do any paragraphs seem unclear in their purpose or unrelated to the rest of the essay? If so, explain why.

Developing Details

- As you review the paper paragraph by paragraph, look for any vague or general "code words" or phrases that you can find. Write questions in the margins asking for elaboration of these terms (for instance, "What made your grandmother's stories 'interesting'?" "What are some of the 'delicious dishes' that are served on this holiday? Do they have any special significance?"). If you notice any sections that seem particularly vague or general, try to suggest to the writer what additional details you would find useful as a reader.

Explain your responses as fully as possible on your revision response sheet. A reasonable goal is to write at least a full page in response to each draft you read. Once you've completed your responses and annotated the draft with your notes and questions, take some time to discuss each paper as a group. After you've received your readers' responses, use them to help you decide what parts of your essay are strongest and which need to be reworked. In order to do a thorough job of revision, you may need to return to some of the strategies you practiced in the drafting phase: visualizing, freewriting, brainstorming, listing, drawing, clustering, outlining, and so on. Keep in mind that these are tools that you can use whenever they're helpful for clarifying or refining your ideas—not just exercises that you go through once and then abandon.

**J O U R N A L
O P T I O N**

Evaluating Your Writing Process

Before you turn in your revised paper, stop a moment to reflect on your writing process for this essay. What gave you the most trouble? What was easiest? Which aspects of the finished paper do you like best and which are you least sure of? What questions do you have about this paper that you'd particularly like your instructor to address? Attach this journal entry to your finished paper when you turn it in so that your instructor can respond to your concerns in her comments.

PART TWO

How Stories Shape Us

CHAPTER 5

Cultural Collisions

Prisoners of Memory

You're sweating your way through an exam in biology. The clock ticks its way toward the end of the hour, and no matter how hard you try, you just can't remember the name of the organelle that generates energy in the cell. You stare at the diagram in the test booklet and try to visualize the sketch you made for your study notes. You mentally review the list of key concepts you wrote out last night. You even try free-associating words in the hope that the answer will appear by itself. What college student hasn't wished for the gift of a perfect memory, for a mind that could instantly and accurately recall all the information taught in college courses?

You might wish you had a perfect memory, but memory can be a problem as well as a gift. In the mid-1920s Russian psychologist Alexander Luria began working with a young man with a very special problem. A failed musician and journalist, "S," as Luria referred to him in his book *The Mind of a Mnemonist* (1968), had the uncanny ability to remember everything he experienced. He could reproduce random lists of words, letters, or numbers regardless of length, backwards as well as forwards. He could repeat complicated tables of nonsense syllables including as many as seventy items, and even identify a specific syllable when given its position in the table. Most impressively, Luria's "mnemonist" could recall any information he was given, no matter how random or meaningless, even decades after he first encountered it. He had, by Luria's account, an inexhaustible memory, a memory that "had no distinct limits."[1]

"S" was capable of such mental feats because his mind was a prodigious maker of stories. When he committed a string of sixty or seventy nonsense syllables to memory, he didn't just "burn them in" by visualizing them; he wove them into a visual narrative—a kind of mental movie—that he could play backwards or forwards at will. He might place a sequence of numbers at particular points along the route he walked home from work at night: to remember the numbers all he had to do was to walk mentally along the route again, "picking up" the numbers where he left them. In his mind a table of nonsense syllables suggested an episode about his landlady, each meaningless sound becoming associated with an object in the story. All of his experiences, all of the books he read, everything he saw or heard was incorporated into a vast network of stories that he could call up at a moment's notice.

The problem that brought "S" to Luria was that he didn't know how to forget. The stories kept permanently on file in his memory were so vivid and real they made it hard for him to stay focused on the here and now: his past experiences constantly threatened to sweep him away from the people and events of his present. Reading was a particularly difficult challenge: "S" struggled to comprehend even relatively straightforward passages because every word he encountered would suggest a story he had read before or a memory of an earlier experience. If the piece he was reading began with "An old man was walking down the road," he would immediately see a specific old man, in full detail, who "lived" in a book he may have read years before. As one memory led to another and story led to story, he would be carried so far from the meaning of the text he was reading that he'd simply give up in confusion. Until Luria helped "S" learn to force himself to forget, he remained a prisoner of the stories his mind could hold.

The story of Luria's "S" continues to interest us half a century later, because, to a certain extent, we are all prisoners of the stories we tell. The difference between the average person and "S" is simply a matter of degree. The stories that snared "S" were perceptual: when he read a word he "saw" an image of a specific person and then got trapped by the details of that specific person's story. Our stories work more subtly. As every student knows, we readily forget the details of what we read, study, and experience. Unlike "S," we are able to sweep insignificant information aside and retain only general outlines of events and relationships. When you enter a restau-

[1] A. R. Luria, *The Mind of a Mnemonist*, trans. Lynn Solotaroff (Cambridge, Mass.: Harvard University Press, 1968), p. 11.

rant you don't have to dredge up specific memories of past meals out to tell you what to do and to expect; you have a generalized story—a script—that does this for you. This ability to create general stories from specific experiences—based on our tendency to forget unimportant details—lies at the heart of all abstract learning and thinking.

We create many of these scripts ourselves from direct personal experience, but we borrow many more from the cultures we grow up in. The story frames provided by our cultures tell us what's important, what we should pay attention to, and what we should shun. They remind us what we should expect to happen in a given situation and what, in turn, is expected of us. Without these cultural scripts and story frames we'd end up much like Luria's "S," easily confused by even the simplest social situation and unable to make sense of what we read. Every time we walked into a classroom we'd have to compare the present situation with specific past memories in order to know how to behave and what to expect. Every day would, in a sense, be as disorienting and embarrassing as our first day in elementary school. By handling all of this work unconsciously and effortlessly, your conceptual scripts and story frames make it possible for you to attend to more important matters—like sizing up your professor or the person sitting next to you.

In a monocultural society, this gift of generalization might seem to be a prescription for harmony and efficiency. If everyone told themselves exactly the same stories and had matching expectations, you might think society would hum along like a well-oiled machine. But cultures never exist in a vacuum: even the most homogeneous cultural group is criss-crossed by subcultures based on age, class, gender, profession, and other factors. Whether we choose to acknowledge it or not, we live in a multicultural world, a world where the drawbacks of being trapped in one set of stories are becoming increasingly apparent. Every day, students on America's college campuses meet people from different geographical regions, socioeconomic classes, and ethnic backgrounds. Every day, you have to negotiate your way through a world where your stories fail to mesh smoothly with those around you—a world where even the way you wave hello may be seen as an affront or insult. In a multicultural world like ours, the unconscious conceptual stories our minds spin can imprison us as surely as the stories that tormented Luria's mnemonist.

This chapter is dedicated to exploring cultural collisions. In it we'll examine how culturally familiar stories lead us to understand and sometimes to misunderstand one another. We begin with a brief selection by a famous student of culture and cultural conflict. A professor of anthropology at Harvard University, Clyde Kluckhohn (1905–1960) wrote many academic essays during his career, most of them focusing on Navajo Indian culture. In this excerpt from his book *Mirror for Man* (1960), Kluckhohn offers a nutshell explanation of how culture shapes our perceptions, our ideas, even our feelings and tastes.

Before Reading

Write a journal entry about your understanding of the word *culture*. What do you associate with the idea of culture? What does culture include? What does culture do?

Designs for Living
Clyde Kluckhohn

Why do the Chinese dislike milk and milk products? Why would Japanese [soldiers] die willingly in a Banzai charge that seemed senseless to Americans? Why do some nations trace descent through the father, others through the mother, still others through both parents? Not because different peoples have different instincts, not because they were destined by God or Fate to different habits, not because the weather is different in China and Japan and the United States. Sometimes shrewd common sense has an answer that is close to that of the anthropologist: "because they were brought up that way." By "culture" anthropology means the total life way of a people, the social legacy the individual acquires from his group. Or culture can be regarded as that part of the environment that is the creation of human beings.

This technical term has a wider meaning than the "culture" of history and literature. A humble cooking pot is as much a cultural product as is a Beethoven sonata. In ordinary speech a man of culture is a man who can speak languages other than his own, who is familiar with history, literature, philosophy, or the fine arts. In some cliques that definition is still narrower. The cultured person is one who can talk about James Joyce, Scarlatti, and Picasso. To the anthropologist, however, to be human is to be cultured. There is culture in general, and then there are the specific cultures such as Russian, American, British, Hottentot, Inca. The general abstract notion serves to remind us that we cannot explain acts solely in terms of the biological properties of the people concerned, their individual past experience, and the immediate situation. The past experience of other people in the form of culture enters into almost every event. Each specific culture constitutes a kind of blueprint for all of life's activities.

One of the interesting things about human beings is that they try to understand themselves and their own behavior. While this has been particularly true of Europeans in recent times, there is no group which has not developed a scheme or schemes to explain human actions. To the insistent human query "why?" the most exciting illumination anthropology has to offer is that of the concept of culture. Its explanatory importance is comparable to categories such as evolution in biology, gravity in physics, disease in medicine. A good deal of human behavior can be understood, and indeed predicted, if we know a people's design for living. Many acts are neither accidental nor due to personal peculiarities nor caused by supernatural forces nor simply mysterious. Even those of us who pride ourselves on our individualism follow most of the time a pattern not of our own making. We brush our teeth on arising. We put on pants—not a loincloth or a grass skirt. We eat three meals a day—not four or five or two. We sleep in a bed—not in a hammock or on a sheep pelt. I do not have to know the individual and his life history to be able to predict these and countless other regularities, including many in the thinking process, of all Americans who are not incarcerated in jails or hospitals for the insane.

To the American woman a system of plural wives seems "instinctively" abhorrent. She cannot understand how any woman can fail to be jealous and uncomfortable if she must share her husband with other women. She feels it "unnatural" to accept such a situation. On the other hand, a Koryak woman of Siberia, for example, would find it hard to understand how a woman could be so selfish and so undesirous of feminine companionship in the home as to wish to restrict her husband to one mate.

Some years ago I met in New York City a young man who did not speak a word of English and was obviously bewildered by American ways. By "blood" he was as American as you or I, for his parents had gone from Indiana to China as missionaries. Orphaned in infancy, he was reared by a Chinese family in a remote village. All who met him found him more Chinese than American. The facts of his blue eyes and light hair were less impressive than a Chinese style of gait, Chinese arm and hand movements, Chinese facial expression, and Chinese modes of thought. The biological heritage was American, but the cultural training had been Chinese. He returned to China.

Another example of another kind: I once knew a trader's wife in Arizona who took a somewhat devilish interest in producing a cultural reaction. Guests who came her way were often served delicious sandwiches filled with a meat that seemed to be neither chicken nor tuna fish yet was

5

reminiscent of both. To queries she gave no reply until each had eaten his fill. She then explained that what they had eaten was not chicken, not tuna fish, but the rich, white flesh of freshly killed rattlesnakes. The response was instantaneous—vomiting, often violent vomiting. A biological process is caught in a cultural web.

A highly intelligent teacher with long and successful experience in the public schools of Chicago was finishing her first year in an Indian school. When asked how her Navaho pupils compared in intelligence with Chicago youngsters, she replied, "Well, I just don't know. . . . The other night we had a dance in the high school. I saw a boy who is one of the best students in my English class standing off by himself. So I took him over to a pretty girl and told them to dance. But they just stood there with their heads down. They wouldn't even say anything." I inquired if she knew whether or not they were members of the same clan. "What difference would that make?"

"How would you feel about getting into bed with your brother?" The teacher walked off in a huff, but, actually, the two cases were quite comparable in principle. To the Indian the type of bodily contact involved in our social dancing has a directly sexual connotation. The incest taboos between members of the same clan are as severe as between true brothers and sisters. The shame of the Indians at the suggestion that a clan brother and sister should dance and the indignation of the white teacher at the idea that she should share a bed with an adult brother represent equally nonrational responses, culturally standardized unreason.

All this does not mean that there is no such thing as raw human nature. The very fact that certain of the same institutions are found in all known societies indicates that at bottom all human beings are very much alike. . . . All people undergo the same poignant life experiences such as birth, helplessness, illness, old age, and death. The biological potentialities of the species are the blocks with which cultures are built. Some patterns of every culture crystallize around focuses provided by the inevitables of biology: the difference between the sexes, the presence of persons of different ages, the varying physical strength and skill of individuals. The facts of nature also limit culture forms. No culture provides patterns for jumping over trees or for eating iron ore.

There is thus no "either-or" between nature and that special form of nurture called culture. Culture determinism is as one-sided as biological determinism. The two factors are interdependent. Culture arises out of human nature, and its forms are restricted both by man's biology and by natural laws. It is equally true that culture channels biological processes—vomiting, weeping, fainting, sneezing, the daily habits of food intake and waste

10

elimination. When a person eats, he is reacting to an internal "drive," namely, hunger contractions consequent upon the lowering of blood sugar, but his precise reaction to these internal stimuli cannot be predicted by physiological knowledge alone. Whether a healthy adult feels hungry twice, three times, or four times a day and the hours at which this feeling recurs is a question of culture. *What* he eats is of course limited by availability, but is also partly regulated by culture. It is a biological fact that some types of berries are poisonous; it is a cultural fact that, a few generations ago, most Americans considered tomatoes to be poisonous and refused to eat them. Such selective, discriminative use of the environment is characteristically cultural. In a still more general sense, too, the process of eating is channeled by culture. Whether a person eats to live, lives to eat, or merely eats and lives is only in part an individual matter, for there are also cultural trends. Emotions are physiological events. Certain situations will evoke fear in people from any culture. But sensations of pleasure, anger, and lust may be stimulated by cultural cues that would leave unmoved someone who has been reared in a different social tradition. . . .

A culture is learned by individuals as the result of belonging to some particular group, and it constitutes that part of learned behavior which is shared with others. It is our social legacy, as contrasted with our organic heredity. It is one of the important factors which permits us to live together in an organized society, giving us ready-made solutions to our problems, helping us to predict the behavior of others, and permitting others to know what to expect of us.

Culture regulates our lives at every turn. From the moment we are born until we die there is, whether we are conscious of it or not, constant pressure upon us to follow certain types of behavior that other men have created for us. Some paths we follow willingly, others we follow because we know no other way, still others we deviate from or go back to most unwillingly. Mothers of small children know how unnaturally most of this comes to us — how little regard we have, until we are "culturalized," for the "proper" place, time, and manner for certain acts such as eating, excreting, sleeping, getting dirty, and making loud noises. But by more or less adhering to a system of related designs for carrying out all the acts of living, a group of men and women feel themselves linked together by a powerful chain of sentiments. Ruth Benedict[1] gave an almost complete definition of the concept when she said, "Culture is that which binds people together."

---

[1] **Ruth Benedict** (1887–1948): a well-known anthropologist.

Issues for Discussion

1. What does Kluckhohn mean by *culture?* How does he distinguish this definition from other meanings of the word? How do you think most people view the notion of culture today?
2. What, according to Kluckhohn, is the relationship between culture and what he calls "raw human nature" (paragraph 9)?
3. Ideas about culture and cultural conflict have changed since Kluckhohn wrote this selection nearly half a century ago. To what extent do you think his views and assumptions about American culture are still accurate?
4. Do you find Kluckhohn's characterizations of other cultures fair and accurate? How would you describe his attitude toward cultural groups that lie outside what he considers "American" culture?

JOURNAL OPTIONS

Sampling Your Cultural Scripts

1. According to Kluckhohn, culture gives us a "design for living," a pattern that determines most of what we do. The cultures we participate in define a set of scripts for us—scripts that specify many of our daily actions and activities and even many of our ideas and conversations. Make an inventory identifying all of the behaviors and verbal exchanges you participate in during a typical morning or afternoon that could be described as culturally "scripted." How often do you step outside of these culturally prescribed roles?
2. If you've finished the first option and would like to try an exercise in imagination, describe your typical morning or afternoon, imagining what would have happened if you had violated the behavior patterns expected by the cultural groups you belong to. What would the consequences have been of these departures? What do we do that is *not* specified in some way by our cultural scripts?

Cultures as Interpretive Communities

We commonly think of a culture as the sum total of things produced by a particular group of people, things like works of art, pieces of music, language, books, varieties of trade and business, different foods, and styles of dress. Kluckhohn's definition of culture subtly challenges this view. According to Kluckhohn, culture is not a passive product or a collection of artifacts; he sees culture as a kind of template that imposes a vast network of mutual expectations and behavioral patterns on its members. Cultures generate these patterns and expectations through the story frames and scripts that they provide, and because these cultural stories are at work in our minds even before we enter a fast-food restaurant or a college classroom or go out on a date, they act as automatic interpreters of all of our experiences. Everything we think, feel, say, or do is filtered through the story frames of our culture—even before we are consciously aware of our thoughts, feelings, intentions, and desires. Our cultures interpret the world for us: they act as automatic translators, telling us what's natural, what's good, what's valuable, and what is to be shunned. Often they shape our perceptions and reactions even before we have the chance to think, and that's why cultural conflicts sometimes turn deadly.

In March of 1991, Latasha Harlins, a fifteen-year-old African American girl, was shot and killed in a South-Central Los Angeles convenience store because she was suspected of stealing a $1.79 bottle of orange juice. The woman who killed her, Soon Ja Du, was a recent Korean immigrant and a fifty-one-year-old grandmother who ran the store for her family. For weeks after this incident local television news shows broadcast graphic footage from the store's security camera—videotape that showed Du and Harlins exchanging words, Du grabbing Harlins by the jacket, Harlins responding by striking Du's face, and ultimately, Du reaching behind the counter for a loaded .38 caliber handgun to shoot Harlins as she walked away. Stunned by the senselessness of the act, civic leaders wondered aloud how a child could be killed for a bottle of orange juice. One way to begin understanding this violent encounter is to see it as a clash of cultural expectations. When Du accused Harlins of shoplifting and grabbed her jacket, she had no way of knowing that she had violated a cultural script about what it takes for a young girl to survive in a tough section of Los Angeles. As African American poet and journalist Wanda Coleman later observed, Du probably had no idea that Harlins was a mere child, because Harlins was playing a part that was scripted for her by life in a racist culture and life on the streets:

> The price black girls pay for not conforming to white standards of physi-cal beauty is extracted in monumental amounts, birth to death. We bend our personalities, and sometimes mutilate our bodies, in defense. Some-times that bent is "bad attitude," perhaps accompanied by a hair-trigger temper, ready to go off at the mildest slight: Neck-wobbling, hands to hips, we exhibit boisterous, hostile, "niggerish" behavior. Latasha, in-sulted by Du's mistaken assumption that she was a thief, went into her attitude. Then Du unwittingly violated a code of street conduct: You do not put your hands on me without a fight—win, lose, or draw.[2]

When Du grabbed Harlins's jacket, she couldn't have known how disas-trously she had misread Harlins's cultural scripts. When Harlins responded by acting out the part prescribed by the cultures she lived in, she couldn't

---

[2] Wanda Coleman, "Blacks, Immigrants, and America," *Nation*, February 15, 1993, p. 187.

have realized how irrevocably she had violated a traditional Korean story frame asserting the absolute supremacy of age and authority. And, undoubtedly, other cultural story frames made it easy for Du to pull the trigger — racist story frames alive in American culture that dehumanize African Americans and stereotype them as violent and dangerous. Both Harlins and Du were victims of their respective interpretive communities: before they had the chance to think, to be reasonable and see things differently, the story frames of their cultures assigned them roles and responses that brought them into conflict.

Fortunately, most culture clashes aren't as serious as the Harlins tragedy. In fact, as long as different cultures have struggled to coexist, cultural misreadings and misinterpretations have been a staple of comedy. The following excerpt from Amy Tan's popular novel *The Joy Luck Club* (1989) offers an example of a cultural collision. In this selection Lena, a young Chinese American woman, tells the story about the first encounter between her Anglo fiancé, Rich, and her very traditional family. Tan was born in Oakland, California, in 1952, two years after her parents immigrated to the United States. *The Joy Luck Club* resulted from her attempts to understand the cultural and generational tensions between herself and her mother. Her second novel, *The Kitchen God's Wife* (1991), was a worldwide best-seller and has been translated into more than twenty-four languages. Her most recent novel, *The Hundred Secret Senses*, was published in 1996.

Before Reading

Write a brief entry in your journal describing a time when you felt like an outsider. Maybe it was the first time you had slept over at a friend's house or when you transferred to a new school. To what extent was your uneasiness due to a conflict of cultural scripts?

Four Directions

Amy Tan

After much thought, I came up with a brilliant plan. I concocted a way for Rich to meet my mother and win her over. In fact, I arranged it so my mother would want to cook a meal especially for him. I had some help from Auntie Suyuan. Auntie Su was my mother's friend from way back. They were very close, which meant they were ceaselessly tormenting each other with boasts and secrets. And I gave Auntie Su a secret to boast about.

After walking through North Beach one Sunday, I suggested to Rich that we stop by for a surprise visit to my Auntie Su and Uncle Canning. They lived on Leavenworth, just a few blocks west of my mother's apartment. It was late afternoon, just in time to catch Auntie Su preparing Sunday dinner.

"Stay! Stay!" she had insisted.

"No, no. It's just that we were walking by," I said.

"Already cooked enough for you. See? One soup, four dishes. You don't eat it, only have to throw it away. Wasted!" 5

How could we refuse? Three days later, Auntie Suyuan had a thank-you letter from Rich and me. "Rich said it was the best Chinese food he has ever tasted," I wrote.

And the next day, my mother called me, to invite me to a belated birthday dinner for my father. My brother Vincent was bringing his girlfriend, Lisa Lum. I could bring a friend, too.

I knew she would do this, because cooking was how my mother expressed her love, her pride, her power, her proof that she knew more than Auntie Su. "Just be sure to tell her later that her cooking was the best you ever tasted, that it was far better than Auntie Su's," I told Rich. "Believe me."

The night of the dinner, I sat in the kitchen watching her cook, waiting for the right moment to tell her about our marriage plans, that we had decided to get married next July, about seven months away. She was chopping eggplant into wedges, chattering at the same time about Auntie Suyuan: "She can only cook looking at a recipe. My instructions are in my fingers. I know what secret ingredients to put in just by using my nose!" And she was slicing with such a ferocity, seemingly inattentive to her sharp cleaver, that I was afraid her fingertips would become one of the ingredients of the red-cooked eggplant and shredded pork dish.

I was hoping she would say something first about Rich. I had seen her 10 expression when she opened the door, her forced smile as she scrutinized him from head to toe, checking her appraisal of him against that already given to her by Auntie Suyuan. I tried to anticipate what criticisms she would have.

Rich was not only *not* Chinese, he was a few years younger than I was. And unfortunately, he looked much younger with his curly red hair, smooth pale skin, and the splash of orange freckles across his nose. He was a bit on the short side, compactly built. In his dark business suits, he looked nice but easily forgettable, like somebody's nephew at a funeral. Which was why I didn't notice him the first year we worked together at the firm. But my mother noticed everything.

"So what do you think of Rich?" I finally asked, holding my breath.

She tossed the eggplant in the hot oil and it made a loud, angry hissing sound. "So many spots on his face," she said.

I could feel the pinpricks on my back. "They're freckles. Freckles are good luck, you know," I said a bit too heatedly in trying to raise my voice above the din of the kitchen.

"Oh?" she said innocently.   15

"Yes, the more spots the better. Everybody knows that."

She considered this a moment and then smiled and spoke in Chinese: "Maybe this is true. When you were young, you got the chicken pox. So many spots, you had to stay home for ten days. So lucky, you thought."

I couldn't save Rich in the kitchen. And I couldn't save him later at the dinner table.

He had brought a bottle of French wine, something he did not know my parents could not appreciate. My parents did not even own wineglasses. And then he also made the mistake of drinking not one but two frosted glasses full, while everybody else had a half-inch "just for taste."

When I offered Rich a fork, he insisted on using the slippery ivory   20
chopsticks. He held them splayed like the knock-kneed legs of an ostrich while picking up a large chunk of sauce-coated eggplant. Halfway between his plate and his open mouth, the chunk fell on his crisp white shirt and then slid into his crotch. It took several minutes to get Shoshana to stop shrieking with laughter.

And then he had helped himself to big portions of the shrimp and snow peas, not realizing he should have taken only a polite spoonful, until everybody had had a morsel.

He had declined the sautéed new greens, the tender and expensive leaves of bean plants plucked before the sprouts turn into beans. And Shoshana refused to eat them also, pointing to Rich: "He didn't eat them! He didn't eat them!"

He thought he was being polite by refusing seconds, when he should have followed my father's example, who made a big show of taking small portions of seconds, thirds, and even fourths, always saying he could not re-sist another bite of something or other, and then groaning that he was so full he thought he would burst.

But the worst was when Rich criticized my mother's cooking, and he didn't even know what he had done. As is the Chinese cook's custom, my mother always made disparaging remarks about her own cooking. That night she chose to direct it toward her famous steamed pork and preserved vegetable dish, which she always served with special pride.

"Ai! This dish not salty enough, no flavor," she complained, after tast-   25
ing a small bite. "It is too bad to eat."

This was our family's cue to eat some and proclaim it the best she had
ever made. But before we could do so, Rich said, "You know, all it needs is a
little soy sauce." And he proceeded to pour a riverful of the salty black stuff
on the platter, right before my mother's horrified eyes.

And even though I was hoping throughout the dinner that my mother
would somehow see Rich's kindness, his sense of humor and boyish charm,
I knew he had failed miserably in her eyes.

Rich obviously had had a different opinion on how the evening had
gone. When we got home that night, after we put Shoshana to bed, he said
modestly, "Well. I think we hit it off *A-o-kay.*" He had the look of a dalma-
tian, panting, loyal, waiting to be petted.

"Uh-hmm," I said. I was putting on an old nightgown, a hint that I was
not feeling amorous. I was still shuddering, remembering how Rich had
firmly shaken both my parents' hands with that same easy familiarity he
used with nervous new clients. "Linda, Tim," he said, "we'll see you again
soon, I'm sure." My parents' names are Lindo and Tin Jong, and nobody,
except a few older family friends, ever calls them by their first names.

"So what did she say when you told her?" And I knew he was referring   30
to our getting married. I had told Rich earlier that I would tell my mother
first and let her break the news to my father.

"I never had a chance," I said, which was true. How could I have told
my mother I was getting married, when at every possible moment we were
alone, she seemed to remark on how much expensive wine Rich liked to
drink, or how pale and ill he looked, or how sad Shoshana seemed to be.

Rich was smiling. "How long does it take to say, Mom, Dad, I'm getting
married?"

"You don't understand. You don't understand my mother."

Rich shook his head. "Whew! You can say that again. Her English was
so bad. You know, when she was talking about that dead guy showing up
on *Dynasty,* I thought she was talking about something that happened in
China a long time ago."

Issues for Discussion

1. What individual mistakes does Rich make during his evening with
   Lena's parents? How should this meeting with Lena's family have gone,
   according to the story frames of Rich's culture? What role would he
   have played? How should Lena's parents have responded?
2. What cultural expectations did Lena's family seem to bring with them
   to this dinner with their daughter's fiancé? What roles did they expect
   to play? How did they expect Rich to behave?

Your Culture-Clash Story

1. Write a story in your journal about a time when you were involved in a clash of cultures or about a time when you committed a *faux pas*—literally a "false step" or culturally inappropriate action—that obviously violated the expectations of those around you. If you can't come up with a story of your own, tell the story of a culture clash involving someone you've known. Try to describe the situation as fully as possible. What was it that you or the people around you failed to understand? What happened as a result? Was there anything you could have done to avoid this misunderstanding?

2. After you've finished with your story, try to reconstruct the story frames that came into conflict in the situation you described. What were your expectations of the situation when you entered it? In other words, what cultural expectations or assumptions did you try to impose on the situation? How was the story supposed to unfold from the perspective of those you came into conflict with?

Cultural Blindness and Stereotypes

We often think that misunderstandings happen because we've failed to express ourselves clearly—perhaps because we didn't choose the right words or because we simply didn't "say" exactly what we had in mind. But cultural collisions usually have more to do with failures of interpretation than with failures of self-expression. Rich misunderstands Lena's parents and they misunderstand—and probably misjudge—him not because they misspoke or did something by mistake but because they expected their encounter to tell different stories. Their differing expectations produced differing interpretations of their roles and relationships—interpretations that give totally different meanings to their actions, words, and intentions. Our story frames help us make sense of the world around us, but they extract a price: they also limit our ability to appreciate alternative points of view. Rich is literally blinded by his own culturally conditioned expectations: his story frame for "Dinner with Your Fiancée's Family" eclipses the reality of what transpires at Lena's house.

Does Rich's cultural blindness make him a racist? There's no doubt that Rich is insensitive to the cultural gap that yawns between his world and that of Lena's parents, and it's equally clear that he's so lost in his own cultural stories that he can't begin to appreciate how badly he's blundered. Like Luria's "S," Rich is imprisoned by his story frames. But Rich's misadventures with Lena's family are the result of insensitivity and inexperience, not necessarily signs of racial prejudice. Racism, like other forms of prejudicial behavior, involves a malfunction of the mind's storytelling machinery. Much of our knowledge relies on stereotyping: you know what to do in a classroom because you have a stereotyped script that outlines what generally happens in educational settings. You also have stereotypes for who professors are, how they act, what they like, and what to expect from them. Some of the specific expectations in these stereotypical scripts may be mistaken, but in general the overall script is accurate enough to help you deal effectively with your teachers in and out of class. If you encounter a professor whose behavior or attitudes contradict your expectations, you're likely to make a mental note—consciously or unconsciously—to be alert for similar behavior in the future. If other professors depart from your script in similar ways, you'll revise it and establish a new set of expectations.

This ability to change distinguishes the stereotypes that form the basis of knowledge from those that underlie prejudice. It's true that Rich is blinded by his cultural story frames, but it's also likely that if he continues to see Lena—and he isn't a victim of prejudice—he'll eventually learn to amend his script and create a new set of expectations for "dinner with Chinese future in-laws." By contrast, prejudicial stereotypes like those based on differences of race, class, gender, or age resist revision. The stereotypical stories that feed prejudice flourish when there is limited contact between groups and where there is a climate of fear or insecurity. All of these conditions make us unwilling to question our own assumptions, to change, and to learn. We cling to the stories of our cultures most tightly when we feel threatened and vulnerable ourselves.

The dangers of cultural blindness and prejudicial stereotypes are illustrated in the next selection. In the title story from the collection *The Language We Use Up Here* (1991), Philip Gambone gives us a clear example of how we try to "read" the words and actions of people from different cultural groups and how this effort often goes awry. The story of Gambone's Robert and Bunkie, like that of Tan's Rich and Lena, is built around clashing cultural expectations—expectations that bespeak differences of race, class, and sexual style. If you've never had much contact with gay cultures, you may find your own reactions to Gambone's story revealing. Gambone has published his short stories in over a dozen magazines and anthologies. He teaches at the Park School in Brookline, Massachusetts.

Before Reading

Write a brief paragraph in your journal describing some of the stereotypes that are commonly associated with gay people and gay culture. Why do you think stereotypical images of gays are still considered entertaining in movies, television shows, and other forms of popular culture?

The Language We Use Up Here

Philip Gambone

Bunkie and I had been dancing together for a good half-hour before we ever spoke a word. I'm not sure I'd even asked him if he wanted to dance; it was just a matter of giving this cute black kid standing next to me a smile and a nod, and off we'd gone, boogying our buns off. Actually, we said a lot to each other that first night on the disco floor, but it was all through our bodies. We played out an entire conversation in gestures and looks, in the casual but deliberate movements of our hips, and chests, and shoulders.

I said things like: I think you're very hot. And he said: No one's ever told me that before. I said: I love the way you move your ass. He said: I'm really pretty shy. I said: Don't get me wrong, I'm not a trashy person. I can be shy, too. And romantic, and funny, and kind. He said: I can tell, that's why I'm dancing with you. I said: I'd like to get to know you better. He said: Let's stop dancing.

As we moved off the disco floor, I ran my hand up and down his back and introduced myself.

"Pleased to meet you, Robert Garthside." He spoke with a Southern accent that I immediately found charming. Even the way he repeated my whole name seemed charming, and almost foreign, as if the nuances of the language, the language we use up here, weren't quite in his mastery yet. He shook my hand vigorously. "I'm Bunkie Williams. Bunkie with a i-e at the end." He pronounced the letters *ah-ee*.

"Bunkie," I repeated. I loved the way he wanted me to get the spelling   5 right, and I wondered what he was telling me in that.

"It comes from my daddy," Bunkie went on. "Daddy being Thurnell Bunker Williams the *Third*. Thurnell Bunker was Daddy's daddy's name, and his daddy before that." He rattled off the genealogy, then giggled, a little stifled-cough sound at the back of his throat. "Yessir, Robert, I might have had quite some bodacious name: Thurnell Bunker Williams the Fourth."

"That would have been some name all right," I said, guiding him toward the railing that penned in the disco area. He seemed oblivious to everything but the story he was delivering, and for a minute I wondered if I'd misread his body English while we were dancing.

"Except that Daddy up and died," Bunkie continued. "Just before I was born. So that's when Mama got determined to break with the family tradition. Superstition, I guess. I suppose she didn't want no son of hers inheriting Daddy's misfortune along with his name. Yessir, she put a stop to me being the Fourth."

The way Bunkie went on and on, I guessed that maybe he was on speed. But when I learned that he was new to Boston—he interrupted himself to tell me he'd moved up at the end of the summer from a place called Dothan in Alabama—that seemed to explain it all. We stepped off the platform and into the crowd near the bar.

"I'm the only son," he said. "I've got six sisters, all older than me. Naturally, everyone was waiting for a boy to come along"—and he laughed again—"so as to carry on the family name. Still, three previous generations of Thurnell Bunker Williamses, it sure is hard to ignore, and that's how Mama and my sisters they come to compromise on Bunkie. Bunkie's my actual baptized Christian name."

A broad grin plumped his cheeks and accentuated his tiny ears. I realized that Bunkie wasn't high at all. It was just that he was happy: happy to make my acquaintance. And unsuspicious, too, in the way that strangers to a new city often are, not yet knowing what's to be wary of. I think he would have been just as friendly to anyone that night. He was the indiscriminate friendly type, a type I find very sexy and—I can admit it now—a little threatening.

I looked at him. Sweat was tracing silver lines down his brown forehead, across his temples and down his neck. His close-cropped hair was glistening, too, from the perspiration and the gelled lights that kept altering the hues in his face: blue-black, red-brown, yellow. He looked exhilarated, almost too exhilarated for this place of choreographed poses. I think right then and there I started falling in love with him.

We smiled at each other, the way you do when the only thing to say next is too obvious, or too embarrassing, or both. And then I saw Bunkie's eyes move back to the dance floor. I looked. There, dancing like a couple of bleached-blond show girls, their bodies as loose as seaweed, were two queens. Young kids, about Bunkie's age—twenty, twenty-one—they wore blousy shirts fastened at the waist with cummerbunds, gaucho pants, and too much jewelry: chains and ear studs and rings on both hands, which they splayed out as if they were demonstrating the aftereffects in a liquid detergent commercial.

"Really," I said, in that way that's taken the place of: Give me a break.

Bunkie looked back at me. He seemed puzzled.

"Queens," I explained, figuring this was part of the vocabulary he'd not yet encountered.

"That's Ted and Jeremy," Bunkie said. "They're friends of my Uncle Carl."

"Uncle Carl?"

"My uncle I live with," Bunkie said.

And that's how I came to learn of Carl.

A lot of my friends have told me that it's just as well things didn't work out with Bunkie and me. They talk about the age difference, the fact that Bunkie was from the South, and once someone even brought up the black-white thing. But eventually they all get around to Uncle Carl.

Because I work for the city housing authority—I'm an administrative type—I've had plenty of experience with good-intentioned liberals. In fact, I guess you'd have to call me a liberal, too. I know how to recognize racism when I see it, enough to admit that I'm not altogether innocent there either. But what happened between Bunkie and me involved something else. Supposedly I was introducing him to the possibility of a dignified life, a dignified gay life. What could have been more politically correct than that?

And that's where, my friends tell me, Uncle Carl comes in.

"What did you expect," they say, "when the kid's only adult role model was someone like *her?*"

That first night—we'd ordered drinks and sat down at a table—Bunkie   25
went on and on about Uncle Carl.

"My uncle's a chef at a big restaurant downtown," he told me, and then, typically, his story went off in several different directions: about how Ted and Jeremy were waiters at the restaurant where Uncle Carl cooked; about how he, Bunkie, had been in town only a few weeks, working days in a bakery and studying at one of the community colleges in the evening; how it was his uncle who'd found him the job and put him up rent-free; how Uncle Carl was his Mama's little brother.

"But Mama isn't speaking with him anymore," Bunkie said. "Mama's been saying for years how Uncle Carl sold his soul in the North."

He told me how Carl had run off when he was twenty and made his way to Boston, where he eventually became a chef.

"Mama came up here to visit him once—I must have been about eleven—and when she came back she announced as how he'd been *intirely* corrupted. I remember she kept shaking her head, and my sisters, they all shook their heads, too. And then Mama said that he didn't seem to want to find himself a wife either, and everyone shook their heads again. It sure seemed peculiar to me."

"Peculiar until you started putting the facts into place, right?" I winked   30
at him. "I mean, isn't that why you came North? Isn't that why you're living with your uncle?" I reached across the table and stroked his arm.

"To tell the truth, Robert, I hadn't much thought about coming North." Bunkie touched me back, a shy, friendly "An' how're you?" touch. "It was Miss Allyn who encouraged me to come up here."

"Who was Miss Allyn?" Bunkie was weaving so many strands into this tale, but I would have listened to an epic as long as it allowed me to keep talking to him.

Bunkie told me that Miss Allyn was his senior English teacher. A white woman and a New Englander, she apparently took quite a liking to Bunkie and pushed him to apply to schools up here.

"She'd have me over for tea," Bunkie explained, "and she and Miss Roberts—that was her lady friend that she lived with—they'd read through the catalogs with me and later helped me polish up the applications. She was the one that suggested I could come North and live with my uncle."

"What did Miss Allyn know about your uncle?" I asked.   35

"Oh, Mama gave her quite a earful," Bunkie said. "When Miss Allyn came to call one afternoon, Mama wanted nothing to do with any plans for my going to school up North and living with Uncle Carl. *Oo-ee!* It took quite a lot of convincing on Miss Allyn's part to get Mama to agree."

"She was a clever dyke, wasn't she" I said.

Bunkie shook the ice in his glass and gave me a confused look.

"Dyke?"

"Don't you see? Miss Allyn saw how it would all work out if you came   40
North. She guessed that you were cut from the same cloth as she and your Uncle Carl. That you needed space to grow—gay space." I watched him for a reaction; I loved introducing Bunkie to these new phrases.

"But what's a dyke?" he said.

We were interrupted by the arrival of the two queens I'd seen on the dance floor, Ted and Jeremy.

"Bunkie!" they shouted practically in unison as they came rushing over to our table.

One of them—I didn't particularly care to learn which was which— gave me the once over, then turned his attention back to Bunkie. I was being written off. Maybe they were jealous of my hair being naturally blond, or maybe the understated preppie look turned them off. Who knows. I've heard all the theories about why queens and straight-appearing gays don't get along. I didn't care. They turned me off, too, and that's all that seemed to matter.

They hovered over Bunkie, spilling out gossipy little stories with manic   45
energy, like a popcorn machine at climax. Even though they were Bunkie's age, it became clear as I listened that Ted and Jeremy were actually Uncle Carl's friends, that Bunkie was someone they'd met only a few times. I watched Bunkie reacting to them. He seemed amused, but awkward, too, and I realized he wasn't sure when he was supposed to laugh or how exactly to react to some of the outrageous tidbits they were throwing out. But with

that indiscriminate friendliness of his he did his best to pick up the cues, to become conversant with their campy style.

Then, in a flutter, Ted and Jeremy were gone. Bunkie smiled again.

"Really," I said.

We didn't go home together that first night. Nor the second time we met. Something told me to go slow with Bunkie. It was hard to tell just how inexperienced he was. I wasn't even sure he'd ever slept with another guy; it was certainly difficult to imagine he could have done so under the watchful eye of his Mama and six sisters. But the more we talked—for we'd agreed to meet regularly at Flash for dancing and talk—the more I picked up that his Uncle Carl was taking Bunkie in hand. Carl had given him a tour of the discos during Bunkie's second week in town. He'd thrown a dinner party to introduce Bunkie to some of his friends. The last week in September, Carl had even taken a day off from work and the two of them made a day trip to Provincetown on the ferry.

"Your uncle sounds terrific," I told him. It was our third Friday night at Flash, our third Friday of dancing and conversation. I kept expecting that Bunkie would want to play the field, but he seemed perfectly happy just spending the whole evening with me. "I mean," I said, "it's got to be every gay man's dream: a gay uncle who'll show him the ropes."

Bunkie blushed.   50

"Uncle Carl even gave me the birds and bees talk," he said. "Not the regular one." He laughed. "You know, the other one, the gay one, and about how to do it safely." For the first time since we'd met, the look he gave me did not seem shy.

I reached across the cocktail table and ran my hand along his cheek.

"Robert," he said, "Robert Garthside. There's so much I don't understand."

"I know, Bunk," I told him. "There's a lot I don't understand either. Maybe all I'm saying is that it would be nice not to understand things together."

I still remember the first time I ever went home with another man. I was   55
eighteen, which makes it a good fourteen years ago. It was the spring of my senior year in high school and I'd gone to town to buy records. As I was browsing through the bins—Mozart, Brahms, Ella Fitzgerald—I noticed this guy kept looking at me. At first I was scared, but then, when I figured out why he was staring, I just looked up at him and nodded my head. He took me to his apartment, somewhere in town, to a section I didn't know. What I most remember is not the sex, which I'd been imagining for quite some time, but the being in a strange neighborhood, a strange home, not

my own. I kept looking at everything—the furniture, the appliances, the bed. It was all very different from the furnishings I'd grown up with, and yet familiar, too. And I got scared again.

That's why I agreed to go to Bunkie's house. I was trying to protect him from feeling overwhelmed the first time.

Bunkie directed me to a neighborhood in Dorchester.

"Turn right," he said after we'd driven a while down the main avenue. "Now right again. This is my street."

One block long, the street fanned out around both sides of an oval park that was lined with tall trees, even an elm or two. It still surprises me to find elms that the blight hasn't reached. Large Victorian houses, each with a front porch, circled the park, in the middle of which someone had planted a flower garden. Even though it was late October, marigolds and dahlias were still blooming.

"That's Uncle Carl's garden," Bunkie said. "I mean, he plants it and   60
weeds it. He calls it his gift to the neighborhood. He's always doing stuff like that. And this"—he pointed— "is our house. Number twenty."

I parked the car, all the while thinking, Is this how it will be from now on, coming here on weekends, watching the progress of autumn, the leaves falling and these overarching elms going bare, the garden collapsing with the first frost; Christmas here, too, and I bet the neighbors all put up lights, and then waking up some January morning with Bunkie next to me and finding it snowing outside; and probably Uncle Carl has planted bulbs, too, so that when spring comes crocus and daffodils will come up; and summers sitting on his porch and being lazy together. I thought about how normal all this was and how much I wanted that, for both of us.

"Twenty's my lucky number," Bunkie continued. "Twenty was how old Uncle Carl was when he came North, twenty is how old I am, and twenty is the number we live at. How about you, Robert? Anything twenty about you?"

"Only that sometimes I wish I were twenty again." As he led me up the front stairs I twisted my finger in his back.

He put his key in the lock, then turned around to me. "Why do you want to be twenty again?"

"Because it wasn't much fun the first time around. I'd like to go   65
through all that stuff I went through at twenty but get it right this time."

"Seems to me you've gotten it all right," he said.

"You think so?" I said.

The house was dark except for a single table lamp in the hall, an overly dramatic thing in crystal and brass—the kind of piece decorators call a "statement." It cast a soft, boudoirlike light against the wall, which had been papered in paisley. Next to the lamp sat a cheap marble copy, about eighteen inches tall, of Michelangelo's David.

"A famous Italian artist made that," Bunkie said, acknowledging the statuette. "It's David. You know, from David and Goliath? Uncle Carl says the man that made this wanted to show how proud and brave David was. He has nothing to hide, that's what him wearing no clothes means."

Bunkie pulled a chain on the lamp and another light went on.   70

"Uncle Carl goes out with his friends after work on Friday nights. This is our special signal to each other: one light on means no one's home, two means one of us is home."

"And how do you signal that I'm here?"

Bunkie chuckled. "I don't know."

"I hope your uncle won't be too surprised," I told Bunkie. "I'm actually looking forward to meeting him."

"He wants to meet you too, Robert. I've told him a lot about you."   75

"Like what?"

"Like how similar you two are. You are, you know. You both know a lot; you're both fun to be with; you both like nice things, and you both care about other people."

"We care about you," I told him. "Except I care in a different way."

The living room was even more of a statement than the hallway. It was papered in gold and black vertical stripes, over which hung framed pages from *Très Parisien* and menus from famous steamliners of the twenties and thirties. There were gilded French Empire chairs and a Victorian love seat upholstered in purple velvet. Between them was a coffeetable carved from an enormous piece of driftwood, highly shellacked and polished, and under it an imitation bokhara in fire engine red. To the left and right of the mantel, a piece of ornate cabinetry that enclosed nothing but the heating grate, stood two tall Chinese vases stuffed with plumes of pampas grass. And on every available surface *objets d'art:* porcelain figurines, enameled ashtrays, a collection of sentimental bibelots. I thought about what Bunkie had said about his uncle and me "liking nice things," and decided that next week I'd show him my place.

He turned on the stereo system, took an album from the top of a pile   80
on the floor, and put it on.

"I want you to hear something," he said. I sat down on the love seat.

As the needle came down on the disk, it picked up a lot of the surface noise on what must have been a well-played record. I put my head back and closed my eyes.

Then a timpani roll, a rush of strings, a chorus of *ahs,* and finally a choked-up voice singing "I'll follow the boys."

Dear Lord, I thought.

"Do you know who this is?" Bunkie asked.   85

I opened my eyes. He was looking at me full of happiness. I nodded my head wearily. "Another famous Italian artiste."

"Uncle Carl has all her albums."

"What a surprise," I told him.

He sat down next to me and stretched back. "Isn't she wonderful?"

"What do you like about her?" I asked him, putting my head on his   90 shoulder.

Bunkie leaned forward suddenly. "Can't you feel it?" he said.

"What I'm feeling," I told him, running my fingers slowly down his cheek, "has nothing to do with Connie Francis."

We heard the front door open and close. From the hallway a falsetto voice joined Connie for the final refrain. Bunkie jumped up from the sofa.

"That's Uncle Carl."

I turned around just as Carl appeared in the parlor entrance. He was an   95 older version of Bunkie, just as lithe, with the same diminutive ears, the same button nose, but his hair was thin and peppered with gray. He was removing a tailored leather jacket trimmed around the collar in white rabbit's fur. He gave us both a broad grin just like Bunkie's.

"Well now," he said, tossing the jacket onto one of the Empire chairs with a certain studied flourish, "you must be my nephew's friend Robert. What a distinct pleasure to meet you."

He wore a Chinese red kimono shirt, cinctured at the waist, and baggy black pants. There were gold bracelets, a lot of them, around his wrists. His face, which was remarkably wrinkle-free considering his age, was highlighted with a blush of rouge on both cheeks, and a little diamond in each earlobe finished off the effect. He and the two bleached-blond numbers probably shopped together.

As I got up to shake his hand, he held his out, divalike.

"How do you do, Uncle Carl," I said. I tried putting some grip into my shake.

"Uncle!" he exclaimed, drawing back and touching his bejeweled right   100 hand to his chest. "Please, just call me Carl. Sugar, I'm not the grandmother, you know." He looked over at Bunkie and winked.

Connie was now onto a perky castanet and electric mandolin arrangement of "Tonight's My Night." She sang about wanting to laugh, wanting to love, wanting to throw her cares away.

"I *love* this lady!" Carl said, swaying to Connie's rhythms. "*We* love this lady." He nodded to Bunkie, then sighed. "Key West. Ah, that spring of nineteen seventy-eight. Just before my fortieth birthday. That album. I listened to it every morning, sitting on my balcony, sipping fresh squeezed orange juice and watching the ocean. The man I was with gave me that album." He paused theatrically. "At least I still have the album."

He moved over to the stereo, his hands held slightly aloft, as if the bracelets would slip from his wrists if he dropped his arms to his sides. "But enough of this sad reminiscing." He picked the tone arm off the record as if he were picking a tea sandwich from a silver tray. "I don't want this child to grow up thinking all affairs end in sadness."

Throwing out his arms, Carl clasped Bunkie's head to his chest. "You re-member that, child. There's plenty of goodness in this world, and lots of good folk." This last—"*Lots* of good folk!"—he repeated while he gave me a scrutinizing stare.

Bunkie seemed perfectly relaxed with his uncle. I thought about all the 105 folks back home in Dothan—his mama, his sisters, and poor unsuspecting Miss Allyn—and wondered what they'd say right now. Carl motioned for us to sit.

"You know," I said, taking the sofa again, "I've eaten at Dolcissimo sev-eral times. What a coincidence that you should turn out to be a chef there."

"*The* chef," Carl corrected. "I've been head chef for five years now." He raised his eyebrows. "I am, you know, one of the reigning stars of the restaurant world here."

I guessed he could be a first-class bitch when he needed to be. I could tell that he was studying me carefully, trying to decide whether I'd be admitted into his court. I was sure Ted and Jeremy had given him a bad report on me.

"Bunkie's told me a lot about you," Carl said, "but I still feel I don't know you very well." He'd crossed his legs in a studied pose that, along with the kimono shirt, made him look like a thirties actress at an informal photo session.

I glanced over at Bunkie. He was leaning forward in his chair, elbows on 110 his knees, studying his uncle with keen fascination. I turned back to Carl.

"What do you want to know?"

"Oh, the usual," Carl said, suddenly putting on an exaggerated Brah-min accent. "Your lineage, where you prepped, what clubs you belong to."

"I'm afraid you've got me pegged wrong," I told him. "That's not my scene."

Carl broke into a hearty cackle, and Bunkie laughed, too.

"Sugar, relax," Carl said. "Ah ain't gonna bite cha." He had switched to 115 a mock Aunt Jemima dialect. He looked at Bunkie. "*Mmm-mm.* Yessir, a lot of people want to see this child do well. A lot of people tryin' to teach him 'bout the world. But you know what ah thinks, Mr. Robert? I thinks he gotta learn it on his own."

In the morning, when I woke up, Bunkie was not in bed, but I could smell bacon frying and heard the whir of a blender. It felt late, maybe as late as noontime.

I found a bathrobe, white terrycloth with a royal blue C monogrammed on the breast pocket, and went in search of the kitchen: down the stairs and past the hideous David again.

Standing over the stove was Uncle Carl. He was wearing a Japanese cotton robe in shades of indigo and blue, and rush sandals. The kitchen radio was playing a Broadway showtune.

"Mornin'," he said, pushing strips of bacon around the skillet and sleepily humming to the song. "Orange juice is on the table." He turned from the stove and nodded over to the kitchen table.

"Thanks," I said. I poured myself a glass and sat down, pulling the terrycloth robe closer together over my chest. "Where's Bunkie?" 120

Carl turned around and gave me a stare, the kind that says, What's the matter with my company?

"Taking his bubble bath."

"Bubble bath!"

"Relax, sugar. He's out buying muffins for his overnight guest. How you like your bacon, crispy or fatty?"

"I don't eat bacon," I told him. "It's bad stuff." 125

"Lordy, Lordy." Carl was into his Aunt Jemima act again. "You mighty careful, ain'tcha? Every once in a while's not gonna kill you, sugar. You gotta learn to relax." He laughed, an older, sarcastic version of Bunkie's back-of-the-throat laugh.

Bunkie came into the kitchen carrying a bakery bag and a dozen flaming pink gladiolas.

"Hi!" he said, smiling and winking at me.

"Child, what have we here?" Uncle Carl exclaimed. He set down the long-handled fork and put his hands on his hips. "My, my. You takin' after your Uncle Carl, bringin' all these pretty flowers home." He looked at me. "What you think about that, Mr. Robert? Bunkie's gonna grow up to be just like his Uncle Carl."

Bunkie was standing between us, the bunch of glads in his arms, beaming first at Carl, then at me. When Carl took the bouquet, I got up from the 130 table and gave Bunkie a kiss and a long embrace.

"I love you," I whispered into his ear. I had not said that to him during the night, even during the most passionate moments of our lovemaking. In two years I had not said "I love you" to anyone, but I felt I had to say it now.

The rest of the story—the part about how it didn't work out with Bunkie and me—well, I've told you my friends' theories: how the end was practically predetermined by the differences between us—race and age and all—and by Bunkie's being under the influence of Uncle Carl. I saw all that, but I told myself that we could overcome those differences and that, as far as Uncle Carl went, what I had to offer Bunkie he'd come to recognize in time.

And so we saw each other the rest of the fall and into the winter, gradually weaning ourselves away from Flash, and Uncle Carl. We spent most weekends just the two of us, taking drives into the country, hiking, and, when it got too cold, going to museums. In the evenings, we went to the movies and once in a while to the theater. Bunkie loved the theater and was considering transferring to a four-year college where he could major in drama. When we slept together, it was now at my place.

Then, one Saturday in February, Bunkie and I decided to go skating. He had to spend the morning studying, so I agreed to pick him up after lunch. When I rang the bell, Carl answered the door.

"Well, Happy New Year, sugar," he said. "You been hidin' from Uncle   135
Carl?" He was holding a silk scarf, threaded with gold, which he demurely held up to his chest. Then, extending it out, he ushered me inside.

It was almost Valentine's Day, and, on the entrance hall table, he'd placed a large red cardboard heart edged in lace behind the statuette of David. I followed Carl into the living room. Seated on the purple velvet loveseat were Ted and Jeremy puffing on cigarettes and listening to one of Carl's Connie Francis albums.

"Hi, Robert," one of them said and wiggled his fingers at me.

"Is Bunkie ready?" I asked Carl.

"Not quite. You know how long these bubble baths take."

Ted and Jeremy giggled. I was being mocked.   140

"So what do you fellows have planned for this afternoon?" I asked, trying to keep the conversation innocuous.

"Sugar, we's goin' skatin' wich you."

The boys giggled again. Apparently they found his Aunt Jemima routine quite amusing.

Bunkie came running down the hall stairs and into the living room. He was wearing the new Brooks Brothers sweater I'd given him for Christmas.

"Child, you look divine," Carl said. Holding the silk scarf by the ends,   145
he cast it around Bunkie's neck and roped him for a kiss on the forehead. When he let go, the silk scarf was still around Bunkie's neck.

Bunkie looked at me. It was that same half-amused, half-uncertain look I'd seen him give Ted and Jeremy the night we met at Flash. I figured it was now or never.

"Look," I said, pulling the scarf off Bunkie and throwing it back at Carl. "How about easing up on the queeny stuff?"

Ted and Jeremy made little outraged squealy noises.

"And that ridiculous Aunt Jemima act. Christ, don't you have any self-respect?"

Carl gave me an amused look. I turned directly to Bunkie. 150

"I'm sorry, Bunkie, but there are things you need to learn. Things you have to be made to see."

And then I just let it out:

"Your uncle's a queen, Bunkie. Do you know what that is?" I grabbed him by the shoulders. "A queen." I was trying to sear it into his brain. "You've got to learn these words. It's the language we use up here."

He looked at me, then past me, at his uncle.

"I know he's family," I said. "I know he's been good to you, but there's 155 a bigger family out there. It doesn't have to be all this. . . ." I tossed my head over to where the vases of pampas grass stood. "All this froufrou, all this self-mockery. Think of Miss Allyn, think of *me*. There's another world out there, Bunkie."

By now I was kneading my thumbs hard into his shoulders. I stared right into Bunkie's eyes. Whatever else happened I didn't want to catch sight of Carl's amused grin again. Or to see Ted and Jeremy, sitting side by side like a couple of doves and now very quiet. There was pain in Bunkie's eyes.

Pain, I thought. Why does growing up have to involve so much pain? Here you have someone with everything going for him: intelligence, beauty, talent, energy. And still there are things he has to learn the hard way. He'd cut himself off from all that bullshit in Dothan, only to buy into more bullshit up here.

"Stereotypes, Bunkie. Ah, now there's another word for you." I looked back at Carl and glared. "They're no good, Bunkie. You've been a victim of them all your life. Take your mother, for instance: her notions about the North, they're all stereotypes. And her ridiculous fears about you living with. . . ."

I caught myself, but not before Bunkie's eyes widened. For a second he looked panicked.

I must have started to correct myself, but he interrupted me. 160

"No, Robert," he said, "I hear you." There was still all that wonderful generosity in his voice, but something else now, too. Something I'm still trying to put a name to: anger maybe, a sense of betrayal. Or maybe just clarity.

He shrugged my hands off his shoulders and with his finger started tracing circles around my heart. "I get it. Stereotypes." The pressure increased—his fingers were digging into the terrycloth—and then he looked over at Uncle Carl. "Yes, that's a good word, Robert. Now I see what you're telling me."

Issues for Discussion

1. What is it that attracts Robert to Bunkie? How would Bunkie have wanted to tell the story of his relationship with Robert? What roles would he and Robert play in his version? How would this story have ended? How would it differ from the version that Uncle Carl might tell?

2. What do the reproduction of Michelangelo's *David* in Uncle Carl's living room and his collection of vintage Connie Francis records represent to Robert? What do you think they mean to Carl? How might Carl interpret the Brooks Brothers sweater that Robert gives Bunkie for Christmas? What would it represent for Robert? What cultural differences underlie these different points of view?

3. How do you interpret the story's conclusion? What does Robert mean when he says that stereotypes are "no good" and that Bunkie has been a victim of them his whole life? What does Bunkie seem to mean by the word *stereotypes* when he tells Robert that he finally "understands" him?

JOURNAL OPTIONS Examining Stereotypes

1. Write about a person you've known who entertained stereotypical ideas based on race, gender, class, age, or physical ability. What made it possible for this person to maintain these stereotypes? What conditions in his or her life made this stereotypical thinking resistant to change? What other factors, besides those mentioned above, do you think contribute to the maintenance of prejudicial stereotypes?

2. Write the story of a time when you or someone you have known overcame or amended a prejudicial stereotype. What circumstances led up to this change in thinking? In what specific ways was the stereotypical script revised? To what extent do you think it is possible to "erase" the stereotypical story frames we absorb from our cultures?

Listening for Difference

Getting to Know You

What do we mean when we say that we know someone? Think of a person you really know well—a family member or friend. What do you really know about this person? Our knowledge of others is embodied in all the stories we've collected about them. We know stories about a friend's personal history, likes and dislikes, weaknesses and strengths. If we know the person very well, we know the scripts that regulate his daily routines and even the stories he knows about us and mutual friends. You sense that you really understand someone when your collection of stories for that person becomes so rich—so complete—that it allows you to anticipate his desires and responses.

It's often easy to get to know people who share your cultural background because you start with a broad base of shared stories. But when you try to connect with someone with a different background your own cultural stories may work against you. As we've seen, the scripts and story frames of your culture can create an invisible wall between you and those who are culturally "other." This chapter is an extended experiment in cross-cultural communication. In it you'll learn more about how cultural assumptions interfere with comprehension. You'll also have the chance to interview and write an extended profile of someone whose cultural background differs from yours. You'll learn some basic approaches to conducting oral interviews, and you'll even explore what we'll call "conversational etiquette"—the peculiar notions our cultures provide us about how we should talk to each other.

Cross-Cultural Storytelling and Condensed Stories

In the 1920s English psychologist Sir Frederick Bartlett designed an experiment to see how people remember stories from other cultures. Bartlett asked his subjects, all British citizens, to read a North American Indian folk tale about a young man who joins a group of strangers in a war canoe, battles against an unfamiliar tribe, and returns home apparently unharmed only to die, mysteriously, the following morning.[1] Bartlett asked his subjects to repeat the story from memory fifteen minutes after reading it and again at intervals ranging from one day to several years later. Most of his subjects produced remarkably detailed versions of the story, but nearly all of these versions differed from the original story in predictable ways. Men who had recently served in World War I tended to reconstruct the tale as a story about the tragedies of warfare. Other readers reshaped the story to fit the framework of a murder mystery. One reader, some six and a half years after encountering the original folk tale, recalled it as a religious quest that ended in ritual self-sacrifice. In almost every case, Bartlett's readers unconsciously attempted to "make sense" of the Indian folk tale by imposing on it the story frames available within their own European culture. Like the characters in the selections by Amy Tan and Philip Gambone in the last chapter, they responded to cultural "otherness" by rereading it in terms of their own cultural stories.

Sometimes a single word was enough to inspire Bartlett's subjects to misread the tale. At one point in the story, the young warrior says that the men he fought with were "ghosts" because although he had been hit by an arrow he was not wounded. This word caused the greatest difficulty for Bartlett's subjects. Several transformed the story into a "ghost story," reading the entire tale as the saga of a group of supernatural beings and emphasizing the spookiness of the ending. For these readers, the word *ghosts* was enough to conjure up an entire interpretive framework. We generally think of words as simple patterns of sound we use to "point to" the objects or feelings or ideas we want to express. Conditioned to think of words as things in dictionaries, we assume a word means nothing more than its definition. *Webster's Dictionary* reduces a word like *ghost* to something like "the soul of a dead person believed to be an inhabitant of an unseen world or to appear in bodily form to living people." But words are rarely this simple or

---

[1] Sir Frederick C. Bartlett, *Remembering: A Study in Experimental and Social Psychology* (Cambridge: Cambridge University Press, 1954), pp. 63–94.

this docile. As Leslie Marmon Silko reminds us in her account of language in Pueblo culture, "each word . . . has a story of its own." A word like *ghost* can evoke a whole collection of cultural stories, including stories about what ghosts are, what they look like, what they do, what they're made of, why they exist, what they fear, where you're likely to find them, how to get rid of them, and who believes in them. The same word also reminds us of dozens of cultural associations—from the short stories of Edgar Allan Poe to popular movies like *Ghostbusters* and *Casper*—all of which contribute to our knowledge of ghostliness. Dictionary definitions are misleading because they reduce word meaning to a few essential features. They tell us an important part of the story behind each word, but they don't give us the whole story. In reality, every word contains a collection of condensed stories: every word has the power to summon up a whole series of stories from the cultural encyclopedia we carry in our heads.

Roger Schank, an expert in the field of Artificial Intelligence, has explored the way that different cultural groups use condensed stories to communicate. According to Schank, even the most casual conversation involves a network of implied or assumed stories. Here's an example Schank offers, excerpted from a conversation between two teenagers:

> Wait, I have to tell you something really funny before I forget. OK, you know I went to see Sting. So I got to see Sting. And Alison pulls, first of all I was in a bitchy mood when we left, 'cause you know how Alison is, you know Alison repeatedly lies, schemes, does things that completely irritate me, and they're always forgivable because for some reason she gets away with it. So, here we are Sunday morning. We had plans, no joke, to leave for Lake Compounce at 6 A.M. Like completely serious plans because we did want to be able to staple ourselves to Sting's leg. So we leave. I call Alison. She calls me the day before. She's like, do you mind if Sue comes? Sue is Alison's friend who I know who I don't dislike, but this was my graduation present from Alison, the tickets, and it's kind of like Alison was supposed to go to the concert with me when I was a sophomore, and she never got to go, and so it was kind of like our rain check. It was delayed. It's hard to explain. It was kind of like a displaced thing. It was like a reenactment of what should have happened when I was a sophomore because we bought the tickets together.[2]

[2] Roger C. Schank, *Tell Me a Story: A New Look at Real and Artificial Memory* (New York: Charles Scribner's Sons, 1990), p. 198.

As Schank observes, this story, told in conversation, actually contains many condensed stories—stories that the teller *assumes* her listener knows. There's the story about Sting, the story about rock megaconcerts and the difficulty of getting tickets, the story about Alison and "how she is," the story about Lake Compounce, the story about rock star/fan relationships, the story about high school graduation, the story about a specific incident that happened in sophomore year, the story about rain checks, and the story about the speaker's special relationship to Alison. The meaning of each of these condensed stories is completely available only to those who are familiar with the American teen culture of Schank's speaker. If you're not a fan of pop music, you may have only a vague idea about Sting's identity, and you might well be puzzled by the speaker's excitement about getting some tickets. If you aren't familiar with American high school graduation rituals, you probably wouldn't understand the significance of the tickets as a present. If you hadn't grown up in a country where baseball games were frequently rained out, you certainly would be confused by the notion of a "rain check." And if you aren't a personal acquaintance of the speaker, you can't really know all the details about the speaker's "bitchy moods" or how the speaker feels about Alison.

Friendships, families, and whole cultures are held together by these networks of mutual assumptions: every time we communicate we rely on the fact that our listener will recognize and understand the condensed stories in literally thousands of concepts and ideas. The ability to make such assumptions lies at the heart of verbal communication. When you read even a sentence as simple as "After the taxi stopped at the curb, the man paid and got out" you know that the man in question was a passenger in the cab because you understand what taxis are and the mutual expectations of taxi drivers and passengers. To the members of a given culture, its condensed stories are so clear they are almost invisible. They play such an all-pervasive role in shaping our ideas and perceptions and are so utterly familiar that we scarcely notice them at work: they become nearly automatic, unconscious. And that's why they're so dangerous in cross-cultural situations. The cultural knowledge embedded in condensed stories is so readily available to all members in a cultural group that it's hard to tell when we've misread them. Bartlett's subjects were unaware that their interpretations of the word *ghost* differed from cultural assumptions made by the American Indians who created the original story. In much the same way, the bottle of French wine is "read" by Rich in Amy Tan's "Four Directions" as a symbol of elegance, graciousness, taste, and perhaps even prosperity, while from the cultural perspective of Lena's parents it might conjure up images of wastefulness, drunkenness, and poor judgment. Every culture and subculture imposes its own set of assumptions on the world it inhabits: failure to grasp the difference between the condensed stories you recognize in a word and those discovered by another is a prescription for cultural miscommunication.

OPTIONAL
ACTIVITIES

Identifying Condensed Stories

1. Working in pairs, reread a page or so of Beverly Donofrio's "Trouble" (p. 9), or Philip Gambone's "The Language We Use Up Here" (p. 130) and list all the condensed stories you can find in your selection. Then choose one of the condensed stories from your list and freewrite all the personal and cultural associations it suggests to you. Compare your results with those of your classmates.

2. Tape-record a casual conversation between two people in your dorm, at home, or on the job. Choose two or three minutes of the tape that seem the richest and transcribe them in dialogue form. Then examine your transcript carefully, trying to identify as many condensed stories as you can. Remember that condensed stories may assume many forms: they may appear as obvious references to specific events, people, or occasions—any of which could easily take the shape of a narrative account. Or they may appear in an abbreviated form, even as single words that contain within themselves cultural ideas or cultural knowledge. At your next class meeting, pair up and compare the results of your analysis: To what extent do you both agree in your identification of the transcript's condensed stories? How might you account for any discrepancies that arise?

JOURNAL
OPTION

Retelling Stories across Cultures

Without reviewing the original version, freewrite as much as you can remember of the "Waithia story" told by Leslie Marmon Silko in Chapter 1 (p. 21). Try to include as much detail as you can and to make your retelling as close to the original as possible. Compare your retellings of "Waithia" in small groups, noting how you and your classmates tended to change the story, which elements you left out, which you amplified, and which, if any, you added. How might you account for any specific transformations that occurred in your retellings?

What do your retellings of "Waithia" suggest about your own cultural assumptions or story frames?

Active Listening

Learning about another culture means learning to listen for what you don't understand. When you encounter ideas or ways of thinking or feeling that don't mesh with the story frames, scripts, and condensed stories of your own culture, the two most common responses are to ignore and forget them or unconsciously misread them so that they conform to your own cultural expectations and predispositions. Either way you remain a prisoner of your own stories. To move beyond the interpretations imposed by your culture, you have to learn to listen actively. Because comprehension usually involves recognizing what we already know, most listening, like most reading, is a relatively lazy affair: we hear what we recognize and skip the rest. Genuine curiosity just takes too much effort. When you listen actively, you work against the mind's programmed inertia by deliberately looking for questions to ask and answer. Most important, the kind of questioning involved in active listening goes both ways: to listen for the differences that exist between you and a person who stands outside your cultural context, you have to begin by questioning your own assumptions, by examining the stories you tell and the story frames you impose on the world around you.

The following selection illustrates how active listening can begin to bridge the gap between cultures. Originally a chapter from Mick Fedullo's *Light of the Feather: Pathways through Contemporary Indian America* (1992), this selection recounts the author's difficulty in trying to communicate with Elenore Cassadore, an influential member of the San Carlos Apache tribe and a senior bilingual instructor at the high school where he taught. Born in Pennsylvania in 1949, Fedullo lived and worked on the Gila River Indian Reservation in Arizona from 1979 to 1984. Since then he has taught creative writing on the Crow, Rocky Boy, and Blackfeet reservations in Montana and on the San Carlos Apache and Navajo reservations in Arizona.

Before Reading

Write a paragraph describing some common stereotypes of the "Indian." What features are usually involved in these stereotypic images? Where do most Americans learn these stereotypes?

Mrs. Cassadore

Mick Fedullo

Mrs. Cassadore and Apache Students

Elenore Cassadore, an elder of the San Carlos Apache, was employed in the bilingual program at the high school in Globe. Because she didn't drive, she rode with a fellow aide each school day from San Carlos to Globe and back, a round trip of over forty miles. I met Mrs. Cassadore at the beginning of a four-week stint working with the Apache high school students. Because there was no high school on the reservation, the students were bused to Globe. Sometimes, when Mrs. Cassadore's ride was unavailable, she joined the kids on the bus.

I knew from the moment I met her that I wanted to spend time talking with her; I could learn much about the San Carlos Apaches from this intelligent and wise woman. Mrs. Cassadore was of medium height and build, with salt-and-pepper hair. Her weathered face looked quiet, firm, sad. I never saw her in anything but traditional, ankle-length Apache camp dresses.

When I was first introduced to her, I explained what I hoped to accomplish with the students. We would, I said, put together a manuscript of poems, stories, articles, and drawings about Apache life, past and present—all composed by the students. I would also conduct several sessions on "survival skills"—that is, comfortable or at least practical ways for young Indian adults to get by in the non-Indian world. I added that it would be an honor if she sat in on some of the classes.

Mrs. Cassadore nodded and said, "Sounds good."

I pressed: "I hope you *will* be able to attend."

"In the morning classes," she answered. "Afternoons I'm busy in the office. But the mornings are okay. Those two classes are the ones I sometimes teach anyway."

In my enthusiasm to develop an acquaintanceship, I said, "I would really enjoy your company at dinner some evening. Maybe we could go to a restaurant. I'd like to talk to you about the students and the bilingual program here. My treat." What I really wanted was to talk to Mrs. Cassadore about her and her tribe. I had lied. A *white* lie.

Mrs. Cassadore nodded and said nothing. I sensed that I had been too abrupt.

The following day, I saw Mrs. Cassadore walking down the hallway toward the bilingual office. All the students were in class, and we were the only two people in the oak-floored, echoey corridor.

5

"Excuse me, Mrs. Cassadore," I said. "Have you thought about that din-   10
ner? Is any particular night best for you?"

"I've thought about it," she said. "There's nothing I can tell you over
dinner that I can't just as well tell you here at the school."

I staggered under the weight of this rejection. Forget it, she had told
me. And with a voice as soft and sweet as a mother's. If that quiet voice
didn't echo in the hallway, it more than bounced around inside my skull.

"Oh," I said. Then, trying to regain my composure: "You're right, but
the offer still holds."

My own Anglo need to be immediately accepted had been thumped on,
and, ridiculously, it hurt. I spent that night repeatedly reliving the corridor
scene, and winced every time Mrs. Cassadore's words replayed in my mind.

The next morning I almost said to Mrs. Cassadore, "Another thing I'd   15
like to talk to you about is . . . well, I'd like to share some of my ideas about
Indian education. And I'd like to learn about your tribe. I'd like to learn
about you." That's how I sort of planned my words. But in the end I held
my tongue. I had already been pushy enough. And now I was remembering
what I had learned in Sacaton from the Whitmans and other Pimas about
friendship. Observe the other person. Be patient. Assume nothing. Determine if there are common grounds. Open up only when the time is appropriate. And once you've decided to open up, and only then, commit yourself to an understanding of relationship—maybe of friendship.

I was trying to see things from Mrs. Cassadore's point of view, from an
Indian point of view. Malinda Powsky, the Hualapai with whom I had developed a friendship rather quickly, had known about me and my work before I met her. She had seen me work with the Hualapai children, and we
had spent hours talking to each other before she invited me for the drive
into the Grand Canyon. Mrs. Cassadore, on the other hand, had never set
eyes on me until yesterday; she didn't know where I had come from, or
anything about my work, and we had never spent a moment talking to
each other.

This elder from the San Carlos Apache tribe had been introduced to
(had to shake the hand of) a tall (intimidating) white man who wore a
sports jacket over a sweatshirt (dressed like a businessman *and* a hippie),
and whose face was covered with a beard (unnatural growth). Before she
knew it, this man had invited (cornered) her into making a decision about
spending time alone with him so he could learn about (exploit) Globe's
bilingual program and the Apaches. Thinking of it from Mrs. Cassadore's
point of view, I was suddenly and definitely put off by this image of myself.

"Good morning," I said to Mrs. Cassadore. This time I spoke with the
quiet respect I knew should be given a person older than I was. At our first

meeting, I had acted disrespectfully, forgetting the rules of Indian friendship and acquaintanceship. It's not easy, after all, to unlearn social habits that have been practiced over a lifetime. I was now behaving toward Mrs. Cassadore not from instinct, as I had yesterday, but from the knowledge I had gained about appropriate social intercourse in the Indian world. I was consciously unlearning, and relearning. I had no right to assume that this Apache woman should be comfortable with, or even aware of, the twists and turns of my Anglo forwardness. I would merely do my best to behave in a way that demonstrated the genuine respect I felt for her, and I hoped that she had not already completely shut out the possibility of some kind of relationship.

I offered, as I said good morning to Mrs. Cassadore, another show of respect by avoiding eye contact with her, instead glancing down at the floor. Among many Indians, quickly establishing direct eye contact is regarded as rude and aggressive, if not downright confrontational.

Mrs. Cassadore's sweet, motherly voice answered, "Good morning." 20 Then we passed each other and walked in opposite directions through the cement corridor.

Be patient, I told myself. Patient and respectful. If it is meant for the two of us to know each other better, it will happen—when the time is appropriate.

My classes with the Apache students were both exciting and rewarding. Particularly interesting were the survival-skills sessions, since they involved more open discussion. Each group I saw was composed of students from all four high school grades, pooled from their English classes. Half of the students already knew and were comfortable with me, since I had worked with them when they were seventh- and eighth-graders at the elementary school on the reservation. At our initial meetings, as I entered the classrooms, the freshmen and sophomores exclaimed, "It's Mick!" "All right!" "You followed us to the high school!" The juniors and seniors, never having seen me before, were quietly curious and suspicious of this white man's presence.

In the first class I conducted, Mrs. Cassadore sat at the back of the room on an old pine chair pressed against the back wall, as far away from me as possible. In the following weeks, she would attend most of my morning classes sitting in the same distant spot. I was especially pleased, however, that she showed up at the beginning of the classes and witnessed the students' welcoming cheers. If nothing else, this would indicate to her the kind of rapport I developed with Indian students—with *Apache* students.

I waited until the third week to begin the survival-skills sessions, giving the older students time to become relaxed in my presence. The first and most important rule of these classes was that, aside from me, no non-Indians were allowed in the classroom. I wanted the Apache students to be open and honest about the problems they perceived in their encounters with the Anglo world. I felt that my established relationship with the younger students would make the discussions not only possible but productive.

And I tried to keep realistic expectations. There was no way I could   25
make survival in two different cultures easy. These Apache students, as well as Indian students in general, had two major tasks challenging them: the maintenance of their own Indian culture and the acquisition of skills that would enable them to function, when they had to, in mainstream non-Indian society. What separated them from other minorities, and made their task more difficult, was the fact that the nature of the differences between their culture and Anglo culture was so extreme. So, coping in the Anglo world meant, as it does today, not a *reconciliation* of opposites, but an *adjustment* to the very existence of profound opposites—an adjustment that must include the development of behaviors that often seem strange to the young Indian. True biculturalism also includes the maintenance of basic Indian cultural patterns and deep-rooted beliefs. As difficult as this may be to accomplish, it remains for Indians a realistic, attainable goal.

Not all the Apache students at Globe High School would become Hartman Lomawaimas, the assistant director of the Lowie Museum in Berkeley, but in our classes we could at least discuss specific problems and various ways to handle them.

Subjects for our discussions ranged from Anglo "time" as a concept different from Indian "time," to the analysis of Anglo behaviors the Apache students found odd or intimidating. I constantly reinforced the idea that the students, in learning survival skills, did not have to give up being Indian; they did not have to become *assimilated.*

The irony, or course, was that at the same time that I was conducting these classes, I was also adjusting my own behaviors to conform to acceptable Indian ways in my encounters with Mrs. Cassadore. Cross-cultural understanding is a two-way street. The non-Indian in contact with Indians has a responsibility to learn about their world and make the same adjustment to profound opposites that is expected of the Indian in reverse situations. When I talked to Mrs. Cassadore, usually in the bilingual office, I kept my side of the conversations brief and to the point, spoke in a soft voice, and never tried to establish prolonged eye contact.

On Wednesday of the second week, I began the morning class by saying, "Today we're going to talk a little bit about racial prejudice toward Indians, toward you guys. Can anyone define what the word 'prejudice' means?"

Tom, a sophomore, said, "It's like when white people look at you funny   30
'cause they don't like Indians."

Marie, also a sophomore, chimed in, "They get suspicious of you, and
some of them just hate us."

"Okay. Why don't we talk about ways that some white people act toward Indians that might show prejudice, and how you can try to tell if
those actions really do show prejudice. And we should talk about the ways
you respond, and other possible responses. Someone tell me something that
some whites do that might show prejudice."

"When they stare at us real long," offered an eleventh-grader named
Sean. "You look away, but every time you look back, they're still staring."
The class stirred, the students nodding and mumbling in agreement.

Sean added, "It's like they don't even blink their eyes, kinda like snakes
or somethin'." Everyone chuckled.

This was a perfect start, I thought. The students had opened up quickly,   35
and even some humor had been injected; a relaxed but honest tone had
been set. I said, "Staring. How about their expressions when they stare? Can
you tell what they're feeling, like anger or hatred or, as Marie pointed out,
suspicion?"

"Sometimes they look like they're mad."

"Or like they think you're gonna steal something."

"Usually just a stare, kinda blanklike."

More students were joining in. I said, "Okay, so let's talk about the situations in which staring occurs. When and where do whites stare?"

"Like last week," a tall, muscular senior said. "Me and my family were at   40
a restaurant here in Globe. We was real quiet, like good Indians." He snickered as he said this, and the class laughed again, acutely aware of the image
many Indians believe they should project when in non-Indian public. "But
this old white man and his wife just kept starin' at us. He even had to look
partway over his shoulder to get a good view." More chuckles.

I said, "Let me tell you right off. Some white people like to stare, even
though it may be rude. Many times it *is* from prejudice. Sometimes it's
not. Staring itself doesn't *always* indicate prejudice. Do you think those
old people were staring because they were prejudiced, or could there have
been some other reason?" This idea had obviously not occurred to most
of the students. Several moments of silence passed as they considered
it. Then I said, "Can you think of any kind of staring that's really not
prejudice?"

The muscular boy pulled his sunglasses down from the top of his head
and over his eyes as he said, "Yeah. On the street, if it's a woman who's
starin', it's 'cause she thinks I'm sexy." The whole class roared.

"Are you all laughing because white women get turned on when they see him, or because so many white women are blind?" The volume of the laughter increased.

When the students settled, I said, "But there you have it. There's a reason why some whites stare at an Indian that's kind of the opposite of prejudice." I pointed to the boy; he was smiling from behind his sunglasses. "Just look at him," I said. "He's a handsome, sexy dude." The kids laughed again, but I knew they were getting the point. "I'll bet every one of you has seen a white kid here at school that you thought was attractive. Maybe you even kind of stared at him or her. Maybe secretly. Maybe not so secretly." Little waves of giggles spread through the classroom. "Give me one good reason why a woman, any woman, wouldn't find this young man attractive. He may have been joking, but he was also right."

Our discussion lasted the full hour and would have to be continued the next day. The students had identified other situations in which staring clearly represented racial prejudice. The fierce, suspicion-filled glare of a store proprietor the minute a young Indian walks into a store—"It makes you feel like a criminal even though you wasn't gonna do nothin' wrong in the first place." The venomous stares of a group of young whites on a street corner challenging a young Indian to some form of perverted, one-sided combat—"They scared the shit outta me." Concerning the old couple in the restaurant, the students concluded it was impossible to determine the motive for their rudeness. They might have been locals who disliked Indians, or they might as easily have been tourists from the hinterlands of the Midwest who had never laid eyes on a real-honest-to-goodness "Injun." 45

During that first hour we had discussed the students' responses to their own individual situations; they had decided no *single* way of dealing with someone whose eyes are fixed on you suits every such encounter. In some cases, the students decided, it was better to ignore the stares. In others, they felt that staring back was justified, if only to embarrass guilty eyes enough to turn them away. A few situations seemed to call for actual verbal or physical responses. One brassy young man told of an experience at a hardware store in which, when the clerk leveled her sights on her Apache target, he pulled out his wallet, raised his arms, looked back into the clerk's eyes, and said, "I got money, lady. I got money." This uncharacteristic response had been applauded by the other students, but most of them, especially the young women, said they personally preferred to ignore stares altogether. We had also discussed at length the fact that different individuals, even of the same tribe, may react differently to similar situations. The important thing, we concluded, was to respond in a manner that felt as comfortable as possible, and at the same time maintain a sense of personal and tribal dignity.

After the bell had sounded its old-fashioned clang, I stood at the doorway saying good-bye to the students individually as they filed out. We all looked forward to the next day's session. It was good, and rare, for these Apache students to have shared such personal experiences with an Anglo who was sympathetic and who could offer legitimate, sometimes new, perspectives. It was good for *this* Anglo as well.

After the last student passed into the corridor, I took a deep breath, at once savoring the moment, giving the moment up, and readying myself to start the whole process over again with another group of kids. I felt exhilarated.

Then Mrs. Cassadore came from her usual spot at the back of the room. "That was good," she said. "We need more of that kind of thing."

"Thank you," I said, looking down.   50

Mrs. Cassadore had watched me interact with the Apache students for two-and-a-half weeks now. She had read their poems and articles. And she had just offered a compliment. I wondered if the time might be right to ask her to dinner again. If she accepted, I would be delighted; if she turned me down, well, I could handle it gracefully and resign myself to knowing her only within the context of our high school meetings.

Looking down at the floor, I said, "You know, I would still enjoy your company for dinner some evening." I braced myself.

Mrs. Cassadore thought for a moment. I readied myself to say something like, "That's okay. It's not that important." Then I glanced up.

Mrs. Cassadore raised her head. In the same sweet voice she used with everyone, she said, "How about tonight?"

Dinner with Mrs. Cassadore

The stereotype of the silent, stoic Indian was created by non-Indians   55
who had never gotten to the first stage of the Indian manner of coming to an understanding of relationship. Had those non-Indians used the Indian approach of quiet, patient, cautious observation, and finally been accepted with trust and friendship, they would have experienced quite a different Indian, one who joked and laughed much of the time, one who loved to talk and share stories with an obsessive attention to detail, one who valued loyalty.

Over dinner, I witnessed a different Mrs. Cassadore, one who had decided I was okay and could be trusted. We had gone to a Mexican restaurant near the high school and sat down in a window booth next to a neon Coors sign that glowed like an electric-stove burner. Brightly colored piñatas hung from the ceiling, and south-of-the-border serapes covered the stucco walls. I ordered chicken enchiladas, rice, beans, and a Dos Equis beer. Mrs. Cassadore asked for combination number one—the basic taco, tamale, and enchilada served with beans and rice—and an iced tea.

We talked for a while about Indian education. I told her about the poetry books and calendars I had edited at Sacaton, the calendar of Apache student writings we had produced at the elementary school in San Carlos, and expressed my hope that the bilingual program at Globe High School would be able to publish the manuscript we were now putting together. The point, I said, was to demonstrate to the students the importance of sharing with the community their written creations while giving them the sense of pride that comes with seeing one's writing in published form.

Mrs. Cassadore said, "But there's a problem with that for some Apaches." I had no idea what she was talking about. Publishing student work and distributing it among the children's parents and throughout the community had always seemed an essential part of my writing program.

"What do you mean?" I asked.

"Well, some Apaches don't think books are important." My face must have registered the same kind of surprise that earlier I had seen on the faces of the high school students when I had said that not all staring by Anglos reflected racial prejudice. Mrs. Cassadore went on, "Some think that written words are kind of evil." 60

I stared at Mrs. Cassadore, confused and curious. My own experience in San Carlos had indicated the opposite. In fact, after we had published the poetry calendar, I had learned of a wonderful example of the benefit of written communication. An eighth-grader named Dawn Casuse had written a simple and elegant description of herself waiting to go through the Sunrise Dance Ceremony, the traditional puberty rite held for young Apache women. The poem appeared on the calendar. I assumed at the time that the girl had already gone through the ritual. A year later, when I returned to San Carlos, I was told by one of her aunts that before writing her poem, Dawn had never expressed an interest in the Sunrise Ceremony, and that whenever her parents had asked her about it, she had told them she didn't want one. Then they saw the poem on the calendar and wondered why she would write about the ceremony if she had no interest in it. They confronted her. Dawn then confessed to them the real reason she had acted indifferent—she feared that they could not afford the expense and didn't want them to feel guilty. Part of the ceremony involves the parents conducting a giveaway in which those in attendance receive blankets and food costing the family hundreds of dollars. Once her parents knew what Dawn was really thinking and feeling, they immediately arranged for her to have a Sunrise Dance Ceremony. Had Dawn not written that poem, and had it not been published, her parents would never have known that she secretly wanted the ritual. Dawn Casuse would have gone through life having never been initiated into adulthood in a way she believed important.

The Dawn Casuse story was one example of the positive side of printing students' work, but now Mrs. Cassadore was telling me that some Apaches viewed printed materials not only as unimportant, but as evil. "I'm lost," I said to her. "Can you explain?"

"Yes." Mrs. Cassadore sipped at her iced tea. I took a long pull from my Dos Equis, squinting into the orange neon glow to my left. "You know a lot of young Apaches," she said. "And you know some of their parents. But there's a lot of parents and grandparents you don't know, and they probably wouldn't want to know you, unless maybe they saw how you are with their kids. They been to school in their day, and what that usually meant was a bad BIA[1] boarding school. And all they remember about school is that there were all these Anglos trying to make them forget they were Apaches; trying to make them turn against their parents, telling them that Indian ways were evil.

"Well, a lot of those kids came to believe that their teachers were the evil ones, and so anything that had to do with 'education' was also evil — like books. Those kids came back to the reservation, got married, and had their own kids. And now they don't want anything to do with the white man's education. The only reason they send their kids to school is because it's the law. But they tell their kids not to take school seriously. So, to them, printed stuff is white-man stuff."

"But Indian education is changing," I said. "Assimilation is not official policy anymore. The school in San Carlos has an Apache school board." 65

"Doesn't matter. Education for some Apache adults means what it always meant. *They* haven't changed. They shut education out a long time ago, and they don't want to hear anything about it. So of course they don't see the changes in the schools. And they don't read a poetry calendar from the school, either."

I said, "That means that we — I mean people working in Indian education, people working for change — have got to get out there and talk to those parents. We've got to show them how things like writing can be important, how education can be used in a positive way."

"You're right. The more Indians you talk to, the more that'll change. But it won't happen all at once. One or two families at a time. A lot probably still won't trust you. Us Apaches don't trust too many outsiders. Too much bad blood between us and Anglos. And it doesn't just go back to Geronimo's day. Things still happen, even today."

---

[1] **BIA:** Bureau of Indian Affairs.

"I'm sure," I said. "I know that's true at Gila River. Could you give me an example, though?"

"I'll give you a good one. It's one of the reasons I really didn't like you for a couple days." 70

"Oh," I said, again startled. "I knew you weren't sure of me, but I didn't know you actually didn't like me."

Mrs. Cassadore continued, "Well, I didn't. You see, something happened to me a long time ago that I never forgot." She hesitated.

"Yeah?"

"When I was raising my family, one time I got sick. Like the flu. I coughed a lot, and my lungs hurt. And I was really tired. For a couple weeks, I stayed in bed most of the time. I didn't want to go to the clinic; I didn't trust Anglo medicine. But I got worse. Finally, I figured I had no choice, so I went to see a doctor.

"He was a young man, just outta school. Those young doctors that bor- 75 rowed money from the government could pay their loans off by going out to an Indian reservation and working for the Indian Health Service for a couple years. That's how they staffed Indian hospitals.

"Well, he told me they had to do some tests, so I stayed at the hospital most of the day. Then he told me to go home, rest, and come back a few days later. When I went back, he took me into an office and closed the door. I didn't like that. Then he told me I had tuberculosis.

"I knew about that disease; I knew it was bad. That doctor said he was sorry, but I couldn't go home, I might spread it around to my children and my husband and other people. He said there was a place in Tucson called a sanatorium, and that I had to go there right away and stay till I got better. But I knew there was more to it than he was saying; I knew he really meant I'd stay there till I got better *or* till I died. I got really upset. Not about dying, but about not seeing my children and husband, not even being able to say good-bye. That same day they took me to Tucson.

"That sanatorium was awful. All these poor Indians just sitting there, or lying there, some of them dying. Coughing and coughing, that's what I remember. I thought if tuberculosis didn't kill me, being in that place would.

"Soon I felt better. I thought I was getting over it. But they kept telling me I couldn't leave. I couldn't understand why I had to stay if I wasn't coughing no more, if I didn't feel sick like all those people around me.

"Then one day someone told me to go to one of the doctors' offices. 80 When I got there, the doctor said, very politely, 'Please sit down.' I was thinking, *What now?*

"He told me that something had gone wrong, that some tests they took showed I didn't have tuberculosis after all, and that the tests they took last week, to make sure, proved it. I wasn't sick.

"I was so happy I cried. I thought of my children and my husband; now I could be with them again. I asked the doctor when I could go home.

"Just like that first doctor in San Carlos, he said, 'I'm sorry.' I knew something wasn't right. Then he told me that there was a chance I had picked up tuberculosis while I was there. I had to stay at least a few more weeks, in another ward, just to make sure I hadn't caught it.

"Every day and every night, all I could think about was that they had sent me away from home, to this terrible place, because of a disease I never had but might have gotten while I was there. If I got it and died, then the IHS[2] killed me. Some white person had made a mistake that killed an In-dian, and I'd be buried, and whoever it was that killed me wouldn't have to answer to anyone. I kept thinking about that young doctor in San Carlos. He should have checked. He should have made sure. It was his fault, really."

Mrs. Cassadore fell silent. She stared at the twisted napkin in her hand, visibly upset.

Shocked into numbness, I could muster no more than a few words. "How long were you in that sanatorium?"

Mrs. Cassadore mumbled, "Half my life." Though she had been incar-cerated for at least weeks, at most months, I knew what she meant.

"When did this happen?"

"In 1973."

I knew that things like that had happened in the 1800s, and maybe in the early part of this century, but I never would have imagined that they were still occurring as late as 1973. How wrong I had been in my supposi-tion. Perhaps things like this happened yet.

Mrs. Cassadore glanced up. "You see, that's why I didn't like you when I first saw you."

I still didn't get it.

"Well, that doctor at the hospital in San Carlos—he looked just like *you.* Tall, curly hair, beard. When I saw you, I saw him. All my memories flooded back. You were that young doctor. You were the one who almost killed me."

After a long silence, I whispered, "And now?"

"Now, I think you're okay."

"What changed?"

[2] **IHS:** Indian Health Service.

"That doctor couldn't be trusted. But you—I've watched you awhile. I think you can be trusted."

"I hope I'm worthy of your trust," I said, again looking down.

Mrs. Cassadore chuckled. "Well, let me put it this way, I've lived long enough, as of tonight, to know I shouldn't judge a white man by his face hair. That's a first for me."

Issues for Discussion

1. What "mistakes" does Fedullo make in his approach to Mrs. Cassadore? How did he probably expect their relationship to develop? What condensed story does Mrs. Cassadore read in Fedullo's dress and appearance? What stereotype underlies this story?
2. How do the Apache students in Fedullo's class "read" the stares of the white people they meet? What cultural assumptions underlie their interpretations of these looks? How does Fedullo challenge the condensed stories that they find in a prolonged stare?
3. In what ways does Fedullo appear to practice active listening? What questions does he put to himself about his failed encounter with Mrs. Cassadore?

JOURNAL OPTION

What Makes a Good Listener?

Write a journal entry about someone you've known whom you might consider a "great listener." What made this person so good at listening to others? What personal qualities or characteristics may have contributed to this talent for listening? Was this person, like Fedullo, particularly good at seeing herself from different points of view?

ESSAY OPTIONS

Interviewing Others

Learning to recognize your own cultural assumptions and to appreciate how they differ from those around you is an essential step in the process of becoming a critically aware reader and writer. The following assignment invites you to try your hand at listening for difference. Choose one of the following topics, but before you begin working, be sure to finish reading the hints on interviewing and conversational etiquette that conclude this chapter.

Topic 1. Interview someone whose background is significantly different from your own and whose professional work, community involvement, political activity, personal experience, way of life, or philosophy interests you. Your interviewee should be someone whose background differs from yours in terms of race, class, ethnicity, gender, sexual orientation, religion, or physical disability. Use information from your interview to write a formal profile in which you present this person's experiences and opinions and explore how they challenge or complicate your own attitudes and assumptions.

Topic 2. Interview someone whose background differs significantly from yours in order to learn about a specific cultural clash this person has experienced. Learn as much as you can about the circumstances that surrounded the incident in question, including any contributing factors as well as the incident's outcome. Try to determine how your interviewee "reads" this clash, how she explained it to herself at the time and how she explains it today. Use your interview as the basis for a paper in which you present a detailed account of this cultural collision, your analysis of the conflicting story frames or cultural assumptions it involved, and your reflections on how your interviewee's perspective challenges or complicates your own attitudes and assumptions.

Successful Interviewing

Because this assignment involves getting information from another person, it's important to plan carefully before you begin. Here are some suggestions for designing and conducting your interview and transforming it into a final paper.

Choosing a Person to Interview.   Your choice of interviewee can make or break your profile. If you choose someone who has little in the way of interesting experience or ideas to offer, chances are that you'll have a hard time finding something interesting to say about this person. You can also run into trouble if you choose someone who's particularly reserved or too busy to give you much information. You may find that an employer, a co-worker, or a neighbor would make a suitable interviewee. Or you may want to consider a classmate, a counselor, a college staff member, or someone living in your dorm or apartment building. Above all, your choice should reflect your interests: choose someone who really piques your curiosity or who seems to have something to teach you.

Focusing on a Purpose.   Before you begin, you need to think about the focus of your interview. Clearly, you'll want to explore how your interviewee's background has shaped her ideas and experiences. It wouldn't make much sense, then, to focus your questions on her taste in cars or what she thinks about the United Nations. Instead, ask yourself what this particular person has to teach you. Are you primarily interested in how her background has affected her professionally? Do you want to focus on her family relationships or the dating and marriage customs of her culture? If the person you're interviewing is a recent immigrant or a foreign student, you might want to know his responses to life in the United States or what it's like for him to attend an American college. If it's someone whose class or racial background differs from yours, you may want to explore her feelings about issues like affirmative action, or her assumptions about people like you. Focusing the purpose of your interview will help you develop your questions and help you organize your thoughts when it comes time to write the profile.

Preparing the Questions.   Once you know what you'll be focusing on, you should plan the specific questions you'll ask during your interview. Since you want to elicit as much information—and as many stories—as possible during the interview, it's generally a good idea to avoid questions that invite "yes" and "no" answers. Instead, try to make your questions "open-ended"—the kind that encourage reflection and detailed responses. You might begin, for example, by simply asking your interviewee to tell about how her background has influenced or affected her, and then move to more specific questions as the occasion arises. Here are a few additional examples of open-ended questions:

- What led you to become interested/involved in _____?

- How would you describe your beliefs or attitudes toward _____?

- In what ways has your ethnicity, gender, and so forth been an advantage to you in your work/activities/personal development?

- Can you tell me about a time when you encountered bias, opposition, or conflict in your work/activities/development because of your ethnicity, gender, and so forth?

- What, if anything, would you like to change about your work/activities/life/world?

- What are your goals for the future?

Arranging the Interview.   Make sure you set a specific date for the interview and allow enough time for detailed responses and follow-up questions. Choose a location that is free from the distractions of street noise, phone calls, drop-by visitors, and so forth. A dorm room, for example, with stereo blasting and friends coming and going probably isn't an ideal setting. And be sure that you give your subject plenty of notice.

Preparing to Tape.   If you have access to a tape recorder, you'll probably want to use it. A tape offers you a permanent record of your interviewee's responses, in case you want to check the accuracy of your memory or quote a particularly interesting response verbatim. Audiotape, unlike handwritten notes, has the additional advantage of being able to capture the mood of your interviewee and the tone of his responses. Finally, taping also allows you to concentrate on interacting with the person you're interviewing. It frees you to respond to his ideas, monitor his facial expressions, and plan follow-up questions. Of course, you'll want to get your interviewee's permission to be taped when you arrange the interview. You should also take some time to practice taping before you meet. If you're borrowing a cassette recorder from a friend, make sure you know how to use all of its functions, and even if you're familiar with the machine, be sure the batteries are fresh and that the sound quality is good when you record. You'll want to check the sound quality again just before beginning the formal interview so you can be certain that your interviewee's voice comes through clearly and that you aren't picking up too much background noise. Given the quality of today's electronic gadgetry and your experience with everything from VCRs to computers, all of these precautions might not seem necessary, but taping a live interview is trickier than it seems, and there's usually no second chance if your tape comes up empty a few days before your paper is due.

Conducting the Interview.   Even if you know the person well, interviews can be awkward, so you'll want to do whatever you can to put her at ease. A cup of coffee or tea and something to eat usually helps, as does a few minutes of casual conversation before getting down to business. You should, of course, be sure to explain why you're conducting the interview, what it will focus on, and how it will be used in your class.

Your ability to listen actively can make or break your interview. As your interviewee talks, you should be constantly putting questions to yourself. Have you really understood what she said? What, exactly, is the significance of the ideas she expresses? Are there any condensed stories in her answers that you might want to learn more about? The most interesting information gained during an interview rarely surfaces in response to prepared questions: the person you're interviewing is more likely to open up to you if you've listened carefully and asked interesting follow-up questions. Finally, you'll want to check your tape recorder periodically during the interview, just to be sure everything's going smoothly.

Prewriting the Profile.   At this point you need to begin shaping the information you've gathered into a finished profile. The first step is to listen to the tape and take notes: a careful review of everything that was said can help you "see" ideas, assumptions, and inferences that may have escaped you during the interview. As you work through the tape, make note of the footage when the topic changes or when you come across a particularly interesting idea or response. These notes will help you locate specific information when you're drafting your paper. You should also pause to jot down ideas that strike you as you listen. After you've reviewed the tape, you can apply some of the prewriting strategies introduced in Chapter 2 (p. 54). You may want to brainstorm lists of words that occur to you in response to your interviewee's experiences and ideas. You might try to freewrite some tentative conclusions about the experience, or about how your interviewee's ideas challenge your own. This is a good time to begin thinking about how you'll structure your essay: how much information does your reader need to know about your interviewee to appreciate the purpose of your paper? Should you explain why you selected this person in the opening paragraph? How should you organize the information you collected? Is it all relevant? What conclusions about this person do you want to emphasize? You may even want to sketch a rough outline of how you'll shape the information you want to present. Prewriting will help you transform the raw responses of your interview into a thoughtful and well-organized paper. If you omit this step, chances are that your profile will be little more than a summary of what your interviewee said.

Conversational Etiquette

Calvin and Hobbes   by Bill Watterson

Our personal and cultural story frames don't just shape our expectations and ideas; they also tell us how to talk. In the cartoon above, Calvin explains his own peculiarly aggressive approach to conversational etiquette. Language for Calvin is a matter of scoring points: the more you dominate the conversation—and your partner—the better your chances of winning. This might seem like a strange way to view communication, but according to linguist Deborah Tannen, men frequently subscribe to Calvin's aggressive style of self-expression. According to Tannen, males tend to view conversation as a contest, a kind of verbal sparring or performance that creates a stage for "self-display" and opportunities for bonding. Tannen notes that women, by contrast, are more likely to avoid direct verbal confrontation and, instead, use language in a way that minimizes difference and tension. Male talk is filled with commands and silences, female talk with questions, requests, and explanations. Men present facts; women exchange feelings.

The different conversational cultures of men and women can lead to serious misunderstandings. In her best-selling study of female/male communication patterns, *You Just Don't Understand* (1990), Tannen provides the following brief example of a conversational clash between a husband and wife planning a dinner party:

> *Maureen:* The only weekend we seem to have free is October tenth.
> *Philip:* That's the opening of hunting season.
> *Maureen:* Well, let's do it Saturday or Sunday evening.
> *Philip:* Okay, make it Saturday.
> *Maureen:* Wouldn't you want to be able to hunt later on the first day of hunting?
> *Philip:* [Annoyed] I said Saturday, so obviously that's the day I prefer.
> *Maureen:* [Now also annoyed] I was just trying to be considerate of you. You didn't give a reason for choosing Saturday.
> *Philip:* I'm taking off Thursday and Friday to hunt, so I figure I'll have had enough by Saturday night.
> *Maureen:* Well, why didn't you say that?
> *Philip:* I didn't see why I had to. And I found your question very intrusive.
> *Maureen:* I found your response very offensive.[3]

As Tannen sees it, this dispute occurs because Maureen misreads Philip's decision to choose Saturday night for the party. Imposing her own story frame on him, she assumes he's trying to "accommodate" her needs by sacrificing his own. When she tries to suggest they hold the party later—in order to be considerate of his desires—he becomes offended: he expects to give orders,

---

[3] Deborah Tannen, *You Just Don't Understand: Women and Men in Conversation* (New York: Ballentine Books, 1990), pp. 158–159.

not reasons, and thus he reads her attempts to be caring as "intrusive" badgering.

Differences in verbal etiquette also show up between other cultural groups. Comparative linguists like Tannen have shown that ethnic groups differ in their tolerance of emotion and anger in conversation. Mediterranean peoples, for example, often engage in heated verbal exchanges and debates that would dismay many Americans. What might seem to be a knock-down/drag-out fight between an Italian or Greek couple may only be an enjoyable conversational ritual. Conversely, the direct and "friendly" conversational style of many Americans—like the approach Mick Fedullo initially took with Mrs. Cassadore—may strike peoples of more formal cultures as rude and offensive. In some cultures direct eye contact, the use of first names, and even smiles are signs of ill-breeding during a first encounter. In others it's an insult if you don't stand within a few inches of your listener. Some groups interpret elaborate politeness and indirection as a sign of insincerity; others have specific conventions for determining who should speak first.

Before you replenish the batteries in your tape recorder and plunge into your interview, it probably would be a good idea to reflect for a moment on the scripts that govern your assumptions about conversation. Clearly, if you set out with an approach that's close to Calvin's, you might be setting yourself up for a social disaster. As we mentioned earlier, to become an active listener you have to start by listening to your own stories—to the habits, assumptions, and mental frameworks that shape your actions and reactions. A bit of self-analysis now may help you communicate more effectively on the day of your interview.

OPTIONAL
ACTIVITIES

Exploring Conversational Etiquettes

As you look over the list of statements below, try to think of yourself in different conversational situations. To what extent does each statement apply to you and your cultural group? Compare your responses with those of your classmates. Can you find predictable patterns of agreement or disagreement? As a class, discuss other examples of unusual conversational cultural styles you've noticed.

1. Look people in the eye when talking to them because that will indicate you are friendly and have nothing to hide.
2. Looking at people in the eye is impolite because you seem to be challenging them.
3. Get close to the person you're talking to or he'll think you're unfriendly.

4. Don't crowd the person you're talking to or she'll feel uncomfortable.
5. Try to make a joke when you meet someone to put him at ease.
6. Ask personal questions to help get the conversation going and to show you're interested in the other person.
7. Talking about yourself is a good way to put the person you're talking to at ease and to get her to open up.
8. Don't express your personal opinions or talk too much about yourself because it seems egotistical.
9. Casually touching the person you're talking to will put him at ease and let him know you're friendly.
10. Talking in a full, loud voice indicates . . . ?
11. Talking in a soft, restrained voice indicates . . . ?

CHAPTER 7

Academically Speaking: Investigating College Culture(s)

What's the Story Here?

By the time you reach college, you've had at least twelve years of experience with school culture. As an insider, you know the cultural scripts: you know what the rules are, what the bells mean, and what will happen if you ignore them; you can predict what a typical hour in Senior English might bring. But as you've undoubtedly noticed by now, college violates many of these familiar cultural scripts. Socially, college offers you new friends, new opportunities, and fewer formal rules. Yet while you're in class for only a few hours a day, and nobody reminds you to do your homework, you're expected to learn more and learn it faster than you ever have before. Intellectually, the culture of higher education can be even more disorienting. On the one hand, American college culture is conservative in its preoccupation with academic prestige, its concern with cultural and intellectual traditions, and its reliance on established methods of analysis. On the other hand, American colleges are frequently portrayed as hotbeds of radical thinking; while this image is grossly exaggerated, it's true that most scholars are dedicated to posing new problems and questioning received wisdom. This willingness to probe any issue and to challenge time-honored beliefs is one of the most distinctive—and potentially unsettling—traits of American higher education. Take a moment to think about your experience of this new culture.

Observing College Culture

1. Brainstorm a list of the differences you've noticed between high school and college or draw visual representations of yourself as a high school student and as a college student; then write a paragraph interpreting these lists or drawings. Comparing your observations with classmates, do you find any consensus about the differences you see? About the best and worst aspects of high school versus college? What underlying values do these differences reflect?

2. From what you've seen so far, how would you describe the culture of your college or university to a complete outsider? What rules would she or he need to know in order to behave appropriately in class and outside of class? What rules govern interactions with professors and with other students? How did you learn these rules yourself?

Academic culture can be strange, confusing, and sometimes alienating for newcomers. One source of difficulty for many students is the wide variety of attitudes, expectations, and conventions they encounter in different classes. Although academics in all fields share a basic belief in the value of intellectual life and scholarship, the goals and methods of this scholarship vary tremendously from one discipline to the next. College is less a single, coherent culture than a loose collection of subcultures. As you move from psychology to biochemistry to ethnomusicology, you'll have to learn different types of research and analysis as well as new subject matter. Even within a single field of study, you'll encounter passionate differences of opinion about what's worthwhile or true. But first, lets concentrate on some of the basic values and practices that unify academic culture—the frequently unspoken assumptions that you need to understand in order to find your own place in the complex culture that surrounds you.

Academic Inquiry: Getting beyond Formulas

Nearly every college instructor has at one time or another experienced the frustration of the history professor in the following *Doonesbury* cartoon. But while the cartoonist seems to blame the students for behaving like nothing more than extremely polite sheep ("BAA, SIR"), we'd argue that scholastic sheep are made, not born. If the schools these dutiful students attended are

like most schools in the United States, much of the precollege education they offered consisted of following rules and learning to give the correct answers to predictable questions. Brazilian educator and philosopher Paulo Freire calls this style of teaching "banking education": the teacher possesses knowledge that she "deposits" in the students, who store the information until the teacher requests a "withdrawal" on an exam or in a paper.[1] The student's role in a "banking" classroom is essentially passive; even if the material is hard to remember or the rules are complicated, the goal is clear—find the correct answer or follow the prescribed procedure and you're home free. The behavior of the students in Trudeau's cartoon really isn't surprising: in carefully taking down everything the professor says—no matter how outrageous or bizarre—they're just being good students, according to their prior training. But as the history professor's vain attempts to stimulate discussion demonstrate, life in college isn't always so straightforward. You'll still encounter the "banking" method in some of your college classes, but serious academic inquiry requires a very different approach.

---

[1] Paulo Freire, *Pedagogy of the Oppressed* (New York: Continuum, 1989), p. 58.

Many of your professors will expect you to take a more active role in your learning: instead of behaving like a bank vault or an empty vessel waiting to be filled up, you'll need to act more like a detective trying to solve a mystery, an attorney arguing a case, or a policymaker weighing the potential consequences of proposed legislation. You may have to define a good (that is, difficult) question and wrestle with it, or propose and defend your own answer to an open-ended question. The goal may be less to come up with a predetermined "correct" response than to demonstrate your ability to reason through a problem on your own. In order to do this well, you'll need to sharpen your powers of observation, reflection, and intellectual curiosity, not just rely on established authority or convention.

The following passage tells the story of one student's first experience with a teacher who challenged his class to think independently. The author, Robert M. Holland (b. 1938), teaches at the University of Akron, where he served as director of composition from 1978 to 1984. He has published a number of articles on teaching writing; this selection comes from an essay that appeared in *Audits of Meaning* (1988), edited by Louise Z. Smith.

Before Reading

Think about a time you encountered a baffling idea or an unexpected result while you were doing an assignment for class. What was the situation and how did you respond to it?

Discovering the Forms of Academic Discourse
Robert M. Holland, Jr.

Plato has Socrates define the ideal of academic discourse in the *Phaedrus:* "true written rhetoric" must not be a creation of fantasy or something aimed merely at creating belief without any attempt at instruction by question and answer; it must be more than a record or mnemonic device; it is written by one who has knowledge of the truth he writes, who can defend what he has written by submitting to an interrogation on the subject, and who makes it evident as soon as he speaks how comparatively inferior are his writings. A scholar teaches what he knows; inquires, through dialectic, into what he does not know; and not only submits to but *seeks* the best interrogation, refutation, or criticism that may be developed by other scholars. Academic discourse, at its best, is both dialectic and didactic.

Such is the case with ideal academic discourse. In the world of school, however, from the earliest "sharing" or pre-school through doctoral dissertations, the academic writer may choose an *eidolon*, a "dream-image" of academic discourse; furthermore, he or she may be quite unaware of having made such a choice. Format and formula may become primary, for they often appear to be the observable determiners of esteem or success. Teachers also (whether aware of it or not) may invite either the idea or the eidolon of academic discourse by the way they design their writing assignments.

Let me illustrate this concept of eidolon with a story from my own early schooling. In September of 1955 our high school chemistry class went to the chemistry laboratory for the first time. We had been told that there was to be no talking while we were in the lab; we were to follow the written instructions on how to work with the material assembled at our stations and to submit a written report before leaving the lab. At each station were four numbered beakers containing clear liquid, two pads of litmus paper (blue, pink), and this assignment: "Use only the litmus paper to find out what you can about the contents of the beakers. Write a report of your findings and what you think those findings mean."

Of course, none of us was entirely in the dark at that point: we had had some experience with "chemistry sets," we "knew" the simple magic of litmus. We set to work, systematically dipping little strips of blue and pink litmus into the series of beakers. For me, as I recall, it went like this: with beaker #1, the pink litmus became blue and the blue litmus became merely damp; with beaker #2, the pink litmus became damp and the blue litmus became pink; with beaker #3, both the blue and the pink litmus paper became damp, neither of them changing color; with beaker #4, both the blue and pink litmus paper turned white.

Now, I hadn't the slightest idea what was happening with beaker #4. I peeked about the lab to see how my classmates were doing and found them peeking about, too: we all had before us, from one or another of our beakers, pink and blue litmus paper strips which had both turned white. Since we had been prohibited from discussing our work, we each turned to the task of composing a written report.

Though puzzled by the whitened litmus, we did know something about writing reports. We each drew up a chart or table (columns for the beakers, rows for the litmus, that sort of thing) and wrote in our findings. We added an introduction, repeating the written instructions at our stations, and we made some sentences about how we had done what we had been told to do. But here is the curious part: *not one of us included the information about both the blue and the pink litmus strips turning white.* (I believe I wrote in my report of both blue and pink litmus for beaker #4: "No change." Others wrote, "Both became damp," or, "Nothing happened.")

The following day, the chemistry teacher began by asking each of us in turn what we had experienced with the litmus and the liquid in a particular beaker (he asked me, of course, about beaker #4). One after another we stated not what we had seen, but what we had written in our reports. The teacher then asked whether any of us had noticed litmus paper turning white. Well, we all had, and now we said so. But none of us, he pointed out, had reported that; how, he asked, did we account for this phenomenon of our concurrence in a fiction? Why had we all written what was untrue?

We replied as best we could, explaining that we had been afraid of being wrong and admitting a shared belief that every finding must be explained; since we had no idea of what was happening with the whitened litmus, we had chosen to describe that occurrence by redefining it. Our replies, taken all together, made clear to us that our reports were not academic discourse but an imitation of academic discourse. While none of us had pretended not to see the litmus paper turn white, we all had pretended so in our reports.

We had missed the point of the laboratory assignment, which had been designed to enable us to discover for ourselves the dialectic of chemistry, and we had chosen to substitute our eidolon of academic discourse. Having assumed that the true subject of our exercise was "Using Litmus Paper," we then formulated our "learning" to fit our expectations. We formatted our findings to fit the fantasy of our waking dream of science—*in spite of* our first-hand experience that called into question the very tool we imagined we had mastered. (Beaker #4, it turned out, contained commercial bleach, which subverted the dye system of the litmus paper itself.)

We had used format and formulation to excuse ourselves from the learning of form, creating an illusion of knowledge based on an absurd and unspoken premise: "What you do not understand, hide." In imitating scientists, we had behaved as no true scientist ever would. What made the exercise nonetheless useful for us, in spite of our failure, was that our reports were in writing: having created ignorance (or, more generously, having made a predictable student error), we had to confront, in the written testimony of our reports, the consequences of our creation. Written discourse made possible a scene for learning that would have been impossible through vocal discussion. By discovering ourselves as a community of *non*-scholars we were able to see what it might mean to become a community of scholars.

The lesson was not learned all at once, of course. In another year, doing physics, we went about the business of heating metal rods, viewing salt and

10

other things in a flame, and rolling steel balls down troughs—and then looked up in handbooks the correct coefficient of expansion or wavelength of light or acceleration of gravity and worked our calculations backwards, leaving what we called a "margin of error." In biology we knew better than to try to draw precisely the protozoa we tracked through our microscopes; no, we traced perfect circles into our laboratory reports and drew within them adaptations of what our textbooks showed. If you were "seeing" a paramecium, it better have a fringe of cilia all around; if an amoeba, include one contractile vacuole.

And so it went in other school subjects: we told back history as it was told to us—never mentioning an open question or an unresolved doubt, and never imagining that it was all right *not* to know the significance of everything. We wrote school discourse, not academic discourse but an eidolon of academic discourse. We dealt in formulas and format, not in form, not in meaning-making dialectic.

Issues for Discussion

1. Why do you think the students in Holland's chemistry class were so afraid to risk being wrong?
2. How much of your education so far has consisted of memorizing information or following set rules and formulas?
3. Did any of your high school classes ask you to participate in the kind of "meaning-making dialectic" that Holland describes? If so, what were the assignments and how did you respond to them?

O P T I O N A L
A C T I V I T Y

Types of Thinking in College Assignments

Review the exam questions and written assignments you've received in your college classes so far: How many call for simple recall of information and how many call for some kind of independent judgment, analysis, or argument? How many assignments or exams were evaluated only on the correctness of your responses and how many also evaluated the quality of your thinking? Compare your assignments with those your classmates have encountered: What types of assignments have you found most challenging and why? How well did your prior education prepare you for the kinds of thinking and studying expected of you now?

Cultural Values and "Good" Writing

Like every aspect of academic life, what's considered effective writing is determined by cultural values that often remain unspoken—assumptions so ingrained that they're rarely explained. Sometimes it takes the perspective of an outsider to see such values and conventions clearly. In the next essay, Fan Shen, a graduate student from mainland China, compares the assumptions of his American and his Chinese teachers about what a "good" essay should look and sound like. Before coming to the United States, Shen worked for seven years in an aircraft factory and was forced to do farm labor during China's Cultural Revolution. He later attended Lanzhou University, where he received a B.A. in literature and linguistics, and ultimately left China to continue his studies abroad. Shen wrote "The Classroom and the Wider Culture" while pursuing a Ph.D. in English at Marquette University; he now teaches English at Rockland Community College in New York. The essay was first published in the journal *College Composition and Communication* (December 1989).

Before Reading

What characteristics do you associate with "good" writing? Have you ever encountered a different definition? If so, what was it and how would you explain the difference?

The Classroom and the Wider Culture: Identity as a Key to Learning English Composition
Fan Shen

One day in June 1975, when I walked into the aircraft factory where I was working as an electrician, I saw many large-letter posters on the walls and many people parading around the workshops shouting slogans like "Down with the word 'I'!" and "Trust in masses and the Party!" I then remembered that a new political campaign called "Against Individualism" was scheduled to begin that day. Ten years later, I got back my first English composition paper at the University of Nebraska-Lincoln. The professor's first comments were: "Why did you always use 'we' instead of 'I'?" and "Your paper would be stronger if you eliminated some sentences in the passive voice." The clashes between my Chinese background and the requirements of English composition had begun. At the center of this mental struggle, which has lasted several years and is still not completely over, is the prolonged, uphill battle to recapture "myself."

In this [paper] I will try to describe and explore this experience of reconciling my Chinese identity with an English identity dictated by the rules of English composition. I want to show how my cultural background shaped—and shapes—my approaches to my writing in English and how writing in English redefined—and redefines—my *ideological* and *logical* identities. By "ideological identity" I mean the system of values that I acquired (consciously and unconsciously) from my social and cultural background. And by "logical identity" I mean the natural (or Oriental) way I organize and express my thoughts in writing. Both had to be modified or redefined in learning English composition. Becoming aware of the process of redefinition of these different identities is a mode of learning that has helped me in my efforts to write in English, and, I hope, will be of help to teachers of English composition in this country. In presenting my case for this view, I will use examples from both my composition courses and literature courses, for I believe that writing papers for both kinds of courses contributed to the development of my "English identity." Although what I will describe is based on personal experience, many Chinese students whom I talked to said that they had had the same or similar experiences in their initial stages of learning to write in English.

IDENTITY OF THE SELF: IDEOLOGICAL AND CULTURAL

Starting with the first English paper I wrote, I found that learning to compose in English is not an isolated classroom activity, but a social and cultural experience. The rules of English composition encapsulate values that are absent in, or sometimes contradictory to, the values of other societies (in my case, China). Therefore, learning the rules of English composition is, to a certain extent, learning the values of Anglo-American society. In writing classes in the United States I found that I had to reprogram my mind, to redefine some of the basic concepts and values that I had about myself, about society, and about the universe, values that had been imprinted and reinforced in my mind by my cultural background, and that had been part of me all my life.

Rule number one in English composition is: Be yourself. (More than one composition instructor has told me, "Just write what *you* think.") The values behind this rule, it seems to me, are based on the principle of protecting and promoting individuality (and private property) in this country. The instruction was probably crystal clear to students raised on these values, but, as a guideline of composition, it was not very clear or useful to me when I first heard it. First of all, the image or meaning that I attached to the word "I" or "myself" was, as I found out, different from that of my English teacher. In China, "I" is always subordinated to "We"—be it the working class, the Party, the country, or some other collective body. Both political pressure and literary tradition require that "I" be somewhat hidden or buried in writings and speeches; presenting the "self" too obviously would give people the impression of being disrespectful of the Communist Party in political writings and boastful in scholarly writings. The word "I" has often been identified with another "bad" word, "individualism," which has become a synonym for selfishness in China. For a long time the words "self" and "individualism" have had negative connotations in my mind, and the negative force of the words naturally extended to the field of literary studies. As a result, even if I had brilliant ideas, the "I" in my papers always had to show some modesty by not competing with or trying to stand above the names of ancient and modern authoritative figures. Appealing to Mao or other Marxist authorities became the required way (as well as the most "forceful" or "persuasive" way) to prove one's point in written discourse. I remember that in China I had even committed what I can call "reversed plagiarism"—here, I suppose it would be called "forgery"—when I was in middle school: willfully attributing some of my thoughts to "experts" when I needed some arguments but could not find a suitable quotation from a literary or political "giant."

Now, in America, I had to learn to accept the words "I" and "Self" as something glorious (as Whitman did), or at least something not to be ashamed of or embarrassed about. It was the first and probably biggest step I took into English composition and critical writing. Acting upon my professor's suggestion, I intentionally tried to show my "individuality" and to "glorify" "I" in my papers by using as many "I's" as possible—"I think," "I believe," "I see"—and deliberately cut out quotations from authorities. It was rather painful to hand in such "pompous" (I mean immodest) papers to my instructors. But to an extent it worked. After a while I became more comfortable with only "the shadow of myself." I felt more at ease to put down *my* thoughts without looking over my shoulder to worry about the attitudes of my teachers or the reactions of the Party secretaries, and to speak out as "bluntly" and "immodestly" as my American instructors demanded.

But writing many "I's" was only the beginning of the process of redefining myself. Speaking of redefining myself is, in an important sense, speaking of redefining the word "I." By such a redefinition I mean not only the change in how I envisioned myself, but also the change in how *I* perceived

5

the world. The old "I" used to embody only one set of values, but now it had to embody multiple sets of values. To be truly "myself," which I knew was a key to my success in learning English composition, meant *not to be my Chinese self* at all. That is to say, when I write in English I have to wrestle with and abandon (at least temporarily) the whole system of ideology which previously defined me in myself. I had to forget Marxist doctrines (even though I do not see myself as a Marxist by choice) and the Party lines imprinted in my mind and familiarize myself with a system of capitalist/ bourgeois values. I had to put aside an ideology of collectivism and adopt the values of individualism. In composition as well as in literature classes, I had to make a fundamental adjustment: if I used to examine society and literary materials through the microscopes of Marxist dialectical materialism and historical materialism, I now had to learn to look through the microscopes the other way around, i.e., to learn to look at and understand the world from the point of view of "idealism." (I must add here that there are American professors who use a Marxist approach in their teaching.)

The word "idealism," which affects my view of both myself and the universe, is loaded with social connotations, and can serve as a good example of how redefining a key word can be a pivotal part of redefining my ideological identity as a whole.

To me, idealism is the philosophical foundation of the dictum of English composition: "Be yourself." In order to write good English, I knew that I had to be myself, which actually meant not to be my Chinese self. It meant that I had to create an English self and be *that* self. And to be that English self, I felt, I had to understand and accept idealism the way a Westerner does. That is to say, I had to accept the way a Westerner sees himself in relation to the universe and society. On the one hand, I knew a lot about idealism. But on the other hand, I knew nothing about it. I mean I knew a lot about idealism through the propaganda and objections of its opponent, Marxism, but I knew little about it from its own point of view. When I thought of the word "materialism"—which is a major part of Marxism and in China has repeatedly been "shown" to be the absolute truth—there were always positive connotations, and words like "right," "true," etc., flashed in my mind. On the other hand, the word "idealism" always came to me with the dark connotations that surround words like "absurd," "illogical," "wrong," etc. In China "idealism" is depicted as a ferocious and ridiculous enemy of Marxist philosophy. Idealism, as the simplified definition imprinted in my mind had it, is the view that the material world does not exist; that all that exists is the mind and its ideas. It is just the opposite of Marxist dialectical materialism which sees the mind as a product of the material world. It is not too difficult to see that idealism, with its idea that mind is of primary importance, provides a philosophical foundation for the Western emphasis on the value of individual human minds, and hence individual human beings. Therefore, my final acceptance of myself as of primary importance—an importance that overshadowed that of authority figures in English composition—was, I decided, dependent on an acceptance of idealism.

My struggle with idealism came mainly from my efforts to understand and to write about works such as Coleridge's *Biographia Literaria* and Emerson's "Over-Soul." For a long time I was frustrated and puzzled by the idealism expressed by Coleridge and Emerson—given their ideas, such as "I think, therefore I am" (Coleridge obviously borrowed from Descartes) and "the transparent eyeball" (Emerson's view of himself)—because in my mind, drenched as it was in dialectical materialism, there was always a little voice whispering in my ear "You are, therefore you think." I could not see how human consciousness, which is not material, could create apples and trees. My intellectual conscience refused to let me believe that the human mind is the primary world and the material world secondary. Finally, I had to imagine that I was looking at a world with my head upside down. When I imagined that I was in a new body (born with the head upside down) it was easier to forget biases imprinted in my subconsciousness about idealism, the mind, and my former self. Starting from scratch, the new inverted self—which I called my "English Self" and into which I have transformed myself—could understand and *accept,* with ease, idealism as "the truth" and "himself" (i.e., my English Self) as the "creator" of the world.

Here is how I created my new "English Self." I played a "game" similar to ones played by mental therapists. First I made a list of (simplified) features about writing associated with my old identity (the Chinese Self), both ideological and logical, and then beside the first list I added a column of features about writing associated with my new identity (the English Self). After that I pictured myself getting out of my old identity, the timid, humble, modest Chinese "I," and creeping into my new identity (often in the form of a new skin or a mask), the confident, assertive, and aggressive English "I." The new "Self" helped me to remember and accept the different rules of Chinese and English composition and the values that underpin these rules. In a sense, creating an English Self is a way of reconciling my old cultural values with the new values required by English writing, without losing the former.

An interesting structural but not material parallel to my experiences in this regard has been well described by Min-zhan Lu in her important article, "From Silence to Words: Writing as Struggle" (*College English* 49 [April 1987]: 437–48). Min-zhan Lu talks about struggles between two selves, an

10

open self and a secret self, and between two discourses, a mainstream Marxist discourse and a bourgeois discourse her parents wanted her to learn. But
her struggle was different from mine. Her Chinese self was severely con-
strained and suppressed by mainstream cultural discourse, but never inter-
fused with it. Her experiences, then, were not representative of those of the
majority of the younger generation who, like me, were brought up on only
one discourse. I came to English composition as a Chinese person, in the
fullest sense of the term, with a Chinese identity already fully formed.

IDENTITY OF THE MIND: ILLOGICAL AND ALOGICAL

In learning to write in English, besides wrestling with a different ideological system, I found that I had to wrestle with a logical system very different from the blueprint of logic at the back of my mind. By "logical system" I mean two things: the Chinese way of thinking I used to approach
my theme or topic in written discourse, and the Chinese critical/logical way
to develop a theme or topic. By English rules, the first is illogical, for it is
the opposite of the English way of approaching a topic; the second is alogical (non-logical), for it mainly uses mental pictures instead of words as a
critical vehicle.

The Illogical Pattern. In English composition, an essential rule for the
logical organization of a piece of writing is the use of a "topic sentence." In
Chinese composition, "from surface to core" is an essential rule, a rule
which means that one ought to reach a topic gradually and "systematically"
instead of "abruptly."

The concept of a topic sentence, it seems to me, is symbolic of the values of a busy people in an industrialized society, rushing to get things done,
hoping to attract and satisfy the busy reader very quickly. Thinking back, I
realized that I did not fully understand the virtue of the concept until my
life began to rush at the speed of everyone else's in this country. Chinese
composition, on the other hand, seems to embody the values of a leisurely
paced rural society whose inhabitants have the time to chew and taste a
topic slowly. In Chinese composition, an introduction explaining how and
why one chooses this topic is not only acceptable, but often regarded as
necessary. It arouses the reader's interest in the topic little by little (and this
is seen as a virtue of composition) and gives him/her a sense of refinement.
The famous Robert B. Kaplan "noodles" contrasting a spiral Oriental
thought process with a straight-line Western approach ("Cultural Thought
Patterns in Inter-Cultural Education," *Readings on English as a Second Language,* Ed. Kenneth Croft, 2nd ed., Winthrop, 1980, 403–10) may be too
simplistic to capture the preferred pattern of writing in English, but I think
they still express some truth about Oriental writing. A Chinese writer often

clears the surrounding bushes before attacking the real target. This bush-clearing pattern in Chinese writing goes back two thousand years to Kong Fuzi (Confucius). Before doing anything, Kong says in his *Luen Yu* (*Analects*), one first needs to call things by their proper names (expressed by his phrase "Zheng Ming"正名). In other words, before touching one's main thesis, one should first state the "conditions" of composition: how, why, and when the piece is being composed. All of this will serve as a proper foundation on which to build the "house" of the piece. In the two thousand years after Kong, this principle of composition was gradually formalized (especially through the formal essays required by imperial examinations) and became known as "Ba Gu," or the eight-legged essay. The logic of Chinese composition, exemplified by the eight-legged essay, is like the peeling of an onion: layer after layer is removed until the reader finally arrives at the central point, the core.

Ba Gu still influences modern Chinese writing. Carolyn Matalene has an excellent discussion of this logical (or illogical) structure and its influence on her Chinese students' efforts to write in English ("Contrastive Rhetoric: An American Writing Teacher in China," *College English* 47 [November 1985]: 789–808). A Chinese textbook for composition lists six essential steps (factors) for writing a narrative essay, steps to be taken in this order: time, place, character, event, cause, and consequence (*Yuwen Jichu Zhishi Liushi Jiang* [*Sixty Lessons on the Basics of the Chinese Language*], Ed. Beijing Research Institute of Education, Beijing Publishing House, 1981, 525–609). Most Chinese students (including me) are taught to follow this sequence in composition.

The straightforward approach to composition in English seemed to me, at first, illogical. One could not jump to the topic. One had to walk step by step to reach the topic. In several of my early papers I found that the Chinese approach—the bush-clearing approach—persisted, and I had considerable difficulty writing (and in fact understanding) topic sentences. In what I deemed to be topic sentences, I grudgingly gave out themes. Today, those papers look to me like Chinese papers with forced or false English openings. For example, in a narrative paper on a trip to New York, I wrote the forced/false topic sentence, "A trip to New York in winter is boring." In the next few paragraphs, I talked about the weather, the people who went with me, and so on, before I talked about what I learned from the trip. My real thesis was that one could always learn something even on a boring trip.

The Alogical Pattern. In learning English composition, I found that there was yet another cultural blueprint affecting my logical thinking. I found from my early papers that very often I was unconsciously under the influence of a Chinese critical approach called the creation of "yijing," which is

15

totally nonWestern. The direct translation of the word "yijing" is: yi, "mind or consciousness," and jing, "environment." An ancient approach which has existed in China for many centuries and is still the subject of much discussion, yijing is a complicated concept that defies a universal definition. But most critics in China nowadays seem to agree on one point, that yijing is the critical approach that separates Chinese literature and criticism from Western literature and criticism. Roughly speaking, yijing is the process of creating a pictorial environment while reading a piece of literature. Many critics in China believe that yijing is a creative process of inducing oneself, while reading a piece of literature or looking at a piece of art, to create mental pictures, in order to reach a unity of nature, the author, and the reader. Therefore, it is by its very nature both creative and critical. According to the theory, this nonverbal, pictorial process leads directly to a higher ground of beauty and morality. Almost all critics in China agree that yijing is not a process of logical thinking—it is not a process of moving from the premises of an argument to its conclusion, which is the foundation of Western criticism. According to yijing, the process of criticizing a piece of art or literary work has to involve the process of creation on the reader's part. In yijing, verbal thoughts and pictorial thoughts are one. Thinking is conducted largely in pictures and then "transcribed" into words (Ezra Pound once tried to capture the creative aspect of yijing in poems such as "In a Station of the Metro." He also tried to capture the critical aspect of it in his theory of imagism and vorticism, even though he did not know the term "yijing.") One characteristic of the yijing approach to criticism, therefore, is that it often includes a description of the created mental pictures on the part of the reader/critic and his/her mental attempt to bridge (unite) the literary work, the pictures, with ultimate beauty and peace.

In looking back at my critical papers for various classes, I discovered that I unconsciously used the approach of yijing, especially in some of my earlier papers when I seemed not yet to have been in the grip of Western logical critical approaches. I wrote, for instance, an essay entitled "Wordsworth's Sound and Imagination: The Snowdon Episode." In the major part of the essay I described the pictures that flashed in my mind while I was reading passages in Wordsworth's long poem, *The Prelude*.

> I saw three climbers (myself among them) winding up the mountain in silence "at the dead of night," absorbed in their "private thoughts." The sky was full of blocks of clouds of different colors, freely changing their shapes, like oily pigments disturbed in a bucket of water. All of a sudden, the moonlight broke the darkness "like a flash," lighting up the

mountain tops. Under the "naked moon," the band saw a vast sea of mist and vapor, a silent ocean. Then the silence was abruptly broken, and we heard the "roaring of waters, torrents, streams/Innumerable, roaring with one voice" from a "blue chasm," a fracture in the vapor of the sea. It was a joyful revelation of divine truth to the human mind: the bright, "naked" moon sheds the light of "higher reasons" and "spiritual love" upon us; the vast ocean of mist looked like a thin curtain through which we vaguely saw the infinity of nature beyond; and the sounds of roaring waters coming out of the chasm of vapor cast us into the boundless spring of imagination from the depth of the human heart. Evoked by the divine light from above, the human spring of imagination is joined by the natural spring and becomes a sustaining source of energy, feeding "upon infinity" while transcending infinity at the same time. . . .

Here I was describing my own experience more than Wordsworth's. The picture described by the poet is taken over and developed by the reader. The imagination of the author and the imagination of the reader are thus joined together. There was no "because" or "therefore" in the paper. There was little *logic*. And I thought it was (and it is) criticism. This seems to me a typical (but simplified) example of the yijing approach. (Incidentally, the instructor, a kind professor, found the paper interesting, though a bit "strange.")

In another paper of mine, "The Note of Life: Williams's 'The Orchestra,'" I found myself describing my experiences of pictures of nature while reading William Carlos Williams's poem "The Orchestra." I "painted" these fleeting pictures and described the feelings that seemed to lead me to an understanding of a harmony, a "common tone," between man and nature. A paragraph from that paper reads:

20

The poem first struck me as a musical fairy tale. With rich musical sounds in my ear, I seemed to be walking in a solitary, dense forest on a spring morning. No sound from human society could be heard. I was now sitting under a giant pine tree, ready to hear the grand concert of Nature. With the sun slowly rising from the east, the cello (the creeping creek) and the clarinet (the rustling pine trees) started with a slow overture. Enthusiastically the violinists (the twittering birds) and the French horn (the mumbling cow) "interpose[d] their voices," and the bass (bears) got in at the wrong time. The orchestra did not stop, they continued to play. The musicians of Nature do not always play in harmony. "Together, unattuned," they have to seek "a common tone" as they play along. The symphony of Nature is like the symphony of human life: both consist of random notes seeking a "common tone."

> For the symphony of life
> Love is that common tone
>   shall raise his fiery head
>   and sound his note.

Again, the logical pattern of this paper, the "pictorial criticism," is illogical to Western minds but "logical" to those acquainted with yijing. (Perhaps I should not even use the words "logical" and "think" because they are so conceptually tied up with "words" and with culturally based conceptions, and therefore very misleading if not useless in a discussion of yijing. Maybe I should simply say that yijing is neither illogical nor logical, but alogical.)

I am not saying that such a pattern of "alogical" thinking is wrong—in fact some English instructors find it interesting and acceptable—but it is very non-Western. Since I was in this country to learn the English language and English literature, I had to abandon Chinese "pictorial logic," and to learn Western "verbal logic."

If I Had to Start Again

The change is profound: through my understanding of new meanings of words like "individualism," "idealism," and "I," I began to accept the underlying concepts and values of American writing, and by learning to use "topic sentences" I began to accept a new logic. Thus, when I write papers in English, I am able to obey all the general rules of English composition. In doing this I feel that I am writing through, with, and because of a new identity. I welcome the change, for it has added a new dimension to me and to my view of the world. I am not saying that I have entirely lost my Chinese identity. In fact I feel that I will never lose it. Any time I write in Chinese, I resume my old identity, and obey the rules of Chinese composition such as "Make the 'I' modest," and "Beat around the bush before attacking the central topic." It is necessary for me to have such a Chinese identity in order to write authentic Chinese. (I have seen people who, after learning to write in English, use English logic and sentence patterning to write Chinese. They produce very awkward Chinese texts.) But when I write in English, I imagine myself slipping into a new "skin," and I let the "I" behave much more aggressively and knock the topic right on the head. Being conscious of these different identities has helped me to reconcile different systems of values and logic, and has played a pivotal role in my learning to compose in English.

Looking back, I realize that the process of learning to write in English is in fact a process of creating and defining a new identity and balancing it with the old identity. The process of learning English composition would have been easier if I had realized this earlier and consciously sought to compare the two different identities required by the two writing systems from two different cultures. It is fine and perhaps even necessary for American composition teachers to teach about topic sentences, paragraphs, the use of punctuation, documentation, and so on, but can anyone design exercises sensitive to the ideological and logical differences that students like me experience—and design them so they can be introduced at an early stage of an English composition class? As I pointed out earlier, the traditional advice "Just be yourself" is not clear and helpful to students from Korea, China, Vietnam, or India. From "Be yourself" we are likely to hear either "Forget your cultural habit of writing" or "Write as you would write in your own language." But neither of the two is what the instructor meant or what we want to do. It would be helpful if he or she pointed out the different cultural/ideological connotations of the word "I," the connotations that exist in a group-centered culture and an individual-centered culture. To sharpen the contrast, it might be useful to design papers on topics like "The Individual vs. The Group: China vs. America" or "Different 'I's' in Different Cultures."

Carolyn Matalene mentioned in her article (789) an incident concerning American businessmen who presented their Chinese hosts with gifts of cheddar cheese, not knowing that the Chinese generally do not like cheese. Liking cheddar cheese may not be essential to writing English prose, but being truly accustomed to the social norms that stand behind ideas such as the English "I" and the logical pattern of English composition—call it "compositional cheddar cheese"—is essential to writing in English. Matalene does not provide an "elixir" to help her Chinese students like English "compositional cheese," but rather recommends, as do I, that composition teachers not be afraid to give foreign students English "cheese," but to make sure to hand it out slowly, sympathetically, and fully realizing that it tastes very peculiar in the mouths of those used to a very different cuisine.

Issues for Discussion

1. In what ways do the different conventions of writing in English and in Chinese reflect the values of the "wider cultures," according to Shen?
2. Why do you think the transition from "the Chinese Self" to "the American Self" is so painful for Shen? If you have ever had to make a similar transition, what made the process easy or difficult for you?
3. Shen describes a number of specific characteristics that he finds typical of "American" and "Chinese" writing styles. Which of these characteristics do you find in "The Classroom and the Wider Culture"?

JOURNAL
OPTION

Classroom Identity

Shen explains that he had to construct a new identity, a different "I," in order to write the kinds of papers demanded by his U.S. English instructors. Do you have a distinctive classroom identity apart from the rest of your life? Freewrite on your "I" inside and outside of class.

Direct and Indirect Style

Fan Shen found that in U.S. academic culture, "good" writing is generally assumed to be assertive, direct, and logical: his teachers advised him to express his opinion; to emphasize his individuality, his "I"; to get straight to the point of his argument and build his paragraphs around "topic sentences"; to stick to his subject (in this case poetry) and avoid "alogical" associations. Although you may have encountered similar advice in writing classes, Shen's initial confusion demonstrates that these values are neither self-evident nor universal. Helen Fox, a writing specialist who has worked extensively with international students, explains why much of the world fails to share the narrowly focused, linear model of "good" writing held by academics in the United States:

> Most "non western" societies are holistic; they emphasize and value how things are interconnected, the roles that people play, the relationships they have to each other and to the natural world. In such a system, you can't understand something very well in isolation, in the abstract; thus the tendency is for speakers or writers to give contextual and emotional information, to fill the audience in on the big picture, to help them feel the way the author felt in such a situation.[2]

Studies by linguists, as well as the stories of students and writers from many cultural backgrounds, show the wide variety of forms "good" writing can take. We saw in Chapter 1 how Leslie Marmon Silko contrasts the linear organization of traditional storytelling in English to the weblike structure of Pueblo storytelling. In many African cultures the sound of a speaker's or writer's words can be as important as the words' meaning, and audiences admire verbal play; someone who goes directly to the main point is seen as having little style or skill in language. Likewise, writers of Spanish and Por-

---

[2] Helen Fox, *Listening to the World: Cultural Issues in Academic Writing* (Urbana, Ill.: NCTE, 1994), p. 27.

tuguese often favor more ornate language, may consciously digress from the main point, and tend to repeat important ideas for emphasis. Formal non-linear structures are popular in both Japanese and Korean writing: four-part essay forms, called *ki-shoo-ten-ketsu* in Japan and *ki-sung-chon-kyul* in Korea, devote the third part of the essay to digressions from the main theme. Arabic writing is frequently organized by metaphor and association rather than linear logic; following the model of the Qu'ran, poetry is considered the highest and most persuasive form of argument a Saudi writer can present. Writers in these cultures can think just as logically as anyone else, but straightforward logic and linear organization may seem rather uninteresting or even simpleminded to them.

Because cultural values differ so widely, the definition of effective writing will vary tremendously depending on where you are and who you're writing for. Here, for example, are the first few sentences of the prefaces to two introductory college physics texts, one American and one Chinese:

> University Physics is intended to provide a broad introduction to physics at the beginning college level for students in science and engineering who are taking an introductory calculus course concurrently.

> Nature is infinitely wide, prosperous and colorful, in which all matter of all kinds and forms are in constant motion and change. What is matter? Big as heavenly bodies such as the sun, the moon and the stars; small as tiny particles, atoms, electrons are all matter.[3]

Given your acquaintance with your own college textbooks and with Fan Shen's essay, you probably easily identified the first passage as the American example and the second passage as the Chinese. The American author gets down to nuts and bolts immediately, identifying the book's purpose, naming its target audience, and even specifying another course the reader ought to be enrolled in. The Chinese author, on the other hand, chooses to "walk step by step to reach the topic," as Shen describes; this preface doesn't even mention physics explicitly until the third paragraph.

Which introduction is better? It depends on your values and expectations. If you don't want to waste any time on unnecessary information, you probably appreciate the American writer's conciseness. On the other hand, if you prefer to be drawn in gradually, to get a sense of the larger context of physics as a field of study, you may prefer the Chinese writer's approach. We actually prefer the Chinese passage. And this illustrates what makes a

---

[3] Both texts quoted by Nancy Duke S. Lay and Gao Jie, "Chinese Rhetorical Patterns Re-examined." Unpublished manuscript.

writer's job tricky: as American academics, we should favor straightforward prose—and in general we do—but as nonphysicists we're not automatically intrigued by the subject of this textbook, and our interest needs to be aroused. Moreover, as people who study language and literature, we appreciate the Chinese writer's way with words—his flowing sentences and appealing imagery. So knowing something about your specific audience is just as important as knowing something about the general culture you're writing in. This brings us back to the importance of flexibility, of getting beyond formulas. The best strategy for you as a writer is not to look for one set of rules to apply in every situation but to develop a variety of strategies to use depending on what's likely to be effective in the particular context. Here's an activity to help you expand your range of strategies.

OPTIONAL ACTIVITY

Trying a New Style

Review your earlier drafts and essays: Do you tend to write in a more direct or a more indirect style? Do you plunge right into the subject or lead into it gradually? Do you assert your ideas forcefully or avoid taking a stand? Is your "I" bold or modest? Do you spell out ideas explicitly or express them through images and metaphors? If it's too hard to identify these characteristics in your own writing, exchange papers with a partner and inventory each other's use of direct and indirect strategies.

Once you've completed your inventory, choose a paragraph that shows particularly strong evidence of your typical style and try rewriting it in the opposite way. Try a more direct or a more gradual beginning. If your language is very literal, try expressing the same idea through metaphors or images; if you're typically metaphoric, "translate" the figures of speech into direct prose. If your "I" is everywhere, try toning it down; if it's hard to find, make it more visible and assertive.

Share the direct and indirect versions of your paragraph in small groups, or do a read-around. Which version do your readers prefer and why? Can you think of different situations in which each version might be appropriate?

Beyond the Five-Paragraph Essay

Preference for the direct style of self-expression has deep roots in American culture. The Puritans, who founded Plymouth Plantation in 1621, were particularly fond of a direct, unadorned approach in sermons and religious tracts. They rebelled against the elaborate, self-consciously witty style of religious writing popular in seventeenth-century Europe. Instead, they adopted a "plain style" in their sermons. Aiming at clarity rather than elaboration, they wrote in the common, everyday language of farmers, merchants, and craftsmen. Likewise, they structured their sermons as simply and directly as possible, most often in three parts. Sermons began with a straightforward statement of a religious "truth" or ideal, frequently taken directly from the Bible. Next came several arguments expanding on and supporting this main lesson. Finally, the conclusion offered a series of practical suggestions for applying the lesson in daily life.

Four centuries later, American students are still taught to write a form of essay that bears an uncanny resemblance to these early Puritan sermons—the five-paragraph essay. It's such a familiar formula that you may readily recognize a five-paragraph essay even if you've never written one. The short version of the formula is, "Tell 'em what you're going to say, say it, then tell 'em what you just said." The slightly more elaborate version goes like this:

Paragraph 1: Introduce the general subject of the essay, state your thesis or argument, and list three supporting points you will develop in the body of the essay.

Paragraphs 2–4: Devote each body paragraph to one of the three points mentioned in the introduction. A topic sentence should state the main point of each paragraph, and that point should be supported by one or more specific examples. The body paragraphs can be linked by introducing them with words or phrases indicating sequence, such as "First, . . . Second, . . . Third, . . ." or "For example, . . . Furthermore, . . . In addition, ..."

Paragraph 5: Signal your conclusion ("In conclusion, . . ."), restate your thesis, and summarize the three points you made in the body of the essay.

Many teachers, recognizing that their students need to learn a direct linear style for academic purposes, recommend the five-paragraph essay as a model of that style. Established patterns of writing, because they're familiar and recognizable, can facilitate communication—they can help the reader understand your purpose and follow you more readily. However, such patterns can also become traps. When followed too closely, they can become empty formalities. The five-paragraph essay is a case in point. It is what Robert Holland refers to as an *eidolon* or false image of academic style. Following this formula may ensure that your essay will be clearly organized, but it's also likely to inhibit careful thinking and critical analysis. At its worst it becomes an empty form to be filled up, like the falsified lab reports in Holland's chemistry class.

To demonstrate what we mean, we've reworked Fan Shen's complex essay to show you what it might look like if he had confined himself to the five-paragraph formula. As much as possible, the sentences and sequence of ideas are taken directly from Fan Shen. Take a few minutes to skim the original essay so that it's clear in your memory as you read this version. Besides length, what differences do you see between the two?

The Classroom and the Wider Culture

(five-paragraph version)

In this paper I will try to describe and explore the experience of reconciling my Chinese identity with an English identity dictated by the rules of English composition. I want to show how my cultural background shaped--and shapes--my approaches to my writing in English and how writing in English redefined--and redefines--my identity. Starting with the first English paper I wrote, I found that learning the rules of English composition is, to a certain extent, learning the values of Anglo-American society. These rules and values conflicted with three aspects of my identity: the image or meaning that I attached to the word "I" or "myself," the Chinese way of thinking I used to approach my theme or topic in written discourse, and the Chinese critical/logical way to develop a theme or topic.

Rule number one in English composition is: Be yourself. The values behind this rule, it seems to me, are based on the principle of protecting and promoting individuality (and private property) in this country. In China, on the other hand, "I" is always subordinated to "We"--be it the working class, the Party, the country, or some other collective body. For a long time the words "self" and "individualism" have had nega-

tive connotations in my mind. Now, in America, I had to learn
to accept the words "I" and "Self" as something glorious. To
be truly "myself," which I knew was a key to my success in
learning English composition, meant not to be my Chinese self
at all.

In English composition, a second essential rule for the
logical organization of a piece of writing is the use of a
"topic sentence." The concept of a topic sentence, it seems to
me, is symbolic of the values of a busy people in an industrialized society, rushing to get things done, hoping to attract
and satisfy the reader very quickly. Chinese composition, on
the other hand, seems to embody the values of a leisurely
paced rural society whose inhabitants have the time to chew
and taste a topic slowly. In Chinese composition, an introduction explaining how and why one chooses this topic is not only
acceptable, but often regarded as necessary. It arouses the
reader's interest in the topic little by little (and this is
seen as a virtue of composition) and gives him/her a sense of
refinement. In several of my early papers I found that the
Chinese approach--the bush-clearing approach--persisted, and I
had considerable difficulty writing (and in fact understanding) topic sentences.

In learning English composition, I found that there was
still another cultural blueprint affecting my logical thinking. I found from my early papers that very often I was unconsciously under the influence of a Chinese critical approach
called the creation of "yijing," which is totally non-Western.
Roughly speaking, yijing is the process of creating a pictorial environment while reading a piece of literature. Almost
all critics in China agree that yijing is not a process of
logical thinking--it is not a process of moving from the
premises of an argument to its conclusion, which is the foundation of Western criticism. In yijing, thinking is conducted

largely in pictures and then "transcribed" into words. In looking back at my critical papers for various classes, I discovered that I unconsciously used the approach of yijing. But since I was in this country to learn the English language and English literature, I had to abandon Chinese "pictorial logic" and to learn Western "verbal logic."

In conclusion, I began to accept the underlying concepts and values of American writing: I learned new meanings for words like "I," learned to use topic sentences, and learned to write about literature using verbal logic. In doing this, I feel that I am writing through, with, and because of a new identity.

What's wrong with this? In many ways it's a very good essay: it's clearly organized; it establishes the main theme right away (the close connection between culture, writing style, and identity); and it then illustrates this theme through three interesting examples of culturally based differences between Chinese and American writing. But when you look back at the original, you can begin to see how dramatically the five-paragraph format simplifies Shen's thoughtful, complex essay. Because the five-paragraph version is so much shorter, the ideas are by definition less fully developed. In particular, this formula doesn't allow for the extended examples Shen includes in his essay—examples that illustrate the profound differences between the two identities he must learn to project in his writing. The one-paragraph treatment of yijing can give only an abstract idea of the "pictorial logic" of Chinese literary criticism, while the original essay includes passages that clearly demonstrate this form of analysis in action. The five-paragraph format also fails to examine the connections between the ideas set out in its three body paragraphs; the discussion of topic sentences and the description of yijing, for example, are treated as completely separate "points" of difference between Chinese and American writing. In the longer essay, though, Shen is able to link both points to an underlying cultural difference in Chinese and American patterns of logic. The disconnectedness of the five-paragraph essay is again a weakness that's built into the formula itself: it's essentially nothing more than a three-item list expanded into three paragraphs and bracketed by an introduction and a conclusion. With little imagination, you could turn a grocery list into the outline for a five-paragraph essay: instant coffee, Whammo Flakes, toilet paper. But to engage in academic analysis, you'd need to explore the significance of the grocery list, to discover connections between these apparently unrelated items and then use them to make a clear point—perhaps about the history of consumer culture or the environmental cost of "convenience" products.

Experimenting with Form: Parody

In order to probe the strengths and limitations of a particular form of writing—or to free themselves from it—professional writers will sometimes parody that form. A parody imitates and critiques a well-known form of writing or art by making fun of its conventions. Parodists target everything from high art to popular culture: television comedy shows like *Saturday Night Live* and *MAD TV* spend much of their time parodying popular TV formats like game shows, talk shows, and infomercials. Movie parodies like the *Police Academy* series have been around for decades; even rock music has its parodists, thanks to performers like Randy Newman and Weird Al Yankovich. Here's a chance to try your hand at a parody of the five-paragraph essay.

OPTIONAL
ACTIVITY

Five-Paragraph Parody

Work in pairs to draft a mock five-paragraph essay on the topic of how college differs from high school. Be sure to follow all of the form's conventions: focus on a single main idea, stated in the introduction; then devote three body paragraphs to the three "points" illustrating your main idea; finish up with a summary or restatement of your theme.

Now critique the product: What aspects of your experience did the five-paragraph format force you to simplify or omit? Was forcing yourself to follow the formula helpful in any way? Compare notes with your classmates: How did this form of writing shape or limit your thinking?

ESSAY
OPTIONS

Academic Profile

Now it's time to do some in-depth investigation of an aspect of academic culture that you'd like to know more about. This set of writing options, like those in the last chapter, asks you to interview and profile a cultural insider—this time someone who's part of the academic community. As we mentioned before, the quality of the interview can make or break the essay. Please review the suggestions for "Successful Interviewing" in Chapter 6 (p. 161) before you set up an appointment with the person you plan to profile.

Topic 1. Interview a professor or graduate student who works in an academic discipline that interests you and write a profile of your interviewee as a professional in her or his field.

Topic 2. Interview one or more advanced students who consider themselves academically successful. According to your informants, what constitutes academic success? What conflicts or obstacles has college life posed and how have they addressed them?

Topic 3. Some colleges require students to do community service as part of their degree programs. Interview one or more students who have been active in a community service project for a year or more. Based on your informants' experiences, what would you say are some of the benefits and drawbacks (personal, academic, or otherwise) of being involved in community service as a college student?

Preparing for the Academic Profile

As in your preparation for the cultural interview, you'll need to think carefully about the questions you want to ask, no matter which of the essay options you choose. Because the focus of the profile in Topic 1 is more specialized, though, your questions should concentrate more narrowly on your interviewee's academic life. To help you get started, here are some sample interview questions for the first topic:

- What initially attracted you to this area of study? Can you recall a particular teacher or experience that motivated you?

- Why is it important for people to study or do research in your field?

- What kinds of misconceptions do people have about your field?

- What kind of research are you currently doing? What do you hope to find?

- What are some of the important current debates among scholars in this field? What's your position?

Work in groups to brainstorm further interview questions for this topic and for each of the other essay options.

In addition to the interview itself, you might ask your informant to allow you to observe her or him at work. If you're interviewing a professor or graduate student, try to visit her classroom, laboratory, or studio or look up an article she's published and peruse it. If your interviewee is a successful undergraduate, see if you can sit in on a study group with him. If you're talking to a student involved in community service, find out if it's possible to assist her for an hour or two in her volunteer work. This kind of firsthand observation can provide insights into your interviewee's personality and professional life that you might not get from an interview alone; it can also give you the kinds of details that lend interest and depth to a profile. For example, Andrew Thanh Tran effectively uses observed detail to introduce his profile of a biochemistry student:

> Young Nguyen was frustrated by the complex process of separating DNA sequence. For two long hours in the laboratory, he was still trying to figure out what went wrong with his result. He is a meticulous man, always trying to follow exactly the procedure from his lab guidance manual. He knew his data were inconsistent with what he had predicted. Young decided to run the experiment again on the gel electrophoresis, a device which separates DNA sequence into small fragments. Carefully placing his sample into a test tube, he proceeded with care to the gel electrophoresis machine. He then laid it on a disk and switched on the power of the electrophoresis. The disk started to spin centrifugally, accelerating quickly for 15 minutes and then slowly coming to a stop. Young removed his sample from the gel-phoresis, placed it on his labtop desk, and added a few drips of chemical liquid onto a glass slide to form a thin film. Then he began to scrutinize his specimen under a microscope. . . . What he saw is still fascinating and exciting to him today.

Tran has skillfully woven together material from his interview—the story of Nguyen's past experience with a difficult DNA experiment—with his firsthand observation of Nguyen performing a similar procedure in the lab. Beginning the essay like this took not only skill but some imagination and perhaps a little courage. Tran could have begun with an explicit statement of his thesis, as the five-paragraph formula dictates: "In this paper, I will show the challenges and demands of biochemical research through the experience of Young Nguyen, a graduate student in biochemistry." Instead he chooses a different approach, one more like the "you are there" style of a magazine or newspaper writer. In this case, the risk pays off. The immediacy of the lab scene gets the reader involved in the subject, and the descriptive style is appropriate for a profile, which aims to give a close-up view of an individual's character, life, or work.

By opening with this vivid example of biochemical research in action, Tran introduces the reader both to Nguyen and to some of the methods of biochemistry as an academic field. We see the patience and precision Nguyen must have in order to obtain accurate results from his experiment, the double-checking of data required by scientific procedure, and the excitement of studying DNA. Without stating his purpose explicitly, Tran clearly lets the reader know that his paper is going to focus on Young Nguyen's work as a biochemist. Unlike the passage from the American physics text quoted earlier (p. 187), which illustrates the direct style at its dullest, this paragraph demonstrates that it's possible to write both directly and engagingly about academic concerns. As you work on the drafts of your academic profile, remember that direct style has more to do with choosing and maintaining a clear focus than with following a particular formula. In the revision workshop that follows, we'll show you how several student writers worked to develop and clarify their own profiles.

CHAPTER 8

Revision Workshop: Writing for Others

Writing across Differences

Have you ever had the experience of agonizing for hours over a short paper for an American history or English class and then, maybe even the same day, dashing off a long letter to a cousin or a friend with no difficulty at all? Why is it so much easier to write a letter than a formal paper? There's obviously a lot less pressure: your friend isn't about to give you a grade and probably won't complain if you misspell a few words. And you probably have a much clearer image of the reader in mind when you write to a friend: you already know her background, her likes and dislikes, her sense of humor—you even have a relatively accurate idea about what she knows about and expects from you. Writing to someone who shares your experience and values is often relatively easy, because you have a strong intuitive sense of what your reader knows and believes.

But the situation changes when you write to someone you don't know as well—someone whose background or interests or point of view may be very different from your own. Some students try to sidestep these differences by confining themselves to polite generalizations that most readers would recognize and accept as conventional wisdom. But in a culture that values assertiveness and individual opinion, this is likely to be a losing strategy. Other students optimistically assume, or hope, that the reader is a lot like they are and will therefore understand them perfectly, or they write as if they were addressing a super-reader—someone, like a teacher, who knows more about the writer's topic than the writer herself. In practice, however, writing and reading seldom work this way. People usually resort to writing because they feel or know something that may be valuable to the reader, and—at least in Western culture—it's valuable precisely because the reader *doesn't* already know it. Readers steeped in the culture of individualism seek out what's new and original. Who, they reason, would bother to read a book containing absolutely no surprises, nothing to be learned, no mysteries to be solved? In this situation, then, writers and readers face each other across a cultural divide: a writer has knowledge that makes her part of a special community of "knowers" of intellectual culture; a reader is an outsider, an "other" who wants to gain access to that culture. It's the writer's task to guide the reader as she moves into unfamiliar territory and to help her make sense of the terrain.

The essay options offered in Chapters 6 and 7 challenge you to bridge this cultural divide. If you've interviewed a Tongan immigrant or someone who teaches archeology or mathematics (as the student writers in this chapter have done), you almost certainly understand that person's experiences, values, and ideas better than your writing instructor and classmates would. Your job, then, is to help your teacher and your peers grasp the significance of what you learned from your interviewee—to help your readers, in effect, share the knowledge you gained. The rest of this chapter addresses some of the challenges you face when you write to "others," and it also offers some suggestions for revising your paper with the reader in mind.

OPTIONAL ACTIVITY

The Reader as "Other"

Do a series of freewrites describing what your interviewee has to teach your teacher, your classmates, and other readers who are unfamiliar with the person's life or work but who might have some interest in the subject.

The Need to Know: Defining and Explaining

During your interview, you may have had to ask your interviewee to explain a term or clarify a concept that was unfamiliar to you. But what happens when you run across something you don't understand while you're reading and the author isn't there to explain it? Think about a time when you picked up an article on an unfamiliar subject and tried to read it. Maybe it was about computers or basketball or the art world. How much did the writer take for granted that you would know about the subject? Was the article written for novices or experts? Did the writer define specialized terminology or just assume that you were familiar with the language of computers, sports, or art? Did your prior knowledge help you understand the article, or did lack of familiarity with the subject interfere with your understanding? In a sense, specialized terms are condensed stories. But as we've seen, even a few pages of writing or a short conversation can contain many possible condensed stories. Which condensed story or stories you choose to open up, the way you explain them, and how much detail you include—all these choices depend on what you think your reader knows and what you're trying to accomplish in your paper.

Earlier we talked about writer responsibility in academic culture—the writer's obligation to make the reader's job easier. This often involves defining terms and explaining concepts that may be new to your audience. In a sense, you need to spell out the condensed stories that specialized language contains. In academic life, people tend to be very knowledgeable in specialized areas and often converse with each other in language that's confusing or opaque to outsiders. Even terms that you think you know may have different connotations in a particular academic field. For example, any psychologist immediately understands that "projection" refers to the unconscious attribution of one's own feelings or motives to someone else. To an economist or a film historian, though, "projection" means something entirely different. If you know that you're addressing a group of fellow specialists or cultural insiders—people who share the same knowledge and vocabulary—there's probably no need to define your terms. However, if your readers might include cultural outsiders—nonspecialists, or specialists from different fields—you'll need to spell things out. Let's look at how and why some of the writers we've encountered have chosen to explain particular terms for their readers.

How Can I Explain It? Some Strategies

1. One of the simplest and most direct approaches is to offer a more familiar **synonym** for the specialized term, as Robert Holland does here:

> "the academic writer may choose an *eidolon,* a 'dream image' of academic discourse; furthermore, he or she may be quite unaware of having made such a choice."

Holland assumes (with good reason) that relatively few of us share his knowledge of classical Greek literature, so he politely and unobtrusively lets us know that *eidolon* means "dream image." What effect would a longer or less subtle explanation have in this passage? For example, Holland could have written "the academic writer may choose an *eidolon* of academic discourse. *Webster's* defines *eidolon* as 'an image without real existence; phantom; apparition.' Furthermore, he or she may be quite unaware of having made such a choice." Which strategy works better and why?

2. Another strategy, one used by Andrew Tran in the introduction to his academic profile, is to explain something unfamiliar by describing its **purpose:**

> "Young decided to run the experiment again on the gel electrophoresis, a device which separates DNA sequence into small fragments."

In this case, giving a simple synonym—like *eidolon* = dream image—wouldn't work because you can't explain electrophoresis in a word or two. Here's how *Webster's* describes it: "the movement of colloidal particles suspended in a fluid toward the electrodes in the fluid, through which an electric current is passed, with the resulting collection of the particles at the electrodes." Aside from the bulkiness of this definition, why do you think Tran chose to emphasize the purpose of the experiment (separating DNA) rather than simply repeat the dictionary definition of "electrophoresis"?

3. In the next passage, Clyde Kluckhohn defines by **contrast**, distinguishing the specialized anthropological meaning of the word *culture* from a more common one:

> This technical term has a wider meaning than the "culture" of history and literature. A humble cooking pot is as much a cultural product as is a Beethoven sonata. In ordinary speech "people of culture" are those who can speak languages other than their own, who are familiar with history, literature, philosophy, or the fine arts. To the anthropologist, however, to be human is to be cultured.

4. Kluckhohn also illustrates the difference between the two meanings of "culture" with an **example** (the cooking pot versus the sonata), a strategy he repeats throughout the essay and one of the most effective methods of explanation. If you remember anything at all about Kluckhohn's essay, you probably remember his examples: the American boy who was culturally Chinese, the woman who served her guests rattlesnake meat. Notice that Kluckhohn spends a lot more time explaining *culture* than Tran devotes to *electrophoresis,* even though the scientific term is probably familiar to fewer readers: Is Kluckhohn just being a long-winded professor? What other reasons might he have for including so much detail?

5. In defining *yijing,* Fan Shen first translates the term from Chinese to English, much as Holland "translates" *eidolon* into more familiar language:

> "The direct translation of the word 'yijing' is: yi, 'mind or consciousness,' and jing, 'environment.'"

Like Kluckhohn, Shen also defines by contrast and example, distinguishing the "pictorial logic" of yijing from the Western verbal logic his readers are likely to be familiar with and illustrating the difference with extended passages from his own yijing-style essays. However, he also bolsters his explanation by referring to established **authority**—Chinese scholars who have studied the subject:

> Many critics in China believe that yijing is a creative process of inducing oneself, while reading a piece of literature or looking at a piece of art, to create mental pictures, in order to reach a unity of nature, the author, and the reader. Therefore, it is by its very nature both creative and critical. According to the theory, this nonverbal, pictorial process leads directly to a higher ground of beauty and morality. Almost all critics in China agree that yijing is not a process of logical thinking—it is not a process of moving from the premises of an argument to its conclusion, which is the foundation of Western criticism.

Why do you think Shen refers to the opinions of "many critics" and "almost all critics," while Kluckhohn doesn't rely on authorities in the same way? Note that Kluckhohn does briefly quote anthropologist Ruth Benedict at the end of his own discussion of culture. How does this citation of another scholar differ from Shen's? Both writers offer extended, elaborate definitions of a single term: Do you think they do this for the same reasons? How might their purposes differ?

OPTIONAL
ACTIVITY

Working with Definitions

Find a term in one of your drafts that you think is likely to be unfamiliar to the readers you want to address. Try defining or explaining it several different ways: try out some of the individual strategies illustrated above, then write a more extended explanation using several strategies in combination, as Kluckhohn and Shen do in their essays. Share your definitions in a small group and evaluate which ones are clearest and most useful. Is there any consensus among the readers about which of your definitions works the best?

Revision Case Study: Clarifying for Readers

Let's take a look at the way one student, Christie Sanchez, revised a passage in her academic profile in order to help nonspecialist readers understand the professional work of Rebecca Scarpelli, a graduate student in public health education. In these two paragraphs, Sanchez describes the role of science and scholarship in the field of public health education.

Draft

```
    Since public health education basically deals with dis-
ease, its distribution in the population, and its prevention,
epidemiology is an important factor in this field of work. It
is also important to study the many types of social problems
which play a major role in these people's health or risk of
disease.
    In order for scientists to support an argument or find
validity in this field of work, they use morbidity and mortal-
ity rates and study if these rates decrease in number. Also, a
decrease in illness or in death would help to show if the pro-
grams helped . . .
```

Unless you're already familiar with the field of public health education, these paragraphs raise more questions than they answer. What is epidemiology? How is it an "important factor" in public health education? What are the "social problems" that affect public health, and how do they play a role in "risk of disease"? What are morbidity and mortality rates? What's their connection to the "programs" mentioned in the last line? What programs is she referring to? In her revision, Sanchez is careful to define specialized terms and give examples that clarify the relationship between epidemiological studies and the work done by public health educators like Scarpelli.

Now take a close look at the passage as Sanchez revised it: Where and how does she answer each of the questions raised by the draft? As a reader, do you have any other questions that she fails to address? If so, how would you revise the passage further in order to address them?

Revision

```
    Since public health education basically deals with dis-
ease, its distribution in the population, and its prevention,
```

epidemiology is an important factor in this field of work because it studies the distribution and causes of disease in population groups rather than in individuals. Epidemiologists also study the variations of disease in relation to factors such as age, sex, race, occupational and social characteristics, place of residence, susceptibility, exposure to specific agents, or other factors. Then from these studies, the educators can distinguish which groups are at greater risk so they can in turn educate those at high risk.

In order for scientists to support an argument or find validity in this field of work, they use morbidity and mortality rates and study if these rates decrease in number after the programs are established. The number of people in a community with heart attacks, lung cancer, high blood pressure, or AIDS would be an example of morbidity rates. The number of deaths in a community would be an example of mortality rates. Public health educators would study these rates to see which of the problems in the community have the highest morbidity and mortality rates and then plan their programs accordingly. For example, if 40 percent of the problem in a community was lung cancer, they would plan programs to educate smokers about the dangers of smoking and the different ways to quit before it is too late. There are many types of programs for exercise, diet, smoking, and so forth in the East Los Angeles community hospital where Rebecca works. Here, patients are referred to her by doctors who feel that their patients need proper education through these programs. A decrease in illness or in death would help to show if the programs helped . . .

The examples Sanchez has added work hard: they not only illustrate the meanings of terms like *epidemiology, morbidity rates,* and *mortality rates* but also enhance the profile of Scarpelli by giving us a clearer image of what her work involves and why it's important. The revision elaborates and explains the connections among several stories that are crucial to understanding what Scarpelli does—stories that were so condensed in the draft that they were invisible. For instance, there's a story about smokers who need to learn more about the dangers of lung cancer, one about doctors who refer patients to programs that educate them about the risks of smoking, and another about public health educators who study information about disease and death in a community in order to plan programs that will improve public health. What other condensed stories has Sanchez clarified in her revision, and how do they contribute to the portrait of Rebecca Scarpelli and her work?

Revising Your Draft: Expanding and Connecting

Working with a partner, exchange drafts of your cultural portraits or academic profiles. As you read through your partner's draft, jot down any questions you have about terms that need to be defined, condensed stories that require explanation, or connections that need to be clarified. Then revise your draft, trying to respond to your reader's questions by defining, explaining, and giving examples as Sanchez does in her revision.

Reader-Friendly Paragraphs: Shaping and Focusing

Paragraphs serve as another aid to readers by separating the text on the page into more manageable chunks and giving visual cues about how the various parts of your paper relate to each other. You might think of yourself as a chef and your paper as a multicourse meal: you probably wouldn't serve appetizer, soup, salad, pasta, vegetable, fish, wine, fruit, cheese, cake, and coffee by throwing everything together in a big pot and plunking the whole mess in front of your horrified guests. Some of the flavors wouldn't blend; others would be entirely lost in the jumble. And aside from this assault on the taste buds, the mere size of the concoction would make most diners queasy. Organizing your paper into paragraphs is a bit like serving a meal in courses: each dish contains only ingredients that work well together; the sequence of different foods creates an interesting variety; and each portion is big enough to be satisfying but small enough to be easily digested.

So how do you become a skillful chef of the written word—what makes a paragraph a paragraph? Paragraph divisions are often described as a way to indicate a "new idea," but this definition can be more confusing than helpful. If every paragraph truly introduced a brand-new idea, the paper would have little focus. So if everything in the paper clearly relates to a central point (as it should in the direct style), then how can you tell where one idea ends and a "new" one begins? Often, especially in academic papers, you'll need to discuss a complex idea that requires lengthy explanation: Does that mean that you just keep going without a paragraph break for as long as it takes to explain the point? In this situation, writers following the "new idea" definition of the paragraph can end up with paragraphs two or three pages long! The "new idea" test can also lead to the opposite problem—short, choppy paragraphs. Since every sentence should add a little new information (otherwise a paper will never get anywhere), writers who interpret very slight shifts of direction as "new ideas" can end up with a string of one-sentence paragraphs.

It's more accurate, and more useful, to think of a new paragraph as a graphic aid that tells readers to pause for a moment before reading on; all you need is a reason to pause and a sensible place to do it. Let's take a closer look at why and where you might make a paragraph break.

Why Paragraph?

To highlight relationships between ideas. When you cluster a series of sentences into a paragraph, you're saying that they relate to each other in a particular way. So beginning a new paragraph may indicate that you want readers to stop and notice a change in the direction, focus, or emphasis of the essay, or to reflect on one point before moving on to the next. Any slight shift of attention in the text can be a logical place to begin a new paragraph: a change in time or place, a movement from general discussion to specific example (or vice versa), a shift of focus from one example to a different one, from one aspect of a topic to another—all of these present possible places to start a new paragraph. But just because a new paragraph is possible, that doesn't mean it's always necessary.

To emphasize a particularly important point. By putting a crucial definition, question, description, or statement in a paragraph by itself, you effectively call readers' attention to it, especially if this paragraph is noticeably shorter than those that surround it.

To provide a visual break. You may simply pause in order to give readers' eyes and attention a brief rest in a lengthy discussion. The length of the "average" paragraph depends on the context you're writing in. Newspaper journalists typically write very short paragraphs to make it easy for casual readers to skim a story and pick up the essential information quickly. Scholars writing in academic journals usually compose much bulkier paragraphs because they can assume that their readers are more willing to devote time and effort to keeping up with new ideas in their field.

To conform to a typographic convention. Finally, there are times when you insert a paragraph break simply because it's customary and expected—after the greeting in a letter, for example. Also, when you're writing or transcribing a conversation, it's conventional in English to begin a new paragraph each time the speaker changes—it helps readers keep track of who's saying what.

Paragraphs and Paragraph Clusters

In order to see how these principles work in practice, let's look at a passage from Rodney Guerrero's academic profile of Julia Sanchez, a graduate student in archaeology. As you can see from the three versions that follow, the passage could work as a single paragraph, or two, or three.

One-Paragraph Version

Archaeology is a very intense profession. In order to analyze collected data, which includes pieces of pottery, sharpened stones, and remains of structures, archaeologists must have an understanding of many other fields. For example, archaeologists trying to develop a hypothesis about what a certain culture hunted or gathered must have an understanding of zoology and botany. They would then be able to identify the animal or plant a specific bone or seed originated from. A reconnaissance team is sent into a possible dig site before the actual equipment and supplies. Their goal is to scan the ground for clues, such as large mounds of soil, to where artifacts are possibly buried. Experienced archaeologists can sometimes even determine if an area was occupied by simply examining the different layers of soil. In Belize, a site where Julia worked to study the Mayan culture, excavation turned up a number of broken ceramics. After using microscopes to examine the burnt material on these pieces of pottery, her crew was able to determine that the Mayans ate maize. What might seem to be an ordinary chipped rock can possibly give archaeologists clues about what a former culture hunted. This is possible, for if it is determined that the stone was once used as a spear point, then the size of the rock will give clues to the size of the animal that was being hunted.

Two-Paragraph Version

Archaeology is a very intense profession. In order to analyze collected data, which includes pieces of pottery, sharpened stones, and remains of structures, archaeologists must have an understanding of many other fields. For example, archaeologists trying to develop a hypothesis about what a certain culture hunted or gathered must have an understanding of zoology and botany. They would then be able to identify the animal or plant a specific bone or seed originated from.

A reconnaissance team is sent into a possible dig site before the actual equipment and supplies. Their goal is to scan the ground for clues, such as large mounds of soil, to where artifacts are possibly buried. Experienced archaeologists can sometimes even determine if an area was occupied by simply examining the different layers of soil. In Belize, a site where Julia worked to study the Mayan culture, excavation turned up a number of broken ceramics. After using microscopes to examine the burnt material on these pieces of pottery, her crew was able to determine that the Mayans ate maize. What might seem to be an ordinary chipped rock can possibly give archaeologists clues about what a former culture hunted. This is possible, for if it is determined that the stone was once used as a spear point, then the size of the rock will give clues to the size of the animal that was being hunted.

Three-Paragraph Version

Archaeology is a very intense profession. In order to analyze collected data, which includes pieces of pottery, sharpened stones, and remains of structures, archaeologists must have an understanding of many other fields. For example, archaeologists trying to develop a hypothesis about what a certain culture hunted or gathered must have an understanding of zoology and botany. They would then be able to identify the animal or plant a specific bone or seed originated from.

A reconnaissance team is sent into a possible dig site before the actual equipment and supplies. Their goal is to scan the ground for clues, such as large mounds of soil, to where artifacts are possibly buried. Experienced archaeologists can sometimes even determine if an area was occupied by simply examining the different layers of soil.

In Belize, a site where Julia worked to study the Mayan culture, excavation turned up a number of broken ceramics. After using microscopes to examine the burnt material on these pieces of pottery, her crew was able to determine that the Mayans ate maize. What might seem to be an ordinary chipped rock can possibly give archaeologists clues about what a former culture hunted. This is possible, for if it is determined that the stone was once used as a spear point, then the size of the rock will give clues to the size of the animal that was being hunted.

In the first version of this passage, the opening statement, "Archaeology is a very intense profession," is clearly the central point—the organizing idea of the paragraph as a whole. All the details, including the kinds of data archaeologists study, the knowledge they must have of fields like zoology and botany, their methods of finding sites and analyzing artifacts, become examples of the wide-ranging, complex work that makes archaeology "intense." The second version separates the discussion of archaeologists' academic training (knowledge of other fields like zoology and botany) from the description of their work in the field (identifying a dig site, excavating and analyzing artifacts). The third version breaks things down even further by dividing the description of fieldwork into two stages: one paragraph is devoted to preparation for the dig (the reconnaissance team searches for mounds and examines soil strata for evidence of former inhabitation), while the next paragraph focuses on the excavation itself and what archaeologists learn from the artifacts they find (like Mayan pottery or a stone spear point).

What rationales can you think of for the paragraph divisions in each version? What's the effect of breaking down the description of archaeological work into smaller components? Do certain details stand out more in one version than in another? Does the paragraph in the first version seem too long? Do the paragraphs in the second or third versions seem too short? Which version do you prefer and why?

Notice that in the two- and three-paragraph versions, the statement, "Archaeology is a very intense profession," still serves as an introduction to the whole passage—in effect, it leads into a pair or a cluster of closely related paragraphs. If you have trouble breaking up long passages into more manageable paragraphs because everything seems so closely related, it might make your job easier to think in terms of paragraph pairs and clusters rather than individual paragraphs.

OPTIONAL ACTIVITY

Playing with Paragraphs

Here's another passage from a student paper, this time a cultural profile. For this paper, Erica Montiel interviewed her friend Manu Langi, whose family immigrated to the United States from the Pacific Islands nation of Tonga. The original paragraph divisions have been removed. Where would you insert paragraph breaks and why? Do you see any potential paragraph pairs or clusters in this passage?

Parents in Tonga have a distinct authoritative role in raising their children. Tongan parents take the responsibility of child-rearing very seriously because children in Tonga are seen as a direct reflection of their parents. A misbehaved child is not blamed for his/her actions; it is the child's parents who are looked down upon for not raising their child responsibly. Tongan children are therefore raised to respect and obey their parents. A child's misbehavior is reprimanded through strict disciplinary actions, which can include hitting. Ironically, Tongan families have very close bonds which Manu attributes to the amount of respect children give to their parents, respect gained through a certain amount of fear and love. Growing up in America Manu was exposed to American parenting, which made Tongan parenting seem very strict. As a teenager, Manu found it difficult living by his parents' rules in American society. Manu was never allowed to go out whenever he pleased, and often times he had to stay home with his family on the weekends while all of his friends were going out. Manu's friends would often remark that his parents "treated him like a girl." Although Manu resented the criticism from his peers, he always managed to maintain the Tongan values of parental respect and obedience. In comparison to American culture, Tongan culture places a higher value on respect, which is the foundation for their social structure. This difference seems to underlie the many differences between the two cultures. The roles of the old and young in Tongan culture are directly related to the value Tongans place on respect. Elders are valued for their wisdom gained through experience, and are always to be respected. It is considered extremely disrespectful to ignore an elder's advice or to disobey an elder's wishes. Because elders play such an integral part in guiding the young, the generations have an extremely close relationship in Tongan culture. Manu remembers an incident once as a child when he challenged his grandfather's authority. Manu's grandfather told him to clean his bedroom. Not particularly wanting to clean his room that very moment, Manu complained and asked his grandfather why he couldn't let it wait a day. Manu's grandfather, surprised by the protest, responded that Manu should do as he was told without any questions. His grandfather later told Manu that regardless of whether he was right or wrong, there was always something to be learned from what he said, because he had lived a long life and had experienced many things Manu had not. From that point on, Manu was able to appreciate his grandfather's wisdom and never questioned him.

Where did you insert paragraph breaks in this passage and what were the reasons for your decisions? Compare your choices and reasons with those of your classmates: How much agreement do you find?

Paragraph Focus and the Myth of the Topic Sentence

Another bit of common wisdom suggests that each paragraph must begin with a topic sentence—a general statement or assertion that announces the main idea of the paragraph. If you look at the five-paragraph version of Fan Shen's essay (p. 190), the topic sentences fairly leap off the page: "Rule number one in English composition is: Be yourself"; "In English composition, a second essential rule for the logical organization of a piece of writing is the use of the topic sentence." As Shen himself might note, each paragraph begins in good, direct Anglo-American style by "knocking the topic right on the head." Subtlety and complexity are sacrificed in this approach for textbook-style clarity. But like the five-paragraph essay itself, the top-down topic sentence formula is too rigid to work for every paragraph. For the sake of contrast, let's also look at how Shen shaped one of his own paragraphs:

But writing many "I's" was only the beginning of the process of re-defining myself. Speaking of redefining myself is, in an important sense, speaking of redefining the word "I." By such a redefinition I mean not only the change in how I envision myself, but also the change in how *I* perceived the world. The old "I" used to embody only one set of values, but now it had to embody multiple sets of values. To be truly "myself," which I knew was a key to my success in learning English composition, meant *not to be my Chinese self* at all. That is to say, when I write in English I have to wrestle with and abandon (at least temporarily) the whole system of ideology which previously defined me in myself. I had to forget Marxist doctrines (even though I do not see myself as a Marxist by choice) and the Party lines imprinted in my mind and familiarize myself with a system of capitalist/bourgeois values. I had to put aside an ideology of collectivism and adopt the values of individualism. In composition as well as literature classes, I had to make a fundamental adjustment: if I used to examine society and literary materials through the microscopes of Marxist dialectical materialism and historical materialism, I now had to learn to look through the microscopes the other way around, i.e., to learn to look at and understand the world from the point of view of "idealism." (I must add here that there are American professors who use a Marxist approach in their teaching.)

The first line looks something like a topic sentence, but if you look closely you'll see that it really doesn't introduce a new "main idea" as such: it merely indicates that his paragraph will have something to do with further self-redefinition—the topic of the entire essay. The second sentence might also be a candidate for topic sentence, but the idea of re-defining the "I" also runs throughout the essay; it's not the sole domain of this paragraph. A better possible topic sentence comes exactly where it's least likely to, according to conventional wisdom—square in the mid-dle of the paragraph: "That is to say, when I write in English I have to wrestle with and abandon (at least temporarily) the whole system of ide-ology which previously defined me in myself." But even this sentence can hardly be considered a guide to the paragraph's "main point," because it actually introduces an idea that will be elaborated for at least five more paragraphs.

Like the five-paragraph essay, the topic sentence is really only an *eidolon*—an artificial form that has no exact counterpart in most writing outside the classroom. Instead of worrying about the generality and loca-tion of their topic sentences, writers tend to be more pragmatic: they tend to see the paragraph as a rather arbitrary boundary surrounding ideas or observations that appear to share a common focus. In the case of Shen's paragraph above, the focus is something like "changing self = changing ide-ology." And in the one-sentence paragraph that follows the long one quoted above, Shen doesn't really introduce a "new idea" so much as he subtly shifts this thematic focus:

> The word "idealism," which affects my view of both myself and the universe, is loaded with social connotations, and can serve as a good ex-ample of how redefining a key word can be a pivotal part of redefining my ideological identity as a whole.

Shen's focus is still "changing self = changing ideology," and, in fact, he's still talking about an idea he took up in the previous paragraph—the West-ern concept of "idealism." He begins a new paragraph here not to signal the discussion of a new idea but to help the reader understand that he is now narrowing his focus to consider this one aspect of his self-redefinition: the impact of Western idealism on his identity. He also uses the visibility of this short paragraph (in contrast to the long ones that surround it) to highlight the importance of this point. The shape and content of a paragraph, then, isn't usually dictated by the domination of a single, all-inclusive topic sentence. Rather, a paragraph represents a cluster of ideas that share a common thematic connection — a sense of relatedness that makes it possible to mark them off as a single, coherent unit. Try to think of paragraphs not as rigid containers for displaying a series of "new ideas" but as flexible boundary markers that can be used to help your readers understand more clearly your own patterns of thought.

OPTIONAL ACTIVITIES

Paragraph Shape and Focus

1. Reread the two-paragraph and the three-paragraph versions of the passage by Rodney Guerrero. Which paragraphs, if any, have topic sentences? If one or more of these paragraphs does not have a topic sentence you can identify, try writing one that sums up the main idea or purpose and add it to the text. Does the addition improve the paragraph's clarity, make it less interesting or effective, or make no difference? Compare your responses in small groups.

2. Reread a few pages of the essays by Kluckhohn (p. 118), Holland (p. 171), or Shen (p. 175) and summarize the focus or purpose of each paragraph in a phrase or short sentence. Compare your results in small groups: Do you agree about the focus of each paragraph? If you find a paragraph with a topic sentence, do you agree on which sentence it is? Do you see any patterns in the way the writer structures his paragraphs?

Revision Case Study: Paragraph Focus

Identifying the central focus of paragraphs is a useful revision tool. If you can sum up the point of a paragraph in a short sentence of your own, you can then check the rest of the paragraph to see if everything in it clearly relates to that focus. If you have a hard time identifying the central idea of a particular paragraph, that may mean you need to delete unnecessary information or define your purpose more clearly. Here's an example: this passage shows how writer Jasmine Yoon reworked the beginning of her paper both to clarify the focus of the paragraphs and to talk comprehensibly about a complex, abstract subject — calculus — to readers who may be unfamiliar with the subject. The paper is based on Yoon's interview with Jon Rogwasky, a mathematics professor at UCLA.

Draft

   At nine o'clock sharp, Professor Rogwasky begins his lecture. He draws two hundred fifty students' minds into the
world of mathematics. One might think of mathematics only as a
set of numbers and formulas, however, Professor Rogwasky says,
"Mathematics is an art form."

   Professor Rogwasky says that teaching is very rewarding.
He gives lectures on Calculus 31B in fall quarter of 1993.
This course basically focuses on "Integral Calculus." The integral was found in motivation to define and calculate the
area of the region lying between the graph of a positive-
valued function f and the x-axis over a closed interval [a, b].
While its application has a significance in other physical
sciences and the engineering field, Professor Rogwasky emphasizes its conceptual viewpoint. "The beauty of the fundamental
theorem is ...," Professor Rogwasky says in class. Who would
find "beauty" in a mathematical theorem? It is impossible for
many students who dislike mathematics and think it to be a
practice of memorization of formulas. But it is possible for
those who, like Professor Rogwasky, look at the deep inside of
the conceptual aspect. According to him, the beauty of the
fundamental theorem of calculus is based on the relationship
between differentiation and integration. People had earlier
calculated areas which are equivalent to integrals and tangent
line slopes equivalent to derivatives. It was Newton and Leibnitz who discovered the inverse relationship between differentiation and integration. "Who could think that the area under
the curve and the slope of the curve are closely connected
with each other?" Professor Rogwasky asks students to give
them the essential idea of the theorem. In his lecture, he
tries to show not only how to calculate numbers to get an accurate answer but also how to think of the fragments of theo-
rems as one big picture of a concept. Also, he shares his

mathematical view with individual students during his office
hour or appointment time. Students are lined up after lecture
in front of his office. Some have questions about the lecture
of the day and occasionally about other interests. Professor
Rogwasky gives sincere answers and even gives extra materials
for enthusiastic students.

Professor Rogwasky has been working on a research project
for over ten years. The research subject is "The Theory of Automorphic Forms." . . .

In this version of the profile, it's very hard to pin down the focus of the
opening paragraphs. The first, short paragraph briefly raises two issues: Professor Rogwasky's compelling lecture style ("He draws two hundred fifty
students' minds into the world of mathematics") and his belief in math as
an art form. Neither idea is elaborated (How does he capture his students'
interest? How is math like art?), and the connection between them is not
explained. The next paragraph opens by emphasizing Rogwasky's love of
teaching ("teaching is very rewarding") and then devotes several sentences
to the details of a specific course he's teaching. However, none of these details helps to explain why he enjoys teaching or how he makes it interesting
to students; in fact, most of this information would be meaningful only to
cultural insiders—UCLA students who know what kind of course Calculus
31B is and people who already understand specialized terms like *the integral,
a positive-valued function f, the x-axis,* and *a closed interval [a, b]*. Next, there
are several sentences that return to the idea of math as art and beauty, some
information on the history of calculus, and, finally, a few more sentences
that focus on Rogwasky's concern for students.

In her revision, Yoon deletes unnecessary details and refocuses her
opening paragraphs: the first paragraph now concentrates on explaining
Rogwasky's view of the relationship between mathematics and art, while
the second centers on his teaching—how he communicates his enthusiasm
for the artistry of math to his students.

Revision

At nine o'clock sharp, Professor Rogwasky begins his lecture. He draws two hundred fifty students' minds into the
world of mathematics. Professor Rogwasky emphasizes a concep-

tual viewpoint that Newton and Leibnitz, the two founders of calculus, originally brought up:

> The beauty of the fundamental theorem is based on the relationship between differentiation and integration. Two things [differentiation and integration] we thought were completely unrelated to each other turned out to have the reverse relation that can be summarized in a few lines of formula. It is a beautiful structure the old mathematicians have discovered.

Professor Rogwasky expresses his excitement in the class. This is something very special about him: his excitement for mathematics. Who would find "beauty" in a mathematical theorem? How could he think an arrangement of signs and numbers a "beautiful structure"? It is impossible for those who think of mathematics only as a set of numbers and formulas and the practice of memorizing formulas. However, the beauty is the motivation to study mathematics for those who look deep inside to the concepts like Professor Rogwasky. Professor Jon Rogwasky says, "Mathematics is an art form."

Professor Rogwasky likes to share his mathematical view with students. He wants to show his students what is marvelous and exciting in mathematics that led him to be a mathematician in his college years. Also, he challenges his students, tossing out essential questions like, "Who could think that the area under the curve and slope of the curve are closely connected with each other?" In his office hour, students are lined up in front of his office. Whatever level the questions may be, Professor Rogwasky gives sincere answers and he cares about his students' understanding of his lecture.

Professor Rogwasky has been researching the "Theory of Automorphic Forms" for over ten years....

Try your hand at glossing these revised paragraphs—that is, coming up with a short sentence that sums up the central focus of each. Now check each sentence in the paragraph to see how it relates to the paragraph as a whole. Is the relationship clear in every case? If not, how could the passage be revised to make the connections clearer throughout?

Revising Your Draft: Paragraphing for Clarity and Readability

- Reformat one of your own drafts so that there are no paragraph breaks. Exchange papers with a partner and mark all the places you would put paragraphs. Compare your paragraphing decisions and discuss any differences of opinion about where or why to insert paragraph breaks.

- Exchange drafts with a partner or members of your response group and number the paragraphs. Read each paragraph carefully and try to identify the central idea; then write a brief gloss in the margin—a short sentence summarizing the main theme or purpose of the paragraph. Now check each sentence in the paragraph to see if it relates to the central theme or purpose. Underline any sentence that doesn't seem to fit. If the paragraph as a whole seems to lack a clear focus, circle the whole paragraph. On a separate piece of paper, explain why the sentences and paragraphs you marked appear disconnected: Why does a particular sentence seem unnecessary or unrelated to the rest of the paragraph? What different ideas do you find in an unfocused paragraph and why don't they seem to fit together?

Use your classmates' questions and responses to guide you in revising your draft.

JOURNAL OPTION

Evaluating Your Writing Process

Before you turn in your revised paper, take a few minutes to reflect on your writing process for this essay. What gave you the most trouble? What was easiest? Now think about your virtual readers: What aspects of the finished paper are you confident that readers will understand most clearly? What passages, if any, are you uncertain about, and why? Attach this journal entry to your finished paper when you turn it in so that your instructor can respond to your concerns in her comments.

PART THREE

Framing Language

CHAPTER 9

Speech Communities

One English or Many?

In the last two sections we've explored some of the assumptions you may have brought with you to college about the rules governing writing and the idea of correctness. We even urged you to break some of these rules and to take some risks with your writing. Why is it that we expect English to amount to a collection of rules? It should be clear to anyone who's ever struggled to squeeze an idea into words that the English language is a mess. Maybe it's a powerful mess, a mess capable of expressing the most subtle ideas and emotions, but a mess just the same. Subjects, verbs, and objects break their grammatical moorings easily and drift at will through sentences, often leaving us to wonder who did what to whom; and as anyone who has suffered through the initiation rite of elementary school spelling drills can tell you, English spelling is even more chaotic. A logical language would offer consistent spellings for the same sound. For example, you wouldn't expect the sound "f" to show up in a word as "ph." English is full of these spelling anomalies: How can you trust a language that offers you at least thirteen different ways to spell the sound "sh"—*shoe, sugar, issue, mansion, mission, nation, suspicion, ocean, conscious, chaperon, schist, fuchsia,* and *pshaw.*[1] To make matters worse, many of the most successful professional

[1]Robert McCrum, William Cran, and Robert MacNeil, *The Story of English* (New York: Penguin Books, 1986), p. 46. Much of the historical information in this section comes from this source and Robert Burchfield, *The English Language* (New York: Oxford University Press, 1986).

writers break or simply disregard the rules of grammar and usage whenever it suits their purpose, and a great many accomplished writers claim that they were never taught any rules at all.

Perhaps we're fascinated with the possibility of reducing English to a set of learnable rules or conventions because the living language itself has always resisted regulation and uniformity. It's actually a mistake to speak of English as if it were a single language, for there are, and have always been, many different Englishes, each one perfectly suited to the cultural group that has developed and used it. Modern English is like a tapestry: it is woven of many different strands, each strand contributing its own peculiar weight, texture, and color to create the impression—a fiction, a trick of the mind—that presents us with a unified whole. Since the birth of the language, there have been hundreds, perhaps thousands, of different Englishes. The story of English is the story of diversity.

Mother Tongues

Actually, the early history of English would make a terrific "B" movie. During its first five hundred years, English was the language of warring tribes, bloodthirsty adventurers, and murderous invaders. The first on the scene were the Anglii, a tribe of fiercely independent Germanic "barbarians" who successfully resisted Roman domination for several centuries, worshipped the Earth Mother, and practiced human sacrifice. In 449 C.E.[2] they left their homeland in present-day Denmark and Holland and made their way, along with two related tribes—the Saxons and Jutes—to an island known to the Romans as *Britan*. The record they kept of their adventures, the *Anglo-Saxon Chronicle*, tells of the resistance they met from the Celts and their leader, King Artorius, the model for the legendary King Arthur. Over the next 150 years, the Anglii and their fellow tribesmen waged a war of systematic destruction against the Celts. In modern English there are few traces left of Gaelic—the original Celtic language, a testament to the brutality of the Anglii's campaign of "ethnic cleansing." The remaining Celts were pushed to the western and northern fringes of Britan, settling eventually in present-day Wales and Ireland.

By 750 C.E. the new inhabitants of Britan were known as the *Angelcynn* (Anglii Kin) and their language was called *Englisc,* the language of the Anglii. The Anglo-Saxons were an agricultural people; they lived close to the

---

[2]The designation A.D. (Anno Domini: Latin, in the year of the Lord) assumes an exclusively Christian point of view. We will be using C.E. (Common Era) in its place.—Aus.

earth, and their language, simple in form and expression, reflected their way of life. The one hundred most common words in contemporary English can be traced back to the tongue of these Germanic invaders, indispensable words like *the, is, you, here,* and *there* and common words like *man, house, boat, drink, earth, ground, bone, cloth, plough, sheep, ox, swine, dog, wood, field, work, fight, glee,* and *laughter.* The simple power of these ancient Anglo-Saxon words gave English its roots, and their influence is still being felt in writing classrooms all over the world. For decades students have been told that if they want their writing to be clear, concise, and powerful, they should rely on straightforward, salt-of-the-earth Anglo-Saxon English.

By 793 C.E. the invaders became the invaded as a new tribal group, collectively known as the Vikings or Norsemen, spread out from present-day Scandinavia to claim territory across the North Atlantic. Contrary to the "Conan the Barbarian" treatment they've received in pop culture, the Vikings were a relatively peaceable group, at least by the apparently brutal standards of the Anglii. They learned to coexist with the Anglo-Saxons, eventually merging with them through commerce and intermarriage. Perhaps because they did "marry into the family," the Vikings also had a sizable impact on the language. They brought a host of new Scandinavian words into English—words like *get, take, want, same, hit, low, root, angry, awkward,* and *wrong.* Almost every word in English that begins with "sk"—words like *skin, sky,* and *skirt*—are of Norse origin. In all, we've inherited more than nine hundred everyday words from the Vikings. But their influence wasn't limited to the addition of new words. During the centuries that they lived side by side, mixing their families, cultures, and affairs, the Vikings and Anglo-Saxons were forced to communicate.

With time, the tongue of the Anglo-Saxons won out, but in the process it was radically changed. To ease communication across cultures, the Vikings and Anglo-Saxons simplified the original Old English of the Angelcynn; they began to speak a "pidgin," a pared-down version of the language that left out many of the grammatical forms and conventions that had been typical of the original Englisc. This is why English words are not inflected— why they do not change endings depending on their role in a sentence as subject, object, or object of a preposition, as do words in German, Russian, or Greek. The Viking invasion was the first of the English language's many great cross-cultural experiences: it transformed English into a language made to be spoken by foreigners, and, in a sense, transformed us all into speakers of English as a Second Language.

Three hundred years after the Vikings' arrival, the Norman French invaded and defeated English-speaking King Harold at the Battle of Hastings in 1066 C.E. Led by William the Conqueror, the Normans imposed a state of linguistic apartheid on England that was to fracture British society for the next three hundred years. The Normans, themselves descendants of Danish invaders who had colonized northern France centuries before, divided England into two social groups: the peasantry spoke their mother tongue, the English they learned in their homes, and the ruling class spoke French and Latin, the language of Christianity. To speak English was to identify yourself as a second-class citizen, someone who was powerless and fit only to serve. But English also became an emblem of resistance and rebellion. As the language of the masses, the ordinary people, English was spoken as an act of defiance; even as late as 1525 the act of translating the Bible into "the Angle not the angel language" was considered a crime punishable by death at the stake. It is one of history's ironies that out of this confrontation, English, not French, emerged as the language of love: like the Vikings, the French eventually intermarried with their subjects and adopted English as the language of hearth, home, and, with time, government as well.

Like their Viking predecessors, the French also left their mark, giving English an expressive range and richness of vocabulary that are among its most distinctive characteristics. Nearly all of our words for government, law, statecraft, and religion derive from French and Latin, words like *advise, command, country, people, peer, realm, reign, court, royalty, govern, sovereign, battle, victory, glory, honor, destitute, poverty, poor, judge, jury, larceny, felony, bailiff,* and *perjury.* In a great many cases, French and Latin words duplicated English words that had come from Norse or Anglo-Saxon roots. This layering of languages has given English a wealth of near-synonyms that makes it capable of differentiating many shades of meaning: thus, in English you can *go up, rise, mount,* or *ascend* depending on the situation or how hard you want to impress your reader. In the right mood, you can be *kingly, queenly, royal, regal,* or even *sovereign.* Should you get the urge, you can *ask, question, inquire,* or *interrogate.* If the spirit moves you, you can think deeply about your *time,* your *age,* your *era,* or your *epoch.* Thanks to those lusty intermarrying French, we have at our disposal the vocabularies of several different languages and several different cultures—all rolled into one.

The many varieties of English that emerged from the melding of Old English, French, and Latin—known collectively as Middle English—were rich, colorful, and almost completely unbowed by rule or regulation. Every town and village spoke its own distinct dialect. Every writer, it seems, spelled and punctuated as he saw fit. This diversity of Englishes was the bane of early publishers like William Caxton, who, like bookmakers in all ages, wanted to appeal to the widest possible audience and boost his sales. An accomplished writer himself, Caxton translated many French "bestsellers" of his day and printed them on the press he brought to England in

1476, the first of its kind on the island. In the prologue to one of his translations, Caxton tells a brief story about the troubles of a traveling merchant trying to order food at an inn to illustrate the bewildering variety of English dialects spoken in fourteenth-century England. We've reproduced this anecdote in its original form to give you a taste of the peculiarity of Caxton's Middle English:

> In so moche that in my dayes happened that certayn marchauntes were in a shippe in tamyse, for to have sayled over the see into zelande, and for lack of wynde, thei taryed atte forlond, and wente to lande for to refreshe them. And one of theym named Sheffelde, a mercer, cam in-to an hows and axed for mete; and spcyally he axyd for eggys. And the goode wyf answerde, that she coude speke no frenshe. And the marchaunt was angry, for he also coude speke no frenshe, but wolde have hadde eggess, and she understode hym not. And thenne at laste a nother sayd that he wolde have eyren. Then the good wyf sayd that she understod hym wel. Loo, what sholde a man in thyse dayes now wryte, egges or eyren? Certaynly it is harde to playse every man by cause of dyversity & chaunge of langage. For in these days every man that is in ony reputacyon in his countre, wyll utter his commynycacyon and maters in suche maners & termes that fewe men shall understonde theym.[3]

Caxton chose to print his words—and the works of popular writers like Geoffrey Chaucer and Thomas Malory—in the London dialect of English, the tongue he felt had the broadest appeal. This choice had two consequences: by committing English to print during its formative years, Caxton and other early publishers fixed spellings before scholars had the chance to regularize the spelling system, leaving us with thirteen ways to spell "sh." The second result of Caxton's printing press was even more far-reaching: by favoring his own dialect—the English spoken in London—above all others, Caxton took an early step toward making it the "standard" dialect, a single, universal, and "correct" form of English that could be imposed on speakers of Englishes everywhere.

During the next 250 years, England and English boomed. Between 1500 and 1650 London grew from a town of 75,000 to a metropolis of 450,000. Fueled by natural resources from British colonies in Asia, Africa, and America, modern industries began emerging across the English countryside. In London peasants and aristocrats flocked to new open-air theaters to see plays by William Shakespeare. As political and economic might began to centralize in the hands of a rising capitalist class, pressure grew to unify and

---

[3] *The Story of English,* p. 86.

standardize the language as well. The first dictionaries appeared in the late sixteenth century. In 1596 Edmund Cook published *The English Scholmaister,* an early textbook containing advice on grammar and vocabulary. Eager to erase the memory of their humble beginnings, the rising merchant class promoted the idea of a "correct" Mother Tongue that could be regulated, like a business, by a body of rules and taught in schools. In the eighteenth and nineteenth centuries, the movement toward universal public education and a torrent of increasingly sophisticated and authoritarian dictionaries and grammar books attempted to silence the many Englishes that had been spoken across England, Ireland, Scotland, and Wales for centuries.

American Englishes

But this is only half the story. The same political and economic forces that created the demand for linguistic conformity in England were also laying the groundwork for an explosion of new Englishes abroad. As military and industrial power grew in London, England dispatched armies, merchants, and missionaries to administer its affairs from India to the Americas. At the same time as the grammarians and lexicographers were trying to halt the mixing of languages that had fueled the rapid development of English since the Viking invasions, British invaders were trying to impose their language and culture on indigenous peoples across the globe. For three hundred years, colonization extended England's economic might, but in the end colonization itself subverted any attempts to control the English language. Within months of their landing in 1620, William Bradford, second governor of the Plymouth Plantation, recorded contact between the newly arrived Pilgrims and an American Indian named Samoset who spoke "to them in broken English, which they could well understand but marveled at." English, it seems, arrived in the New World even before the Pilgrim colonists. Passed along by sailors, fishermen, merchants, and slave traders who plied the Atlantic coast during the early 1600s and who seasoned their speech with Spanish, Portuguese, Indian, and African words, ideas, rhythms, and intonations, English was already on the way to becoming "many Englishes" again.

Throughout its history, America has been a breeding ground of competing and complementary languages. What we call American English has grown out of this language mix, bringing together the words, idioms, expressions, and ideas of those who sought opportunity and freedom and those who found only bondage and disenfranchisement in the "New World." Contemporary American English still reflects these diverse contributions. From the many languages spoken by American Indians, we've adopted words like *chipmunk, moose, skunk, raccoon, moccasin, pow-wow,* and *squash.* The Spanish-speaking inhabitants of the western territories gave us *barbecue, chocolate, tomato, plaza, tornado, alligator, canyon, patio, cafeteria,* and *marijuana.* From the original Dutch settlers of New York we get *waffle, coleslaw, cookie, landscape, caboose, sleigh, boom, snoop, Yankee,* and *Santa Claus.* From the German immigrants who settled in Pennsylvania we inherited *dumb, bummer, check, cookbook, ecology, fresh, hoodlum, mix, phooey, rifle,* and *scram* and expressions like *and how, no way,* and *will do.* The Jewish families that fled the pogroms of Eastern Europe brought Yiddish words like *chutzpah, shlep, kosher, shlock, shtick, mensch,* and *yenta.* The French settlers of Louisiana offered *bayou, praline, depot, cent, dime, butte,* and *chowder.* Words have come into the language from our national obsessions and pastimes. The railroads that were so vital to national expansion have lent us hundreds of colorful expressions, including ideas and concepts like *streamlined, the gravy train, getting sidetracked, going first class, being in the clear, making the grade, having the right of way, backtracking,* and *reaching the end of the line.* We've even been influenced by our national weakness for gambling: you can still hear the voice of the riverboat cardsharp in common phrases like *pass the buck, ante up, call your bluff, new deal, fair deal, square deal,* and *raw deal.* At one time or another, we've all had the cards stacked against us, yet even when the chips were down, we probably still dreamed of hitting the jackpot.

But American English may have gained some of its most distinctive features from the African Americans who originally came to this country against their will. During the infamous Middle Passage—the voyage from Africa to the Americas—African captives were treated worse than animals, penned or forced to lie in inhumanely narrow berths below decks for weeks on end, and subject to disease, malnutrition, and physical abuse. The possibility of resistance and rebellion during a long sea voyage was a constant threat to slave-trading captains. To discourage organized uprisings slavers learned to separate family members and to mix captives from different tribal groups. Deprived of a common language, their captives found resistance almost impossible. As early as 1744 Captain William Smith recommended the strategy of verbal domination when he suggested that if his fellow slave traders carry ". . . some of every Sort on board, there will be no more Likelihood of their succeeding in a Plot, than of finishing the Tower of Babel."[4]

[4]J. L. Dillard, *Black English: Its History and Usage in the United States* (New York: Random House, 1972), p. 73.

Unable to communicate in their native languages, African captives were forced to adopt the language of their captors. By the time they arrived in port, many had already mastered a simplified form of English. By the 1800s this "pidginized" English had developed into a full-blown language, a distinct variety of English with its own grammar and vocabulary. For more than a hundred years, scholars refused to acknowledge that Black English had any influence on the development of American English as a whole. Today, however, the contributions of Black English are inescapable: there can be no doubt about the impact that Black English has had and is having on all of the many "Englishes" spoken in America. Without Black English we wouldn't have words for gospel, the blues, jazz, rock 'n roll, or rap. We wouldn't know a *high five* from a *slam dunk*. We owe Black English some of our coolest concepts, conveyed in words and expressions like *hip, hot, bad, heavy, mean, chilling, fresh, uptight, hang loose, hung up, square, doing your own thing, ripped off, busted, blast, jive, jam,* and *kicks*. Linguists now even suggest that the distinctive accent and style of southern American dialect derives from the influence of Black English. Certainly, there's no doubt that in the age of electronic media, megasports, and mass entertainment, Black English has given our language a sense of *soul* that sets it apart from the English spoken anywhere else in the world.

OPTIONAL
ACTIVITIES

Exploring the Englishes We Speak

1. Because English is a mix of several different languages—including Anglo-Saxon, Norse, Latin, and French—it frequently offers us a range of synonyms for a single concept. As noted above, synonymous words like *ask, question,* and *interrogate* each set their own particular tone and bear their own shade of meaning or "connotation": interrogating someone is a more elaborate—and a more formal—process than merely questioning them, and because interrogations are associated with legal and police proceedings, the act of interrogating someone also suggests an unequal power relation between interviewer and interviewee. Working in small groups, try to explain the differences in tone and meaning between the pairs of words listed below. In what contexts or situations would you expect to find these words used? Before you compare your conclusions, try to think of some other synonym pairs or combinations on your own.

   - pay, compensation
   - hatred, aversion
   - divinity, god
   - food, nourishment
   - trepidation, fear
   - discover, find
   - edifice, building
   - view, panorama
   - combine, mix
   - dung, excrement

2. Return to the story told by William Caxton (p. 225) and translate it into contemporary English. Compare your translations when finished. How would you describe the differences between Caxton's Middle English and the English we currently speak?

What Are Speech Communities?

It would be tempting to think that American English is a kind of melting pot where the contributions of different ethnic groups have simmered into a single savory stew. But history tells us that there has never been a single English language—not even a single American English. Take a look at the two bits of conversation below, originally reported by the same student, Henry Sum:

Dude #1: Hey, brah! How is it?
Dude #2: Pretty good. 'Bout 3–4 feet. Little bit blown out, but should be getting better as the tide gets higher.
Dude #1: Cool. At least there aren't any fuckin' kooks out!
Dude #2: Yeah. Hopefully the surfers will stay home too.
Dude #1: Goin' out?
Dude #2: Yeah. See ya out there, dude.
Dude #1: Damn, that paddle out was hard! I thought I was never gonna make it out.
Dude #2: Saw you get hammered by that death set. EEEEE!!! I'm on this left!!
Dude #1: Yeah! Git on it!

Homie #1: Hey! Sup, homie?
Homie #2: Chillin', man. Sup wit you?
Homie #1: Nuttin. Just kickin' it for now. Whatcha gonna do tonight?
Homie #2: Ain't got no plans right now. Why? Wuz sup?
Homie #1: We gonna go to party.
Homie #2: Yeah? Any hotties gonna be there?
Homie #1: Hell, yeah!
Homie #2: Then it's on. You wanna get some grub first?
Homie #1: Cooool. Spot me on some ends?
Homie #2: Yeah. Broke ass fool!

It's obvious that these two conversations are both in English: they both use elements of the same grammatical system and share a number of words in common. But in many ways speech on the street and in the surf represent two distinct languages—two different brands of English—each with its own style, rules, and vocabulary. In reality, no one speaks just one kind of English. There are literally hundreds of different kinds of American English, and every one of us participates in literally hundreds of different "speech communities" that employ their own peculiar vocabulary, style, accent, and way of looking at the world. We shift between these speech communities instinctively and unconsciously. When you talk to members of your family around the breakfast table, you adopt a certain familiar tone and use language that is part of your family culture. Your language, tone, and style change when you meet your friends on the street and will change again if a police officer stops you to ask a question. Later, in class, you'll make yet another adjustment, accommodating yourself to the demands made by the academic speech community represented by a college course. Each of these social groups specializes in its own brand of English. Some are full of slang and inside jokes; others are formal and carefully controlled. Some allow for intense self-expression; others demand scrupulous self-effacement. The cultural worlds we live in are composed of interwoven networks of these language relationships.

In the following selection, Paul Roberts explains some of the forces that cause languages to change and to develop a variety of distinct speech communities. Growing up, Roberts suggests, involves us in the constant acquisition of new languages: as our experience of the world around us broadens, we continually increase the number of speech communities we participate in. The author of several books on linguistics, Paul Roberts taught English at San Jose State University in California and Columbia University in New York. "Speech Communities" is from *Understanding English* (HarperCollins, 1958).

Before Reading

Write a brief entry in your journal, speculating about why you think a language like English has changed into so many different "Englishes" over time. What forces or factors cause language to change?

Speech Communities
Paul Roberts

Imagine a village of a thousand people all speaking the same language and never hearing any language other than their own. As the decades pass and generation succeeds generation, it will not be very apparent to the speakers of the language that any considerable language change is going on. Oldsters may occasionally be conscious of and annoyed by the speech forms of youngsters. They will notice new words, new expressions, "bad" pronunciations, but will ordinarily put these down to the irresponsibility of youth, and decide piously that the language of the younger generation will revert to decency when the generation grows up.

It doesn't revert, though. The new expressions and the new pronunciations persist, and presently there is another younger generation with its own new expressions and its own pronunciations. And thus the language changes. If members of the village could speak to one another across five hundred years, they would probably find themselves unable to communicate.

Now suppose that the village divides itself and half the people move away. They move across the river or over a mountain and form a new village. Suppose the separation is so complete that the people of New Village have no contact with the people of Old Village. The language of both villages will change, drifting away from the language of their common ancestors. But the drift will not be in the same direction. In both villages there will be new expressions and new pronunciations, but not the same ones. In the course of time the language of Old Village and New Village will be mutually unintelligible with the language they both started with. They will also be mutually unintelligible with one another.

An interesting thing—and one for which there is no perfectly clear explanation—is that the rate of change will not ordinarily be the same for both villages. The language of Old Village changes faster than the language of New Village. One might expect that the opposite would be true—that the emigrants, placed in new surroundings and new conditions, would undergo more rapid language changes. But history reports otherwise. American English, for example, despite the violence and agony and confusion to which the demands of a new continent have subjected it, is probably essentially closer to the language of Shakespeare than London English is.

Suppose one thing more. Suppose Old Village is divided sharply into an upper class and a lower class. The sons and daughters of the upper class go to preparatory school and then to the university; the children of the lower class go to work. The upper-class people learn to read and write and develop a flowering literature; the lower-class people remain illiterate. Dialects develop, and the speech of the two classes steadily diverges. One might suppose that most of the change would go on among the illiterate, that the upper-class people, conscious of their heritage, would tend to preserve the forms and pronunciations of their ancestors. Not so. The opposite is true. In speech, the educated tend to be radical and the uneducated conservative. In England one finds Elizabethan forms and sounds not among Oxford and Cambridge graduates but among the people of backward villages.

A village is a fairly simple kind of speech community—a group of people steadily in communication with one another, steadily hearing one another's speech. But the village is by no means the basic unit. Within the simplest village there are many smaller units—groupings based on age, class, occupation. All these groups play intricately on one another and against one another, and a language that seems at first a coherent whole will turn out on inspection to be composed of many differing parts. Some forces tend to make these parts diverge; other forces hold them together. Thus the language continues in tension.

THE SPEECH COMMUNITIES OF THE CHILD

The child's first speech community is ordinarily his family. The child learns whatever kind of language the family speaks—or, more precisely, whatever kind of language it speaks to him. The child's language learning, now and later, is governed by two obvious motives: the desire to communicate and the desire to be admired. He imitates what he hears. More or less successful imitations usually bring action and reward and tend to be repeated. Unsuccessful ones usually don't bring action and reward and tend to be discarded.

But since language is a complicated business it is sometimes the unsuccessful imitations that bring the reward. The child, making a stab at the word *mother,* comes out with *muzzer.* The family decides that this is just too cute for anything and beams and repeats *muzzer,* and the child, feeling that he's scored a bull's eye, goes on saying *muzzer* long after he has mastered *other* and *brother.* Baby talk is not so much invented by the child as sponsored by the parent.

Eventually the child moves out of the family and into another speech community—other children of his neighborhood. He goes to kindergarten and immediately encounters speech habits that conflict with those he has learned. If he goes to school and talks about his *muzzer,* it will be borne in on him by his colleagues that the word is not well chosen. Even *mother* may not pass muster, and he may discover that he gets better results and is altogether happier if he refers to his female parent as his ma or even his old lady.

Children coming together in a kindergarten class bring with them language that is different because it is learned in different homes. It is all to some degree unsuccessfully learned, consisting of not quite perfect imitations of the original. In school all this speech coalesces, differences tend to be ironed out, and the result differs from the original parental speech and differs in pretty much the same way.

10

The pressures on the child to conform to the speech of his age group, his speech community, are enormous. He may admire his teacher and love his mother; he may even—and even consciously—wish to speak as they do. But he *has* to speak like the rest of the class. If he does not, life becomes intolerable.

The speech changes that go on when the child goes to school are often most distressing to parents. Your little Bertram, at home, has never heard anything but the most elegant English. You send him to school, and what happens? He comes home saying things like "I done real good in school today, Mom." But Bertram really has no choice in the matter. If Clarence and Elbert and the rest of the fellows customarily say "I done real good," then Bertram might as well go around with three noses as say things like "I did very nicely."

Individuals differ of course, and not all children react to the speech community in the same way. Some tend to imitate and others tend to force imitation. But all to some degree have their speech modified by forces over which neither they nor their parents nor their teachers have any real control.

Individuals differ too in their sensitivity to language. For some, language is always a rather embarrassing problem. They steadily make boners, saying the right thing in the wrong place or the wrong way. They have a hard time fitting in. Others tend to change their language slowly, sticking stoutly to their way of saying things, even though their way differs from that of the majority. Still others adopt new language habits almost automatically, responding quickly to whatever speech environment they encounter.

Indeed some children of five or six have been observed to speak two or more different dialects without much awareness that they are doing so. Most commonly, they will speak in one way at home and in another on the playground. At home they say, "I did very nicely" and "I haven't any"; these become, at school, "I done real good" and "I ain't got none." 15

The Class as a Speech Community

Throughout the school years, or at least through the American secondary school, the individual's most important speech community is his age group, his class. Here is where the real power lies. The rule is conformity above all things, and the group uses its power ruthlessly on those who do not conform. Language is one of the chief means by which the school group seeks to establish its entity, and in the high school this is done more or less consciously. The obvious feature is high school slang, picked up from the radio, from other schools, sometimes invented, changing with bewildering speed. Nothing is more satisfactory than to speak today's slang; nothing more futile than to use yesterday's.

There can be few tasks more frustrating than that of the secondary school teacher charged with the responsibility of brushing off and polishing up the speech habits of the younger generation. Efforts to make *real* into *really*, *ain't* into *am not*, *I seen him* into *I saw him*, *he don't* into *he doesn't* meet at best with polite indifference, at worst with mischievous counterattack.

The writer can remember from his own high school days when the class, a crashingly witty bunch, took to pronouncing the word *sure* as *sewer*. "Have you prepared your lesson, Arnold?" Miss Driscoll would ask. "Sewer, Miss Driscoll," Arnold would reply. "I think," said Miss Driscoll, who was pretty quick on her feet too, "that you must mean 'sewerly,' since the construction calls for the adverb not the adjective." We were delighted with the suggestion and went about saying "sewerly" until the very blackboards were nauseated. Miss Driscoll must have wished often that she had left it lay.

Confronting the Adult World

When the high school class graduates, the speech community disintegrates as the students fit themselves into new ones. For the first time in the experience of most of the students the speech ways of adult communities begin to exercise real force. For some people the adjustment is a relatively simple one. A boy going to work in a garage may have a good deal of new lingo to pick up, and he may find that the speech that seemed so racy and won such approval in the corridors of Springfield High leaves his more adult associates merely bored. But a normal person will adapt himself without trouble.

For others in other situations settling into new speech communities may be more difficult. The person going into college, into the business world, into scrubbed society may find that he has to think about and work on his speech habits in order not to make a fool of himself too often.

College is a particularly complicated problem. Not only does the freshman confront upperclassmen not particularly disposed to find the speech of Springfield High particularly cute, but the adult world, as represented chiefly by the faculty, becomes increasingly more immediate. The problems of success, of earning a living, of marriage, of attaining a satisfactory adult life loom larger, and they all bring language problems with them. Adaptation is necessary, and the student adapts.

The student adapts, but the adult world adapts too. The thousands of boys and girls coming out of the high schools each spring are affected by the speech of the adult communities into which they move, but they also affect that speech. The new pronunciation habits, developing grammatical

20

features, different vocabulary do by no means all give way before the disapproval of elders. Some of them stay. Elders, sometimes to their dismay, find themselves changing their speech habits under the bombardment of those of their juniors. And then of course the juniors eventually become the elders, and there is no one left to disapprove.

THE SPACE DIMENSION

Speech communities are formed by many features besides that of age. Most obvious is geography. Our country was originally settled by people coming from different parts of England. They spoke different dialects to begin with and as a result regional speech differences existed from the start in the different parts of the country. As speakers of other languages came to America and learned English, they left their mark on the speech of the sections in which they settled. With the westward movement, new pioneers streamed out through the mountain passes and down river valleys, taking the different dialects west and modifying them by new mixtures in new environments.

Today we are all more or less conscious of certain dialect differences in our country. We speak of the "southern accent," the "Brooklyn accent," the "New England accent." Until a few years ago it was often said that American English was divided into three dialects: Southern American (south of the Mason-Dixon line); Eastern American (east of the Connecticut River); and Western American. This description suggests certain gross differences all right, but recent research shows that it is a gross oversimplification.

The starting point of American dialects is the original group of colonies. 25 We had a New England settlement, centering in Massachusetts; a Middle Atlantic settlement, centering in Pennsylvania; a southern settlement, centering in Virginia and the Carolinas. These colonies were different in speech to begin with, since the settlers came from different parts of England. Their differences were increased as the colonies lived for a century and a half or so with only thin communication with either Mother England or each other. By the time of the Revolution the dialects were well established. Within each group there were of course subgroups. Richmond speech differed markedly from that of Savannah. But Savannah and Richmond were more like each other than they were like Philadelphia or Boston.

The Western movement began shortly after the Revolution, and dialects followed geography. The New Englanders moved mostly into upper New York State and the Great Lakes region. The Middle Atlantic colonists went down the Shenandoah Valley and eventually into the heart of the Midwest. The southerners opened up Kentucky and Tennesseee, later the lower Mississippi Valley, later still Texas and much of the Southwest. Thus new speech communities were formed, related to the old ones of the seaboard, but each developing new characteristics as lines of settlement crossed.

New complications were added before and after the Revolution by the great waves of immigration of people from countries other than England: Swedes in Delaware, Dutch in New York, Germans and Scots-Irish in Pennsylvania, Irish in New England, Poles and Greeks and Italians and Portuguese. The bringing in of Negro slaves had an important effect on the speech of the South and later on the whole country. The Spanish in California and the Southwest added their mark. In this century movement of peoples goes on: the trek of southern Negroes to northern and western cities, the migration of people from Arkansas, Oklahoma, and Texas to California. All these have shaped and are shaping American speech.

We speak of America as the melting pot, but the speech communities of this continent are very far from having melted into one. Linguists today can trace very clearly the movements of the early settlers in the still living speech of their descendants. They can follow an eighteenth century speech community west, showing how it crossed this pass and followed that river, threw out an offshoot here, left a pocket there, merged with another group, halted, split, moved on once more. If all other historical evidence were destroyed, the history of the country could still be reconstructed from the speech of modern America.

SOCIAL DIFFERENCES

The third great shaper of speech communities is the social class. This has been, and is, more important in England than in America. In England, class differences have often been more prominent than those of age or place. If you were the blacksmith's boy, you might know the son of the local baronet, but you didn't speak his language. You spoke the language of your social group, and he that of his, and over the centuries these social dialects remained widely separated.

England in the twentieth century has been much democratized, but the language differences are far from having disappeared. One can still tell much about a person's family, his school background, his general position in life by the way he speaks. Social lines are hard to cross, and language is perhaps the greatest barrier. You may make a million pounds and own several cars and a place in the country, but your vowels and consonants and nouns and verbs and sentence patterns will still proclaim to the world that you're not a part of the upper crust.

In America, of course, social distinctions have never been so sharp as they are in England. We find it somewhat easier to rise in the world, to

30

move into social environments unknown to our parents. This is possible, partly, because speech differences are slighter; conversely, speech differences are slighter because this is possible. But speech differences do exist. If you've spent all your life driving a cab in Philly and, having inherited a fortune, move to San Francisco's Nob Hill, you will find that your language is different, perhaps embarrassingly so, from that of your new acquaintances.

Language differences on the social plane in America are likely to correlate with education or occupation rather than with birth—simply because education and occupation in America do not depend so much on birth as they do in other countries. A child without family connection can get himself educated at Harvard, Yale, Princeton. In doing so, he acquires the speech habits of the Ivy League and gives up those of his parents.

Exceptions abound. But in general there is a clear difference between the speech habits of the college graduate and those of the high school graduate. The cab driver does not talk like the Standard Oil executive, the college professor like the carnival pitch man, or an Illinois merchant like a sailor shipping out of New Orleans. New York's Madison Avenue and Third Avenue are only a few blocks apart, but they are widely separated in language. And both are different from Broadway.

It should be added that the whole trend of modern life is to reduce rather than to accentuate these differences. In a country where college education becomes increasingly everybody's chance, where executives and refrigerator salesmen and farmers play golf together, where a college professor may drive a cab in the summertime to keep his family alive, it becomes harder and harder to guess a person's education, income, and social status by the way he talks. But it would be absurd to say that language gives no clue at all.

GOOD AND BAD

Speech communities, then, are formed by many features: age, geography, education, occupation, social position. Young people speak differently from old people, Kansans differently from Virginians, Yale graduates differently from Dannemora graduates. Now let us pose a delicate question: aren't some of these speech communities better than others? That is, isn't better language heard in some than in others? 35

Well, yes, of course. One speech community is always better than all the rest. This is the group in which one happens to find oneself. The writer would answer unhesitatingly that the noblest, loveliest, purest English is that heard in the Men's Faculty Club of San Jose State College, San Jose, California. He would admit, of course, that the speech of some of the younger members leaves something to be desired; that certain recent immigrants from Harvard, Michigan, and other foreign parts need to work on the laughable oddities lingering in their speech; and that members of certain departments tend to introduce a lot of queer terms that can only be described as jargon. But in general the English of the Faculty Club is ennobling and sweet.

As a practical matter, good English is whatever English is spoken by the group in which one moves contentedly and at ease. To the bum on Main Street in Los Angeles, good English is the language of other L.A. bums. Should he wander onto the campus of UCLA, he would find the talk there unpleasant, confusing, and comical. He might agree, if pressed, that the college man speaks "correctly" and he doesn't. But in his heart he knows better. He wouldn't talk like them college jerks if you paid him.

If you admire the language of other speech communities more than you do your own, the reasonable hypothesis is that you are dissatisfied with the community itself. It is not precisely other speech that attracts you but the people who use the speech. Conversely, if some language strikes you as unpleasant or foolish or rough, it is presumably because the speakers themselves seem so.

To many people, the sentence "Where is he at?" sounds bad. It is bad, they would say, in and of itself. The sounds are bad. But this is very hard to prove. If "Where is he at?" is bad because it has bad sound combinations, then presumably "Where is the cat?" or "Where is my hat?" are just as bad, yet no one thinks them so. Well, then, "Where is he at?" is bad because it uses too many words. One gets the same meaning from "Where is he?" so why add the *at*? True. Then "He going with us?" is a better sentence than "Is he going with us?" You don't really need the *is,* so why put it in?

Certainly there are some features of language to which we can apply the terms *good* and *bad, better* and *worse.* Clarity is usually better than obscurity; precision is better than vagueness. But these are not often what we have in mind when we speak of good and bad English. If we like the speech of upper-class Englishmen, the presumption is that we admire upper-class Englishmen—their characters, culture, habits of mind. Their sounds and words simply come to connote the people themselves and become admirable therefore. If we heard the same sounds and words from people who were distasteful to us, we would find the speech ugly.

This is not to say that correctness and incorrectness do not exist in speech. They obviously do, but they are relative to the speech community—or communities—in which one operates. As a practical matter, correct speech is that which sounds normal or natural to one's comrades. Incorrect speech is that which evokes in them discomfort or hostility or disdain.

40

Issues for Discussion

1. Summarize the claims that Roberts makes about how languages change. To what extent do you agree with him? Can you think of any examples of language change that challenge his ideas?
2. According to Roberts, what speech communities will an individual move through during her lifetime?
3. What factors help to shape and define speech communities? To what extent do you agree with Roberts's assertion that "correct" speech is the speech we're most accustomed to? What kind of language comes to mind when you think of "correct" speech?
4. How has American English changed since Roberts wrote this essay? What specific words, phrases, and references mark his language as dated?

JOURNAL OPTIONS

Exploring Your Speech Communities

1. Brainstorm all the speech communities you participate in. How would you describe the speech communities you belong to by virtue of your age, gender, ethnicity, economic background, religion, personal interests, job skills, geographic location, and so forth? Chances are you'll find that you belong to several communities within each category. Most people, for example, are members of several distinct geographic speech communities, defined by their region, state, city, and even their neighborhood. And remember that almost any relationship or activity can represent a speech community of sorts: Would you consider your family a distinct speech community? How many separate speech communities would you be able to describe among your friends and fellow students? Would participation in a hobby or sport include you in a particular speech community? Try to make your list of speech communities as complete and as inclusive as possible. At your next class meeting, work in small groups to compare and discuss your lists. Based on this comparison, try to create your own definition of a speech community. Would this class qualify as one?
2. Write sample dialogues, like the ones quoted at the beginning of this section (p. 229), for two or more of the speech communities you belong to.

C H A P T E R   1 0

Negotiating Multiplicity

The Dream of a Common Language

It may be a fact that we inhabit many different speech communities, but the idea of language diversity hasn't always been greeted with enthusiasm. In the Old Testament, not long after God flooded the earth to purge it of humanity's corruption, a new problem sprang up: human cooperation. The story of Babel attempts to teach an object lesson on the power of a common language and the dangers of language diversity. Able to speak a "single speech," humanity could pool its knowledge and build a tower tall enough to challenge God's authority in the heavens. Recognizing the power of this dream, God thwarts his creatures by confusing their speech:

> And the Lord said, Behold, the people is one, and they have all one language; and this they begin to do: and now nothing will be restrained from them, which they have imagined to do.
>
> Go to, let us go down, and there confound their language, that they may not understand one another's speech. (Genesis 11:5–6)

The moral is clear: a common language means strength; a babel of tongues, chaos. It's an idea that has influenced attitudes toward language diversity for several millennia. Whenever large numbers of new speakers have entered the English-speaking world—through immigration, colonization, or slavery—leaders and intellectuals have wrung their hands over the condition of the language. In the eighteenth century, as England extended its hold over most of the globe and English began to diversify at an increasing rate, this sentiment found a champion in Jonathan Swift, the famous playwright and social critic best known for his satirical novel *Gulliver's Travels* (1735). An archconservative with a self-acknowledged dread of progress, Swift published a pamphlet in 1712 calling for the formation of an "English Academy," an association of scholars and writers that would guarantee that no further changes or "corruptions" would be tolerated in the language:

> But what I have most at hart is, that some method should be thought on for ascertaining and fixing our language for ever, after such alterations are made in it as shall be thought requisite. For I am of the opinion it is better a language should not be wholly perfect, than that it should be perpetually changing; and we must give over at one time, or at length infallibly change for the worse.[1]

The recommendations Swift made in his *Proposal for Correcting, Improving, and Ascertaining the English Tongue* were never acted on by Parliament, but the idea of a single correct form of English won the day. Since the 1800s educators, writers, politicians, and other self-appointed protectors of the English language have cranked out a steady stream of grammars, stylebooks, handbooks, pronunciation guides, and vocabulary builders—all in the cause of advancing linguistic conformity. Playing to the insecurity of their audience, the "Language Bosses," as linguist Robin Lakoff has called them, offer us "rules" of correct usage and hints on improving our style as they belittle the "improper" or "ungrammatical" speech of the "uneducated." In place of the many Englishes spoken on the streets of New York and Los Angeles, or on the farms and reservations of the Dakotas and the deep South, the bosses offer "Standard English," a hypercorrect, artificially sanitized form of the language that's "spoken" only in schoolbooks and on television news programs.

"Standard English" exists not because it is better, more beautiful, or more expressive than the other Englishes we speak but because it is the language of power. As Lakoff has suggested, the central issue for the Language Bosses—and the central aim of the "Standard English" they endorse—is social, not linguistic, control:

> As reality speeds up, language spins ever more dizzily to keep up with it. It is then a natural tendency for those fearful of the changes they observe in concrete reality to turn on language and see its evolution as the villain: the cause of their own distress, the motive force behind the threatening changes they encounter in real life (although it is reality

---

[1] Jonathan Swift, *A Proposal for Correcting, Improving, and Ascertaining the English Tongue,* quoted in Robin Tolmach Lakoff, *Talking Power: The Politics of Language* (New York: Basic Books, 1990), p. 286.

change that creates language change, not vice versa). Their rage is directed against language itself: the young are speaking in a code they can't understand, much less use; changes in the way of life they might otherwise be able to ignore leap out at them from every TV commercial in neologisms and slangy verbal expressions. . . . To them, innovations are a barrier to clear thought, since for them clear thought is expressed otherwise. But for those young or flexible enough to adjust their grammars to keep up with innovation, nothing is lost, and the language and its speakers have gained: the language matches its user's reality, as it must if it is to be an effective vehicle of communication.[2]

Those in power have long understood the link between social and linguistic control. Not long after Swift submitted his proposal to Parliament, England began an all-out assault on Gaelic, the original language of his native Ireland. After the 1803 Act of Union, which made Ireland part of the United Kingdom, Gaelic, "the pagan tongue," was banned in public schools. To keep track of the times they lapsed into their native speech, Irish students were forced to wear "tally-sticks" around their necks: at the end of each week the sticks were read and punishment was meted out accordingly. Particularly stubborn cases were required to wear wooden "gags." Within a hundred years this program of linguistic genocide reduced the number of Irish citizens who claimed Gaelic as their sole language to a few thousand. Today, the spirit of linguistic intolerance flourishes on this side of the Atlantic. "English-only" measures are appearing on public ballots across the country in response to the same fear of cultural "fragmentation" and ethnic "difference" that motivated the British two centuries ago. Behind the dream of a common language lurks a fantasy of cultural and political domination: the most expedient way to erase difference in others is to remake them in one's own image.

For those lucky enough to be born into a speech community that approximates the "mother tongue" of "Standard English," this process of remaking costs little. But for those whose home languages are full of expressive "nonstandard" constructions—or who grew up in families that spoke a mixture of languages—there's no need to theorize about the political consequences of language standardization. For decades, kids who entered California and Texas schools speaking Spanish were routinely punished or shunted into special classes for the learning disabled. Working-class students who weren't savvy enough to eliminate street slang from their vocabularies and clean up their pronunciation were "tracked" away from the "college curriculum" into vocational programs. During the 1960s and 1970s, when Chicano and African American students began to arrive at American universities in historically unprecedented numbers, special departments—bearing

---

[2] Lakoff, *Talking Power*, p. 295.

names like "Developmental Communications," "Learning Skills," or "Preparatory Writing"—were often created to segregate them from the "regular" English students and faculty. And vestiges of this system of linguistic apartheid still exist on many college campuses today. Anyone who has endured the "House of Correction" approach fostered in "remedial" English understands that, as linguist Deborah Cameron has noted, efforts to subdue the many Englishes we speak, in fact, frequently mask attempts to subdue the people who speak them.[3]

The following poems express some of the personal costs of being a casualty in America's language wars. In "I Recognize You," Rosario Morales reminds us that the price of joining the speech community of "Standard English" sometimes includes the loss of important cultural voices and values. Ramón Galván's response to Morales's poem offers another perspective on the tension that exists between home speech communities and "Standard English." Rosario Morales (b. 1930) grew up in New York City among the children of Irish, European Jewish, Puerto Rican, and southern black and Afro-Caribbean migrants. In addition to her work as a writer, she farmed for five years in Puerto Rico, has done ecological and other scientific work, and holds an M.A. in anthropology from the University of Chicago. Her publications include *Getting Home Alive* (1986), a collection of poems and prose that she co-authored with her daughter, Aurora Levins Morales. Ramón Galván wrote "I Recognize Myself" as a journal entry in a first-year writing class at UCLA. He graduated from UCLA in 1994 and is currently studying law at Stanford University.

Before Reading

Try to remember a time when you felt that your language marked you as "different." What was the situation? How would you describe the experience of being a linguistic outsider?

I Recognize You

Rosario Morales

I recognize you. Spitting out four, five, six-syllable English words, your tongue turning a tight grammatical sentence, flipping adjectives and adverbs into line faster than you can say *Oxford Unabridged Dictionary*

---

[3] Deborah Cameron, *Verbal Hygiene* (London: Routledge, 1995), pp. 22–23.

and pinning all of it in place with commas, colons, semicolons, and parentheses.

You were one I couldn't beat at spelling bees, the other girl who got *A* in grammar two semesters in a row. You're the one who went on to college, or maybe didn't, but took classes after work, who reads and reads and worries whether you're reading enough or the right thing.

I know without meeting you that you're working class, or a woman of color, or an immigrant, or child of immigrants. That you keep your mama language for the kitchen, hardly ever pronounce it in public, never on the written page.

You're proud. You've done this by yourself, or with your family behind you. And I'm impressed. You can make the English language roll over, bark on command, sit up and beg, you—who were raised on spuds, grits, rice, or tortillas.

But I'm sad, too. For the English language robbed of the beat your home talk could give it, the words you could lend, the accent, the music, the word-order reordering, the grammatical twist. I'm sad for you, too, for the shame with which you store away—hide—a whole treasure box of other, mother, language. It's too rough-mannered, you say, too strange, too exotic, too untutored, too low class. 5

You're robbing us, robbing the young one saying her first sentence, reading her first book, writing her first poem. You're confirming her scorn of her cradle tongue. You're robbing her of a fine brew of language, a stew of words and ways that could inspire her to self-loving invention.

And you're robbing yourself . . . no, we're robbing ourselves, of selfness, of wholeness, of the joys of writing with *all* our words, of the sound of your Mama's voice, my Papa's voice, of the smell of the kitchen on the page.

STUDENT WRITING

I Recognize Myself
Ramón Galván

```
I recognize myself
I am the one spitting out four, five, six-syllable
     English words
My tongue barely knows the flavor
```

of the culture I might be a part of.
My skin, hair, and eyes are dark
       but to you I am as white as the paper I write on.
I have not betrayed you
I have been robbed
I have been robbed of a language
       you hold so close
Robbed of an identity you hold so dear
There has been no thief
But yet I feel robbed.
And now you nod your head
Whispering !Menso! (stupid)
You are trying to rob me of my pride.
You have mastered Spanish and have
       trouble with English--with me
You speak of envy.
But it is I who envy you
       because of the bond you seem
       to share with other Chicano/as
A bond that leaves me feeling
       alone.
I recognize myself
My strengths, my weaknesses
I recognize that there is NOT
       ONE
Chicano experience
I recognize that this is mine.

Issues for Discussion

1. Who is the "you" that Morales addresses in this poem? What do we learn about this person? How would you describe the speaker's attitude toward her?
2. Who is "robbing" who of what in "I Recognize You"?
3. What is Galván's attitude toward the speaker of Morales's poem? What is Galván's view of "Standard English" and Chicano culture?

J O U R N A L
O P T I O N S

Fitting In or Speaking Out?

1. Write your own imitation of Morales's poem, based on an experience you've had fitting into a particular speech community or cultural group.
2. Write a letter of reply to Morales from the "you" of her poem. How might Morales's "you" respond to the charges leveled against her?

Internalized Speech Communities: The Plural Self

THE FAR SIDE   By GARY LARSON

The Lone Ranger, long since retired,
makes an unpleasant discovery.

The Lone Ranger in the Gary Larson cartoon above has fallen into the trap of "Standard English": to someone like Rosario Morales or Ramón Galván, the cost of learning the dominant language involves the struggle to maintain one's cultural identity, but the cost of speaking the language of power—and only the language of power—is ignorance. In Chapter 5 we examined how our story frames hinder cross-cultural communication by blinding us to the stories that other people tell. If the stories we rely on to interpret the world keep us from comprehending those told in other cultures, how can we ever learn to communicate with someone whose background is different from ours? The Language Bosses who insist that election ballots be printed only in English or that books containing "nonstandard" dialects be banned from school libraries think they can solve the problem of cross-cultural communication by imposing a single language—and a single culture—on everyone. But the futility of this scheme, as Paul Roberts points out in "Speech Communities" (p. 230), should be obvious to anyone who understands that sometimes "good" is "bad" and "hot" is "cool." We aren't hamstrung by problems of cross-cultural communication because we all participate in many different speech communities. Speaking across cultures is possible because, like our ancestors, we're good at adapting to the expectations of many different speech communities. Every time we enter a new stage in our lives, start a new job, make a new acquaintance, or move into a new neighborhood, we have the chance to add to the varieties of English we speak. College itself can be seen as a clearinghouse for membership in many new speech communities. Every course you take introduces you to the terms, concepts, story frames, and styles of a new intellectual culture, an academic community that helps you see the world in a new light. Take a course in physics and the solid surface of your writing desk becomes an illusion generated by a whir of subatomic particles. Take one in social psychology and the rock concert you attended becomes an opportunity for teens to express repressed sexual drives. Take one in artificial intelligence and the mind turns into a sophisticated machine. Our ability to participate in multiple cultures and to speak many different "languages" is what keeps daily life from disintegrating into an endless series of cultural collisions. Refuse to learn a new language, to adapt yourself to new voices, styles, and ways of thinking, and you end up like the Lone Ranger—a real horse's ass.

But acquiring a new speech community isn't like adding a new book to your home library or buying some new software for your computer. Books sit passively on shelves until they are read; software programs run, in an orderly manner, one at a time. Our multichannel, multicultural minds are never this logical or this peaceful. Whether we like it or not, language is soaked in power and politics, and the many Englishes we speak bear their political tensions and conflicts with them into our thoughts and feelings. Like Hollywood agents or mental lobbyists, the story frames and scripts of our speech communities contend for our allegiance and attention. Official dialects like "Standard English" tell us tales of power and authority; they woo us with images of success, status, and importance. Home language asserts an authority of a different kind: filled with accents and associations from our past, it reminds us of our families, cultural ties, and the meanings of our past. Every speech community we belong to contributes a story or a set of stories to our identity: each one tells us something about who we are, who we have been, and who we might become.

Most of us have little trouble negotiating the competing claims of these internal agents; we attune ourselves to our surroundings, picking out the "frequency" of words, style, and story that best fits the situation we're in. We change ourselves by shifting into the language of a different speech community as the need arises. But it's also true that every one of us has experienced conflict between our speech communities—times when we've felt "torn" between two ways of seeing and reacting to an event, torn between speaking in the voice we'd like to speak in and in the one that seems "appropriate." When our speech communities conflict, we're forced to make a choice between them. But when the cultures involved are powerful or deeply rooted in our identities, no simple choice is available. When this happens we feel silenced, as if an internalized censor were holding back our words, keeping us from thinking, speaking, and writing.

In the following selection, Chicana writer Gloria Anzaldúa dissects her own plural cultural identity, exploring the multiple speech communities she participates in and trying to assess what each contributes to her sense of self. Born and raised in the Rio Grande Valley in southwestern Texas, Anzaldúa grew up in a world that was divided along cultural and linguistic borders, a world that forced her to speak many languages and participate in many different speech communities. As Anzaldúa notes, speaking multiple languages and dialects can be a source of both pleasure and pain: participating in many speech communities can enrich your understanding of the world around you and lend you strength, but it can also lead to frustration, anger, and silence. In addition to writing poetry and fiction, Anzaldúa is an accomplished editor and cultural theorist whose work focuses on the experiences of multiethnic women in a society that is becoming more culturally and ethnically diverse. Like all her writings, this selection from her book *Borderlands/La Frontera: The New Mestiza* (1984) blends argument, poetry, personal stories, history, and political theory, as well as English and Spanish.

Before Reading

Try to recall one or two occasions you spoke with a "wild tongue." What was the situation you found yourself in? What were the consequences?

How to Tame a Wild Tongue

Gloria Anzaldúa

"We're going to have to control your tongue," the dentist says, pulling out all the metal from my mouth. Silver bits plop and tinkle into the basin. My mouth is a motherlode.

The dentist is cleaning out my roots. I get a whiff of the stench when I gasp. "I can't cap that tooth yet, you're still draining," he says.

"We're going to have to do something about your tongue," I hear the anger rising in his voice. My tongue keeps pushing out the wads of cotton, pushing back the drills, the long thin needles. "I've never seen anything as strong or as stubborn," he says. And I think, how do you tame a wild tongue, train it to be quiet, how do you bridle and saddle it? How do you make it lie down?

> "Who is to say that robbing a people of
> its language is less violent than war?"   —Ray Gwyn Smith[1]

I remember being caught speaking Spanish at recess—that was good for three licks on the knuckles with a sharp ruler. I remember being sent to the corner of the classroom for "talking back" to the Anglo teacher when all I was trying to do was tell her how to pronounce my name. If you want to be American, speak 'American.' If you don't like it, go back to Mexico where you belong."

"I want you to speak English. *Pa' hallar buen trabajo tienes que saber hablar el inglés bien. Qué vale toda tu educación si todavía hablas inglés con un* accent," my mother would say, mortified that I spoke English like a Mexican. At Pan American University, I, and all Chicano students were required to take two speech classes. Their purpose: to get rid of our accents.

Attacks on one's form of expression with the intent to censor are a violation of the First Amendment. *El Anglo can cara de inocente nos arrancó la lengua.* Wild tongues can't be tamed, they can only be cut out.

Overcoming the Tradition of Silence

Ahogadas, escupimos el oscuro.
Peleando con nuestra propia sombra
el silencio nos sepulta.

En boca cerrada no entran moscas. "Flies don't enter a closed mouth" is a saying I kept hearing when I was a child. *Ser habladora* was to be a gossip and a liar, to talk too much. *Muchachitas bien criadas,* well-bred girls don't answer back. *Es una falta de respeto* to talk back to one's mother or father. I

5

remember one of the sins I'd recite to the priest in the confession box the few times I went to confession: talking back to my mother, *hablar pa' 'tras, repelar. Hocicona, repelona, chismosa,* having a big mouth, questioning, carrying tales are all signs of being *mal criada.* In my culture they are all words that are derogatory if applied to women—I've never heard them applied to men.

The first time I heard two women, a Puerto Rican and a Cuban, say the word, *"nosotras,"* I was shocked. I had not known the word existed. Chicanas use *nosotros* whether we're male or female. We are robbed of our female being by the masculine plural. Language is a male discourse.

> And our tongues have become
> dry   the wilderness has
> dried out our tongues   and
> we have forgotten speech.   —Irena Klepfisz[2]

Even our own people, other Spanish speakers *nos quieren poner candados en la boca.* They would hold us back with their bag of *reglas de academia.*

OYÉ COMO LADRA: EL LENGUAJE DE LA FRONTERA

Quien tiene boca se equivoca.   —Mexican saying

"Pocho, cultural traitor, you're speaking the oppressor's language by   10
speaking English, you're ruining the Spanish language," I have been accused by various Latinos and Latinas. Chicano Spanish is considered by the purist and by most Latinos deficient, a mutilation of Spanish.

But Chicano Spanish is a border tongue which developed naturally. Change, *evolución, enriquecimiento de palabras nuevas por invención o adopción* have created variants of Chicano Spanish, *un nuevo lenguaje. Un lenguaje que corresponde a un modo de vivir.* Chicano Spanish is not incorrect, it is a living language.

For a people who are neither Spanish nor live in a country in which Spanish is the first language; for a people who live in a country in which English is the reigning tongue but who are not Anglo; for a people who cannot entirely identify with either standard (formal, Castillian) Spanish nor standard English, what recourse is left to them but to create their own language? A language which they can connect their identity to, one capable of communicating the realities and values true to themselves—a language with terms that are neither *español ni inglés,* but both. We speak a patois, a forked tongue, a variation of two languages.

Chicano Spanish sprang out of the Chicanos' need to identify ourselves as a distinct people. We needed a language with which we could communicate with ourselves, a secret language. For some of us, language is a home-land closer than the Southwest—for many Chicanos today live in the Midwest and the East. And because we are a complex, heterogeneous people, we speak many languages. Some of the languages we speak are:

1. Standard English
2. Working class and slang English
3. Standard Spanish
4. Standard Mexican Spanish
5. North Mexican Spanish dialect
6. Chicano Spanish (Texas, New Mexico, Arizona and California have regional variations)
7. Tex-Mex
8. *Pachuco* (called *caló*)

My "home" tongues are the languages I speak with my sister and brothers, with my friends. They are the last five listed, with 6 and 7 being closest to my heart. From school, the media and job situations, I've picked up standard and working class English. From Mamagrande Locha and from reading Spanish and Mexican literature, I've picked up Standard Spanish and Standard Mexican Spanish. From *los recién llegados*, Mexican immigrants, and *braceros*, I learned the North Mexican dialect. With Mexicans I'll try to speak either Standard Mexican Spanish or the North Mexican dialect. From my parents and Chicanos living in the Valley, I picked up Chicano Texas Spanish, and I speak it with my mom, younger brother (who married a Mexican and who rarely mixes Spanish with English), aunts and older relatives.

With Chicanas from *Nuevo México* or *Arizona* I will speak Chicano Spanish a little, but often they don't understand what I'm saying. With most California Chicanas I speak entirely in English (unless I forget). When I first moved to San Francisco, I'd rattle off something in Spanish, unintentionally embarrassing them. Often it is only with another Chicana *tejana* that I can talk freely.   15

Words distorted by English are known as anglicisms or *pochismos*. The *pocho* is an anglicized Mexican or American of Mexican origin who speaks Spanish with an accent characteristic of North Americans and who distorts and reconstructs the language according to the influence of English.[3] Tex-Mex, or Spanglish, comes most naturally to me. I may switch back and forth from English to Spanish in the same sentence or in the same word. With my sister and my brother Nune and with Chicano *tejano* contemporaries I speak in Tex-Mex.

From kids and people my own age I picked up *Pachuco*. *Pachuco* (the language of the zoot suiters) is a language of rebellion, both against

Standard Spanish and Standard English. It is a secret language. Adults of the culture and outsiders cannot understand it. It is made up of slang words from both English and Spanish. *Ruca* means girl or woman, *vato* means guy or dude, *chale* means no, *simón* means yes, *churro* is sure, talk is *periquiar*, *pigionear* means petting, *que gacho* means how nerdy, *ponte águila* means watch out, death is called *la pelona*. Through lack of practice and not having others who can speak it, I've lost most of the *Pachuco* tongue.

Chicano Spanish

Chicanos, after 250 years of Spanish/Anglo colonization, have developed significant differences in the Spanish we speak. We collapse two adjacent vowels into a single syllable and sometimes shift the stress in certain words such as *maíz/maiz, cohete/cuete*. We leave out certain consonants when they appear between vowels: *lado/lao, mojado/mojao*. Chicanos from South Texas pronounce *f* as *j* as in *jue (fue)*. Chicanos use "archaisms," words that are no longer in the Spanish language, words that have been evolved out. We say *semos, truje, haiga, ansina*, and *naiden*. We retain the "archaic" *j*, as in *jalar*, that derives from an earlier *h* (the French *halar* or the Germanic *halon* which was lost to standard Spanish in the 16th century), but which is still found in several regional dialects such as the one spoken in South Texas. (Due to geography, Chicanos from the Valley of South Texas were cut off linguistically from other Spanish speakers. We tend to use words that the Spaniards brought over from Medieval Spain. The majority of the Spanish colonizers in Mexico and the Southwest came from Extremadura—Hernán Cortés was one of them—and Andalucía. Andalucians pronounce *ll* like a *y*, and their *d's* tend to be absorbed by adjacent vowels: *tirado* becomes *tirao*. They brought *el lenguaje popular, dialectos y regionalismos*.)[4]

Chicanos and other Spanish speakers also shift *ll* to *y* and *z* to *s*.[5] We leave out initial syllables, saying *tar* for *estar*, *toy* for *estoy*, *hora* for *ahora* (*cubanos* and *puertorriqueños* also leave out initial letters of some words). We also leave out the final syllable such as *pa* for *para*. The intervocalic *y*, and *ll* as in *tortilla, ella, botella*, gets replaced by *tortia* or *tortiya, ea, botea*. We add an additional syllable at the beginning of certain words: *atocar* for *tocar*, *agastar* for *gastar*. Sometimes we'll say *lavaste las vacijas*, other times *lavates* (substituting the *ates* verb endings for the *aste*).

We use anglicisms, words borrowed from English: *bola* from ball, *carpeta*   20
from carpet, *máchina de lavar* (instead of *lavadora*) from washing machine. Tex-Mex argot, created by adding a Spanish sound at the beginning or end of an English word such as *cookiar* for cook, *watchar* for watch, *parkiar* for park, and *rapiar* for rape, is the result of the pressures on Spanish speakers to adapt to English.

We don't use the word *vosotros/as* or its accompanying verb form. We don't say *claro* (to mean yes), *imagínate,* or *me emociona,* unless we picked up Spanish from Latinas, out of a book, or in a classroom. Other Spanish-speaking groups are going through the same, or similar, development in their Spanish.

Linguistic Terrorism

Deslenguadas. Somos los del españñol deficiente. We are your linguistic nightmare, your linguistic aberration, your linguistic *mestisaje,* the subject of your *burla.* Because we speak with tongues of fire we are culturally crucified. Racially, culturally and linguistically *somos huérfanos*—we speak an orphan tongue.

Chicanas who grew up speaking Chicano Spanish have internalized the belief that we speak poor Spanish. It is illegitimate, a bastard language. And because we internalize how our language has been used against us by the dominant culture, we use our language differences against each other.

Chicana feminists often skirt around each other with suspicion and hesitation. For the longest time I couldn't figure it out. Then it dawned on me. To be close to another Chicana is like looking into the mirror. We are afraid of what we'll see there. *Pena.* Shame. Low estimation of self. In childhood we are told that our language is wrong. Repeated attacks on our native tongue diminish our sense of self. The attacks continue throughout our lives.

Chicanas feel uncomfortable talking in Spanish to Latinas, afraid of their censure. Their language was not outlawed in their countries. They had a whole lifetime of being immersed in their native tongue; generations, centuries in which Spanish was a first language, taught in school, heard on radio and TV, and read in the newspaper.

If a person, Chicana or Latina, has a low estimation of my native tongue, she also has a low estimation of me. Often with *mexicanas y latinas* we'll speak English as a neutral language. Even among Chicanas we tend to speak English at parties or conferences. Yet, at the same time, we're afraid the other will think we're *agringadas* because we don't speak Chicano Spanish. We oppress each other trying to out-Chicano each other, vying to be the "real" Chicanas, to speak like Chicanos. There is no one Chicano language just as there is no one Chicano experience. A monolingual Chicana whose first language is English or Spanish is just as much a Chicana as one who speaks several variants of Spanish. A Chicana from Michigan or Chicago or Detroit is just as much a Chicana as one from the Southwest. Chicano Spanish is as diverse linguistically as it is regionally.

25

By the end of this century, Spanish speakers will comprise the biggest minority group in the U.S., a country where students in high schools and colleges are encouraged to take French classes because French is considered more "cultured." But for a language to remain alive it must be used.[6] By the end of this century English, and not Spanish, will be the mother tongue of most Chicanos and Latinos.

So, if you want to really hurt me, talk badly about my language. Ethnic identity is twin skin to linguistic identity—I am my language. Until I can take pride in my language, I cannot take pride in myself. Until I can accept as legitimate Chicano Texas Spanish, Tex-Mex and all the other languages I speak, I cannot accept the legitimacy of myself. Until I am free to write bilingually and to switch codes without having always to translate, while I still have to speak English or Spanish when I would rather speak Spanglish, and as long as I have to accommodate the English speakers rather than having them accommodate me, my tongue will be illegitimate.

I will no longer be made to feel ashamed of existing. I will have my voice: Indian, Spanish, white. I will have my serpent's tongue—my woman's voice, my sexual voice, my poet's voice. I will overcome the tradition of silence.

> My fingers
> move sly against your palm
> Like women everywhere, we speak in code. . . .
> —Melanie Kaye/Kantrowitz[7]

"*Vistas*," *corridos, y comida:* My Native Tongue

In the 1960s, I read my first Chicano novel. It was *City of Night* by John Rechy, a gay Texan, son of a Scottish father and a Mexican mother. For days I walked around in stunned amazement that a Chicano could write and could get published. When I read *I Am Joaquín*[8] I was surprised to see a bilingual book by a Chicano in print. When I saw poetry written in Tex-Mex for the first time, a feeling of pure joy flashed through me. I felt like we really existed as a people. In 1971, when I started teaching High School English to Chicano students, I tried to supplement the required texts with works by Chicanos, only to be reprimanded and forbidden to do so by the principal. He claimed that I was supposed to teach "American" and English literature. At the risk of being fired, I swore my students to secrecy and slipped in Chicano short stories, poems, a play. In graduate school, while working toward a Ph.D., I had to "argue" with one advisor after the other, semester after semester, before I was allowed to make Chicano literature an area of focus.

Even before I read books by Chicanos or Mexicans, it was the Mexican 30 movies I saw at the drive-in—the Thursday night special of $1.00 a carload—that gave me a sense of belonging. *"Vámonos a las vistas,"* my mother would call out and we'd all—grandmother, brothers, sister and cousins—squeeze into the car. We'd wolf down cheese and bologna white bread sandwiches while watching Pedro Infante in melodramatic tearjerkers like *Nosotros los pobres,* the first "real" Mexican movie (that was not an imitation of European movies). I remember seeing *Cuando los hijos se van* and surmising that all Mexican movies played up the love a mother has for her children and what ungrateful sons and daughters suffer when they are not devoted to their mothers. I remember the singing-type "westerns" of Jorge Negrete and Miquel Aceves Mejía. When watching Mexican movies, I felt a sense of homecoming as well as alienation. People who were to amount to something didn't go to Mexican movies, or *bailes* or tune their radio to *bolero, rancherita,* and *corrido* music.

The whole time I was growing up, there was *norteño* music sometimes called North Mexican border music, or Tex-Mex music, or Chicano music, or *cantina* (bar) music. I grew up listening to *conjuntos,* three- or four-piece bands made up of folk musicians playing guitar, *bajo sexto,* drums and button accordion, which Chicanos had borrowed from the German immigrants who had come to Central Texas and Mexico to farm and build breweries. In the Rio Grande Valley, Steve Jordan and Little Joe Hernández were popular, and Flaco Jiménez was the accordion king. The rhythms of Tex-Mex music are those of the polka, also adapted from the Germans, who in turn had borrowed the polka from the Czechs and Bohemians.

I remember the hot, sultry evenings when *corridos*—songs of love and death on the Texas-Mexican borderlands—reverberated out of cheap amplifiers from the local *cantinas* and wafted in through my bedroom window.

Corridos first became widely used along the South Texas/Mexican border during the early conflict between Chicanos and Anglos. The *corridos* are usually about Mexican heroes who do valiant deeds against the Anglo oppressors. Pancho Villa's song, *"La cucaracha,"* is the most famous one. *Corridos* of John F. Kennedy and his death are still very popular in the Valley. Older Chicanos remember Lydia Mendoza, one of the great border *corrido* singers who was called *la Gloria de Tejas.* Her *"El tango negro,"* sung during the Great Depression, made her a singer of the people. The everpresent *corridos* narrated one hundred years of border history, bringing news of events as well as entertaining. These folk musicians and folk songs are our chief cultural myth-makers, and they made our hard lives seem bearable.

I grew up feeling ambivalent about our music. Country-western and rock-and-roll had more status. In the 50s and 60s, for the slightly educated and *agringado* Chicanos, there existed a sense of shame at being caught listening to our music. Yet I couldn't stop my feet from thumping to the music, could not stop humming the words, nor hide from myself the exhilaration I felt when I heard it.

There are more subtle ways that we internalize identification, especially   35
in the forms of images and emotions. For me food and certain smells are tied to my identity, to my homeland. Woodsmoke curling up to an immense blue sky; woodsmoke perfuming my grandmother's clothes, her skin. The stench of cow manure and the yellow patches on the ground; the crack of a .22 rifle and the reek of cordite. Homemade white cheese sizzling in a pan, melting inside a folded *tortilla*. My sister Hilda's hot, spicy *menudo, chile colorado* making it deep red, pieces of *panza* and hominy floating on top. My brother Carito barbequing *fajitas* in the backyard. Even now and 3,000 miles away, I can see my mother spicing the ground beef, pork and venison with *chile*. My mouth salivates at the thought of the hot steaming *tamales* I would be eating if I were home.

> *SI LE PREGUNTAS A MI MAMÁ, "¿QUÉ ERES?"*
>
> "Identity is the essential core of who
> we are as individuals, the conscious
> experience of the self inside."   —Kaufman[9]

Nosotros los Chicanos straddle the borderlands. On one side of us, we are constantly exposed to the Spanish of the Mexicans, on the other side we hear the Anglos' incessant clamoring so that we forget our language. Among ourselves we don't say *nosotros los americanos, o nosotros los españoles, o nosotros los hispanos*. We say *nosotros los mexicanos* (by *mexicanos* we do not mean citizens of Mexico; we do not mean a national identity, but a racial one). We distinguish between *mexicanos del otro lado* and *mexicanos de este lado*. Deep in our hearts we believe that being Mexican has nothing to do with which country one lives in. Being Mexican is a state of soul—not one of mind, not one of citizenship. Neither eagle nor serpent, but both. And like the ocean, neither animal respects borders.

> *Dime con quien andas y te diré quien eres.*
> (Tell me who your friends are and I'll tell you who
> you are.)   —Mexican saying

Si le preguntas a mi mamá. "¿Qué eres?" te dirá, "Soy mexicana." My brothers and sister say the same. I sometimes will answer *"soy mexicana"* and at others will say *"soy Chicana" o "soy tejana."* But I identified as *"Raza"* before I ever identified as *"mexicana"* or "Chicana."

As a culture, we call ourselves Spanish when referring to ourselves as a linguistic group and when copping out. It is then that we forget our predominant Indian genes. We are 70–80% Indian.[10] We call ourselves Hispanic[11] or Spanish-American or Latin American or Latin when linking ourselves to other Spanish-speaking peoples of the Western hemisphere and when copping out. We call ourselves Mexican-American[12] to signify we are neither Mexican nor American, but more the noun "American" than the adjective "Mexican" (and when copping out).

Chicanos and other people of color suffer economically for not acculturating. This voluntary (yet forced) alienation makes for psychological conflict, a kind of dual identity—we don't identify with the Anglo-American cultural values and we don't totally identify with the Mexican cultural values. We are a synergy of two cultures with various degrees of Mexicanness or Angloness. I have so internalized the borderland conflict that sometimes I feel like one cancels out the other and we are zero, nothing, no one. *A veces no soy nada ni nadie. Pero hasta cuando no lo soy, lo soy.*

When not copping out, when we know we are more than nothing, we   40
call ourselves Mexican, referring to race and ancestry; *mestizo* when affirming both our Indian and Spanish (but we hardly ever own our Black ancestry); Chicano when referring to a politically aware people born and/or raised in the U.S.; *Raza* when referring to Chicanos; *tejanos* when we are Chicanos from Texas.

Chicanos did not know we were a people until 1965 when César Chávez and the farmworkers united and *I Am Joaquín* was published and *la Raza Unida* party was formed in Texas. With that recognition, we became a distinct people. Something momentous happened to the Chicano soul—we became aware of our reality and acquired a name and a language (Chicano Spanish) that reflected that reality. Now that we had a name, some of the fragmented pieces began to fall together—who we were, what we were, how we had evolved. We began to get glimpses of what we might eventually become.

Yet the struggle of identities continues, the struggle of borders is our reality still. One day the inner struggle will cease and a true integration take place. In the meantime, *tenémos que hacer la lucha. ¿Quién está protegiendo los ranchos de mi gente? ¿Quién está tratando de cerrar la fisura entre la india y el blanco en nuestra sangre? El Chicano, si, el Chicano que anda como un ladrón en su propia casa.*

Los Chicanos, how patient we seem, how very patient. There is the quiet of the Indian about us.[13] We know how to survive. When other races have given up their tongue, we've kept ours. We know what it is to live under the hammer blow of the dominant *norteamericano* culture. But more than we count the blows, we count the days the weeks the years the centuries the eons until the white laws and commerce and customs will rot in the deserts they've created, lie bleached. *Humildes* yet proud, *quietos* yet wild, *nosotros los mexicanos-Chicanos* will walk by the crumbling ashes as we go about our business. Stubborn, persevering, impenetrable as stone, yet possessing a malleability that renders us unbreakable, we, the *mestizas* and *mestizos,* will remain.

NOTES

1. Ray Gwyn Smith, *Moorland Is Cold Country*, unpublished book.
2. Irena Klepfisz, *"Di rayze aheym/*The Journey Home," in *The Tribe of Dina: A Jewish Women's Anthology*, Melanie Kaye/Kantrowitz and Irena Klepfisz, eds. (Montpelier, VT: Sinister Wisdom Books, 1986), 49.
3. R. C. Ortega, *Dialectología Del Barrio*, trans. Hortencia S. Alwan (Los Angeles, CA: R. C. Ortega Publisher & Bookseller, 1977), 132.
4. Eduardo Hernandéz-Chávez, Andrew D. Cohen, and Anthony F. Beltramo, *El Lenguaje de los Chicanos: Regional and Social Characteristics of Language Used by Mexican Americans* (Arlington, VA: Center for Applied Linguistics, 1975), 39.
5. Hernandéz-Chávez, xvii.
6. Irena Klepfisz, "Secular Jewish Identity: Yidishkayt in America," in *The Tribe of Dina*, Kaye/Kantrowitz and Klepfisz, eds., 43.
7. Melanie Kaye/Kantrowitz, "Sign," in *We Speak In Code: Poems and Other Writings* (Pittsburgh, PA: Motheroot Publications, Inc., 1980), 85.
8. Rodolfo Gonzales, *I Am Joaquín/Yo Soy Joaquín* (New York, NY: Bantam Books, 1972). It was first published in 1967.
9. Kaufman, 68.
10. Chávez, 88–90.
11. "Hispanic" is derived from *Hispanis* (*España,* a name given to the Iberian Peninsula in ancient times when it was a part of the Roman Empire) and is a term designated by the U.S. government to make it easier to handle us on paper.
12. The Treaty of Guadalupe Hidalgo created the Mexican-American in 1848.
13. Anglos, in order to alleviate their guilt for dispossessing the Chicano, stressed the Spanish part of us and perpetrated the myth of the Spanish Southwest. We have accepted the fiction that we are Hispanic, that is, Spanish, in order to accommodate ourselves to the dominant culture and its abhorrence of Indians. Chávez, 88–91.

Issues for Discussion

1. What's the significance of the story about the dentist that Anzaldúa uses to begin her essay?
2. In what ways is Anzaldúa "silenced" by her family and the cultures she grows up in?
3. How does Anzaldúa characterize each language community that she belongs to? What qualities or powers does she ascribe to each? What, in particular, does her home culture—Chicano culture—contribute to her personal identity?

4. How do you react to the unusual mix of languages that Anzaldúa uses in this excerpt? Do you find it strange, intriguing, poetic, or just confusing? What do you think she's trying to achieve by writing in this way?

JOURNAL OPTIONS

Responding to "How to Tame a Wild Tongue"

1. Write a letter to Anzaldúa describing your reactions to her language and ideas. (If your home language isn't English, try imitating Anzaldúa's bilingual style in your response to her essay.)
2. Write about a time when you felt that someone in authority tried to silence you or criticized the way you spoke.
3. In discussing the various terms used to define her ethnicity (Spanish, Hispanic, Latino, Chicano, and so forth), Anzaldúa suggests that the words you choose to describe your heritage have political consequences. Why does such naming matter? What does she mean when she claims that when people use some of these terms they are "copping out"? Do you agree? List all the terms that people of your own ethnic group use to define themselves, then freewrite about which of these words you prefer, and why. After freewriting, discuss your responses in class.

ESSAY OPTION

Comparing Your Speech Communities

Becoming aware of the many speech communities you participate in is an important part of becoming a proficient writer. Your choice of words, attitude, style, tone—even the kinds of stories you tell and assume your reader understands—depend on the speech community you are addressing. In addition, you may experience conflicts between "Standard English" and one of the languages or styles of English you speak at home or with your friends. This assignment gives you the chance to examine two of your own speech communities, to explore what they mean to you, and to assess how they are interrelated.

Write a paper in which you compare *two* of the speech communities or social groups you belong to. As you decide which group to focus on, try to go beyond preconceived ideas about how speech communities are defined. You may discover that one of your most memorable speech communities was centered in the kitchen of a favorite aunt, the garage where your cousins fixed old cars, a neighborhood hangout, a club you were a member of, or a particular workplace. Most important, try to select speech communities or social groups that have a special meaning or importance for you. You should describe both of these groups in detail and explain what makes them significant to you. You might refer to Gloria Anzaldúa's essay for a possible model. Anzaldúa associates speaking Chicano Spanish with the "crack of a .22 rifle" and "white cheese sizzling in a pan." She "hears" her speech community in the polkas of Flaco Jiménez "the accordion king" and in the *corridos*—or folk ballads—that celebrate Mexican heroes. These are a few of the many details, associations, and "condensed stories" she offers to explain what speaking Spanish and being a Chicana mean to her.

As you prewrite and plan your essay, you may want to consider some of the following questions: What stories, memories, or associations are connected with your speech communities? How do your language and behavior change as you move from one group to the other? Have there been times in your experience when the values and expectations of these two groups conflicted? If so, how did you balance or choose between these competing demands? What does inclusion in these two speech communities mean to you? How does each group contribute to your identity?

CHAPTER 11

Academically Speaking: Audience, Language, Power

Talking in Class: School Voice

Calvin and Hobbes

by Bill Watterson

In the cartoon above, Calvin seems to have figured out the key to successful academic writing. The way he sees it, academic writing has less to do with clear thinking and common sense than it does with highfalutin theories and multisyllabic head-scratchers. Like many students before him, Calvin's model of academic "voice" derives from a common stereotype about intellectuals and academic discourse: from his perspective, teachers want to read something that "sounds" intellectual—something that is so "intimidating and impenetrable" that it's just got to be smart—even if it all adds up to verbal gobbledygook. In Calvin's view, teachers speak a secret language of power, a language that is clear only to those who are lucky enough and intelligent enough to belong to the secret society of academia. When he imitates the pretentious language of this academic club—the verbal equivalent of a secret handshake—Calvin becomes a pompous, self-important, middle-aged academic windbag; in short, he becomes exactly like the audience he thinks he's addressing.

Why is this model of academic voice so common? In part, it derives from the years we spend poring over textbooks that often present even the most exciting ideas as dull formulas or dry facts. Cultural stereotypes also contribute: by the time you enter college, you've already encountered enough mass-media parodies of boring intellectuals and pompous professors to write a good one yourself. Another source is the "rules" of writing you pick up in school—rules like "Never use 'I'" or "Don't fill your paper with personal opinion." When you've been taught that academic writing is supposed to be abstract and impersonal, it's easy to imagine it sounding like something produced by a machine. And, to be honest, there's more than a hint of truth in Calvin's parody: freighted with highly specialized vocabulary and obsessed with theory and precision, much academic writing does tend to sound like computer-generated nonsense to someone outside the discipline it's written for. Take a glance at the following example from the introduction to a book about narrative:

> The specific situation of this book is our staging of the encounter of semiotics, cognitive science, and psychoanalysis—the superimposing of these discourses within the same interpretive context that we have constructed for studying scientific and humanist discourse.

All the elements of academic voice at its worst are on display here: long-windedness, hundred-dollar vocabulary, and mind-numbing abstraction; like Calvin's parody, this kind of writing seems to work hard at sounding rigid, impersonal, and intimidating. It seems, in fact, more interested in making an impression than in communicating ideas that may be important, moving, or meaningful to a reader.

The good news is that you don't have to think and write like a cyborg to become a successful academic writer. Many professional academics write in styles and voices that are personal, down-to-earth, and at times even dramatic. The bad news is that this *eidolon,* this false image of academic voice, can wreak havoc with your work when you're learning how to write for academic purposes. Trying to "sound educated" can cut you off from one of your greatest assets as a developing writer; when you mimic the abstract style that's commonly associated with academic writing, you lose touch with the many languages and voices that you already have at your disposal.

Voice is one of the most important qualities of any piece of writing. A powerful story or speech becomes inseparable in our memories from the sound of the speaking voice: for anyone who has listened to the famous tape, the phrase "I have a dream" instantly conjures up the tone and texture of Martin Luther King's unforgettable oratory; his voice is woven into our cultural memory. Most of us have strong associations with particular voices from our own lives, too: Remember your best friend's hushed, ominous voice when she told you the ghost story that terrified you one night when you were ten, or the ringing voice of the speaker whose fire and conviction riveted the attention of 1,500 restless high school students? Of course, when you're reading words on a page, there's no live voice to listen to; all you experience is an approximation of a spoken voice. But some written approximations can move you as if you're hearing a good speaker — the words on the page seem to have life and personality — while others seem flat, distant, boring. You may repeatedly doze off over your U.S. history text but spend hours devouring *The Autobiography of Malcolm X*. Why? The answer lies, at least partially, in voice.

We begin our exploration of voice with a reading that challenges most of our common preconceptions about the tone and style of academic discourse. In the following short but powerful personal essay, A. S. (anonymous student) who attended Los Angeles City College, chooses to reject the safe, formal *eidolon* of school voice and to risk something livelier and more personal.

Before Reading

Take a few moments to think about some memorable experiences you've had in which someone was speaking to you — alone or as part of a group or crowd. Maybe it was the sweetest voice you ever heard, or the most stirring, or the dullest or most annoying. Visualize the scene and try to recapture your feelings as you recall the voice's quality and tone, the expression and attitude of the speaker. What words come to mind when you think of this voice? Compare your responses with those of your classmates, pooling your responses to create a "dictionary" of terms for describing voice.

I Come from Everywhere
A. S.

I come from Alcoholism. I come from Drug Addiction. I come from Welfare. I come from a place where babysitters don't exist. I hail from a city of too much responsibility. I ran in sophisticated streets, baby, and I can hold my own. I come from everywhere--and no place at all. I was a grownup at six, with all of the independence but none of the freedom.

I come from 1967, Summer of love. I had parents that married young. They made two babies in two years, then divorced. I come from this place where Daddies are vague weekenders, looming large in the darkness, and Mommies dig the nightlife, like to "party down," don't bake no cookies. I lived in thirty-seven houses before I saw my fourteenth year. I can't remember all the schools. Can't remember!

I raised my little sister; she still calls me "mama." I made scrambled eggs for dinner, breakfast, and lunch. I was the one with the chipped-tooth grin and the angry, old eyes.

I was sent to my Dad, C.O.D., when I was a freshman in high school. His third wife made do, but when push came to shove, as it always does, she said, "You kids go, or you go." So us kids went.

Mom didn't want no two, tall teenagers, so she walked. Said, "I don't owe you a fucking thing." Said, "I can't take it, adoption's the option." Foolishly, brave Aunt Sandy, as white as her sister was black, stepped in. Took in the two tall ones; now she had five. I come from Sandy, who made sixteen bearable. At 17, on the edge of graduation from the fifth high school, Mom says, "I want in!"

All of a sudden, I come from REHABILITATION. Sweet Jesus, hold everything! Turn back the clock on all damage done! Tried to make room for the woman in my head, but wasn't much left after all. Mom spends five years clean and sober, making amends.

5

I split to another town. Came alone, with two suitcases. I came with strength. I came with pride. I carried the weight of a lifetime in the crease of my brow.

I am somebody. I keep my family at a distance. I hold my friends in my heart like newborn babies. I am a motherless child, a childless mother. I'm the one they didn't think could do it. I am an open wound, but <u>I</u> am the doctor. And baby, I'll win this war.

I come from destruction, yet still I live! I come from hopelessness, but I believe. I come from neglect, I bear the scar, yet I am able to love and protect. I come from devastation, yet I create. I came from the mouth of death, and I survived. Look at me: I come from nowhere, but here I am, tall, proud, and in your face.

Issues for Discussion

1. How would you describe the "voice" of this essay? What specific elements contribute to it?
2. How does A. S.'s voice compare with Paul Roberts's (p. 230)? With Gloria Anzaldúa's (p. 249)? Which do you prefer and why?

JOURNAL OPTION

Exploring Academic Voice

Write two versions of a note describing an imaginary (or real) bad day you've had recently and explaining why you had to turn in a paper (also real or imaginary) late. Address the first version to a friend and the second to the professor whose deadline you missed. How would you describe the difference in the voices you used in these two notes? Which do you prefer and why?

Capturing Voice in Writing

Voice is something we rarely think about when we speak; in casual conversation, our voice—the style, tone, vocabulary, accent, and attitude of our speech—is determined in large part by the speech community we're operating in at a given moment. We're all highly skilled at adapting our voices to suit our audience: most of us, for example, probably wouldn't use exactly the same words, tone, and style when talking to a parent, a teacher, a friend, or a police officer. We're so accomplished at this art of conversational audience analysis that we usually take it for granted. When you speak to someone directly, you can communicate through facial expressions, hand gestures, and body movements. You can raise or lower your voice, alter your tone, slow down, speed up, and pause dramatically. Perhaps most importantly, you can watch your listeners' faces for signs of interest, confusion, or boredom, and act accordingly. When you're writing, though, you have only the words on the page to rely on—and they need to do much heavier work. How do you begin to express a scowl, a smile, a high five, a conspiratorial whisper, an angry bellow, a defiant hand on a hip—in short, how do you convey your personality and style—in words alone?

The most useful resource a writer has for creating the illusion of voice in writing is the knowledge she gains from belonging to many different speech communities. Every speech community has its own distinctive voice or accent, its own rich vocabulary, tonal patterns, established attitudes, and vocal styles. If, like Gloria Anzaldúa, you can recite a dozen *corridos* from memory, you'll have no problem identifying the rhythms and intonations of Tejano Spanish; if you can rap, you have access to a whole different set of vocal patterns and gestures. The trick lies in your ability to capture these living, changing vocal patterns in the relatively static patterns offered by written words. To convey the voice they want to project in a particular situation, writers frequently rely on two aspects of written English: vocabulary and sentence shape.

Vocabulary

The kind of language you use—street language, textbook language, TV news anchor language—conveys your style, level of formality, and attitude toward your readers. Compare these two sentences from A.S. and Leslie Marmon Silko:

> I come from this place where Daddies are vague weekenders, looming large in the darkness, and Mommies dig the nightlife, like to "party down," don't bake no cookies.

> Where I come from, the words that are most highly valued are those which are spoken from the heart, unpremeditated and unrehearsed.

Both writers are talking about their backgrounds—some of the habits and values that surrounded them as they grew up—and both sentences are clear, direct, and skillfully written. But the language creates a very different voice in each case. A.S. is informal ("I come from *this place*"), conversational ("Daddies," "Mommies," "weekenders"), uses slang ("dig," "party down"), plays with language ("looming large in the darkness"), and doesn't worry about being grammatically correct all the time ("don't bake no cookies"). She is confiding in you, talking as she would to a friend; you could be sitting on the floor late at night, sharing a pizza and swapping stories. Silko is more formal and correct ("Where I come from, . . ." "those which are spoken"), her words more professorial ("highly valued," "unpremeditated," "unrehearsed"). She sounds as if she's addressing a group of well-educated people, some or all of whom may be strangers; perhaps she's standing at a podium or sitting behind a table at the front of a classroom or lecture hall; she's not condescending or unfriendly, but she places herself at a greater distance from you than A.S. does.

Some readers strongly prefer one of these voices to the other: some respond to the lively sense of drama of A.S. while others are drawn to Silko's reflectiveness and dignity. However, both styles are effective (and therefore "correct") in the right situation and for the right audience. In a highly personal essay like "I Come from Everywhere," an informal voice is perfectly appropriate: it conveys a sense of her personality more vividly than a more "proper" style would be able to do. If you "cleaned up" the sentence above, for example, you might end up with a bland, lifeless statement like this: "I come from an area where fathers visit only on weekends and mothers enjoy attending parties and do not bake any cookies." Ugh—this sounds like a robot speaking, not a person.

On the other hand, Silko's more scholarly topic (analyzing the function of language and literature in the Pueblo culture) calls for a more formal style. But while Silko sounds more academic, she doesn't sound stiff and bloodless like our "translation" of A.S. She also speaks in the first person, and she tells stories as well as analyzing them. Her observations about Pueblo storytelling are based not only on the traditional myths and tales that are part of the Pueblo culture as a whole, but also on her Aunt Suzie's storytelling style and her own experience as a guest speaker in a high school English class. In fact, Silko is very conscious in her essay of modifying formal conventions to reflect her own values and cultural traditions: "I have intentionally not written a formal paper to read to this session . . . because I want you to hear and to experience English in a nontraditional structure, a structure that follows patterns from the oral tradition." A really skillful writer has a range of voices at her command, and she carefully shapes her voice to suit the occasion and the audience, but as Silko demonstrates, even a formal, academic voice doesn't have to sound dull or mechanical; it, too, can reflect the writer's beliefs and purposes.

Sentence Shape and Rhythm

Sentence length and structure can suggest a particular pace and attitude—both components of a writer's voice. A series of very short or incomplete sentences can make the writer sound like someone who's in a hurry. Rushed, impatient, abrupt. No time to explain. Gotta go. Short sentences can also sound strong and dramatic, as in the opening paragraph of "I Come from Everywhere":

> I come from Alcoholism. I come from Drug Addiction. I come from Welfare. I come from a place where babysitters don't exist. I hail from a city of too much responsibility. I ran in sophisticated streets, baby, and I can hold my own.

The brevity of the first three sentences highlights the dangers and difficulties the writer has faced in her life—alcoholism, addiction, welfare—and the repeated phrase "I come from . . ." sounds direct and no-nonsense. The next few sentences are a little longer; the writer varies her rhythm and phrasing to prevent monotony: "I come from . . . I hail from . . . I ran in . . ."

By contrast, longer, more grammatically complex sentences evoke a different feeling. They can, for example, suggest a speaker who is trying to discover words that will do justice to a complex idea or set of ideas. You hear this kind of intellectual rhythm in the following passage from Gloria Anzaldúa:

> For a people who are neither Spanish nor live in a country in which Spanish is the first language; for a people who live in a country in which English is the reigning tongue but who are not Anglo; for a people who cannot entirely identify with either standard (formal, Castillian) Spanish nor standard English, what recourse is left to them but to create their own language? A language which they can connect their identity to, one capable of communicating the realities and values true to themselves—a language with terms that are neither *español ni ingles,* but both.

Instead of the dramatic starts and stops in "I Come from Everywhere," Anzaldúa's writing moves slowly, repeating the same phrase ("For a people who . . .") again and again and building momentum before coming to the climactic question "What recourse is left to them but to create their own language?" She follows up with three phrases that play off her initial sentence, each one elaborating the idea of language she is presenting ("A language . . . ," "one capable of . . . ," "a language with . . ."). This kind of measured and balanced repetition gives her writing a sense of gravity and importance. Her voice sounds serious and weighty—much like the kind of voice you might expect from a formal declaration or a political manifesto.

Of course, long sentences don't always generate tones of seriousness and solemnity. Longer sentences with a "looser" grammatical structure can evoke completely different feelings. They can, for example, suggest a speaker who is relaxed and reflective; listen to the rhythm of this sentence from David Mura's family story in Chapter 2:

> From classical records to Japanese pottery and prints, from children's books to various Japanese foods, my aunt's house was filled with objects exotic to me, that embodied some alternative to my parents' all-American suburbia of bridge, golf, and television.

In contrast to the energy of A.S. and Anzaldúa's seriousness, Mura creates a tone in this long sentence that's personal, informal, and reflective. It's almost as if he's taking us along on a leisurely stroll through his aunt's home, noting what he sees there in his memory as he goes. In this instance, his use of a longer sentence creates an atmosphere of intimacy, not formality.

OPTIONAL
ACTIVITIES

Experimenting with Voice

1. Find examples of formal and informal writing and share them in class. Work in pairs to "translate" a short paragraph from a formal to an informal voice and vice versa. Read the originals and the revised versions aloud and compare their effects. Do the translations sound strange? If so, why?
2. Return to one of the family or school stories you wrote earlier in the course. Rewrite one paragraph using all short, simple sentences; write another version of the same paragraph using longer, more complex sentences; finally, do a third version mixing short and long sentences depending on the mood you want to create or the ideas you want to emphasize. Compare notes on the effects of each version.

Virtual Realities

Earlier we explored some of the problems that arise from assumptions that writers commonly make about readers. If you assume your reader knows more than you do—that she's a super-reader who can almost literally read your mind—you're likely to skimp on introductions and details. If you assume your reader shares your ideas, values, and beliefs, you probably won't bother explaining unusual experiences or concepts. Teachers often try to combat these assumptions by urging students to write for a "general audience" or a "general reader." Defined as the "average" well-educated, literate adult, the general reader was cooked up to get students to look past the teacher as reader. A general reader is a remarkable fiction: it's someone who's sharp enough to catch every grammar mistake but dull enough to need a detailed explanation of every point you make.

The problem is that the general reader is *too* general: if your model of the reader is someone who speaks "Standard English" and knows a little bit about everything, how do you know what to explain and what to leave out? How do you know what a general reader will enjoy, or laugh at, or find insulting—particularly since most of what seems humorous, enjoyable, or hurtful is so intimately bound up with the cultures we belong to? The school-created fiction of the general reader, like the fiction of "Standard English," hides the fact that every audience is different. Readers, like all human beings, have specific likes and dislikes; they have values, beliefs, pet peeves, politics, and hang-ups of their own. Readers, like writers, have their own cultures and speech communities, and a great deal of a writer's energy goes into adjusting her language, voice, and approach in response to the expectations of her audience.

So where do these expectations come from? How do you figure out the pet peeves, politics, and language preferences of your audience? Lacking a face-to-face, flesh-and-blood listener, writers are forced to fall back on imagination. Every time a writer puts pen to paper, she builds an imaginary mental model—consciously or unconsciously—of the reader she wants to address. In some limited situations—for example, when you write a letter to a friend—the intended reader is a specific individual, someone you know and for whom you probably already have a well-developed mental model. Your knowledge of your friend guides the way you shape the stories you tell in your letter, helps you know what you need to explain in detail, and tells you what your reader will agree with, doubt, abhor, or laugh at. In a sense, the letter you write results from a collaborative dialogue between yourself as writer and the model of your friend that lives in your imagination.

Writing to a specific individual is relatively easy because your mental model of a friend, relative, or boss is well developed. But most writers don't usually enjoy the luxury of a personal relationship with their audience. In most writing situations the reader exists only as a virtual reader—an anonymous, generalized image that represents a whole group of potential readers. The writer constructs this model reader from stereotypical ideas about the target audience's interests, values, and beliefs—from everything that the reader knows about the *type* of person the reader is likely to be and about the background knowledge the reader is likely to possess. If, for example, you're writing a review of a rock concert for your campus newspaper, you might assume that your reader is somewhere between seventeen and twenty-five years old, is interested in rock music, can distinguish between rap, rock, metal, pop, punk, and alternative, recognizes a number of major bands by name, and knows something about the latest tours and releases. Your virtual reader would probably also be familiar with a range of pop cultural figures and events—from MTV and the latest music videos to what's hot in fashion and at the box office. Armed with this knowledge, you'd be in a good position to predict what your reader might think is cool, funny, bogus, or boring. You'd know which details to include and which to leave out. And you'd even have a good sense about the way your voice should sound: chances are you wouldn't kick off your article with a line like, "Recently I had the immense pleasure of attending a popular music function at the Palladium highlighting the work of Nine Inch Nails."

In part, your image of this virtual "rock reader" may derive from your own knowledge of pop culture, but it also includes your understanding of what other rock fans like, how they behave, and what they know or understand. In fact, you may not even agree with all the ideas or share all the values of your virtual audience: after all, you may worship seventies disco music, but that doesn't stop your virtual reader from being enthralled by the rock of the moment. The virtual readers we create in our minds are useful to us because they don't simply reproduce our own knowledge and expectations: they help us anticipate our readers' needs, expectations, and reactions precisely because they model the differences between us and the readers we address.

The flip side of the virtual reader is the virtual writer. When we read a piece of writing we do more than simply decode the words on the page or add them up to capture the overall meaning of the text. When we approach a piece of writing attentively and critically, we try to grasp the author's intention—the purpose underlying the author's words. In order to understand the writer's motivation, we draw on all the information we can glean from the text to construct a mental image of the writer. Every statement, choice of words, and assumption provides us with clues about the author's views, experience, values, and beliefs. The approach the author takes to her topic, the arguments she makes, her attitudes toward her audience, her voice, and even the things she chooses not to say add to the image of the virtual writer that we build in our minds as we read. Think back for a moment to Beverly Donofrio's "Trouble" (p. 9). The image of the writer that emerges from this personal memoir is someone who understands rebellion and questions authority, but she's also someone who remembers crucial details from teen life in the early 1960s—things like the name of a popular hair spray or the cultural importance of Pat Boone. Bits of information like these, plus knowledge about Donofrio's working-class Italian background and the facts we garner about her family situation, come together to create an image of who she is as a person, a writer, and a thinker. As soon as we identify some of the key qualities of our virtual writer—a smart-talking, tough, intelligent, independent, working-class Italian American woman who rejects parental authority and grows up on the streets—we connect her with a reservoir of ideas and associations that help us understand her actions and her thinking. What kind of job do you think Donofrio would be more likely to have in her mid-twenties—florist or bartender? Who do you think she'd be more likely to vote for—a Democrat or a Republican? All of the hunches we make about a text—including the inferences we make about the author's intentions, his attitude toward his topic, and his view of his readers—depend on the virtual writer we create in our minds as we read.

OPTIONAL ACTIVITIES

Identifying Virtual Readers and Writers

1. Return to Paul Roberts's "Speech Communities" in Chapter 9 (p. 230). Working in pairs, try to identify in as much detail as possible the virtual writer that emerges from Roberts's text. What image of Roberts do you get from your rereading of "Speech Communities"? What does he look like? What socioeconomic class or group would you identify him with? How do you think he sees himself? How does he seem to want us to view him and his ideas? What would you imagine some of his central ideas, values, and beliefs to be? As you detail your picture of Roberts's virtual writer, think, too, about the virtual audience that's implied in this essay. Who is Roberts writing for? How can you tell?

2. Again working in pairs, try to develop a similar model of the virtual writer in Gloria Anzaldúa's "How to Tame a Wild Tongue" (p. 249). Brainstorm a list of qualities, characteristics, values, and beliefs that you associate with the virtual writer of "Wild Tongue." Who is Anzaldúa's virtual audience? How would you describe her attitude toward her reader? How does her attitude compare with Roberts's attitude toward his audience?

3. Take another look at Leslie Marmon Silko's essay on language and Pueblo culture in Chapter 1 (p. 21). To what extent does Silko's virtual writer identify with or resist identification with her audience? How can you tell?

Voice and Audience

As Gloria Anzaldúa reminds us, there's a life-and-death connection between language and identity. Your voice—the vocabulary you use, the formality of your tone, the intimacy or grandeur of your style—tells the reader who you are or who you want to be. But your choice of voice isn't a free decision: the language you choose to write is determined by your aims and purposes *and* by the values, tastes, and expectations of the audience—or audiences—you're addressing. In academic settings, questions of voice, audience, and identity become particularly thorny. When you write to a teacher, do you have to emulate the language of power—do you have to erase all traces of your home speech communities and languages? Is there any way to master the conventions of "Standard English" and academic writing and not sacrifice all of the spunk, insight, and creativity you derive from the words and stories you learn at home or on the street? Or, like Calvin in the cartoon at the beginning of this chapter, do you have to become a pseudo-intellectual windbag to make it in college?

The relation between audience, power, and voice is the theme of the following essay by African American activist, poet, and teacher June Jordan. "Nobody Mean More to Me than You and the Future Life of Willie Jordan" tells the story of Jordan's decision to teach Black English in a college poetry course and her students' struggle when confronted with the need to speak the language of power. A professor of English at SUNY Stony Brook when she wrote this essay, Jordan now teaches African American Studies at the University of California, Berkeley. She has authored several collections of essays, including *On Call* (1986), the source of this selection; *Naming Our Destiny* (1989); and *Technical Difficulties* (1992). Her most recent volume of poetry, *Haruko Love Poems: New and Selected Love Poems,* appeared in 1994.

Before Reading

Take a few moments to jot down what you know about Black English. How would you describe the differences in style, tone, and expressiveness between Black English and "Standard English"? Where have you encountered Black English? How many forms of Black English are you aware of?

Nobody Mean More to Me than You[1] and the Future Life of Willie Jordan
June Jordan

Black English is not exactly a linguistic buffalo; as children, most of the thirty-five million Afro-Americans living here depend on this language for our discovery of the world. But then we approach our maturity inside a larger social body that will not support our efforts to become anything other than the clones of those who are neither our mothers nor our fathers. We begin to grow up in a house where every true mirror shows us the face of somebody who does not belong there, whose walk and whose talk will never look or sound "right," because that house was meant to shelter a family that is alien and hostile to us. As we learn our way around this environment, either we hide our original word habits, or we completely surrender our own voice, hoping to please those who will never respect anyone different from themselves: Black English is not exactly a linguistic buffalo, but we should understand its status as an endangered species, as a perishing, irreplaceable system of community intelligence, or we should expect its extinction, and, along with that, the extinguishing of much that constitutes our own proud, and singular, identity.

What we casually call "English," less and less defers to England and its "gentlemen." "English" is no longer a specific matter of geography or an element of class privilege; more than thirty-three countries use this tool as a means of "intranational communication."[2] Countries as disparate as Zimbabwe and Malaysia, or Israel and Uganda, use it as their non-native currency of convenience. Obviously, this tool, this "English," cannot function inside thirty-three discrete societies on the basis of rules and values absolutely determined somewhere else, in a thirty-fourth other country, for example.

In addition to that staggering congeries of non-native users of English, there are five countries, or 333,746,000 people, for whom this thing called "English" serves as a native tongue.[3] Approximately 10% of these native speakers of "English" are Afro-American citizens of the U.S.A. I cite these numbers and varieties of human beings dependent on "English" in order, quickly, to suggest how strange and how tenuous is any concept of "Standard English." Obviously, numerous forms of English now operate inside a natural, and uncontrollable, continuum of development. I would suppose "the standard" for English in Malaysia is not the same as "the standard" in Zimbabwe. I know that standard forms of English for Black people in this country do not copy that of whites. And, in fact, the structural differences between these two kinds of English have intensified, becoming more Black, or less white, despite the expected homogenizing effects of television[4] and other mass media.

Nonetheless, white standards of English persist, supreme and unquestioned, in these United States. Despite our multi-lingual population, and despite the deepening Black and white cleavage within that conglomerate, white standards control our official and popular judgements of verbal proficiency and correct, or incorrect, language skills, including speech. In contrast to India, where at least fourteen languages co-exist as legitimate Indian languages, in contrast to Nicaragua, where all citizens are legally entitled to formal school instruction in their regional or tribal languages, compulsory education in America compels accommodation to exclusively white forms of "English." White English, in America, is "Standard English."

This story begins two years ago. I was teaching a new course, "In Search   5
of the Invisible Black Woman," and my rather large class seemed evenly divided between young Black women and men. Five or six white students also sat in attendance. With unexpected speed and enthusiasm we had moved through historical narratives of the 19th century to literature by and about Black women in the 20th. I had assigned the first forty pages of Alice Walker's *The Color Purple,* and I came, eagerly, to class that morning:
"So!" I exclaimed, aloud. "What did you think? How did you like it?"
The students studied their hands, or the floor. There was no response. The tense, resistant feeling in the room fairly astounded me.
At last, one student, a young woman still not meeting my eyes, muttered something in my direction:
"What did you say?" I prompted her.
"Why she have them talk so funny. It don't sound right."   10
"You mean the language?"
Another student lifted his head: "It don't look right, neither. I couldn't hardly read it."
At this, several students dumped on the book. Just about unanimously, their criticisms targeted the language. I listened to what they wanted to say and silently marvelled at the similarities between their casual speech patterns and Alice Walker's written version of Black English.
But I decided against pointing to these identical traits of syntax; I wanted not to make them self-conscious about their own spoken language — not while they clearly felt it was "wrong." Instead I decided to swallow my astonishment. Here was a negative Black reaction to a prize winning accomplishment of Black literature that white readers across the country had selected as a best seller. Black rejection was aimed at the one irreducibly Black element of Walker's work: the language — Celie's Black English. I wrote the opening lines of *The Color Purple* on the blackboard and asked the students to help me translate these sentences into Standard English:

You better not never tell nobody but God. It'd kill your mammy.
Dear God,
    I am fourteen years old. I have always been a good girl. Maybe you can give me a sign letting me know what is happening to me.
    Last spring after Little Lucious come I heard them fussing. He was pulling on her arm. She say it too soon, Fonso. I ain't well. Finally he

leave her alone. A week go by, he pulling on her arm again. She say, Naw, I ain't gonna. Can't you see I'm already half dead, an all of the children.[5]

Our process of translation exploded with hilarity and even hysterical, shocked laughter: The Black writer, Alice Walker, knew what she was doing! If rudimentary criteria for good fiction include the manipulation of language so that the syntax and diction of sentences will tell you the identity of speakers, the probable age and sex and class of speakers, and even the locale—urban/rural/southern/western—then Walker had written, perfectly. This is the translation into Standard English that our class produced:

Absolutely, one should never confide in anybody besides God. Your secrets could prove devastating to your mother.
Dear God,
     I am fourteen years old. I have always been good. But now, could you help me to understand what is happening to me?
     Last spring, after my little brother, Lucious, was born, I heard my parents fighting. My father kept pulling at my mother's arm. But she told him, "It's too soon for sex, Alfonso. I am still not feeling well." Finally, my father left her alone. A week went by, and then he began bothering my mother, again: Pulling her arm. She told him, "No, I won't! Can't you see I'm already exhausted from all of these children?"

(Our favorite line was "It's too soon for sex, Alphonso.")   15
Once we could stop laughing, once we could stop our exponentially wild improvisations on the theme of Translated Black English, the students pushed me to explain their own negative first reactions to their spoken language on the printed page. I thought it was probably akin to the shock of seeing yourself in a photograph for the first time. Most of the students had never before seen a written facsimile of the way they talk. None of the students had ever learned how to read and write their own verbal system of communication: Black English. Alternatively, this fact began to baffle or else bemuse and then infuriate my students. Why not? Was it too late? Could they learn how to do it, now? And, ultimately, the final test question, the one testing my sincerity: Could I teach them? Because I had never taught anyone Black English and, as far as I knew, no one, anywhere in the United States, had ever offered such a course, the best I could say was "I'll try."

He looked like a wrestler.
He sat dead center in the packed room and, every time our eyes met, he quickly nodded his head as though anxious to reassure, and encourage, me.

Short, with strikingly broad shoulders and long arms, he spoke with a surprisingly high, soft voice that matched the soft bright movement of his eyes. His name was Willie Jordan. He would have seemed even more unlikely in the context of Contemporary Women's Poetry, except that ten or twelve other Black men were taking the course, as well. Still, Willie was conspicuous. His extreme fitness, the muscular density of his presence underscored the riveted, gentle attention that he gave to anything anyone said. Generally, he did not join the loud and rowdy dialogue flying back and forth, but there could be no doubt about his interest in our discussions. And, when he stood to present an argument he'd prepared, overnight, that nervous smile of his vanished and an irregular stammering replaced it, as he spoke with visceral sincerity, word by word.

That was how I met Willie Jordan. It was in between "In Search of the 20 Invisible Black Woman" and "The Art of Black English." I was waiting for Departmental approval and I supposed that Willie might be, so to speak, killing time until he, too, could study Black English. But Willie really did want to explore Contemporary Women's Poetry and, to that end, volunteered for extra research and never missed a class.

Towards the end of that semester, Willie approached me for an independent study project on South Africa. It would commence the next semester. I thought Willie's writing needed the kind of improvement only intense practice will yield. I knew his intelligence was outstanding. But he'd wholeheartedly opted for "Standard English" at a rather late age, and the results were stilted and frequently polysyllabic, simply for the sake of having more syllables. Willie's unnatural formality of language seemed to me consistent with the formality of his research into South African apartheid. As he projected his studies, he would have little time, indeed, for newspapers. Instead, more than 90% of his research would mean saturation in strictly historical, if not archival, material. I was certainly interested. It would be tricky to guide him into a more confident and spontaneous relationship both with language and apartheid. It was going to be wonderful to see what happened when he could catch up with himself, entirely, and talk back to the world.

September, 1984: Breezy fall weather and much excitement! My class, "The Art of Black English," was full to the limit of the fire laws. And, in Independent Study, Willie Jordan showed up, weekly, fifteen minutes early for each of our sessions. I was pretty happy to be teaching, altogether!

I remember an early class when a young brother, replete with his ever present pork-pie hat, raised his hand and then told us that most of what he'd heard was "all right" except it was "too clean." "The brothers on the street," he continued, "they mix it up more. Like 'fuck' and 'motherfuck.'

Or like 'shit.'" He waited. I waited. Then all of us laughed a good while, and we got into a brawl about "correct" and "realistic" Black English that led to Rule 1.

Rule 1: *Black English is about a whole lot more than mothafuckin.*

As a criterion, we decided, "realistic" could take you anywhere you want to go. Artful places. Angry places. Eloquent and sweetalkin places. Polemical places. Church. And the local Bar & Grill. We were checking out a language, not a mood or a scene or one guy's forgettable mouthing off.

It was hard. For most of the students, learning Black English required a fallback to patterns and rhythms of speech that many of their parents had beaten out of them. I mean *beaten.* And, in a majority of cases, correct Black English could be achieved only by striving for *incorrect* Standard English, something they were still pushing at, quite uncertainly. This state of affairs led to Rule 2.

Rule 2: *If it's wrong in Standard English it's probably right in Black English, or, at least, you're hot.*

It was hard. Roommates and family members ridiculed their studies, or remained incredulous, "You *studying* that shit? At school?" But we were beginning to feel the companionship of pioneers. And we decided that we needed another rule that would establish each one of us as equally important to our success. This was Rule 3.

Rule 3: *If it don't sound like something that come out somebody mouth then it don't sound right. If it don't sound right then it ain't hardly right. Period.*

This rule produced two weeks of compositions in which the students agonizingly tried to spell the sound of the Black English sentence they wanted to convey. But Black English is, preeminently, an oral/spoken means of communication. *And spelling don't talk.* So we needed Rule 4.

Rule 4: *Forget about the spelling. Let the syntax carry you.*

Once we arrived at Rule 4 we started to fly because syntax, the structure of an idea, leads you to the world view of the speaker and reveals her values. The syntax of a sentence equals the structure of your consciousness. If we insisted that the language of Black English adheres to a distinctive Black syntax, then we were postulating a profound difference between white and Black people, *per se.* Was it a difference to prize or to obliterate?

There are three qualities of Black English—the presence of life, voice, and clarity—that testify to a distinctive Black value system that we became excited about and self-consciously tried to maintain.

1. Black English has been produced by a pre-technocratic, if not anti-technological, culture. More, our culture has been constantly threatened by annihilation or, at least, the swallowed blurring of assimilation. Therefore, our language is a system constructed by people constantly needing to insist

that we exist, that we are present. Our language devolves from a culture that abhors all abstraction, or anything tending to obscure or delete the fact of the human being who is here and now/the truth of the person who is speaking or listening. Consequently, *there is no passive voice construction possible in Black English.* For example, you cannot say, "Black English is being eliminated." You must say, instead, "White people eliminating Black English." The assumption of the presence of life governs all of Black English. Therefore, overwhelmingly, *all action takes place in the language of the present indicative.* And every sentence assumes the living and active participation of at least two human beings, the speaker and the listener.

2. A primary consequence of the person-centered values of Black English is the delivery of voice. If you speak or write Black English, your ideas will necessarily possess that otherwise elusive attribute, *voice.*   35

3. One main benefit following from the person-centered values of Black English is that of *clarity.* If your ideas, your sentence, assumes the presence of at least two living and active people, you will make it understandable because the motivation behind every sentence is the wish to say something real to somebody real.

As the weeks piled up, translation from Standard English into Black English or vice versa occupied a hefty part of our course work.

> Standard English (hereafter S.E.): "In considering the idea of studying Black English those questioned suggested—"
> (What's the subject? Where's the person? Is anybody alive in there, in that idea?)
> Black English (hereafter B.E.): "I been asking people what you think about somebody studying Black English and they answer me like this:"

But there were interesting limits. You cannot "translate" instances of Standard English preoccupied with abstraction or with nothing/nobody evidently alive, into Black English. That would warp the language into uses antithetical to the guiding perspective of its community of users. Rather you must first change those Standard English sentences, themselves, into ideas consistent with the person-centered assumptions of Black English.

GUIDELINES FOR BLACK ENGLISH

1. Minimal number of words for every idea: This is the source for the aphoristic and/or poetic force of the language; eliminate every possible word.
2. Clarity: If the sentence is not clear it's not Black English.

3. Eliminate use of the verb *to be* whenever possible. This leads to the deployment of more descriptive and therefore, more precise verbs. 40

4. Use *be* or *been* only when you want to describe a chronic, ongoing state of things.

> He *be* at the office, by 9. (He is always at the office by 9.)
> He *been* with her since forever.

5. Zero copula: Always eliminate the verb *to be* whenever it would combine with another verb, in Standard English.

> S.E.: She is going out with him.
> B.E.: She going out with him.

6. Eliminate *do* as in:

> S.E.: What do you think? What do you want?
> B.E.: What you think? What you want?

Rules number 3, 4, 5, and 6 provide for the use of the minimal number of verbs per idea and, therefore, greater accuracy in the choice of verb.

7. In general, if you wish to say something really positive, try to formulate the idea using emphatic negative structure. 45

> S.E.: He's fabulous.
> B.E.: He bad.

8. Use double or triple negatives for dramatic emphasis.

> S.E.: Tina Turner sings out of this world.
> B.E.: Ain nobody sing like Tina.

9. Never use the *-ed* suffix to indicate the past tense of a verb.

> S.E.: She closed the door.
> B.E.: She close the door. Or, she have close the door.

10. Regardless of intentional verb time, only use the third person singular, present indicative, for use of the verb to *have,* as an auxiliary.

> S.E.: He had his wallet then he lost it.
> B.E.: He have him wallet then he lose it.
> S.E.: We had seen that movie.
> B.E.: We seen that movie. Or, we have see that movie.

11. Observe a minimal inflection of verbs. Particularly, never change from the first person singular forms to the third person singular.

> S.E. Present Tense Forms: He goes to the store.
> B.E.: He go to the store.

> S.E.: Past Tense Forms: He went to the store.
> B.E.: He go to the store. Or, he gone to the store. Or, he been to the store.

12. The possessive case scarcely ever appears in Black English. Never use an apostrophe ('s) construction. If you wander into a possessive case component of an idea, then keep logically consistent: *ours, his, theirs, mines*. But, most likely, if you bump into such a component, you have wandered outside the underlying world-view of Black English.

> S.E.: He will take their car tomorrow.
> B.E.: He taking they car tomorrow.

13. Plurality: Logical consistency, continued: If the modifier indicates plurality then the noun remains in the singular case.

> S.E.: He ate twelve doughnuts.
> B.E.: He eat twelve doughnut.
> S.E.: She has many books.
> B.E.: She have many book.

14. Listen for, or invent, special Black English forms of the past tense, such as: "He losted it. That what she felted." If they are clear and readily understood, then use them.

15. Do not hesitate to play with words, sometimes inventing them: e.g. "astropotomous" means huge like a hippo plus astronomical and, therefore, signifies real big.

16. In Black English, unless you keenly want to underscore the past tense nature of an action, stay in the present tense and rely on the overall context of your ideas for the conveyance of time and sequence.

17. Never use the suffix *-ly* form of an adverb in Black English.

> S.E.: The rain came down rather quickly.
> B.E.: The rain come down pretty quick.

18. Never use the indefinite article *an* in Black English.

> S.E.: He wanted to ride an elephant.
> B.E.: He want to ride him a elephant.

19. Invarient syntax: in correct Black English it is possible to formulate an imperative, an interogative, and a simple declarative idea with the same syntax:

> B.E.: You going to the store?
> You going to the store.
> You going to the store!

50

55

Where was Willie Jordan? We'd reached the mid-term of the semester. Students had formulated Black English guidelines, by consensus, and they were now writing with remarkable beauty, purpose, and enjoyment:

I ain hardly speakin for everybody but myself so understan that.

— Kim Parks

Samples from student writings:

Janie have a great big ole hole inside her. Tea Cake the only thing that fit that hole . . .

That pear tree beautiful to Janie, especial when bees fiddlin with the blossomin pear there growin large and lovely. But personal speakin, the love she get from starin at that tree ain the love what starin back at her in them relationship. (Monica Morris)

Love is a big theme in, *They Eye Was Watching God.* Love show people new corners inside theyself. It pull out good stuff and stuff back bad stuff . . . Joe worship the doing uh his own hand and need other people to worship him too. But he ain't think about Janie that she a person and ought to live like anybody common do. Queen life not for Janie. (Monica Morris)

In both life and writin, Black womens have varietous experience of love that be cold like a iceberg or fiery like a inferno. Passion got for the other partner involve, man or woman, seem as shallow, ankle-deep water or the most profoundest abyss. (Constance Evans)

Family love another bond that ain't never break under no pressure. (Constance Evans)

You know it really cold / When the friend you / Always get out the fire / Act like they don't know you / When you in the heat. (Constance Evans)

Big classroom discussion bout love at this time. I never take no class where us have any long arguin for and against for two or three day. New to me and great. I find the class time talkin a million time more interestin than detail bout the book. (Kathy Esseks)

As these examples suggest, Black English no longer limited the students, in any way. In fact, one of them, Philip Garfield, would shortly "translate" a pivotal scene from Ibsen's *Doll House,* as his final term paper:

Nora: I didn't gived no shit. I thinked you a asshole back then, too, you make it so hard for me save mines husband life.

> *Krogstad:* Girl, it clear you ain't any idea what you done. You done exact
> what I once done, and I losed my reputation over it.
> *Nora:* You asks me believe you once act brave save you wife life?
> *Krogstad:* Law care less why you done it.
> *Nora:* Law must suck.
> *Krogstad:* Suck or no, if I wants, judge screw you wid dis paper.
> *Nora:* No way, man. (Philip Garfield)

But where was Willie? Compulsively punctual, and always thoroughly 60
prepared with neatly typed compositions, he had disappeared. He failed to
show up for our regularly scheduled conference, and I received neither a
note nor a phone call of explanation. A whole week went by. I wondered if
Willie had finally been captured by the extremely current happenings in
South Africa: passage of a new constitution that did not enfranchise the
Black majority, and militant Black South African reaction to that affront. I
wondered if he'd been hurt, somewhere. I wondered if the serious workload
of weekly readings and writings had overwhelmed him and changed his
mind about independent study. Where was Willie Jordan?

One week after the first conference that Willie missed, he called: "Hello,
Professor Jordan? This is Willie. I'm sorry I wasn't there last week. But something has come up and I'm pretty upset. I'm sorry but I really can't deal
right now."

I asked Willie to drop by my office and just let me see that he was okay.
He agreed to do that. When I saw him I knew something hideous had happened. Something had hurt him and scared him to the marrow. He was all
agitated and stammering and terse and incoherent. At last, his sadly jum-
bled account let me surmise, as follows: Brooklyn police had murdered his
unarmed, twenty-five-year-old brother, Reggie Jordan. Neither Willie nor
his elderly parents knew what to do about it. Nobody from the press was interested. His folks had no money. Police ran his family around and around,
to no point. And Reggie was really dead. And Willie wanted to fight, but he
felt helpless.

With Willie's permission I began to try to secure legal counsel for the
Jordan family. Unfortunately Black victims of police violence are truly numerous while the resources available to prosecute their killers are truly
scarce. A friend of mine at the Center for Constitutional Rights estimated
that just the preparatory costs for bringing the cops into court normally approaches $180,000. Unless the execution of Reggie Jordan became a major
community cause for organizing, and protest, his murder would simply become a statistical item.

Again, with Willie's permission, I contacted every newspaper and media person I could think of. But the William Bastone feature article in *The Village Voice* was the only result from that canvassing.

Again, with Willie's permission, I presented the case to my class in Black English. We had talked about the politics of language. We had talked about love and sex and child abuse and men and women. But the murder of Reggie Jordan broke like a hurricane across the room.

There are few "issues" as endemic to Black life as police violence. Most of the students knew and respected and liked Jordan. Many of them came from the very neighborhood where the murder had occurred. All of the students had known somebody close to them who had been killed by police, or had known frightening moments of gratuitous confrontation with the cops. They wanted to do everything at once to avenge death. Number One: They decided to compose personal statements of condolence to Willie Jordan and his family written in Black English. Number Two: They decided to compose individual messages to the police, in Black English. These should be prefaced by an explanatory paragraph composed by the entire group. Number Three: These individual messages, with their lead paragraph, should be sent to *Newsday*.

The morning after we agreed on these objectives, one of the young women students appeared with an unidentified visitor, who sat through the class, smiling in a peculiar, comfortable way.

Now we had to make more tactical decisions. Because we wanted the messages published, and because we thought it imperative that our outrage be known by the police, the tactical question was this: Should the opening, group paragraph be written in Black English or Standard English?

I have seldom been privy to a discussion with so much heart at the dead heat of it. I will never forget the eloquence, the sudden haltings of speech, the fierce struggle against tears, the furious throwaway, and useless explosions that this question elicited.

That one question contained several others, each of them extraordinarily painful to even contemplate. How best to serve the memory of Reggie Jordan? Should we use the language of the killers—Standard English—in order to make our ideas acceptable to those controlling the killers? But wouldn't what we had to say be rejected, summarily, if we said it in our own language, the language of the victim, Reggie Jordan? But if we sought to express ourselves by abandoning our language wouldn't that mean our suicide on top of Reggie's murder? But if we expressed ourselves in our own language wouldn't that be suicidal to the wish to communicate with those who, evidently, did not give a damn about us/Reggie/police violence in the Black community?

At the end of one of the longest, most difficult hours of my own life, the students voted, unanimously, to preface their individual messages with a paragraph composed in the language of Reggie Jordan. *"At least we don't give up nothing else. At least we stick to the truth: Be who we been. And stay all the way with Reggie."*

It was heartbreaking to proceed, from that point. Everyone in the room realized that our decision in favor of Black English had doomed our writings, even as the distinctive reality of our Black lives always has doomed our efforts to "be who we been" in this country.

I went to the blackboard and took down this paragraph, dictated by the class:

> . . . YOU COPS!
> WE THE BROTHER AND SISTER OF WILLIE JORDAN, A FELLOW STONY BROOK STUDENT WHO THE BROTHER OF THE DEAD REGGIE JORDAN. REGGIE, LIKE MANY BROTHER AND SISTER, HE A VICTIM OF BRUTAL RACIST POLICE, OCTOBER 25, 1984. US APPALL, FED UP, BECAUSE THAT ANOTHER SENSELESS DEATH WHAT OCCUR IN OUR COMMUNITY. THIS WHAT WE FEEL, THIS, FROM OUR HEART, FOR WE AIN'T STAYIN' SILENT NO MORE:

With the completion of this introduction, nobody said anything. I asked for comments. At this invitation, the unidentified visitor, a young Black man, ceaselessly smiling, raised his hand. He was, it so happens, a rookie cop. He had just joined the force in September and, he said, he thought he should clarify a few things. So he came forward and sprawled easily into a posture of bar-room, or fireside, nostalgia:

"See," Officer Charles enlightened us, "Most times when you out on the street and something come down you do one of two things. Over-react or under-react. Now, if you under-react then you can get yourself kilt. And if you over-react then maybe you kill somebody. Fortunately it's about nine times out of ten and you will over-react. So the brother got kilt. And I'm sorry about that, believe me. But what you have to understand is what kilt him: Over-reaction. That's all. Now you talk about Black people and white people but see, now, I'm a cop myself. And (big smile) I'm Black. And just a couple months ago I was on the other side. But see it's the same for me. You a cop, you the ultimate authority: the Ultimate Authority. And you on the street, most of the time you can only do one of two things: over-react or under-react. That's all it is with the brother. Over-reaction. Didn't have nothing to do with race."

That morning Officer Charles had the good fortune to escape without being boiled alive. But barely. And I remember the pride of his smile when I read about the fate of Black policemen and other collaborators, in South Africa. I remember him, and I remember the shock and palpable feeling of shame that filled the room. It was as though that foolish, and deadly, young man had just relieved himself of his foolish, and deadly, explanation, face to face with the grief of Reggie Jordan's father and Reggie Jordan's mother. Class ended quietly. I copied the paragraph from the blackboard, collected the individual messages and left to type them up.

Newsday rejected the piece.

The Village Voice could not find room in their "Letters" section to print the individual messages from the students to the police.

None of the tv news reporters picked up the story.

Nobody raised $180,000 to prosecute the murder of Reggie Jordan.   80

Reggie Jordan is really dead.

I asked Willie Jordan to write an essay pulling together everything important to him from that semester. He was still deeply beside himself with frustration and amazement and loss. This is what he wrote, un-edited, and in its entirety:

> Throughout the course of this semester I have been researching the effects of oppression and exploitation along racial lines in South Africa and its neighboring countries. I have become aware of South African police brutalization of native Africans beyond the extent of the law, even though the laws themselves are catalyst affliction upon Black men, women and children. Many Africans die each year as a result of the deliberate use of police force to protect the white power structure.
>
> Social control agents in South Africa, such as policemen, are also used to force compliance among citizens through both overt and covert tactics. It is not uncommon to find bold-faced coercion and cold-blooded killings of Blacks by South African police for undetermined and/or inadequate reasons. Perhaps the truth is that the only reasons for this heinous treatment of Blacks rests in racial differences. We should also understand that what is conveyed through the media is not always accurate and may sometimes be construed as the tip of the iceberg at best.
>
> I recently received a painful reminder that racism, poverty, and the abuse of power are global problems which are by no means unique to South Africa. On October 25, 1984 at approximately 3:00 p.m. my brother, Mr. Reginald Jordan, was shot and killed by two New York City policemen from the 75th precinct in the East New York section of Brooklyn. His life ended at the age of twenty-five. Even up to this current point in time the Police Department has failed to provide my family, which consists of five brothers, eight sisters, and two parents, with a plausible reason for Reggie's death. Out of the many stories that were

given to my family by the Police Department, not one of them seems to hold water. In fact, I honestly believe that the Police Department's assessment of my brother's murder is nothing short of ABSOLUTE BULLSHIT, and thus far no evidence had been produced to alter perception of the situation.

Furthermore, I believe that one of three cases may have occurred in this incident. First, Reggie's death may have been the desired outcome of the police officers' action, in which case the killing was premeditated. Or, it was a case of mistaken identity, which clarifies the fact that the two officers who killed my brother and their commanding parties are all grossly incompetent. Or, both of the above cases are correct, i.e., Reggie's murderers intended to kill him and the Police Department behaved insubordinately.

Part of the argument of the officers who shot Reggie was that he had attacked one of them and took his gun. This was their major claim. They also said that only one of them had actually shot Reggie. The facts, however, speak for themselves. According to the Death Certificate and autopsy report, Reggie was shot eight times from point-blank range. The Doctor who performed the autopsy told me himself that two bullets entered the side of my brother's head, four bullets were sprayed into his back, and two bullets struck him in the back of his legs. It is obvious that unnecessary force was used by the police and that it is extremely difficult to shoot someone in his back when he is attacking or approaching you.

After experiencing a situation like this and researching South Africa I believe that to a large degree, justice may only exist as rhetoric. I find it difficult to talk of true justice when the oppression of my people both at home and abroad attests to the fact that inequality and injustice are serious problems whereby Blacks and Third World people are perpetually short-changed by society. Something has to be done about the way in which this world is set up. Although it is a difficult task, we do have the power to make a change.

—Willie J. Jordan Jr.
EGL 487, Section 58, November 14, 1984

It is my privilege to dedicate this book to the future life of Willie J. Jordan Jr.
August 8, 1985

NOTES

1. Black English aphorism crafted by Monica Morris, a Junior at S.U.N.Y. at Stony Brook, October, 1984.
2. *English is Spreading, But What Is English?* A presentation by Professor S. N. Sridahr, Dept. of Linguistics, S.U.N.Y. at Stony Brook, April 9, 1985: Dean's Conversation Among the Disciplines.

3. Ibid.
4. *New York Times,* March 15, 1985, Section One, p. 14: Report on study of Linguistics at the University of Pennsylvania.
5. Alice Walker, *The Color Purple,* p. 11, Harcourt Brace, N.Y.

Issues for Discussion

1. How might Paul Roberts explain Jordan's claim that Black English has become increasingly different from "Standard English"? Can you offer any additional explanations for this phenomenon?
2. What, according to Jordan, are the deepest cultural differences between Black English and "Standard English"? Do you agree that Black English expresses a more vital "presence of life" than "Standard English"?
3. If you had been a student in Jordan's class, would you have opted to write your letter of protest in "Standard" or Black English? Why?
4. How would you describe Jordan's audience? What do you imagine are her virtual reader's level of education, class background, political sympathies, values, and beliefs? How would you describe the virtual writer that emerges from this essay?

J O U R N A L   O P T I O N S

Exploring Voice and Audience

1. Translate any of the longer passages of Black English in Jordan's essay into "Standard English." What, if anything, is gained or lost in this translation?
2. Write a pro/con dialogue in your journal on whether it is appropriate for professors like Jordan to teach Black English—or any variety of English other than "Standard English"—in their classes. Share these dialogues with your classmates in small groups and try to reach a consensus on the issue.

E S S A Y   O P T I O N S

Addressing Different Audiences

Every time you address a different audience you become a different kind of writer: you adjust the assumptions you make about what your reader knows and understands according to the audience's level of education and variety of experience; you may adopt a different voice or writing style depending on the speech community your reader belongs to; you may even find yourself changing the way you present your ideas to accommodate the reader's cultural and political biases. The following essay options give you the chance to observe how you adapt your language and approach for different audiences.

Topic 1. Investigate an issue on your campus that you're interested in or personally involved with—it might concern student/faculty relations, affirmative action, fraternity/sorority issues, tensions between various student groups, a proposed new course requirement, or anything that affects you directly. Do some informal research on the issue by reading news items and interviewing students, faculty members, or administrators who are actively involved in the debate. You might want to share the burden by working in small groups: each person can take responsibility for gathering information from a particular source or exploring a particular perspective.

Once you've gathered information, write two versions of a brief editorial (two to three pages) about your issue, one addressing a fairly broadly defined audience—like all the professors and students at your college—and another (a revised version of the first) addressing a narrower speech community in which you participate. The point of this revision isn't to change your opinion on the issue but to present the same opinion in a different way, using strategies that appeal to the language, values, attitudes, and assumptions of each audience. When you've completed drafts of each version, distribute them in your read-around groups and let your group members see if they can determine the target audience of each editorial. Read-around group members might also want to speculate about the nature of the virtual writer that emerges from each version.

Topic 2. Find a newspaper editorial on a public issue that you're familiar with and have strong feelings about and write two letters of response to it, each directed to a different audience. Again, before writing you may want to do some informal research by reading additional news articles on your issue and by talking to classmates, friends, or co-workers to get their opinions and perspectives. The audiences you select should represent two of the groups that are most involved in the public debate you're addressing. If, for example, you're writing responses to an editorial on affirmative action, you might want to direct one to a local minority-rights interest group like MALDEF (Mexican American Legal Defense and Education Fund) or the NAACP and the other to a political interest group organized against affirmative action policies. Again, as in the case of Topic 1, your purpose isn't to present two opinions on the issue but to present the same opinion using strategies that appeal to the language, values, attitudes, and assumptions of each audience. Each response should be from two to three pages long.

CHAPTER 12

Revision Workshop: Shaping Structure, Shaping Voice

What's the Alternative?

THE FAR SIDE   By GARY LARSON

Edgar Allan Poe in a moment of writer's block.

What if Poe *had* written "The Telltale Bladder" instead of "The Telltale Heart"? The cartoon above plays on our sense of the inevitability of Poe's title—the familiarity of the tale makes the title appear self-evidently "right"; the idea of Poe agonizing over "The Telltale Duodenum" seems ridiculous. Much of our school experience in the United States conditions us to assume that there's always a single "right" choice: multiple choice and true/false exams, answer keys in textbooks, a proliferation of standardized achievement tests like the SAT. Because education so often means finding the right answer, it's no wonder that when students sit down to write, they long for a correct answer or surefire method that, if only they could find it, would make writing a breeze. Unfortunately, we don't have a magic formula to share. Language and communication are slippery things that require careful thought, not ready-made answers. Good writers constantly consider alternatives and play with a variety of options before choosing the strategy or approach that they think will be most effective for their particular purpose and audience. Writer and teacher Donald Murray notes that, as he prepared to write a new article, he would often try out up to 150 different titles for the piece to help him focus his ideas and think through the subject.[1] So although it seems unlikely that Poe ever seriously considered calling his short story "The Telltale Spleen," he undoubtedly did consider a number of alternatives before settling on the title we all recognize. This revision workshop encourages you to consider alternatives of structure and voice as you rework your drafts for the "Speech Communities" and "Multiple Audiences" assignments in the previous two chapters.

Structuring Comparisons

The essay option that calls for an extended comparison of two speech communities poses a question of structure: How do you go about organizing and unifying your discussion of both speech communities? Sometimes writers include a brief comparison—say, several sentences or paragraphs—in a longer essay in order to develop an idea or illustrate a point. For instance, June Jordan in "Nobody Mean More to Me than You and the Future Life of Willie Jordan" supports her criticism of the dominance of "white standards of English" in the United States by quickly contrasting American attitudes toward linguistic diversity to the attitudes in India and Nicaragua:

> Despite our multi-lingual population, and despite the deepening Black and white cleavage within that conglomerate, white standards control our official and popular judgments of verbal proficiency and correct, or

---

[1] Donald Murray, *Write to Learn,* 4th ed. (San Diego: Harcourt Brace, 1993), p. 102.

> incorrect, language skills, including speech. In contrast to India, where at least fourteen languages co-exist as legitimate Indian languages, in contrast to Nicaragua, where all citizens are legally entitled to formal school instruction in their regional or tribal languages, compulsory education in America compels accommodation to exclusively white forms of "English." (paragraph 4)

In Jordan's paragraph, the comparison is so brief that there's not much to organize; it's true that she might have reversed the order of the Indian and Nicaraguan examples, or she might have discussed the linguistic tolerance of these countries at the beginning or the end of the paragraph rather than in the middle. However, the point of the comparison (the remarkable rigidity of American linguistic "standards") can be made very succinctly, so the writer's options are fairly limited.

In "Speech Communities," Paul Roberts includes a four-paragraph comparison of British and American English in his discussion of social class distinctions and speech. Here's the gist of those paragraphs:

> The third great shaper of speech communities is the social class. This has been, and is, more important in England than in America. . . .
>
> England in the twentieth century has been much democratized, but the language differences are far from having disappeared. One can still tell much about a person's family, his school background, his general position in life by the way he speaks. . . .
>
> In America, of course, social distinctions have never been so sharp as they are in England. . . . But speech differences do exist. . . .
>
> Language differences on the social plane in America are likely to correlate with education or occupation rather than with birth—simply because education and occupation in America do not depend so much on birth as they do in other countries. . . .

As you can see, Roberts organizes his comparison in two blocks, first devoting two paragraphs to England and then another two paragraphs to the United States. However, he could have chosen to structure the discussion differently, by alternating the British and American examples throughout the passage. Nearly any extended comparison can be organized according to either block or alternating structure, and students often ask which approach is best. There's no hard-and-fast answer—that's the kind of judgment a writer has to make on a case-by-case basis. Let's take a close look at two essays to see how two writers chose to structure their comparisons differently. The first essay, by Kosuke Will Tanaka, compares the polite speech community of a restaurant where he works as a waiter to the rougher speech community of the basketball court that he shares with his friends. Tanaka is an English major who has recently given up waitering in order to work as a writing tutor in the Academic Advancement Program at UCLA.

STUDENT
WRITING

Taking the Journey through Speech
Kosuke Will Tanaka

Living in different speech communities is a part of life's journey. To survive in this competitive and diverse world, adjusting my language and changing my appearance to the people in a certain speech community is a necessity. I belong to two of the most distinct speech communities--one in a family restaurant where the atmosphere asks for formal speaking and passive behavior and the other on the blacktop basketball court where the action calls for street talk and aggressive, physical moves. The two environments have given me the experience of relating with people--to help me face the challenges of the real world and to help prepare me for a career.

Making the transitions into the restaurant and basketball speech communities, respectively, was difficult at first. When I was first exposed to the family restaurant scene, where I work as a waiter, I had to completely adjust my language into a more gentle and passive tone and change my appearance by wearing a nice clean dress shirt and a bow tie to please the customers. Even when I am in the worst of moods, about to take an order, I force a nice, big, phony smile and say with pre- tended enthusiasm, "Hi, how are you doing tonight? May I take your order? Couple more minutes? Sure. I'll be back when you're ready." And I leave with a persistent smile. Inside, I am really saying, "Can't you people make up your mind? You're messing up my routine."

On the contrary, when I am on the basketball court with my "b-ball" buddies, I feel I can speak in a more natural and comfortable way than in the restaurant. I put on my Nikes and "b-ball" shorts and roll my socks down to the ankles--I am ready to "ball." When I play basketball, I am a lot more involved in the action, so my language becomes more passionate. For example, when the game is really intense and I want my teammates to play good defense, I yell, "Hey guys, let's pick it up! It's point up so we gotta stick our man. Let's just 'D' it up, baby!" I get really pumped up and zealously express my feelings. On the blacktop, I don't speak formal English. I speak the "Language of the Playground," consisting of slang and street talk to get an emotional feel for the game.

On the other hand, when my speech community is the restaurant, I feel that I am holding in many of my feelings and therefore my body language is passive and gentle. For instance, when I know that a customer is completely finished with a meal, I pass by the table and hesitantly sneak my hand near the empty plate, but appearing unsure of myself about whether to take the plate, until the customer gives the sign to take it away. Or if I am passing out the dinner plates, I very gently set them down, so softly that the plates make no sound on the glass table. I act this way so the customers know that I am not forceful or aggressive towards them and they could feel like they have control. My body language represents my personality as a waiter and shows the customers how I will be serving them.

On the blacktop, it is quite a different manner. The competitiveness of the game demands assertive and aggressive action. The physical atmosphere the blacktop creates gives me the freedom to fully manifest my emotions. When I am really fired up, dribble-driving towards the basket and I see a monstrous, muscular defender just thirsting to block my shot, I

5

go straight at him attempting to make my shot. But it is a risk I take because on several occasions that I did drive in, I have ended up with a sprained ankle, bruised knee or a slight concussion. Nevertheless, these injuries are part of the game. That's life on the blacktop.

Although the speech communities of the family restaurant and the basketball court are unique, they both have rules to follow--rules of my boss and rules of the court. As a waiter, I am prohibited to wear anything but a tuxedo uniform and address the customers only in an eloquent and polite way--treating them like royalty. Consequently, if I don't follow the rules, I will be fired. On the basketball court, if I wear dress shoes and slacks, it will be breaking the dress code of basketball, and I will not be able to even step on the court. Shorts and sneakers are required on the blacktop. The court doesn't accept formal speech, so if I talk in an eloquent style, I will be told to "get out of the house," meaning "talk the 'b-ball' language or don't play." After I became a part of these speech communities, I gradually adapted to them. I conform my language and behavior because I want to be accepted in each of the communities. Being a waiter and a basketball player made me realize that every speech society has its own rules and if I do not follow them, I face the consequence of not being accepted in the community.

Waitering and playing basketball have given me the mind and skills to help prepare me for the future--in relating with people, giving interviews, and training for a career. In both communities, there is a great level of competition and they give me the experience to deal with many kinds of pressures which I will face a lot more of in the future. In the restaurant, I have to constantly compete with other waiters and waitresses for tips by giving the customers the best service I can provide. Some days it gets so competitive that waiters and

waitresses get in arguments over who will get the large table
with the ten businessmen dressed in Armani suits and who will
be the less fortunate one to serve the teenage couple with the
grunge look. On the court, competition is just part of the
game, but it is a different kind of competitiveness from the
waitering job. Teams compete against each other to decide
which teams remain on the court to be labeled the "king of
the court" for the day. Each individual player competes for
respect--respect as a "helluva baller" from the other players.
But I learned to handle the different kinds of pressure and
these levels of competition give me some background about the
challenges I will face in the future. In the working world,
there will always be the struggle for the competitive edge,
trying to get the promotions and leap ahead of everyone else.

The two communities I am engaged in also provide me the
experience to deal with different kinds of people. Every day
at work, I am dealing with new faces and I approach each customer with respect and courtesy. There are customers who are
outgoing and respond very friendly to me, but there are the
ones who complain and protest about the taste or constantly
nag me for more ketchup. But no matter what personalities the
customers have--either friendly and courteous or nasty and
disrespectful--I treat them all in a similar way as if they
were all one nice person--that is my job. Unlike the customers, I view each of the "b-ballers" with their own unique
attributes and characteristics. One player could be tall and
muscular but play "soft" and seldom show emotions. Another
player could be short and stubby, but really runs his mouth
until he finishes playing for the day. In basketball, contrary
to waitering, I deal with each personality in my unique way,
depending on the situation. For example, if the strong but
passive player is on the opposing team I will "attack" him
with the ball because I know that he will not aggressively

challenge my shot, but if he is on my team I will encourage
him to use his strength and play with more emotion. The second
player is labeled the "trash talker" and if he is on my team,
I will tell him to calm down, but if I am playing against him,
I will try to make him eat his words by guarding him tightly
and making some offensive moves over him.

The ability to deal with different kinds of people in
certain situations and adapt to their styles is a necessary
skill when going into the work force. My future co-workers
will all have different personalities--some friendly, some intimidating, and others just darn annoying--but I will eventually have to deal with that. When I am negotiating deals with
businesspeople, I will have to maintain a keen mind and know
how to deal with pushy people as well as dishonest ones. The
basketball and restaurant communities have helped me develop
these abilities by interacting with all kinds of people. I
learned that in different speech communities, I treat the people in a way that conforms to the specific environment. As a
waiter I treat everyone in a similar manner and as a basketball player I treat each personality in a different way. I
firmly believe that the experience in working with people and
the challenges I face from the competitiveness has greatly
helped me in developing invaluable tools to confidently look
toward my future.

Alternating Comparison Structure

As this essay shows, alternating structure involves identifying *categories* of
comparison—in this case, general characteristics shared by both speech
communities, such as language, appearance, behavior, rules, competition,
and interaction with people. Then within each category, Tanaka discusses
specific similarities or differences between the two communities. So the
focus shifts back and forth, or alternates, between the two speech communities throughout the essay. Here's a schematic outline that highlights this
alternating structure:

I. Introduction: Speech communities of the restaurant (formal speech, passive behavior) and the basketball court (street talk, physical aggression) help one prepare for a future career.

II. Speech and appearance
   A. restaurant: dress formally, please customers, hide real feelings
   B. basketball court: dress casually, play with intensity, express feelings

III. Behavior
   A. restaurant: be quiet, unobtrusive
   B. basketball court: compete aggressively, even risk injury

IV. Rules
   A. restaurant: conform to boss's rules to keep job
   B. basketball court: conform to peers' rules to be accepted

V. Competition
   A. restaurant: compete for tips
   B. basketball court: compete to win

VI. Interaction with people
   A. restaurant: treat everyone with same courtesy
   B. basketball court: respond differently to individuals as part of game strategy

VII. Conclusion: Skills learned in both speech communities will help in dealing with diverse co-workers and negotiating deals in the competitive business world.

Although alternating structure can be fairly formal, there's still room for flexibility. Notice, for example, that in some categories the comparison takes up two paragraphs while in others it takes only one. In the discussion of behavior, Tanaka devotes one entire paragraph to behavior in the restaurant and a second one to behavior on the court. In the discussion of rules, on the other hand, he discusses both speech communities in the same paragraph. Tanaka makes the reader's job easier by paragraphing for the eye: he breaks the text into manageable chunks when he has a lot to say about each speech community and combines his observations to avoid choppiness when there's less to say. Alternating structure doesn't commit you to producing a certain number of paragraphs for each category of comparison. In fact, it can work on nearly any scale—from alternating chapters in a book to alternating sentences in a paragraph. The message, finally, is not to let some predetermined form dictate the length or shape of your paper but rather to use form to help you organize, develop, and clarify your ideas.

Because a paper based on extended comparison often follows a relatively predictable pattern, it's easy to get caught up in the details of the analysis—the identification of similarities and differences—and forget that the comparison needs to make a larger point. Tanaka, for example, could have begun his essay by stating, "There are differences and similarities between the speech communities of the restaurant where I work and the basketball court where I play with my friends." The essay could have continued by pointing out that while speech, appearance, and behavior differ between the two communities, they share an emphasis on rules and competition. An essay like this would still be readable and well-organized, but it would seem pretty pointless: What's the significance of these similarities and differences? One of the strengths of Tanaka's paper is that his comparison has a clear purpose: besides detailing the differences in his language and behavior as he moves from the restaurant to the basketball court, he argues that adapting to both speech communities gives him valuable experience dealing with people and helps to prepare him for a career. A paragraph-by-paragraph summary shows how he develops his analysis:

Paragraph 1: Introduction: Speech communities of the restaurant (formal speech, passive behavior) and the basketball court (street talk, physical aggression) help one prepare for a future career.

Paragraph 2: Speech and appearance in the restaurant demand formal dress and polite speech; pleasing customers is paramount, even if this means hiding your real feelings.

Paragraph 3: Speech and appearance on the basketball court are casual and unrestrained, reflecting players' passionate involvement in the game.

Paragraph 4: Behavior in the restaurant must be quiet and unobtrusive, giving customers a sense of being in control.

Paragraph 5: Behavior on the court is competitive, leading to physical aggression, risk-taking, and occasional injury.

Paragraph 6: Rules in the restaurant and on the court both require conformity to win acceptance (break your boss's rules and risk losing your job; break peers' rules and risk their rejection).

Paragraph 7: Competition for tips in the restaurant and for winning on the court helps one prepare for competition in the work world.

Paragraph 8: Different people skills required in the restaurant and on the court help one develop flexibility for dealing with different kinds of people on the job.

Paragraph 9: Conclusion: Skills learned in both speech communities will help in dealing with diverse co-workers and negotiating deals in the competitive business world.

Instead of settling for an arbitrary list of differences and similarities, Tanaka unifies these observations by arguing that *all* the skills he's learning—the ability to adhere to rules, compete, and adapt to a variety of people—will be useful to him in the future. How persuasively do you think he builds his case? Are you convinced that both speech communities provide good preparation for a career? Which aspects of the essay do you find most and least persuasive and why?

Block Comparison Structure

Now let's look at a different strategy for shaping comparisons. In her analysis of speech communities, Amy Yang chooses to organize her material in two blocks rather than following the alternating format of Tanaka's essay. Yang is currently a junior majoring in psychobiology.

STUDENT
WRITING

My Speech Communities
Amy Yang

"Good-da Morn-lin," my mom whispered with her accented English, "Wen-Tieng, e gen chi dein le, ne jin tean bu yung sung shar ma?" (Amy, it's seven o'clock already; don't you need to go to school?)

Lingering in my dream world, I answered her back, "Ma, wuo jin tean may yo zhou ker, so e bu yung na ma zhou che lie." (Mom, I don't have a morning class today, so I don't have to wake up so early.)

"Thai young e jen zhou dou pee coo le, kwi dein che lie zhez block-face," mom called. (The sun is shining. Get up and get your breakfast!)

"Okee, ma," I replied and went back to sleep.

Ten minutes later, I was annoyed by another soul trying to wake me up from my slumber.

"Wake up, you lazy bum," my sister yelled into my ears.

5

"What, What?!" I jumped up from the bed, "Oooh, shit! you scared the heck outa me--are you crazy, trying to give me a heart attack? You butthead!"

"S-way zu (you pig)," Sis replied laughingly. "It's seven o'clock already, shitface. Don't be such a pig--get to class. I know you have one!"

"You're such an asshole," I mumbled annoyingly. "Of all the sisters in the world, why do I have to be stuck with you?"

"And I love you too, dear!" my sister replied.   10

People rarely realize that in a single day, they engage in as many as six speech communities. Switching from one community to the next is usually done unconsciously--for example: do you consciously switch from one code to another when speaking to your mom in Spanish or Chinese, and then to your closest friend in English? Do you consciously realize the differences in speech between your teachers and your peers? People adapt to numerous speech communities due to the environment they are in and the audience they are interacting with.

As a Chinese immigrant to this country, I was forced to learn a new language in order to communicate with the speech communities of my adopted country. But at the same time, it is important for me to maintain my mother language in order to communicate with my parents and my native people. By maintaining my mother language, I am also keeping in sight my identity as a Chinese and the values that come with it. As the dialogue with my mom shows, when speaking to her, I reject all horseplay language, slang and curses. The speech I use around her shows her of my honor and love for her because her position as my mom demands speech that is educated and respectful.

Being Chinese, I was taught at an early age the value of respect for elders. To the Chinese people, respect is a discipline one must teach to a child at the earliest age. If children should talk back to their elders or show any disrespect by way of their expression in language, punishment will be given. As a child growing up in the riches of Chinese custom, I knew that punishment extended beyond a mere grounding period of a few weeks, like the American custom. Instead, punishment was given in the form of kneeling in front of your ancestors for two hours, repenting your sins, or washing your mouth vigorously with soap ten times. I remember the first time I was punished with this crude fate. That afternoon, I was playing tack-ball with my sister and some of my friends in the back yard. The objective of the game was not to end up with the ball, and the only way to pass it on was to tack the ball at someone who eventually gets it. At the end, my sister and I won the game, but the opposing team wasn't too happy, because the next thing I knew the ball ended up in my face.

"Ta ma the, ne men pu fue che, zhea ley e zhe yea!" I yelled. (Fuck, you sour losers. You want to play it over?)

Unfortunately for me, my mom was within earshot when I   15
yelled out the words. The next thing I knew, I was being hurled into the bathroom with a bar of soap in my mouth.

"A lady doesn't use such language," my mom said (in Mandarin), "and certainly not around me."

The usage of "proper language" has its rewards. I remember the numerous occasions when my mom would take me to visit an aunt or a neighbor. Paying my respects and acting like a "sweet little girl" won me many treats of candies, hugs, and compliments that would inevitably produce a smile from my mom. In this speech community of elders, as with my mom, I would never raise my voice when speaking; I would never speak in a language they don't comprehend, such as slang or English, nor would I speak in broken sentences. With my parents, conversation is carried out with a certain level of formality and always in a mellow tone of voice that reflects respect and good manners. If I speak to my mom in the same fashion I use with my sister, not only will I be punished with the ritual of mouth washing, but I will also feel very uncomfortable because the audience I am interacting with does not fit into the kind of speech community I share with my peers. Try to imagine speaking to your best friend as you would with your mom. Would you feel a little bit weird? If so, then you are experiencing a conscious switch between speech communities. If your audience requires speech that is informal and rough, using speech that is formal and rigid will repel your audience and communication will be hindered.

The speech community I shared with my sister is very different from that of my mom. With my sister, I am not restrained by the rules of "proper language." I am free to raise my voice when I am feeling annoyed or mad; I can use slang to show that I am "cool" and "in with the crowd." I can also use curses, in a playful manner, to show my sister affection. The story behind this is as follows: When my family first moved to the United States, my sister and I were both struggling with the English language. I remember our first day in an American school. Everything and everyone seemed so intimidating and foreign. During lunch time, a dark-skin kid came up to us and taught us to pronounce the word "Fuck," saying that it is the way Americans greet each other. So my sister and I walked around the school yard, greeting people we'd just met with this new word we'd learned. Later on, when we found out what the word meant, my sister and I laughed and marveled at the miracle that we were still alive and unharmed. From then on, it became our ritual to pick out a word from TV, books, or from the people around us. And, after checking its meaning, we would practice using that word around each other. Even to this day, we still greet each other with "Fuck" and call each other names. I call her "butthead" and she calls me "shitface" be-

```
cause these are the words we have picked up from our environ-
ment and they contribute to the memory of the days we've
struggled with the American language.

      My sister and I belong to a speech community that allows
us to share secrets with each other--whispering words in Eng-
lish that are incomprehensible to my mom, and Chinese that
is unfathomable to our group of friends. With this community,
my sister and I form a bond that is unique to us, just as
other teenagers create their own bond through their individual
language of slang, curses, and name-calling. Language can be
boring and uninteresting without these groups of people who
make up these speech communities that transform language into
different expressions and give it an identity of its own.
```

It's immediately clear that the differences between Tanaka's and Yang's essays go beyond the way the writers structure their comparisons. The first paper is direct and thesis-driven: the writer makes the point of his essay clear in the first paragraph and carefully lines up supporting evidence throughout the rest of the essay. The second paper is indirect and exploratory: it presents a series of thematically linked personal stories woven together with analysis of the stories' significance and reflections on speech communities in general. The essay begins not with a statement of purpose but with a dialogue that demonstrates how differently Yang speaks to her mother and her sister. Next comes a paragraph that defines speech communities and explains the kind of code-switching illustrated by the opening dialogue. Not until the second paragraph following the dialogue does Yang arrive at the central point of the comparison—that for her, speaking English is a matter of survival, but continuing to speak Chinese is an expression of personal values and identity. In this essay, Yang seems less concerned with marshalling evidence to prove a point than with exploring the subject to see where it leads.

Despite the apparently spontaneous or natural flow of ideas in this essay, you can see how carefully structured it is if you look a little more closely. First, there is the unifying theme of "proper" versus "improper" language that underlies the discussion of both Chinese and English speech communities. The two "blocks" of the comparison also have a loosely parallel structure. As Yang examines each speech community, she first defines some of its values (tradition and respect in the Chinese-speaking community; freedom and being "cool" in the English-speaking community); next, she tells a story about a painful experience that reflects those values (getting her mouth washed out with soap for using improper language in front of her traditional Chinese mother; being tricked by an American classmate into using obscene language because she doesn't understand English); then she describes some of the pleasures or rewards of belonging to the speech community (compliments, treats, and a sense of honor for being properly respectful to elders; a special bond with her sister having survived the ordeal of learning English together). Verbal links further help to unify the essay: each story is introduced by the repeated phrase "I remember," thus connecting the stories structurally as well as thematically. In addition, each new paragraph is clearly linked to the previous one either by the repetition of a key word or phrase or by a transitional sentence that shows the relationship between the paragraphs.

A schematic outline of Yang's essay might look like this:

I. Introduction
    A. Prelude: Conversation with mother and with sister
    B. Definitions of speech communities and code switching
II. Chinese speech community: Shared with mother
    A. Speak English for survival; speak Chinese "mother language" to maintain a sense of identity and values—for example, respect, honor, and love of parents and culture
    B. Failure to show proper respect leads to punishment (story about mother washing mouth out with soap)
    C. Proper respect of elders is rewarded with compliments and treats; good manners in this community also mean more effective communication, because elders may be unfamiliar with English or with American slang
III. English speech community: Shared with sister
    A. No rules of "proper" language—free to express anger, to be "cool" by using slang, and to curse as a sign of affection
    B. Early experience learning English was painful and embarrassing (story about being tricked into thinking that "Fuck" meant "Hello"); affectionate cursing thus recalls sisters' shared struggles with English
    C. Reward of belonging to this speech community is a special bond with sister; ability to switch languages gives them a private code apart from both Chinese-speaking parents and English-speaking friends

Now that you've seen both alternating and block comparison structure in action, we return to the original question: Which is better? Many American college professors would undoubtedly find the alternating form more attractive or more satisfying because it breaks the subject up into conceptual categories and looks more analytical. But as Yang's essay demonstrates, block comparison requires at least as much careful thought, as much skill with language and form as the more obviously "academic" alternating comparison. In fact, it might be harder to write a really good essay in block form. Papers following this structure often end up looking like two separate essays because the two "blocks" aren't clearly enough related; the writers haven't provided the thematic, structural, and verbal links that unify Yang's essay. Other block comparisons end up sounding repetitious because the links are *too* obvious—the writers cover the same territory twice. Which of the two speech community essays do you prefer? Which do you find easier to read? Which is more interesting? Which approach appeals to you more— the direct, argumentative style of Tanaka's essay or the more indirect, reflective style of Yang's?

Revising Your Draft: Outlining as a Revision Tool

As you can see from the preceding examples, outlining a paper after it's been drafted can be as useful as outlining before writing—maybe even more so. Outlining your draft gives you an overview of the whole essay: it can help you see connections between ideas, notice gaps in development, and detect unnecessary repetition. It's easier to see the paper's structure when you look at an outline, because you don't get bogged down in detail or distracted by questions of editing. A paragraph-by-paragraph summary (see p. 299) can give you an idea how well the ideas connect to one another and to your overall purpose, while a more schematic outline (see pp. 298 and 305) is good for revealing structural gaps and organizational problems.

Working in your peer response groups, try out one or both forms of outlining on your partners' drafts. When you've finished outlining a draft, read through the outline and write responses to the following questions:

Questions for the "Exploring Your Speech Communities" Essay Options (p. 259)

- What strategy is each writer using to structure her comparison? If the strategy is unclear or seems to shift, point out where you get lost.

- What is the purpose of the comparison? Try to sum up the point of the paper in a single sentence.

- If the writer is using alternating structure, what are the categories of comparison? How do they relate to the overall purpose of the essay?

- If the writer is using block structure, how does she link the two "halves" of the essay? If the "blocks" seem relatively disconnected, suggest some specific ways the writer might unify them.

- Does the comparison—however it's structured—avoid unnecessary repetition of ideas? Point out any passages where the writer seems to be spinning his wheels.

- What do you like best about the draft? What's the writer doing particularly well?

Questions for the "Addressing Different Audiences" Essay Options (p. 288)

- What's the writer's overall purpose? Try to summarize it in a sentence.

- Does the sequence of ideas in the draft make sense? Do you see any gaps or unnecessary repetitions? Do you see any ideas that don't seem to belong at all or that would work better in a different part of the essay?

- How does each paragraph help to develop or support the main point of the essay?

- What do you like best about the draft? What's the writer doing particularly well?

Compare your questions and suggestions with those of other group members and discuss.

Revision Case Study: Addressing Audience Concerns

As we've seen in the discussion of speech communities, everyone has access to a variety of voices. Some voices feel comfortable and natural while others may feel awkward or artificial, especially when you're still learning the ins and outs of a new speech community. But all the voices you develop, whether they're absorbed unconsciously or learned with great effort, become part of who you are. In writing, these voices become resources that can help you communicate effectively in a variety of situations and with a wide range of audiences. Essayist and scholar bell hooks describes how she learned to value multiple voices in her own writing through an immersion in the works of multivocal African American poets and musicians:

> In part, attending all-black segregated schools with black teachers meant that I had come to understand black poets as being capable of speaking in many voices, that the Dunbar of a poem written in dialect was no more or less authentic than the Dunbar writing a sonnet. Yet it was listening to black musicians like Duke Ellington, Louis Armstrong, and later John Coltrane that impressed upon [my] consciousness a sense of versatility—they played all kinds of music, had multiple voices. So it was with poetry. The black poet, as exemplified by Gwendolyn Brooks and later Amiri Baraka, had many voices—with no single voice being identified as more or less authentic.[2]

It's exactly this versatility or flexibility that good writers work hard to cultivate. But having access to many voices isn't enough in itself—you also need to consider which of your voices will be most appropriate or most powerful in a given situation.

Which voice or voices you decide to call upon depends on the virtual reader you picture yourself addressing. In a sense, you negotiate your voice as a virtual writer in response to your image of the virtual reader. But remember that adapting to virtual readers doesn't mean simply telling them what you think they want to hear. That's not only cynical and dishonest, but likely to backfire: if you're arguing for something you don't believe in, your efforts could easily end up sounding half-hearted, forced, or just plain phoney. The point is to say what *you* want to say in a voice that will win the attention and respect of your readers. This means selecting the voice (among your many voices) and highlighting the aspects of your story most likely to appeal to their values and interests. As you plan your approach, try to keep these three questions in mind:

1. *What do the virtual readers know about the subject?* If you think that some or all of your readers may know less than you do about the subject, you'll need to explain terms and concepts and provide the background information or context that they need to understand your point. (Review pp. 199–201 for specific approaches to defining and explaining.)
2. *What attitudes are virtual readers likely to have about you or your subject?* Can you assume that your readers will be interested in the subject and sympathetic to your ideas? If so, all you have to do is make your point as clearly and emphatically as possible. However, if some readers are likely to be indifferent, you'll have to work harder at winning their interest; if they're unsympathetic, you'll have to be more diplomatic and

---

[2]bell hooks, *Talking Back: Thinking Feminist, Thinking Black* (Boston: South End Press, 1989), p. 11.

may need to anticipate and respond to potential misconceptions or objections.

3. *How can you appeal to virtual readers' interests and goals (without compromising your own)?* If you can show that your ideas serve readers' interests in some way or that your motives are at least partially consistent with theirs, you're more likely to gain and hold their attention.

In the next essay, Mohamed Awad adapts his voice skillfully as he addresses first a homeowners' group and then the engineering team for a construction project, trying in each case to persuade his audience to abandon plans to build a new school in an environmentally sensitive area. To avoid unnecessary repetition, we've reprinted only the first three paragraphs of the second version. The environmental study he describes here was done as a group project for a geography class, called "People and the Earth's Ecosystems," that he had taken the previous term.

STUDENT
WRITING

To Build or Not to Build? (versions 1 and 2)
Mohamed Awad

Version 1 (to Homeowners)

As an energy and air quality specialist evaluating the proposed school site located on Mulholland Drive off of the 405 freeway, I have analyzed the construction plans and have come to the conclusion that the harmful effects associated with building a school in this area far outweigh the benefits. I understand that convenience and time-saving are high priorities for the typical parent. The completion of a school in this beautiful area would not only mean shorter trips, but it would mean safety and security, as your kids would be much nearer to home, as well as other benefits, such as the increased value of your property. However, I cannot allow in good conscience the construction of a school in this area, because unfortunately I, more than most people, know the full effects on both the taxpayer and on the environment. Let me attempt to summarize these effects for you.

Although the environment is a concern on everyone's mind, there are certain things that strike closer to home, and more specifically, closer to the pocketbook. If the project were to be built, there would be crews working day and night to finish construction. This would cause great noise throughout the course of the day, as well as horrible traffic during rush hour times. Also, the cost for construction and operation of the school in this area is relatively high in comparison to other similar projects. One of my colleagues has estimated that the school would cost the average taxpayer living within a two-mile radius of the site about 75 cents per day. This may not seem like much, but numbers such as these add up quickly. These are some of the reasons I feel the project in this area is not worth the results to the average person.

The first severe change that would have to take place at the site is grading. Grading is a process by which land is clear-cut and leveled off so that it may be usable for roads, buildings, and other things. Since the land around the school site is naturally hilly, grading would have profound impacts on the area. First, it would destroy much of the beautiful wildlife in the region, and expose the site to twice as much sunlight as is now. This causes high surface temperatures necessary for air pollution.

Another major impact of the proposed school site is the introduction of inorganic building materials. Asphalt, cement, and glass, to name a few, also increase the temperature of the area by changing the balance of radiation that exists naturally in the region. Since there will be little vegetation to absorb the incoming light, it will be reflected by the light-colored buildings in the area, thus causing a temperature increase. Because of this increase, the school will have to consume more energy and electricity. Buildings need lighting for

activities and air-conditioning, which would require power
lines running through the beautiful natural terrain.

We have thus far looked at the damage done through the
perspective of energy, but now the effects of this on air
quality will be analyzed. Let us sum up the situation. The
area in question is one of high air pollution potential because air pollutants are trapped near the ground. Up to now,
the area has managed to self-sustain, balancing the amount of
radiation coming in with that going out, and using the natural
vegetation of the region to control levels of air pollutants.
With the introduction of a school, this balance is upset.
Grading takes place, which exposes the area to more sunlight,
idealizing conditions for ozone production. Vegetation is removed and replaced by inorganic materials, increasing the
overall temperature during the day. At the school site, light
winds and surrounding hilly terrain trap air pollutants near
the ground. This will lead to production of harmful gases,
such as ozone. Although ozone in the stratosphere enables life
to flourish on Earth, near the ground it is still poisonous
and caustic to human tissue. Ozone formation requires adequate
sunshine, of which this area has plenty, and high surface temperature, which would be increased by the school. So your kids
would be breathing this toxin day in and day out.

Finally, increased numbers of automobiles and people increase the levels of poisonous gases in the area. In particular, carbon dioxide and other greenhouse gases are relatively
transparent to sunshine but trap heat by more efficiently absorbing the longer-wavelength infrared radiation released by
the earth. This is known as the greenhouse effect: certain
gases, including water vapor and carbon dioxide, allow light
and radiation to enter into a certain area, but as this radiation is converted to long-wave, these gases trap it and re-
reflect it to the earth, in the form of heat, thus causing a

mild but significant increase in temperature. In the areas near the school, this effect would be multiplied by the fact that there is tremendous emission of greenhouse gases by people and automobiles.

To conclude therefore, I hope I have shown you that the damage caused by this school is much too great to risk in the area. From air quality to energy, I must recommend that all construction plans be rejected as soon as possible so that an environmental disaster does not occur here.

VERSION 2 (TO ENGINEERS)

As an energy and air quality specialist consulting on the construction of the designated school site 24602 (Mulholland-405 intersection), I have analyzed the construction project and have arrived at the definite conclusion that project 24602 should not be completed. Changes in grading and land restructuring, introduction of foreign inorganic materials into the region, increased energy consumption coupled with decreased energy efficiency, and overall increases in temperature argue for an environmentally conscious decision to relocate the 24602 construction.

The first significant change in the region would be grading. Grading would involve the clear-cutting and leveling of over 2563 acres, meaning the obliteration of 15 newly discovered sub-ecosystems. In addition, grading would have a significant impact on the amount of sunlight reaching the soil of the region. Whereas now each side of a certain hill receives partial sun, this new exposure would enable the sun to reach the area all day long, causing unnaturally high temperatures, changing Q_{total} of 24602, and rendering the landscape of the region permanently damaged. Clearly, no mitigation measures can be implemented to counter these adverse effects in 24602.

Another major impact of the proposed school site is the introduction of foreign inorganic materials. Such materials

include a surface area of 54,980 square meters of asphalt and
cement for the 220-car parking lot, 10 tons of glass, and 20
tons of other building materials. These materials would change
the albedo of the region, and cause an estimated 4 degree increase in temperature over the span of the day. During the
daytime, energy, in the form of radiation that would have been
absorbed by the dark natural vegetation of the region and used
for photosynthesis, would reflect off of the light-colored
materials and be trapped between buildings and automobiles.
This would cause a "heat island" around area 24602. During the
nighttime, the artificial blackbodies, such as asphalt and
metal objects, emit nearly all of the radiation they absorbed
during the day, causing a temperature increase as well....

In the first paragraph of version 1, Awad appeals to the homeowners by
demonstrating that he understands their interests and goals: he acknowledges that they might favor the school project because it seems to offer convenience for them, safety for their children, and increased value for their
property. Then, in the rest of the essay, he demonstrates how the school
project could actually controvert these goals by creating inconveniences
like construction noise and heavier traffic, degrading the natural beauty of
the area, raising property taxes, and posing environmental dangers to families. His strategy thus anticipates some resistance to his position and addresses the audience's concerns directly. Many writers hesitate to admit that
a position different from their own has any value, because they fear that
such a concession will weaken their argument. However, as you can see
here, this strategy strengthens rather than weakens Awad's position. If the
homeowners feel that he's a reasonable fellow who understands their interests, they're more likely to be receptive to his ideas. This strategy of concession and reasoned counterargument is a very common and generally effective way to deal with differences that you perceive between your virtual
readers' attitudes and your own.

In his address to the engineers, Awad adapts his voice to acknowledge
the technical expertise of his audience. While many of us would be mysti-
fied by his references to Q_{total}, *mitigation measures, albedo, heat islands,* and
artificial blackbodies, the specialized jargon is appropriate for this audience
because it tells the engineers that Awad speaks their language and understands their work. He realizes that, unlike the homeowners, who may

require some explanation of construction processes, the engineers don't need to have terms like *grading* and *foreign inorganic materials* defined for them. Awad also addresses their interest in precise data by specifying the measurements and calculations that he bases his conclusions on. But does he acknowledge the attitudes and goals of the engineers—particularly their economic interest in the project—as effectively as he addresses the concerns of the homeowners? What further strategies might he use in his effort to persuade the engineers to abandon the school project?

Now read the opening paragraphs of both versions of Kristy Rios's essay, "Offensive Song Lyrics Hurt." The essay refers to an incident that occurred at UCLA several years ago. A student moving into an apartment near campus found a photocopied fraternity songbook—filled with raunchy, violent, and sexually explicit lyrics—left behind by the previous resident. An editorial in the feminist student newspaper condemned the fraternity and reprinted the lyrics of a particularly grotesque song entitled "Lupe." The article, and the song, generated tremendous debate. In the first version of her essay, Rios addresses an audience of peers—Chicanas and Latinas attending UCLA. In the second version, she addresses a general university audience, including faculty, staff, administrators, and students of all ethnicities. How does she adapt her voice for each audience?

STUDENT
WRITING

Offensive Song Lyrics Hurt (versions 1 and 2)
Kristy Rios

VERSION 1 (TO PEERS)

Ask me who I am, and I'll tell you. Ask me why I chose UCLA, and I'll explain. Ask me for an apology, and you'll never get one from me. I am Hispanic, Mexican, Latina, or Chicana, whichever is more politically correct these days. I have been branded by society as a minority, to be judged primarily by a label rather than by my qualities, sort of like a second-hand department store in Downtown L.A. But no one can deny that statistics show my race will soon grow to be the majority. I know this may be difficult for some to accept, but society will have to adapt.

I guess it is evident in Theta Xi's songbook that not everyone is going to accept us so easily, and that is what hurts. The lyrics to "Lupe," glorifying the rape and murder of an eight-year-old "Mexican whore," are intolerable--too downright racist to be included in a fraternity songbook. The frat boys say to ignore it: "Hey, it's only a song." The Administration say they're investigating, but they're really just waiting for the bad press to die down, and then maybe the fraternity will get a slap on the hand.

Then there is militant MEChA (Movimiento Estudiantil Chicano de Aztlan), waving around the Mexican flag, demanding a Chicana/o studies department at the same time they protest for complete disaffiliation with all Greek fraternities and sororities at UCLA. And they say they have my best interests in mind. Who are they kidding? What about me? Where do I stand? I'm the one who has to walk around campus feeling self-conscious for being a minority. I'm the one who feels I have to whip out my SAT and GPA scores like a gun fighter at the O.K. Corral. I'm the one with "Affirmative Action" branded on my forehead just waiting for someone to tell me I got here the easy way. But I'm also the one who has to remain silent and hope this incident will just go away if I don't want to be accused of being militant or branded a "Greek basher." But what about all the pain and anger and disgust? What am I supposed to do now? Where do I aim all of this frustration?...

Version 2 (to Faculty, Staff, Administrators, Students)

I am proud of my heritage and hide that fact from no one. This is why I feel I owe no one an apology for attending UCLA because I am a minority. To many, I am just another Mexican-American filling a quota. Yes, an underprivileged youth whom others feel has gotten an easy ride to a prestigious school because of the color of her skin and a government handout called affirmative action. But I refuse to spend the next four years explaining to everyone I meet that I have as much right to be at UCLA as everyone else. Nor do I feel I need to flash my SAT scores to fit in with the academic elite.

Unfortunately, fraternity members from Theta Xi are making my road to acceptance that much bumpier. A recent songbook, considered an educational manual for the Theta Xi fraternity, is known to contain explicit and derogatory lyrics aimed at minorities, specifically Hispanics, women, and gays. One such song, entitled "Lupe," graphically exploits a young Mexican girl. The lyrics speak of her as a whore whose eventual rape and murder becomes glorified because these actions are executed by "Theta Xi Men." This fraternity tries to justify their actions by saying that "Lupe" is only a song, so what harm can come from it? "Freedom of speech" and "First Amendment rights" have echoed loudly throughout this campus. Administrative action seems to have stalled. No action seems to be taking place.

But I can't say that I know of the perfect punishment against this fraternity. What I do know is that this issue cannot be ignored. Because of the insecurity I feel about myself on this campus, I don't know if things will ever be the same. I constantly find myself on the defensive. These lyrics went straight to the heart. I can't tell you how devastated I felt. These lyrics have made me feel like I have no place in this society. I lost faith in this school and in the entire Greek system. . . .

OPTIONAL
ACTIVITIES

Evaluating Voice

1. Working in pairs or groups, list all the differences you can find between the two versions of Rios's opening paragraphs. What details are included or excluded? How do the focus and style of the two versions vary? What assumptions does Rios seem to make about the knowledge, attitudes, and interests of each audience?

2. How do the voices you hear in Rios's paragraphs compare with those in the two versions of Mohamed Awad's essay? How would you describe each of these voices? How would you describe Amy Yang's and Kosuke Will Tanaka's voices? Which voice or voices appeal to you most strongly and why?

3. Take a close look at one of the student essays or passages that you particularly like. Try to identify some of the characteristics of language and structure the writer uses to create a distinctive voice. Can you produce the same effects? Take a sentence or two from your draft and try rewriting the passage in different voices.

Revising Your Draft: Voice

Work with one or more of the following peer response options in order to check your own sense of voice against the impressions of another reader or readers. Based on the responses you receive, revise your draft to create a more compelling or appropriate voice throughout the essay.

- Number the paragraphs of your draft. Reread the draft and choose the paragraph where you think the voice is most effective and the paragraph where you feel that it is least effective. Don't mark the draft itself but note the paragraph numbers on the back of the draft. Exchange drafts with a partner and read to find the paragraphs with the most and least effective use of voice. Mark these "most" and "least" in the margins. Compare your responses with your partner's: Did you choose the same passages? Talk about the reasons you made the choices you did.

- On a separate sheet of paper, write a description of the virtual readers you had in mind as you wrote your essay: What did you assume about their knowledge of the subject, their attitudes toward you or your topic, their interests and goals? Now exchange drafts with a partner and read: What assumptions does the writer seem to make about her or his audience? Jot down your impressions, then compare your notes with the writer's description of the virtual readers she was trying to address.

- Do a read-around, paying particular attention to voice. (To preserve anonymity, remove cover sheets or fold over corners where names appear.) After your group has read a set of your classmates' drafts, discuss which voice or voices are most appealing to you or most appropriate for the audience the writer has identified. Select a few particularly strong passages to share with the rest of the class.

First Things: Motivating Readers

The way you choose to begin and end an essay help to define both the structure and voice of the piece as a whole. The introduction sets the tone and establishes readers' expectations about what will follow. The conclusion completes the structure of the essay and gives you a chance to leave readers with a strong final impression. The final sections of this revision workshop are designed to help you shape the beginnings and endings of your essays more effectively.

In Chapter 3 we talked about the need to provide focus, context, and a sense of direction at the beginning of your essay. The introduction—whether it's a paragraph, a page, or a whole chapter in a book—gives readers the information they need to comprehend the writing that follows. It offers a kind of road map—an overview of where the essay or article is going. However, the introduction serves another purpose, as well—to get readers' attention and motivate them to read further. It can engage readers by appealing to their reason, curiosity, sympathy, fear, patriotism, self-interest, moral outrage, sense of humor—in short, any motive or feeling they're likely to respond to. In this sense, you might think of introductions as movie previews designed not only to give you a general idea what the film is about but also to grab your attention and motivate you to see the whole thing. No matter what analogy you prefer, your introduction needs to orient readers to the subject you're writing about, give them an idea where the paper is going, and make them want to continue reading. Here's a short checklist to help you evaluate your opening strategy:

A good introduction should	*. . . and address these questions*
focus	What's the paper about?
inform	What background or context do readers need?
forecast	Where is the paper going? What is its point or purpose?
motivate	Why should readers care?

Lisette Parra neatly combines these four functions in a short paragraph introducing each version of her "two audiences" essay. The essay describes a volunteer outreach program, Latinas Guiding Latinas, first to potential sponsors and then to the high school girls it's designed to assist. How does Parra focus, inform, forecast, and motivate in each version? What information does she include in both versions? How and why do her strategies change for each audience?

STUDENT
WRITING

Version 1 (To Sponsors)

Latinas Guiding Latinas (LGL), formed in 1987, is an organization that provides academic assistance and a mentorship program to young Chicana/Latina high school girls. The main goal
is to motivate young girls to attain a higher education for
themselves. The program consists of college visits, educational conferences, parent conferences, and social activities.
LGL empowers girls to believe in themselves and have self-
confidence that a Latina in today's society can make it
through college. The program makes them aware of what awaits
them in the future with a higher education. As a previous
mentee, and now as a mentor, I know how important it is for
young girls to participate in a program that can provide the
special attention they deserve.

Version 2 (To High School Students)

How would you like to join a club that will teach you how to
become a lawyer, engineer, doctor, accountant--and have fun at
the same time? If you have been wanting to join such a club,
then Latinas Guiding Latinas (LGL) is for you. LGL helps young
Latinas like yourself get a higher education. The program offers college tours, one-on-one counseling, parent conferences,
and social events. Our goal is to make you feel proud of who
you are and believe that someone like yourself, a Latina, can
and will make it into college. As a former high school member
of LGL, and now as an LGL volunteer, I guarantee it will be a
profitable and exciting program to join.

OPTIONAL
ACTIVITY

Introductions at Work

Scan the introductions to the stories in a current newspaper or news magazine:
Which openers catch your attention and make you want to read further? How
do they do it? What kinds of background information do they include? Compare notes with classmates: Are they drawn to the same types of beginnings?

Compare the news story openers with some chapter introductions in your textbooks. What do they do differently and why? What strategies and functions do they share?

Last Things: Crafting Conclusions

Coming up with a good conclusion can be the hardest part of your job as a writer. By the time you get there, you're usually bone tired and may feel as if you've already said everything you possibly can about the subject. It's tempting to just stop writing and let it go at that—or maybe dash off a quick summary of the paper with the words "Finally" or "In conclusion" tacked on for effect. But the ending of an essay is a critical part of its structure: if the introduction is a road map, the conclusion is the destination; if the introduction is a movie preview, the conclusion is the final scene of the film—where plot lines converge, conflicts are resolved, and mysteries are explained. As you look over what you've written, ask yourself what it adds up to: ask yourself, "So what?" The conclusion should answer that question.

We're not saying you should never summarize. The summary can be useful, particularly if the paper is long or complex and the reader's memory needs to be jogged. And a very brief summary—say, a sentence or two—can be a useful part of the conclusion even in a shorter paper. But summary alone is seldom enough, and a point-by-point summary of a short essay is just plain redundant and boring. A good conclusion should seem like a logical completion or extension of the essay. It can

- return to an anecdote or story told at the beginning of the essay with new insight or greater understanding.

- answer a question or resolve a conflict posed at the beginning of the essay.

- present a new idea—something you've learned or decided based on what you've written.

- recommend action or advocate a change of perspective based on your argument.

- predict consequences of results based on your analysis.

- pose a question raised by your discussion for readers to ponder.

- place the subject in a larger perspective or context.

Manuel Ruiz revised the conclusion of his speech communities paper in order to integrate it more effectively with the rest of the essay. Here's his opening paragraph:

As a child, I grew up in two different worlds--the colorful world of the streets and the intellectual world of my family. Raised in the projects (government-run apartment buildings) in cities such as Pacoima and Sylmar and then taking
trips to the suburban houses of my wealthy, conservative
uncles, I learned at a young age that you are expected to talk
to different people in different ways if you want to be respected. I found out that I couldn't use the language I picked
up from the streets to talk to my grandmother and expect her
to understand what I was trying to say to her. I could say
something like, "That shit was fresh!" and she would probably
look on the floor for some kind of animal droppings.

And this is how he ended the paper in his first draft:

Whenever a relative from the suburbs would decide to go
by our house and visit, they would always be surprised by the
raw language used in my neighborhood. It would make them
uncomfortable when they heard all the profanity and slang in
this speech community. Sometimes my grandparents would ask,
"Why do they talk like that?" or "Don't their parents ever
discipline them?" They just couldn't understand why so much
profanity was needed in a conversation to get a point across.
I'd always had to make sure that a cuss word would not slip
out while they were there. If somehow one did slip out,
though, I would just try to play it off (pretend I said something else) and say that I said, "Fudge." Never would I admit
that I cussed to my family; I would rather lie to them than be
nagged about the truth. No way would they understand that profanity is a really important way of expressing ourselves in
our community.

> As you can observe, English has many different languages
> in itself. It may seem that education has a big impact on
> speech communities, and it may have, but there are many other
> factors that isolate certain speech communities. The way a
> person would talk to his professor would be extremely differ-
> ent than the way someone would talk to his friend. Just the
> subject in general of what the conversation is about would be
> totally different. It comes down to this: even when you talk
> to different friends, you talk to each of them in different
> languages--whether it is your best friend or someone you met
> yesterday, it doesn't matter. It is inevitable that every two
> people who share a conversation share their own distinct lan-
> guage.

If you read this concluding paragraph by itself, it looks pretty good. Ruiz makes some valid points about speech communities and illustrates them clearly with the examples about speaking to professors and friends; the paragraph also has a nice air of finality ("It comes down to this . . . "). How-ever, keep in mind that direct style favors a narrow focus on the topic: while the generalizations here may be true, they're pointless, because they have little to do with the rest of the essay. The conclusion seems arbitrarily stuck on; it doesn't relate in any specific way to Ruiz's central focus on the difference between his family's speech and the street talk of his neighbor-hood. The effect is to leave readers asking, "So what?"

In his revision, Ruiz made no changes in the next-to-last paragraph, but he completely rethought the concluding paragraph:

> As you can tell, I feel a lot more comfortable using the
> speech community that comes from the streets rather than that
> of my family. My family's speech community is so constrained
> that I really can't express myself as much as I would like to.
> Unlike that of my family, the speech community from the
> streets has many more colorful words and meanings that I can
> choose from to express myself fully. A big part of my point is
> being able to swear. Profanity is just so much more powerful
> than the average word. "Fuck no!" puts so much more into say-
> ing "No" and meaning it than "No, darn it!" "Fuck no!" just

makes the sentence so much livelier. Having a good job and
money gives my uncles all the authority they want. They can do
what they want when they want to do it. They have the power to
make changes. The speech community from the streets, on the
other hand, is used mainly by people who don't have very much
wealth or power. Their words are the only power they have, so
they make the most of what they got. Because most of the time,
it's all they got.

This new conclusion follows more clearly from the rest of the essay. Ruiz continues his discussion of family talk versus street talk, but he goes beyond simply summarizing the differences. Here he discloses how he feels about each speech community and, even more important, offers an explanation for the most salient difference between the two—the pervasive profanity of street talk in contrast to the polite restraint of well-to-do relatives. In the next-to-last paragraph, Ruiz asserts that profanity is an "important way of expressing ourselves" in the streets. While the first draft leaves that assertion unsupported, the revision develops it by placing street talk in the larger context of power relations: the street community's lack of economic or political power ("the power to make changes") means that they assert power where they can, through their talk. If a reader is put off by Ruiz's language here, the reaction only underlines his point that profanity has a certain raw power—if only the power to offend.

OPTIONAL
ACTIVITIES

Alternative Endings

1. As a class project, collect short editorials that illustrate a variety of endings; refer to the list on page 320 to give you an idea of some particular strategies to look for, but don't confine yourself to these. Share your examples with classmates: Which ones do you find most effective and why?
2. Even strong writers can have trouble with endings. Working with a partner, reread one of the complete student essays in this chapter ("Taking the Journey through Speech," "My Speech Communities," or "To Build or Not to Build?" version 1), paying particular attention to its conclusion. What might make the ending more effective? Try writing a couple of alternative endings for this essay and compare notes with others who wrote alternative conclusions to the same piece.

Revising Your Draft: Beginnings and Endings

Working in your peer response groups, comment on each draft's introduction and conclusion, keeping these questions in mind:

- What are the subject and purpose of the paper, according to the introduction? How accurately does the opening describe the essay's subject and purpose?

- What background information does the writer include? Do you need to know anything more? Does any of the background seem unnecessary?

- Does the introduction motivate you to read further? If so how, and if not why not?

- How does the conclusion relate to the rest of the essay?

- What does the conclusion do beyond summarizing what's already been said?

- If you feel that either the introduction or the conclusion could be stronger, try to come up with some specific alternatives and discuss them with the writer.

JOURNAL
OPTION

Evaluating Your Writing Process

Before you turn in your revised paper, take a few minutes to reflect on your writing process for this essay. What gave you the most trouble? What was easiest? What aspects of the essay's structure (beginning, ending, overall organization) satisfy you most and least? How would you describe your voice or voices in this essay? Attach this journal entry to your finished paper when you turn it in so that your instructor can respond to your concerns in her comments.

PART FOUR

Framing Ideas: Analytic Storytelling

CHAPTER 13

Framing: Interpretation and Explanation Patterns

═══════════════════════════════════════

Just So Stories

Why is it that personal stories often seem to "flow" from pen to paper while writing an analysis or an interpretation can seem like pulling teeth? Often even writers who have a way with words get into trouble when they are asked to interpret or analyze an object, text, or event. One reason that analysis can seem more challenging than straightforward storytelling is that the "story" that holds an analysis together—the explanatory story that gives it its form and meaning—is often hidden behind the actions or objects that are being analyzed. Once you learn to see the explanatory story underlying an analysis or an interpretation, you're on your way to becoming a more proficient academic thinker and writer.

Let's begin our exploration of analytic storytelling with an old Iroquois legend told to explain one of nature's apparent oddities:

Why the Owl Has Big Eyes[1]

Raweno, the Everything-Maker, was busy creating various animals. He was working on Rabbit, and Rabbit was saying: "I want nice long legs and long ears like a deer, and sharp fangs and claws like a panther."

"I do them up the way they want to be; I give them what they ask for," said Raweno. He was working on Rabbit's hind legs, making them long, the way Rabbit had ordered.

---

[1]Richard Erdoes and Alfonso Ortiz, eds., *American Indian Myths and Legends* (New York: Pantheon Books, 1984), p. 398.

Owl, still unformed, was sitting on a tree nearby and waiting his turn. He was saying: "Whoo, whoo, I want a nice long neck like Swan's, and beautiful red feathers like Cardinal's, and a nice long beak like Egret's, and a nice crown of plumes like Heron's. I want you to make me into the most beautiful, the fastest, the most wonderful of all the birds."

Raweno said: "Be quiet. Turn around and look in another direction. Even better, close your eyes. Don't you know that no one is allowed to watch me work?" Raweno was just then making Rabbit's ears very long the way Rabbit wanted them.

Owl refused to do what Raweno said. "Whoo, whoo" he replied, "nobody can forbid me to watch. Nobody can order me to close my eyes. I like watching you, and watch I will!"

Then Raweno become angry. He grabbed Owl, pulling him down from his branch, stuffing his head deep in his body, shaking him until his eyes grew big with fright, pulling at his ears until they were sticking up at both sides of his head.

"There," said Raweno, "that'll teach you. Now you won't be able to crane your neck to watch things you shouldn't watch. Now you have big ears to listen when someone tells you what not to do. Now you have big eyes—but not so big that you can watch me, because you'll be awake only at night, and I work by day. And your feathers won't be red like Cardinal's, but gray like this"—and Raweno rubbed Owl all over with mud—"as punishment for your disobedience." So Owl flew off, pouting: "Whoo, whoo, whoo."

Then Raweno turned back to finish Rabbit, but Rabbit had been so terrified by Raweno's anger, even though it was not directed at him, that he ran off half done. As a consequence, only Rabbit's hind legs are long, and he has to hop about instead of walking or running. Also, because he took fright then, Rabbit has remained afraid of almost everything, and he never got the claws and fangs he asked for in order to defend himself. Had he not run away then, Rabbit would have been an altogether different animal.

As for Owl, he remained as Raweno had shaped him in anger—with big eyes, a short neck, and ears sticking up on the sides of his head. On top of everything, he has to sleep during the day and come out only at night.

Chances are you've heard stories like this, stories about how elephants got trunks or leopards spots, much like the tales in Rudyard Kipling's famous collection of *Just So Stories*. Every culture tells its own "Just So Stories" to explain or interpret the peculiarities of the natural world, and usually the method of explanation is the same: a biological oddity—the rabbit's long hind legs or the owl's glowing eyes—is explained as the result of a mistake made during creation or as the consequence of bad behavior. The inner logic of Just So Stories is simple: we explain the mysteries of the natural world in terms we understand, in terms of human experience. Why would the creator make something as ungainly as an owl? Well, it makes sense if you imagine that the owl's stubby torso and oversized eyes were his punishment. Why would the rabbit's legs be so out of proportion? Nature wouldn't do this on purpose; it's more plausible, and more fun, to think of the rabbit as a botched creation—something like an animal carving left half done by a preoccupied artist. The explanatory strategy of all Just So Stories involves borrowing story frames from the realm of human experience—story frames that make sense to us, like "punishment follows bad behavior"—and imposing them on the peculiarities we find in nature. In fact, the greatest of all Just So Stories, the story of divine creation itself, follows exactly this pattern: in most cultural traditions, animals, plants, and human beings aren't usually seen as popping into existence all by themselves; they are crafted by a god or group of gods who, like celestial artisans, build them out of clay, cinders, mud, wood, plant fiber, or stone. In culture after culture, the wonders of the natural world are explained in the same way: they're interpreted in terms of story frames drawn from the familiar realm of human motives, actions, and interactions.

It may be tempting to dismiss stories like "Why the Owl Has Big Eyes" as examples of flawed thinking: backed up by stories of our own—like the scientific theory of evolution—we might think of Just So Stories as examples of what happens when explanations are based on incomplete knowledge. But Just So Stories are neither misconceptions nor misinterpretations: if anything, they are celebrations of the pleasure people get from the process of explanation. In a sense, all explanations—even scientific ones—are Just So Stories. Every time we analyze, interpret, or explain something that puzzles us, we do exactly what the teller of a good Just So Story does: we use a familiar pattern of experience to make sense of something else that isn't familiar. Suppose you run into your English instructor on the street and she fails to acknowledge you when you give her your friendliest "Hello." You expect teachers to behave in a relatively friendly way; after all, most of your past instructors have been relatively open, congenial types. How do you explain this snub? You begin by searching your memory for similar experiences you've had before—times when teachers acted weird around you in the past. Sure enough, there was a time once in high school when your drama coach cooled toward you after you missed a couple of key rehearsals: maybe your English teacher gave you the cold shoulder because you blew the essay you turned in last Friday. Whenever our expectations are thwarted—whether they are expectations about the appropriate behavior of teachers or the appropriate shape of legs on a rabbit—we search our knowledge of the world for a story frame that will explain what happened: we try to remember familiar patterns that make sense of the puzzles around us.

To keep the distinction clear, let's call the story frame that we impose on our experience when we explain something an "explanation pattern." In "Why the Owl Has Big Eyes," two different explanation patterns are borrowed from the realm of human experience: "punishment follows bad behavior" and "distracted artists botch their work." A single pattern—something like "teachers avoid disappointing students"—is at work in our other example. For symmetry's sake, let's call the thing we're trying to explain the "object of explanation." Discovering an explanation pattern for a given situation is often ridiculously easy. When a football coach tries to explain to the press how he lost the "big game," he'll probably say that the home team just had too many injuries, or that they peaked too soon, or that they were looking ahead to the playoffs, or that they just got too confident. When a politician explains her reasons for throwing her hat in the ring, she's likely to say that she feels she can make a difference, or that she just has to oppose the disastrous policies of her opponent, or that her wealth of experience from running her own business has prepared her for public office. When someone you know decides to file for divorce she might explain her decision by saying that she changed and outgrew her husband, or that she never really knew him in the first place, or that she always felt stifled in the relationship. Usually, when we feel the need to explain our actions or decisions, we draw on a stock of stereotypical explanation patterns we're sure others will recognize and comprehend. A standard explanation like "She's leaving him because he changed" may not really do justice to what actually happened between two of your friends, but it does offer a plausible account that seems to "make sense" of their actions. Stock explanation patterns keep us from spending too much time and effort worrying over things that are either relatively unimportant in the first place (does the television audience really care why the big game was lost?) or things that are too complicated—or too painful—to probe further (do you really want to find out why your marriage failed while you're in the middle of a divorce?) Stock explanation patterns dissolve problems and puzzles by "explaining them away": they give us the impression that we understand events around us—and ourselves—even when we don't.

Much of the story we're telling you right now about explanation patterns and how they work was inspired by the work of artificial intelligence expert Roger Schank. Throughout his career, Schank has studied the way people think and learn, in the attempt to create computer programs that simulate human intelligence. According to Schank, the key to intelligent behavior lies in the appropriate application of explanation patterns. In the passage that follows, excerpted from one of his most accessible books, *Tell Me a Story: A New Look at Real and Artificial Memory,* Schank presents his theory of how explanation patterns—or "skeleton stories" as he calls them here—are used to interpret historical events. The object of explanation in this case is the downing of an Iranian airliner in 1988 by a United States Navy warship on patrol in the Persian Gulf, an incident that cost the lives of 290 civilian passengers and increased tensions across the Middle East. Schank (b. 1946) has authored twelve books on artificial intelligence programming, education, and creativity. He currently directs the Institute for Learning Sciences at Northwestern University, where he is John Evans Professor of Electrical Engineering and Computer Science as well as professor of psychology and of education and social policy. In the past he has served as director of Yale's Artificial Intelligence Project and as professor of linguistics and computer science at Stanford. His most recent book, *The End of Education,* appeared in 1995.

Before Reading

Imagine for a moment that you're the president of the United States and you've been asked to explain why a United States Navy warship mistakenly downed a civilian airliner over international waters: What stock explanation patterns might you use to explain this event?

Story Skeletons and Story-Fitting
Roger C. Schank

SOME SKELETON STORIES

If we construct our own version of truth by reliance upon skeleton stories, two people can know exactly the same facts but construct a story that relays those facts in very different ways. Because they are using different story skeletons, their perspectives will vary. For example, a United States Navy warship shot down an Iranian airliner carrying 290 passengers on July 3, 1988. Let's look at some different stories that were constructed to explain this event. All the stories that follow are excerpts from various *New York Times* reports in the days following this incident:

Mr. Reagan smiled and waved at tourists as he returned to the White House. But in speaking to reporters he remarked on what he had previously called "a terrible human tragedy. I won't minimize the tragedy," Mr. Reagan said. "We all know it was a tragedy. But we're talking about an incident in which a plane on radar was observed coming in the direction of a ship in combat and the plane began lowering its altitude. And so, I think it was an understandable accident to shoot and think that they were under attack from that plane," he said.

In this quotation from Ronald Reagan, the use of skeletons to create stories can be easily seen. Mr. Reagan has chosen a common skeleton: *understandable tragedy*. The skeleton looks something like this:

Actor pursues justifiable goal.

Actor selects reasonable plan to achieve goal.

Plan involves selection of correct action.

Action taken has unintended and unanticipated result.

Result turns out to be undesirable.

Innocent people are hurt by result.

In essence, what Mr. Reagan has done is to select this skeleton and to interpret the events of the shooting down of the airplane in terms of that skeleton. Had he been asked to tell the story of what happened, he would simply have had to fill in each line above with the actual event that matches it. As it is, he merely had to recognize that that skeleton was applicable and to use the phrases "terrible human tragedy" and "understandable accident," which are well-known referents to that skeleton.

Now let's look at some other comments on the event:

After expressing "profound regret" about the attack, Mrs. Thatcher said: "We understand that in the course of an engagement following an Iranian attack on the U.S. force, warnings were given to an unidentified aircraft. We fully accept the right of forces engaged in such hostilities to defend themselves."

Mrs. Thatcher has used a much more specific skeleton, namely the *justifiability of self-defense*. This skeleton proceeds as follows: 5

First actor pursues unjustifiable goal.

First actor selects plan.

Plan has intention of negative effect on second actor.

Second actor is justified in selecting goal.

Second actor selects justifiable plan.

Plan causes action to take place which harms first actor.

Let's look at the other side of the political spectrum now:

Libya's official press agency called the downing "a horrible massacre perpetrated by the United States." It said the attack was "new proof of state terrorism practiced by the American administration" and it called Washington "insolent" for insisting that the decision to down the plane was an appropriate defensive measure.

Here, two different skeletons are invoked. The first is *state terrorism* and the second is *insolence.* The insolence skeleton is an amusing one to invoke, but we shall ignore it and concentrate on the terrorism skeleton:

Actor chooses high-level goal.

Country blocks high-level goal.

Actor chooses secondary goal to harm citizens of country.

Actor endangers or actually harms citizens of country.

Actor expects blockage of high-level goal by country to go away.

"State terrorism" supposedly means that the actor is a country too. But "state terrorism" is not exactly a well-known story skeleton for an American. In fact, Arab leaders refer to this skeleton quite often and we can figure what it must mean and why Arab leaders used it to justify their own actions. Other people's story skeletons, ones that we have not heard before, are usually best understood by analogy to skeletons we already know.

Notice that the events under discussion fit as easily into the state terrorism skeleton as into the above two skeletons. The art of skeleton selection is exactly that—an art. No real objective reality exists here. One can see and tell about events in any way that one wants to. In each case, certain aspects of the story being transmitted are enhanced and certain elements are left out altogether.

The real problem in using skeletons this way is that the storytellers usually believe what they themselves are saying. Authors construct their own reality by finding the events that fit the skeleton convenient for them to believe. They enter a storytelling situation wanting to tell a certain kind of story and only then worrying about whether the facts fit onto the bones of the skeleton that they have previously chosen. This method has almost comic qualities to it when various interpretations of an event are so clearly interpretations independent of the event itself. For example, consider the following comment:

> A newspaper in Bahrain, *Akhbar Al Khalij,* said, "No doubt yesterday's painful tragedy was the result of Iran's insistence in continuing the Iran-Iraq war. The United States as a great power does not lack moral courage in admitting the mistake. This will help contain the effects of the incident."

The remarks above refer to two skeletons: the *justifiable bad effects of war* **10** *on the aggressor* and *moral courage.* Both of these skeletons could have been used to describe nearly any event in the Middle East that the newspaper wanted to comment upon.

The use of new events as fodder for invoking old skeletons is the stuff of which international political rhetoric is made. In the *Times* of the same period, we have another reference to how Reagan commented on a similar situation some years back:

> President Reagan, in a speech after the Korean plane was shot down after straying over Soviet airspace above Sakhalin Island, said: "Make no mistake about it, this attack was not just against ourselves or the Republic of Korea. This was the Soviet Union against the world and the moral precepts which guide human relations among people everywhere.
>
> "It was an act of barbarism," Mr. Reagan went on, "born of a society which wantonly disregards individual rights and the value of human life and seeks constantly to expand and dominate other nations."

While the Americans used the *barbarism* skeleton, where the Koreans were the victim and the Russians the actor, to describe the shooting down of the Korean airliner, the Russians, in describing the Korean Airlines attack, used the *military aggressor* skeleton, where the Koreans were the actor and the Russians the victim. This same discrepancy occurred in the Russian statement about the Iranian airliner:

> The Tass statement said the attack Sunday was the inevitable result of the extensive American military presence in the Persian Gulf.
>
> "The tragedy, responsibility for which is wholly with the American command, has been far from accidental," the agency said. "It has been, in effect, a direct corollary of United States actions over the past year to increase its military presence in the gulf."
>
> It added: "The Soviet Union has repeatedly warned at different forums that the path of military actions cannot lead to a normalized situation. If the warnings had been heeded, the July 3 tragedy would not have occurred."

International politicians are not alone in telling stories by selecting their favorite skeletons and fitting the event to the skeletons. The candidates for president [in the 1988 race] also had something to say:

> Mr. Jackson said there was "no evidence that the U.S. ship was under attack by that plane." But he added, "The issue is not just failed technology, but failed and vague policy for the region." Mr. Jackson argued that the United States should not be in the gulf unilaterally, but as part of a United Nations peacekeeping effort that would have as its prime goal a negotiated settlement of the Iran-Iraq war.
>
> At a Fourth of July address at the Charlestown Navy Yard in Boston today, Mr. Dukakis described the incident as a "terrible accident," adding: "Clearly we have the right to defend our forces against imminent threats. And apparently, the shooting down of the airliner occurred over what appears to have been an unprovoked attack against our forces."

For Mr. Jackson, the appropriate skeletons were *bad technology causes errors,* and *vague policy causes problems.* Mr. Dukakis, on the other hand, looked suspiciously like Mr. Reagan, indicating that he was already acting presidential. Mr. Jackson had already realized that he was not going to be president at this point, but he was still campaigning to be taken seriously. Therefore, he was still raising issues. The Iran incident reminded him of two of his favorite issues, so he chose to see the Iranian airplane event in terms of those issues.

Last, we should look at the Iranian point of view. They, too, have their favorite skeletons in terms of which they can look at this event. First, let us look at the remarks of an exiled Iranian official: 15

> "It must be clear that much of the policies in Iran today are dictated by the internal struggle for power," said Abolhassan Bani-Sadr, the first president of Iran. Mr. Bani-Sadr, who spoke in an interview, lives in exile in Paris and opposes the current regime.
>
> "In that sense," Mr. Bani-Sadr said, "this American act of aggression will increase pressure to steer away from conciliatory policies in favor of radicals inside Iran who want to crush all talk of compromise. I am sure the trend now will be toward more mobilization for more war, although it will get nowhere."

Mr. Bani-Sadr was trying to predict the future rather than retell an old story. Nevertheless, he still relied upon a skeleton to create his new story. The skeleton he chose was *fanatics find fuel to add to fire.* Now look at a comment from inside Iran:

Hojatolislam Rafsanjani, who is the commander of Iran's armed forces, warned today against a hasty response to the American action. In a speech reported by the Teheran radio, he told Parliament, "We should let this crime be known to everyone in the world and be discussed and studied."

The Speaker, who has emerged as Iran's most powerful figure after Ayatollah Khomeini, went on to say that the Americans might "want a clumsy move somewhere in the world so that they can take the propaganda pressure off America and transfer it somewhere else."

Hojatolislam Rafsanjani added that Iran retains the right of taking revenge, but that "the timing is up to us, not America." He called the downing of the airliner "an unprecedented disaster in contemporary history" and said it should be used by Iran to "expose the nature of America," statements indicating that for now the Speaker favors a measured response.

Here again, we have a story about the future. Two skeletons are invoked as possible candidates for the basis of this story. One, *force opponents into bad move,* refers to the intentions of the U.S. as seen by the Iranians and is really a part of a continuing story of conflict between the two countries. The second, *avoid revenge to show up opponent,* is more or less the other side of the same coin. In both cases, we have a kind of conscious admission by Mr. Rafsanjani that the real question is which story skeleton will be followed in the creation of the next set of events. The only problem with this assertion is that Mr. Rafsanjani naively seems to assume that some audience is waiting to see the next act in the play. A more accurate assumption is that, no matter what happens next, all the viewers of the play will retell the story according to skeletons that they have already selected; i.e., they will probably not be moved to reinterpret any new event in terms of some skeleton that they do not already have in mind.

SKELETONS AND MEMORY

Story skeletons can have an important effect on memory. Since we see the world according to the stories we tell, when we tell a story in a given way, we will be likely to remember the facts in terms of the story we have told. This effect on memory has an interesting offshoot. When we select a particular skeleton because we have no real choice from a political point of view, we, most likely, will begin to believe the story we find ourselves telling. Consider the following statement, for example:

Iran Air's senior Airbus instructor, Capt. Ali Mahdaviani, ruled out the possibility of pilot error in the tragedy. He said it was possible that the airliner's captain, Mohsen Rezaian, failed to respond to signals from the American cruiser *Vincennes* because at that stage in the flight he was busy receiving air controller instructions off two radios and from four control towers, Bandar Abbas, Teheran, Dubai, and Qeshon Island in the gulf.

He insisted that the airliner would not have been outside the flight corridor and certainly would not have been descending, as early Pentagon reports said. He attributed the incident to a panicky reaction from the American cruiser, but did concede that the decision to fire the two surface-to-air missiles was made in difficult circumstances. "I think the decision to shoot down the plane was taken in very nervous conditions," he said.

And now consider an opposing statement:

"We have in this briefing all the facts that were made available to the captain when he made his decision," said Senator John Warner, a Virginia Republican and former Navy Secretary. "We are all of the same view, that he acted properly and professionally."

Senator Sam Nunn, the Georgia Democrat who is the chairman of the Armed Services Committee, agreed. "I find nothing to second-guess him on, based on his information," Mr. Nunn said.

He was quick to add, however, that the information that Capt. Will C. Rogers 3d, the commanding officer of the *Vincennes,* was working with might be contradicted by information on the computer tapes, which are believed to have recorded every action taken by the ship's operators, every bit of data picked up by its sensors, and every communication heard in the region during the encounter.

"It is an entirely different matter to second-guess a decision that had to be made in three or four minutes, to second-guess it over a two-week period," Mr. Nunn said, referring to the deadline for Navy investigators looking into the events.

Each of these statements is what might have been expected from the people who made them. Yet how were the memories of the spokesmen affected by the stories they told? In some sense, they told stories that they had to tell. Neither of these spokesmen was necessarily one hundred percent sure that the pilot and/or the captain weren't somewhat wrong in what they did. Situations are rarely that black-and-white. But having made a statement to support his man, each spokesman probably believed more in his man after defending him.

One issue in story understanding, then, is to determine which story skeleton is the right one to choose. Moreover, this issue is important in storytelling and, therefore, in memory as well. We can see an event in so many different ways that we must understand how we decide which story skeleton is applicable. In politics, this decision is easy. Russians or Iranians don't have to debate about which skeleton to choose. Rather, they make choices on the basis of political positions adopted before any story is heard. But for individuals who must decide how to look at a given situation, the possibilities are much larger.

One of the oddities of story-based understanding is that people have difficulty making decisions if they know that they will have trouble constructing a coherent story to explain their decision. In a sense, people tell stories to themselves to see whether they are comfortable enough with telling them for a while. You need to believe your own story in order to tell it effectively. Thus, decision making often depends upon story construction.

A storyteller might be more accurately described as a story-fitter. Telling stories of our own lives, especially ones with high emotional impact, means attempting to fit events to a story that has already been told, a well-known story that others will easily understand. Story-fitting, then, is a kind of deceptive process, one that creates stories that are not always exactly true, that lie by omission. These lies, however, are not necessarily intentional.

A true story could be told but would take much more time. So time, in many ways, is the villain here. Your listener doesn't have hours to listen to your story, so you create a short version that looks more standard, that fits a well-known story skeleton. The problem with this solution, as we have seen, is that the teller himself begins to believe his story. In short, storytelling is a very powerful process. We remember our own stories. Stories replace the memory of events that actually took place. So when people tell the kinds of stories we have seen [here], they usually believe them.

Married couples often comment on a sequence from the Woody Allen 25 movie *Annie Hall*. The sequence involves two scenes, where first the female lead and then the male lead discuss their sex life as a couple with their respective therapists. The woman complains that her boyfriend wants to have sex all the time—two or three times a week. The man complains that they almost never have sex together—only two or three times a week.

This movie scene expresses the essence of story construction. We take the facts and we interpret them in such a way as to create a story. In order to facilitate communication and to allow easy conversation, we use standard story skeletons that we share as a culture. The choice, however, of which skeleton to use is, in essence, a political choice. We choose to see the world according to a view that we find convenient, and we communicate by adopting standard points of view. The stories we tell communicate this view both to others and to ourselves. In the end, we become shaped by the skeletons we use.

Which of the *Annie Hall* characters is right? This question is, of course, absurd. Both characters are right, as are all the politicians quoted earlier. The skeletons we use indicate our point of view. Storytelling causes us to adopt a point of view. With this adoption comes a kind of self-definition, however. We are the stories we tell. We not only express our vision of the world, we also shape our memory by the stories we tell. As we come to rely upon certain skeletons to express what has happened to us, we become incapable of seeing the world in any other way. The skeletons we use cause specific episodes to conform to one another. The more a given skeleton is used, the more the stories it helps to form begin to cohere in memory. Consequently, we develop consistent, and rather inflexible, points of view.

Issues for Discussion

1. Compare the "skeleton stories" or explanation patterns evoked by Ronald Reagan, Margaret Thatcher, the Soviets, Jessie Jackson, and the Libyans to explain why the Iranian airliner was shot down. What purpose does each serve in relation to its teller and audience?
2. What would you have to do to determine which, if any, of these explanation patterns is the most accurate? What other stories might be offered to explain why the airliner was shot down?

J O U R N A L
O P T I O N S

Exploring Explanation Patterns

1. List as many standard or stock explanation patterns as you can for each of the following situations. When you meet again in class, compare your results with those of your classmates.

   - Deciding to go to a small four-year college instead of a large university

   - Deciding to attend a college in a different part of the country

   - Enlisting in the armed services

   - Joining a gang

   - Leaving home to live on your own

   - Deciding to postpone marriage

2. Examine newspaper accounts covering an important event—the deployment of troops, a celebrity trial, a racial conflict, and so forth—over the period of at least a full month. What explanation patterns are commonly

evoked in analyses and interpretations of this event? To what extent do these patterns change over time?

Matters of Perspective

What determines the story we choose to tell about a particular object or event? What guides our choice of the explanation patterns we use to interpret our experiences and explain our decisions? The answer to these questions lies, in part, in the idea of perspective. To see what we're getting at, imagine you're at a typical Saturday afternoon American college football game. Ask the young guy sitting next to you what football means to him, and he might give you an earful about the game embodying the pursuit of excellence or the spirit of competition at its finest. Ask the woman who came with him and you may get a different story: she might see the same game as an unconscious celebration of a particularly primitive brand of male thinking that's obsessed with "defense," "possession," and "scoring." Ask the Brazilian tourist further down the aisle what he thinks, and he might well tell you that American football, with all its huddles and time-outs, is an incredibly boring sport in contrast to the nonstop action of soccer, and that it reminds him of the uptight, rule-bound formality of American society as a whole. Ask the professor of anthropology who's watching the big game on television at home, and she may inform you that football isn't a game at all but an important cultural ritual: as she sees it, football acts out the myth of a classless society with a boundless faith in progress; it represents a world in which blue-collar linesmen work hand in hand with free-wheeling quarterback executive decisionmakers as they collectively strive toward success.

Differences in interpretation like these are usually said to result from different perspectives or points of view. Our all-American football lover sees the game the way it's sold in NFL propaganda—as a competition of champion athletes. The woman he's with sees it from a different point of view, one that reflects her experiences with men and male culture. Further down the aisle, the Brazilian tourist can't help but view the game from the vantage of his own national sport, nor can he help associating it with his judgment of American customs. And our armchair anthropologist has her own distinct point of view on the sport; even if she still gets into the thrill of the game, she's bound to view it from the perspective offered by her own academic training—a perspective that constantly seeks to translate human activities into culturally symbolic meanings.

The notion of perspective or point of view suggests that the way you interpret or analyze things depends on your "position"—not the kind of physical location you occupy when you buy tickets on the fifty-yard line, but the ideological position you occupy by virtue of the cultures you belong to. All the stories you know—stories that shape your values, beliefs, and judgments—also shape the way you analyze and interpret the world around you. If you identify with the popular culture of American sports, you're likely to interpret football as a "competition of champions." This stock explanation pattern is likely to come to mind because that's the way professional sports is sold by sports corporations and the mass media. But if you also belong to the culture of professional anthropologists, you're just as likely to borrow an academic explanation pattern, like the "important cultural ritual" explanation pattern—to explain why grown men chase leather balloons on weekends in America. As we shall see in greater detail in Chapter 14, it's no exaggeration to say that our cultures choose our explanation patterns for us, and these patterns, together with the values and beliefs associated with them, shape the way we interpret our experiences.

Our cultures specify the repertoire of story frames we use to explain our experiences, but ultimately we choose a particular explanation pattern in a given situation because it serves our personal interests and the collective interests of the social groups we identify with. Ronald Reagan could have called on a number of different explanation patterns to explain why a United States Navy vessel had fired on an Iranian airliner: he might have said that the Iranians had used the airliner to provoke an international incident, or that the ship's commander made the right decision because his ship was in a state of military alert, or even that an unfortunate human or technological mistake had been made. But as Roger Schank points out, Reagan chose the "understandable tragedy" story frame because it was in his interests to do so: as commander in chief of the Armed Forces, head of state, and leader of the Republican party, Reagan decided to choose a strategy that would (1) minimize the chance of armed confrontation by expressing sympathy for the dead, (2) "save face" for the United States by excusing American forces of any wrongdoing, and (3) reassure Americans by affirming the basic "correctness" of U.S. actions. Although Jessie Jackson undoubtedly also knew the "understandable tragedy" explanation pattern, his interests and those of his low-income, politically underrepresented constituents were better served by his choice of what we might label the "failed foreign policy" explanation pattern. It was in his interests to interpret the airliner's downing not as a military blunder, or an unforeseeable accident, but as a symptom of bad political leadership. The motive behind any analysis grows out of the interpreter's individual interests—*and* out of the collective interests of the social, political, religious, ethnic, economic, or other groups the writer identifies with.

Like our cultures and speech communities, our perspectives and interests change throughout our lives. That's why kids, teens, and adults seem so often not only to speak different languages but even to see the world through different eyes. That's also why our interpretations of events, objects, people, and relationships change over time: the movie you couldn't get enough of when you were ten may strike you as a piece of commercialized kitty litter by the time you enter college; the grandparent who always seemed like "a lot of fun" when you were a child may come to represent an alternative way of living—or way of life full of snares and pitfalls—when you're twenty. The following story illustrates the way that an intergenerational difference of perspective can lead to clashing interpretations of the same event. In "The Last Word" Judith Ortiz Cofer relates her own version of a childhood memory—one that differs sharply from the family story told by her mother. The conflict between these versions of Cofer's past gives us the chance to see how interests can shape the way we interpret the events of our lives—and even the way we shape interpretations of our identity. Cofer was born in Puerto Rico in 1952. She immigrated to the United States with her family in 1960 and spent much of her childhood shuttling between her home in New Jersey and the small town of Hormigueros, where she was born. Her writings focus on the tensions she experienced growing up between two cultures and two languages. This selection first appeared in *Silent Dancing: A Partial Remembrance of a Puerto Rican Childhood* (1990). Cofer has also authored two books of poetry and the novel *The Line of the Sun* (1989).

Before Reading

Briefly sketch one or two stories told about you as a child that were meant to illustrate what you were like when you were growing up.

The Last Word
Judith Ortiz Cofer

"I did that," says my memory.
"I did not," says my pride; and
memory yields.   —Nietzsche, *Beyond Good and Evil*

My mother opens the photo album to a picture of my father as a very young man in an army uniform. She says to me, "You had not met your father yet when this photograph was taken. He left for Panama when I was a couple of months pregnant with you, and didn't get back until you were two years old."

I have my own "memories" about this time in my life, but I decide to ask her a few questions, anyway. It is always fascinating to me to hear her version of the past we shared, to see what shades of pastel she will choose to paint my childhood's "summer afternoon."

"How did I react to his homecoming?" I ask my mother whose eyes are already glazing over with grief and affection for her husband, my father, dead in a car wreck now for over a decade. There are few pictures of him in middle age in her album. She prefers to remember him as the golden boy she married, forever a young man in military uniform coming home laden with gifts from exotic places for us.

"You were the happiest little girl on the island, I believe," she says smiling down at his picture. "After a few days of getting acquainted, you two were inseparable. He took you everywhere with him."

"Mother . . ." In spite of my resolve, I am jarred by the disparity of our recollections of this event. "Was there a party for him when he returned? Did you roast a pig out in the backyard. I remember a fire . . . and an accident . . . involving me." 5

She lifts her eyes to meet mine. She looks mildly surprised.

"You were only a baby . . . what is it that you think happened on that day?"

"I remember that I was put in a crib and left alone. I remember many people talking, music, laughter." I want her to finish the story. I want my mother to tell me that what I remember is true. But she is stubborn too. Her memories are precious to her and although she accepts my explanations that what I write in my poems and stories is mainly the product of my imagination, she wants certain things she believes are true to remain sacred, untouched by my fictions.

"And what is this accident you remember? What do you think happened at your father's homecoming party?" Her voice has taken on the deadly serious tone that has always made me swallow hard. I am about to be set straight. I decide to forge ahead. *This is just an experiment,* I tell myself. I am comparing notes on the past with my mother. This can be managed without resentment. After all, we are both intelligent adults.

"I climbed out of the crib, and walked outside. I think . . . I fell into 10 the fire."

My mother shakes her head. She is now angry, and worse, disappointed in me. She turns the pages of the book until she finds my birthday picture. A short while after his return from Panama, my father is supposed to have spent a small fortune giving me the fanciest birthday party ever seen in our pueblo. He wanted to make up for all the good times together we had missed. My mother has told me the story dozens of times. There are many photographs documenting the event. Every time I visit a relative someone brings out an album and shows me a face I've memorized: that of a very solemn two-year-old dressed in a fancy dress sent by an aunt from New York just for the occasion, surrounded by toys and decorations, a huge, ornate cake in front of me. I am not smiling in any of these pictures.

My mother turns the album toward me. "Where were you burned?" she asks, letting a little irony sharpen the hurt in her voice. "Does that look like a child who was neglected for one moment?"

"So what really happened on that day, Mami?" I look at the two-year-old's face again. There is a celebration going on around her, but her eyes—and my memory—tell me that she is not a part of it.

"There was a little accident involving the fire that day, Hija," my mother says in a gentler voice. She is the Keeper of the Past. As the main witness of my childhood, she has the power to refute my claims.

"This is what happened. You were fascinated by a large book your fa- 15
ther brought home from his travels. I believe it was a foreign language dictionary. We couldn't pry it away from you, though it was almost as big as you. I took my eyes off you for one moment, *un momentito, nada más, Hija,* and you somehow dragged that book to the pit where we were roasting a pig, and you threw it in."

"Do you know why I did that, Mother?" I am curious to hear her explanation. I dimly recall early mentions of a valuable book I supposedly did away with in the distant past.

"Why do children do anything they do? The fire attracted you. Maybe you wanted attention. I don't know. But," she shakes her finger at me in mock accusation, "if you remember a burning feeling, the location of this fire was your little behind after I gave you some *pan-pan* to make sure you didn't try anything like that ever again."

We both laugh at her use of the baby word for a spanking that I had not heard her say in three decades.

"That is what really happened?"

"*Es la pura verdad,*" she says. "Nothing but the truth." 20

But that is not how *I* remember it.

LESSONS OF THE PAST

For my daughter

I was born the year my father learned to march
   in step
with other men, to hit bull's eyes, to pose for
   sepia photos
in dress uniform outside Panamanian nightspots
    —pictures
he would send home to his pregnant teenage
   bride inscribed:
To my best girl.

My birth made her a madonna, a husbandless
   young woman
with a legitimate child, envied by all the tired
   women
of the pueblo as she strolled my carriage down
   dirt roads,
both of us dressed in fine clothes bought with
   army checks.

           When he came home,
he bore gifts: silk pajamas from the orient for
   her; a pink
iron crib for me. People filled our house to welcome him.
He played Elvis loud and sang along in his new
   English.
She sat on his lap and laughed at everything.
They roasted a suckling pig out on the patio.
   Later,
no one could explain how I had climbed over the
   iron bars
and into the fire. Hands lifted me up quickly,
   but not before
the tongues had licked my curls.

           There is a picture of me
taken soon after: my hair clipped close to my
   head,
my eyes enormous—about to overflow with fear.
I look like a miniature of one of those women
in Paris after World War II, hair shorn,
being paraded down the streets in shame,
for having loved the enemy.

> But then things changed,
> and some nights he didn't come home. I remem-
> ber
> hearing her cry in the kitchen. I sat on the rock-
> ing chair
> waiting for my cocoa, learning how to count, *uno,*
> *dos, tres,*
> *cuatro, cinco,* on my toes. So that when he came
> in,
> smelling strong and sweet as sugarcane syrup,
> I could surprise my *Papasito*—
> who liked his girls smart, who didn't like
> crybabies—
> with a new lesson, learned well.

Issues for Discussion

1. Summarize the different versions that Cofer and her mother offer of the party that Cofer recalls in this selection. What roles do Cofer, her mother, and her father play in each? What explanation patterns seem to shape their recollections of this incident?

2. How might you explain the differences between Cofer's story and that of her mother? What interests, values, or beliefs are reflected in these two different versions of her story?

3. Whose version do you find more plausible? Why?

JOURNAL OPTION

Exploring How Perspective Shapes Stories

Look back at the childhood stories you sketched in your journal before reading Cofer's "The Last Word." To what extent does your memory of these events differ from the stories you heard related about you? How might you account for any differences you notice?

Inside Explanation Patterns: If the Story Fits . . .

Americans never seem to get enough courtroom drama. From *Perry Mason* to *L.A. Law* to *Law and Order,* we never seem to tire of watching shows in which people spend most of their time talking and very little time doing anything else. Why are television programs and movies about judges and lawyers—both standard targets of ridicule in our culture—so popular? One reason may be that besides telling a good story, they're about what it takes to make a story good. If you stop to think about it, the entire judicial system was created for the purpose of settling disputes between conflicting stories. Prosecutors and defense lawyers play the part of expert storytellers: their role is to weave plausible stories out of all the evidence at hand—stories that either condemn or vindicate the accused. The judge is a story referee, enforcing the ground rules in this storytelling contest, determining the aspects of each version the jury is allowed to hear and filtering out details that are considered biased or irrelevant. Juries have the function of deciding which story carries the day—which, ultimately, is the most believable. From the state's perspective, the defendant is a heartless murderer who premeditated his father's death to collect the insurance money; according to the defense, he's the victim of an abusive parent whose daily beatings drove him to the brink of insanity. When all goes right, the story that best "fits" the evidence is the story that wins.

To make an explanation or analysis effective you have to assess the "fit" between the explanation pattern you're using and the evidence it's meant to interpret. As Roger Schank indicates in "Story Skeletons and Story-Fitting" (p. 331), every explanation pattern contains or implies a predictably linked series of ideas and associations. So, for example, the "understandable tragedy" explanation pattern that Ronald Reagan chose to shape his interpretation of the Iranian airliner incident implies the ideas that U.S. troops were pursuing a "justifiable goal" and that their response was "unintended and unanticipated" even if it was "undesirable." Whether or not you find this explanation believable depends on how accurately Reagan's explanation pattern fits the facts surrounding the incident. The same is true for the lawyer who argues that his client is a "victim of abuse" and not a killer. He has to show that there is a reasonable "fit" between the implications involved in the "victim of abuse" explanation pattern and the evidence of the case: if it turns out that his client had rarely complained of ill treatment at home and had shown unusual interest in his father's insurance policy just days before his death, the attorney for the defense might find it hard to convince the jury to believe his version of what happened.

"Fit," however, never involves a perfect match. Reality never lines up with all of our expectations—and our explanation patterns—as neatly as we might hope. Every act of explanation, analysis, or interpretation requires us to shape the evidence somewhat to fit the explanation pattern we've chosen to guide it. It may be true that our murder suspect only rarely complained about the way his father abused him, but that's typical of many victims of abuse—the fact itself doesn't contradict the general pattern of this story. And his drug habit? Well, that was just a result of the terrible situation he had to live with. Every analysis or interpretation subtly emphasizes certain facts and minimizes others. That's why it's possible to retell or reinterpret a story from different points of view: the details associated with any event, text, or object can be selected and shaped to conform to the story frames suggested by many different explanation patterns. When there is a good fit between the implications of a pattern and the details of the object of explanation—when the inner structure of both coincide neatly like those transparent pictures of bones and muscles in an anatomy book—the explanation pattern almost seems to disappear into the object: the explanation seems utterly plausible, even "natural," and we have no trouble believing it. But when the fit seems forced or strained, the grinding gears of interpretation become too obvious and eventually distract us. When there's a bad fit between our explanation pattern and the evidence, the defendant-as-victim story seems like exactly that—an artificial tale that the defense has concocted out of desperation.

You might not expect anyone to try to squeeze an explanation pattern over a Barbie doll, but the author of our next reading does just that. In this selection from *Forever Barbie: The Unauthorized Biography of a Real Doll,* M. G. Lord uses several different explanation patterns to interpret Barbie's significance for two generations of American women. Lord's analysis of Barbie offers you a good chance to see how a writer edits, emphasizes, and omits details to make the object of explanation fit the explanation patterns she's chosen to impose upon it. M. G. Lord is a journalist whose work has appeared in New York *Newsday, The Nation, The American Spectator,* and *The Wall Street Journal.*

Before Reading

Jot down a few sentences that describe ideas you associate with Barbie—or about what you think accounts for Barbie's success.

Interpreting Barbie
M. G. Lord

My mother was, by most people's definitions, a beauty: five feet ten, 132 pounds, and possessed of breasts that in their size and shape resembled Barbie's. They didn't droop or sag; nor did their size—38-C—interfere with her ability to win at sports. Even in her forties she could swim faster and hit a softball harder than people half her age. No doubt you assume that I will write about how her perfection placed me in competition with her and, by extension, all women; how I ached to have 38-C breasts; and how every month when *Vogue* arrived I pored over pictures of Verushka begging, "Dear God, please make me look like her." Nothing, however, could be further from the truth.

When I was eight years old and my mother was forty-six, she had a mastectomy. Her experience with cancer did not have a happy ending. It was a prelude to chemotherapy, more operations, and, six years later, death. This was before the age of reconstructive surgery, political activism, and the life-affirming defiance that one sees among breast-cancer patients today. The illness was shrouded in secrecy, almost shame.

As her health deteriorated, her remaining breast mocked her. It hovered there—flawless—next to her indignant red scar. What it said to me was: You do not want Barbie's breasts; the last thing on earth you want are Barbie's breasts. I associated them with nausea, hair loss, pain, and decay. I associated them with annihilation. I believed myself blessed when nature didn't provide them.

True, at sixteen, when I had my first serious beau, I felt vaguely shabby that his gropings were so meanly rewarded; but the shabby feeling quickly passed. I was alive and hoped to remain so. In my mind, small breasts would make this possible; they seemed somehow less vulnerable. Of course not every little girl's mother has a mastectomy, but many do. Since 1980, 450,000 women have died of breast cancer. In the decade of the nineties, an estimated 1.5 million women will be diagnosed with the disease, and one-third of them will die.

These grim statistics suggest that daughters of breast-cancer patients are far from an insignificant minority. But I suspect, as a consequence of the disease's historical invisibility, the experiences of breast-cancer daughters have often been ignored by so-called body image experts. When I heard *Beauty Myth* author Naomi Wolf say on National Public Radio, "We were all raised on a very explicit idea of what a sexually successful woman was supposed to look like," I wanted to shout that another "we"—millions of breast-cancer daughters—had had a very different experience. When Wolf said "the official breast" was "Barbie's breast," I muttered aloud, "Speak for yourself, lady." Not all women respond in a crazed, competitive, Pavlovian fashion to pictures of models or the body of a doll. And it's demeaning to suggest that they do.

My Barbie play was as idiosyncratic as my childhood. I remembered nothing about it until four years ago when my father got my dolls out of storage and shipped them to me. Tucked away since 1968, the vinyl cases seemed innocuous, yet I kept finding reasons not to open them.

I wonder if archeologists hesitate, mid-dig, before making their discoveries, if they falter outside tombs the way I fumbled with the clasp of Ken's mildewed sarcophagus. When, after several tugs, the latch finally gave, I dropped the case, bouncing Ken onto the floor. I reached for him, then froze. He was wearing Barbie's low-cut, sequined "Solo in the Spotlight."

Nonchalant, he gazed at me, radiating what Susan Sontag has called the "androgynous vacancy" behind Greta Garbo's "perfect beauty." If Mattel had intended to model him on the Swedish actress, it couldn't have done a better job.

My Midge, by contrast, was laid out spartanly in her original carton; a mere sidekick, she didn't have a fancy case. At least she looked comfortable, wearing what I would have worn for twenty years in storage—Ken's khaki trousers, navy blazer, and dress shirt.

Then there was Barbie—blond ponytail Barbie—wearing tennis whites   10 and a sweatshirt in her glossy red valise. Her cruel mouth, still haughty, brought back memories. I remembered a fight after which my mother grudgingly bought me fat-cheeked, blotchy Midge. I remembered a second fight after which she bought me perfect Barbie and Ken. And I remembered Midge's ordeal. Midge didn't seduce Ken—that would have been too obvious. She became his platonic pal, introducing him to a new pastime: looking more Barbie-like than Barbie.

I was tempted to slam the cases, to squelch the memories, but I rummaged farther. My dolls had not been cross-dressed in a vacuum. It had happened during the years of my mother's illness; years of uncertainty, of sleepovers at friends' houses when she was in the hospital; years which, until I opened the boxes, I had forgotten. But as I picked through the miniatures, why I did what I did became less of a mystery.

My Barbie paraphernalia was a museum of my mother's values. Arrayed together, the objects were a nonverbal vocabulary, the sort of language in which John Berger[1] urged women to express themselves. Except for "Solo," which a friend had given me, the language was hers.

A chemist who fled graduate school long before completing a Ph.D., my mother was a casualty of the Feminine Mystique. She had stopped work to become a fifties housewife and hated every minute of it. She didn't tell me, "Housework is thralldom," but she refused to buy Barbie cooking utensils. She didn't say, "Marriage is jail," but she refused to buy Barbie a wedding

[1]**John Berger** (b. 1926) is a well-known novelist, essayist, and art critic.

dress. What she did say often, though, was "Education is power." And in case I missed the point, she bought graduation outfits for each of my dolls.

Nor did she complain about her mastectomy. I sensed the scar embarrassed her, but I never knew how much. Then I unearthed Barbie's bathing suit—a stretched-out maillot onto which my mother had sewn two clumsy straps to keep the top from falling down.

That sad piece of handiwork spoke to me in a way she never had. It spoke not of priggishness or prudery, but of the anguish she had felt poolside and why she rarely ventured into the water. It spoke of how she felt herself watched—how all women feel themselves watched—turning male heads before the operation and fearing male scrutiny after it. It spoke of pain and stoicism and quiet forbearance. It broke her silence and my heart.

When things of aesthetic power—say, the Vietnam Veterans Memorial—have emotional resonance, the resonance feels right. But I cannot tell you how strange it was to ache with grief over a bunch of doll clothes. Or to find in a Barbie case a reliquary of my mother.

I forced myself to study Ken masquerading as Steichen's portrait of Garbo; Midge looking like a refugee from a boys' boarding school; even Barbie looking more Martina than Chrissy.[2] (Barbie wore a tiny tennis skirt, but it was under *Ken's* sweatshirt.) I concluded that I'd been one messed-up kid.

But as I explored the mess, I came to realize that, given my environment, it would have been far flakier not to have cross-dressed the dolls. It wasn't just my mother's message that a woman's traditional role was loathsome; it was all the weirdness and fear floating around the idea of breasts. I don't think Midge's sartorial inspiration was Una Lady Troubridge or Radclyffe Hall. I think it was terror. Femaleness, in my eight-year-old cosmos, equaled disease; I disguised Midge in men's clothes to protect her. If her breasts were invisible, maybe the disease would pass over them. Maybe she'd survive. I even shielded Barbie, permitting her to show her legs but armoring her chest. Only Ken was allowed the luxury of feminine display; he had no breasts to make him vulnerable.

Seeing Barbie ignited a brushfire of ancient emotions; no longer could I dismiss the doll as trivial. Freud, of course, understood that dolls weren't trivial; in his essay on "The Uncanny," he writes about the creepy or "uncanny" feeling dolls or automata provoke in people when such dolls are too lifelike. He also understood that if commonplace or familiar things—like, say, Barbies—trigger the recollection of a repressed memory, they can send shivers down one's spine.

15

---

[2]Martina Navratilova and Chris Evert were top-rated tennis players during the 1970s and 1980s.

In German, "the uncanny" is *das Unheimliche*—that which is weird or 20 foreign. The word is the opposite of *das Heimliche*—that which is familiar, native, of the home. Once "homely" objects, my dolls had become uncanny: they preserved, as if in amber, the forgotten terrors of my childhood. Freud explains: "If psycho-analytic theory is correct in maintaining that every affect belonging to an emotional impulse, whatever its kind, is transformed, if it is repressed, into anxiety, then among instances of frightening things there must be one class in which the frightening element can be shown to be something repressed which *recurs*."

He calls this class of scary things "the uncanny." Consequently, Freud writes, "we can understand why linguistic usage has extended *das Heimliche* ['homely'] into its opposite *das Unheimliche,* for this uncanny is really nothing new or alien, but something which is familiar and old-established in the mind and which has become alienated from it only through the process of repression."

In his essay, Freud pushes the idea of the uncanny much farther than I do. He describes the fantasy of being mistakenly buried alive as "the most uncanny thing of all"—remarking that psychoanalysis has revealed that fantasy to be a transformation of another, originally nonterrifying fantasy qualified "by a certain lasciviousness"—that of intrauterine existence.

Thus the womb, "the former *Heim* [home] of all human beings," is the ultimate *unheimlich* place. This might also suggest why, while not literally a return to the womb, my profound reconnection with my mother—experienced as an adult through my childhood dolls—seemed uncanny.

I was eight when I got my Barbies, well past the age of appropriating them as what psychoanalyst D. W. Winnicott termed "transitional objects." But Mattel's research shows that today kids get Barbies earlier, usually about age three. Thus, Barbies, in the psyches of toddlers, can function as transitional objects—which warrants a closer look at Winnicott's concept.

During the months following birth, a baby doesn't grasp that its 25 mother is separate from itself. Embodied by her ever-nurturing breast, the mother is an extension of the child; she can be magically conjured up by the child whenever the child wants—or so the child believes. As the child develops, however, it must face the fact that this just isn't so—not, for the child, a happy idea. It isn't just the physical weaning, having to give up a stress-free means of satisfying hunger. It's also the trauma of becoming independent, of losing the blissful, boundariless connection to Mom.

This, says Winnicott, is where transitional objects come in. They are, for a child, his or her first "not me" objects. The child imbues them with elements of the self and the mother; and they symbolize, for the child, that relationship, which is coming to an end.

There aren't hard and fast rules about transitional objects: They can be as stereotypical as Linus's security blanket in *Peanuts* or as idiosyncratic as a piece of string. Nor are there rules about the age at which children appropriate them. Sometimes a baby will attach itself to a toy in its crib; sometimes an older child—such as Linus—will endure the ridicule of schoolmates rather than renounce his object. But the objects, Winnicott has pointed out, aren't fetishes; having them, for kids, is normal behavior.

Significantly, though, the transitional object "is not just a 'not me' object, it's a also a 'me' object," said Ellen Handler Spitz, who has written on the phenomenon in *Art and Psyche.* "If she loses it and is put to bed without it, she may have a tantrum and be devastated. Like the transitional object, the Barbie doll leads the child into the future by enabling her to detach, to some extent, from the mother. At the same time, because the doll is a little woman, it represents the relationship with the mother." A transitional object can also be a child's bridge to future aesthetic experiences. This is because the child often sucks, strokes, and mutilates it into "a highly personal object," the way an artist fashions artwork out of clay.

Legally speaking, the Barbie doll *is* a work of art. Mattel copyrighted Barbie's face as a piece of sculpture, not because the doll was intended to be a unique object, but because it wasn't. The manual processes in Barbie's creation—the sewing-on of hair, the painting of lips—might permit a variation or two; thus hair and makeup were not copyrighted. But the duplication of the doll's body was mechanical and, therefore, uniform; hence the registration of the sculpture.

In 1936, when critic Walter Benjamin investigated the idea of *Art in the Age of Mechanical Reproduction,* he focused principally on photographs, which in his view satisfied the masses' craving "to bring things 'closer' spatially and humanly, which is just as ardent as their bent toward overcoming the uniqueness of every reality by accepting its reproduction." 30

In the case of Barbie, however, the reality is the reproduction. Human icons—Elvis, Garbo, Madonna—can only be possessed through film or audiotape; there either was or is an "original" somewhere that forever eludes ownership. But Barbie herself was meant to be owned—not just by a few but by everybody. Issued in editions of billions, she is the ultimate piece of mass art.

Benjamin was writing at the dawn of the age of mechanical reproduction, two decades before the post–World War II boom in synthetics that made Barbie possible. He wrote before the era of plastic, the revolutionary material that did for objects what film did for images. Plastic is a key to understanding Barbie: Her substance is very much her essence.

Hard, smooth, cool to the touch, plastic can hold any shape and reproduce the tiniest of details. It is not mined or harvested; chemists manufacture it. Nor does it return to nature: you can throw it away, but it will not vanish—poof—from the landfill. Time may alter its appearance, as it has with some of the earlier Barbies—dolls with white arms on coral torsos with oily, apricot-colored legs.

To a poet or a child or anyone given to anthropomorphizing, such dolls are victims of vitiligo, the disease from which Michael Jackson claims to suffer. But to a chemist, they are evidence of an inadequate recipe. Never mind the beads of moisture on their mottled thighs, old dolls, a chemist will tell you, don't sweat. But their "plasticizer" (the substance used to make plastic pliable) may begin to separate from their "resin" (the plastic base— polyvinylchloride in Barbie's case). Or their dyes might fade.

In the environmentally conscious nineties, it's hard to remember a time when plastic was considered miraculous. In the fifties, "Better living through chemistry" was the slogan of the plastic pocket protector set, not an ironic catch phrase coined by users of hallucinogenic drugs. Science was inextricably tied up with patriotism. The Soviets launched *Sputnik* in September 1957; we countered four months later with a satellite of our own. Can-do, know-how— these were American things, as were those big acrylic polymers and giant supermolecules. It had been our manifest destiny to tame a big continent; we drove big cars; even on the molecular level, we placed our trust in big.

With the introduction of credit cards, "plastic" became a synonym for money. Diner's Club issued the first universal credit card in 1950, American Express followed in 1958, and by 1968, the best career tip for a youth like Dustin Hoffman in *The Graduate* was simply: "Plastics."

Plastic, Roland Barthes wrote, "is the very idea of its infinite transformation; as its everyday name indicates, it is ubiquity made visible." It is also democratic, almost promiscuously commonplace. In the past, imitation materials implied pretentiousness; they were used to simulate luxuries— diamonds, fur, silver—and "belonged to the world of appearances not to that of actual use." Plastic, by contrast, is a "magical substance which consents to be prosaic"; it is cast, extruded, drawn, or laminated into billions of household things.

But if Barbie's substance is the very essence of the mid-twentieth century, her form is nearly as old as humanity, and it is her form that gives her mythic resonance. Barbie is a space-age fertility symbol: a narrow-hipped mother goddess for the epoch of cesarean sections. She is both relentlessly of her time and timeless. To such overripe totems as the Venus of Willendorf, the Venus of Lespugue, and the Venus of Dolni, we must add the Venus of Hawthorne, California.

Venus of Lespugue. Collection of Musée de L'homme, Paris

Venus of Willendorf. Collection of Naturhistorisches Museum, Wien

But wait, you say, Barbie is no swelling icon of fecundity; thick of waist, round of shoulder, pendulous of breast and bulging of buttock. How can you link her with Stone Age, pre-Christian fertility amulets? The connection rests on her feet, or the relative lack of them.

The Venus of Willendorf is a portable object of veneration. Her legs, like those of other Stone Age "Venuses," taper into prongs at the ankles. For her to stand up, the prong or prongs must be plunged into the earth, an act that, as she is a representation of the Great Mother, completes her. Mother Nature, Great Mother, Mother Goddess, Mother Earth—by any name, the female principle of fecundity is "chthonian," literally "of the earth."

In this context, Barbie's itty-bitty arched feet can be interpreted as vestigial prongs. Their suitability to the wearing of high heels is a camouflage, diverting the modern eye from their ancient function. No one disputes that Barbie has the trappings of a contemporary woman, but, either deliberately or coincidentally, they are arrayed on a prehistoric icon. When I raised the issue with Mattel employees, most responded cryptically with a remark like: "I've heard that said."

Sleek, angular fertility idols are not without precedent. The best-known were produced in the Cyclades, Aegean islands off the coast of Greece, between 2600 and 1100 B.C. The artist who fashioned the Venus of Willendorf conceived of female anatomy as a landscape of dimpled knolls; the Cycladic artists, by contrast, translated breasts and bellies into schematized geometric forms. Like Barbie's, the shoulders of Cycladic dolls are wider than their hips and their bodies are hard and smooth. They are an example of what art historian Kenneth Clark terms a "crystalline Aphrodite"—a stylized descendant of the Neolithic "vegetable Aphrodite." Why Cycladic sculptors streamlined the dolls, however, remains a mystery; scholars, says art historian H. W. Janson, can't "even venture a guess."

Over the years, "dolls"—anthropomorphic sculptures of the human figure—have been used as often in religion as in play. Archeologists who unearth such figures must puzzle out whether they were intended for the temple or the nursery. When first discovered, the ancient Egyptian figures known as *Ushabti* were believed to be dolls; scholars now classify them as funereal statues—miniature versions of a master's slaves buried with the master to serve him after death. Likewise, the Barbie-shaped "snake goddesses" produced in Crete around 1600 B.C. look like dolls but were in fact religious icons.

Then there are dolls that defy classification. Traditionally, Hopi Indian parents give their children kachina figures—cult objects representing various gods—to play with on ceremonial occasions. Barbie is both toy and mythic object—modern woman and Ur-woman—navelless, motherless, an

40

incarnation of "the One Goddess with a Thousand Names." In the reservoir of communal memory that psychologist Carl Jung has termed the "collective unconscious," Barbie is an archetype of something ancient, matriarchal, and profound.

In Barbie's universe, women are not the second sex. Barbie's genesis 45 subverts the biblical myth of Genesis, which Camille Paglia has described as "a male declaration of independence from the ancient mother-cults." Just as the goddess-based religions antedated Judeo-Christian monotheism, Barbie came before Ken. The whole idea of woman as temptress, or woman as subordinate to man, is absent from the Barbie cosmology. Ken is a gnat, a fly, a slave, an accessory of Barbie. Barbie was made perfect: her body has not evolved dramatically with time. Ken, by contrast, was a blunder: first scrawny, now pumped-up, his ever-changing body is neither eternal nor talismanic.

Critics who ignore Barbie's mythic dimension often find fault with her lifestyle. But it is mythologically imperative that she live the way she does. Of course Barbie inhabits a prelapsarian paradise of consumer goods; she has never been exiled from the garden.

Mattel attributes the success of its 1992 "Totally Hair" Barbie, a woolly object reminiscent of Cousin It from *The Addams Family,* to little girls' fascination with "hairplay"—combing, brushing, and generally making a mess of the doll's ankle-length tresses. But since not all Barbie owners become cosmetologists, one has to wonder what "hairplay" is really about. I think it may be a modern reenactment of an ancient goddess-cult ritual.

Witches traditionally muss up their hair when they are preparing to engage in witchcraft. As late as the seventeenth century, civilized Europeans, historian Barbara Walker tells us, actually believed witches "raised storms, summoned demons and produced all sorts of destruction by unbinding their hair." In Scottish coastal communities, women were forbidden to brush their hair at night, lest they cause a storm that would kill their male relatives at sea. St. Paul, one of history's all-time woman-haters, was scared of women's hair; he thought unkempt locks could upset the angels.

The toddler brushing Barbie's hair may look innocent, but who knows, perhaps she is in touch with some ancient matriarchal power. In 1991, a survey of three thousand children commissioned by the American Association of University Women revealed that girls begin to lose their self-confidence at puberty, about the time they give up Barbie. At age nine, the girls were assertive and felt positive about themselves, but by high school, fewer than a third felt that way. Perhaps this could have been avoided had the girls simply hung on to their Barbies. Forget trying to be Barbie; even gorgeous grown people would be hard-pressed to pass for an eleven-anda-half-inch thing. But maybe they should build a shrine to the doll and light some incense.

There is a remarkable amount of pagan symbolism surrounding Barbie.   50
Even the original location of Mattel—Hawthorne—has significance. The Hawthorn, or May Tree, represents the White Goddess Maia, the mother of Hermes, goddess of love and death, "both the ever-young Virgin giving birth to the God, and the Grandmother bringing him to the end of his season." Barbie's pagan identity could also account for Ken's genital abridgment; cults of the Great Mother were ministered to by eunuchs. And it would explain why the housewives in Dichter's[3] study took an immediate dislike to Barbie: "The white goddess is anti-domestic," Robert Graves writes in *The White Goddess: A Historical Grammar of Poetic Myth.* "She is the perpetual 'other woman.'"

Even if it wanted to, Mattel could not assert ignorance of pagan symbolism. This isn't merely because Aldo Favilli, the Italian-born, classically educated former sculpture restorer at Florence's Uffizi Gallery who has run Mattel's sculpture department since 1972, ought to know a thing or two about iconography. In 1979, the company test-marketed two "Guardian Goddesses," "SunSpell," "the fiery guardian of good," and "MoonMystic," "who wears the symbols of night." Identical in size and shape to Barbie, they came with four additional outfits—"Lion Queen," "Soaring Eagle," "Blazing Fire," and "Ice Empress"—sort of Joseph Campbell[4] meets Cindy Crawford. But even stranger than their appearance was what they did. To "unlock" their "powers," you *spread their legs*—or, as their box euphemizes, made them "step to the side." Then they flung their arms upward, threw off their street clothes and controlled nature. Freezing volcanoes, drying up floods, blowing away tornadoes, and halting a herd of stampeding elephants are among the activities suggested on their box.

The goddesses took Barbie's crystalline hardness one step further. They wore plastic breastplates and thigh-high dominatrix boots—outfits created by two female Mattel designers that evoke Camille Paglia's characterization of the Great Mother as "a sexual dictator, symbolically impenetrable." Yet despite their literal virginity, their powers were metaphorically linked to sex. To set the dolls' mechanism, their thighs had to be squeezed together until they clicked. To release it, their legs had to be parted; the box features a drawing of two juvenile hands clutching each foot. Vintage doll dealers speculate that

---

[3]**Ernest Dichter:** a founder of the field of motivational research. He conducted marketing studies in 1959 to predict responses to Barbie.
[4]**Joseph Campbell** (d. 1987) wrote a number of popular and influential books on world mythology.

the goddesses were removed from the market because their mechanism was too delicate. But between their lubricious leg action and pantheistic message, they strike me as having been too indelicate.

If I had to locate the point at which I began to see the ancient archetype within the modern toy, it would be at the home of Robin Swicord, a Santa Monica–based screenwriter whom Mattel commissioned in the 1980s to write the book for a Broadway musical about the doll.

Swicord is not a New Age nut; she's a writer. And even after megawrangles with Mattel's management—the musical was sketched out but never produced—she is still a fan of the doll. "Barbie," she said, "is bigger than all those executives. She has lasted through many regimes. She's lasted through neglect. She's survived the feminist backlash. In countries where they don't even sell makeup or have anything like our dating rituals, they play with Barbie. Barbie embodies not a cultural view of femininity but the essence of woman."

Over the course of two interviews with Swicord, her young daughters played with their Barbies. I watched one wrap her fist around the doll's legs and move it forward by hopping. It looked as if she were plunging the doll into the earth—or, in any event, into the bedroom floor. And while I handle words like "empowering" with tongs, it's a good description of her daughters' Barbie play. The girls do not live in a matriarchal household. Their father, Swicord's husband, Nicholas Kazan, who wrote the screenplay for *Reversal of Fortune,* is very much a presence in their lives. Still, the girls play in a female-run universe, where women are queens and men are drones. The ratio of Barbies to Kens is about eight to one. Barbie works, drives, owns the house, and occasionally exploits Ken for sex. But even that is infrequent: In one scenario, Ken was so inconsequential that the girls made him a valet parking attendant. His entire role was to bring the cars around for the Barbies.

In other informal interviews with children, I began to notice a pattern: Clever kids are unpredictable; they don't cut their creativity to fit the fashions of Mattel. One girl who wanted to be a doctor didn't demand a toy hospital; she turned Barbie's hot pink kitchen into an operating room. Others made furniture—sometimes whole apartment complexes—out of Kleenex boxes and packing cartons. And one summer afternoon in Amagansett, New York, I watched a girl and her older brother act out a fairy tale that fractured gender conventions. While hiking in the mountains, a group of ineffectual Kens was abducted by an evil dragon who ate all but one. He remained trapped until a posse of half-naked Barbies—knights in shining spandex—swaggered across the lawn and bludgeoned the dragon to death with their hairbrushes.

Issues for Discussion

1. What personal story interferes for Lord with the common assumption that Barbie represents an ideal of female physical beauty—that "the official breast" was "Barbie's breast"? What story of beauty does Barbie tell? Who does it include and exclude?

2. What different explanation patterns does Lord use to interpret Barbie's significance?

3. Examine the case Lord makes for Barbie as a "goddess" figure. What specific connections does she make to support the use of this explanation pattern? How persuasive do you find her efforts to "fit" Barbie to this explanation pattern?

JOURNAL
OPTIONS

Evaluating Fit

1. Using Lord's interpretation of Barbie as a model, offer your own interpretation of a popular children's toy, character, superhero, or video game. When you're finished, try to identify the explanation pattern you've used to shape your analysis as well as the series of ideas and associations it implies. Then share your interpretation with your classmates in small groups and let them try to identify your choice of explanation pattern.

2. Think for a moment about a recent, widely publicized court case and analyze the arguments made by the prosecution and the defense. (You may want to refer back to the journal entry you made after reading Roger Schank's "Story Skeletons" (p. 331).) What explanation patterns were evoked by each side? What weaknesses can you find in the "fit" between the explanation patterns and the evidence presented in the case?

Critical Reading: Analyzing Analysis

Most of us don't need help to gauge our gut reaction when we hear an analysis or an interpretation. We "swallow" some explanations pretty easily because they just seem to "make sense." Others are enough to give you a bad case of the cramps: there's almost nothing as upsetting as an explanation that contradicts your sense of reality. Responding critically to a piece of analytic or interpretive writing, however, can involve some serious detective work. To get beyond the messages your gut sends your head about an analysis, you need to examine the interpretive choices an author makes, the

assumptions that are implied in those choices, and the motives that underlie them. Here are some tips for reading and responding critically to analysis
and interpretation.

What's the explanation pattern?   In order to grasp the point of a reading
like Lord's interpretation of Barbie, you have to figure out what story the
author is trying to impose on the object of interpretation. Lord, as you
probably recognized, uses several different explanation patterns to guide
her interpretation of Barbie's appeal, including the explanation pattern that
equates Barbie with ancient earth goddesses. Critical appraisal of her interpretation begins when you are able to identify the specific patterns that she
is attempting to impose on her topic.

Of course, the process of analysis isn't always as obvious — or as playful — as it is in Lord's interpretation of Barbie. Portraying Mattel's plastic
Pollyanna as the earth mother incarnate is a stretch, and it's clear that
Lord enjoys the intellectual challenge of making such a far-fetched connection. In most cases, however, explanation patterns are "effaced" — hidden within or obscured behind the interpretation itself. No self-respecting
lawyer would turn to the jury and say, "I'm going to show that my client's
story fits the well-known story pattern of 'the victim of abuse,' and that
he therefore deserves to go free." Usually, the machinery of interpretation —
the explanation pattern guiding our interpretive efforts — stays hidden behind the scenes: the explanation patterns we choose shape our explanations and specify the points we have to make, but they themselves take a
backseat to the event, object, or person we're trying to analyze. Ronald
Reagan didn't take the time to tell us that he was employing the standard
"understandable tragedy" pattern to shape his explanation of the Iranian
airliner incident (he probably wasn't even aware that his analysis fit a
stock interpretive pattern): he just used it. By contrast, Leslie Marmon
Silko does tell us that the way Pueblo Indians use language "resembles
something like a spider's web — with many threads radiating from a center" (p. 21). But while the image of the web underlies everything she says
about the importance of Pueblo storytelling, she doesn't bother to make it
explicit in every section of her essay — she doesn't take the time to tell us
directly something like "stories connect to other stories like a web" or
"stories connect us to other members of our community and other generations within it like a web." It's up to her reader to reconstruct the "stories
= webwork" explanation pattern from the hints she offers and the overall
pattern of relations and ideas that emerges from her analysis.

How does it "fit"?   Another issue you usually consider when critiquing an analysis or interpretation is the "fit" between the explanation pattern and the object of explanation. A thorough critique of Lord's analysis of Barbie, for example, might question whether Barbie's feet really have anything to do with the "vestigial prongs" of earth goddess figures: Is Barbie literally meant to be "plunged into the earth"? Hawthorne, California, Barbie's birthplace, may indeed be named after the May Tree, a symbol of the goddess of life and death, but are we to assume that Mattel built its toy plant there to exploit the connection? A thoughtful response to Lord's and any other analysis will sift through the individual points that are made, comparing the relation of the ideas implied by the explanation pattern with the features of the object of explanation, acknowledging those that seem meaningful and making note of those that seem implausible or far-fetched.

It may also be important to consider aspects of the explanation pattern that the writer omits. Prehistoric goddess figures are generally supposed to have served as religious objects related to fertility religions: such figures are thought to have been used in rituals meant to assure a bountiful harvest or to increase the birth of children. Lord omits, or perhaps deliberately ignores, this aspect of the "goddess" explanation pattern, perhaps because Mattel has done everything possible to dissociate Barbie from the notion of fertility. Part of what made Barbie so unusual when she appeared on the market in the 1960s was the fact that she was a grown-up doll who was unmarried and childless. Once you've noted an omission like this, you can ask further questions about what *it* means: If Barbie lacks the single most important characteristic of earth goddess figures, can you buy Lord's analysis? Isn't Barbie's lack of fertility—physical or intellectual—her most important feature? How persuasive can Lord's analysis of Barbie be if she leaves this aspect out? The things a writer omits—the major implications of an explanation pattern left unexplored—are often more revealing than any single weakness in the fit between explanation and object.

What other assumptions are implied?   In addition to exploring how well an explanation pattern fits, you'll want to consider the assumptions that a writer makes in linking a particular explanation pattern to a particular object. Some assumptions are glaringly obvious: when Ronald Reagan invoked the "understandable tragedy" pattern to explain the 1988 Iranian airliner incident, he simply *assumed* that it suited the occasion; he didn't bother to detail how accurately it fit the evidence at hand. A careful critique of Reagan's position, then, would have to question the accuracy of this assumption by probing how well the explanation pattern actually did fit this case: you'd have to question whether the U.S. destroyer involved in the incident was, in fact, "justifiably deployed" in the Persian Gulf, whether it was deployed without the intention of provoking a conflict, whether it acted out of self-defense, and so forth.

But analyses and interpretations may also contain more subtle, structural assumptions. Whether it's immediately apparent or not, explanation patterns are rooted in a specific cultural context, a context built up from a network of associations and ideas on a given topic. When an explanation pattern from a particular realm of experience is linked—through analysis or interpretation—with an object belonging to a different one, a kind of mental "short-circuit" happens, and all the ideas, relationships, and associations in them are allowed to mix and mingle. Take, for example, one of the explanation patterns most commonly used to explain how minds work—the computer. For the last couple of decades psychologists and educators have looked to the computer for an explanatory model of brain function and structure. According to the "mind = computer" explanation pattern, perceptions are a kind of "input" from the environment; these "signals" travel along wirelike neuronal pathways to different "parts" of the brain, or "modules" as some experts term them, where they are "processed." Eventually, the brain's central processor—the cerebral cortex—integrates "information" from all "modules" and applies various "routines" for analyzing it. No doubt the "computer = mind" explanation pattern is useful, but it also gives rise to some troublesome assumptions. Does the mind actually have well-defined "parts" like a machine? Is thinking as orderly or as linear as the "processing" that happens in a computer? If the mind is seen as a machine, what happens to emotion and human interaction? This kind of mixing or cross-contamination of associations occurs even when the explanation pattern we're using has become so generalized—so much a part of our stock of standard explanation patterns—that we no longer associate it with a specific context. When Reagan explained that U.S. actions in the Persian Gulf amounted to an "understandable tragedy," he probably wasn't consciously thinking about the history of the stage. But the word *tragedy* still bears associations from its roots in Greek theater, where "tragic" action involved the inevitable destruction of the innocent by forces that were beyond human control. A tragedy, to the Greek mind, was fated by heavenly destiny and not susceptible to mortal intervention. Whether U.S. forces in the Persian Gulf were also beyond human control is an assumption that might be worth looking into.

What's the motive?   Once you've identified the explanation pattern that guides the analysis you're critiquing and evaluated its "fit," you'll want to consider the intentions that led to its choice. As we noted in the last chapter, the motives behind any analysis can be traced to the writer's individual interests *and* to the collective interests of the social, political, religious, ethnic, economic, or other groups the writer identifies with. What purposes could be served by explaining Barbie's appeal in terms of the earth goddess? Well, for one thing, Lord's choice is entertaining, and you can't rule out the desire to make a few bucks by selling some books. But there's also the possibility that Lord was trying to "rehabilitate" Barbie's reputation, particularly among feminist intellectuals: by linking Barbie to a symbol of female power, she may be trying to find something "positive" in a doll that has long been criticized for promoting sexist and stereotypical attitudes about what it means to be a woman. By interpreting Barbie as a source of female empowerment, Lord may be trying to "reclaim" Barbie for liberated women—or even trying to suggest that, despite Mattel's best efforts, girls have always been smart enough to resist common gender stereotypes. And finally, there may be a more personal motive: it's possible that Lord was trying to explain her own childhood fascination with a doll that reminded her of her mother's illness. Understood in this way, the earth goddess explanation pattern transforms Lord's youthful attachment to Barbie from a potentially morbid obsession into an act of personal empowerment. What was Lord's real motive? There's no way of telling for certain. The intention behind a particular explanation or analysis is always a matter of conjecture, but it's one you have to make if you want to understand, as completely as possible, what a particular analysis or interpretation means to you.

Alternatives?   Finally, it never hurts to consider alternative patterns of explanation. There are as many explanation patterns to choose from as there are ways of looking at things, and no one pattern fully explains any object or event. Instead of conceiving the mind in terms of a digital computer that "processes" incoming data in a fairly neat and orderly manner, it might make more sense—you might get a better "fit" between explanation pattern and object—if you think of it as a kind of continuous political convention where diverse groups, each armed with slightly different "versions" of reality and different interests, compete for power and attention. Or how about seeing the mind as a complex biochemical ecosystem that has its own brand of emotional "weather" and strives to assimilate outside intrusions while maintaining a state of equilibrium? Over the centuries any number of models have been used to explain the mind, including a slab of wet clay, a mirror, a blank slate, a bank, a theater, a clock, a hydraulic system, all varieties of electronic gadgets and gizmos, and even subatomic particles in a so-called quantum state. Before you judge the usefulness of any one model, it makes sense to consider at least a few alternatives. And the same is true for any analysis or interpretation: Is it more plausible to interpret Barbie's appeal in terms of her function as a vestige of the earth goddess or in terms of her function as a pop-cultural "drug" used by Mattel to separate parents from their money? What other ways can you see Barbie? Until you ask this final question, your critique remains incomplete.

In summary, then, here are five things you want to consider when you read and respond to an analysis or an interpretation:

1. Choice of explanation pattern
2. The fit between explanation pattern and object of explanation
3. Assumptions underlying the explanation pattern
4. The author's motives or interests
5. Alternative explanations, interpretations, and analyses

Reading Pictures

A picture, like any object you might want to explain, never comes with its meaning prepackaged: even photographs and videotapes have to have their stories told before they become significant. It's tempting to think that a picture "means" what it "looks like": after all, if you see a photo of a man hugging a woman, that's all there is to it. But such literal thinking confuses the facts of what you see—the various details, figures, and actions represented in a photo or a picture—with the way you interpret those facts. As we've suggested, meanings are never simply "there," embedded in facts and details: meanings only emerge when you shape the facts to fit a story of your own, when you *impose* an explanation pattern of your choosing on the facts you see.

The following photographs and pictures allow you to explore how analysis and interpretation generate meanings. The first exhibit in our minigallery is a famous photo by an equally famous photographer, Alfred Eisenstaedt (1898–1995). A photographer for *Life* magazine for more than forty years, Eisenstaedt captured this embrace between strangers on the day that World War II ended on the Pacific front, August 14, 1945. Since it first appeared on the cover of *Life*, this image has been considered a classic of wartime photography, symbolizing for most Americans the joy and relief that greeted V-J Day. In the editorial opinion that follows, Donna Britt, a *Washington Post* columnist, offers her own interpretation of Eisenstaedt's celebrated "embrace." After critiquing Britt's analysis of Eisenstaedt, you can try your hand at reading the gallery of images that follows. As you tell your own stories about these photos and pictures, remember that you're

trying to analyze or interpret the significance or meaning of each image, not simply describe or identify the objects, people, and situations represented in them. Remember, too, that there's no one "right" way to interpret: any analysis is possible as long as it moves us beyond the mere "facts" of the object—*and* if the explanation pattern it relies on fits its object.

Before Reading

Before you read Britt's analysis of Eisenstaedt's "embrace," jot down a few lines explaining what you see in this celebrated photo.

A Kiss May Not Still Be a Kiss
Donna Britt

As a youngster growing up in the 1960s and '70s, I saw it at least a dozen times—Alfred Eisenstaedt's unforgettable *Life* magazine cover shot, taken 50 years ago this month, of a sailor kissing a nurse on V-J Day in Times Square.

To my teen-age eyes, the uniformed pair's embrace represented the perfect picture of wartime romance: spontaneous, passionate, urgently but innocently sexy. The horrors of war, the photo said, are over. Let the good times begin again.

Eisenstaedt's death last week at 96 gave us another glimpse of what became his signature shot. Once again, I admired its perfect composition, how it captured, through people whose faces we never see, a nation's rekindled joy.

But it sparks something different in me today than it did when I was 15. Some classic images—such as Mathew Brady's bleak Civil War compositions—would seem to have a similar impact on viewers of any era. Others suggest different things to different people at different times.

Now, gazing at the Eisenstaedt photo, I found myself wondering: What was the nurse feeling? For the first time, I noticed that she is bent over backward, at a nearly 45-degree angle, with her leg slightly twisted to help her maintain her balance. Because she isn't returning the sailor's hug—her visible arm hangs at her side—it is inaccurate to describe their connection as an embrace. But neither is she pushing him away. The woman appears as impassive as a rag doll—neither reciprocating nor rejecting the advance.

The sailor's physical intent, however, seems clear. You can read his resolve in the way his whole upper body bends hers back, the way one arm encircles her waist while the other forms a crook perfect for positioning a head for a kiss. The clenched elbow ensures that she's not getting away—though there's no real suggestion that she wants to.

Eisenstaedt said that he happened upon the shot while scouring Times Square on that momentous day. He noticed a sailor grabbing, kissing and hugging every woman in sight. Following him, the photographer waited until he grabbed a slim nurse all in white—and then snapped.

Analyzing the resulting photo, reading the sailor's and the nurse's disparate body languages, I wonder. Is she, as I once assumed, as rapturous as the man holding her? Is she as caught up in this moment of liberation, in the longed-for end to a struggle unimaginable to those of us who never lived through it?

Or is she stunned by an intimate liberty being taken by a stranger before dozens of people? Was her impassivity that of someone caught unawares or that of a woman who'd prepared herself for the offering? Could she have felt some strange combination of all those things?

These may be '90s questions forced on a '40s vision, but I wish I knew. [10] Knowing how time and celebrity can alter people's views, I'm not even sure I'd trust whatever the nurse's stated feelings about that moment were.

But somehow, the photo that once suggested only romance to me now whispers complexity. Because it hasn't changed, my eyes must have. The photo illustrates how an act that is tolerated or even lauded in one era might a generation later be regarded as unacceptable. It shows how 50 years—during which terms such as "date rape" became part of the lexicon, record numbers of women learned self-defense and women became "assertive" while men became "angry"—can alter an outlook.

Or maybe it's personal. In the decades between looking at the photo and seeing something wonderful and looking at it and seeing only questions, I have become a woman like many women. We've experienced enough uninvited touches—some that we pretended didn't matter, others that mattered far too much for pretense—to ask questions that once never would have arisen.

And I've met dozens of men who are sick to death of women's fears and suspicions—who, tired of feeling like the enemy, will wonder why anybody would see anything but joy in Eisenstaedt's still-amazing masterpiece.

While part of me wishes things were as simple—for the nation and for me—as they once seemed, most of me is glad for the questions.

And, because vision never stops evolving, I know this: Fifty years from [15] now, I may look at Eisenstaedt's masterpiece and see something else entirely.

Issues for Discussion

1. What explanation pattern does Britt use to interpret the scene in Eisenstaedt's photo? How well do you think this explanation pattern fits the image? Does Britt's interpretation "make sense," or is she "reading" too much into this picture?
2. What interests are served by Britt's analysis of Eisenstaedt's photo? What group does Britt apparently identify with or represent?

OPTIONAL
ACTIVITY

Interpreting Images

Study the following images and choose two to focus on. Write brief, one- to two-page interpretations of each, being sure to explain your view of the "story" told in the images you chose—your version of what each image means. In class, do a read-around of these interpretations in small groups, trying to identify the explanation patterns that underlie each interpretation and evaluating the fit between these patterns and the images to which they're applied.

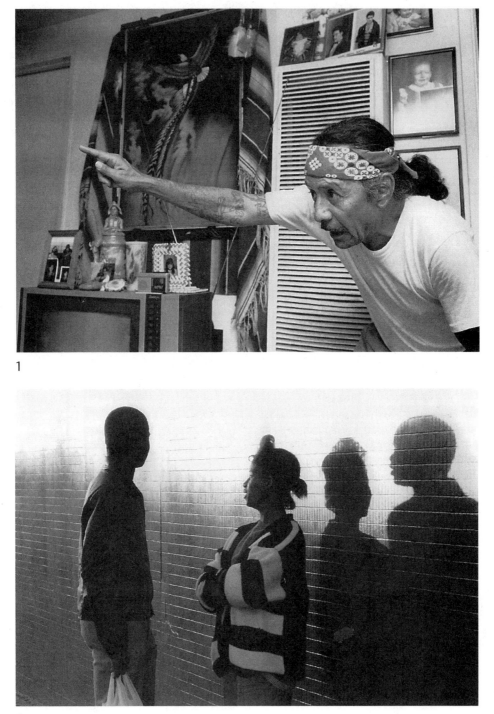

1

2

3

4

Reframing: Talking Back to Official Stories

Twice-Told Tales

Remember the story about the emperor and his new suit of clothes? It's the one about a couple of feudal con artists who dupe the king into buying a new outfit sewn from the most expensive, luxurious, and hard-to-make material in the world: the only hitch is that it's completely invisible. Too proud to admit that he can't see the wonderful suit these crooked tailors pretend to be sweating over for weeks, the emperor agrees to wear it as he parades down the main thoroughfare of his city. All goes well until a child, apparently the only clear-headed person around, shouts out what everyone should be able to see—that the king is as naked as the day he was born. First published by Hans Christian Andersen, this fairy tale is often interpreted as a warning against excessive pride. But it can also be read as a cautionary tale about the danger of mixing stories and power. Andersen's emperor proves a fool not only because his pride leads him to stroll down the street in the buff, but also because he, his ministers, his court, and everyone around him are hypnotized by the story of his infallibility: they all fall for the tailors' trick because none of them can admit that the emperor, in all his majesty, could possibly be wrong. Thus, Andersen's tale isn't about fabric; it's about fabrication—about the way that stories backed by power can distort our sense of what's real.

Stories always have power, but some stories have more power than others. Every culture has its share of "official stories"—famous anecdotes, story frames, and explanation patterns that can dominate thought and stifle alternative points of view. Official stories operate like super explanation patterns: they impose themselves on our experiences and interpret them for us—often before we even realize they're at work. In the case of Andersen's befuddled emperor, only a child has the ability to penetrate the stories that blind the adults around him. His innocence allows him to see the truth behind the official stories of court and culture. But the idea of children's innocence is itself one of the most influential official stories of Western European society. According to the official story of youthful innocence, children live in a world that is psychologically and ethically different from that of adult society. Swaddled in innocence and immune to duplicity and self-deception, children have a natural goodness, an honesty, and a simplicity that inevitably erode in the process of becoming an adult. It's a story that's been repeated in many different versions—from the horde of preadolescent Hollywood heroes who *Free Willy* or defeat evil adults while *Home Alone* to the historical myth of America's "birth" as a fledgling nation, innocent of the decadence, corruption, and class distinctions of the so-called Old World.

Because official stories are repeated so frequently, the ideas they contain take on the status of "common sense." Their "storiness"—the recognition that they are cultural creations made by people to promote certain interests or reinforce specific values—fades away and leaves behind what seems to be simple, natural "fact." The connection between childhood and innocence strikes us as so "natural" that we're shocked when headlines remind us how violent real children can be. The official stories of Western culture are so invisible that many Americans become outraged when we hear that children work and marry like adults in other, non-Western cultures. This shock and outrage are possible, however, only because we tend to forget that the story of childhood innocence is itself just a few hundred years old—even in the West. As historian Philippe Aries notes in his classic work on the subject, before the eighteenth century, children in European society were not seen as living in a special world or having different ways of thinking or perceiving; in fact, from the Middle Ages through the Renaissance, European children were rarely "seen" at all. Considered incomplete adults, their existence was deemed negligible. Little attempt was made to educate or even discipline them, and no pains were taken to shield them from the harsher—and often the cruder—realities of adult life. Indeed, Aries reports that before the eighteenth century children were often treated as if they were sexual toys—cuddly erotic playthings that could be displayed or fondled in public by friends and family. At seven, the so-called "age of reason," children were considered "mature": they typically left home to become apprentices or servants and frequently married by the time they entered their teens.[1]

Just how official stories like the story of childhood innocence get started is a matter of debate. It's clear that some official stories are literally "official," in the sense that they are produced and perpetuated by governments and other powerful cultural institutions. In nineteenth-century America, the official story of "manifest destiny"—the notion that the United States was not only right but fated to expand to the West—was manufactured to justify military aggression against Mexico and genocidal government policies against American Indians. In the 1950s, government-sponsored stories about the benefits of atomic power and the promise of technology paved the way for environmental disasters during the decades that followed. Still, simple straightforward political domination can't account for the persistence of many official stories: otherwise individuals would never be able to reject the teachings of their governments. It's more likely that most official stories owe their longevity to a convergence of cultural, economic, and political interests, not to the efforts of any one narrowly defined group or political faction. The story of childhood innocence, for example, appears to have emerged in eighteenth-century Europe in response to a number of factors. European governments needed larger populations to administer colonial holdings and fill newly created factories; the most immediate way to increase population size was to improve the living conditions of children. At the same time, religious and political leaders were beginning to promote the interests of the individual over those of the clan and the state. The idea of the sanctity of the individual, combined with the need to improve childrearing practices, led to the transformation of the family into an institution dedicated to nurturing children—and to shielding them from the harmful effects of the adult world. Official stories exist because they further collective interests and reinforce shared beliefs and values: think of them as the ideological "glue" that cultures use to bind themselves together.

Invasion of the Body Snatchers

The problem is that the same official stories that *bind* cultures together also *blind* us to new ideas and new ways of thinking. Two decades ago, biologist Richard Dawkins scandalized a number of his fellow scientists by proposing

[1]Philippe Aries, *Centuries of Childhood: A Social History of Family Life,* trans. Robert Baldick (New York: Vintage Books, 1962), pp. 100–127.

a new way of looking at genetics and the function of genes. For years, the official story of genetics had it that genes were something like little chemical tape recorders that helped a species survive by encoding and passing along its biological characteristics. Dawkins took this familiar explanation pattern and turned it inside out: in his highly controversial book, *The Selfish Gene,* Dawkins offered a radical reinterpretation of Darwinian theory. Instead of seeing genes as chemical machines helping species to reproduce and survive, he theorized that genes themselves struggled to reproduce and pass along their information to future generations and that the individual creatures that make up a species were only "survival machines"—artificial environments created to protect genes from a hostile chemical world. This "gene's-eye view" of evolution was daring enough, but Dawkins carried his interpretive play even further: extending the explanation pattern of the "selfish gene" into the realm of culture, he suggested that ideas, songs, values, beliefs—in fact, all cultural creations—exploit people's minds in this "selfish" way to replicate themselves and guarantee their own survival. "Memes," as Dawkins called these cultural replicators, include the jingle from a commercial that you can't get out of your head, your mother's recipe for meatloaf, the internal combustion engine, *Jurassic Park,* the concept of the atom, Einstein's theory of relativity, the idea of God—any cultural artifact that can enter your mind, combine there with other ideas, "reproduce," and be passed along to further generations. As Dawkins himself explains this audacious theory:

> Examples of memes are tunes, ideas, catch-phrases, clothes fashions, ways of making cooking pots or of building arches. Just as genes propagate themselves in the gene pool by leaping from body to body via sperms or eggs, so memes propagate themselves in the meme pool by leaping from brain to brain via a process which, in the broad sense, can be called imitation. If a scientist hears, or reads about, a good idea, he passes it on to his colleagues and students. He mentions it in his articles and his lectures. If the idea catches on, it can be said to propagate itself, spreading from brain to brain. As my colleague N. K. Humphrey neatly summed up an earlier draft of this chapter: ". . . memes should be regarded as living structures, not just metaphorically but technically. When you plant a fertile meme in my mind you literally parasitize my brain, turning it into a vehicle for the meme's propagation in just the way that a virus may parasitize the genetic mechanism of a host cell. And this isn't just a way of talking—the meme for, say, 'belief in life after death' is actually realized physically, millions of times over, as a structure in the nervous systems of [people] the world over."[2]

[2]Richard Dawkins, *The Selfish Gene* (New York: Oxford University Press, 1989), p. 192.

You might be tempted to agree with philosopher Daniel Dennett that the idea of your brain being used as "a sort of dungheap in which the larvae of other people's ideas renew themselves" isn't very attractive.[3] But the concept of the meme does suggest the power that official stories have over our thinking. When an official story, like the story of childhood innocence, is reproduced so frequently and authoritatively that it is mistaken for simple "common sense" or "natural fact," we forget that it represents just one more "version" of reality—one more story or interpretation—told to promote specific purposes. Like Dawkins's memes, such "naturalized" stories colonize our minds, shaping our perceptions and influencing our reactions before we even realize that they're at work. Here's a quick example borrowed from the composition classroom. For decades teachers have taught writing as if they were preparing their students to fight a war or build a house: students were urged to think carefully and "plan strategies of attack" before they wrote, to "take a position" on their topic, to "defend" their position with plenty of evidence, to "anticipate and attack" opposing points of view; alternatively, they were urged to "build" or "structure" their paper around a thesis, to "support" it with strong arguments, and to undergird these arguments with a sound "foundation" of evidence or research.[4] Because the explanation patterns—"writing = war" and "writing = building a physical structure"—underlying these versions of the writing story are hidden or effaced, students rarely pause to question the assumptions about writing that they promote. Once you begin to discuss writing as a matter of "attack and defense," it gets harder to see it from other points of view—as, say, an active dialogue between different cultures or subcultures or as a process of negotiation between parties whose approaches differ but who share many of the same ideas and values. Once you begin to think of writing a paper as "building" a free-standing physical object like a house, it gets harder to imagine the act of writing as entering into a relationship or as a conversation involving a whole community of writers and thinkers on a particular topic. Official stories are "selfish" stories because they impose their interpretations and explanations on us without giving us the chance to recognize their artificiality: we're forced to accept all the hidden explanation patterns and all the values, beliefs, and assumptions they entail, without having the chance to recognize their existence as "just another story" that can be questioned, critiqued, and challenged.

[3]Daniel Dennett, *Darwin's Dangerous Idea: Evolution and the Meanings of Life* (New York: Simon & Schuster, 1995), p. 346. (Dennett, from whom we borrowed the title for this segment, is actually an avid supporter of Dawkins's ideas.)

[4]You can find a more detailed treatment of such metaphors in George Lakoff and Mark Johnson, *Metaphors We Live By* (Chicago: University of Chicago Press, 1980).

Official stories are "selfish" in a second way as well. Take a look at the figure below:

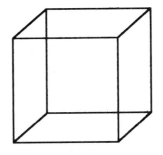

Psychologists use the Necker cube to demonstrate how the mind automatically shapes sensory data into meaningful patterns. If you stare continuously at this image for more than a few moments, you'll notice a remarkable thing: the cube seems to change orientation. One minute it faces down and toward the left; the next it faces up and toward the right. Keep staring and the shape will keep transforming itself. Perhaps the most intriguing feature of this optical trick is that you can't see both versions of the cube at the same time: no matter how hard you try to capture both orientations in a single glance, your eyes deliver just one image at a time. The Necker cube works this way because the mind has trouble making sense of more than one explanation pattern at a time: the lines that make up both interpretations of the Necker cube are right there in front of you, but you can see only one possible interpretation of them or the other—you can't grasp both at once. Stories work in a similar way: once a particular explanation pattern is imposed on an event or object, it becomes increasingly difficult to see it from any other perspective. If you're brought up in a culture that repeatedly tells you that childhood is a special time of innocence, you may have a hard time seeing children in any other light. Your mind "locks on" to the first pattern that seems meaningful, and the dominance of that pattern blocks out alternatives. That's why official stories can be dangerous. Repeated so frequently, so authoritatively, and so uncritically, they are always at hand when you need an explanation, conveniently foreclosing alternative points of view. A good official story can literally stop your thinking before it starts by "explaining away" the puzzles and contradictions you meet before you can question them. Disguised as common sense and armed with the power to silence alternative interpretations, official stories can anesthetize your sense of wonder and transform you, in meme-like fashion, from a thinking individual into a well-oiled, unconscious, interpreting machine.

The only way to avoid becoming a victim of the stories you tell is to self-consciously choose your stories *before* they choose you. The process of consciously choosing and evaluating the explanation patterns you use to analyze and interpret your world is commonly called critical thinking. It's not really all that mysterious: most of the time critical thinking boils down to "talking back" to the official stories that dominate your topic. You're beginning to think critically when you question and seek alternatives to culturally dominant story frames and explanation patterns.

The following reading offers an example of such "talking back" in action. The story of how Rosa Parks inspired the civil rights movement when she refused to give up her bus seat on a sultry Alabama afternoon is one of the most popular tales told in American classrooms. It's become a standard feature of the elementary school curriculum, taking its place beside the signing of the Declaration of Independence and Lincoln's Gettysburg Address. In this selection, educator and social critic Herbert Kohl identifies the official version of the Rosa Parks legend and then offers his own alternative retelling—a revision that he feels is truer to Parks's life, beliefs, and intentions. Herbert Kohl has written more than a dozen books on education, including *Shall We Burn Babar: Essays on Children's Literature and the Power of Stories* (1995), the source of this selection. In the course of his career he has served as director of the Horace Mann–Lincoln Institute for School Experimentation and headed the "Other Ways" experimental educational program conducted in the school district of Berkeley, California.

Before Reading

Freewrite in your journal on Rosa Parks and her role in the civil rights movement. Try to put down everything you know about Parks and her story. Where did you learn your version of the Rosa Parks story?

The Story of Rosa Parks and the Montgomery Bus Boycott Revisited
Herbert Kohl

Racism, and the direct confrontation between African American and European American people in the United States, is an issue that is usually considered too sensitive to be dealt with directly in the elementary school classroom. When confrontation between African Americans and European

Americans occurs in children's literature, it is routinely described as a problem between individuals that can be worked out on a personal basis. In the few cases where racism is addressed as a social problem, there has to be a happy ending. This is most readily apparent in the biographical treatment of Rosa Parks, one of the two names that most children in the United States associate with the Civil Rights movement in the southern United States during the 1960s; the other is Martin Luther King Jr.

Over the past few years, during visits to schools, I've talked with children about the Civil Rights movement. One of the things I ask the children is what they know of Rosa Parks and her involvement in the Montgomery bus boycott. This focus developed after I observed a play about civil rights in a fourth-grade classroom in southern California several years ago. One scene in the play took place on a bus in Montgomery, Alabama. A tired Rosa Parks got on the bus and sat down. The child portraying Mrs. Parks was dressed in shabby clothes and carried two worn shopping bags. She sat down next to the driver, and other children got on the bus until all the seats in front were filled up. Then a boy got on and asked her to move. She refused, and the bus driver told her he didn't want any trouble. Politely he asked her to move to the back of the bus. She refused again and the scene ended. In the next scene we see a crowd of students, African American and European American, carrying signs saying Don't Ride the Buses, We Shall Overcome, and Blacks and Whites Together. One of the students, playing Martin Luther King Jr., addressed the rest of the class, saying something to the effect that African American and European American people in Montgomery got angry because Rosa Parks was arrested for not moving to the back of the bus, and that they were boycotting the buses until all people could ride wherever they wanted. The play ended with a narrator pointing out that the bus problem in Montgomery was solved by people coming together to protest peacefully for justice.

Before talking to the children about their perceptions of Rosa Parks and her motivations, I had a moment to talk with the teacher about a major misrepresentation of facts in the play: there were no European Americans involved in boycotting the buses in Montgomery. The struggle was organized and maintained by the African American community, and to represent it as an interracial struggle was to take the power and credit away from that community. The teacher agreed that the play took some liberty with history but said that since his class was interracial, it was better for all the children to do the play as an integrated struggle. Otherwise, he said, the play might lead to racial strife in the classroom. I disagreed and pointed out that by showing the power of organized African Americans, it might lead all the children to recognize and appreciate the strength oppressed people can show when confronting their oppressors. In addition, the fact that European Americans joined the struggle later on could lead to very interesting discussions about social change and struggles for justice, and could be related to the current situation in South Africa and the resurgence of overt racism in the United States. He disagreed and ended our chat by telling me how hard it was to manage an integrated classroom.

I contented myself with asking the children about Rosa Parks. The girl who played Mrs. Parks, Anna, told me that she imagined "Rosa," as she called Mrs. Parks, to be a poor woman who did tiring and unpleasant work. She added that she imagined Rosa was on her way home to a large family that she had to take care of all by herself when she refused to move to the back of the bus. In other words, Rosa Parks was, in her mind, a poor, single parent with lots of children, and an unskilled worker. I asked her how she got that idea, and she replied that's just the kind of person she felt Rosa Parks must be. She added that nobody had ever told her that her view was wrong, so she never bothered to question it. Her teacher backed her up and claimed that she had made reasonable assumptions about Rosa Parks, ones that he felt were true to the way Rosa Parks was portrayed in the books they had in class. I couldn't argue with that last comment.

I changed the subject and asked Anna why Rosa Parks's arrest led to a boycott. She said she didn't know. Maybe Rosa had a friend who told everybody, or maybe it was in the newspaper. One of the other students suggested that her arrest was on TV and everybody came out to protest because they didn't think it was right to arrest someone just for not moving to the back of the bus. The boycott was, to them, some form of spontaneous action that involved no planning or strategy.

All the children admired Rosa Parks for not moving. Some said she must be a very stubborn person, others that she had to be so angry that she didn't care what happened to her. They agreed that it took a special person to be so courageous and wondered if they would be able to muster such courage. I got the impression that Mrs. Parks's exceptional courage might be an excuse for them to not act.

I decided to push the issue a bit and asked the class why Rosa Parks had to move to the back of the bus anyway. One of the African American children said it was segregated in the South back then, and African Americans and European Americans couldn't do things together. When I asked why there was segregation in those days there was absolute silence. I shifted a bit and asked if the African Americans and European Americans in their classroom could do things together. One of the boys answered, "In school they do, mostly." Since I was just a guest I left it at that. However, it was clear to me that issues of racial conflict were not explicitly discussed in this classroom, and that the play about the Montgomery bus boycott left the children with some vague sense of unity and victory, but with no sense of the risk and courage of the African American people who originated the struggle for civil rights in the United States or of the history and nature of segregation. I have no idea whether there was any racism manifest in the everyday lives of the children in that classroom, but wondered whether they or the teacher were at all prepared to deal with it if it erupted.

The children's visualization of Rosa Parks, whom they felt free to call by her first name, was particularly distressing. As well as poor, they imagined her to be without education or sophistication, a person who acted on impulse and emotion rather than intelligence and moral conviction. There was no sense of her as a community leader or as part of an organized struggle against oppression. I decided to find out how common this view was, and I have been astonished to find that those children's view of Rosa Parks is not at all different from that of most European American adults and almost all the school children I have questioned.

The image of "Rosa the Tired," and the story that goes with it, exists on the level of a national cultural icon in the United States. School textbooks and children's books are major perpetuators of this myth, but none of them I've seen quote sources for their distorted personal information about Mrs. Parks. Yet, most American children's first encounter with the Civil Rights movement comes through these writings. Dozens of children's books and textbooks I've looked at present the same version of Rosa Parks and the Montgomery bus boycott. This version can be reduced to the following generic story, which I fabricated* and could be titled:

"ROSA WAS TIRED: THE STORY OF THE MONTGOMERY BUS BOYCOTT"

Rosa Parks was a poor seamstress. She lived in Montgomery, Alabama, during the 1950s. In those days there was still segregation in parts of the United States. That meant that African Americans and European Americans were not allowed to use the same public facilities such as restaurants or swimming pools. It also meant that whenever it was crowded on the city buses African Americans had to give up seats in front to European Americans and move to the back of the bus.

One day on her way home from work Rosa was tired and sat down in the front of the bus. As the bus got crowded she was asked to give up her seat to a European American man, and she refused. The bus driver told her she had to go to the back of the bus, and she still refused to

---

*See the note on references at the end of this reading for the specific sources I drew upon to create this generic version of Rosa Parks's story.

move. It was a hot day, and she was tired and angry, and became very stubborn.

The driver called a policeman, who arrested Rosa.

When other African Americans in Montgomery heard this they became angry too, so they decided to refuse to ride the buses until everyone was allowed to ride together. They boycotted the buses.

The boycott, which was led by Martin Luther King Jr., succeeded. Now African Americans and European Americans can ride the buses together in Montgomery.

Rosa Parks was a very brave person.

This story seems innocent enough. Rosa Parks is treated with respect   10
and dignity and the African American community is given credit for running the boycott and winning the struggle. It reflects the view of Mrs. Parks often found in adult literature as well as writings for children. For example, in the book by eminent psychiatrist Robert Coles, *The Moral Life of Children* (Boston: Houghton Mifflin, 1986), we find the following quote:

> We had come to know. . . . a group of poor and poorly educated people, who, nevertheless, acquitted themselves impressively in pursuit of significant ethical objectives. I think of Rosa Parks, a seamstress, whose decision to sit where she pleased on a Montgomery, Alabama, bus in the middle 1950s preceded the emergence of the so-called Civil Rights movement and of Dr. King and Ralph Abernathy as leaders of it. (p. 25)

A more recent example of this can be found in Robert Fulghum's bestselling book, *It Was on Fire When I Lay Down on It* (Ivy Books, 1988):

> I write this on the first day of December in 1988, the anniversary of a moment when someone sat still and lit the fuse to social dynamite. On this day in 1955, a forty-two-year-old woman was on her way home from work. Getting on a public bus, she paid her fare and sat down on the first vacant seat. It was good to sit down — her feet were tired. As the bus filled with passengers, the driver turned and told her to give up her seat and move on back in the bus. She sat still. The driver got up and shouted, "MOVE IT!" She sat still. Passengers grumbled, cursed her, pushed at her. Still she sat. So the driver got off the bus, called the police, and they came to haul her off to jail and into history.
>
> Rosa Parks. Not an activist or a radical. Just a quiet, conservative, churchgoing woman with a nice family and a decent job as a seamstress. For all the eloquent phrases that have been turned about her place in the flow of history, she did not get on that bus looking for trouble or trying to make a statement. Going home was all she had in

mind, like everybody else. She was anchored to her seat by her own dignity. Rosa Parks simply wasn't going to be a "nigger" for anybody anymore. And all she knew to do was to sit still. (pp. 109–10)

And here's a current textbook version of the Montgomery bus boycott story written for elementary school children. It comes from the Heath Social Studies series for elementary school, *Exploring My World* by Jeff Passe and Evangeline Nicholas (Lexington, MA: 1991, D.C. Heath, reproduced on page 188 of the Teachers' Guide), and is similar in content to my generic tale:

When Rosa Parks rode on a bus, she had to sit all the way in the back. Her city had a law. It said black people could not sit in the front of a bus.

One day Rosa was tired. She sat in the front. The bus driver told her to move. She did not. He called the police. Rosa was put in jail.

Some citizens tried to help. One of them was Martin Luther King Jr. The citizens decided to stop riding buses until the law was changed.

Their plan worked. The law was changed. Soon, many other unfair laws were changed. Rosa Parks led the way!

The Teachers' Guide to this text informs teachers that "Mrs. Parks' single act brought about the desegregation of buses all over the country." In a lesson plan referring to Rosa Parks's being told to move to the back of the bus, it informs teachers to "tell children they will be reading about a woman who became angry when this happened to her. She decided she was not being treated fairly, and she was not going to put up with that kind of treatment anymore. Have children read to find out how the actions of Rosa Parks helped to change the way black people were treated" (p. 188).

This book was published in 1991 and is certainly still in use. It encourages presenting the Montgomery bus boycott as the single act of a person who was tired and angry. Intelligent and passionate opposition to racism is simply not part of the story. In the entire part of the guide dealing with the Montgomery bus boycott, there is no mention of racism at all. Instead the problem is unfairness, a more generic and softer form of abuse that avoids dealing with the fact that the great majority of White people in Montgomery were racist and capable of being violent and cruel to maintain segregation. Thus we have an adequate picture of neither the courage of Rosa Parks nor the intelligence and resolve of the African American community in the face of racism.

Research into the history of the Montgomery bus boycott, however, reveals some distressing characteristics of this generic story, which misrepresents an organized and carefully planned movement for social change as a

15

spontaneous outburst based upon frustration and anger. The following annotations on "Rosa Was Tired" suggest that we need a new story, one more in line with the truth and directed at showing the organizational intelligence and determination of the African American community in Birmingham, as well as the role of the bus boycott in the larger struggle to desegregate Birmingham and the South.

The Annotated "Rosa Was Tired"

Rosa Parks was a seamstress who was poor. She lived in Montgomery, Alabama, during the 1950s.

Rosa Parks was one of the first women in Montgomery to join the NAACP and was its secretary for years. At the NAACP she worked with E. D. Nixon, vice president of the Brotherhood of Sleeping Car Porters, who was president of the Montgomery NAACP, and learned about union struggles from him. She also worked with the youth division of the NAACP, and she took a youth NAACP group to visit the Freedom Train when it came to Montgomery in 1954. The train, which carried the originals of the U.S. Constitution and the Declaration of Independence, was traveling around the United States promoting the virtues of democracy. Since its visit was a federal project, access to the exhibits could not legally be segregated. Mrs. Parks took advantage of that fact to visit the train. There, Rosa Parks and the members of the youth group mingled freely with European Americans from Montgomery who were also looking at the documents. This overt act of crossing the boundaries of segregation did not endear Rosa Parks to the Montgomery political and social establishment.

Her work as a seamstress in a large department store was secondary to her community work. As she says in an interview in *My Soul Is Rested* by Howard Raines (New York: Bantam, 1978, p. 35), she had "almost a life history of being rebellious against being mistreated because of my color." She was well known to all of the African American leaders in Montgomery for her opposition to segregation, her leadership abilities, and her moral strength. Since 1954 and the Supreme Court's *Brown v. Topeka Board of Education* decision, she had been working on the desegregation of the Montgomery schools. In addition, she was good friends with Clifford and Virginia Durr, European Americans who were well known opponents of segregation. She had also attended an interracial meeting at the Highlander Folk School in Tennessee a few months before the boycott. Highlander was known throughout the South as a radical education center that was overtly planning for the total desegregation of the South, and Rosa Parks was aware of that when she attended the meeting. At that meeting, which dealt with plans for school desegregation in the South, she indicated that she intended to become an active participant in other attempts to break down the barriers of segregation. Finally, Rosa Parks had the active support of her mother and her husband in her civil rights activities. To call Rosa Parks a poor, tired seamstress and not talk about her role as a community leader as well is to turn an organized struggle for freedom into a personal act of frustration. It is a thorough misrepresentation of the Civil Rights movement in Montgomery, Alabama, and an insult to Mrs. Parks as well. Here is a more appropriate way of beginning a children's version of the Montgomery bus boycott:

> It was 1955. Everyone in the African American community in Montgomery, Alabama, knew Rosa Parks. She was a community leader, and people admired her courage. All throughout her life she had opposed prejudice, even if it got her into trouble.

In those days there was still segregation in parts of the United States. That meant that African Americans and European Americans were not allowed to use the same public facilities . . .

The existence of legalized segregation in the South during the 1950s is integral to the story of the Montgomery bus boycott, yet it is an embarrassment to many school people and difficult to explain to children without accounting for the moral corruption of the majority of the European American community in the South. The sentence I composed is one way of avoiding direct confrontation with the moral issues of segregation. First it says, "In those days there was still segregation" as if segregation were no longer an issue. However, as recently as July 1, 1990, an article by Ron Rapaport of the *Los Angeles Daily News* (reprinted in the Santa Rosa, CA, *Press Democrat,* July 1, 1990) focused on the current segregation of private golf clubs in Birmingham and other parts of the United States. In the article he says: 20

> It certainly isn't a secret that Shoal Creek Country Club has no black members because, in the words of its founder, Hall Thompson, "that's just not done in Birmingham."
>
> There are lots of places where it's just not done and not just in the South, either. Many of the golf courses that host PGA (Professional Golfers Association) events are restricted and while it may not often become a public issue, that does not mean people are not aware of it.
>
> As for shame, well, that is a commodity that is in short supply as well.
>
> "The country club is our home," Thompson said, "and we pick and choose who we want."

To this day the club still has only one African American member, who has special status as a guest member. Ironically, in 1994 a young African American golfer won a tournament at the club while other African Americans demonstrated outside its gates protesting the club's segregationist policies.

Locating segregation in the past is a way of avoiding dealing with its current manifestations and implying that racism is no longer a major problem in the United States. This is particularly pernicious at a time when overt racism is once again becoming a common phenomenon and when children have to be helped to understand and eliminate it.

Describing integration passively ("there was still segregation" instead of "European Americans segregated facilities so that African Americans couldn't use them") avoids the issue of activist racist activity on the part of some Whites. Since there was legalized segregation in Alabama, and Mrs. Parks was arrested for a violation of the Alabama state law that institutionalized segregation in public facilities, there must have been racists to have passed those laws. Yet they are absent from the narrative, which doesn't talk overtly about racism. The avoidance of direct discussion of what to do about individuals who are racist is all too characteristic of school programs and children's literature.

This avoidance of dealing directly with racism is also evident in the next sentence, which says that "African Americans and European Americans were not allowed to use the same public facilities." It puts African Americans and European Americans on the same footing, as if there were some symmetry and both were punished by the segregation laws. A more appropriate way of describing the situation would be:

> African American people were prevented by law from using the same public facilities as European Americans. In addition, the African American facilities were vastly inferior to the ones made available to European Americans.

Even this rewriting is too generous given the pervasive, brutal, and absolute nature of segregation in the pre–civil rights South. Perhaps the best analogy that could be used here is apartheid, as legalized segregation in the South hardly differed from South Africa's policy of total separation of the races to ensure White dominance.

I've raised the question with a number of educators, both African American and European American, of how to expose children to the reality of segregation and racism. Most of the European American and a few of the African American educators felt that young children do not need to be exposed to the harsh and violent history of segregation in the United States.

They worried about the effects such exposure would have on race relations in their classrooms, and especially about provoking rage on the part of African American students. The other educators felt that, given the resurgence of overt racism in the United States these days, allowing rage and anger to come out was the only way African American and European American children could work from the reality of difference and separation toward a common life. They felt that conflict was a positive thing that could be healing when confronted directly, and that avoiding the horrors of racism was just another way of perpetuating them. I agree with this second group and believe that some recasting of the third and fourth sentences of "Rosa Was Tired" is called for:

> In those days Alabama was legally segregated. That means that African American people were prevented by the state law from using the same swimming pools, schools, and other public facilities as European Americans. There also were separate entrances, toilets, and drinking fountains for African Americans and European Americans in places such as bus and train stations. The facilities African Americans were allowed to use were not only separate from the ones European Americans used but were also very inferior. The reason for this was racism, the belief that European Americans were superior to African Americans and that therefore European Americans deserved better facilities.

. . . whenever it was crowded on the city buses African Americans had to give up seats in front to European Americans and move to the back of the bus.

Actually African Americans were never allowed to sit in the front of the bus in the South in those days. The front seats were *reserved* for European Americans. Between five and ten rows back the "Colored" section began. When the front of the bus filled up, African Americans seated in the "Colored" section had to give up their seats and move toward the back of the bus. Thus, for example, an elderly African American woman would have to give up her seat to a European American teenage male at the peril of being arrested. Consistent with the comments I've been making so far, and with the truth of the experience of segregation, this sentence should be expanded as follows:

> In those days public buses were divided into two sections, one at the front for European Americans, which was supposed to be "for Whites only." From five to ten rows back the section for African Americans began. That part of the bus was called the "Colored" section.
>
> Whenever it was crowded on the city buses African American people were forced to give up seats in the "Colored" section to European Americans and move to the back of the bus. For example, an elderly

African American woman would have to give up her seat to a European American teenage male. If she refused she could be arrested for breaking the segregation laws.

One day on her way home from work Rosa was tired and sat down in the front of the bus.

Rosa Parks did not sit in the front of the bus. She sat in the front row of the "Colored" section. When the bus got crowded she refused to give up her seat in the "Colored" section to a European American. It is important to point this out, as it indicates quite clearly that it was not her intent, on that day, to break the segregation laws.

At this point the story lapses into the familiar and refers to Rosa Parks as "Rosa." The question of whether to use the first name for historical characters in a factual story is complicated. One argument in favor of doing so is that young children will more readily identify with characters who are presented in a personalized and familiar way. However, given that it was a sanctioned social practice in the South during the time of the story for European Americans to call African American adults by their first names as a way of reinforcing the African Americans' inferior status (African Americans could never call European Americans by their first names without breaking the social code of segregation), it seems unwise to use that practice in the story.

In addition, it's reasonable to assume that Rosa Parks was not any more tired on that one day than on other days. She worked at an exhausting full-time job and was also active full-time in the community. To emphasize her being tired is another way of saying that her defiance of segregation was an accidental result of her fatigue and consequent short temper on that particular day. However, rage is not a one-day thing, and Rosa Parks acted with full knowledge of what she was doing.

It is more respectful and historically accurate to make these changes:

December 1, 1955, on her way home from work, Rosa Parks took the bus as usual. She sat down in the front row of the "Colored" section.

As the bus got crowded she was asked to give up her seat to a European American man, and she refused. The bus driver told her she had to go to the back of the bus, and she still refused to move. It was a hot day, and she was tired and angry, and became very stubborn.

The driver called a policeman, who arrested Rosa.

Rosa Parks described her experiences with buses in her own words (*My Soul Is Rested*):

30

35

I had problems with bus drivers over the years because I didn't see fit to pay my money into the front and then go around to the back. Sometimes bus drivers wouldn't permit me to get on the bus, and I had been evicted from the bus. But, as I say, there had been incidents over the years. One of the things that made this . . . [incident] . . . get so much publicity was the fact that the police were called in and I was placed under arrest. See, if I had just been evicted from the bus and he hadn't placed me under arrest or had any charges brought against me, it probably could have been just another incident. (p. 31)

More recently, in *Voices of Freedom* by Henry Hampton and Steve Fayer (New York: Bantam, 1990), she described her thoughts that day in the following way:

Having to take a certain section [on a bus] because of your race was humiliating, but having to stand up because a particular driver wanted to keep a white person from having to stand was, to my mind, most inhumane.

More than seventy-five, between eighty-five and I think ninety, percent of the patronage of the buses were black people, because more white people could own and drive their own cars than blacks. I happened to be the secretary of the Montgomery branch of the NAACP as well as the NAACP Youth Council adviser. Many cases did come to my attention that nothing came out of because the person that was abused would be too intimidated to sign an affidavit, or to make a statement. Over the years, I had had my own problems with the bus drivers. In fact, some did tell me not to ride their buses if I felt that I was too important to go to the back door to get on. One had evicted me from the bus in 1943, which did not cause anything more than just a passing glance.

On December 1, 1955, I had finished my day's work as a tailor's assistant in the Montgomery Fair Department store and I was on my way home. There was one vacant seat on the Cleveland Avenue bus, which I took, alongside a man and two women across the aisle. There were still a few vacant seats in the white section in the front, of course. We went to the next stop without being disturbed. On the third, the front seats were occupied and this one man, a white man, was standing. The driver asked us to stand up and let him have those seats, and when none of us moved at his first words, he said, "You all make it light on yourselves and let me have those seats." And the man who was sitting next to the window stood up, and I made room for him to pass by me. The two women across the aisle stood up and moved out. When the driver saw me still sitting, he asked if I was going to stand up and I said, "No, I'm not."

> And he said, "Well, if you don't stand up, I'm going to call the police and have you arrested."
>
> I said, "You may do that."
>
> He did get off the bus, and I still stayed where I was. Two policemen came on the bus. One of the policemen asked me if the bus driver had asked me to stand and I said yes.
>
> He said, "Why don't you stand up?"
>
> And I asked him, "Why do you push us around?"
>
> He said, "I do not know, but the law is the law and you're under arrest." (pp. 19, 20)

Mere anger and stubbornness could not account for the clear resolve with which Rosa Parks acted. Nor was she, as Robert Fulghum says in the selection from his book quoted at the beginning of this [essay], "Not an activist or a radical. Just a quiet, conservative, churchgoing woman with a nice family and a decent job as a seamstress." She knew what she was doing, understood the consequences, and was prepared to confront segregation head on at whatever sacrifice she had to make. A more accurate account of the event, taking into consideration Rosa Parks's past history, might be:

> As the bus got crowded the driver demanded that she give up her seat to a European American man, and move to the back of the bus. This was not the first time that this had happened to Rosa Parks. In the past she had refused to move, and the driver had simply put her off the bus. Mrs. Parks hated segregation, and along with many other African American people, refused to obey many of its unfair rules. On this day she refused to do what the bus driver demanded.
>
> The bus driver commanded her once more to go to the back of the bus and she stayed in her seat, looking straight ahead and not moving an inch. He got angry at her and became very stubborn. He called a policeman, who arrested Mrs. Parks.

When other African Americans in Montogomery heard this they became angry too, so they decided to refuse to ride the buses until everyone was allowed to ride together. They boycotted the buses.

The connection between Rosa Parks's arrest and the boycott is a mystery in most accounts of what happened in Montgomery. Community support for the boycott is portrayed as being instantaneous and miraculously effective the very day after Mrs. Parks was arrested. Things don't happen that way, and it is an insult to the intelligence and courage of the African American community in Montgomery to turn their planned resistance to segregation into a spontaneous emotional response. The actual situation was more interesting and complex. Not only Rosa Parks had defied the bus segregation laws in the past: According to E. D. Nixon, in the three months preceding Mrs. Parks's arrest at least three other African American people had been arrested in Montgomery for refusing to give up their bus seats to European American people. In each case, Nixon and other people in leadership positions in the African American community in Montgomery investigated the background of the person arrested. They were looking for someone who had the respect of the community and the strength to deal with the racist police force as well as all the publicity that would result from being at the center of a bus boycott. This leads to the most important point left out in popularized accounts of the Montgomery bus boycott: the boycott had been planned and organized before Rosa Parks was arrested. It was an event waiting to take place, and that is why it could be mobilized so quickly. Rosa Parks's arrest brought it about because she was part of the African American leadership in Montgomery and was trusted not to cave in under the pressure everyone knew she would be exposed to, including threats to her life.

But the story goes back even farther than that. There was an African American women's organization in Montgomery called the Women's Political Council (WPC). It was headed those days by Jo Ann Gibson Robinson, who was a professor of English at Alabama State University in Montgomery, an all-African American university. In 1949 Ms. Gibson was put off a bus in Montgomery for refusing to move from her seat in the fifth row of an almost empty bus to the back of the bus. She and other women in Montgomery resolved to do something about bus segregation. As she says in her book *The Montgomery Bus Boycott and the Women Who Started It: The Memoir of Jo Ann Gibson Robinson* (Knoxville: University of Tennessee Press, 1987), "It was during the period of 1949–1955 that the Women's Political Council of Montgomery—founded in 1946 with Dr. Mary Burks as president and headed from 1950 on by me—prepared to stage a bus boycott when the time was ripe and the people were ready. The right time came in 1955" (p. 17).

This story of collective decision making, willed risk, and coordinated 40 action is more dramatic than the story of an angry individual who sparked a demonstration; it has more to teach children who themselves may have to organize and act collectively against oppressive forces in the future. Here's one way to tell this complex story to young children:

> Mrs. Parks was not the first African American person to be arrested in Montgomery for refusing to move to the back of the bus. In the months before her refusal, at least three other people were arrested for the same reason. In fact, African American leaders in Montgomery were planning to overcome segregation. One way they wanted to do this was to have

every African American person boycott the buses. Since most of the bus riders in the city were African American, the buses would go broke if they refused to let African Americans and European Americans ride the buses as equals.

From 1949 right up to the day Mrs. Parks refused to move, the Women's Political Council of Montgomery prepared to stage a bus boycott because of how African Americans were treated on the bus. African American people in Montgomery were ready to support the boycott. They were just waiting for the time to be ripe. Nineteen fifty-five was the time.

However, none of the people who were arrested before Mrs. Parks was were leaders. She was a leader, and the day she was arrested the leadership called a meeting at the Dexter Avenue Baptist Church. They decided to begin their refusal to ride the buses the next morning. They knew Mrs. Parks had the courage to deal with the pressure of defying segregation and would not yield even if her life was threatened.

The next day the Montgomery bus boycott began.

The boycott, which was led by Martin Luther King Jr., succeeded. Now African American and European Americans can ride the buses together in Montgomery. Rosa Parks was a very brave person.

The boycott was planned by the WPC, E. D. Nixon, and others in Montgomery. Martin Luther King Jr. was a new member of the community. He had just taken over the Dexter Avenue Baptist Church, and when Nixon told him that Rosa Parks's arrest was just what everybody was waiting for to kick off a bus boycott and assault the institution of segregation, King was at first reluctant. However, the community people chose him to lead, and he accepted their call. The boycott lasted 381 inconvenient days, something not usually mentioned in children's books. It did succeed and was one of the events that sparked the entire Civil Rights movement. People who had been planning an overt attack on segregation for years took that victory as a sign that the time was ripe, even though the people involved in the Montgomery boycott did not themselves anticipate such results. Here's one possible way to convey this to children:

There was a young new minister in Montgomery those days. His name was Martin Luther King Jr. People in the community felt that he was a special person and asked him to lead the boycott. At first he wasn't sure. He worried about the violence that might result from the boycott. However, he quickly made up his mind that it was time to destroy segregation and accepted the people's call for him to be their leader.

The Montgomery bus boycott lasted 381 days. For over a year the African American people of Montgomery, Alabama, stayed off the buses. Some walked to work, others rode bicycles or shared car rides. It was very hard for them, but they knew that what they were doing was very important for all African American people in the South.

The boycott succeeded, and by the end of 1956 African Americans and European Americans could ride the buses in Montgomery as equals. However, the struggle for the complete elimination of segregation had just begun.

We all owe a great deal to the courage and intelligence of Rosa Parks and the entire African American community of Montgomery, Alabama. They took risks to make democracy work for all of us.

CONCLUDING THOUGHTS

What remains, then, is to retitle the story. The revised version is still about Rosa Parks, but it is also about the African American people of Montgomery, Alabama. It takes the usual, individualized version of the Rosa Parks tale and puts it in the context of a coherent, community-based social struggle. This does not diminish Rosa Parks in any way. It places her, however, in the midst of a consciously planned movement for social change, and reminds me of the freedom song "We shall not be moved," for it was precisely Rosa Parks's and the community's refusal to be moved that made the boycott possible. For that reason the new title, "She Would Not Be Moved: The Story of Rosa Parks and the Montgomery Bus Boycott" makes sense.

As it turns out, my retelling of the story of Rosa Parks and the Montgomery bus boycott is not the only recent one. In 1990, thirty-five years after the event, we finally have a full, moving, and historically accurate 124-page retelling of the story written for young people. The book, *Rosa Parks: The Movement Organizes* by Kai Friese (Englewood Cliffs, NJ: Silver Burdett, 1990), is one of nine volumes in a series edited by the scholar Eldon Morris entitled *The History of the Civil Rights Movement*. Other volumes in the series, such as those about Ella Baker and Fannie Lou Hamer, also provide a fuller, more accurate look at people's struggles during the Civil Rights movement of the 1960s than has been available to young people until now. These volumes are gifts to all of us from a number of African American scholars who have reclaimed history from the distortions and omissions of years of irresponsible writing for children about the Civil Rights movement. They are models of how history and biography can directly confront racial conflict and illuminate social struggle. This is particularly true of the Rosa Parks volume, which takes us up to date in Mrs. Parks's life and informs us that she remained active over the years, working for social and economic justice in Congressman John Conyer's office in Detroit.

The book, which credits all the people involved in making the Mont-   45
gomery boycott possible, provides a portrait of a community mobilized for
justice. It also leaves us with a sense of the struggle that still needs to be
waged to eliminate racism in the United States.

Rosa Parks has also written an autobiography (with Jim Haskins), which
presents a more personal version of the story given here.

When the story of the Montgomery bus boycott is told merely as a tale
of a single heroic person, it leaves children hanging. Not everyone is a hero
or heroine. Of course, the idea that only special people can create change is
useful if you want to prevent mass movements and keep change from happening. Not every child can be a Rosa Parks, but everyone can imagine her-
or himself as a participant in the boycott. As a tale of a social movement
and a community effort to overthrow injustice, the Rosa Parks story as I've
tried to rewrite it opens the possibility of every child identifying her- or
himself as an activist, as someone who can help make justice happen. And
it is that kind of empowerment that people in the United States desperately
need.

REFERENCES

The following quotes are taken from recent children's books and school textbooks. The
publication date of the earliest of them is 1976; the rest were published in their current
form in the 1980s. However, two of the children's books were copyrighted in 1969 and
reissued in the 1980s with new illustrations. No attempt was made in these two cases to
update the material in the books.

The sample of quotes included is representative of dozens I've read, and cumulatively
represents all the different aspects of the Rosa Parks myth I portrayed in "Rosa Was Tired."
Some of the other texts and the specific lines that related to my text are listed at the end of
this appendix. The passages quoted more fully here are from the most progressive texts and
trade books I've found. I have avoided citing texts no longer in print.

1. From Valerie Schloredt, *Martin Luther King Jr: America's Great Nonviolent Leader in the
   Struggle for Human Rights* (Harrisburg, PA: Morehouse Publishing, 1990).

   On the evening of Dec. 1, 1955, a black lady named Rosa Parks left the downtown
   department store where she worked as a seamstress and walked to the bus stop to
   catch the bus that would take her home.

   The book goes on to describe what happened when Mrs. Parks refused to move
   to the back of the bus:

   Mrs. Parks was tired. She had a long, hard day. . . . Something snapped in Mrs.
   Parks at that moment. Perhaps the patience with which she had endured years of
   subservience and insult. . . . Mrs. Parks didn't look like a person to challenge the
   law of Montgomery. She was a quiet looking lady, wearing small steel rimmed
   spectacles; but like thousands of other black people who rode the buses day after
   day, she was weary of being treated with such contempt.
       Much later she was asked if she had planned her protest. "No," she answered.
   "I was just plain tired, and my feet hurt."

> Mrs. Parks' patience had given way, had she but known it, at the best possible moment. (pp. 19, 20)

2. Here is the Random House version for first- to third-graders from James T. Kay, *Meet Martin Luther King Jr.* (New York: Random House, Step-up Books, 1969), reprinted with new cover in 1989.

> On Dec. 1, 1955, a woman named Rosa Parks did something about the Jim Crow buses.
>
> Mrs. Parks was black. She worked in a department store. That evening she climbed on the bus and sat down.
>
> Each time the bus stopped, more people got on. Soon no seats were left in the white part of the bus.
>
> At the next stop some white people got on. The driver got up and walked over to Mrs. Parks. He told her to give her seat to a white woman.
>
> But Rosa Parks was tired. She did something she had never done before. She just stayed in her seat. . . .
>
> Black people all over the city heard about Rosa Parks. They were very angry. They were mad at the Jim Crow laws. They were mad at the police. They were mad at the bus company. But what could they do?
>
> Then one man said, "Why don't we boycott the buses?" This meant that all the black people would stop riding the buses. Soon the bus company would lose money. Maybe then the owners would be fair to blacks. (not paged)

3. This selection is from Dharathula H. Millender's *Martin Luther King, Jr.: Young Man with a Dream* (New York: Bobbs-Merrill, 1969; Macmillan, Alladin Books, 1986). It is one of the finest of the older children's books about the Civil Rights movement.

> Things came to a head over bus segregation on December 1, 1955. Mrs. Rosa Parks, an attractive negro seamstress, boarded a bus in downtown Montgomery. This was the same bus she had boarded many times after a hard day's work. Today she was tired and eager to get off her aching feet. Accordingly she sat down in the first seat in the Negro section behind the section reserved for white passengers. . . .
>
> At first the driver was surprised (when she refused to move) wondering whether he had heard correctly. When Mrs. Parks clung to her seat, however, and held her head proudly in the air, he realized that he was facing trouble. Accordingly, he stopped his bus, called the police and had her arrested. Her arrest attracted wide attention because she was one of the most respected people in the Negro community. It helped to start a Negro revolt not only in Montgomery but all across the nation. (pp. 148–9)

4. This is from the upper elementary grades social studies textbook *The United States and the Other Americas* by Allan King, Ida Dennis, and Florence Potter, in the Macmillan Social Studies Series (New York: Macmillan, 1982).

> In 1955 Rosa Parks, a black, refused to give up her bus seat to a white in Montgomery, Alabama. She was arrested because of this. Other blacks, led by Dr. Martin Luther King Jr., of Atlanta, Georgia, refused to ride the city buses. The following year a federal court ruled that segregated buses were no longer allowed. (p. 141)

In the teacher's edition the following instructions are given to teachers:

> Have the pupils read the rest of page 413. Draw their attention to the photograph of Rosa Parks. Explain that on December 1, 1955, Rosa Parks boarded a bus in Montgomery, Alabama. Her arms were full of groceries, so she sat in the front row of the section of the bus in which blacks were permitted to sit. As the bus filled up, more white people got on, and the bus driver told Rosa to give up her seat to a white person. Rosa looked out the window and pretended not to hear him. She re-

fused to give up her seat, and because of this she was arrested. In protest against her arrest, the black people of Montgomery refused to ride the bus. They formed car pools, walked, rode mules and horses and buggies. On April 23, 1956, the Supreme Court declared that state and local laws that required segregation of buses were unconstitutional. (p. 413)

5. This is taken from Allan O. Kownslar and William R. Fielder's *Inquiring About American History* (New York: Holt, Rinehart and Winston, 1976), in the Holt Databank System. This is a "modern" series based on inquiry and is considered too liberal for many school districts. It is for upper elementary and junior high students.

> For the black citizens of Montgomery, Alabama, some of the "separate but equal" laws had been changed by 1955. . . . But, in spite of these changes, many people still refused to treat blacks and whites equally. Rosa Parks, a black woman who lived in Montgomery in 1955, had to deal with this problem.
>
> One evening, Rosa Parks was coming home from work on a Montgomery city bus. She had been working hard all day at her job in a downtown department store. Rosa was quite tired. She took a seat toward the back of the bus, where black passengers normally sat. The bus began to fill quickly. As whites got on, they took what seats there were, and soon the bus was full.
>
> Rosa realized that some of the blacks would be asked to give up their seats and move to the back of the bus. They would be asked to stand so that white passengers could sit. She felt that this was unfair. Why should she have to move?
>
> Suddenly the driver turned and asked her, and some other blacks, to move to the rear of the bus. Rosa argued with the driver, but he still insisted that she leave her seat and stand in the back. Rosa paused. She had to make a decision quickly. Should she give up her seat or remain seated?
>
> What would you have done if you had been Rosa Parks? What do you think she did?
>
> Rosa Parks made her choice. She decided to remain seated on the bus. Her action led to the Montgomery Bus Boycott—and eventually, to a Supreme Court ruling against the separation of blacks and whites on all buses. (p. 301)

6. This selection is from another upper elementary text, *The United States and Its Neighbors* by Timothy Helmus, Val Arnsdorf, Edgar Toppin, and Norman Pounds (Morristown, NJ: Silver Burdett, 1984), in the series *The World and Its People*.

> Dr. King gained nationwide fame in Montgomery, Alabama, in 1955. At that time blacks had to sit in the back of public buses. But one day a quiet woman named Rosa Parks decided to sit in the "whites only" part of the bus. She was arrested. Dr. King led a boycott of Montgomery buses to protest her arrest. People who supported Dr. King would not use the buses until anyone could sit wherever she or he pleased. The boycott worked. (p. 248)

Finally, here is a list of quotes from a sampling of texts for all grade levels dealing with Rosa Parks and the Montgomery bus boycott. I've only quoted eighteen of the dozens of books consulted, though I think the unity of their tale comes across quite clearly. The word *racism* was not used in any of them.

1. Karen McAuley et al., *The United States Past to Present,* Teacher's Ed. (Lexington, MA: D. C. Heath, 1987), p. 405. Grade 5.
   "It had been a long, hard day and she was tired."

2. Susan Williams McKay, *The World of Mankind* (Chicago: Follet Publishing, 1973), p. 221. Grade 3.
   "Mrs. Parks sat alone. She was tired. She decided not to move."

3. *The United States: Its History and Neighbors,* Teacher's Ed. (Orlando, FL: Harcourt Brace Jovanovich, 1988), p. 507. Grade 5.
    "On Dec. 1, 1955, Rosa Parks sank wearily to her seat on the bus in Montgomery, Alabama. . . .

    "As the bus filled up, Rosa Parks was asked to give up her seat. She refused. The bus driver called the police, and she was taken to jail."

4. Leonard C. Wood et al., *America: Its People and Values,* Teacher's Ed. 1985, p. 721. Junior High.
    "On that day a black seamstress named Rosa Parks refused to give up her seat in the white section of the bus. . . .

    "There as in many other parts of the south, local laws kept public places strictly segregated. Restaurants, businesses, and all forms of public transportation had separate sections for blacks and whites."

5. Allan O. Kownslar et al., *Inquiring About American History* (New York: Holt, Rinehart and Winston, 1976), p. 301. Grade 5.
    "One evening, Rosa Parks was coming home from work on a Montgomery city bus. She had been working hard all day at her job . . . Rosa was quite tired. . . ."

    "Suddenly, the driver turned and asked her, and some other blacks, to move to the rear of the bus. Rosa argued with the driver . . ."

6. JoAnn Cangemi, *Our History,* 1983, pp. 388–89. Grade 5.
    "In 1955, a black woman named Rosa Parks sat down in the front of the bus in Montgomery, Alabama. Parks refused to get up from the seat so that a white person could sit down and she was arrested."

    "Angry about the arrest, Montgomery Blacks refused to ride city buses."

    "The bus boycott was led by Dr. Martin Luther King, Jr."

7. Beverly J. Armento et al., *This Is My Country* (Boston: Houghton Mifflin, 1991), p. 98. Grade 4.
    "She was tired and her feet hurt"

    "At that time, black and white people had to sit in separate sections on the bus. Other places were divided too, such as restrooms, waiting rooms, movie theatres and restaurants."

8. Henry F. Graff, *America: The Glorious Republic,* vol. 1, 1985, pp. 717–18. Jr./Sr. High.
    "The next day the 50,000 black citizens of Montogomery began a bus boycott of the city's buses: choosing to walk rather than ride under humiliating conditions."

9. Henry F. Graff, *America: The Glorious Republic,* vol. 2, 1986, pp. 349–50. Jr./Sr. High.
    ". . . a seamstress named Rosa Parks took a courageous and fateful step."

    "The next day the 50,000 black citizens of Montgomery began a boycott of city buses."

10. John Edward Wiltz, *The Search for Identity: Modern American History* (Philadelphia: J. B. Lippincott, 1973), p. 684. Jr. High.
    "When Mrs. Parks, a small, soft-spoken woman boarded the Cleveland Avenue bus she was tired and her feet hurt."

11. Beverly Jeanne Armento et al., *Living in Our Country* (River Forest, IL: Laidlaw Brothers, 1988), pp. 417–18. Grade 5.
    "In Montgomery, Alabama, a black woman was arrested for using a seat in the front of a bus."

    "For this reason many black people refused to ride the buses in Montgomery."

12. Glen M. Linden et al., *Legacy of Freedom: A History of the United States,* 1986, p. 670. Jr./Sr. High.

    "Tired after a long day's work, Mrs. Parks boarded a bus for home and refused to give up her seat to a white passenger when asked to do so by the bus driver."

    "The leaders of Montgomery's black community were outraged. Almost at once, they organized a boycott of the Mongomery transit system."

13. Ernest R. May, *A Proud Nation,* Teacher's Ed. (Evanston, IL: McDougal, Littell, 1983), p. 691. Jr. High.

    "On Dec. 1, Rosa Parks, a black woman, refused to give up her seat in the front of a bus to a white person. She had simply worked all day, Parks said, and her feet hurt."

14. Alma Graham et al., *United States: Our Nation and Neighbors* (New York: McGraw-Hill, 1980), p. 340. Grade 5.

    "The bus boycott was led by Dr. Martin Luther King Jr."

15. George Vuicich et al., *United States,* 1983, p. 322. Grade 5.

    "In 1955, a black woman, Rosa Parks, refused to give up her seat on a bus in Montgomery, Alabama. She was arrested. Some people became determined to do something. Blacks in Montgomery began a boycott of the city's buses."

    "The bus boycott was led by Dr. Martin Luther King, Jr., . . ."

16. Henry F. Graff et al., *The Promise of Democracy: The Grand Experiment* (Chicago: Rand McNally, 1978), pp. 365–66. Jr./Sr. High.

    ". . . in many southern communities, black people had to sit at the back of the city buses."

    ". . . and she was tired."

17. Roger M. Berg, *Social Studies* (Glenview, IL: Scott, Foresman, 1979), p. 335. Grade 5.

    "In some cities, blacks were forced to ride in separate parts of buses. In 1955, in Montgomery, Alabama, Rosa Parks wanted to sit in a part of a public bus set aside for whites. She was arrested. The black people of Montgomery refused to ride the city buses until they could sit where they wanted."

18. Richard H. Loftin et al., *Our Country's Communities* (Morristown, NJ: Silver Burdett and Ginn, 1988), p. 246. Grade 3.

    "One day a black woman named Rosa Parks got on a bus and found the back seats filled. She had been working all day and was tired. She sat down in another seat and was arrested."

    "With Dr. King as their leader, the black people of Montgomery refused to ride on the bus until they had the same rights as the other riders."

    "They did as he (King) said and finally won out."

Issues for Discussion

1. How is Rosa Parks portrayed in the official version of her story? What, according to Kohl, does this version of the story leave out? What explanation pattern is imposed on her life and actions in this version?

2. How is Parks portrayed in Kohl's revision of her story? What explanation pattern does Kohl impose on her story? Which version of the Rosa Parks story do you prefer? Why?

Revisiting Rosa Parks

Select a textbook at the elementary school, secondary school, or college level to see how the story of Rosa Parks is depicted. How does the version you examined compare to the "generic" version offered by Herbert Kohl?

Case Study: Stories of Discovery

As the cartoon above suggests, there's more than one way to tell the story of Columbus's "discovery" of America. For decades, kids in elementary school classrooms across the United States were drilled in the official version of the Columbus saga. They read the standard social science textbook account of how Columbus convinced Queen Isabella to back his hunch that the world wasn't flat and that there was a water route to India. They memorized doggerel rhymes to help them remember that "In fourteen hundred and ninety-two, Columbus sailed the ocean blue." They decorated classroom walls with cutouts of the intrepid and poetically named *Nina*, *Pinta*, and *Santa Maria*. Despite some shabby sailing and the indisputable fact that Columbus died penniless and dead wrong, the official story of his "discovery" of the Americas has almost always been told as a heroic legend—the tale of a man who followed his dream, defied common logic, and did something great. Traditionally, Columbus has been depicted as a kind of entrepreneurial visionary who took a huge risk on a big idea, placed his faith in the latest navigational technology, and proved his brethren a pack of backward-thinking fools. In an America entranced by dreams of geographic expansion and economic success, it's little wonder that the story of Columbus's "discovery" became as famous as that of the Boston Tea Party or Lincoln's self-education.

But as the preceding cartoon reminds us, heroism—and storytelling in general—depends on your point of view. The brief case study that follows offers you the chance to compare three different interpretations of the Columbus story and to judge for yourself to what extent each "talks back" to the official story of "discovery." The first selection comes from historian Daniel Boorstin's 1983 best-seller *The Discoverers: A History of Man's Search to Know His World and Himself.* The second is an excerpt from Howard Zinn's classic populist critique of American history, *A People's History of the United States* (1980). The third, an essay by noted Modoc author Michael Dorris, was written in response to the quincentenary of Columbus's first voyage. Daniel Boorstin (b. 1914) has served as director of the Library of Congress, director of the National Museum of American History, and senior historian of the Smithsonian Institution in Washington, D.C. He has published more than fifteen books and is the editor of the thirty-volume *Chicago History of American Civilization.* Howard Zinn (b. 1922) received his Ph.D. in Political Science from Columbia University. An activist as well as an educator, Zinn is currently an associate professor in the Department of Government at Boston University. Michael Dorris (b. 1945), a widely published novelist, short story writer, poet, essayist, scholar, and author of children's books, has served as chair of Native American Studies at Dartmouth College since 1979.

Before Reading

Make a quick list of all the facts you recall being taught about Columbus in school. To what extent has your own version of the Columbus story been influenced by the myth of the hero?

From The Discoverers: A History of Man's Search to Know His World and Himself

Daniel J. Boorstin

Columbus' first voyage had many features of a Caribbean cruise, for he mainly enjoyed the sights and sounds and curiosities which he could witness from the coast, with only occasional short excursions inland. He had speedily coursed through the Bahamas, then skirted the northern coasts of eastern Cuba and of Hispaniola. Just three months after he first sighted the land of "the Indies," the island of San Salvador, his caravels set sail on January 16, 1493, from Samaná Bay on the eastern end of the island of Hispaniola to return home.

After only so brief a journey to the peripheral islands, with so little experience of the interior and such ambiguous clues to the Oriental character of the country, Columbus remained undaunted in his faith. His report revealed no doubt that he had reached "the Indies." And he generalized with all the confidence of the quickie tourist. The natives, he asserted, were "so ingenuous and free with all they have, that no one would believe it who has not seen it; of anything that they possess, if it be asked of them, they never say no; on the contrary, they invite you to share it and show as much love as if their hearts went with it, and they are content with whatever trifle be given them, whether it be a thing of value or of petty worth." "In all these islands, I saw no great diversity in the appearance of the people or in their manners and language, but they all understand one another, which is a very singular thing, on account of which I hope that their Highnesses will determine upon their conversion to our holy faith, towards which they are much inclined." The place he chose for La Villa de Navidad was "in the best district for the gold mines and for every trade both with this continent and with that over there belonging to the Gran Can [Grand Khan], where there will be great trade and profit." To their Catholic Highnesses he promised "as much gold as they want if their Highnesses will render me a little help; besides spices and cotton, as much as their Highnesses shall command; and gum mastic, as much as they shall order shipped . . . and aloe wood, as much as they shall order shipped, and slaves, as many as they shall order, who will be idolaters. And I believe that I have found rhubarb and cinnamon, and I shall find a thousand other things of value, which the people whom I have left there will have discovered, for I have not delayed anywhere, provided the wind allowed me to sail. . . ."

During the next twelve years Columbus undertook three more voyages to "the Indies." They were called voyages of discovery, but more precisely they should have been called voyages of confirmation. For someone less committed they might have produced tantalizing puzzles, planting seeds of doubt. When these successive voyages still failed to connect with the Great Khan or to discover Oriental splendors, it became harder to persuade others back home. Although Columbus was ingenious at inventing new strategies of explanation, as his explanations became increasingly farfetched he once again became a butt of ridicule, a casualty of his own faith.

Only six months after returning from his first voyage, Columbus set out again. This time his expedition was on a far grander scale. Instead of three small caravels he had an armada of seventeen vessels and at least twelve hundred men (still no women), now including six priests to oversee the work of conversion, numerous officials to enforce order and keep books, colonists hoping to make their fortunes in the Indies, and, of course, the crews. While the first voyage could have been called merely exploratory, this second voyage was planned to make the exploration pay off. Columbus was now commissioned to set up a trading post in Hispaniola. He was under greater pressure than ever to prove that he had found the fabled treasure trove of the Indies. This time Columbus' feat of seamanship was even more impressive. While crossing the ocean, he managed to keep the seventeen ships together, and, as Samuel Eliot Morison boasts, "Columbus hit the Lesser Antilles at the exact spot recommended by sailing directions for the next four centuries!" His actual discoveries were also significant, for he found the Lesser Antilles, Jamaica, and Puerto Rico, explored the south coast of Cuba, and established the first permanent European settlement on this side of the Atlantic. Still, for Columbus this was not enough. He demanded the shores of Asia.

On this second trip, as Columbus proceeded through countless small islands of the Lesser Antilles he was encouraged by recalling Sir John Mandeville's observation that there were five thousand islands in the Indies. By the time he reached the southern tip of Cuba he was convinced that he had reached the mainland of Asia. As he coasted Cuba westward from the Gulf of Guacanayabo he was confident that he was following the shores of Marco Polo's Mangi in southern China. When he reached Bahía Cortés, a point where the coast turns sharply toward the south, he knew that he was at the starting point of the eastern shores of the Golden Chersonese (the Malay Peninsula). If he had not yet found the sea passage that Marco Polo said would lead him to the Indian Ocean, he had found the peninsula at the end of which the sea passage would surely appear. But at this point his caravels were leaking, his ships' rigging tattered, his supplies low, and his crew showing signs of mutiny. Columbus decided to turn back. A pity. If he had gone only fifty miles farther, he could have discovered that Cuba was an island.

To protect himself against accusations of timidity or cowardice and to "confirm" his geographic ideas, from the officers and crew of all the three ships which he had detached for this exploring sally he extracted sworn depositions. This was not an unprecedented procedure, as Columbus must have known. Only six years earlier, in 1488, Columbus had been at Lisbon when Dias returned and had to justify his reversing course at the critical moment when he had clear sailing to India. As we have seen, Bartholomeu Dias had taken this same precaution to prove that it was his crew that forced him to return. But while Dias' crew had been asked only to certify Dias' courage and seamanship, Columbus' crew was asked also to certify Columbus' geography. The deposition that all were required to sign declared that the coast they had sailed three hundred and thirty-five leagues from east to west was longer than any island they had seen, that therefore they were certain that this coast must be part of a continent, which was obviously Asia, and that if they had sailed farther, they would have encountered "civilized people of intelligence who know the world." Columbus threatened to prove it by continuing the voyage until they had circumnavigated the globe. As an additional argument, Columbus explained that anyone who refused to sign would be fined ten thousand maravedis and have his tongue cut out. If the obstinate sailor happened to be a boy, he would take a hundred lashes on his bare back.

Columbus, the Indians, and Human Progress
Howard Zinn

There was gold in Asia, it was thought, and certainly silks and spices, for Marco Polo and others had brought back marvelous things from their overland expeditions centuries before. Now that the Turks had conquered Constantinople and the eastern Mediterranean, and controlled the land routes to Asia, a sea route was needed. Portuguese sailors were working their way around the southern tip of Africa. Spain decided to gamble on a long sail across an unknown ocean.

In return for bringing back gold and spices, they promised Columbus 10 percent of the profits, governorship over new-found lands, and the fame that would go with a new title: Admiral of the Ocean Sea. He was a merchant's clerk from the Italian city of Genoa, part-time weaver (the son of a skilled weaver), and expert sailor. He set out with three sailing ships, the largest of which was the *Santa Maria,* perhaps 100 feet long, and thirty-nine crew members.

Columbus would never have made it to Asia, which was thousands of miles farther away than he had calculated, imagining a smaller world. He would have been doomed by that great expanse of sea. But he was lucky. One-fourth of the way there he came upon an unknown, uncharted land that lay between Europe and Asia — the Americas. It was early October 1492, and thirty-three days since he and his crew had left the Canary Islands, off the Atlantic coast of Africa. Now they saw branches and sticks floating in the water. They saw flocks of birds. These were signs of land. Then, on October 12, a sailor called Rodrigo saw the early morning moon shining on white sands, and cried out. It was an island in the Bahamas, the Caribbean sea. The first man to sight land was supposed to get a yearly pension of 10,000 maravedis for life, but Rodrigo never got it. Columbus claimed he had seen a light the evening before. He got the reward.

So, approaching land, they were met by the Arawak Indians, who swam out to greet them. The Arawaks lived in village communes, had a developed agriculture of corn, yams, cassava. They could spin and weave, but they had no horses or work animals. They had no iron, but they wore tiny gold ornaments in their ears.

This was to have enormous consequences: it led Columbus to take some of them aboard ship as prisoners because he insisted that they guide him to the source of the gold. He then sailed to what is now Cuba, then to Hispaniola (the island which today consists of Haiti and the Dominican Republic). There, bits of visible gold in the rivers, and a gold mask presented to Columbus by a local Indian chief, led to wild visions of gold fields.

On Hispaniola, out of timbers from the *Santa Maria,* which had run aground, Columbus built a fort, the first European military base in the Western Hemisphere. He called it Navidad (Christmas) and left thirty-nine crewmembers there, with instructions to find and store the gold. He took more Indian prisoners and put them aboard his two remaining ships. At one part of the island he got into a fight with Indians who refused to trade as many bows and arrows as he and his men wanted. Two were run through with swords and bled to death. Then the *Nina* and the *Pinta* set sail for the Azores and Spain. When the weather turned cold, the Indian prisoners began to die.

Columbus's report to the Court in Madrid was extravagant. He insisted he had reached Asia (it was Cuba) and an island off the coast of China (Hispaniola). His descriptions were part fact, part fiction:

> Hispaniola is a miracle. Mountains and hills, plains and pastures, are both fertile and beautiful . . . the harbors are unbelievably good and there are many wide rivers of which the majority contain gold. . . . There are many spices, and great mines of gold and other metals. . . .

The Indians, Columbus reported, "are so naïve and so free with their possessions that no one who has not witnessed them would believe it. When you ask for something they have, they never say no. To the contrary, they offer to share with anyone. . . ." He concluded his report by asking for a little help from their Majesties, and in return he would bring them from his next voyage "as much gold as they need . . . and as many slaves as they ask." He was full of religious talk: "Thus the eternal God, our Lord, gives victory to those who follow His way over apparent impossibilities."

Because of Columbus's exaggerated report and promises, his second expedition was given seventeen ships and more than twelve hundred men. The aim was clear: slaves and gold. They went from island to island in the Caribbean, taking Indians as captives. But as word spread of the Europeans' intent they found more and more empty villages. On Haiti, they found that the sailors left behind at Fort Navidad had been killed in a battle with the Indians, after they had roamed the island in gangs looking for gold, taking women and children as slaves for sex and labor.

Now, from his base on Haiti, Columbus sent expedition after expedition into the interior. They found no gold fields, but had to fill up the ships returning to Spain with some kind of dividend. In the year 1495, they went on a great slave raid, rounded up fifteen hundred Arawak men, women, and children, put them in pens guarded by Spaniards and dogs, then picked the five hundred best specimens to load onto ships. Of those five hundred, two hundred died en route. The rest arrived alive in Spain and were put up for sale by the archdeacon of the town, who reported that, although the slaves were "naked as the day they were born," they showed "no more embarrassment than animals." Columbus later wrote: "Let us in the name of the Holy Trinity go on sending all the slaves that can be sold."

But too many of the slaves died in captivity. And so Columbus, desperate to pay back dividends to those who had invested, had to make good his promise to fill the ships with gold. In the province of Cicao on Haiti, where he and his men imagined huge gold fields to exist, they ordered all persons fourteen years or older to collect a certain quantity of gold every three months. When they brought it, they were given copper tokens to hang around their necks. Indians found without a copper token had their hands cut off and bled to death.

The Indians had been given an impossible task. The only gold around was bits of dust garnered from the streams. So they fled, were hunted down with dogs, and were killed.

Trying to put together an army of resistance, the Arawaks faced Spaniards who had armor, muskets, swords, horses. When the Spaniards took prisoners they hanged them or burned them to death. Among the Arawaks, mass suicides began, with cassava poison. Infants were killed to save them from the Spaniards. In two years, through murder, mutilation, or suicide, half of the 250,000 Indians on Haiti were dead.

10

Discoveries

Michael Dorris

Imagine the scene: it is an autumn day in the late fifteenth century. On a beach with rose-colored sand, somewhere in the Caribbean, two groups of people, the hosts and their visitors, are about to meet for the first time. Emerging from a small landing boat is a group of men exhausted from a long and frightening ocean voyage. They didn't trust where they were going and now they don't know where they've arrived—but it doesn't look at all like the India described by Marco Polo. They come from Spain and Portugal and Genoa, are Christian and Jewish. The more superstitious and uneducated among them feared that, by sailing west across the Atlantic, they would fall off the edge of the planet.

The men seek treasure and adventure, fame and glory, but the people who greet them—if in fact they are "people" at all—seem, though handsome, quite poor. They are not dressed in fine brocade encrusted with precious jewels, as one would expect of subjects of the great Khan. They are, in fact, not dressed at all, except for a few woven skirts and dabs of ochre. Are they demons? Are they dangerous? Do they know where the gold is hidden?

Watching the boat draw near is a cluster of men, women, and children. They speak a dialect of the Arawak language and are delighted to receive new guests, especially ones who aren't painted white—signifying death. Strangers arrive often, anxious to barter parrot feathers or new foods or useful objects made of stone or shell. These particular visitors look rather strange, it's true: their bodies are covered with odd materials, not at all suited for the warm climate, and they communicate with each other in a tongue as indecipherable as Carib or Nahuatl.

Up close there are more surprises. The group includes no women and some among the hosts speculate why this may be the case. Have their clan mothers expelled these men, banned them to wander alone and orphaned? Has their tribe suffered some disaster? And another thing: they have the strong odor of people who have not had their daily bath. Are they from some simple and rude society that doesn't know how to comport itself?

But all this notwithstanding, guests are guests and should be treated with hospitality. They must be offered food and shelter, must be entertained with stories and music, before the serious business of trade begins.   5

The earth was much larger than Christopher Columbus imagined, its human population far more diverse. The land mass he encountered on his transatlantic voyages was thoroughly inhabited by more than one hundred million people, from the frigid steppes of Patagonia at the farthest extremity of South America to the dark arboreal forests of Newfoundland. In the inhospitable Arctic, Inuits foraged for much of the year in small nuclear or extended family groups, assembling sporadically to carry on the necessary business of marriage, remembrance, or collective action, and only when the availability of food was at its peak. In the lush and verdant jungles of Yucatán and Guatemala, the Mayas had invented agriculture, writing, and an accurate calendar fifteen hundred years before the birth of Christ. Organized in complex, class-oriented societies, they subsisted on a nutritionally balanced diet based on maize, squashes, and beans. In the Andes of northwestern South America early Quechuas domesticated the potato, engineered an intricate system of roads and bridges, and formed a nation in which the state owned all property except houses and movable household goods, and taxes were collected in labor.

The Western Hemisphere was home to literally hundreds of cultures whose people spoke a multiplicity of dialects and languages derived from at least ten mutually exclusive linguistic families. Many societies had well-developed traditions of science and medicine—some 40 percent of the modern world's pharmacopoeia was utilized in America before 1492—and literature, visual art, and philosophy flourished in a variety of contexts. Yet beyond a shared geography, there were few common denominators; due to the haphazard nature and long process by which in-migrating peoples distributed themselves throughout the continents, the Western Hemisphere thrived as a living laboratory of disparate lifestyles, linguistic variety, and cultural pluralism.

Obviously, no single group was directly aware of more than a fraction of the other extant societies—and there was no conception of an overarching group identity. "We" was the family, the community, the tribe, and "they" were everyone else, known and unknown. The fact of cultural diversity, however, was manifest. Within a day's walk of virtually every indigenous population could be found at least one and probably more than one unrelated community whose inhabitants, relative to the visitor, spoke a totally foreign and incomprehensible language, adhered to a unique cosmology, dressed in unusual clothing, ate exotic foods, and had a dissimilar political organization with peculiar variations on age and gender roles.

A native person in most regions of precontact America could and undoubtedly did believe that he or she belonged to the smartest, most tasteful, most accomplished, and most handsome human constellation in the universe, but clearly not the only one. Pluralism, in whichever way it was construed and explained, was inescapably the norm.

It is little wonder, therefore, that for Europeans of the fifteenth and six- 10
teenth centuries, America proved to be much more than a single new world:
it was an unimagined universe. The sheer heterogeneity of Western Hemisphere societies challenged every cherished medieval assumption about the
orderly nature of human origin and destiny. It was as if a whole new set of
potential operating rules were revealed—or, even more disconcerting, the
cultural hodge-podge of America was an ego-threatening intimation that
there were no dependable rules at all. Imagine the shock! To have believed for
a thousand years that everything and everybody of consequence was known
and neatly categorized and then suddenly to open a window and learn that
all along one had been dwelling in a small house with no perspective on the
teeming and chaotic city that surrounded one's accustomed neighborhood—
no map or dictionary provided. How did Cain and Abel fit into this new,
complicated schema? Which Old Testament patriarch begat the Lakota or the
Chibcha? How did the Comanche get from the Tower of Babel to Oklahoma?

The contrasts between the Old World and the Americas were staggering. With only a few minor exceptions, virtually all Europeans spoke languages that sprang from a single linguistic family. Moreover, in the larger
context, Europe's vaunted religious and philosophical divisions were basically variations on a concordant theme. Everyone from the Baltic to the
Balkans to the British Isles professed belief in the same divinity or, in the
case of European Jewry, His father.

As side effects of this theological unity, Latin became a lingua franca for
intellectuals from all sectors, and the Mosaic code formed the basis for practically every ethical or legal philosophy. The broad assumption of male
dominance reigned uncontested, from individual marriage contracts to the
leadership hierarchy of emergent nation-states. The Bible—in particular,
the book of Genesis—was regarded as a literally true and factually accurate
accounting of the origin of everything.

Significantly, in the Adam and Eve story, creation is intentional; a personalized, anthropomorphic God formed man in His image and then threw
in a woman, made out of a nonessential rib, for his company and pleasure.
His word was law and His only token competition came from a fallen angel,
also of His manufacture. After devising, in six days, a universe whose primary purpose was to exist as a backdrop and amusement park for man, the
Divinity set up a test for the objects of his invention—a test that the Divinity, being omniscient as well as omnipotent, must have known all along
man would fail.

Man did.

A nonbeliever attempting to analyze this saga might well find parts of 15
it, while interesting, a bit bizarre. Why were men and women so dispropor-

tionately blessed? Why did God go to all the trouble? For all its paradox, however, the Genesis story did fulfill a function for the Hebraic culture to whom it was initially addressed. It authenticated divine sponsorship for the law of the land and proffered the explanation, so necessary for a poor, threatened minority population, that life was supposed to be pain, that man deserved what he got, and that the only true happiness and peace would come to the just after death.

The disparate creation stories Native Americans believed about themselves—be they emergence myths or earth-diver tales, divine births or great floods—are every bit as pregnant with particular meaning for their specific audiences as was Genesis for the Israelites. Take, for example, a tale found in several Northwest Coast repertoires: According to legend, one day Raven, the androgynous culture hero/Trickster, spies a bush containing a new kind of berry. They are purple and luscious, bursting with sweet juice, and Trickster can't resist. He/she begins to gobble them up and doesn't stop until every one is consumed. His/her breast feathers are stained and his/her belly is bloated, but Raven staggers to the side of a cliff, spreads his/her wings, and careens off into the air.

Suddenly Raven is seized by terrible stomach cramps and immediately experiences the worst case of diarrhea in history. It's terrible: everywhere Raven flies, his/her droppings land, until finally the attack is over, the pain subsides, and with a sigh of relief Raven looks down at the earth to see the mess he/she has made. And there we are, come to life: human beings! Raven beholds these ridiculous creatures, made out of his/her excrement, and laughs. And the ridiculous creatures squint up at Raven—and laugh back!

A society with this irreverent coda has a very different self-concept than one with solemn Genesis as its primary referent. The Raven tale is supposed to be funny, is aimed to entertain and thus be memorable. Creation itself, the story implies, was a totally random act—a fluke. Additionally, the first encounter between creator and createe is maddening for both. Theirs is a relationship without mutual culpability, without guilt, affection, or even clear purpose. As a matter of fact, subsequent chapters in the cycle demonstrate that the joking relationship between Raven and humanity persists and becomes even more perverse over time.

The universe based on such stories was conceived in large part as irrational, not a product of cause and effect, stimulus and response. Events occurred without great purpose and had to be dealt with on their own terms—pragmatically and intelligently. A plague of locusts, an earthquake, a misfortune did not take place because an individual or a people failed to satisfy a demanding and ambiguous Zeus or Jupiter or Jehovah, but rather were regarded as haphazard disruptions in the inevitable course of existence. Humor and fatalism, as opposed to responsibility and recrimination, were the appropriate attitudes toward misfortune. The gods, like everything else, were inscrutable. Harmony, in human communities or in nature as a whole, was best preserved through balance and established custom, and both people and divinities were but elements in a grand, interrelated panorama that encompassed all things.

In historical retrospect, is it unambiguously clear which group was "advanced," which was "primitive"? *Barbarous*—a term many Europeans and their Western Hemisphere descendants eventually used to describe Native American societies—is a relative, superficial designate, as it has been since the days when ancient Greeks judged the sophistication of foreigners on the basis of whether or not they grew beards. The Arawaks of the Caribbean never went to the moon or built a telephone, but they also never waged a war, never depleted the ozone layer with fluorocarbons. They were not saints, but neither were they devils. History remembers them most as beautiful, gentle, and impossible to enslave, not as conquerors or missionaries or industrialists.

Yes, the boys from the boat obviously fulfilled their ambitions: they "won." But in the long run, if we as a species delimit our imaginations, forget or lose touch with the thesaurus of our marvelously diversified past, did *we?*

In conclusion, the plaster stereotypes must be abandoned, not only because they are simplistic and ill informed, but more so because they are far less intellectually engaging, less interesting, less stimulating, and less challenging than the living, breathing, often exasperating, and always complicated reality.

Issues for Discussion

1. Compare the images of Columbus presented by Boorstin and Zinn. How do they each portray him as an explorer and as a human being? How do they depict his values, motives, and character? Which version seems closest to the official story of Columbus's "discovery" of America? Which version seems the most critical? Why?

2. What explanation patterns do Boorstin and Zinn use to shape their versions of the Columbus story? How do these explanation patterns compare with the "Columbus as hero" pattern frequently associated with Columbus in the past? Why do you think they chose to portray Columbus as they did? Whose interests do these portrayals serve?

3. How does Dorris challenge the official story of the European "discovery" of America? What explanation patterns guide his interpretations of European culture and the indigenous cultures of America?

JOURNAL
OPTION

Perspectives on Columbus

Ask two or three people of different generations or ethnic backgrounds to explain to you their understanding of the Columbus story. Write a brief synopsis of each version and compare them in class. What conclusions, if any, can you reach about why certain groups of people tell the story as they do?

ESSAY
OPTIONS

Analyzing Historical Stories

As the readings in the case study you've just completed suggest, history is a breeding ground for competing perspectives and interests. Since the time when scribes figured out how to encode speech sounds on clay tablets, kings have been determined to make sure that history told the "correct" version of their exploits—the version that they liked best. But other voices, visions, and versions have always made themselves heard as well. The following assignments challenge you to explore for yourself the ways that interpretations of historical events and figures are shaped.

Topic 1. Write a paper in which you compare two or more perspectives on a single historical figure or event. You may choose a subject in history that interests you or that has had an impact on you, your family, or your friends. You'll be analyzing and comparing two different sources, one official and one alternative:

Official source: An encyclopedia entry or a chapter from an introductory history textbook (either high school or beginning college level).

Alternative source: A chapter from a revisionist history text; or a chapter from an oral history, autobiography, or other first-person account; or an interview with a person who participated in the event.

Your essay should explain how and why the two sources differ. Here are some questions to consider in your analysis:

- What information is included and what is left out of each account?

- What seems to be the underlying explanation pattern used to shape each version?

- What attitudes and underlying assumptions does each account reflect?

- What cultural or group values does each account reflect?

- Who is the author or speaker in each case? How might the author's or speaker's background influence the way each version is shaped?

- Who is the audience in each case? How might the author's or speaker's intended audience influence the way the story is shaped?

- What are the author's or speaker's motives for telling this particular version of the story?

Topic 2. For a more limited assignment, find and read another account of Christopher Columbus's exploits. You might look for another version of the Columbus story in a high school or college history textbook, an encyclopedia, or an article in a popular magazine (check "Columbus" as a topic in the *Reader's Guide to Periodic Literature* or the periodical data base in your library). Compare this version of the Columbus story with the ones you read by Daniel Boorstin, Howard Zinn, and Michael Dorris. You can use the questions listed under Topic 1 to guide your comparisons.

Survival of the "Fittingest"

It's easy to think that official stories, like Dawkins's memes, have a life and a will of their own, because they often seem remarkably good at self-preservation. Old official stories rarely die without a fight: faced with extinction, they have the habit of mutating and infiltrating new realms of experience. By the end of the eighteenth century, the era of Europe's geographical expansion was drawing toward its end. With the exception of Antarctica, all major land masses had been claimed, mapped, and colonized. Clipper ships had replaced galleons, and adventure had given way to commerce. But the story of conquest and discovery was too resilient to die along with the so-called Age of Exploration. Instead of quietly fading away, the official story of "discovery" leaped from the world of geographical exploration to the realm of scientific inquiry. In the eighteenth century the scientist emerged as spiritual heir to the legacy of the conquistador: armed with revolutionary technological advances, the modern scientist sallied forth to participate in the adventure of discovery, to expand the "frontiers" of knowledge, and to carry "enlightenment" and the rule of law—scientific law—into the mysterious and unruly world of nature.

The story of science is itself the official story of most intellectual inquiry since the eighteenth century, and that story is inextricably connected with the story of European conquest and colonization. Before Columbus left Spain in search of a water route to the Indies in 1492, Europeans looked at nature differently from the way most of us do today. Still adhering to the teachings of the early Greek philosopher Aristotle, medieval Europe didn't think of nature as a world teeming with diverse life forms and incessant activity. Aristotle had divided nature into a rigid system of categories—a collection of ideal "types" that corresponded to the unchanging, eternal "truths" he felt must underlie the universe. The purpose of Aristotelian *scientia* was to study these mathematically precise universal "truths" as they manifested themselves in nature's regularities. Thus, as historian Lorraine Daston has pointed out, before the modern era, science focused only on what was common or typical in nature, not on nature's particular features or oddities.[5] The individual "facts" of the natural world were shunned by science as unimportant and were assigned to the inferior study of "natural history." As Daston indicates in her study of the subject, deviations from the norm of nature—things like comets, earthquakes, floods, the aurora borealis, infestations of insects, plagues, Siamese twins, two-headed cats, ostrich eggs, ship-destroying whirlpools, or women with beards—were seen as unnatural "marvels" or "prodigies." Falling outside the orderly world of nature, such oddities were read as signs or portents of God's divine will: a famine or a plague might be read as a message conveying divine displeasure; a shooting star might be interpreted as a warning that a terribly destructive war was brewing as punishment for sin.

Global exploration and colonization caused European notions of science and nature to implode. The same ships that ferried explorers and armies to strange lands and came home loaded with gold and silver also brought back stories of unheard of customs and cultures and thousands of specimens of unusual plants, animals, and minerals. As science historian Londa Schiebinger has noted, between 1550 and 1700 the number of plant species known in Europe increased fourfold, and this explosion of natural diversity fed Europe's growing appetite for things "exotic."[6] By the mid-1700s, wealthy European families proudly displayed their own cabinets of natural history, filled with "perhaps the brains and genitalia of both sexes, a skeleton, embryos at different stages of development, or a monstrous fetus."[7] Confronted with indisputable evidence of nature's diversity and particularity, European thinkers were forced to reevaluate Aristotelian ideas about the unchanging "universal truth" of natural forms and categories. In 1620 the English statesman and philosopher Sir Francis Bacon had taken the first important step in this effort by redefining the "fact." According to

---

[5]Lorraine Daston, "Marvelous Facts and Miraculous Evidence in Early Modern Europe," in *Questions of Evidence: Proof, Practice, and Persuasion across the Disciplines,* ed. James Chandler, Arnold I. Davidson, and Harry Harootunian (Chicago: University of Chicago Press, 1994), pp. 243–63.

[6]Londa Schiebinger, *Nature's Body: Gender in the Making of Modern Science* (Boston: Beacon Press, 1993), p. 14.

[7]Schiebinger, p. 3.

the theory of science laid out in Bacon's *Novum Organum,* the proper task of science is to study and explain the particular oddities, the "marvels" and "singularities" of nature that defy common sense and break simplistic rules. Modern science began when thinkers like Bacon built a wall between the oddities of the natural world and the stories that had been used to interpret them for hundreds of years. Stripped of the religious stories that had given them meaning, the particular features of nature came to be seen as neutral and objective "facts"—a perspective that has itself become the foundation of modern science.

From its birth, then, modern science has been at odds with storytelling. The whole apparatus of scientific inquiry boils down to a wonderfully complex mechanism for story elimination. You're probably familiar with the basic outline of the scientific method: careful observation of facts leads to the formation of a tentative hypothesis; this hypothesis is rigorously tested by means of a carefully controlled experiment; hypotheses that are repeatedly confirmed in this empirical manner are deemed theories. The whole mechanism is built to ensure that stories in the form of preconceptions, biases, pet theories, and subjective judgments can't interfere with the scientist's direct observation of natural phenomena. The patterns of significance that emerge from these "objective" observations are supposed to arise directly from the particular facts of nature themselves, not from the personal preferences, cultural presuppositions, or explanation patterns that individual scientists bring with them to their work. If a pattern is shown to describe what happens during every observation or experiment—if it "fits" and thus explains every situation it's applied to, it becomes a "law." This story—the story of objective observation and objective thought—is the official story of modern science. It's the story that tells us we can separate what we see from who we are, the story that tells us that nature's "facts" can be divorced from the people who observe them and the cultural explanation patterns that constantly threaten to contaminate their vision.

But trying to keep stories out of thinking is an impossible task: if you don't welcome them at the front door, they'll go around to the back or help themselves in through a window. To appreciate just how open the back door of science has remained to the influence of official stories, let's pause to look at what might be the "fittingest" scientific theory of them all: Darwin's theory of evolution by means of "natural selection." In 1832 Charles Darwin set off on his own voyage of discovery aboard the HMS *Beagle.* Bound for South America, Darwin was to spend the next four years observing plant and animal life as well as geological formations in and around the Galápagos Islands off the coast of Peru. The diverse creatures he encountered convinced him that species were not perfect, unchanging "types" or categories as they had been traditionally seen. In a journal entry while visiting the Galápagos, he questions this Aristotelian view of biological stability:

> When I see these islands in sight of each other, and possessed of but a scanty stock of animals, tenanted by these birds but slightly differentiated in structure filling the same place in Nature, I must suspect they are only varieties. . . . If there is the slightest foundation for these remarks, the zoology of the Archipelagoes will be well worth examining; for such facts would undermine the stability of Species.[8]

When he returned to England, Darwin was determined to explain the mechanism underlying the variations he perceived in animal and plant species. For the next five years he dedicated himself to the search for a plausible explanation. He later described this quest in the introduction to his famous *The Origin of Species* (1859):

> After my return to England it appeared to me that . . . by collecting all facts which bore in any way on the variation of animals and plants under domestication and nature, some light might perhaps be thrown on the whole subject. My first notebook was opened in July 1837. I worked on true Baconian principles and without any theory, collected facts on a wholesale scale. . . . After five years' work I allowed myself to speculate on the subject and drew up some short notes.[9]

The story Darwin offers here agrees with the official story of how science works: the good scientist purges stories from his observations and confronts the "facts" of experience before he even begins to knit his observations into an explanation. In reality, however, as a number of critics and biographers have shown, like most scientists, Darwin had committed himself to a theory—and an explanation pattern—*before* he began searching for the "facts" to support it.[10] Darwin "borrowed" his theory from a highly controversial book on population growth published nearly four decades before he set off on the *Beagle*. According to the ideas outlined in Thomas Malthus's *Essay on the Principle of Population*, all groups of creatures—whether they are composed of yeast cells or human beings—are locked in a "struggle for survival," because their ability to reproduce outruns their supply of natural resources. Having picked up Malthus's

---

[8]Quoted in John Bowlby, *Charles Darwin: A New Life* (New York: Norton Books, 1990), p. 220.

[9]Charles Darwin, *The Origin of Species,* quoted in Arthur Koestler's *The Act of Creation* (New York: Penguin, 1964), p. 134.

[10]See R. C. Lewontin, "Facts and the Factitious in Natural Sciences," in *Questions of Evidence,* p. 491, and Koestler, *The Act of Creation,* p. 135.

book as "pleasure reading" not long after he returned to England, Darwin found there the explanation pattern he needed to account for evolution: if species are locked in permanent competition for resources, this "struggle" could "select" those that were best suited for survival. Darwin didn't "discover" the theory of natural selection in the many "facts" he eventually assembled to confirm it during his lifetime: instead, the story of the "survival of the fittest" discovered him and guided him as he sought to explain the diversity of the natural world.

The theory of evolution is an example of brilliant scientific thinking, but it's also an example of the dangers involved in taking the official story of scientific objectivity too literally. Darwin himself was a progressively minded social thinker who personally opposed slavery and supported the independence of women. But the explanation pattern of "natural competition" he borrowed from Malthus was fraught with cultural associations and value judgments that worked against his own political principles. Since publication of *The Origin of Species* in 1859, the idea of the "survival of the fittest" has been evoked to justify a number of socially reprehensible activities—from racial segregation to anti-immigrant hysteria to restricted educational opportunities and legal rights for women. Once you swallow the idea that scientific thinking is objective, impersonal, and "story-free," you give up your ability to resist the stories that scientific thinking—like all analysis and interpretation—always tells. Modern science is a breeding ground for official stories because it actively denies the fact that it's culturally constructed. Yet, as we've seen in the case of Darwin, stories have a way of slipping into scientific theories through the back door—not because of poor thinking, but because all analytic thinking relies on the patterns that stories and storytelling make possible.

The reading that follows offers another example of the relationship between official cultural stories and scientific thinking. In "The Egg and the Sperm: How Science Has Constructed a Romance Based on Stereotypical Male–Female Roles," anthropologist Emily Martin examines the way that cultural stories about gender have infiltrated scientific interpretations of sexual reproduction. Martin teaches at Princeton University. Her latest research is reported in *Flexible Bodies: Tracking Immunity in America from the Days of Polio to the Age of AIDS* (1994).

Before Reading

Write a brief paragraph in which you tell the story of what you think happens when egg meets sperm.

The Egg and the Sperm: How Science Has Constructed a Romance Based on Stereotypical Male–Female Roles

Emily Martin

> The theory of the human body is always a part of a world-picture. . . .
> The theory of the human body is always a part of a *fantasy*.[1]

As an anthropologist, I am intrigued by the possibility that culture shapes how biological scientists describe what they discover about the natural world. If this were so, we would be learning about more than the natural world in high school biology class; we would be learning about cultural beliefs and practices as if they were part of nature. In the course of my research I realized that the picture of egg and sperm drawn in popular as well as scientific accounts of reproductive biology relies on stereotypes central to our cultural definitions of male and female. The stereotypes imply not only that female biological processes are less worthy than their male counterparts but also that women are less worthy than men. Part of my goal in writing this article is to shine a bright light on the gender stereotypes hidden within the scientific language of biology. Exposed in such a light, I hope they will lose much of their power to harm us.

EGG AND SPERM: A SCIENTIFIC FAIRY TALE

At a fundamental level, all major scientific textbooks depict male and female reproductive organs as systems for the production of valuable substances, such as eggs and sperm.[2] In the case of women, the monthly cycle is described as being designed to produce eggs and prepare a suitable place for them to be fertilized and grown—all to the end of making babies. But the enthusiasm ends there. By extolling the female cycle as a productive enterprise, menstruation must necessarily be viewed as a failure. Medical texts describe menstruation as the "debris" of the uterine lining, the result of necrosis, or death of tissue. The descriptions imply that a system has gone awry, making products of no use, not to specification, unsaleable, wasted, scrap. An illustration in a widely used medical text shows menstruation as a chaotic disintegration of form, complementing the many texts that describe it as "ceasing," "dying," "losing," "denuding," "expelling."[3]

Male reproductive physiology is evaluated quite differently. One of the texts that sees menstruation as failed production employs a sort of breathless prose when it describes the maturation of sperm: "The mechanisms which guide the remarkable cellular transformation from spermatid to mature sperm remain uncertain. . . . Perhaps the most amazing characteristic of spermatogenesis is its sheer magnitude: the normal human male may manufacture several hundred million sperm per day."[4] In the classic text *Medical Physiology,* edited by Vernon Mountcastle, the male–female, productive–destructive comparison is more explicit: "Whereas the female *sheds* only a single gamete each month, the seminiferous tubules *produce* hundreds of millions of sperm each day" (emphasis mine).[5] The female author of another text marvels at the length of the microscopic seminiferous tubules, which, if uncoiled and placed end to end, "would span almost one-third of a mile!" She writes, "In an adult male these structures produce millions of sperm cells each day." Later she asks, "How is this feat accomplished?"[6] None of these texts expresses such intense enthusiasm for any female processes. It is surely no accident that the "remarkable" process of making sperm involves precisely what, in the medical view, menstruation does not: production of something deemed valuable.[7]

One could argue that menstruation and spermatogenesis are not analogous processes and, therefore, should not be expected to elicit the same kind of response. The proper female analogy to spermatogenesis, biologically, is ovulation. Yet ovulation does not merit enthusiasm in these texts either. Textbook descriptions stress that all of the ovarian follicles containing ova are already present at birth. Far from being *produced,* as sperm are, they merely sit on the shelf, slowly degenerating and aging like overstocked inventory: "At birth, normal human ovaries contain an estimated one million follicles [each], and no new ones appear after birth. Thus, in marked contrast to the male, the newborn female already has all the germ cells she will ever have. Only a few, perhaps 400, are destined to reach full maturity during her active productive life. All the others degenerate at some point in their development so that few, if any, remain by the time she reaches menopause at approximately 50 years of age."[8] Note the "marked contrast" that this description sets up between male and female: the male, who continuously produces fresh germ cells, and the female, who has stockpiled germ cells by birth and is faced with their degeneration.

Nor are the female organs spared such vivid descriptions. One scientist writes in a newspaper article that a woman's ovaries become old and worn out from ripening eggs every month, even though the woman herself is still relatively young: "When you look though a laparoscope . . . at an ovary that has been through hundreds of cycles, even in a superbly healthy American female, you see a scarred, battered organ."[9]

5

To avoid the negative connotations that some people associate with the female reproductive system, scientists could begin to describe male and female processes as homologous. They might credit females with "producing" mature ova one at a time, as they're needed each month, and describe males as having to face problems of degenerating germ cells. This degeneration would occur throughout life among spermatogonia, the undifferentiated germ cells in the testes that are the long-lived, dormant precursors of sperm. . . .

The real mystery is why the male's vast production of sperm is not seen as wasteful.[10] Assuming that a man "produces" 100 million (10^8) sperm per day (a conservative estimate) during an average reproductive life of sixty years, he would produce well over two trillion sperm in his lifetime. Assuming that a woman "ripens" one egg per lunar month, or thirteen per year, over the course of her forty-year reproductive life, she would total five hundred eggs in her lifetime. But the word "waste" implies an excess, too much produced. Assuming two or three offspring, for every baby a woman produces, she wastes only around two hundred eggs. For every baby a man produces, he wastes more than one trillion (10^{12}) sperm.

How is it that positive images are denied to the bodies of women? A look at language—in this case, scientific language—provides the first clue. Take the egg and the sperm. It is remarkable how "femininely" the egg behaves and how "masculinely" the sperm.[11] The egg is seen as large and passive.[12] It does not *move* or *journey*, but passively "is transported," "is swept,"[13] or even "drifts"[14] along the fallopian tube. In utter contrast, sperm are small, "streamlined,"[15] and invariably active. They "deliver" their genes to the egg, "activate the developmental program of the egg,"[16] and have a "velocity" that is often remarked upon.[17] Their tails are "strong" and efficiently powered.[18] Together with the forces of ejaculation, they can "propel the semen into the deepest recesses of the vagina."[19] For this they need "energy,"[20] "fuel,"[20] so that with a "whiplashlike motion and strong lurches"[21] they can "burrow through the egg coat"[22] and "penetrate" it.[23]

At its extreme, the age-old relationship of the egg and the sperm takes on a royal or religious patina. The egg coat, its protective barrier, is sometimes called its "vestments," a term usually reserved for sacred, religious dress. The egg is said to have a "corona,"[24] a crown, and to be accompanied by "attendant cells."[25] It is holy, set apart and above, the queen to the sperm's king. The egg is also passive, which means it must depend on sperm for rescue. Gerald Schatten and Helen Schatten liken the egg's role to that of Sleeping Beauty: "a dormant bride awaiting her mate's magic kiss, which instills the spirit that brings her to life."[26] Sperm, by contrast, have a "mission,"[27] which is to "move through the female genital tract in quest of the ovum."[28] One popular account has it that the sperm carry out a "perilous journey" into the "warm darkness," where some fall away "exhausted." "Survivors" "assault" the egg, the successful candidates "surrounding the prize."[29] Part of the urgency of this journey, in more scientific terms, is that "once released from the supportive environment of the ovary, an egg will die within hours unless rescued by a sperm."[30] The wording stresses the fragility and dependency of the egg, even though the same text acknowledges elsewhere that sperm also live for only a few hours.[31]

In 1948, in a book remarkable for its early insights into these matters, Ruth Herschberger argued that female reproductive organs are seen as biologically interdependent, while male organs are viewed as autonomous, operating independently and in isolation:

> . . . The sperm is no more independent of its milieu than the egg, and yet from a wish that it were, biologists have lent their support to the notion that the human female, beginning with the egg, is congenitally more dependent than the male.[32]

An article in the journal *Cell* has the sperm making an "existential decision" to penetrate the egg: "Sperm are cells with a limited behavioral repertoire, one that is directed toward fertilizing eggs. To execute the decision to abandon the haploid state, sperm swim to an egg and there acquire the ability to effect membrane fusion."[33] Is this a corporate manager's version of the sperm's activities—"executing decisions" while fraught with dismay over difficult options that bring with them very high risk. . . .

One depiction of sperm as weak and timid, instead of strong and powerful—the only such representation in Western civilization, so far as I know—occurs in Woody Allen's movie *Everything You Always Wanted to Know about Sex (But Were Afraid to Ask).* Allen, playing the part of an apprehensive sperm inside a man's testicles, is scared of the man's approaching orgasm. He is reluctant to launch himself into the darkness, afraid of contraceptive devices, afraid of winding up on the ceiling if the man masturbates.

The more common picture—egg as damsel in distress, shielded only by her sacred garments; sperm as heroic warrior to the rescue—cannot be proved to be dictated by the biology of these events. While the "facts" of biology may not *always* be constructed in cultural terms, I would argue that in this case they are. The degree of metaphorical content in these descriptions, the extent to which differences between egg and sperm are emphasized, and the parallels between cultural stereotypes of male and female behavior and the character of egg and sperm all point to this conclusion.

NEW RESEARCH, OLD IMAGERY

As new understandings of egg and sperm emerge, textbook gender imagery is being revised. But the new research, far from escaping the stereotypical representations of egg and sperm, simply replicates elements of textbook gender imagery in a different form. The persistence of this imagery calls to mind what Ludwik Fleck termed "the self-contained" nature of scientific thought. As he described it, "the interaction between what is already known, what remains to be learned, and those who are to apprehend it, go to ensure harmony within the system. But at the same time they also preserve the harmony of illusions, which is quite secure within the confines of a given thought style."[34] We need to understand the way in which the cultural content in scientific descriptions changes as biological discoveries unfold, and whether that cultural content is solidly entrenched or easily changed.

In all of the texts quoted above, sperm are described as penetrating the egg, and specific substances on a sperm's head are described as binding to the egg. Recently, this description of events was rewritten in a biophysics lab at Johns Hopkins University—transforming the egg from the passive to the active party.[35]

Prior to this research, it was thought that the zona, the inner vestments of the egg, formed an impenetrable barrier. Sperm overcame the barrier by mechanically burrowing through, thrashing their tails and slowly working their way along. Later research showed that the sperm released digestive enzymes that chemically broke down the zona; thus, scientists presumed that the sperm used mechanical *and* chemical means to get through to the egg.

In this recent investigation, the researchers began to ask questions about the mechanical force of the sperm's tail. (The lab's goal was to develop a contraceptive that worked topically on sperm.) They discovered, to their great surprise, that the forward thrust of sperm is extremely weak, which contradicts the assumption that sperm are forceful penetrators.[36] Rather than thrusting forward, the sperm's head was now seen to move mostly back and forth. The sideways motion of the sperm's tail makes the head move sideways with a force that is ten times stronger than its forward movement. So even if the overall force of the sperm were strong enough to mechanically break the zona, most of its force would be directed sideways rather than forward. In fact, its strongest tendency, by tenfold, is to escape by attempting to pry itself off the egg. Sperm, then, must be exceptionally efficient at *escaping* from any cell surface they contact. And the surface of the egg must be designed to trap the sperm and prevent their escape. Otherwise, few if any sperm would reach the egg.

The researchers at Johns Hopkins concluded that the sperm and egg stick together because of adhesive molecules on the surfaces of each. The egg traps the sperm and adheres to it so tightly that the sperm's head is forced to lie flat against the surface of the zona, a little bit, they told me, "like Br'er Rabbit getting more and more stuck to tar baby the more he wriggles." The trapped sperm continues to wiggle ineffectually side to side. The mechanical force of its tail is so weak that a sperm cannot break even one chemical bond. This is where the digestive enzymes released by the sperm come in. If they start to soften the zona just at the tip of the sperm and the sides remain stuck, then the weak, flailing sperm can get oriented in the right direction and make it through the zona—provided that its bonds to the zona dissolve as it moves in.

Although this new version of the saga of the egg and the sperm broke through cultural expectations, the researchers who made the discovery continued to write papers and abstracts as if the sperm were the active party who attacks, binds, penetrates, and enters the egg. The only difference was that sperm were now seen as performing these actions weakly.[37] Not until August 1987, more than three years after the findings described above, did these researchers reconceptualize the process to give the egg a more active role. They began to describe the zona as an aggressive sperm catcher, covered with adhesive molecules that can capture a sperm with a single bond and clasp it to the zona's surface.[38] In the words of their published account: "The innermost vestment, the *zona pellucida,* is a glyco-protein shell, which captures and tethers the sperm before they penetrate it. . . . The sperm is captured at the initial contact between the sperm tip and the *zona.* . . . Since the thrust [of the sperm] is much smaller than the force needed to break a single affinity bond, the first bond made upon the tip-first meeting of the sperm and *zona* can result in the capture of the sperm."[39]

Experiments in another lab reveal similar patterns of data interpretation. Gerald Schatten and Helen Schatten set out to show that, contrary to conventional wisdom, the "egg is not merely a large, yolk-filled sphere into which the sperm burrows to endow new life. Rather, recent research suggests the most heretical view that sperm and egg are mutually active partners."[40] This sounds like a departure from the stereotypical textbook view, but further reading reveals Schatten and Schatten's conformity to the aggressive-sperm metaphor. They describe how "the sperm and egg first touch when, from the tip of the sperm's triangular head, a long, thin filament shoots out and harpoons the egg." Then we learn that "remarkably, the harpoon is not so much fired as assembled at great speed, molecule by molecule, from a pool of protein stored in a specialized region called the acrosome. The filament may grow as much as twenty times longer than the sperm head itself before its tip reaches the egg and sticks."[41] Why not call this "making a bridge" or "throwing out a line" rather than firing a harpoon? Harpoons pierce prey and injure or kill them, while this filament only sticks. And why not focus, as the Hopkins lab did, on the stickiness of the egg, rather than the stickiness of the sperm? Later in the article, the Schattens replicate the common view of the sperm's perilous journey into the warm darkness of the vagina, this time for the purpose of explaining its journey into the egg itself: "[The sperm] still has an arduous journey ahead. It must penetrate farther into the egg's huge sphere of cytoplasm and somehow locate the nucleus, so that the cells' chromosomes can fuse. The sperm dives down into the cytoplasm, its tail beating. But it is soon interrupted by the sudden and swift migration of the egg nucleus, which rushes toward the sperm with a velocity triple that of the movement of chromosomes during cell division, crossing the entire egg in about a minute."[42]

Like Schatten and Schatten and the biophysicists at Johns Hopkins, another researcher has recently made discoveries that seem to point to a more interactive view of the relationship of egg and sperm. This work, which Paul Wassarman conducted on the sperm and eggs of mice, focuses on identifying the specific molecules in the egg coat (the zona pellucida) that are involved in egg–sperm interaction. At first glance, his descriptions seem to fit the model of an egalitarian relationship. Male and female gametes "recognize one another," and "interactions . . . take place between sperm and egg."[43] But the article in *Scientific American* in which those descriptions appear begins with a vignette that presages the dominant motif of their presentation: "It has been more than a century since Hermann Fol, a Swiss zoologist, peered into his microscope and became the first person to see a sperm penetrate an egg, fertilize it and form the first cell of a new embryo."[44] This portrayal of the sperm as the active party—the one that *penetrates* and *fertilizes* the egg and *produces* the embryo—is not cited as an example of an earlier, now outmoded view. In fact, the author reiterates the point later in the article: "Many sperm can bind to and penetrate the zona pellucida, or outer coat, of an unfertilized mouse egg, but only one sperm will eventually fuse with the thin plasma membrane surrounding the egg proper (*inner sphere*), fertilizing the egg and giving rise to a new embryo."[45]

The imagery of sperm as aggressor is particularly startling in this case: the main discovery being reported is isolation of a particular molecule *on the egg coat* that plays an important role in fertilization! Wassarman's choice of language sustains the picture. He calls the molecule that has been isolated, ZP3, a "sperm receptor." By allocating the passive, waiting role to the egg, Wassarman can continue to describe the sperm as the actor, the one

20

that makes it all happen: "The basic process begins when many sperm first attach loosely and then bind tenaciously to receptors on the surface of the egg's thick outer coat, the zona pellucida. Each sperm, which has a large number of egg-binding proteins on its surface, binds to many sperm receptors on the egg. More specifically, a site on each of the egg-binding proteins fits a complementary site on a sperm receptor, much as a key fits a lock."[46] With the sperm designated as the "key" and the egg the "lock," it is obvious which one acts and which one is acted upon. Could this imagery not be reversed, letting the sperm (the lock) wait until the egg produces the key? Or could we speak of two halves of a locket matching, and regard the matching itself as the action that initiates the fertilization? . . .

Social Implications: Thinking Beyond

All three of these revisionist accounts of egg and sperm cannot seem to escape the hierarchical imagery of older accounts. Even though each new account gives the egg a larger and more active role, taken together they bring into play another cultural stereotype: woman as a dangerous and aggressive threat. In the Johns Hopkins lab's revised model, the egg ends up as the female aggressor who "captures and tethers" the sperm with her sticky zona, rather like a spider lying in wait in her web.[47] The Schatten lab has the egg's nucleus "interrupt" the sperm's dive with a "sudden and swift" rush by which she "clasps the sperm and guides its nucleus to the center."[48] Wassarman's description of the surface of the egg "covered with thousands of plasma membrane-bound projections, called microvilli" that reach out and clasp the sperm adds to the spiderlike imagery.[49]

These images grant the egg an active role but at the cost of appearing disturbingly aggressive. Images of woman as dangerous and aggressive, the *femme fatale* who victimizes men, are widespread in Western literature and culture.[50] More specific is the connection of spider imagery with the idea of an engulfing, devouring mother.[51] New data did not lead scientists to eliminate gender stereotypes in their descriptions of egg and sperm. Instead, scientists simply began to describe egg and sperm in different, but no less damaging, terms.

Can we envision a less stereotypical view? Biology itself provides another model that could be applied to the egg and the sperm. The cybernetic model—with its feedback loops, flexible adaptation to change, coordination of the parts within a whole, evolution over time, and changing response to the environment—is common in genetics, endocrinology, and ecology and has a growing influence in medicine in general.[52] This model has the potential to shift our imagery from the negative, in which the female reproductive system is castigated both for not producing eggs after birth and for producing (and thus wasting) too many eggs overall, to something more positive. The female reproductive system could be seen as responding to the environment (pregnancy or menopause), adjusting to monthly changes (menstruation), and flexibly changing from reproductivity after puberty to non-reproductivity later in life. The sperm and egg's interaction could also be described in cybernetic terms. J. F. Hartman's research in reproductive biology demonstrated fifteen years ago that if an egg is killed by being pricked with a needle, live sperm cannot get through the zona.[53] Clearly, this evidence shows that the egg and sperm *do* interact on more mutual terms, making biology's refusal to portray them that way all the more disturbing. . . .

The models that biologists use to describe their data can have important social effects. During the nineteenth century, the social and natural sciences strongly influenced each other: the social ideas of Malthus about how to avoid the natural increase of the poor inspired Darwin's *Origin of Species*.[54] Once the *Origin* stood as a description of the natural world, complete with competition and market struggles, it could be reimported into social science as social Darwinism, in order to justify the social order of the time. What we are seeing now is similar: the importation of cultural ideas about passive females and heroic males into the "personalities" of gametes. This amounts to the "implanting of social imagery on representations of nature so as to lay a firm basis for reimporting exactly that same imagery as natural explanations of social phenomena."[55]

Further research would show us exactly what social effects are being wrought from the biological imagery of egg and sperm. At the very least, the imagery keeps alive some of the hoariest old stereotypes about weak damsels in distress and their strong male rescuers. That these stereotypes are now being written in at the level of the *cell* constitutes a powerful move to make them seem so natural as to be beyond alteration.

25

NOTES

1. James Hillman, *The Myth of Analysis* (Evanston, Ill.: Northwestern University Press, 1972), 220.
2. The textbooks I consulted are the main ones used in classes for undergraduate premedical students or medical students (or those held on reserve in the library for these classes) during the past few years at Johns Hopkins University. These texts are widely used at other universities in the country as well.
3. Arthur C. Guyton, *Physiology of the Human Body*, 6th edn. (Philadelphia: Saunders College Publishing, 1984), 624.
4. Arthur J. Vander, James H. Sherman, and Dorothy S. Luciano, *Human Physiology: The Mechanisms of Body Function*, 3d edn. (New York: McGraw-Hill, 1980), 483–4.

5. Vernon B. Mountcastle, *Medical Physiology,* 14th edn. (London: Mosby, 1980), 2:1624.

6. Eldra Pearl Solomon, *Human Anatomy and Physiology* (New York: CBS College Publishing, 1983), 678.

7. For elaboration, see Emily Martin, *The Woman in the Body: A Cultural Analysis of Reproduction* (Boston: Beacon, 1987), 27–53.

8. Vander, Sherman, and Luciano, 568.

9. Melvin Konner, "Childbearing and Age," *New York Times Magazine* (27 Dec. 1987), 22–3, esp. 22.

10. In her essay "Have Only Men Evolved?" (in Sandra Harding and Merrill B. Hintikka (eds.), *Discovering Reality: Feminist Perspectives on Epistemology, Metaphysics, Methodology, and Philosophy of Science* (Dordrecht: Reidel, 1983), 45–69, esp. 60–1), Ruth Hubbard points out that sociobiologists have said the female invests more energy than the male in the production of her large gametes, claiming that this explains why the female provides parental care. Hubbard questions whether it "really takes more 'energy' to generate the one or relatively few eggs than the large excess of sperms required to achieve fertilization."

11. See Carol Delaney, "The Meaning of Paternity and the Virgin Birth Debate," *Man,* 21/3 (Sept. 1986), 494–513. She discusses the difference between this scientific view that women contribute genetic material to the fetus and the claim of long-standing Western folk theories that the origin and identity of the fetus comes from the male, as in the metaphor of planting a seed in soil.

12. For a suggested direct link between human behaviour and purportedly passive eggs and active sperm, see Erik H. Erikson, "Inner and Outer Space: Reflections on Womanhood," *Daedalus,* 93/2 (Spring 1964), 582–606, esp. 591.

13. Guyton (n. 3 above), 619; and Mountcastle (n. 5 above), 1609.

14. Jonathan Miller and David Pelham, *The Facts of Life* (New York: Viking Penguin, 1984), 5.

15. Bruce Alberts *et al., Molecular Biology of the Cell* (New York: Garland, 1983), 796.

16. Ibid. 796.

17. See, e.g. William F. Ganong, *Review of Medical Physiology,* 7th edn. (Los Altos, Calif.: Lange Medical Publications, 1975), 322.

18. Alberts *et al.* (n. 15 above), 796.

19. Guyton, 615.

20. Solomon (n. 6 above), 683.

21. Vander, Sherman, and Luciano (n. 4 above), 4th edn. (1985), 580.

22. Alberts *et al.,* 796.

23. All biology texts quoted above use the word "penetrate."

24. Solomon, 700.

25. A. Beldecos *et al.,* "The Importance of Feminist Critique for Contemporary Cell Biology," *Hypatia,* 3/1 (Spring 1988), 61–76.

26. Gerald Schatten and Helen Schatten, "The Energetic Egg," *Medical World News,* 23 (23 Jan. 1984), 51–3, esp. 51.

27. Alberts *et al.,* 796.

28. Guyton (n. 3 above), 613.

29. Miller and Pelham (n. 14 above), 7.

30. Alberts *et al.* (n. 15 above), 804.

31. Ibid. 801.

32. Ruth Herschberger, *Adam's Rib* (New York: Pelligrini & Cudaby, 1948), esp. 84.

33. Bennett M. Shapiro, "The Existential Decision of a Sperm," *Cell,* 49/3 (May 1987), 293–4, esp. 293.

34. Ludwik Fleck, *Genesis and Development of a Scientific Fact,* ed. Thaddeus J. Trenn and Robert K. Merton (Chicago: University of Chicago Press, 1979), 38.

35. Jay M. Baltz carried out the research I describe when he was a graduate student in the Thomas C. Jenkins Department of Biophysics at Johns Hopkins University.

36. Far less is known about the physiology of sperm than comparable female substances, which some feminists claim is no accident. Greater scientific scrutiny of female reproduction has long enabled the burden of birth control to be placed on women. In this case, the researchers' discovery did not depend on development of any new technology. The experiments made use of glass pipettes, a manometer, and a simple microscope, all of which have been available for more than one hundred years.

37. Jay Baltz and Richard A. Cone, "What Force Is Needed to Tether a Sperm?" (abstract for Society for the Study of Reproduction, 1985), and "Flagellar Torque on the Head Determines the Force Needed to Tether a Sperm" (abstract for Biophysical Society, 1986).

38. Jay M. Baltz, David F. Katz, and Richard A. Cone, "The Mechanics of the Sperm–Egg Interaction at the Zona Pellucida," *Biophysical Journal,* 54/4 (Oct. 1988), 643–54.

39. Ibid. 643, 650.

40. Schatten and Schatten (n. 26 above), 51.

41. Ibid. 52.

42. Schatten and Schatten, 53.

43. Paul M. Wassarman, "Fertilization in Mammals," *Scientific American,* 259/6 (Dec. 1988), 78–84, esp. 78, 84.

44. Ibid. 78.

45. Ibid. 79.

46. Ibid. 78.

47. Baltz, Katz, and Cone (n. 38 above), 643, 650.

48. Schatten and Schatten, 53.

49. Paul M. Wassarman, "The Biology and Chemistry of Fertilization," *Science,* 235/4788 (30 Jan. 1987), 553–60, esp. 554.

50. Mary Ellman, *Thinking about Women* (New York: Harcourt Brace Jovanovich, 1968), 140; Nina Auerbach, *Woman and the Demon* (Cambridge, Mass.: Harvard University Press, 1982), esp. 186.

51. Kenneth Alan Adams, "Arachnophobia: Love American Style," *Journal of Psychoanalytic Anthropology,* 4/2 (1981), 157–97.

52. William Ray Arney and Bernard Bergen, *Medicine and the Management of Living* (Chicago: University of Chicago Press, 1984).

53. J. F. Hartman, R. B. Gwatkin, and C. F. Hutchison, "Early Contact Interactions between Mammalian Gametes *In Vitro,*" *Proceedings of the National Academy of Sciences (US),* 69/10 (1972), 2767–9.

54. Ruth Hubbard, "Have Only Men Evolved?" (n. 10 above), 51–2.

55. David Harvey, personal communication, Nov. 1989.

Issues for Discussion

1. How, according to Martin, has the interaction of eggs and sperm traditionally been interpreted in specific writings? What explanation patterns have shaped scientists' view of this interaction? What's wrong with these explanation patterns from Martin's point of view?

2. What alternative explanation pattern does Martin suggest to replace traditional interpretations of what happens during sexual reproduction? What problems might be associated with this explanation?

Thinking Critically about Science

1. Informally survey three or four people—friends, co-workers, relatives, or classmates—to get their views about what happens at the cellular level between eggs and sperm during conception. To what extent do their versions of the egg–sperm interaction reflect the influence of culturally created gender stereotypes?

2. Try to identify and describe as many official stories as you can that are associated with the different academic disciplines you are currently studying. They may include theories like the story of evolution or commonly repeated story frames like the idea of "discovery" in either history or science.

Academically Speaking: Reading and Writing Academic Analysis

Entering the Conversation

Where do ideas come from? Most people's theory of thinking recalls the way that God fashions the universe in the Old Testament. The prototype of the "heroic creative genius," God in the Judeo-Christian tradition works in a vacuum. He's a loner who relies on no one and participates in no culture or community. He looks inside himself, discovers in his mind the divine *logos*—the creative word or idea—expresses it, and the universe is made. This, the standard "genius" or "expressive" model, is the way people often imagine the enterprise of thinking. Ideas, according to this official story, just pop out of the heads of creative thinkers: some people find it easy to generate lots of them—usually wild-eyed artists or scientific types with unruly hairdos—but most people don't.

Actually not all thinkers and creators work alone. For an alternative version of how thinking and creating work, let's turn to an excerpt from another Native American legend: this one, from the Crow culture, tells how Coyote makes the world.

Old Man Coyote Makes the World

How water came to be, nobody knows. Where Old Man Coyote came from, nobody knows. But he was, he lived. Old Man Coyote spoke: "It is bad that I am alone. I should have someone to talk to. It is bad that there is only water and nothing else." Old Man Coyote walked around. Then he saw some who were living—two ducks with red eyes.

"Younger brothers," he said, "is there anything in this world but water and still more water? What do you think?"

"Why," said the ducks, "we think there might be something deep down below the water. In our hearts we believe this."

"Well, younger brothers, go and dive. Find out if there is something. Go!"

One of the ducks dove down. He stayed under water for a long, long time.

"How sad!" Old Man Coyote said. "Our younger brother must have drowned."

"No way has he drowned," said the other duck. "We can live under water for a long time. Just wait."

At last the first duck came to the surface. "What our hearts told us was right," he said. "There is something down there, because my head bumped into it."

"Well, my younger brother, whatever it may be, bring it up."

The duck dived again. A long time he stayed down there. When he came up, he had something in his beak. "Why, this is a root," he said. "Where there are roots, there must be earth. My younger brother, dive again. If you find something soft, bring it up."

The duck went down a third time. This time he came up with a small lump of soft earth in his bill. Old Man Coyote examined it. "Ah, my younger brother, this is what I wanted. This I will make big. This I will spread around. This little handful of mud shall be our home."

Old Man Coyote blew on the little lump, which began to grow and spread all over. "What a surprise, elder brother!" said the ducks. "This is wonderful! We are pleased."

Old Man Coyote took the little root. In the soft mud he planted it. Then things started to grow. Grasses, plants, trees, all manner of food Old Man Coyote made this way. "Isn't this pretty?" he asked. "What do you think?"

"Elder brother," answered the ducks, "this is indeed very pretty. But it's too flat. Why don't you hollow some places out, and here and there make some hills and mountains. Wouldn't that be a fine thing?"

"Yes, my younger brothers. I'll do as you say. While I'm about it, I will also make some rivers, ponds, and springs so that wherever we go, we can have cool, fresh water to drink."

"Ah, that's fine, elder brother," said the ducks after Old Man Coyote had made all these things. "How very clever you are."[1]

[1]"Old Man Coyote Makes the World," in Richard Erdoes and Alfonso Ortiz, eds., *American Indian Myths and Legends* (New York: Pantheon Books, 1984), p. 88.

Coyote isn't a lone "creative genius"—one of those gods who magically plucks the universe out of an empty hat. In this tribal story, nature exists, paradoxically enough, even before it's made, and the creator—a rather amiable old fellow—isn't above asking for help and following a good suggestion when he hears one. Creative thinking from this point of view is a collaborative process, one that involves the active contribution of a community of thinkers and makers working together. The idea of the universe doesn't just pop into Coyote's brain fully formed; it takes root and grows there in response to suggestions made by his fellow creatures. From Coyote's perspective, creative thinking is an active, collaborative process; it results from a communal dialogue of ideas—a give and take of suggestions, visions, and revisions—and not from a lone heroic effort.

Most academic thinkers operate more like Coyote than Yahweh when it comes to cooking up their ideas. Portrayals of scholarly thinking in popular movies or books tend to follow the outlines of the "heroic creative genius" model: writers are depicted sequestered in their bedrooms, isolated on romantic tropical islands, or cut off from human contact in jail. Scientists are always rogues and loners who make earthshaking discoveries or diabolical inventions secreted away in homemade laboratories. But outside of Hollywood and pulp fiction, academic thinkers are a remarkably collaborative group. Scientists, historians, psychologists, and literary critics almost never think in isolation. When a scientist wants to explain a puzzling phenomenon, the first thing she does is to familiarize herself with all of the ideas and explanations that have been offered on the subject; when a historian wants to reexamine a particular era or event, he begins by consulting earlier interpretations that have been particularly influential; when a psychologist wants to explain a facet of human behavior, she turns first to the many theories that have shaped how psychologists have traditionally understood her subject. Every academic discipline, every field of academic inquiry, really amounts to an ongoing dialogue, a continuous exchange of analyses, interpretations, and explanations about the world and how it works. And it's this ongoing conversation of ideas that usually provides academic thinkers with their most productive and insightful ideas.

Herbert Kohl's essay on Rosa Parks in the last chapter (p. 378) offers a model of this kind of dialogical academic thinking at work. Before Kohl presents his own version of Rosa Parks's story, he begins by identifying the official versions of the tale that dominate elementary school classrooms. Kohl recognizes that he is not writing or thinking in a vacuum. He realizes that there are various versions of Rosa Parks's story, different interpretations of her life and actions, and that these versions existed and shaped discussion of his topic even before he decided to write about it. To engage his subject critically he had to enter into the ongoing conversation of stories that surrounds the historical figure of Rosa Parks and identify the culturally dominant explanation patterns — the official stories — that shape the way people generally think of her. M. G. Lord does much the same thing at the beginning of her analysis of Barbie's popularity (p. 348). Before plunging into her "earth goddess" theory, Lord acknowledges the dominant interpretation of Barbie's popularity: the idea that women want to imitate the myth of female beauty they see in Barbie, the idea that, as Lord puts it, women "respond in a crazed, competitive, Pavlovian fashion to pictures, models or the body of a doll." Once she has disposed of this common explanation pattern, Lord can move on to present her own reading of Barbie's significance. And although it may not be as apparent, in her essay on Laguna Pueblo storytelling (p. 21) Leslie Marmon Silko surveys the dominant conception of stories and storytelling in much the same way: throughout her essay, she contrasts her view of what stories mean in Pueblo Indian culture with "common" notions about storytelling — like the idea that stories are told at specific times or are meant primarily for children. She also contrasts her notion of storytelling with common academic approaches to the subject — like the distinction anthropologists frequently make between "old and sacred and traditional" stories and contemporary family stories. Before you can begin to think and write critically, you have to recognize that you never think alone: you have to realize that every topic — whether it's Rosa Parks, Barbie's popularity, the nature of childhood, or the function of storytelling — is surrounded by an ongoing conversation of ideas. Academic thinkers and writers enter this conversation by identifying the official stories that are already being told about their subject before they venture their own analyses and interpretations. In fact, their own ideas often arise as responses to or revisions of the theories that have dominated their topic. In this sense, academic analysis always involves intellectual revision — the reevaluation and reshaping of stories that have come before.

Once you've identified the theories, explanation patterns, or official stories that dominate the conversation of ideas surrounding your topic, you need to acknowledge their strengths and expose their limitations. Lord rejects the "Pavlovian" explanation pattern for Barbie's popularity because she notes that it doesn't "fit" her own personal experience, and in general she finds it "demeaning" to women. Kohl offers a much more systematic and rigorous critique of the Rosa Parks stories he samples. By comparing the official version of the Parks legend to information he culls from other historical accounts — like the book *My Soul Is Rested* — Kohl demonstrates how poorly the "Rosa Was Tired" story pattern fits the facts of Parks's biography. And he doesn't stop there: by speculating at length about the motives that underlie specific omissions and editings in the official account, he "denaturalizes" it, exposing its artificiality and the fact that it is simply one of many ways of telling the Parks story. By demonstrating how "Rosa Was Tired" discourages the kind of active political participation needed to effect real social change, Kohl exposes this official story as simply another cultural construct meant to reinforce certain cultural values and forward certain group interests. Once Kohl has freed himself and his reader from the influence of the official version of Parks's story, he can "talk back" to it by offering his own revision — one that better fits his understanding of what happened to Rosa Parks *and* one that reflects his own particular perspective, beliefs, and values. Critical analysis boils down to three simple steps:

- Identify and briefly summarize dominant stories/interpretations/analyses.

- Critique or evaluate these official explanation patterns.

- Present and explain your own analysis.

The following selection offers another example of an academic thinker who enters into the conversation of ideas in her field as she engages her subject. In "Kochinnenako in Academe," Paula Gunn Allen surveys common approaches to interpreting a Native American legend and then presents an alternative version, a retelling based on her own cultural experience. "Kochinnenako" is an ancient tribal story about Yellow Woman, the Corn Mother of the Keres tribe, who brings about the rebirth of nature in the spring. Born in New Mexico in 1939, Allen is a Laguna Pueblo/Sioux Indian with a distinguished reputation as a novelist, poet, essayist, and literary critic. She currently teaches English at the University of California, Los Angeles.

Before Reading

Briefly preview the text of "Kochinnenako," paying particular attention to the subheadings that Allen uses to identify the major sections of her essay and skimming the first paragraph of each section. Where do you think Allen identifies and critiques official interpretations of the Kochinnenako story in her essay? Whose point of view do you expect these official interpretations to represent? Where in the text does Allen appear to begin presenting her own interpretation?

Kochinnenako in Academe: Three Approaches to Interpreting a Keres Indian Tale

Paula Gunn Allen

I became engaged in studying feminist thought and theory when I was first studying and teaching American Indian literature in the early 1970s. Over the ensuing fifteen years, my own stances toward both feminist and American Indian life and thought have intertwined as they have unfolded. I have always included feminist content and perspectives in my teaching of American Indian subjects, though at first the mating was uneasy at best. My determination that both areas were interdependent and mutually significant to a balanced pedagogy of American Indian studies led me to grow into an approach to both that is best described as tribal-feminism or feminist-tribalism. Both terms are applicable: if I am dealing with feminism, I approach it from a strongly tribal posture, and when I am dealing with American Indian literature, history, culture, or philosophy I approach it from a strongly feminist one.

A feminist approach to the study and teaching of American Indian life and thought is essential because the area has been dominated by paternalistic, male-dominant modes of consciousness since the first writings about American Indians in the fifteenth century. This male bias has seriously skewed our understanding of tribal life and philosophy, distorting it in ways that are sometimes obvious but are most often invisible.

Often what appears to be a misinterpretation caused by racial differences is a distortion based on sexual politics. When the patriarchal paradigm that characterizes western thinking is applied to gynecentric tribal modes, it transforms the ideas, significances, and raw data into something that is not only unrecognizable to the tribes but entirely incongruent with their philosophies and theories. We know that materials and interpretations amassed by the white intellectual establishment are in error, but we have not pinpointed the major sources of that error. I believe that a fundamental source has been male bias and that feminist theory, when judiciously applied to the field, makes the error correctible, freeing the data for reinterpretation that is at least congruent with a tribal perceptual mode.

To demonstrate the interconnections between tribal and feminist approaches as I use them in my work, I have developed an analysis of a traditional Kochinnenako, or Yellow Woman story of the Laguna-Acoma Keres, as recast by my mother's uncle John M. Gunn in his book *Schat Chen*.[1] My analysis utilizes three approaches and demonstrates the relationship of context to meaning, illuminating three consciousness styles and providing students with a traditionally tribal, nonracist, feminist understanding of traditional and contemporary American Indian life.

SOME THEORETICAL CONSIDERATIONS

Analyzing tribal cultural systems from a mainstream feminist point of view allows an otherwise overlooked insight into the complex interplay of factors that have led to the systematic loosening of tribal ties, the disruption of tribal cohesion and complexity, and the growing disequilibrium of cultures that were anciently based on a belief in balance, relationship, and the centrality of women, particularly elder women. A feminist approach reveals not only the exploitation and oppression of the tribes by whites and white government but also areas of oppression within the tribes and the sources and nature of that oppression. To a large extent, such an analysis can provide strategies for ameliorating the effects of patriarchal colonialism, enabling many of the tribes to reclaim their ancient gynarchical,[2] egalitarian, and sacred traditions.

At the present time, American Indians in general are not comfortable with feminist analysis or action within the reservation or urban Indian enclaves. Many Indian women are uncomfortable with feminism because they perceive it (correctly) as white-dominated. They (not so correctly) believe it is concerned with issues that have little bearing on their own lives. They are also uncomfortable with it because they have been reared in an anglophobic world that views white society with fear and hostility. But because of their fear of and bitterness toward whites and their consequent unwillingness to examine the dynamics of white socialization, American Indian women often overlook the central areas of damage done to tribal tradition by white Christian and secular patriarchal dominance. Militant and "progressive" American Indian men are even more likely to quarrel with feminism; they have benefited in certain ways from white male-centeredness, and while those benefits are of real danger to the tribes, the individual rewards are compelling.

It is within the context of growing violence against women and the concomitant lowering of our status among Native Americans that I teach and write. Certainly I could not locate the mechanisms of colonization that have led to the virulent rise of woman-hating among American Indian men (and, to a certain extent, among many of the women) without a secure and determined feminism. Just as certainly, feminist theory applied to my literary studies clarifies a number of issues for me, including the patriarchal bias that has been systematically imposed on traditional literary materials and the mechanism by which that bias has affected contemporary American Indian life, thought, and culture.

The oral tradition is more than a record of a people's culture. It is the creative source of their collective and individual selves. When that well-spring of identity is tampered with, the sense of self is also tampered with; and when that tampering includes the sexist and classist assumptions of the white world within the body of an Indian tradition, serious consequences necessarily ensue.

The oral tradition is a living body. It is in continuous flux, which enables it to accommodate itself to the real circumstances of a people's lives. That is its strength, but it is also its weakness, for when a people finds itself living within a racist, classist, and sexist reality, the oral tradition will reflect those values and will thus shape the people's consciousness to include and accept racism, classism and sexism, and they will incorporate that change, hardly noticing the shift. If the oral tradition is altered in certain subtle, fundamental ways, if elements alien to it are introduced so that its internal coherence is disturbed, it becomes the major instrument of colonization and oppression.

Such alterations have occurred and are still occurring. Those who trans-   10
late or "render" narratives make certain crucial changes, many unconscious. The cultural bias of the translator inevitably shapes his or her perception of the materials being translated, often in ways that he or she is unaware of. Culture is fundamentally a shaper of perception, after all, and perception is shaped by culture in many subtle ways. In short, it's hard to see the forest when you're a tree. To a great extent, changes in materials translated from a tribal to a western language are a result of the vast difference in languages; certain ideas and concepts that are implicit in the structure of an Indian language are not possible in English. Language embodies the unspoken assumptions and orientations of the culture it belongs to. So while the problem is one of translation, it is not simply one of word equivalence. The differences are perceptual and contextual as much as verbal.

Sometimes the shifts are contextual; indeed, both the context and content usually are shifted, sometimes subtly, sometimes blatantly. The net effect is a shifting of the whole axis of the culture. When shifts of language and context are coupled with the almost infinite changes occasioned by Christianization, secularization, economic dislocation from subsistence to industrial modes, destruction of the wilderness and associated damage to the biota, much that is changed goes unnoticed or unremarked by the people being changed. This is not to suggest that Native Americans are unaware of the enormity of the change they have been forced to undergo by the several centuries of white presence, but much of that change is at deep and subtle levels that are not easily noted or resisted.

John Gunn received the story I am using here from a Keres-speaking informant and translated it himself. The story, which he titles "Sh-ah-cock and Miochin or the Battle of the Seasons," is in reality a narrative version of a ritual. The ritual brings about the change of season and of moiety among the Keres. Gunn doesn't mention this, perhaps because he was interested in stories and not in religion or perhaps because his informant did not mention the connection to him.

What is interesting about his rendering is his use of European, classist, conflict-centered patriarchal assumptions as plotting devices. These interpolations dislocate the significance of the tale and subtly alter the ideational context of woman-centered, largely pacifist people whose ritual story this is. I have developed three critiques of the tale as it appears in his book, using feminist and tribal understandings to discuss the various meanings of the story when it is read from three different perspectives.

In the first reading, I apply tribal understanding to the story. In the second, I apply the sort of feminist perspective I applied to traditional stories, historical events, traditional culture, and contemporary literature when I began developing a feminist perspective. The third reading applies what I call a feminist-tribal perspective. Each analysis is somewhat less detailed than it might be; but as I am interested in describing modes of perception and their impact on our understanding of cultural artifacts (and by extension our understanding of people who come from different cultural contexts than our own) rather than critiquing a story, they are adequate.

YELLOW WOMAN STORIES

The Keres of Laguna and Acoma Pueblos in New Mexico have stories   15
that are called Yellow Woman stories. The themes and to a large extent the motifs of these stories are always female-centered, always told from Yellow Woman's point of view. Some older recorded versions of Yellow Woman tales (as in Gunn) make Yellow Woman the daughter of the hocheni. Gunn translates *hocheni* as "ruler." But Keres's notions of the hocheni's function and position are as cacique or Mother Chief, which differ greatly from Anglo-European ideas of rulership. However, for Gunn to render *hocheni* as "ruler" is congruent with the European folktale tradition.[3]

Kochinnenako, Yellow Woman, is in some sense a name that means Woman-Woman because among the Keres, yellow is the color for women (as pink and red are among Anglo-European Americans), and it is the color ascribed to the Northwest. Keres women paint their faces yellow on certain ceremonial occasions and are so painted at death so that the guardian at the gate of the spirit world, Naiya Iyatiku (Mother Corn Woman), will recognize that the newly arrived person is a woman. It is also the name of a particular Irriaku, Corn Mother (sacred corn-ear bundle), and Yellow Woman stories in their original form detail rituals in which the Irriaku figures prominently.

Yellow Woman stories are about all sorts of things—abduction, meeting with happy powerful spirits, birth of twins, getting power from the spirit worlds and returning it to the people, refusing to marry, weaving, grinding corn, getting water, outsmarting witches, eluding or escaping from malintentioned spirits, and more. Yellow Woman's sisters are often in the stories (Blue, White, and Red Corn) as is Grandmother Spider and her helper Spider Boy, the Sun God or one of his aspects, Yellow Woman's twin sons, witches, magicians, gamblers, and mothers-in-law.

Many Yellow Woman tales highlight her alienation from the people: she lives with her grandmother at the edge of the village, for example, or she is in some way atypical, maybe a woman who refuses to marry, one who is known for some particular special talent, or one who is very quick-witted and resourceful. In many ways Kochinnenako is a role model, though she possesses some behaviors that are not likely to occur in many of the women who hear her stories. She is, one might say, the Spirit of Woman.

The stories do not necessarily imply that difference is punishable; on the contrary, it is often her very difference that makes her special adventures possible, and these adventures often have happy outcomes for Kochinnenako and for her people. This is significant among a people who value conformity and propriety above almost anything. It suggests that the behavior of women, at least at certain times or under certain circumstances, must be improper or nonconformist for the greater good of the whole. Not that all the stories are graced with a happy ending. Some come to a tragic conclusion, sometimes resulting from someone's inability to follow the rules or perform a ritual in the proper way.

Other Kochinnenako stories are about her centrality to the harmony, balance, and prosperity of the tribe. "Sh-ah-cock and Miochin" is one of these stories. John Gunn prefaces the narrative with the comment that while the story is about a battle, war stories are rarely told by the Keres because they are not "a war like people" and "very rarely refer to their exploits in war."

20

Sh-ah-cock and Miochin or
the Battle of the Seasons

In the Kush-kut-ret-u-nah-tit (white village of the north) was once a ruler by the name of Hut-cha-mun Ki-uk (the broken prayer stick), one of whose daughters, Ko-chin-ne-nako, became the bride of Sh-ah-cock (the spirit of winter), a person of very violent temper. He always manifested his presence by blizzards of snow or sleet or by freezing cold, and on account of his alliance with the ruler's daughter, he was most of the time in the vicinity of Kush-kut-ret, and as these manifestations continued from month to month and year to year, the people of Kush-kut-ret found that their crops would not mature, and finally they were compelled to subsist on the leaves of the cactus.

On one occasion Ko-chin-ne-nako had wandered a long way from home in search of the cactus and had gathered quite a bundle and was preparing to carry it home by singeing off the thorns, when on looking up she found herself confronted by a very bold but handsome young man. His attire attracted her gaze at once. He wore a shirt of yellow woven from the silks of corn, a belt made from the broad green blades of the same plant, a tall pointed hat made from the same kind of material and from the top of which waved a yellow corn tassel. He wore green leggings woven from kow-e-nuh, the green stringy moss that forms in springs and ponds. His moccasins were beautifully embroidered with flowers and butterflies. In his hand he carried an ear of green corn.

His whole appearance proclaimed him a stranger and as Ko-chin-ne-nako gaped in wonder, he spoke to her in a very pleasing voice asking her what she was doing. She told him that on account of the cold and drouth, the people of Kush-kut-ret were forced to eat the leaves of the cactus to keep from starving.

"Here," said the young man, handing her the ear of green corn. "Eat this and I will go and bring more that you may take home with you."

He left her and soon disappeared going towards the south. In a short time he returned bringing with him a big load of green corn. Ko-chin-ne-nako asked him where he had gathered corn and if it grew nearby. "No," he replied, "it is from my home far away to the south, where the corn grows and the flowers bloom all the year around. Would you not like to accompany me back to my country?" Ko-chin-ne-nako replied that his home must be very beautiful, but that she could not go with him because she was the wife of Sh-ah-cock. And then she told him of her alliance with the Spirit of Winter, and admitted that her husband was very cold and disagreeable and that she did not love him. The strange young man urged her to go with him to the warm land of the south, saying that he did not fear Sh-ah-cock. But Ko-chin-ne-nako would not consent. So the stranger directed her to return to her home with the corn he had brought and cautioned her not to throw away any of the husks out of the door. Upon leaving he said to her, "you must meet me at this place tomorrow. I will bring more corn for you."

Ko-chin-ne-nako had not proceeded far on her homeward way ere she met her sisters who, having become uneasy because of her long absence, had come in search of her. They were greatly surprised at seeing her with an armful of corn instead of cactus. Ko-chin-ne-nako told them the whole story of how she had obtained it, and thereby only added wonderment to their surprise. They helped her to carry the corn home; and there she again had to tell her story to her father and mother.

When she had described the stranger even from his peaked hat to his butterfly moccasins, and had told them that she was to meet him again on the day following, Hut-cha-mun Ki-uk, the father, exclaimed:

"It is Mi-o-chin!"

"It is Mi-o-chin! It is Mi-o-chin!" echoed the mother. "Tomorrow you must bring him home with you."

The next day Ko-chin-ne-nako went again to the spot where she had met Mi-o-chin, for it was indeed Mi-o-chin, the Spirit of Summer. He was already there, awaiting her coming. With him he had brought a huge bundle of corn.

Ko-chin-ne-nako pressed upon him the invitation of her parents to accompany her home, so together they carried the corn to Kush-kut-ret. When it had been distributed there was sufficient to feed all the people of the city. Amid great rejoicing and thanksgiving, Mi-o-chin was welcomed at the Hotchin's (ruler's) house.

In the evening, as was his custom, Sh-ah-cock, the Spirit of the Winter, returned to his home. He came in a blinding storm of snow and hail and sleet, for he was in a boisterous mood. On approaching the city, he felt within his bones that Mi-o-chin was there, so he called in a loud and blustering voice:

"Ha! Mi-o-chin, are you here?"

For answer, Mi-o-chin advanced to meet him.

Then Sh-ah-cock, beholding him, called again,

"Ha! Mi-o-chin, I will destroy you."

"Ha! Sh-ah-cock, I will destroy you," replied Mi-o-chin, still advancing.

Sh-ah-cock paused, irresolute. He was covered from head to foot with frost (skah). Icycles [*sic*] (ya-pet-tu-ne) draped him round. The fierce, cold wind proceeded from his nostrils.

As Mi-o-chin drew near, the wintry wind changed to a warm summer breeze. The frost and icycles melted and displayed beneath them, the dry, bleached bulrushes (ska-ra-ru-ka) in which Sh-ah-cock was clad.

Seeing that he was doomed to defeat, Sh-ah-cock cried out:

"I will not fight you now, for we cannot try our powers. We will make ready, and in four days from this time, we will meet here and fight for supremacy. The victor shall claim Ko-chin-ne-nako for his wife."

With this, Sh-ah-cock withdrew in rage. The wind again roared and shook the very houses; but the people were warm within them, for Mi-o-chin was with them.

The next day Mi-o-chin left Kush-kut-ret for his home in the south. Arriving there, he began to make his preparations to meet Sh-ah-cock in battle.

First he sent an eagle as a messenger to his friend, Ya-chun-ne-ne-moot (a kind of shaley rock that becomes very hot in the fire), who lived in the west, requesting him to come and help to battle Sh-ah-cock. Then he called together the birds and the four legged animals — all those that live in sunny climes. For his advance guard and shield he selected the bat (pickikke), as its tough skin would best resist the sleet and hail that Sh-ah-cock would hurl at him.

Meantime Sh-ah-cock had gone to his home in the north to make his preparations for battle. To his aid he called all the winter birds and all of the four legged animals of the wintry climates. For his advance guard and shield he selected Shro-ak-ah (a magpie).

When these formidable forces had been mustered by the rivals, they advanced, Mi-o-chin from the south and Sh-ah-cock from the north, in battle array.

Ya-chun-ne-ne-moot kindled his fires and piled great heaps of resinous fuel upon them until volumes of steam and smoke ascended, forming enormous clouds that hurried forward toward Kush-kut-ret and the battle ground. Upon these clouds rode Mi-o-chin, the Spirit of Summer, and his vast army. All the animals of the army, encountering the smoke from Ya-chun-ne-ne-moot's fires, were colored by the smoke so that, from that day, the animals from the south have been black or brown in color.

Sh-ah-cock and his army came out of the north in a howling blizzard and borne forward on black storm clouds driven by a freezing wintry wind. As he came on, the lakes and rivers over which he passed were frozen and the air was filled with blinding sleet.

When the combatants drew near to Kush-kut-ret, they advanced with fearful rapidity. Their arrival upon the field was marked by fierce and terrific strife.

Flashes of lightning darted from Mi-o-chin's clouds. Striking the animals of Sh-ah-cock, they singed the hair upon them, and turned it white, so that, from that day, the animals from the north have worn a covering of white or have white markings upon them.

From the south, the black clouds still rolled upward, the thunder spoke again and again. Clouds of smoke and vapor rushed onward, melting the snow and ice weapons of Sh-ah-cock and compelling him, at length, to retire from the field. Mi-o-chin, assured of victory, pursued him. To save himself from total defeat and destruction, Sh-ah-cock called for armistice.

This being granted on the part of Mi-o-chin, the rivals met at Kush-kut-ret to arrange the terms of the treaty. Sh-ah-cock acknowledged himself defeated. He consented to give up Ko-chin-ne-nako to Mi-o-chin. This concession was received with rejoicing by Ko-chin-ne-nako and all the people of Kush-kut-ret.

It was then agreed between the late combatants that, for all time thereafter, Mi-o-chin was to rule at Kush-kut-ret during one-half of the year, and Sh-ah-cock was to rule during the remaining half, and that neither should molest the other.[4]

John Gunn's version has a formal plot structure that makes the account seem to be a narrative. But had he translated it directly from the Keres, even in "narrative" form, as in a storytelling session, its ritual nature would have been clearer.

I can only surmise about how the account might go if it were done that way, basing my ideas on renderings of Keres rituals in narrative forms I am acquainted with. But a direct translation from the Keres would have sounded more like the following than like Gunn's rendition of it:

Long ago. Eh. There in the North. Yellow Woman. Up northward she went. Then she picked burrs and cactus. Then here went Summer. From the south he came. Above there he arrived. Thus spoke Summer. "Are you here? How is it going?" said Summer. "Did you come here?" thus said Yellow Woman. Then answered Yellow Woman. "I pick these poor things because I am hungry." "Why do you not eat corn and melons?" asked Summer. Then he gave her some corn and melons. "Take it!" Then thus spoke Yellow Woman, "It is good. Let us go. To my house I take you." "Is not your husband there?" "No. He went hunting deer. Today at night he will come back."

Then in the north they arrived. In the west they went down. Arrived then they in the east. "Are you here?" Remembering Prayer Sticks said. "Yes" Summer said. "How is it going?" Summer said. Then he said, "Your daughter Yellow Woman, she brought me here." "Eh. That is good." Thus spoke Remembering Prayer Sticks.

The story would continue, with many of the elements contained in Gunn's version but organized along the axis of directions, movement of the participants, their maternal relationships to each other (daughter, mother, mother chief, etc.), and events sketched in only as they pertained to directions and the division of the year into its ritual/ceremonial segments, one belonging to the Kurena (summer supernaturals or powers who are connected to the summer people or clans) and the other belonging to the Kashare, perhaps in conjunction with the Kopishtaya, the Spirits.

Summer, Miochin, is the Shiwana who lives on the south mountain, and Sh-ah-cock is the Shiwana who lives on the north mountain.[5] It is interesting to note that the Kurena wear three eagle feathers and ctc'otika' feathers (white striped) on their heads, bells, and woman's dress and carry a reed flute, which perhaps is connected with Iyatiku's sister, Istoakoa, Reed Woman.

A KERES INTERPRETATION

When a traditional Keres reads the tale of Kochinnenako, she listens   25 with certain information about her people in mind: she knows, for example, that Hutchamun Kiuk (properly it means Remembering Prayer Sticks, though Gunn translates it as Broken Prayer Sticks)[6] refers to the ritual (sacred) identity of the cacique and that the story is a narrative version of a ceremony related to the planting of corn. She knows that Lagunas and Acomas don't have rulers in the Anglo-European sense of monarchs, lords, and such (though they do, in recent times, have elected governors, but that's another matter) and that a person's social status is determined by her mother's clan and position in it rather than by her relationship to the cacique as his daughter. (Actually, in various accounts, the cacique refers to Yellow Woman as his mother, so the designation of her as his daughter is troublesome unless one is aware that relationships in the context of their ritual significance are being delineated here.)

In any case, our hypothetical Keres reader also knows that the story is about a ritual that takes place every year and that the battle imagery refers to events that take place during the ritual; she is also aware that Kochinnenako's will, as expressed in her attraction to Miochin, is a central element of the ritual. She knows further that the ritual is partly about the coming of summer and partly about the ritual relationship and exchange of primacy between the two divisions of the tribe, that the ritual described in the narrative is enacted by men, dressed as Miochin and Sh-ah-cock, and that Yellow Woman in her Corn Mother aspect is the center of this and other sacred rites of the Kurena, though in this ritual she may also be danced by a Kurena mask dancer. (Gunn includes a drawing of this figure, made by a Laguna, and titled "Ko-chin-ne-nako—In the Mask Dances.")

The various birds and animals along with the forces such as warm air, fire, heat, sleet, and ice are represented in the ritual; Hutchamun Kiuk, the timekeeper or officer who keeps track of the ritual calendar (which is intrinsically related to the solstices and equinoxes), plays a central role in the ritual. The presence of Kochinnenako and Hutchamun Kiuk and the Shiwana Miochin and Sh-ah-cock means something sacred is going on for the Keres.

The ritual transfers the focus of power, or the ritual axis, held in turn by two moieties whose constitution reflects the earth's bilateral division between summer and winter, from the winter to the summer people. Each moiety's right to power is confirmed by and reflective of the seasons, as it is reflective of and supported by the equinoxes. The power is achieved through the Iyani (ritual empowerment) of female Power,[7] embodied in Kochinnenako as mask dancer and/or Irriaku. Without her empowering mediatorship among the south and north *Shiwana,* the *cacique,* and the village, the season and the moiety cannot change, and balance cannot be maintained.

Unchanging supremacy of one moiety/season over the other is unnatural and therefore undesirable because unilateral dominance of one aspect of existence and of society over another is not reflective of or supported by reality at meteorological or spiritual levels. Sh-ah-cock is the Winter Spirit or Winter Cloud, a *Shiwana* (one of several categories of supernaturals), and as such is cold and connected to sleet, snow, ice, and hunger. He is not portrayed as cold because he is a source of unmitigated evil (or of evil at all, for that matter).

Half of the people (not numerically but mystically, so to speak) are Winter, and in that sense are Sh-ah-cock; and while this aspect of the group psyche may seem unlovely when its time is over, that same half is lovely indeed in the proper season. Similarly, Miochin will also age—that is, pass his time—and will then give way for his "rival," which is also his complement. Thus balance and harmony are preserved for the village through exchange of dominance, and thus each portion of the community takes responsibility in turn for the prosperity and well-being of the people. 30

A Keres is of course aware that balance and harmony are two primary assumptions of Keres society and will not approach the narrative wondering whether the handsome Miochin will win the hand of the unhappy wife and triumph over the enemy, thereby heroically saving the people from disaster. The triumph of handsome youth over ugly age or of virile liberality over withered tyranny doesn't make sense in a Keres context because such views contradict central Keres values.

A traditional Keres is satisfied by the story because it reaffirms a Keres sense of rightness, of propriety. It is a tale that affirms ritual understandings, and the Keres reader can visualize the ritual itself when reading Gunn's story. Such a reader is likely to be puzzled by the references to rulers and by the tone of heroic romance but will be reasonably satisfied by the account because in spite of its westernized changes, it still ends happily with the orderly transfer of focality between the moieties and seasons accomplished in seasonal splendor as winter in New Mexico blusters and sleets its way north and summer sings and warms its way home. In the end, the primary Keres values of harmony, balance, and the centrality of woman to maintain them have been validated, and the fundamental Keres principal of proper order is celebrated and affirmed once again.

A Modern Feminist Interpretation

A non-Keres feminist, reading this tale, is likely to wrongly suppose that this narrative is about the importance of men and the use of a passive female figure as a pawn in their bid for power. And, given the way Gunn renders the story, a modern feminist would have good reason to make such an inference. As Gunn recounts it, the story opens in classic patriarchal style and implies certain patriarchal complications: that Kochinnenako has married a man who is violent and destructive. She is the ruler's daughter, which might suggest that the traditional Keres are concerned with the abuses of power of the wealthy. This in turn suggests that the traditional Keres social system, like the traditional Anglo-European ones, suffer from oppressive class structures in which the rich and powerful bring misery to the people, who in the tale are reduced to bare subsistence seemingly as a result of Kochinnenako's unfortunate alliance. A reader making the usual assumptions western readers make when enjoying folk tales will think she is reading a sort of Robin Hood story, replete with a lovely maid Marian, an evil Sheriff, and a green-clad agent of social justice with the Indian name Miochin.

Given the usual assumptions that underlie European folktales, the Western romantic view of the Indian, and the usual antipatriarchal bias that characterizes feminist analysis, a feminist reader might assume that Kochinnenako has been compelled to make an unhappy match by her father the ruler, who must be gaining some power from the alliance. Besides, his name is given as Broken Prayer Stick, which might be taken to mean that he is an unholy man, remiss in his religious duties and weak spiritually.

Gunn's tale does not clarify these issues. Instead it proceeds in a way best calculated to confirm a feminist's interpretation of the tale as only another example of the low status of women in tribal cultures. In accordance with this entrenched American myth, Gunn makes it clear that Kochinnenako is not happy in her marriage; she thinks Sh-ah-cock is "cold and disagreeable, and she cannot love him." Certainly, contemporary American women will read that to mean that Sh-ah-cock is an emotionally uncaring, perhaps cruel husband and that Kochinnenako is forced to accept a life bereft of warmth and love. A feminist reader might imagine that Kochinnenako, like many women, has been socialized into submission. So obedient is she, it seems, so lacking in spirit and independence, that she doesn't seize her chance to escape a bad situation, preferring instead to remain obedient to the patriarchal institution of marriage. As it turns out (in Gunn's tale), Kochinnenako is delivered from the clutches of her violent and

35

unwanted mate by the timely intervention of a much more pleasant man, the hero.

A radical feminist is likely to read the story for its content vis à vis racism and resistance to oppression. From a radical perspective, it seems politically significant that Sh-ah-cock is white. That is, winter is white. Snow is white. Blizzards are white. Clearly, while the story does not give much support to concepts of a people's struggles, it could be constructed to mean that the oppressor is designated white in the story because the Keres are engaged in serious combat with white colonial power and, given the significance of storytelling in tribal cultures, are chronicling that struggle in this tale. Read this way, it would seem to acknowledge the right and duty of the people in overthrowing the hated white dictator, who by this account possesses the power of life and death over them.

Briefly, in this context, the story can be read as a tale about the nature of white oppression of Indian people, and Kochinnenako then becomes something of a revolutionary fighter through her collusion with the rebel Miochin in the overthrow of the tyrant Sh-ah-cock. In this reading, the tale becomes a cry for liberation and a direct command to women to aid in the people's struggle to overthrow the colonial powers that drain them of life and strength, deprive them of their rightful prosperity, and threaten them with extinction. An activist teacher could use this tale to instruct women in their obligation to the revolutionary struggle. The daughter, her sisters, and the mother are, after all, implicated in the attempt to bring peace and prosperity to the people; indeed, they are central to it. Such a teacher could, by so using the story, appear to be incorporating culturally diverse materials in the classroom while at the same time exploiting the romantic and moral appeal Native Americans have for other Americans.

When read as a battle narrative, the story as Gunn renders it makes clear that the superiority of Miochin rests as much in his commitment to the welfare of the people as in his military prowess and that because his attempt to free the people is backed up by their invitation to him to come and liberate them, he is successful. Because of his success he is entitled to the hand of the ruler's daughter, Kochinnenako, one of the traditional Old World spoils of victory. Similarly, Sh-ah-cock is defeated not only because he is violent and oppressive but because the people, like Kochinnenako, find that they cannot love him.

A radical lesbian separatist might find herself uncomfortable with the story even though it is so clearly correct in identifying the enemy as white and violent. But the overthrow of the tyrant is placed squarely in the hands of another male figure, Miochin. This rescue is likely to be viewed with a jaundiced eye by many feminists (though more romantic women might be satisfied with it, since it's a story about an Indian woman of long ago), as Kochinnenako has to await the coming of a handsome stranger for her salvation, and her fate is decided by her father and the more salutary suitor Miochin. No one asks Kochinnenako what she wants to do; the reader is informed that her marriage is not to her liking when she admits to Miochin that she is unhappy. Nevertheless, Kochinnenako acts like any passive, dependent woman who is exploited by the males in her life, who get what they want regardless of her own needs or desires.

Some readers (like myself) might find themselves wondering hopefully   40 whether Miochin isn't really female, disguised by males as one of them in order to buttress their position of relative power. After all, this figure is dressed in yellow and green, the colors of corn, a plant always associated with Woman. Kochinnenako and her sisters are all Corn Women and her mother is, presumably, the head of the Corn Clan; and the Earth Mother of the Keres, Iyatiku, is Corn Woman herself. Alas, I haven't yet found evidence to support such a wishful notion, except that the mask dancer who impersonates Kochinnenako is male, dressed female, which is sort of the obverse side of the wish.

A FEMINIST-TRIBAL INTERPRETATION

The feminist interpretation I have sketched—which is a fair representation of one of my early readings from what I took to be a feminist perspective—proceeds from two unspoken assumptions: that women are essentially powerless and that conflict is basic to human existence. The first is a fundamental feminist position, while the second is basic to Anglo-European thought; neither, however, is characteristic of Keres thought. To a modern feminist, marriage is an institution developed to establish and maintain male supremacy; because she is the ruler's daughter, Kochinnenako's choice of a husband determines which male will hold power over the people and who will inherit the throne.[8]

When Western assumptions are applied to tribal narratives, they become mildly confusing and moderately annoying from any perspective.[9] Western assumptions about the nature of human society (and thus of literature) when contextualizing a tribal story or ritual must necessarily leave certain elements unclear. If the battle between Summer Spirit and Winter Spirit is about the triumph of warmth, generosity, and kindness over coldness, miserliness, and cruelty, supremacy of the good over the bad, why does the hero grant his antagonist rights over the village and Kochinnenako for half of each year?

The contexts of Anglo-European and Keres Indian life differ so greatly in virtually every assumption about the nature of reality, society, ethics, female roles, and the sacred importance of seasonal change that simply telling a Keres tale within an Anglo-European narrative context creates a dizzying series of false impressions and unanswerable (perhaps even unposable) questions.

For instance, marriage among traditional Keres is not particularly related to marriage among Anglo-European Americans. As I explain in greater detail in a later essay, paternity is not an issue among traditional Keres people; a child belongs to its mother's clan, not in the sense that she or he is owned by the clan, but in the sense that she or he belongs within it. Another basic difference is the attitude toward conflict; the Keres can best be described as a conflict-phobic people, while Euro-American culture is conflict-centered. So while the orderly and proper annual transference of power from Winter to Summer people through the agency of the Keres central female figure is the major theme of the narrative from a Keres perspective, the triumph of good over evil becomes its major theme when it is retold by a white man.

Essentially what happens is that Summer (a mask dancer dressed as   45
Miochin) asks Kochinnenako permission, in a ritual manner, to enter the village. She (who is either a mask dancer dressed as Yellow Woman, or a Yellow Corn Irriaku) follows a ritual order of responses and actions that enable Summer to enter. The narrative specifies the acts she must perform, the words she must say, and those that are prohibited, such as the command that she not "throw any of the husks out of the door." This command establishes both the identity of Miochin and constitutes his declaration of his ritual intention and his ritual relationship to Kochinnenako.

Agency is Kochinnenako's ritual role here; it is through her ritual agency that the orderly, harmonious transfer of primacy between the Summer and Winter people is accomplished. This transfer takes place at the time of the year that Winter goes north and Summer comes to the pueblo from the south, the time when the sun moves north along the line it makes with the edge of the sun's house as ascertained by the hocheni calendar keeper who determines the proper solar and astronomical times for various ceremonies. Thus, in the proper time, Kochinnenako empowers Summer to enter the village. Kochinnenako's careful observance of the ritual requirements together with the proper conduct of her sisters, her mother, the priests (symbolized by the title Hutchamun Kiuk, whom Gunn identifies as the ruler and Yellow Woman's father, though he could as properly—more properly, actually—be called her mother), the animals and birds, the weather, and the people at last brings summer to the village, ending the winter and the famine that accompanies winter's end.

A feminist who is conscious of tribal thought and practice will know that the real story of Sh-ah-cock and Miochin underscores the central role that woman plays in the orderly life of the people. Reading Gunn's version, she will be aware of the vast gulf between the Lagunas and John Gunn in their understanding of the role of women in a traditional gynecentric society such as that of the western Keres. Knowing that the central role of woman is harmonizing spiritual relationships between the people and the rest of the universe by empowering ritual activities, she will be able to read the story for its western colonial content, aware that Gunn's version reveals more about American consciousness when it meets tribal thought than it reveals about the tribe. When the story is analyzed within the context to which it rightly belongs, its feminist content becomes clear, as do the various purposes to which industrialized patriarchal people can put a tribal story.

If she is familiar with the ritual color code of this particular group of Native Americans, a feminist will know that white is the color of Shipap, the place where the four rivers of life come together and where our Mother Iyatiku lives. Thus she will know that it is appropriate that the Spirit of Woman's Power/Being (Yellow Woman) be "married" (that is, ritually connected in energy-transferring gestalts) first with Winter who is the power signified by the color white, which informs clouds, the Mountain Tse-pina, Shipap, originating Power, Koshare, the north and northwest, and that half of the year, and then with Summer, whose color powers are yellow and green, which inform Kurena, sunrise, the growing and ripening time of Mother Earth, and whose direction is south and southeast and that portion of the year.

A feminist will know that the story is about how the Mother Corn Iyatiku's "daughter," that is, her essence in one of its aspects, comes to live as Remembering Prayer Sticks' daughter first with the Winter people and then with the Summer people, and so on.

The net effect of Gunn's rendition of the story is the unhappy wedding   50 of the woman-centered tradition of the western Keres to patriarchal Anglo-European tradition and thus the dislocation of the central position of Keres women by their assumption under the rule of the men. When one understands that the hocheni is the person who tells the time and prays for all the people, even the white people, and that the Hutchamun Kiuk is the ruler only in the sense that the Constitution of the United States is the ruler of the citizens and government of the United States, then the Keres organization of women, men, spirit folk, equinoxes, seasons, and clouds into a balanced and integral dynamic will be seen reflected in the narrative. Knowing this, a feminist will also be able to see how the interpolations of patriarchal thinking distort all the relationships in the story and, by extension, how such impositions of patriarchy on gynocracy disorder harmonious social and spiritual relationships.

A careful feminist-tribal analysis of Gunn's rendition of a story that would be better titled "The Transfer of Ianyi (ritual power, sacred power) from Winter to Summer" will provide a tribally conscious feminist with an interesting example of how colonization works, however consciously or unconsciously, to misinform both the colonized and the colonizer. She will be able to note the process by which the victim of the translation process, the Keres woman who reads the tale, is misinformed because she reads Gunn's book. Even though she knows that something odd is happening in the tale, she is not likely to apply sophisticated feminist analysis to the rendition; in the absence of real knowledge of the colonizing process of story-changing, she is all too likely to find bits of the Gunn tale sticking in her mind and subtly altering her perception of herself, her role in her society, and her relationship to the larger world.

The hazard to male Keres readers is, of course, equally great. They are likely to imagine that the proper relationship of women to men is subservience. And it is because of such a shockingly untraditional modern interpretation, brought on as much by reading Gunn as by other, perhaps more obvious societal mechanisms, that the relationships between men and women are so severely disordered at Laguna that wife-abuse, rape, and battery of women there has reached frightening levels in recent years.

POLITICAL IMPLICATIONS OF NARRATIVE STRUCTURE

The changes Gunn has made in the narrative are not only changes in content; they are structural as well. One useful social function of traditional tribal literature is its tendency to distribute value evenly among various elements, providing a model or pattern for egalitarian structuring of society as well as literature. However, egalitarian structures in either literature or society are not easily "read" by hierarchically inclined westerners.

Still, the tendency to equal distribution of value among all elements in a field, whether the field is social, spiritual, or aesthetic (and the distinction is moot when tribal materials are under discussion), is an integral part of tribal consciousness and is reflected in tribal social and aesthetic systems all over the Americas. In this structural framework, no single element is foregrounded, leaving the others to supply "background." Thus, properly speaking, there are no heroes, no villains, no chorus, no setting (in the sense of inert ground against which dramas are played out). There are no minor characters, and foreground slips along from one focal point to another until all the pertinent elements in the ritual conversation have had their say.

In tribal literature, the timing of the foregrounding of various elements is dependent on the purpose the narrative is intended to serve. Tribal art functions something like a forest in which all elements coexist, where each   55 is integral to the being of the others. Depending on the season, the interplay of various life forms, the state of the overall biosphere and psychosphere, and the woman's reason for being there, certain plants will leap into focus on certain occasions. For example, when tribal women on the eastern seaboard went out to gather sassafras, what they noticed, what stood out sharply in their attention, were the sassafras plants. But when they went out to get maple sugar, maples became foregrounded. But the foregrounding of sassafras or maple in no way lessens the value of the other plants or other features of the forest. When a woman goes after maple syrup, she is aware of the other plant forms that are also present.

In the same way, a story that is intended to convey the importance of the Grandmother Spirits will focus on grandmothers in their interaction with grandchildren and will convey little information about uncles. Traditional tales will make a number of points, and a number of elements will be present, all of which will bear some relationship to the subject of the story. Within the time the storyteller has allotted to the story, and depending on the interests and needs of her audience at the time of the storytelling, each of these elements will receive its proper due.

Traditional American Indian stories work dynamically among clusters of loosely interconnected circles. The focus of the action shifts from one character to another as the story unfolds. There is no "point of view" as the term is generally understood, unless the action itself, the story's purpose, can be termed "point of view." But as the old tales are translated and rendered in English, the western notion of proper fictional form takes over the tribal narrative. Soon there appear to be heroes, point of view, conflict, crisis, and resolution, and as western tastes in story crafting are imposed on the narrative structure of the ritual story, the result is a western story with Indian characters. Mournfully, the new form often becomes confused with the archaic form by the very people whose tradition has been re-formed.

The story Gunn calls "Sh-ah-cock and Mi-o-chin or The Battle of the Seasons" might be better termed "How Kochinnenako Balanced the World," though even then the title would be misleading to American readers, for they would see Kochinnenako as the heroine, the foreground of the story. They would see her as the central figure of the action, and of course that would be wrong. There is no central figure in the tale, though there is a central point. The point is concerned with the proper process of a shift in focus, not the resolution of a conflict. Kochinnenako's part in the process is agency, not heroics; even in Gunn's version, she does nothing heroic. A situation presents itself in the proper time, and Yellow Woman acts in accordance with the dictates of timing, using proper ritual as her mode. But the people cannot go from Winter into Summer without conscious acceptance of Miochin, and Yellow Woman's invitation to him, an acceptance that is encouraged and supported by all involved, constitutes a tribal act.

The "battle" between Summer and Winter is an accurate description of seasonal change in central New Mexico during the spring. This comes through in the Gunn rendition, but because the story is focused on conflict rather than on balance, the meteorological facts and their intrinsic relationship to human ritual are obscured. Only a non-Indian mind, accustomed to interpreting events in terms of battle, struggle, and conflict, would assume that the process of transfer had to occur through a battle replete with protagonist, antagonist, a cast of thousands, and a pretty girl as the prize. For who but an industrialized patriarch would think that winter can be vanquished? Winter and Summer enjoy a relationship based on complementarity, mutuality, and this is the moral significance of the tale.

Tribal Narratives and Women's Lives

Reading American Indian traditional stories and songs is not an easy   60
task. Adequate comprehension requires that the reader be aware that Indians never think like whites and that any typeset version of traditional materials is distorting.

In many ways, literary conventions, as well as the conventions of literacy, militate against an understanding of traditional tribal materials. Western technological-industrialized minds cannot adequately interpret tribal materials because they are generally trained to perceive their entire world in ways that are alien to tribal understandings.

This problem is not exclusive to tribal literature. It is one that all ethnic writers who write out of a tribal or folk tradition face, and one that is also shared by women writers, who, after all, inhabit a separate folk tradition. Much of women's culture bears marked resemblance to tribal culture. The perceptual modes that women, even those of us who are literate, industrialized, and reared within masculinist academic traditions, habitually engage in more closely resemble inclusive-field perception than excluding foreground-background perceptions.

Women's traditional occupations, their arts and crafts, and their literature and philosophies are more often accretive than linear, more achronological than chronological, and more dependent on harmonious relationships of all elements within a field of perception than western culture in general is thought to be. Indeed, the patchwork quilt is the best material example I can think of to describe the plot and process of a traditional tribal narrative, and quilting is a non-Indian woman's art, one that Indian women have taken to avidly and that they display in their ceremonies, rituals, and social gatherings as well as in their homes.

It is the nature of woman's existence to be and to create background. This fact, viewed with unhappiness by many feminists, is of ultimate importance in a tribal context. Certainly no art object is bereft of background. Certainly the contents and tone of one's background will largely determine the direction and meaning of one's life and, therefore, the meaning and effect of one's performance in any given sphere of activity.

Westerners have for a long time discounted the importance of background. The earth herself, which is our most inclusive background, is dealt with summarily as a source of food, metals, water and profit, while the fact that she is the fundamental agent of all planetary life is blithely ignored. Similarly, women's activities—cooking, planting, harvesting, preservation, storage, homebuilding, decorating, maintaining, doctoring, nursing, soothing, and healing, along with the bearing, nurturing, and rearing of children—are devalued as blithely. An antibackground bias is bound to have social costs that have so far remained unexplored, but elite attitudes toward workers, nonwhite races, and women are all part of the price we pay for overvaluing the foreground.

In the western mind, shadows highlight the foreground. In contrast, in the tribal view the mutual relationships among shadows and light in all their varying degrees of intensity create a living web of definition and depth, and significance arises from their interplay. Traditional and contemporary tribal arts and crafts testify powerfully to the importance of balance among all elements in tribal perception, aesthetics, and social systems.

Traditional peoples perceive their world in a unified-field fashion that is very different from the single-focus perception that generally characterizes western masculinist, monotheistic modes of perception. Because of this, tribal cultures are consistently misperceived and misrepresented by nontribal folklorists, ethnographers, artists, writers, and social workers. A number of scholars have recently addressed this issue, but they have had little success because the demands of type and of analysis are, after all, linear and fixed, while the requirements of tribal literatures are accretive and fluid. The one is unidimensional, monolithic, excluding, and chronological while the other is multidimensional, achronological, and including.

How one teaches or writes about the one perspective in terms of the other is problematic. This essay itself is a pale representation of a tribal understanding of the Kochinnenako tale. I am acutely aware that much of what I have said is likely to be understood in ways I did not intend, and I am also aware of how much I did not say that probably needed to be said if the real story of the transfer of responsibility from one segment of the tribe to the other is to be made clear.

In the end, the tale I have analyzed is not about Kochinnenako or Shah-cock and Miochin. It is about the change of seasons and it is about the centrality of woman as agent and empowerer of that change. It is about how a people engage themselves as a people within the spiritual cosmos and in an ordered and proper way that bestows the dignity of each upon all with careful respect, folkish humor, and ceremonial delight. It is about how everyone is part of the background that shapes the meaning and value of each person's life. It is about propriety, mutuality, and the dynamics of socioenvironmental change.

NOTES

1. John M. Gunn, *Schat Chen: History, Traditions and Narratives of the Queres Indians of Laguna and Acoma* (Albuquerque, N. Mex.: Albright and Anderson, 1917; reprint, New York: AMS, 1977). Gunn, my mother's uncle, lived among the Lagunas all his adult life. He spoke Laguna (Keres) and gathered information in somewhat informal ways while sitting in the sun visiting with older people. He married Meta Atseye, my great-grandmother, years after her husband (John Gunn's brother) died and may have taken much of his information from her stories or explanations of Laguna ceremonial events. She had a way of "translating" terms and concepts from Keres into English and from a Laguna conceptual framework into an American one, as she understood it. For example, she used to refer to the Navajo people as "gypsies," probably because they traveled in covered wagons and the women wear long, full skirts and head scarves and both men and women wear a great deal of jewelry.

2. In a system where all persons in power are called Mother Chief and where the supreme deity is female, and social organization is matrilocal, matrifocal, and matrilineal, gynarchy is happening. However, it does not imply domination of men by women as patriarchy implies domination by ruling class males of all aspects of a society.

3. His use of the term may reflect the use by his informants, who were often educated in Carlisle or Menaul Indian schools, in their attempt to find an equivalent term that Gunn could understand to signify the deep respect and reverence accorded the hocheni tyi'a'muni. Or he might have selected the term because he was writing a book for an anonymous non-Keres audience, which included himself. Since he spoke Laguna Keres, I think he was doing the translations himself, and his renderings of words (and contexts) was likely influenced by the way Laguna themselves rendered local terms into English. I doubt, however, that he was conscious of the extent to which his renderings reflected European traditions and simultaneously distorted Laguna-Acoma ones.

   Gunn was deeply aware of the importance and intelligence of the Keresan tradition, but he was also unable to grant it independent existence. His major impulse was to link the western Keres with the Sumerians, to in some strange way demonstrate the justice of his assessment of their intelligence. An unpublished manuscript in my possession written by John Gunn after *Schat Chen* is devoted to his researches and speculations into this area.

4. Gunn, *Schat Chen*, pp. 217–222.

5. Franz Boas, *Keresan Texts*, Publications of the American Ethnological Society, vol. 8, pt. 1 (New York: American Ethnological Society, 1928), writes, "The second and the fourth of the shiwana appear in the tale of summer and winter . . . Summer wears a shirt of buckskin with squash ornaments, shoes like moss to which parrot feathers are

tied. His face is painted with red mica and flowers are tied on to it . . . Winter wears a shirt of icicles and his shoes are like ice. His shirt is shiny and to its end are tied turkey feathers and eagle feathers" (p. 284).

6. Boas, *Keresan Texts,* p. 288. Boas says he made the same mistake at first, having misheard the word they used.

7. When my sister Carol Lee Sanchez spoke to her university Women's Studies class about the position of centrality women hold in our Keres tradition, one young woman, a self-identified radical feminist, was outraged. She insisted that Sanchez and other Laguna women had been brainwashed into believing that we had power over our lives. After all, she knew that no woman anywhere has ever had that kind of power; her feminist studies had made that fact quite plain to her. The kind of cultural chauvinism that has been promulgated by well-intentioned but culturally entranced feminists can lead to serious misunderstandings such as this and in the process become a new racism based on what becomes the feminist canon. Not that feminists can be faulted entirely on this—they are, after all, reflecting the research and interpretation done in a patriarchal context, by male-biased researchers and scholars, most of whom would avidly support the young radical feminist's strenuous position. It's too bad, though, that feminists fall into the patriarchal trap!

8. For a detailed exposition of what this dynamic consists of, see Adrienne Rich, "Compulsory Heterosexuality and Lesbian Existence," *Signs: Journal of Women in Culture and Society,* vol. 5, no. 4 (Summer 1980). Reprinted in 1982 as a pamphlet with an updated foreword, Antelope Publications, 1612 St. Paul, Denver, CO 80206.

9. Elaine Jahner, a specialist in Lakota language and oral literature, has suggested that the western obsession with western plot in narrative structure led early informant George Sword to construct narratives in the western fashion and tell them as Lakota traditional stories. Research has shown that Sword's stories are not recognized as Lakota traditional stories by Lakotas themselves; but the tribal narratives that are so recognized are loosely structured and do not exhibit the reliance on central theme or character that is so dear to the hearts of western collectors. As time has gone by, the Sword stories have become a sort of model for later Lakota storytellers who, out of a desire to convey the tribal tales to western collectors have changed the old structures to ones more pleasing to American and European ears. Personal conversations with Elaine Jahner.

Education in western schools, exposure to mass media, and the need to function in a white-dominated world have subtly but perhaps permanently altered the narrative structures of the old tales and, with them, the tribal conceptual modes of tribal people. The shift has been away from associative, synchronistic, event-centered narrative and thought to a linear, foreground-centered one. Concurrently, tribal social organization and interpersonal relations have taken a turn toward authoritarian, patriarchal, linear, and misogynist modes—hence the rise of violence against women, an unthinkable event in older, more circular, and tribal times.

Issues for Discussion

1. What "official" interpretations of the Kochinnenako story does Allen identify? How would you describe the explanation pattern that each of these interpretations imposes on the story?

2. What social or cultural interests does each of these common interpretations serve, according to Allen? What values or beliefs underlie these different cultural interests?

3. In what respects does Allen's "Feminist-Tribal Interpretation" differ from the dominant readings of the story she discusses earlier? How would you describe the explanation pattern she uses to guide her own interpretation? How does her interpretation differ from the interpretations she critiques? What evidence does she provide to demonstrate a better "fit" for her interpretation?

Hearing Voices: The Archaeology of Academic Texts

The collaborative, dialogical nature of academic analysis gives academic writing one of its most distinctive features: academic texts almost always contain a layering of several competing stories, theories, perspectives, or voices. In contrast to straightforward personal stories told from a single point of view, academic analyses and interpretations are multivocal: they contain a number of voices and relate a number of different—and sometimes even contradictory—stories. In "Kochinnenako in Academe" Paula Gunn Allen underscores the different perspectives she discusses by devoting an entire subsection of her essay to each. Before she gets around to her own "feminist-tribal" interpretation of the Corn Mother story, she relates two competing versions—one originally told by the white male anthropologist John Gunn; the other a composite of typical "feminist" interpretations. M. G. Lord does much the same thing, although she's not nearly as obvious or methodical as Allen. Before she presents her own "earth goddess" theory, she introduces several "common" explanations for Barbie's popularity, among them the idea that Barbie reinforces cultural stereotypes of beauty, Freud's theory of "*das Unheimliche,*" and the psychological concept of "transitional objects." A reader who is used to the relatively straightforward approach of personal storytelling might have trouble sorting out which of these explanation patterns Lord endorses; in fact, inexperienced readers often assume that every idea expressed in a piece of writing "belongs to" the writer. But more savvy readers who understand the multivocal nature of academic writing will be on the lookout for the "official stories" that Lord will be talking back to in her analysis. They know that academic writers usually begin by "entering the dialogue of ideas" on their subject, and so they expect Lord to discuss one or more theories or explanation patterns that she may only partially agree with—or totally reject—before she presents her own analysis. Like archaeologists, seasoned readers approach academic texts expecting to discover multiple layers of stories—different versions, interpretations, or explanations—that must be identified and held in mind in order to appreciate the writer's own analysis and point of view.

To help readers cope with the multilayered nature of their texts, academic writers usually pay special attention to the way they "attribute" the ideas, theories, or explanations they discuss. Attributions clarify whose perspective is whose; they tell us whose ideas or explanation patterns are being presented at a particular moment. Often they involve little more than simple formulaic phrases like "According to Freud . . ." or "Freud claims that . . ."; other times, however, attributive references are woven throughout an entire paragraph. Here's the way Lord introduces the "transitional object" explanation pattern:

> I was eight when I got my Barbies, well past the age of appropriating them as what psychoanalyst D. W. Winnicott termed "transitional objects." But Mattel's research shows that today kids get Barbies earlier, usually about age three. Thus, Barbies, in the psyches of toddlers, can function as transitional objects—which warrants a closer look at Winnicott's concept.
>
> During the months following birth, a baby doesn't grasp that its mother is separate from itself. Embodied by her ever-nurturing breast, the mother is an extension of the child. . . . (paragraphs 24–25)

In this brief passage Lord makes sure her reader understands that the theory she's presenting belongs to D. W. Winnicott and does not necessarily represent her point of view. Her careful attribution allows her to describe a theory that is commonly used to explain children's attachment to their toys, but it also makes it clear that this is *not* her theory. By repeatedly attributing the "transitional object" theory to Winnicott, Lord informs us that the explanation pattern she is about to describe in detail ("During the months following birth. . .") is only one way to explain her subject, and not necessarily her way. Attributions help readers sort out whose story is being told at any particular moment in a piece of critical writing. Use them well and your reader will have little trouble figuring out whose point of view you're discussing; neglect them and your reader will assume that all the ideas mentioned in your writing belong to you and you alone.

The multivoiced, multilayered complexity of critical discourse shows up most clearly when you summarize a piece of critical analysis or interpretation. Take a look at the following section from a one-page summary of Kohl's analysis of the Rosa Parks story:

The traditional version of the story of Rosa Parks, according to Kohl, presents her as a simple, hard-working woman who never planned to get involved with protests or boycotts when she got on that Montgomery bus. *According to this version of the story,* which Kohl calls "Rosa Was

Tired," Parks was "Just a quiet, conservative, churchgoing woman with a nice family and a decent job." *In this version,* Parks was just minding her own business when she got on the bus that day and probably wouldn't have protested anything—or become a hero—if she hadn't been so tired and the day hadn't been so hot.

Kohl argues that this version of Parks's story is wrong because it leaves out the truth about who Parks really was. *Kohl's research shows* that Parks was an activist long before she got on the bus on December 1, 1955. She was one of the first women in Montgomery to join the . . .

The writer of this summary works hard to identify the multiple voices contained in Kohl's original essay. Phrases like "The traditional version of the story of Rosa Parks" tell us that we're dealing with the official story of Rosa Parks's life—the version Kohl constructed from a number of elementary school textbooks—and not Kohl's revised version. Every time a specific version of the story is mentioned, it is identified with an attributive phrase. And it's also worth noting how conscientiously the writer of this summary reminds us that even the official version of Parks's story is told "according to Kohl"—that it's the result of Kohl's own interpretation of what the schoolbooks say and thus is itself open to question and debate. After all, who's to say how accurately Kohl did his homework? It's possible that if you read all of the sources he covered in his research, you might come up with a different interpretation—not only of what happened to Rosa Parks back in 1955 but of how her story is commonly retold and interpreted in American schools. Becoming an expert reader of academic discourse means learning to identify the multiple stories and multiple voices in any piece of academic writing—but it also means recognizing that ideas, theories, and explanations are inseparable from the perspective and the interests of the person who puts them down on paper.

OPTIONAL ACTIVITIES

Exploring the Multiple Voices of Academic Analysis

1. Return to the first few pages of Herbert Kohl's analysis of the Rosa Parks legend (p. 378), M. G. Lord's interpretation of Barbie's popularity (p. 348), and Emily Martin's critique of how science has portrayed the "romance" of sexual reproduction (p. 417) and identify all of the different voices, stories, or explanation patterns they contain. Also note any phrases that serve as attributions and help guide the reader through these multivoiced academic texts.

2. Try your own hand at writing a brief, one- to two-page summary of Kohl, Lord, or Martin's stories, paying special attention to the way you identify the various theories, versions, or perspectives they contain.

Thinking in Theory

The official stories that academic thinkers use to explain or interpret things are known as *theories.* In economics there's the theory of supply and demand; in physics there's the theory of thermodynamics; in political science there's the notion of the "social contract"; in psychology there are theories about transitional objects, childhood trauma, and repressed memory. Every academic discipline contains scores of theories that offer academic thinkers powerful explanation patterns they can use to explore and answer the questions they raise. The unusual explanatory power of academic theories stems, in part, from their high level of generality: the story frame implied in the economic theory of "supply and demand," for example, can be used to analyze almost any market transaction—from the exchange of baseball cards among kids on a playground to the sale of stocks and bonds on Wall Street. The theory of thermodynamics can be used to interpret the responses of billiard balls in a pool hall just as successfully as it does the motion of planets in the solar system. Academic theories acquire this high level of generality because they are tested—systematically, repeatedly, and publicly—in a variety of specific situations. You might form a personal explanation pattern like "teachers avoid contact with you when they're disappointed" on the basis of a couple of observations, but the explanation pattern contained in an academic theory has usually survived repeated tests and trials: a good deal of a scholar's time is devoted to testing how well the theories in her discipline "fit" the world as she sees it.

Learning how to apply theoretical explanation patterns is also the most important—and often the most challenging—part of being a college student. Much of the thinking you're asked to do in college involves the application of theoretical story frames to specific cases. Every time you're asked to explain an academic concept, you're really being asked to summarize the explanation pattern it contains and to demonstrate how this pattern "fits" a particular situation—an exemplary case offered to clarify how the concept actually works. In an economics course you might explain the concept of "supply and demand" along the following lines:

> *Explanation Pattern Summary* According to the theory of supply and demand, prices are determined by market forces: when the supply of goods is great, prices fall; when demand for goods is great, prices rise.

Sample Case   If, for example, a shortage of silicon causes the supply of microchips available for sale to decline, computer users should expect their price to rise according to the theory of supply and demand. When, however, silicon supplies are restored, the price of microchips should return to its original level.

Theoretical thinking and writing usually conforms to this simple pattern: first, the general outline of a theory is described; then it's followed by one or more clarifying examples, demonstrating the "fit" between theory and practical experience.

For a closer look at how theoretical explanation works in academic writing, let's examine a passage from a popular social psychology textbook. In the following selection from *The Social Animal,* Elliot Aronson presents four different theories of prejudice—theories meant to explain why particular individuals harbor biased attitudes and opinions about others. Take notes as you read and try to identify the explanation patterns that underlie these theories of prejudiced behavior. A professor of psychology at the University of California, Santa Cruz, Aronson has won national awards for his teaching, writing, and research.

Before Reading

Freewrite about what you think causes prejudice.

The Causes of Prejudice
Elliot Aronson

ECONOMIC AND POLITICAL COMPETITION

Prejudice can be considered to be the result of economic and political forces. According to this view, given that resources are limited, the dominant group might attempt to exploit or derogate a minority group in order to gain some material advantage. Prejudiced attitudes tend to increase when times are tense and there is conflict over mutually exclusive goals. This is true whether the goals are economic, political, or ideological. Thus, prejudice has existed between Anglo and Mexican American migrant workers as a function of a limited number of jobs, between Arabs and Israelis over disputed territory, and between Northerners and Southerners over the abolition of slavery. The economic advantages of discrimination are all too clear when one looks at the success certain craft unions have had, over the years, in denying membership to women and members of ethnic minorities, thus keeping them out of the relatively high-paying occupations the unions control. For example, the decade between the mid-1950s and the mid-1960s was one of great political and legal advancement for the civil rights movement. Yet in 1966 only 2.7 percent of union-controlled apprenticeships were filled with black workers—an increase of only 1 percent over the preceding ten years. Moreover, in the mid-1960s, the U.S. Department of Labor surveyed four major cities in search of minority-group members serving as apprentices among union plumbers, steamfitters, sheetmetal workers, stone masons, lathers, painters, glaziers, and operating engineers. In the four cities, they failed to find a single African American thus employed. Clearly, prejudice pays off for some people.[1] While the 1970s and 1980s have produced significant changes in many of these statistics, they also show that the situation remains far from equitable for minority groups.

Discrimination, prejudice, and negative stereotyping increase sharply as competition for scarce jobs increases. In one of his classic early studies of prejudice in a small industrial town, John Dollard documented the fact that, although there was initially no discernible prejudice against Germans in the town, it came about as jobs became scarce:

> Local whites largely drawn from the surrounding farms manifested considerable direct aggression toward the newcomers. Scornful and derogatory opinions were expressed about these Germans, and the native whites had a satisfying sense of superiority toward them. . . . The chief element in the permission to be aggressive against the Germans was rivalry for jobs and status in the local woodenware plants. The native whites felt definitely crowded for their jobs by the entering German groups and in case of bad times had a chance to blame the Germans who by their presence provided more competitors for the scarcer jobs. There seemed to be no traditional pattern of prejudice against Germans unless the skeletal suspicion against all outgroupers (always present) can be invoked in its place.[2]

Similarly, the prejudice, violence, and negative stereotyping directed against Chinese immigrants in the United States fluctuated wildly throughout the nineteenth century—spurred largely by changes in economic competition. For example, when the Chinese were attempting to mine gold in California, they were described as "depraved and vicious . . . gross gluttons . . . bloodthirsty and inhuman."[3] However, just a decade later, when they were willing to accept dangerous and arduous work building the transcontinental railroad—work that Caucasian Americans were unwilling to undertake— they were generally regarded as sober, industrious, and law-abiding. Indeed, Charles Crocker, one of the western railroad tycoons, wrote: "They are equal to the best white men. . . . They are very trusty, very intelligent and they live up to their contracts."[4] After the completion of the railroad, however, jobs became more scarce; moreover, when the Civil War ended, there was an influx of former soldiers into an already tight job market. This was immediately followed by a dramatic increase in negative attitudes toward the Chinese: The stereotype changed to "criminal," "conniving," "crafty," and "stupid."

These data suggest that competition and conflict breed prejudice. Moreover, this phenomenon transcends mere historical significance—it seems to have enduring psychological effects as well. In a survey conducted in the 1970s, most antiblack prejudice was found in groups that were just one rung above the blacks socioeconomically. And as we might expect, this tendency was most pronounced in situations in which whites and blacks were in close competition for jobs.[5] At the same time, there is some ambiguity in interpreting the data, because in some instances the variables of competition are intertwined with such variables as educational level and family background.

In order to determine whether competition causes prejudice in and of itself, an experiment is needed. But how can we proceed? Well, if conflict and competition lead to prejudice, it should be possible to produce prejudice in the laboratory. This can be done by the simple device of (1) randomly assigning people of differing backgrounds to one of two groups, (2) making those two groups distinguishable in some arbitrary way, (3) putting those groups into a situation in which they are in competition with each other, and (4) looking for evidence of prejudice. Such an experiment was conducted by Muzafer Sherif and his colleagues[6] in the natural environment of a Boy Scout camp. The subjects were normal, well-adjusted, twelve-year-old boys who were randomly assigned to one of two groups, the *Eagles* and the *Rattlers*. Within each group, the youngsters were taught to cooperate. This was largely done through arranging activities that made each group highly intradependent. For example, within each group, individuals cooperated in building a diving board for the swimming facility, preparing group meals, building a rope bridge, and so on.

After a strong feeling of cohesiveness developed within each group, the stage was set for conflict. The researchers arranged this by setting up a series of competitive activities in which the two groups were pitted against each other in such games as football, baseball, and tug-of-war. In order to increase the tension, prizes were awarded to the winning team. This resulted in some hostility and ill will during the games. In addition, the investigators devised rather diabolical devices for putting the groups into situations specifically designed to promote conflict. In one such situation, a camp party was arranged. The investigators set it up so that the *Eagles* were allowed to arrive a good deal earlier than the *Rattlers*. In addition, the refreshments consisted of two vastly different kinds of food: About half the food was fresh, appealing, and appetiz-

5

ing; the other half was squashed, ugly, and unappetizing. Perhaps because of the general competitiveness that already existed, the early arrivers confiscated most of the appealing refreshments, leaving only the less interesting, less appetizing, squashed, and damaged food for their adversaries. When the *Rattlers* finally arrived and saw how they had been taken advantage of, they were understandably annoyed—so annoyed they began to call the exploitive group rather uncomplimentary names. Because the *Eagles* believed they deserved what they got (first come, first served), they resented this treatment and responded in kind. Name calling escalated into food throwing, and within a very short time a full-scale riot was in progress.

Following this incident, competitive games were eliminated and a great deal of social contact was initiated. Once hostility had been aroused, however, simply eliminating the competition did not eliminate the hostility. Indeed, hostility continued to escalate, even when the two groups were engaged in such benign activities as sitting around watching movies. Eventually, the investigators succeeded in reducing the hostility.

The "Scapegoat" Theory of Prejudice

In the preceding chapter, I made the point that aggression is caused, in part, by frustration and such other unpleasant or aversive situations as pain or boredom. In that chapter, we saw there is a strong tendency for a frustrated individual to lash out at the cause of his or her frustration. Frequently, however, the cause of a person's frustration is either too big or too vague for direct retaliation. For example, if a six-year-old boy is humiliated by his teacher, how can he fight back? The teacher has too much power. But this frustration may increase the probability of his aggressing against a less-powerful bystander—even if the bystander had nothing to do with his pain. By the same token, if there is mass unemployment, who is the frustrated, unemployed worker going to strike out against—the economic system? The system is much too big and much too vague. It would be more convenient if the unemployed worker could find something or someone less vague and more concrete to blame. The president? He's concrete, all right, but also much too powerful to strike at with impunity.

The ancient Hebrews had a custom that is noteworthy in this context. During the days of atonement, a priest placed his hands on the head of a goat while reciting the sins of the people. This symbolically transferred the sin and evil from the people to the goat. The goat was then allowed to escape into the wilderness, thus cleansing the community of sin. The animal was called a scapegoat. In modern times the term *scapegoat* has been used to describe a relatively powerless innocent who is made to take the blame for something that is not his or her fault. Unfortunately, the individual is not allowed to escape into the wilderness but is usually subjected to cruelty or even death. Thus, if people are unemployed, or if inflation has depleted their savings, they can't very easily beat up on the economic system—but they can find a scapegoat. In Nazi Germany, it was the Jews; in nineteenth-century California, it was Chinese immigrants; in the rural South, it was black people. Some years ago, Carl Hovland and Robert Sears[7] found that, in the period between 1882 and 1930, they could predict the number of lynchings in the South in a given year from a knowledge of the price of cotton during that year. As the price of cotton dropped, the number of lynchings increased. In short, as people experienced an economic depression, they probably experienced a great many frustrations. The frustrations apparently resulted in an increase in lynchings and other crimes of violence.

Otto Klineberg,[8] a social psychologist with a special interest in the cross-cultural aspects of prejudice, describes a unique scapegoating situation in Japan. The Burakumin are a group of two million outcasts, scattered throughout Japan. Although there are no inherited racial or physical differences between the Burakumin and other Japanese, they are considered unclean and fit only for certain undesirable occupations. As you might imagine, the Burakumin usually live in poor, slum areas. Their IQ scores were, on average, some sixteen points lower than that of other Japanese. Burakumin children were absent from school more often and their delinquency rate was three times higher than other Japanese children. According to Klineberg, it was considered taboo for a member of the Burakumin to marry outside of his or her group. They are an invisible race—an outgroup defined more by social class than by any physical characteristics. They can only be identified because of their distinctive speech pattern (which has developed from years of nonassociation with other Japanese) and their identity papers. Although their historical origins are unclear, they probably occupied the lower rungs of the socioeconomic ladder until an economic depression led to their complet expulsion from Japanese society. Now the Japanese consider the Burakumin to be "innately inferior," thus justifying further scapegoating and discrimination.

It is difficult to understand how the lynching of blacks or the mistreatment of the Burakumin could be due only to economic competition. There is a great deal of emotion in these actions that suggests the presence of deeper psychological factors in addition to economics. Similarly, the zeal with which Nazis carried out their attempt to erase all members of the Jewish ethnic group (regardless of economic status) strongly suggests that the phenomenon was not exclusively economic or political, but was (at least in part) psychological.[9] Firmer evidence for the existence of psychological processes comes from a well-controlled experiment by Neal Miller and Richard Bugelski.[10] Individuals were asked to state their feelings about various minority groups. Some of the subjects were then frustrated by being deprived of an opportunity to attend a film and were given an arduous and difficult series of tests instead.

10

They were then asked to restate their feelings about the minority groups. These subjects showed some evidence of increased prejudicial responses following the frustrating experience. A control group that did not go through the frustrating experience did not undergo any change in prejudice.

Additional research has helped to pin down the phenomenon even more precisely. In one experiment,[11] white students were instructed to administer a series of electric shocks to another student as part of a learning experiment. The subjects had the prerogative to adjust the intensity of the shocks. In actuality, the learner was an accomplice of the experimenter and (of course) was not really connected to the apparatus. There were four conditions: The accomplice was either black or white; he was trained to be either friendly or insulting to the subject. When he was friendly, the subjects administered slightly less intense shocks to the black student; when he insulted them, they administered far more intense shocks to the black student than to the white student. In another experiment,[12] college students were subjected to a great deal of frustration. Some of these students were highly anti-Semitic; others were not. The subjects were then asked to write stories based on pictures they were shown. For some subjects, the characters in these pictures were assigned Jewish names; for others, they were not. There were two major findings: (1) After being frustrated, anti-Semitic subjects wrote stories that directed more aggression toward the Jewish characters than did people who were not anti-Semitic; and (2) there was no difference between the anti-Semitic students and the others when the characters they were writing about were not identified as Jewish. In short, frustration or anger leads to a specific aggression—aggression against an outgroup member.

The laboratory experiments help to clarify factors that seem to exist in the real world. The general picture of scapegoating that emerges is that individuals tend to displace aggression onto groups that are disliked, that are visible, and that are relatively powerless. Moreover, the form the aggression takes depends on what is allowed or approved by the ingroup in question: In society, lynchings of blacks and pogroms against Jews were not frequent occurrences, unless they were deemed appropriate by the dominant culture or subculture.

I used the past tense in the preceding sentence because it is comforting to believe that extreme forms of scapegoating are a thing of the past. But, in the present decade, events have taken place that have caused many of us a great deal of consternation. For example, when the Soviet Union fell apart, we were momentarily encouraged as all of Eastern Europe gained its freedom. Unfortunately, in much of the region, this new freedom was accompanied by increased feelings of nationalism, which have, in turn, produced additional prejudice and hostility against outgroups. Thus, in the Balkans, for example, intense nationalism led to eruptions of hostility between Serbs and Croats, between Azerbaijanis and Uzbekistanis, and between Christians and

Muslims in Bosnia. In addition, economic hardship and frustrated expectations throughout Eastern Europe produced a sharp rise in anti-Semitism.

THE PREJUDICED PERSONALITY

As we have seen, the displacement of aggression onto scapegoats may 15 be a human tendency, but not all people do it to a like degree. We have already identified socio-economic status as a cause of prejudice. Also, we have seen that people who dislike members of a particular outgroup are more apt to displace aggression onto them than are people who do not dislike members of that outgroup. We can now carry this one step further. There is some evidence to support the notion of individual differences in a general tendency to hate. In other words, there are people who are predisposed toward being prejudiced, not solely because of immediate external influences, but because of the kind of people they are. Theodor Adorno and his associates[13] refer to these individuals as "authoritarian personalities." Basically, authoritarian personalities have the following characteristics: They tend to be rigid in their beliefs; they tend to possess "conventional" values; they are intolerant of weakness (in themselves as well as in others); they tend to be highly punitive; they are suspicious; and they are respectful of authority to an unusual degree. The instrument developed to determine authoritarianism (called the *F* scale) measures the extent to which each person agrees or disagrees with such items as these:

> Sex crimes such as rape and attacks on children deserve more than mere imprisonment; such criminals ought to be publicly whipped, or worse.

> Most people don't realize how much our lives are controlled by plots hatched in secret places.

> Obedience and respect for authority are the most important virtues children should learn.

A high degree of agreement with such items indicates authoritarianism. The major finding is that people who are high on authoritarianism do not simply dislike Jews or dislike blacks, but rather, they show a consistently high degree of prejudice against *all* minority groups.

Through an intensive clinical interview of people high and low on the *F* scale, Adorno and his colleagues have traced the development of this cluster of attitudes and values to early childhood experiences in families characterized by harsh and threatening parental discipline. Moreover, people high on the *F* scale tend to have parents who use love and its withdrawal as their major way of producing obedience. In general, authoritarian personalities, as children, tend to be very insecure and highly dependent on their parents; they fear their parents and feel unconscious hostility toward them. This combination sets the stage for the emergence of an adult with a high degree of anger, which, because of fear and insecurity, takes the form of displaced aggression against powerless groups, while the individual maintains an outward respect for authority.

It is instructive to note that, in a recent study of authoritarianism in the former Soviet Union, Sam McFarland and his colleagues[14] found that people high on the *F* scale tend to be in favor of overthrowing their newly acquired democracy and restoring the former communist regime. Ideologically, this is quite different from U.S. authoritarians who tend to be anticommunist. The common linkage, of course, is not a specific ideological belief but, rather, a kind of conventionalism and respect for authority. In other words, both U.S. and Russian authoritarians are linked by a common need to conform to the traditional values of their culture and a tendency to be suspicious of new ideas and of people who are different from themselves.

Although research on the authoritarian personality has added to our understanding of the possible dynamics of prejudice, it should be noted that the bulk of the data are correlational. That is, we know only that two variables are related—we cannot be certain what causes what. Consider, for example, the correlation between a person's score on the *F* scale and the specific socialization practices he or she was subjected to as a child. Although it is true that adults who are authoritarian and highly prejudiced had parents who tended to be harsh and to use "conditional love" as a socialization technique, it is not necessarily true that this is what caused them to develop into prejudiced people. It turns out that the parents of these people tend, themselves, to be highly prejudiced against minority groups. Accordingly, it may be that the development of prejudice in some people is due to conformity through the process of identification. That is, a child might consciously pick up beliefs about minorities from his or her parents because the child identifies with them. This is quite different from, and much simpler than, the explanation offered by Adorno and his colleagues, which is based on the child's unconscious hostility and repressed fear of his or her parents.

This is not to imply that, for some people, prejudice is not rooted in unconscious childhood conflicts. Rather, it is to suggest that many people may have learned a wide array of prejudices on Mommy's or Daddy's knee. Moreover, some people may conform to prejudices that are limited and highly specific, depending upon the norms of their subculture. Let's take a closer look at the phenomenon of prejudice as an act of conformity. 20

PREJUDICE THROUGH CONFORMITY

It is frequently observed that there is more prejudice against blacks in the South than in the North. This often manifests itself in stronger attitudes against racial integration. For example, in 1942, only 4 percent of all southerners were in favor of the desegregation of transportation facilities, while 56 percent of all northerners were in favor of it.[15] Why? Was it because of economic competition? Probably not; there is more prejudice against blacks in those southern communities in which economic competition is low than in northern communities in which economic competition is great. Are there relatively more authoritarian personalities in the South than in the North? No. Thomas Pettigrew[16] administered the *F* scale widely in the North and in the South and found the scores about equal for northerners and southerners. In addition, although there is more prejudice against blacks in the South, there is less prejudice against Jews in the South than there is in the nation as a whole; the prejudiced personality should be prejudiced against everybody—the southerner isn't.

How then do we account for the animosity toward blacks that exists in the South? It could be due to historical causes: The blacks were slaves, the Civil War was fought over the issue of slavery, and so on. This could have created the climate for greater prejudice. But what sustains this climate? One possible clue comes from the observation of some rather strange patterns of racial segregation in the South. One example, a group of coal miners in a small mining town in West Virginia, should suffice. The black miners and the white miners developed a pattern of living that consisted of total and complete integration while they were under the ground, and total and complete segregation while they were above the ground. How can we account for this inconsistency? If you truly hate someone, you want to keep away from him— why associate with him below the ground and not above the ground?

Pettigrew has suggested that the explanation for these phenomena is conformity. In this case, the white miners are simply conforming to the norms that exist in their society (above the ground!). The historical events of the South set the stage for greater prejudice against blacks, but it is conformity that keeps it going. Indeed, Pettigrew believes that, although economic competition, frustration, and personality needs account for some prejudice, the greatest proportion of prejudiced behavior is a function of slavish conformity to social norms.

How can we be certain conformity is responsible? One way is to determine the relation between a person's prejudice and that person's general pattern of conformity. For example, a study of interracial tension in South Africa[17] showed that those individuals who were most likely to conform to a great variety of social norms also showed a higher degree of prejudice against blacks. In other words, if conformists are more prejudiced, the suggestion is that prejudice may be just another thing to conform to. Another way to determine the role of conformity is to see what happens to people's prejudice when they move to a different area of the country. If conformity is a factor in prejudice, we would expect individuals to show dramatic increases in their prejudice when they move into areas in which the norm is more prejudicial, and to show dramatic decreases when they are affected by a less prejudicial norm. And that is what happens. In one study, Jeanne Watson[18] found that individuals who had recently moved to New York City and had come into direct contact with anti-Semitic people became more anti-Semitic themselves. In another study, Pettigrew found that, as southerners entered the army and came into contact with a less discriminatory set of social norms, they became less prejudiced against blacks.

The pressure to conform can be relatively overt. On the other hand, conformity to a prejudicial norm might simply be due to the unavailability of accurate evidence and a preponderance of misleading information. This can lead people to adopt negative attitudes on the basis of hearsay. Examples of this kind of stereotyping behavior abound in literature. For example, consider Christopher Marlowe's *The Jew of Malta* or William Shakespeare's *The Merchant of Venice*. Both of these works depict the Jew as a conniving, money-hungry, cringing coward. We might be tempted to conclude that Marlowe and Shakespeare had had some unfortunate experiences with unsavory Jews, which resulted in these bitter and unflattering portraits — except for one thing: The Jews had been expelled from England some three hundred years before these works were written. Thus, it would seem that the only thing with which Marlowe and Shakespeare came into contact was a lingering stereotype. Tragically, their works not only reflected the stereotype but undoubtedly contributed to it as well.

Even casual exposure to bigotry can affect our attitudes and behavior toward a group that is the victim of prejudice. For example, research has demonstrated that merely overhearing someone use a derogatory label — such as a racial or ethnic epithet — toward a given group can increase our likelihood of viewing someone from that group, or someone merely associated with that group, in a negative light. In one experiment,[19] Shari Kirkland and her co-researchers asked subjects to read a transcript of a criminal trial in which a white defendant was represented by a black attorney, whose picture was attached to the trial transcript. While reading the transcript, the subject "overhears" a brief exchange between two experimental confederates, who are posing as subjects. Some subjects hear the first confederate call the black lawyer a "nigger," while other subjects hear the confederate call him a "shyster." In both conditions, the second confederate expresses agreement with the first confederate's derogatory opinion of the black lawyer. With this conformity dynamic in place, the experimenters then asked the subject to evaluate the attorney and the defendant. An analysis of these ratings revealed that subjects who overheard the racial slur rated the black lawyer more negatively than those who overheard a derisive comment that was not related to the lawyer's race. Moreover, the white defen-

25

dant received particularly harsh verdicts and highly negative evaluations from subjects who heard the racial slur against the black attorney. This latter finding indicates that conformity to the prejudiced norms can have damaging effects that extend beyond the initial target of racism.

Bigoted attitudes can also be fostered intentionally by a bigoted society that institutionally supports these attitudes. For example, a society that supports the notion of segregation through law and custom is supporting the notion that one group is inferior to another. A more direct example: One investigator[20] interviewed white South Africans in an attempt to find reasons for their negative attitudes toward blacks. He found that the typical white South African was convinced that the great majority of crimes were committed by blacks. This was erroneous. How did such a misconception develop? The individuals reported they saw a great many black convicts working in public places—they never saw any white convicts. Doesn't this prove blacks are convicted of more crimes than whites? No. In fact, the rules forbade white convicts from working in public places! In short, a society can *create* prejudiced beliefs by its very institutions. In our own society, forcing blacks to ride in the back of the bus, keeping women out of certain clubs, preventing Jews from staying at exclusive hotels are all part of our recent history—and create the illusion of inferiority or unacceptability.

NOTES

1. Levitas, M., *America in Crisis* (New York: Holt, Rinehart and Winston, 1969).
2. Dollard, J., Hostility and fear in social life, *Series Forces, 17* (1938), 15–26.
3. Roberts, E., quoted by P. Jacobs and S. Landau, *To Serve the Devil* (Vol. 2, p. 71) (New York: Vintage Books, 1971).
4. Crocker, C., quoted by P. Jacobs and S. Landau, *To Serve the Devil* (Vol. 2, p. 81) (New York: Vintage Books, 1971).
5. Greeley, A., and P. Sheatsley, The acceptance of desegregation continues to advance, *Scientific American, 225*(6) (1971), 13–19. See also R. D. Vanneman and T. F. Pettigrew, Race and relative deprivation in the urban United States, *Race, 13* (1972), 461–486.
6. Sherif, M., O. J. Harvey, B. J. White, W. Hood, and C. Sherif, *Intergroup Conflict and Cooperation: The Robbers Cave Experiment* (Norman: University of Oklahoma Institute of Intergroup Relations, 1961).
7. Hovland, C., and R. Sears, Minor studies of aggression: Correlation of lynchings with economic indices, *Journal of Psychology, 9* (1940), 301–310.
8. Klineberg, O., Black and white in international perspective, *American Psychologist, 26* (1971), 119–128.
9. Speer, A., *Inside the Third Reich: Memoirs* (R. Winston and C. Winston, Trans.) (New York: Macmillan, 1970).
10. Miller, N., and R. Bugelski, Minor studies in aggression: The influence of frustrations imposed by the in-group on attitudes expressed by the out-group, *Journal of Psychology, 25* (1948), 437–442.
11. Rogers, R., and S. Prentice-Dunn, Deindividuation and anger-mediated interracial aggression: Unmasking regressive racism, *Journal of Personality and Social Psychology, 41* (1981), 63–73.
12. Weatherly, D., Anti-Semitism and the expression of fantasy aggression, *Journal of Abnormal and Social Psychology, 62* (1961), 454–457.

13. Adorno, T., E. Frenkel-Brunswick, D. Levinson, and R. N. Sanford, *The Authoritarian personality* (New York: Harper, 1950).

14. McFarland, S. M., V. S. Ageyev, and M. A. Abalakina-Paap, Authoritarianism in the former Soviet Union, *Journal of Personality and Social Psychology, 63* (1992), 1004–1010.

15. Greeley and Sheatsley, Acceptance of desegregation.

16. Pettigrew, T. F., Regional differences in anti-Negro prejudice, *Journal of Abnormal and Social Psychology, 59* (1959), 28–36.

17. Pettigrew, T. F., Personality and sociocultural factors and intergroup attitudes: A cross-national comparison, *Journal of Conflict Resolution, 2* (1958), 29–42.

18. Watson, J., Some social and psychological situations related to change in attitude, *Human Relations, 3* (1950), 15–56.

19. Kirkland, S. L., J. Greenberg, and T. Pyszczynski, Further evidence of the deleterious effects of overheard derogatory ethnic labels: Derogation beyond the target, *Personality and Social Psychology Bulletin, 13* (1987), 216–227.

20. MacCrone, I., *Race attitudes in South Africa* (London: Oxford University Press, (1937).

Issues for Discussion

1. How would you summarize each of the four theories of prejudice that Aronson presents?

2. Which of the examples and illustrations that Aronson offers seem the most helpful to you? Are there any that strike you as particularly weak or unhelpful? In general, what makes an example or illustration effective?

Fitting Evidence to Theory

Look back for a moment at the opening paragraph of Aronson's explanation of how economic and political competition generates prejudice. Once he has announced the general idea that "Prejudice can be considered to be the result of economic and political forces," he begins to outline the "competition" explanation pattern. The basic framework of the "competition" theory of prejudice might be summarized as follows:

Prejudice can arise when

- economic resources are limited.

- a dominant group uses its power to gain economic advantages.

- competition or tension between groups increases.

Aronson structures his explanation around these three ideas—all central components of the "competition" theory of prejudice. These ideas provide him with a framework that organizes his explanation. Next, he fleshes out this conceptual framework with specific examples drawn from actual historical or experimental contexts. He notes that economic competition has led to the development of prejudice in several different cases, including conflicts between Anglo and Mexican migrant workers, Arabs and Israelis, and Northerners and

Southerners during the Civil War. He then follows up with a detailed example of how craft unions have conspired against women and minority groups to preserve high-paying jobs for white males. In the second paragraph he focuses more narrowly on the idea that increased competition leads to increased prejudice. Once Aronson repeats this idea in the first sentence, he follows again with two extended examples: one based on John Dollard's early study of anti-German prejudice in a small industrial town, and the other addressing changes in attitudes toward Chinese immigrants during the nineteenth century. The remaining paragraphs offer further examples that show how the "competition" theory of prejudice "fits" and thus explains specific historical cases of discrimination. Aronson even offers a detailed account of an elaborate experiment designed to create prejudice through competition under "controlled" laboratory conditions. Finally, it's important to note that Aronson doesn't simply list or name examples or illustrations; he takes considerable pains to show us how well each example "fits" the "competition" model of prejudice. Mentioning that attitudes toward Chinese immigrants "fluctuated wildly during the nineteenth century" in response to changes in competition isn't enough; Aronson takes the time to tell us the story of how these attitudes changed from decade to decade, demonstrating along the way how neatly the competition theory "fits" and thus explains the Chinese experience.

Connecting with Theory

Thinking theoretically can seem like an awfully chilly and unwelcoming activity. Many people see theoretical thinking as something that only guys in white coats do—or professors who smoke pipes in ivory towers and read tomes as big as phone books. Theoretical thinking can seem threatening for a number of reasons. For one, theory is usually associated with "big," intimidating ideas like Einstein's theory of relativity or Freud's theory of psychoanalysis. And theory can also be off-putting because it seems so impersonal, abstract, and emotionless—so distant from the practical, down-to-earth concerns of everyday life. In fact, as a number of researchers have noted over the past two decades, many college women often feel alienated by the kind of critical analysis involved in abstract theoretical thinking; women often prefer "connected knowing"—knowing that builds on truth "that is personal, particular, and grounded in first-hand experience."[1]

[1]Mary Field Belenky et al., *Women's Ways of Knowing: The Development of Self, Voice, and Mind* (New York: Basic Books, 1986), p. 113.

But thinking through theory doesn't necessarily have to be an exercise in alienation and intimidation. Not all theories are as mysterious as $E = mc^2$. Actually, just about any generalized assertion of truth qualifies as a theory, even statements as apparently direct and uncomplicated as "Many college women are put off by formal academic analysis" or "Women and men tend to think differently about relationships." The only difference between generalizations like these and formal theory is a matter of context: express ideas like these over coffee between classes and they amount to little more than opinions; include them in a formal paper or assert them during an academic presentation and they leave the realm of opinion and become theories—publicly verifiable claims of truth. What separates theory from personal opinion is the fact that every theory invites active public scrutiny.

In college it's easy to forget that the theories you're learning are meant to be questioned and tested. You can get so wrapped up in memorizing theories for tests that you no longer see them as a bunch of really good hunches and begin instead to regard them as a series of distant, immutable "laws." When that happens, education stops being fun and becomes indoctrination: After all, who enjoys listening to official stories without having the chance to talk back? One way to bring theory down to earth is by drawing on your own experiences and your knowledge of the world to see how well the theories you learn actually "fit" the things they are meant to explain. Once you recognize that academic theories are only "rough drafts" of knowledge open to revision and rebuttal and that your own knowledge is an important measure of a theory's worth, you begin to bridge the gap between personal and academic ways of thinking.

The following reading selection gives you a theoretical perspective you can use to "enter the conversation" of academic analysis for yourself. In "Images of Power and Powerlessness," Hilary M. Lips claims that over the past twenty years media portrayals of women haven't come as far as we might like to think and that men still dominate media images associated with power, status, and control. Lips is a professor of psychology and director of the Center for Gender Studies at Radford University.

Before Reading

Freewrite for a few minutes about one or two specific media images of women—from a magazine, television show, or movie—that come to mind. How are these women portrayed? Do they seem powerful to you?

Images of Power and Powerlessness

Hilary M. Lips

One February morning in 1989, newspapers featured an arresting image on the front page: A woman in bishop's clothing. The woman was black and middle-aged. The article said that she had been divorced, and that she had written "liberal" things about such topics as homosexuality and American policy in Central America. But the most striking thing about her was that she was joyful, for she, Barbara Harris, had just been consecrated as the first female bishop in the Episcopalian church, the first, in fact, in the 2000-year history of any of the "catholic" branches of Christianity. The shock value of the image of a woman—a black woman, at that—arrayed in full bishop's regalia, miter on her head and staff in her hand, was obviously not lost on newspaper editors who gave this picture so prominent a place. As a society we are still not accustomed to seeing women, especially women of color, wearing the accoutrements of power; we are still jolted by the confluence of our images of power with our images of people who are not supposed to have it.

So upsetting was the prospect of the elevation of a female to the rank of bishop that the Reverend Harris' initial election had touched off months of debate, with some church members arguing, even during the ceremony, that her consecration would be a sacrilege. Boston's Roman Catholic cardinal refused an invitation to attend the ceremony, saying that it had "serious ecumenical implications because it departs from a common tradition in regard to sacramental orders" (Diamond, 1989, p. 2A). Traditionalists insisted that because the first apostles were men the position of bishop should rightfully go only to men. This argument, backed by the full power of the church, has successfully kept women out of the Roman Catholic priesthood. And until Barbara Harris, had worked to keep the few Episcopalian women priests from rising in the hierarchy. In this instance, the conservative forces were insufficient to exclude Barbara Harris, despite their appeals to truth and tradition, but there is much to be learned from their desperation to do so—and from their tactics.

The first important thing to note about this story is the intense personal discomfort experienced by certain individuals when confronted with the idea of a female bishop. The second is the scarcity of comparable images of powerful women in our culture. The third is the way that those resisting the inclusion of women in the priestly hierarchy have used a supposedly objective "truth" as the basis for their position. In this [essay], we will come to see that these three things are interconnected.

I am indebted to Leslie Campbell for some of the ideas in this essay.

First, many people are genuinely uncomfortable with images of female power because these images do not conform with their own *schemas,* or mental frameworks, for power and for femininity. Second, the reason individuals find the images of femininity and power incongruous is that the culture's dominant collective knowledge or set of accepted myths portrays femininity and power as falling on opposite sides of a duality, and either gives no prominence to powerful women (even though there have been many of them) or includes them only as examples of distortions of what is natural. Third, the shape of this collective knowledge—what we sometimes think of as truth—is strongly influenced by authorities in positions of relative power who say they are objective but who have a (sometimes unacknowledged) vested interest in the status quo. These three processes work together to ensure that only "appropriate" images of power are absorbed into and expressed in our culture's accepted mythology. Together, they make it difficult for images of female power to be viewed with comfort and approval.

THE INDIVIDUAL DILEMMA: VISIONS OF POWER THAT DO NOT FIT

Powerful Images

The term *power* calls forth a host of stereotypic images. For example, the Judeo-Christian image of god is of a being who is supernatural and all-powerful: present everywhere, seeing and knowing everything, able to change anything. Some of the awe that people accord to supernatural power is also accorded to individuals believed to have a special link to that power: priests, prophets, evangelists, gurus, faith healers, witches, sorcerers, mystics. Another image associated with power is physical strength and skill. The champion boxer, the hockey star, the world-class runner, the discus thrower—all are surrounded with an aura of power. In the areas of politics and business, individuals who hold formal authority or who control vast resources are seen as powerful. Still other people are viewed as powerful because of a certain personal magnetism or charisma that allows them to charm others. Another image called up by the notion of power is that of the expert: the individual who understands what others do not, who has access to information that is beyond the reach of others.

Although the above images are stereotypic, or perhaps because they are stereotypic, they provide an outline of the schema of power that predominates in our culture and that organizes the way many of us think about power. Thinking is a complex process with which we make sense of the information that surrounds us, impose some mental order on it, and also have our minds changed by it. Schemas play a part in this process. Accord-

5

ing to cognitive psychologists, a schema is a mental structure, a kind of outline that we hold in our minds of an idea or concept. A schema develops as we learn about a concept and begin to think about it. Once it has begun to form, it filters the information we are constantly taking in, keeping or absorbing what seems to fit the schema, ignoring or rejecting what does not, sometimes subtly changing itself in response to new information. For example, when a child is introduced to the concept *family*, she or he may begin to form mental rules for distinguishing when a group of people is or is not a family. These rules form a pattern, or outline—a schema—against which to assess whether or not new groups encountered are families. The schema itself may change gradually over time as the child encounters more and more instances of groups defining themselves as families that did not fit the original schema. However, what will usually happen when the child encounters an instance of a family that does not fit the current schema is that the information will be ignored or quickly forgotten because it cannot easily be integrated into the family schema. In other words, the family that deviates significantly from the child's family schema may not be classified as a family at all.

Psychologists use the term *schema* as an attribute of the thought processes of particular individuals. Many schemas, however, are shared among the members of a culture, since they are constructed from the information that surrounds most of us. They are not necessarily shared across groups exposed to different information and experiences; for example, European-Americans and African-Americans, for whom the role of women has historically been somewhat different, may have overlapping but far from identical schemas for the concept of *femininity*.

Most of us probably have a schema for the concept of power. Indeed, early studies of the shades of meaning that people attach to words and concepts show that one of the three major dimensions people use in characterizing a variety of images is potency, or power (Osgood, Suci, & Tannenbaum, 1957). Power, it seems, is an important component of people's evaluation of roles, activities, and other people they encounter. But whether an individual sees a particular behavior or a particular person as powerful, and how well she or he remembers a particular instance of powerful behavior, or a powerful person, depends to a large extent on whether the behavior or person in question fits that individual's schema for power. If we have learned through our culture that powerful leaders do not compromise, we may characterize as powerless or weak a politician who tries to negotiate a peace settlement or an employer who works hard to reach a mutually agreeable wage settlement with employees—even if those actions require great risk-taking and stamina. And if we have learned that women do not generally wield most kinds of power, we may find it difficult to call to mind the instances of women's powerful behavior that we have observed: We have not integrated the information into our existing schemas for power (or for women).

Gender and the Images of Power

In reviewing stereotypic images of power, most readers will find that the examples of powerful people brought to mind are male. The image of God in Christian, Jewish, and Moslem religions is definitely male, as are most of the people thought to hold spiritual power by virtue of a special link to God. Examples of people who are physically powerful are also generally male, despite the widespread media attention given to such exceptions to that rule as Olympic athletes Jackie Joyner-Kersee, Florence Griffith-Joyner, and tennis star Martina Navratilova. In politics and business, when most people think of a president, prime minister, chairperson of the board, bank manager, or corporate chief executive, they think of a man, even though women sometimes hold these positions. And in the realm of expertise, masculine images still hold sway. It is men—mostly white men—who are pictured knee-deep in printouts in computer advertisements (Marshall & Bannon, 1988); the typical image of a scientist is still a man in a white lab coat; and female physicians, lawyers, professors, auto mechanics, plumbers, and accountants are still trusted less than their male counterparts. Perhaps only in the realm of power based on attractiveness, charisma, and personal magnetism do female power images compete with male ones: A beautiful, charming woman is said to be able to "wrap a man around her little finger."

Both sexes generally attribute more power to males than females, al- 10 though women show this pattern less strongly. In one study in which university students were asked to list the most powerful person they knew, 91% of the males and 69% of the females named a man (Lips, 1985). The template for this tendency to see males as powerful more often than females may be laid down in the family: About one quarter of the male and female respondents in the study cited their father as the most powerful person they knew, but only 16% of the females and 2% of the males named their mothers.

The high proportion of male to female powerful images is not at all surprising when considered in the light of research on gender stereotypes. A large body of research in psychology has shown that men and women are often thought of as opposite sides of a duality: Men are strong, independent, worldly, aggressive, ambitious, logical, and rough; women are weak, dependent, passive, naive, not ambitious, illogical, and gentle (Broverman, Vogel, Broverman, Clarkson, & Rosenkrantz, 1972; Edwards & Williams, 1980). The most positively valued masculine traits have to do with activity and competence; highly valued feminine traits emphasize warmth and expressiveness, qualities not generally associated with power.

Portrayals of women and men based on the stereotypic notions of masculine strength and feminine weakness bombard us through the media. In any given week we can find numerous examples of tough guys on television: cool (but caring) cops, steely eyed and stubble-faced detectives, gung-ho Marines. Where are the tough gals? New York policewomen Cagney and Lacey, now gone from the screen, were the only reliable representatives. We are surrounded with the message that masculine males can be powerful, but feminine females cannot, or that women's only effective source of feminine influence is beauty and sex appeal. When the media does present an exception to the rule of the powerless woman, she is often portrayed as a tragic, bitter figure, like Dian Fossey in the film *Gorillas in the Mist,* or as an evil, twisted character, like the other woman in the film *Fatal Attraction.*

These media messages have such a self-fulfilling quality that it is difficult to say how and when the stereotypes got started and how the cycle can be broken. Are women seldom elevated to positions of power because they are stereotyped as weak and passive, or are they stereotyped as weak because they are rarely seen in powerful positions? Both processes operate together, creating a vicious circle that reaches back for hundreds, even thousands, of years.

Our society's notions of power and gender are so intertwined that it is next to impossible to separate the two. Any major alteration of our thinking about the relationship between the two concepts requires a radical change in our schemas for both. In fact, a number of researchers and writers have argued that gender differences and power differences are irretrievably confounded with each other because females are automatically given lower status than males (Hacker, 1951; Henley, 1977; MacKinnon, 1987).

The almost automatic status differential between women and men is one of the keys to understanding why the image of a powerful woman causes discomfort in so many people. There is a tendency for people to attribute a relative *status*—position in a hierarchy of power relations within a social group—to others they encounter. This attributed status helps to guide their interactions with the other person: Should they defer to that other? Treat her or him as an equal? Assume superiority? Attributed status is based on both *achievement* (the role one performs and how well one performs it) and *ascription* (personal characteristics such as age, race, social class, sex, appearance). Research shows clearly that the status ascribed to females is consistently lower than that of males (Berger, Rosenholtz, & Zelditch, 1980). The effect is so strong that when women are seen to be invading a particular high-status occupation, the status of that occupation drops significantly (Touhey, 1974). 15

Since people use sex as an indicator of *ascribed* status, they are likely to attribute different statuses to males and females performing the same roles. A male flight attendant may be ascribed more status than a female flight attendant, a male police officer may be seen as having more authority than a female police officer, and a woman complaining about poor service in a store or restaurant may get a slower response than a man making a similar complaint. In each case, the person ascribed higher status, the man, is more likely to be listened to, to be treated with respect, and to be taken seriously. Moreover, the woman who holds a role that gives her high *achieved* status finds herself in a position of *status incongruity:* The high achieved status of her role conflicts with the low ascribed status of her sex. Others who encounter her may feel uncomfortable with this double status message. Why? First, it jeopardizes their carefully constructed categories for the roles associated with women and men, forcing them to do more mental work. Second, in the absence of old and familiar rules for relating to women and men, they feel awkward about relating to her—and everyone hates feeling awkward. Third, her violation of the unspoken rules of social structure by achieving too high a status for a woman may be seen and resented as an implicit threat to their own position in the status hierarchy.

Of course, sex is not the only source of ascribed status. Status ascribed according to sex can and does interact with status ascribed according to other characteristics such as race or sexual orientation. A man who is suspected of being gay may be ascribed less status than a female colleague, and white women may be ascribed more status than their nonwhite counterparts.

One of the reasons why power in the hands of a woman is sometimes regarded as sinister and dangerous is that women are seen to exert power in different ways than men. Women sometimes rely on less direct forms of influence than men because they have less access to traditional avenues of power and have been encouraged to use feminine charms and wiles to get their way. When the successful use of power is covert or manipulative, we are likely to view the power wielder as duping others, and we judge the person's behavior as unfair.

Such supposed differences in the styles of power exertion do not, however, account for the negative reaction to and portrayal of women who are powerful—women such as England's former Prime Minister, Margaret Thatcher—in the same way as men are powerful. Journalists often refer to Thatcher as "the iron maiden" and "Attila the Hen." Such epithets, even if they were masculinized, would not be applied to a man behaving in a similar fashion. Their use seems to represent an uneasy attempt to trivialize or make ridiculous the notion of a woman holding so much formal power. Although powerful male politicians are often caricatured, their masculinity is seldom called into question in public, whereas slurs upon the femininity of a powerful female politician are frequent. The masculinity of male politicians is, on the other hand, questioned only if they appear weak.

The Cultural Mythology of Power and Gender

It is all very well to note that individuals feel uncomfortable when images challenge their schemas for power or for gender and to say that status incongruity is the explanation for the discomfort. But why do people tend to ascribe lower status to females than to males? Why do so many individuals develop schemas for femininity that are incongruous with powerful behavior or position? Part of the reason is that for centuries many Western cultures have mythologized the images of male and female as opposing sides of a duality in which male was equated with strength, activity, aggression, and light; whereas female was equated with weakness, passivity, subtlety, and darkness. This mythology of dualism, of opposites, has become so much a part of our consciousness, and is reinforced so extensively that it is difficult to conceive of gender in any other way. Within the framework of this dualism, a woman seen acting in a powerful way is seen to be acting like a man, and thus, by definition, not like a woman. Therefore, women holding powerful positions or behaving in powerful ways risk being viewed as unwomanly or unfeminine. Because of the cultural habit of thinking dualistically, the concept of power just does not fit with the concept of woman. When the two concepts are forced together, the result is the contradiction of the unwomanly woman. Powerful women are subjected to extremely pejorative labels: castrating bitch, ball-breaker, iron maiden, witch.

20

REFERENCES

Berger, Joseph, Rosenholtz, Susan J., & Zelditch, Morris, Jr. (1980). Status organizing processes. *Annual Review of Sociology, 6,* 479–508.

Broverman, Inge K., Vogel, Susan R., Broverman, Donald M., Clarkson, Frank E., & Rosenkrantz, Paul S. (1972). Sex-role stereotypes: A current appraisal. *Journal of Social Issues, 28,* 59–78.

Diamond, John (1989, February). Episcopalians install the first woman bishop. *Arizona Daily Star,* February 12, pp. 1A, 2A.

Edwards, John R., & Williams, John E. (1980). Sex-trait stereotypes among young children and young adults: Canadian findings and cross-national comparisons. *Canadian Journal of Behavioural Science, 12,* 210–220.

Hacker, Helen M. (1951). Women as a minority group. *Social Forces, 30,* 60–69.

Henley, Nancy M. (1977). *Body politics: Power, sex, and nonverbal communication.* Englewood Cliffs, NJ: Prentice-Hall.

Lips, Hilary M. (1985). Gender and the sense of power: Where are we and where are we going? *International Journal of Women's Studies, 8* (5), 483–489.

MacKinnon, Catherine (1987). *Feminism unmodified: Discourses on life and law.* Cambridge, Mass.: Harvard University Press.

Marshall, Jon C., & Bannon, Susan (1988). Race and sex equity in computer advertising. *Journal of Research on Computing in Education, 21* (1), 15–27.

Osgood, Charles E., Suci, George J., & Tannenbaum, Percy H. (1957). *The measurement of meaning.* Urbana, Ill.: University of Illinois Press.

Touhey, John C. (1974). Effects of additional women professionals on rating of occupational prestige and desirability. *Journal of Personality and Social Psychology, 29,* 86–89.

Issues for Discussion

1. What, in Lips's view, is the dominant "schema" for power in American society? To what extent do you agree with her assertion that "both sexes generally attribute more power to males than females"?
2. How, according to Lips, are men and women typically portrayed by the media? What evidence does she present to support her interpretation of media imagery? How does she account for exceptions to these portrayals?

E S S A Y
O P T I O N S

Entering the Conversation of Ideas

The following two essay options invite you to explore academic analysis for yourself. The first asks you to analyze how you think women are portrayed by the media and gives you the chance to test Hilary Lips's theory of media stereotyping. The second, a more ambitious assignment, challenges you to analyze an intergroup conflict you've experienced, studied, or read about, in light of the theories of prejudice outlined by Elliot Aronson.

Topic 1. Survey a specific form of popular media (such as video games, ads in women's or men's magazines, action-adventure films, situation comedies, or television cartoons for children) and write an essay in which you analyze the way that women are represented. Once you've chosen a focus, you should plan to do some informal research by examining several representative games, issues, or shows. You can "enter the conversation" on your topic by discussing and evaluating the position Hilary Lips presents in "Images of Power and Powerlessness." To what extent does your survey of media imagery confirm or challenge Lips's theory? How might you qualify or revise Lips's position in light of your own analysis of media gender images?

Topic 2. Write a three- to five-page essay in which you analyze the cause of a recent intergroup conflict in your community or on your campus. This conflict may focus on a specific incident or it may involve long-standing tensions between two social groups. The groups you consider may be defined by race, ethnicity, gender, economic status, age, sexual orientation, or other factors. As part of your prewriting for this paper, you may want to do some informal research by reading news accounts or editorials on the conflict you're examining. In your essay you should offer a brief history of this conflict, including details about specific clashes or issues that have generated tension. The primary purpose of your essay, however, is to explain the cause or causes of this conflict. Use Elliot Aronson's "The Causes of Prejudice" (p. 460) as your starting point — the point where you "enter into the conversation" of ideas on this topic. Which of the four theories of prejudice that Aronson describes best accounts for the conflict?

Which aspects of the conflict refuse to fit any of the theories Aronson presents? Can you think of alternative explanations?

As you work on your paper, keep in mind that academic analysis is both critical and dialogical: you should feel free to "talk back" to Lips and Aronson. Don't hesitate to "think against" the explanations and interpretations they present in order to develop your own analysis.

Cohesion: Story Hunger

One of the most difficult parts of analytic writing is getting the sections of your essay to come together as a unified whole. Cohesion—that feeling of unity you get when a piece of writing "flows" smoothly from section to section—is relatively easy to come by when you're writing a straightforward story, like the family or personal stories you wrote in the first section of this book. If you stick to a straightforward sequence of events and if your story has a single "point" to make, it will probably hang together just fine. Personal stories seem to cohere all by themselves; the very fact that you remember an experience as a "story" means that it's been shaped into some kind of a coherent and meaningful event. But when you're asked to analyze something, you lose the organizational power of story structure. Without a good story to tell, how do you satisfy your story hunger? How do you get your writing to come together as a coherent, unified whole?

One way to improve the coherence of your writing is to build clear bridges between the various parts of your paper. Composition textbooks usually offer a menu of techniques for smoothing out the "transitions" between paragraphs. Here are some of the most common.

Key words.   The most obvious way to develop cohesion in an essay is by repeating words, concepts, or phrases that are central to your topic. It should come as no surprise, for example, that the words most frequently repeated in Elliot Aronson's explanation of the "competition" theory of prejudice include *prejudice, economic, competition, conflict, stereotyping,* and *discrimination.* By repeating these terms as he introduces the main idea or focus of every paragraph, Aronson constantly reminds the reader about his topic and strengthens the connection of paragraph to paragraph.

The danger with the key word approach to coherence is that repeating a given term over and over can be deadly for your reader. Our interest in the "competition" theory of prejudice would probably wane pretty quickly if Aronson started out every paragraph with the sentence "Another aspect of the economic and political competition theory of prejudice is . . ." Instead of repeating the same words or phrases again and again, experienced writers like Aronson vary their choice of words by using synonyms and near synonyms like *conflict* and *tension* for *competition,* and *discrimination* or *stereotyping* for *prejudice.*

Signposts. Verbal signposts offer another simple way to build coherence in your writing. There's nothing more disconcerting to a reader than being catapulted from idea to idea between paragraphs. Maybe you've had the experience yourself: you're reading along, following the writer's train of thought, then a new paragraph comes up and suddenly you feel as if you've stumbled into a whole new paper. One way to smooth out rough transitions between paragraphs is to use a verbal "signpost"—a word or phrase that clarifies the logical relation between upcoming and preceding ideas. Here's a brief catalogue of common verbal signposts.

Signposts showing continuation, similarity, or elements in a series:

in addition	similarly	first . . . second . . . etc.
additionally	like	next
moreover	likewise	later
another	in the same way	eventually
furthermore		

Signposts showing cause and effect relation between ideas:

as a result	consequently	because
as a consequence	in response to	since

Signposts showing contradiction or contrasting ideas:

however	despite	by contrast
but	although	conversely
		on the one hand/
		on the other hand

Signposts showing logical conclusion or summary:

thus	finally	in conclusion
therefore	ultimately	in summary
		to sum up

In addition to using key words, Aronson also uses an occasional signpost term to give his writing coherence. In paragraph two he discusses anti-German attitudes in America during the nineteenth century. The first word of the next paragraph tells the reader that another example of how competition fuels prejudice is about to follow: *"Similarly,* the prejudice, violence, and negative stereotyping directed against Chinese immigrants in the United States fluctuated wildly throughout the nineteenth century." The first word of this transitional sentence establishes a clear expectation of what Aronson plans to do in the following paragraph. That's why signposts are so useful: they give readers hints about writers' intentions and set up expectations that writers can fulfill. An essay that consistently establishes clear expectations about what's coming up and then fulfills those expectations is bound to have a strong sense of coherence.

Just one word of caution. Signposts can help you smooth the transition between paragraphs, but they need to be used sparingly. If you kick off every paragraph with an "in addition," a "moreover," or a "by contrast," your writing will start to sound too mechanical and formulaic. A good rule of thumb is to use signposts only when they seem especially appropriate. They're no substitute for real, content-based cohesion.

Bridge sentences.   The most effective way of linking two paragraphs is to connect them with one or more bridge sentences. Bridge sentences are designed to link the main ideas of two different paragraphs or sections of an essay. Let's return to Aronson again for a quick example. His fifth paragraph focuses on an experiment showing that prejudice can be created under laboratory conditions. Aronson could have introduced this topic simply by saying something like "Prejudice has even been created artificially in the laboratory" or "Muzafer Sherif and his colleagues created prejudice in the natural environment of a Boy Scout camp." Either of these sentences would have clarified the focus of the new paragraph for the reader. But neither would have provided a clear understanding of how the upcoming information relates to what Aronson has said in earlier paragraphs. Aronson makes this connection in the bridge sentences he uses to get this paragraph started: "In order to determine whether competition causes prejudice in and of itself, an experiment is needed. But how can we proceed? Well, if conflict and competition lead to prejudice, it should be possible to produce prejudice in the laboratory." In these three sentences Aronson gently reminds the reader of what he's been saying in the first four paragraphs—that competition causes prejudice—and then he goes on to indicate how this idea connects logically with the information he's about to present: to prove that prejudice is caused by competition you need an experiment that rules out other factors. Aronson's bridge sentences create coherence by introducing the focus of the upcoming paragraph and by clarifying how this focus relates to what's come before.

Sometimes its easy to build a bridge between two paragraphs using a single sentence that links the content of both. Aronson does this in the fifth paragraph of the section "The 'Scapegoat' Theory of Prejudice": "Additional research has helped to pin down the phenomenon even more precisely." Here, he tells the reader that the upcoming paragraph will describe "additional" research studies that offer even more detailed information about how frustration leads to scapegoating—the "phenomenon" that he discussed in the preceding paragraph. At other times you may need to use a number of sentences to build a bridge, particularly if you are trying to link major sections of a paper or major ideas. Aronson uses six sentences to open paragraph 16:

> As we have seen, the displacement of aggression onto scapegoats may be a human tendency, but not all people do it to a like degree. We have already identified socio-economic status as a cause of prejudice. Also, we have seen that people who dislike members of a particular outgroup are more apt to displace aggression onto them than are people who do not dislike members of that outgroup. We can now carry this one step further. There is some evidence to support the notion of individual differences in a general tendency to hate. In other words, there are people who are predisposed toward being prejudiced, not solely because of immediate external influences, but because of the kind of people they are. . . .

Extended bridges like this are useful when you want to remind the reader about important ideas you've developed earlier in your writing. The first three sentences in this bridge summarize the two theories of prejudice that Aronson has already presented—the "competition" and "scapegoat" models. They also help to reinforce the structure of Aronson's presentation: when he says it's time to carry the discussion "one step further," he's signaling that a third theory of prejudice is coming up. In the next two sentences he introduces this theory—the model of the "prejudiced personality"— and clarifies the focus of the next section of his presentation.

Finding an explanation pattern.   The strategies outlined in this section will help improve the coherence in your writing, but by themselves they can't really satisfy your story hunger or make a collection of disjointed ideas or observations hang together. If your analysis or interpretation has no story to tell—if it isn't built on a clear, recognizable explanation pattern— then no amount of tinkering will pull it together into a coherent whole. Often when students have trouble with coherence it's not because they haven't used enough verbal "glue" to stick their paragraphs together; it's because there's no coherent relationship between the paragraphs and the ideas they contain to begin with.

Real coherence isn't something you can tack on to an essay; it grows directly out of the explanation pattern that structures its form and content. The explanation pattern specifies not only the content of each section of the paper but the paper's logical sequence as well. If, for example, you're analyzing a local intergroup conflict in terms of the "competition" theory of prejudice, the structure of the "competition" explanation pattern specifies the structure of your analysis: you're bound by the "competition" explanation pattern to demonstrate how the groups involved struggle for a limited resource, and you're bound to show how one group uses its dominant position to its own advantage. To demonstrate that the conflict in question arose through competition and not because of another factor like "social learning," you'd probably also have to show, as Aronson does, that conflict increases when competition increases. The structure of the explanation pattern underlying your analysis sets up a series of expectations in your reader's mind about the content and logical order of your paper. If you follow through on this order and fulfill the reader's expectations, your essay will seem coherent, logical, and complete. If you don't follow through on the expectations established by the explanation pattern you've chosen, you run the risk of giving a case of story hunger to your reader.

In courses in the so-called "hard" sciences like physics or biology, and even in social science classes like psychology, sociology, and anthropology, finding an explanation pattern to structure your analysis or interpretation usually isn't much of a problem. Science courses tend to teach theories directly, and science teachers usually expect students to apply standard or "official" theories when they interpret data. But the situation is more complicated in the humanities, particularly in literary studies or history courses where the official story of the self-expressive classroom dominates. When a teacher asks you to offer your own interpretation of a character in a novel or your own analysis of a historical event, she is setting you up for a serious bout of story hunger. Students who excel in such "open-ended" assignments are usually those who already know some of the standard explanation patterns—the official stories—associated with the discipline in question, and they use this knowledge to create well-organized and creative interpretations and analyses. If, for example, your English instructor asks you to write your own interpretation of the character Celie in Alice Walker's novel *The Color Purple*, you might well end up generating a disjointed series of paragraphs, each focusing on a different observation about Celie's character. But if you recognize in Celie an explanation pattern that's common in the discipline of literary studies—that is, if you see her as a "hero," as a woman who overcomes apparently insurmountable obstacles and helps herself and those around her—you're on your way to writing a paper that "makes sense" in the academic culture of your classroom. Every course contains a stock of commonly used explanation patterns—whether or not they are made explicit—often disguised as deceptively simple concepts like "hero," "antagonist," "revolutionary," "feminist," and so forth. Entering into the culture of a particular discipline means becoming aware of the theories and explanation patterns that structure thinking within it.

OPTIONAL ACTIVITY

Mapping Transitions

Working in pairs, return to Elliot Aronson's "The Causes of Prejudice" (p. 460), Hilary M. Lips's "Images of Power and Powerlessness" (p. 474), or any of the selections you have read in this section and analyze how the author creates coherence in a passage of at least two to three pages. Identify the explanation pattern at work in the passage, underline all key words and verbal signposts you can find, and note which sentences act as bridge sentences between paragraphs. Does the author do anything else to foster coherence?

CHAPTER 16

Revision Workshop: Writing for an Academic Audience

Establishing Authority in Academic Culture

What gives a piece of writing authority and power? As we've emphasized throughout this book, that depends a great deal on cultural context—the values and expectations of the audience or speech community you're addressing. To gain credibility with an academic audience, you need to demonstrate that you share, or at least understand and respect, the values that are important to them. In the cartoon below, Calvin drastically misjudges the expectations of the classroom and (as usual) loses any shreds of credibility he might have had.

CALVIN AND HOBBES By Bill Watterson

On the playground, Calvin's approach could have some persuasive power. If a popular kid declares contemptuously that bubble gum is "totally bogus" it might be enough to convince some of his friends that chewing the pink stuff is hopelessly uncool. But in the classroom, self-confident opinion and aggressive assertion—even combined with personal charisma—generally aren't enough to carry the day. Academics demand reasons, evidence, elaboration, and support before they'll accept a writer's assertions. In this revision workshop we'll take a closer look at the assumptions and strategies that inform academic analysis.

Evaluating Sources

Much of an academic writer's authority depends on the quality of the sources she relies on, and one of the first things to consider is whether a source is primary or secondary. *Primary sources* are texts, works of art, or data that become the objects of explanation and analysis: works of literature, manuscripts, music, paintings and photos, films, field notes, lab notes, original research results, raw statistics. In historical research, where the object of explanation may be an event or time period, primary sources would include original documents and testimony by witnesses, participants, or others who lived during the time in question. Such testimony can take the form of news stories, letters, diaries, autobiographies, interviews, and oral histories. *Secondary sources* are works of scholarship and analysis based on primary sources or on other secondary sources; they include academic books and articles, monographs, theses, dissertations, conference papers, encyclopedias, textbooks, reviews, editorials, documentaries, and so forth. In academic culture, these sources are sometimes considered less valuable than primary sources because they're a step or two removed from the object of explanation. You might recall the childhood game of "gossip," where a message is whispered from one person to the next until it reaches the last person, at which point it seldom bears much resemblance to the original message. Secondary sources often carry less authority for precisely that reason: because they involve more layers of interpretation, they present more opportunities for error and distortion. Thus Herbert Kohl (p. 378) relies on the power of primary sources—the testimony of Rosa Parks herself and of a Montgomery bus boycott leader—to convince us that the secondary sources we're familiar with (textbooks, children's books, best-sellers) are inaccurate and misleading.

Primary sources aren't invariably more authoritative than secondary sources, though. Autobiography is a case in point. You would assume that the best-informed source about an individual's life would be the person himself, but autobiographers have a habit of softening, suppressing, or even flatly denying unpleasant facts about themselves. In a famous example, novelist Mary McCarthy once commented of Lillian Hellman (perhaps best known for her autobiographical memoir *Pentimento*), "Every word she writes is a lie, including 'a' and 'the.'" While the accusation was extreme, so was Hellman's prevarication, according to evidence that has emerged since her death.[1] In this instance, as well as less dramatic ones, secondary sources can be more trustworthy even though—or maybe *because*—they're distanced from the subject.

So whether the source is primary or secondary, it must be carefully evaluated. No source is infallible: each one reflects the personal and cultural assumptions of the people who produced it, so there's plenty of room to question its authority. When you're trying to determine the credibility of a source, four of the most important questions to ask are these:

Is the author reliable?   Does she seem well-informed about the subject? Is she a recognized authority in the field? M. G. Lord herself isn't a household name, but she cites big names like Freud and Jung in order to give her analysis more weight. If you're not familiar with the author's reputation, there are other signs of academic reliability you can look for. Academics tend to trust other academics, so an author who teaches at a respected college or university would generally be assumed to be reliable. Books published by academic presses and articles in scholarly journals are usually considered reputable sources, because they're reviewed by other experts in the field before being accepted for publication. It's a good sign of intellectual honesty if an author invites verification by other scholars by documenting his sources so they can be checked for accuracy. Note that both Hilary Lips and Emily Martin carefully cite many sources to help establish their credibility as scholars. Likewise, writers reporting research results are expected to describe their methods in detail so that other researchers can replicate their experiments or studies in order to test the validity of the results.

Is the information current?   Because scholars in every field are continually coming up with new theories, discoveries, and research, it's vital that information be up to date. Martin, for example, faults biology textbooks for neglecting recent research that challenges traditional accounts of fertiliza-

---

[1]Joan Mellen, *Hellman and Hammett* (New York: HarperCollins, 1996).

tion. Conversely, Lips refers to a 1988 study which concluded that white men predominate in ads for computers, but is this still true almost ten years later? The most recent source isn't always or automatically the best, however. Depending on the topic, you may find that certain historical materials or "classic" works are still useful.

Is the evidence representative?   Evidence isn't very persuasive if it can be easily dismissed as an exception. Martin emphasizes that the medical textbooks she criticizes are representative, describing them as "widely used" and referring to one as a "classic text." If they were obscure or atypical texts, they wouldn't support her larger argument that gender stereotypes are pervasive in the field of biology. You could ask whether Herbert Kohl's "generic" version of the Rosa Parks story is truly representative, since he concocted it himself. Are the real-life examples he quotes (Robert Fulghum and others) as typical as he claims? Why does he construct this hypothetical Rosa Parks story instead of responding to a specific text?

Is the perspective free of major bias — or at least fair-minded?   Every writer has a purpose and perspective; the point is to determine what the perspective is and whether or not it significantly skews the writer's conclusions. Paula Gunn Allen (p. 434), for instance, criticizes earlier interpretations of the Kochinnenako tale as culturally biased and therefore highly inaccurate and misleading. To determine perspective, look for direct statements of purpose, particularly in introductions and conclusions; pay attention to selection and emphasis (What information is included and excluded? What ideas, opinions, or events are emphasized and deemphasized?); be alert to tone (Does the writer use more sympathetic or more judgmental language when referring to particular people, ideas, or events?).

OPTIONAL
ACTIVITY

Evaluating Authority

Work in groups to evaluate the academic credibility of *one* of the following essays: M. G. Lord, "Interpreting Barbie" (p. 348); Herbert Kohl, "The Story of Rosa Parks and the Montgomery Bus Boycott Revisited" (p. 378); Emily Martin, "The Egg and the Sperm" (p. 417); Paula Gunn Allen, "Kochinnenako in Academe" (p. 434); Elliot Aronson, "The Causes of Prejudice" (p. 460); and Hilary Lips, "Images of Power and Powerlessness (p. 474). Some questions to consider include:

- What are the strengths and weaknesses of the writer's sources?

- What does the writer do to establish her or his credibility?

- Is the supporting evidence current and representative?

- What is the writer's perspective?

- Does bias get in the way here?

- How persuasive do you find the essay overall?

Don't be surprised if group members come to different conclusions, even after you've looked at the same evidence. However, do your best to come to a consensus and report your conclusions to the class.

Case Study: When Sources Conflict

What do you do when sources disagree? This question may have come up as you confronted the two texts for your historical analysis essay. Some discrepancies are easy to explain: the brevity of encyclopedia entries means that they necessarily exclude many details that you'd find in more specialized books; a U.S. history text that discusses the Vietnam War will most likely focus on large political and economic issues, whereas an oral history of American foot soldiers in that war will emphasize the day-to-day hardships and horrors of combat; a Cuban history text may paint a heroic portrait of Fidel Castro, while an interview with a Cuban refugee in the United States will undoubtedly produce a less flattering picture of Castro's political leadership and economic policies. But other cases are tougher. The writer of the following paper, Shant Kazazian, tackled a subject that has generated heated debate among scholars for decades — the Armenian genocide. While Kazazian, an Armenian American student, was from the start sympathetic to the Armenian side of the debate, he also recognized the possibility of bias in both his sources. As a result, he was initially reluctant to take a clear position; his first draft concluded that "the truth of the event must lie somewhere in between all of its different explanations."

Many students resort to "splitting the difference" when they're confronted by conflicting information or arguments, or they may conclude that "everyone's entitled to an opinion" and leave it at that. These strategies are often well-intentioned attempts to be diplomatic and to avoid offending readers who favor one side or the other. However, academic readers interpret these moves differently: they assume that smart people have opinions and values, enjoy intellectual challenge, and can use their minds to sort through complex or conflicting information. So when they encounter a writer who seems reluctant to weigh the evidence and take a position, they tend to assume that she's either incapable of doing so or unwilling to make the effort. In either case, the unfortunate writer, like Calvin at the beginning of this chapter, loses her credibility. In his revision, Kazazian avoids this pitfall: although he still acknowledges the potential bias of both sources, he weighs the evidence and explains why he ultimately finds one account more credible than the other.

STUDENT
WRITING

The Armenian Genocide: Two Dynamically Different Accounts
Shant Kazazian

Amid the terror and destruction of World War I lies the story of what many people refer to as the Armenian genocide. This story ended with over a million Armenians dead--a reality that stands undisputed. The fact, though, of what actually occurred to lead to this conclusion is to this day unresolved. The following excerpts from two historical texts demonstrate how differently this story is told:

> The panic in the city was terrible. The Armenians felt that the Government was determined to exterminate the Armenian race, and they were powerless to resist. The people were sure that the men were being killed and the women kidnapped. (Report of the American Committee on Armenian Atrocities, qtd. in Toynbee, p. 50)
>
> The Turkish atrocities in the district of Bitlis are indescribable. After having massacred the whole male population of this district, the Turks collected 9,000 women and children from the surrounding villages, and drove them in upon Bitlis. Two days later they marched them out to the bank of the Tigris, shot them all, and threw the 9,000

corpses into the river. (Russian news story, qtd. in Toynbee, p. 94)

An inquiry has proved that out of a thousand who
started, scarcely 400 have reached the place from which I
am writing [Anatolia]. Out of the 600 to be accounted for,
380 men and boys above 11 years of age, as well as 85
women, have been massacred or drowned outside the town
walls by the gendarmes who conducted them; 120 young women
and girls and 40 boys have been kidnapped, so that among
all these deported people one does not see a single pretty
face. Among the survivors, 60 percent are sick; they are
shortly to be forwarded to another specified locality,
where certain death awaits them . . . (letter from a witness, qtd. in Toynbee, pp. 101-2)

Armenian terrorist activities and direct involvement by
European powers in the internal affairs of the Ottoman Empire reached a peak during the First World War.

. . . In response to the open Armenian uprising as
well as the threat of further revolts, the Ottoman authorities concluded they had no alternative but to relocate
the Armenians from the eastern front region to the Southern provinces of the Empire.

. . . The claim that the Ottoman government had em-
barked on a course of deliberate extermination of the Armenian people is false. The Armenian people in many villages led violent revolts which erupted into several
battles. Any and all deaths of the Armenians occurred during the context of war. (Elekdag, p. 33)

The first three passages are personal accounts from witnesses of the genocide contained in <u>Armenian Atrocities</u>: <u>The
Murder of a Nation</u> (1917) by Arnold J. Toynbee, an English
historian. In it we find many writers expressing their belief

that there actually was a planned, premeditated Armenian genocide led by the Turkish government--a massacre aimed to eliminate non-Muslims within its realm. The second set of passages
is a historical account of the Armenian genocide taken from a
letter written to the editor of the Wall Street Journal in
1983 by Sukru Elekdag, ambassador of Turkey. In it he rules
out the possibility that the deportation of the Armenians was
planned by pointing to the mounting factors that finally
caused the Turkish government to order the deportation. He
further claims it was not a genocide; it was the outcome of
war.

Evidence of such different explanations of one certain
historical event suggests that little objective reality exists
in historical texts. Events are illustrated through the eyes
of writers and interpreted in such ways that they find appropriate. It is evident that the former passages weave an image
of the blatant violation of human rights, while the latter depict a justified deportation of the Armenian people, which led
to killings through war. Based on the same facts, both authors
produced dynamically different reports. At one extreme we find
a condemnation of the Turkish government for committing such
an unjustifiably cruel act, and at the other we are told that
the blame is shifted toward the Armenian people, who left the
leaders of the Turkish government no choice but to act. This
paper will, in effect, venture to determine why such different
stories of this event exist, and to which of the two accounts
we can assign greater merit.

Truth cannot possibly fit into two opposed explanations.
Writers will consequently spin stories in many different ways
to justify their cause, stressing certain aspects of the
event to draw a conclusion. Toynbee, in his historical account of the event, makes no mention of the "Armenian terrorist activities" that, according to Elekdag, were the cause of

the deportations. By the same token, Elekdag fails to mention
or address any sort of genocide or massacres of the "powerless
Armenians" by the Turkish government. Whereas witnesses quoted
in Toynbee refer to the actions taken by the Turkish government as a "forced evacuation," Elekdag simply calls it a
"relocation."

The two authors also differ in their interpretations as   5
to why this event occurred. Toynbee claims that although Armenians represented only about 8 percent of the population of
Turkey, "their commercial genius gave them a virtual monopoly
of trade, and a correspondingly large share in the wealth of
the country" (p. 34). By proposing this viewpoint, Toynbee establishes a motive on the part of the Turkish government to
plan the genocide. This would in effect support his claim that
the massacres were premeditated to rid the country of all Armenians. Elekdag dismisses this claim as absurd, stating that
the deportations were decided upon in order to prevent any
possible threat the Armenians could pose to a country that was
involved externally in the world war. He goes on to claim that
this decision was made during the war, not planned:

> The tragedies of 1915 during World War One brought immense
> suffering to all ethnic groups living in Anatolia under
> the Ottoman Empire. That warfare in eastern Turkey, to-
> gether with famine and epidemics, resulted in the suffer-
> ing and deaths of members of all ethnic groups, including
> 2 million Turks, is not in doubt. However, allegations
> that the slaughter of Armenian civilians on any scale was
> systematically planned, organized, or carried out by the
> Ottoman authorities cannot be sustained by the historical
> evidence. (p. 33)

From these two historical accounts emerge two different
"virtual writers," each unique in their intentions, motivation, and use of explanation patterns in expressing their

views. The author who collected the first set of personal accounts was a contemporary of the genocide. In 1915, Toynbee
was already recognized as a "brilliant" young historian at Oxford University: "shocked like the rest of the civilized world
at the stark brutality of the genocide, he put his skills to
work . . . in establishing and publicizing its true picture"
("Foreword," Toynbee, pp. 18-19). As a result, he interviewed
witnesses of the genocide who use terms like "terrible," "ex-
terminate," and "powerless" to describe events that took place
during this time in history, and he explains them using the
planned exploitation of the powerless as his explanation pattern. We thus find him using a "skeleton story" involving two
parties: one party attains greater power than the other, and
as a result oppresses and kills the weaker. He finds this explanation pattern and "skeleton story" most appropriate in
conveying these horrible events to the public. The passages he
has presented must be given credit because they are firsthand
accounts of the event. These people wrote what they saw; they
did not write from what they had heard about the event. Interpreting this event through his explanation pattern, involving
the exploitation of the weak, Toynbee does not mention any
possible justification for the actions taken by the Turks. But
this was not his intention in writing, and perhaps he was correct in leaving out this explanation. He did not believe anything would warrant what the Turks did to the Armenians. With
this belief, he labeled the event as a genocide, sharing the
group values of all Armenian people across the world who find
no justification for this outcome.

The second virtual writer, in writing his letter to Washington in 1983, felt it necessary to press his own case before
the bar of public opinion, for it was during this time in history that Armenian activists brought the Armenian genocide
back into public light. Because this letter comes from the pen
of the Turkish ambassador to the United States, we may take it

as an official statement of Turkey's version of the events of 1915 and deserving of attention. As a matter of fact, Elekdag has brought together in one place all the arguments given by this government over the decades--first to deny and then by a twist of logic to justify what took place. His motivation and intentions are very clear--to justify the occurrence of the genocide, what he referred to as war, in order to clear up any and all misconceptions about the atrocities the Turkish government was said to have committed. His explanation pattern consequently involves that of the justified measures taken by a government during wartime and turmoil. He thus claims that the Turkish government, faced with World War I on the international level and Armenian revolts internally, had to act. It ordered the deportation of the Armenians, who were treated fairly and humanely throughout. He claims that the only source of Armenian deaths came upon resistance led by the people-- resistance that exploded into battles. He thus vindicates the actions taken by the Turks by using a familiar explanation that had been used by his government since the event took place. In doing so, Elekdag does not mention any occurrence that would not fit into his explanation of the actions taken by his government. He therefore leaves out any possibility that there occurred unjustified and unlawful actions by his government during this time in history.

Analysis of these two writers points to which account we can tend to assign greater validity. On the one hand, we have someone whose motive is to expose the atrocity, someone whose only relation to the parties involved is that he, too, is a human. On the other hand, we have someone who is giving a secondhand account of the event with the ulterior motive to clear his government of the burden of committing a genocide. Given this motive, he must make the event fit into certain patterns that lead him into further trouble. Surely, Elekdag would say that Armenians died because of the war. But when did war involve the massacre of women and children and the mounting of severed heads of priests on sticks? Toynbee provides photographs of these atrocities taken by witnesses.[1] Toynbee's history of the Armenian genocide, which admittedly is presented through his perspective and assumptions, may commit the common bias perpetuated by all historians--to present what they understand. However, Toynbee's interpretation definitely gives a more legitimate account of the event compared to Elekdag's, given the motives I presented on behalf of both writers. The common bias committed by historians was most likely unintentional on the part of Toynbee and most probably intentional for Elekdag: the bad reputation of Elekdag's government had to be cleared. As a result, it is much easier for the latter to have been motivated to misrepresent the event.

After viewing such contrasting accounts of history stemming from a certain collection of facts, I realize that reality is a matter of judgment. One historian will judge a certain event within a framework he decides to set forth and another historian will do the same in a different fashion, each with his unique motives. Given this reality, we must appreciate the fact that we can find various accounts of historical events. Because of these many versions of history, we will not be held captive by the viewpoints of one storyteller.

WORKS CITED

Elekdag, Sukru. "Armenians vs. Turks: The View From Istanbul." <u>Wall Street Journal</u>, September 21, 1983, p. 33.

Toynbee, Arnold J. <u>Armenian Atrocities: The Murder of a Nation</u>. 1917. Foreword Dr. Fred Assadourian. New York: Tankian Publishing, 1975.

[1]The reprint of Toynbee's book used by Kazazian includes photographs and political cartoons from the period; these did not appear in the original edition.

Weighing Conflicting Evidence

In this essay, Kazazian works to establish academic authority through both organization and method of analysis. Following the general structure of critical analysis described in Chapter 15, he begins by clearly summarizing the two historical accounts that he's comparing; he highlights the major discrepancies between them and evaluates the credibility of each source; finally he presents his own interpretation—that Toynbee's account is more believable than Elekdag's. Throughout the essay, he supports his analysis with specific evidence from both texts, and although he clearly favors Toynbee's version of events, he treats Elekdag's account with respect. Kazazian's case focuses on two arguments: that Toynbee's compilation of eyewitness reports (primary sources) has more authority than Elekdag's "secondhand" information, and that Elekdag is more prone to bias than Toynbee because, as a Turkish government official, he has a stronger motive for distorting the facts. Do you find his argument convincing?

OPTIONAL ACTIVITIES

Reviewing Evidence and Sources

Working in teams, look up and evaluate Kazazian's sources; Toynbee's book should be readily available, and past issues of the *Wall Street Journal* can usually be found on microfiche. Do you find additional evidence that would support his position, conflicting evidence that he overlooked, or both? After reviewing the sources for yourself, do you come to the same conclusion as Kazazian?

Alternatively, look up accounts of the Armenian genocide in recent encyclopedias and histories of World War I (published in or after 1990): What version(s) of events do you find in these sources?

Revising Your Draft: Sources

Review the draft of your historical comparison to evaluate the reliability of your sources. What indications do you find that the authors or informants are reliable? How recently were the texts published? Does the information they present seem representative or atypical? What evidence can you find of the writer's or interview subject's perspective? Does bias undermine the credibility of either source?

If time allows, share your sources (texts or interview notes) as well as your draft with a partner. Work together to determine whether there is more evidence you could use to support your analysis of the two sources. Is there conflicting evidence that you overlooked? Do you take a clear position in explaining the differences you see in the two accounts?

Developing and Supporting an Analysis

When writing an academic analysis, you need to do more than simply report the information you find in your sources: you need to put your own spin on the subject. You might wonder how on earth you're supposed to do more than explain what the experts have already written—after all, they've probably spent more time studying the subject than you have. But American academic culture values innovation, individual perspective, and lively debate: it demands active participation. Besides, you don't have to develop an earthshaking theory; you just need to come up with a different angle. As we suggested in Chapter 15, doing academic work means engaging in an ongoing conversation of ideas: writers enter the conversation by building on previous work, by challenging it, or both.

Building on Established Knowledge

Three common ways to build on previous work are (1) to elaborate on another writer's ideas or add new support for an established theory; (2) to show new relationships between ideas or synthesize information from a variety of sources; and (3) to apply prior knowledge in a new way. Hilary Lips demonstrates several of these approaches in her essay (p. 474). Her study of college students' perceptions of powerful people supports earlier psychological studies that showed a connection between gender and power status. She draws connections between scholarship in psychology and gender images in popular culture. And she uses the familiar psychological concept of status incongruity in a novel way—to explain jokes about Margaret Thatcher. Notice, too, that while Lips is building her analysis of gender and power, she's also establishing her own academic credibility: her citations of research in psychology include studies ranging from the 1950s up through much more current scholarship; in effect, she's demonstrating her command of the field, her expertise.

However, you don't always have to be an ace researcher to demonstrate expertise and build on the ideas of established scholars. Don't forget that you already possess a wealth of information that you've gained by being an observant, intelligent person with interests and experiences of your own. Bringing your personal knowledge and expertise into dialogue with the theories and disciplines you encounter in your classes can generate lively, powerful analysis. That's what John Tuan Ho does in this passage from his essay on images of women and power in video games.

> The largest target consumers of video games are teenage boys. This is the period when puberty occurs and curiosity about women is high. Knowing this, producers of video games make it a point to include a buxom female character. The lone female warrior in *Mortal Kombat*, Sonya, is the embodiment of male fantasy--beautiful, blond, big-breasted, and thin. Sonya also embodies the sexist images of female power in this form of entertainment. All princesses need rescuing and all female warriors must be beautiful. Any female short of astonishing must settle for the role of the evil witch or hag. Good is associated with beauty. This male-dominated society enjoys the beauty of women and is willing to pay for a product that promotes this fantasy of women. The success of the magazine *Playboy*, which features beautiful nude women, is a testament to the popularity of this fantasy.
>
> Video game producers know that in order to make more money, they have to promote sexist images. The male warriors in *Mortal Kombat* have uniforms that represent their type of combat (Lui Kang is a Bruce Lee-type fighter and Scorpion is a Ninja), while Sonya, who is representing the armed forces, is not dressed in camouflage but in a tight aerobics outfit. Furthermore, the special finishing moves called "fatalities" have elements of sexism. While the male warriors have fatalities displaying their strength, such as ripping the fallen warrior's head from his/her body, Sonya kisses her opponent, who perishes. Her fatality isn't based on her strength like the male warriors'; rather, it is a display of her femininity that is the final reward of her victory. As Lips says, "We are surrounded with the message that masculine males can be powerful, but feminine females cannot, or that women's only effective source of feminine influence is beauty and sex appeal."

In these two paragraphs, Ho demonstrates how Lips's analysis of gender images and power can be applied to video games—a medium that Lips herself doesn't discuss. Thus, he develops a strong, original analysis by building on her ideas—extending them into a new area. Moreover, he does so by tapping his own expertise in video games. In building his analysis, Ho uses his personal knowledge in much the same way he would use a written source: he illustrates his observations about sexist images with plenty of specific evidence from the "text"—the video game. He describes details of Sonya's body, dress, and combat style that support Lips's assertion that women are expected to exert power only through physical beauty; he also illustrates the very different power possessed by the male video characters. Like Lips, he shows how stereotypic images of female power are embedded in the larger culture—in popular magazines like *Playboy* and in the powerful economic incentive for video game producers to continue creating female fantasy figures for adolescent boys. Of course your own knowledge of video games may not support Ho's analysis. Can you think of any female video game characters who do not fit the pattern he describes?

Challenging Prior Work

It's a central paradox of academic analysis that while you're supposed to build on prior work, you're also expected to challenge it. As we've seen, Herbert Kohl (p. 378), Emily Martin (p. 417), and Paula Gunn Allen (p. 434) offer extended critiques of other writers' work. Their essays point out many of the most common academic "sins," including error, bias, misrepresentation, exaggeration, omission, inconsistency, and failure to acknowledge recent research. Although all three writers point out multiple weaknesses in the texts they discuss, each also has a larger explanation pattern that unifies these criticisms. For example, Kohl argues that white Americans' reluctance to confront the realities of racism leads to pervasive distortions in mainstream accounts of Rosa Parks and the Montgomery bus boycott. Allen attributes the errors in John Gunn's interpretation of the Kochinnenako story to cultural bias or ethnocentrism, and Martin exposes the sexist bias that perpetuates gender stereotypes in scientific descriptions of egg fertilization.

However, challenging another writer's ideas doesn't have to involve the detailed criticism that you see in the essays by Kohl, Martin, and Allen. An analysis may offer only a single point of disagreement. Connie Chang, using Aronson's discussion of prejudice to analyze the homophobic attitudes of an acquaintance, offers a clear example of this approach. She concentrates on the conformity theory of prejudice, and throughout most of her analysis she demonstrates a clear "fit" between Aronson's discussion and her friend's experience. But at the end of the essay, she also challenges Aronson by suggesting that he may have neglected a key element in anti-gay prejudice. Here is her final paragraph:

> Taking the explanations given by Aronson in his "prejudice through conformity" theory, I have been able to conclude that Tom's* prejudice against homosexuals is best accounted for by his misguidance by parents, lack of education, and perception of what society deems to be normal behavior. However, I also believe that his prejudice comes from fear, an idea not touched upon by Aronson. The prejudice Tom carries is in fact an outward expression of a deeper feeling he has towards gays: fear. Some straights fear that homosexuals will harm them, based on the mistaken notion that they are highly susceptible to contracting AIDS from gays and on the perceived threat to their sexuality by gays. The only way most homophobics know how to react is through aggression. Taking on a bigoted attitude allows for the feelings of insecurity and fear to become masked. A rewarding sense of relief from fear and anger is gained when people avoid or destroy outsiders, and an equally rewarding sense of pride, self-righteousness, respect, and approval by their parents, family, neighborhood, class, nation, and race. Fear will always be built upon other fears. When all these fears create one large overriding fear, it is painted over with prejudice.

Chang successfully builds on Aronson's ideas by demonstrating how the concept of prejudice through conformity applies to the specific case of her friend's homophobia; however, she takes her analysis a step further by pointing out what she sees as an omission in Aronson's approach to prejudice. Although Chang constructs a logical explanation of how prejudice is unconsciously used to mask fear and rationalize aggression, she doesn't offer any specific evidence that her friend feels threatened by gays or by irrational fears of AIDS. Do you think this omission weakens her analysis?

*(Tom is a pseudonym.)

Does she succeed in convincing you that Aronson unduly neglects the role of fear in prejudice?

Acknowledging Complexity

As Chang's paragraph suggests, academic analysis can, and often does, build on and challenge prior work simultaneously. Analyzing "fit," as the essay options responding to Lips and Aronson require, almost invariably produces complex results: you'll find that some details fit the theory perfectly, whereas others are just a little off or don't fit at all. Writers new to academic analysis often get confused and frustrated when they notice these messy results; they may be tempted simply to ignore the examples that don't neatly fit the theory or to dismiss the theory as useless if it fails to explain everything. After all, it may appear that an absolute position is a strong one. Most academic readers, however, prefer writing that acknowledges the complexity of the subject — that recognizes shades of gray, not just black and white. So writers need to figure out ways to accommodate or explain mixed results, as Vy Le does in her response to Aronson. Le chose to analyze a debate about welfare that she and her roommate had with two of their friends. She finds that Aronson's discussion of conformity and displaced aggression works well to explain her friends' prejudice against welfare recipients, but when she tries to explain their attitudes using the theory of economic competition, the results are more complicated. Here's her introduction:

> In apartment 416, a heated and violent debate occurred on the topic of welfare; the participants included my friends Tammy, Mark, Renée*, and me. On one side were Tammy and Mark, who believe that the welfare system should be abolished, while Renée and I support the system. Since Tammy and Mark wrongly believe that over ninety-five percent of the people on welfare are African Americans or Hispanics, their prejudice against welfare recipients ultimately stems from their prejudice against these minority groups. Their discrimination can be explained using Elliot Aronson's theories about the causes of prejudice. In <u>The Social Animal</u>, he argues that economic com-

*(pseudonyms)

petition, displaced aggression, personality needs, and conformity to existing social norms are the four basic causes of
prejudice. In the case of Tammy and Mark, conformity best describes the cause of their bias against welfare recipients,
but displaced aggression also plays an important role. Although Aronson's theory that direct economic competition
causes prejudice does not explain Tammy and Mark's attitude
toward welfare, the loss of economic profits contributes to
their prejudice.

Now here's her discussion of economic competition, which appears later in
the essay:

Aronson states that prejudice can also be explained by
economic competition. He argues that prejudice often increases
when competition over similar economic goals increases. However, in the welfare example, Tammy's prejudice stems purely
from economic resentment and not economic competition. Because
welfare recipients receive money from the government as aid,
Tammy believes that the welfare system basically steals money
from her. Her discrimination against welfare recipients increases as her parents find themselves paying more and more
taxes. Although people on welfare are not threatening to her
socioeconomic status, she still feels that they are taking
away from her parents' economic profits. Thus not only can
economic competition increase prejudice, but a decrease in
economic profits can also cause discrimination against a minority group such as people on welfare.

Le responds to the imperfect fit between Aronson's discussion of prejudice
and her friend's situation by proposing a qualification and extension of the
theory of economic competition. Her analysis, like Chang's, offers a qualified endorsement of Aronson's work.

   Careful qualification is, in fact, one of the most consistent characteristics of academic writing. In everyday conversation we may exaggerate for
emphasis or dramatic effect, as in *"Everyone* is into body piercing now," or
"I wish we could just send the entire Congress into orbit and start over from

scratch!" However, academic writers, knowing that their ideas are open to challenge, have to be more concerned with accuracy. The trouble with absolute statements and sweeping generalizations is that they're so easy to disprove by citing an exception or two: if you leave yourself open to such obvious challenges, your authority and your analysis will suffer. So any academic worth her salt will be careful to acknowledge alternative perspectives, qualify generalizations, and tone down absolutes. Herbert Kohl offers a case in point when he argues against the practice of referring to Rosa Parks as "Rosa" in children's books:

> The question of whether to use the first name for historical characters in a factual story is complicated. *One argument in favor* of doing so is that young children will more readily identify with characters who are presented in a personalized and familiar way. *However,* given that it was a sanctioned social practice in the South during the time of the story for European Americans to call African American adults by their first names as a way of reinforcing the African Americans' inferior status . . . it seems unwise to use that practice in the story. (p. 388)

Kohl anticipates a common argument for using Parks's first name but then goes on to explain why he feels that other, more serious considerations outweigh this rationale. Kohl thus strengthens his analysis in two ways: he acknowledges the complexity of the issue by recognizing an alternative perspective and at the same time develops the argument for his own view.

Hilary Lips provides another example of how a writer can deal with complex subject matter. Arguing that images of power in Western culture are typically male, Lips concedes that there are exceptions to this rule but asserts that they are atypical:

> Examples of people who are physically powerful are . . . *generally* male, *despite* the widespread media attention given to *such exceptions* to that rule as Olympic athletes Jackie Joyner-Kersee, Florence Griffith-Joyner, and tennis star Martina Navratilova. In politics and business, when *most* people think of a president, prime minister, chairperson of the board, bank manager, or corporate chief executive, they think of a man, *even though* women *sometimes* hold these positions. (p. 477)

Lips's strategy makes it clear that she has considered conflicting evidence and thus deflects easy challenges to her analysis. In the process, she demonstrates two simple but effective ways to acknowledge complexity. She subordinates evidence that doesn't support her analysis and uses qualifying words in place of absolutes. Subordination uses verbal cues like *despite, in spite of, even though,* and *although* to indicate that one point is less important than another. As you can see in the examples that follow, whatever follows the subordinating cue is the subordinate point:

[Major Point], *despite* [Minor Point]

Most people picture corporate executives as men, *despite* the growing number of women in business.

Although [Minor Point], [Major Point]

Although more women are succeeding in business, most people still picture CEOs as men.

Qualifiers allow you to make generalizations while still recognizing that there are exceptions to every rule. Here are some common absolutes and their more cautious substitutes:

Absolute	Qualified
always	usually, often, frequently, sometimes
never	seldom, rarely, infrequently
everyone, all	most, many, some
no one, no, none	few, lacking, little

Examples

Everyone goes to action movies, although there are *no* strong female characters.	Action movies *usually* draw *huge crowds,* despite the *lack* of strong female characters.
Television comedies *always* portray women as airheads.	*Many* television comedies portray women as airheads.
	or
	Television comedies *often* portray women as airheads.

O P T I O N A L   A C T I V I T Y

Absolute and Qualified Language

Working in small groups, choose a carefully qualified passage from one of the academic essays in the last few chapters or from the text of this chapter. Circle all the qualifiers and write in absolutes instead. Read the altered passage aloud: How does this revision affect the tone and authority of the passage?

Revising Your Draft: Developing and Qualifying

Exchange drafts with a partner and write responses to each other's essays, focusing particularly on these questions:

- What strategies does the writer use to develop her analysis? Can you suggest further ways she could either build on or challenge her sources in order to strengthen the essay?

- To what extent does she acknowledge complexity? Does she recognize alternative views and exceptions without sounding wishy-washy?

- Circle any overgeneralizations or absolutes that could be easily challenged. Can you suggest more carefully qualified language?

- What parts of the analysis work particularly well and why?

Can You Own an Idea? Plagiarism and Academic Culture

In academic circles, conspiring to burn down the administration building or plotting to murder a professor might be considered a more serious crime than plagiarism—but then again, it might not. What is plagiarism and why do college professors take it so seriously? Plagiarism is usually understood as the use of another writer's words or ideas as if they were your own or without appropriate citation of the source. It makes little difference whether the illegitimate borrowing is intentional or unintentional; the consequences can be severe: students can be disciplined and even expelled, and tenured professors can be fired if they're found guilty of plagiarism. But since virtually no idea is absolutely new, and scholars almost always build on each other's work, determining what's "original" and what's "borrowed" can be tricky. Furthermore, in other contexts and cultures, borrowing is expected and even honored. American journalists routinely take information verbatim from press releases and wire service stories without quoting and footnoting. In China, the ability to use set phrases from classic works is a sign of education and refinement, not moral turpitude.[2]

Even in Western academic culture, the concept of plagiarism as we understand it today is a relatively recent development. Before the invention of the printing press and the lending library, scholars had access to books only

---

[2]Carolyn Matalene, "Contrastive Rhetoric: An American Writing Teacher in China," *College English* 47, no. 8 (December 1985): 803–804.

by copying them longhand. Copyists would sometimes add their own commentary to the text, and punctuate however it suited them, so that the "copy" might differ significantly from the original text by the time it was finished. After printing made it possible to produce and sell multiple exact copies, texts became a commodity. Early copyright laws were enacted for the benefit of the publisher, not the author, and the value of protecting ownership of the text was purely economic.[3] In today's academic culture, texts have both monetary and intellectual value: knowledge and ideas are the gold standard, determining who wins jobs, promotions, respect, and status. So establishing "ownership" of ideas becomes crucial, and "stealing" another scholar's ideas is like stealing his livelihood and self-worth.

Students are often advised to cite the source of any information that's not "common knowledge." The trouble is, what's common knowledge to one person or speech community may be absolutely new to another. The concept of punctuated equilibrium, for example, is familiar to anyone who's studied evolutionary biology, just as the Sapir-Whorf hypothesis is common knowledge among linguists. But outside these fields, references to such theories would probably require documentation because they're not part of the shared body of knowledge that most people take for granted. Moreover, an individual's store of common knowledge changes over time. Say you're a first-year college student taking Introduction to American History and you decide to write a paper about the civil rights movement. Before you begin your research, your knowledge of the subject may consist of little more than a general sense that Rosa Parks refused to give up her seat on a bus and that Martin Luther King, Jr., led some marches and gave an influential speech called "I Have a Dream" at a rally in Washington, D.C. As you're browsing in the library, you run across Herbert Kohl's essay on Rosa Parks and decide that your paper should mention the extensive planning that went into the Montgomery bus boycott. Because this information is new to you, you should certainly cite Kohl in your essay—or better still, look up the primary sources that he refers to and cite them. But if your professor gives a lecture on the role Highlander Folk School played in training civil rights activists like Rosa Parks, you're free to use that information without citation because it's part of the "common knowledge" of the classroom community. Later, you become a history major with a special interest in the civil rights movement. As you develop your expertise in this area, more and more of the material becomes common knowledge to you. At that point, you certainly wouldn't document the mere fact of Parks's activism or cite

---

[3]Ron Scollon, "Plagiarism and Ideology: Identity in Intercultural Discourse," *Language in Society* 24, no. 1 (1995): 24.

Kohl, a nonhistorian, as a source. Like many other issues in writing, the question of when to document is contextual; if you're unsure whether to cite a source, talk to your instructor.

Quoting Sources Skillfully

One of the surest ways to distinguish an expert from an academic beginner is to look at her skill in quoting sources. If you can quote accurately, select and edit quoted material effectively, and incorporate quotations seamlessly into your own prose, you'll be well on your way to sounding like a pro. We're concerned here not with details of citation form, but with how to use quoted text to support your analysis. For advice on the conventions of bibliographic form, footnotes, and parenthetical citations, consult a recent handbook. The sample quotations in the following paragraphs relate to this short passage from M. G. Lord's essay:

> In Barbie's universe, women are not the second sex. Barbie's genesis subverts the biblical myth of Genesis, which Camille Paglia has described as "a male declaration of independence from the ancient mother-cults." Just as the goddess-based religions antedated Judeo-Christian monotheism, Barbie came before Ken. The whole idea of woman as temptress, or woman as subordinate to man, is absent from the Barbie cosmology. Ken is a gnat, a fly, a slave, an accessory of Barbie. Barbie was made perfect: her body has not evolved dramatically with time. Ken, by contrast, was a blunder: first scrawny, now pumped-up, his ever-changing body is neither eternal nor talismanic. (p. 357)

Represent your sources fairly and accurately.   The way you use sources reflects on your own credibility. If you misquote other writers' words or misrepresent their ideas, you'll look as if you're either careless or dishonest, and your readers will have good reason to distrust you. Often writers who aren't used to relying on sources misrepresent them unintentionally. The most common pitfall is distorting someone's words or ideas by taking them out of context. How does each of the following examples misrepresent Lord's text, and how would you revise to avoid the problem?

> *Misrepresented:* Concerned parents should boycott the Mattel Company because, as M. G. Lord points out, Barbie "subverts . . . Judeo-Christian monotheism" (p. 357).

> *Misrepresented:* I believe that Barbie symbolizes "the whole idea of woman as temptress" (Lord, p. 357).

Be careful to distinguish direct quotation from paraphrase.   Quoting means borrowing another writer's words and putting them in quotation marks to indicate that they aren't your own; paraphrasing means borrowing another writer's idea, but putting it in your own words. In either case, you must cite the source of the quotation or the idea.

> *Quotation:* M. G. Lord suggests that Barbie is a feminist icon: "The whole idea of woman as temptress, or woman as subordinate to man, is absent from the Barbie cosmology. Ken is a gnat, a fly, a slave, an accessory of Barbie" (p. 357).

> *Paraphrase:* According to Lord, Barbie can be seen as a feminist icon—clearly superior to the bland Ken (p. 357).

Note that merely changing a few words doesn't constitute legitimate paraphrase; in fact, it's considered a form of plagiarism—even if you cited the source. In order to avoid the appearance of plagiarism, either thoroughly rephrase the idea in your own words or clearly indicate quoted passages by using quotation marks:

> *Plagiarized:* M. G. Lord argues that in Barbie's universe, women are not subordinate to men: Ken is a nothing, a mere accessory of Barbie.

This sentence follows the original passage far too closely: it reproduces the same sequence of ideas and even retains some of Lord's phrasing.

> *Paraphrased:* In "Interpreting Barbie" M. G. Lord argues that women are dominant in Barbie's world: Ken is clearly a secondary character.

This sentence restates Lord's general idea without copying her organization or phrasing. Because Lord talks about Ken's subordinate status throughout the essay, there's no need to cite a specific page number here.

> *Paraphrased and quoted:* M. G. Lord argues that women are dominant in Barbie's world—that Ken is merely "an accessory of Barbie" (p. 357).

This sentence paraphrases the general idea of the original paragraph but clearly indicates that the description of Ken is taken directly from Lord; because of this specific reference, the page number is included.

Make sure that quotations are completely accurate.   When you enclose words in quotation marks, you're telling the reader, "This is exactly what the author said." Even a slight change in the wording makes a quotation inaccurate:

Inaccurate: M. G. Lord points out that Barbie's body, unlike Ken's, "has not changed dramatically over time" (p. 357).

Even though the change of wording here is minor and does not affect meaning ("changed" is substituted for "evolved"), the quotation is misleading because it doesn't represent the author's exact words.

Accurate: M. G. Lord points out that Barbie's body, unlike Ken's, "has not evolved dramatically with time" (p. 357).

Keep quotations tightly focused.   Quote only as much of the text as you need in order to fairly represent the writer's meaning and to support the specific point you're making.

Unfocused: Lord asserts that because Barbie was created before her male companion, Ken, her story reverses the story of Genesis:

> Just as the goddess-based religions antedated Judeo-Christian monotheism, Barbie came before Ken. The whole idea of woman as temptress, or woman as subordinate to man, is absent from the Barbie cosmology. Ken is a gnat, a fly, a slave, an accessory of Barbie. Barbie was made perfect: her body has not evolved dramatically with time. Ken, by contrast, was a blunder: first scrawny, now pumped-up, his ever-changing body is neither eternal nor talismanic. (p. 357)

This long quotation includes material about Barbie's and Ken's bodies that has little or nothing to do with the writer's main point—the idea that "the Barbie cosmology" turns Genesis on its head. In the sample revision that follows, this irrelevant material is deleted and the quotation helps readers to follow the writer's analysis rather than distracting them with unnecessary detail:

Focused: M. G. Lord asserts that because Barbie was created before her male companion, Ken, her story reverses the story of Genesis: "Barbie came before Ken. The whole idea of woman as temptress, or woman as subordinate to man, is absent from the Barbie cosmology" (p. 357).

Besides boring or confusing readers, long, rambling quotations can be the sign of a writer with more serious problems. They might suggest that the writer doesn't fully understand the text he's quoting. They may indicate that the writer isn't quite sure what he's trying to accomplish and thus can't identify which parts of the quoted text are relevant and irrelevant. Or they could just be acting as filler—big chunks of text the writer included to avoid doing the harder work of careful analysis. So what may look like a purely technical concern can end up having an enormous impact on your authority as a writer.

Integrate quotations smoothly with your own text. Quotations should be seamlessly worked into your sentences and paragraphs: you should be able to read them as if they were structurally part of your own writing.

> *Bumpy:* I completely disagree with Lord's point about "just as the goddess-based religions antedated Judeo-Christian monotheism, Barbie came before Ken" (p. 357) because this is offensive.

> *Smooth:* Lord claims that "just as the goddess-based religions antedated Judeo-Christian monotheism, Barbie came before Ken" (p. 357). I think this comparison of religions to toys is offensive.

> *Bumpy:* M. G. Lord has a quote that says, "the biblical myth of Genesis, which Camille Paglia has described as 'a male declaration of independence from the ancient mother-cults'" (p. 357).

> *Smooth:* M. G. Lord cites Camille Paglia's description of Genesis as "a male declaration of independence from the ancient mother-cults" (p. 357).

You can make minor editorial changes in quotations if you clearly indicate what changes you've made. Sometimes, in order to make a quoted passage flow smoothly, you may need to omit an inessential phrase, add a word or make some other small change in the text. It's OK to make changes like these if they don't alter the meaning of the original passage and if you show the reader what you've changed.

> *Mark an omission with ellipses (. . .):* Lord observes that "Barbie was made perfect . . . ; Ken, by contrast, was a blunder" (p. 357).

> *Mark an addition or change in a word by putting square brackets [ ] around the alteration:* Ken's body has changed over the years; Lord points out that although he was "first scrawny, [he is] now pumped up" (p. 357).

Revising Your Draft: Quoting Text for Support

Reread your draft and mark all of the quotations and paraphrased ideas. Then ask yourself the following questions:

- Do you represent your sources fairly and accurately? Make sure you don't misquote or misrepresent the text.

- Do you enclose all quotations in quotation marks and indicate the source of any idea that you paraphrased?

Now work with a partner and review each other's drafts with these questions in mind:

- Are quotations brief and relevant to the point the writer is making? If quoted material seems unfocused, offer suggestions for editing the quotation or clarifying the analysis.

- Does the writer integrate quotations seamlessly into her own prose? Do the quotations clearly help her to develop her analysis or do they interrupt the flow of ideas? If quotations are awkward or disconnected from the surrounding sentences, explain how the writer might incorporate them more smoothly or link her ideas more effectively.

- Where is the writer making particularly good use of her sources?

JOURNAL OPTION

Evaluating Your Writing Process

Before you turn in your revised paper, take a few minutes to reflect on your writing process for this essay. What was most challenging about this paper? What aspects of your essay do you think will appeal most to an academic audience and why? Which parts are you least confident about? Attach this journal entry to your finished paper when you turn it in so that your instructor can respond to your concerns in her comments.

Acknowledgments continued from copyright page

Index of Authors and Titles